D0148301

The Rise of Anthropological Theory

The Rise of

A History of Theories of Culture

Thomas Y. Crowell Company

NEW YORK ESTABLISHED 1834

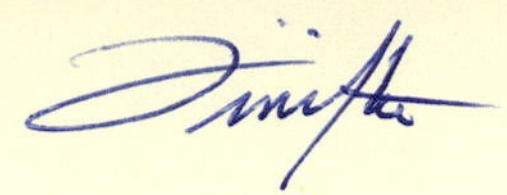

Anthropological Theory

Marvin Harris

COLUMBIA UNIVERSITY

Library of Congress Catalog Card Number: 68–17392
Designed by Judith Woracek Barry. Manufactured in the United States of America.

Acknowledgments are gratefully made to the following authors and publishers who have granted permission to use selections from copyrighted publications.

BOAS, F., *Race, Language and Culture* (New York: The Macmillan Company, 1940). Copyright © 1940 by Franz Boas.

DUBOIS, C., ed., *Lowie's Selected Papers in Anthropology* (Berkeley: University of California Press, 1960).

DURKHEIM, É., *The Elementary Forms of Religious Life*, trans. J. W. Swain (London: George Allen & Unwin Ltd., 1915).

DURKHEIM, É., *The Rules of Sociological Method,* trans. S. Solovay and J. Mueller (Glencoe, Ill.: The Free Press, 1938). Copyright © 1938 by George Catlin.

FORDE, C. D., *Habitat, Economy and Society* (London: Methuen & Company, Ltd.; New York: E. P. Dutton, Inc., 1934).

KROEBER, A., *The Nature of Culture* (Chicago: The University of Chicago Press, 1952). Copyright © 1952 by The University of Chicago Press.

LÉVI-STRAUSS, C., *Totemism,* trans. R. Needham (Boston: Beacon Press, 1963). Copyright © 1962 by Presses Universitaires de France; translation copyright © 1963 by Beacon Press.

LOWIE, R., *History of Ethnological Theory* (New York: Farrar and Rinehart, 1937).

MURDOCK, G. P., Social Structure (New York: The Macmillan Company, 1949). Copyright © 1949 by The Macmillan Company.

PIKE, K., *With Heart and Mind* (Grand Rapids, Mich.: Wm. B. Eerdmans Publishing Company, 1962).

RADCLIFFE-BROWN, A. R., *Structure and Function in Primitive Society* (London: Cohen and West Ltd.; New York: The Macmillan Company, 1952).

SAPIR, E., "Review of W. H. R. Rivers 'Instinct and the Unconscious: A Contribution to a Biological Theory of Psycho-Neurosis,' " ed. D. Mandelbaum, *Selected Writings of Edward Sapir* (Berkeley: University of California Press, 1949).

STEWARD, J., "The Economic and Social Basis of Primitive Bands," ed. R. Lowie, *Essays in Anthropology Presented to A. L. Kroeber* (Berkeley: University of California Press, 1936).

STEWARD, J., and F. SELTZER, "Function and Configuration in Archaeology," *American Antiquity,* IV (1938), 4–10.

SUMNER, W. G., and A. G. KELLER, *The Science of Society* (New Haven: Yale University Press, 1927).

TYLOR, E. B., *Primitive Culture* (New York: Harper Torchbooks, 1958).

Acknowledgments

When an author has completed his book, it would seem a simple task to thank those who have helped him in its preparation. In actuality the task is not an easy one at all. Apart from all the advice and assistance received from colleagues, I am indebted in many ways to those men and women whose ideas and conclusions are the subject of this book. It was their writings and research that helped shape and define the discipline of anthropology; and though I disagree with many of their formulations, this book is in a sense a result of these disagreements.

It is not possible to name all those who have helped in the preparation of this volume, but I would like to single out those who made specific suggestions for the improvement of the manuscript. I benefited especially from the contributions of Elman Service, Robert Carneiro, Morton Fried, Harvey Pitkin, Eric R. Wolf, Robert Cumming, Victor Barnouw, Abraham Rosman, Robert Murphy, Nan Pendrell, Alexander Alland, Michael Harner, William Willis, Alexander Lesser, and Barbara Price.

I should also like to thank my students and associates for their help and encouragement, especially Rolf Knight, Richard Davis, and Adrian DeWind for their invaluable assistance in all matters pertaining to references and the bibliography, and to Amelia Hess and Esther Modell for their general patience and fortitude.

Contents

Introduction 1

Anthropology began as the science of history. Inspired by the triumphs of the scientific method in the physical and organic domains, nineteenth-century anthropologists believed that sociocultural phenomena were governed by discoverable lawful principles. This conviction joined their interests with the aspiration of a still earlier period, extending back before the social sciences had been named, to the epochal stirrings of the eighteenth-century Enlightenment and the vision of a universal history of mankind. Whatever the weaknesses of the theories propounded by the early anthropologists under the sway of nineteenth-century scientism, we must concede that the issues addressed—origins and causes—gave their writings an enduring significance. Commencing with the twentieth century, however, and continuing through the early forties, efforts were made to alter the strategic premise upon which the scientism of anthropological theory depended. Almost simultaneously, there arose in England, France, Germany, and the United States, schools of anthropology that in one way or another rejected the scientific mandate. It came to be widely believed that anthropology could never discover the origins of institutions or explain their causes. In the United States, the dominant school flatly asserted that there were no historical laws and that there could not be a science of history.

It has been said in defense of this period that anthropological theory had become overspeculative and that an interval of intense dedication to the collection of empirical data was precisely what was most needed at the time. In retrospect, however, it is apparent that the data were not collected without theoretical bias, or theoretical consequence. While ostensibly operating within a restricted theoretical frame, conclusions of the widest possible significance bearing on the nature of history and culture were formulated. These spread to adjacent disciplines and were incorporated into the intellectual prospectus of the public at large. On the basis of partial, incorrect, or misinterpreted ethnographic evidence, there emerged a view of culture that exaggerated all the quixotic, irrational, and inscrutable ingredients in human life. Delighting in diversity of pattern, anthropologists sought out divergent and incomparable events. They stressed the inner, subjective meaning of experience to the exclusion of objective effects and relations. They denied historical determinism in general, and above all, they denied the determinism of the material conditions of life. By emphasizing inscrutable values, vain prestige, irrational motives, they discredited the economic interpretation of history. Anthropology came increasingly to concern itself with idiographic phenomena, that is, with the study of the unique and the nonrepetitive aspects of history.

This state of affairs did not for long go unchallenged. A strong countercurrent tending toward the reinstatement of *nomothetic*—that is, generalizing—interests was already making itself felt in the 1930's. Since then, the interest in regularities has spread, and the form, if not the substance, of scientism is once more in the ascendancy. Yet, it remains uncertain to what extent anthropology is about to resume its eminence as the science of history. The resistance to this formulation of the grand strategy of anthropological research has acquired the strength of habit. Many anthropologists find it sufficient to apply themselves to limited problems cast in an ostensibly scientific idiom but deliberately detached from questions of causality and origins. Various strategems have been introduced that avoid statements of causality, while conveying the impression that an explanation is being offered. Rather than explanations of sociocultural differences and similarities in terms of true nomothetic principles, we have so-called functional explanations; we have correlations in which it is not known how the causal arrow points, and we have "accounting for" in terms of paradigmatic cognitive frames, which are accepted as givens, although nothing is known about how long they have existed.

My main reason for writing this book is to reassert the methodological priority of the search for the laws of history in the science of man. There is an urgency associated with this rededication, which grows in direct proportion to the increase in the funding and planning of anthropological research and especially to the role anthropologists have been asked to assume in the planning and carrying out of international development programs. A general theory of history is required if the expansion of disposable research funds is to result in something other than the rapid growth in the amount of trivia being published in the learned journals. The publishing of more and more about less and less is an acceptable consequence of affluence only if specialization does not lead to an actual neglect or even obfuscation of fundamental issues.

Needless to say, if the anthropological contribution to international development programs continues without benefit of a general theory of sociocultural change, the consequences could be disastrous in a more literal sense. It may be possible to defend the so-called middle-range theories in relation to pure research, the idea being that work can proceed on an eclectic, piecemeal basis in the expectation that the fragments will eventually fall into place when macro-theory is created. But the middle-range, piecemeal approach to directed cultural change exposes anthropologists to the charge of irresponsibility. Actually, there is little to commend the idea of middle-ground theory, even without the possible onus of development programs that result in underdevelopment. In theoretical as well as applied anthropology, eclecticism is frequently nothing more than a convenient excuse for not having to bother with the question of the scientific importance of a particular research option.

Were mere exhortation on behalf of macro-theory the subject of this volume, I should not have troubled myself with its writing. But the matter is considerably more advanced. The burden of my argument is that the basic principle of a macro-theory of sociocultural evolution is already known. This is not to say that it is known in the form that is familiar to us from physics—as the Newtonian laws of motion, or as the laws of quantum mechanics—but rather in a fashion that closely approximates the kind of principle that has governed research in evolutionary biology since the time of Darwin. The kind of principle to which I refer, in other words, has its precise analogue in the doctrine of natural selection. In this analogy, the meaning of "principle" is not equivalent to the statement of the specific "laws" of evolution, but rather to the statement of a basic research strategy, from the application of which there is an expectation that a nomothetic causal understanding of sociocultural phenomena may be achieved. Darwin's contribution, which we shall have occasion to discuss later on, was to direct attention to the general conditions responsible for bio-evolution, namely, differential reproductive success. It remains for the biological researcher to discover the particular concatenation of causes in any given instance of speciation responsible for the reproductive success of later over earlier forms.

I believe that the analogue of the Darwinian strategy in the realm of sociocultural phenomena is the principle of techno-environmental and techno-economic determinism. This principle holds that similar technologies applied to similar environments tend to produce similar arrangements of labor in production and distribution, and that these in turn call forth similar kinds of social groupings, which justify and coordinate their activities by means of similar systems of values and beliefs. Translated into research strategy, the principle of techno-environmental, techno-economic determinism assigns priority to the study of the material conditions of sociocultural life, much as the principle of natural selection assigns priority to the study of differential reproductive success.

The strategy in question will at once strike the sensitized reader as a form of materialism, and, indeed, I shall refer to it throughout this book as the strategy of "cultural materialism." Although I am tempted to avoid the term "materialism" in deference to the reflexive opprobrium which it elicits among the public at large as well as among many social scientists, to do so would be pusillanimous.

It may be said that one of the central purposes of the present volume is to decontaminate, so to speak, the materialist approach to history. This result can be achieved only if the strategy of cultural materialism is carefully separated from philosophical materialism on the one hand, and dialectical materialism on the other. In the former case, we deal with metaphysical disputations concerning the essence of being—the question of the ontological priority of matter over mind. This issue may well be left to the philosophers, since it has no direct bearing on the statement of the laws of sociocultural evolution. To take a position concerning the direction of the causal arrow in sociocultural systems does not oblige us to enter into a discussion of the ultimate nature of reality. In the case of dialectical materialism, however, there is much that requires our closest attention. Dialectical materialism is a sub-case of cultural materialism, which has been incorporated into the political creed of Marxist communism. The dialectical and revolutionary components in this brand of materialism have not been confirmed by anthropological research. Indeed, the mystification of world historical processes under dialectical materialism is no less severe than under bourgeois cultural idealism. My aim has been resolutely to steer a course independent of the ideologues of the cold war. I shall recognize in the writings of Marx and Engels achievements of unparalleled importance for a science of man; but I shall also insist on the error of Marx and Engels's attempt to shackle cultural materialism to the spooks of Hegel's dialectic. I am convinced that the coming generation of social scientists is prepared to say to party hacks and bourgeois toadies, "a plague on both your houses," and to get on with the business of seeking the truth, wherever the search may lead.

In order to achieve a fair hearing for the cultural-materialist strategy, we are compelled to embark upon an historical survey of the development of anthropological theories of culture. The reason for thus passing in review the major anthropological theories of the past two hundred years is to prove that the principle of techno-economic and techno-environmental determinism has never been consistently applied across the range of phenomena with which anthropologists are familiar, despite the fact that anthropologists have played a crucial role in discrediting this option. I shall demonstrate that the failure to apply the cultural-materialist strategy resulted not from any reasonable program of oriented research, but from the covert pressures of the sociocultural milieu in which anthropology achieved its disciplinary identity. This failure is all the more remarkable in view of the admitted and demonstrable inability of the science of man to develop a viable alternative to the prematurely discredited strategy, and in view of the passion with which anthropologists have argued that they have remained free of ideological bias.

The reader has now been forewarned that, while this book is a history of anthropological theories, it is intended to prove a point rather than to provide an encyclopedic inventory of all the figures who have in any degree ever made suggestions concerning the causes of sociocultural phenomena. While there are useful purposes to be fulfilled by a compendium approach, it appears to me far more urgent for anthropologists and all those who feel the need for resuming and carrying forward the search for the principles governing the trajectory of sociocultural evolution to devote themselves to a critique, rather than a summary, of where we have come from and where we are going.

This larger enterprise obliges us to view anthropology in a fashion to which its practitioners have all too readily grown unaccustomed. As a discipline which above all others is competent to concern itself with the fundamental questions of sociocultural causality, anthropology must cease to regard itself as being somehow outside of and detached from and above the main currents of Western thought. During the idiographic interlude at the beginning of this century, an image of anthropology as a new discipline contributed greatly to the élan of the pioneering fieldworkers. The achievements of the present were stressed almost to the complete neglect of the historical conditions out of which the discipline had arisen. The result has been that many anthropologists have suffered a form of deculturation—they have been cut off from their own cultural roots. The penalty for this discontinuity is a form of naïveté similar to ethnocentrism. The "culture" of the latest research design and practice is taken as natural, while alternatives are barely considered or remain unimagined. The provincialism of this situation is intensified by the scientific community's disposition to regard research as the *summum bonum* of all scientific activity. A kind of pragmatism has resulted, in which it is held that a bit of research is to be judged only on its own merits—that is, for what it has accomplished. But by returning to the historical sources of our discipline, we shall come to understand that research must be evaluated not only by what it has done, but also by what it has not done. One might argue that the choice of a particular research topic and research strategy does not prevent others from making a different set of choices. But the limitations on deployable time and manpower oblige us to consider carefully the relative contributions of alternative research options and strategies to the development of nomothetic theory. It is only by a study of how currently acceptable fashions in anthropological research developed within the wider intellectual habitat that we shall learn to appreciate what has been achieved as well as what has not been achieved in anthropological theory.

It follows from the importance of an ample vision of the history of ideas that the selection of key figures in the history of anthropological theory should be guided by criteria of intellectual relevance and influence, as well as by disciplinary identity. For this reason, certain explicitly anthropological personalities have been omitted, while philosophers, economists, historians, etc., are discussed at length. A certain amount of calculated indifference to disciplinary boundaries is absolutely essential for an understanding of the viewpoint of the period which predated the formal crystallization of social-science specialties. It would undoubtedly be useful to sustain this coverage through to the present moment, since many features of contemporary anthropological theory are shared by adjacent disciplines. Most regrettable in this regard is the omission of relevant twentieth-century sociological theory. But the prospect of further enlarging the present volume acted as a deterrent, giving rise to a result which the reader may wish to regard as a merciful inconsistency.

I should like to take this opportunity to apologize for what may appear at times as unnecessarily severe criticism of venerated colleagues, in both present and past generations. Although I have sought to avoid *ad hominem* discussions, it has seemed to me at this particular moment in the development of anthropological theory that critical judgments deserve priority over polite ones. It has certainly not been my intention to be disrespectful of the men and women who have devoted themselves, frequently with great personal courage and sacrifice, to the ideal of furthering the understanding of the ways of mankind. My interest throughout the writing of this book has been to advance the theoretical standing of anthropology among the social sciences. Nothing said herein may properly be construed as demeaning anthropology's universalistic and comparative mission, nor as detracting from the personal stature of the extraordinarily talented, enlightened, and humanly involved scholars with whom anthropology has always been so well endowed.

Enlightenment

2

The rise of anthropological theory began during that hallowed epoch in Western culture known as the Enlightenment—the period roughly coincident with the one hundred years from the writing of John Locke's *An Essay Concerning Human Understanding* (1690) to the outbreak of the French Revolution. Yet the importance of this epoch in the formation of the science of culture has gone unrecognized, principally because of the prolonged influence of anthropologists who were uninterested in such a science or who denied that it was possible. For there have been many anthropologists who believed that the human actor's free will, the uncertainties of national character, and the tangle of chance and circumstance in history thwart all scientific efforts in this domain. Those who believe that it is man's unique destination to live outside the determinate order of nature will not concede the importance of the eighteenth century. Many contemporary anthropologists regard the scientific aspirations of the Enlightenment as the very quintessence of that vanity to which the prophet of Ecclesiastes referred all new ideas. Thus, Margaret Hodgen (1964:484) has written about the eighteenth century as if it were a mere "aftermath" to the Middle Ages, asserting furthermore that "recent centuries have witnessed little that warrants the title of theoretical innovation." But for Hodgen and the anthropologists upon whom she relied for her misunderstanding of contemporary theories of culture, all scientism in sociocultural matters is a delusion. This book is predicated on a contrary belief; and hence, for us, all that is new in anthropological theory begins with the Enlightenment. We shall see in the present chapter how the social philosophers of the eighteenth century first brought the central issues of contemporary anthropology into focus, and how they sought resolutely, but without success, to formulate the laws governing the course of human history and the evolution of sociocultural differences and similarities.

The issues of sociocultural inquiry brought forth during the Enlightenment embrace most of the themes that serve either as the foundation of contemporary theory or as the basic frame of reference in terms of which modern sociocultural research is still being carried out. In the present chapter, we shall review these contributions as they relate to vitally important aspects of modern theory. We shall inquire into the degree of success with which the Enlightenment philosophers were able to identify the sociocultural domain as a distinct field of inquiry characterized by a uniquely human elaboration of culturally determined behavior; to what extent and upon what philosophical and epistemological grounds the proto-anthropologists of the Enlightenment believed that sociocultural phenomena were a legitimate domain for scientific study; the extent to which ideas concerning the nature and direction of sociocultural evolution were set forth in the Enlightenment, a hundred years before Darwin. Finally, we shall describe and evaluate the first halting approximations to a theory of sociocultural causation based on naturalistic premises.

THE ENLIGHTENMENT AND THE CULTURE CONCEPT

According to Alfred Kroeber and Clyde Kluckhohn, the concept of culture, in the sense of a "set of attributes and products of human societies, and therewith of mankind, which are extrasomatic and transmissible by mechanisms other than biological heredity . . . did not exist anywhere in 1750" (1952:145). Although these authors recognize and cite the use of the term "culture" (only in the Germanic *Kultur* form) and "civilization" (in both French and English) during the eighteenth century, they postpone the emergence of the modern concept until well into the nineteenth century. They concede only that "By 1850 it was de facto being held in some quarters in Germany, though never quite explicitly . . ." (*ibid.*).

There is actually no reason why a definition of culture must or should emphasize the extrasomatic and nonhereditary factors, even though most twentieth-century anthropologists regard these as essential to the concept. Since we have yet to discover how to separate hereditary from acquired influences in a given human or infrahuman population's entire repertory of behavior, we can scarcely hope to delimit an operationally valid cultural field of inquiry in such theoretical terms. The definition that Kroeber and Kluckhohn propose is one step beyond a mere concept of culture; it is rather a theory of culture, namely, an explanation of how the features of a particular population's behavioral repertory are established, i.e., by learning rather than by genetic processes. It is not particularly vital in the present context, however, to argue whether the prevailing formula is a concept of culture or a partial theory of culture; rather let us determine to what extent the ideas to which Kroeber and Kluckhohn refer are anticipated in the years preceding the French Revolution.

A more generous concern with *de facto* or implicit, as opposed to formal or explicit, definitions justifies a much earlier historical threshold for the culture concept than that set by these two authors. The principal defect in their history of the concept is that they fail to locate its development within the main currents of the scientific awakening. They neglect to point out that the implicit, or *de facto*, formulation was not a mere appendage of an occasional interest in customs and institutions, which has to be ferreted out of obscure passages in the collected works of forgotten authors. On the contrary, from our vantage point, it is apparent that a nascent version of the concept and theory of culture was *the* major theme in the intellectual ferment that preceded the French Revolution. Indeed, these ideas have always had revolutionary political, as well as intellectual, auspices and consequences. Not only is the modern culture concept implicit in the ideological antecedents of the French Revolution (and of the American Revolution as well), but the very substance of the revolutionary program proclaimed the validity of the concept and testified to its importance.

THE EMPTY CABINET

It was actually the seventeenth-century English philosopher John Locke who provided the metaphysical foundation upon which anthropologists over two hundred years later were to rear the first formal definitions of culture. In fact, Locke's *An Essay Concerning Human Understanding* was the midwife of all those modern behavioral disciplines, including psychology, sociology, and cultural anthropology, which stress the relationship between conditioning environment and human thought and actions. "He stood in relation to the eighteenth century much as Freud and Marx stand to ours. Even his enemies were obliged to employ his terms" (HART 1964:6). What Locke attempted to prove was that the human mind at birth was an "empty cabinet" (LOCKE 1894 I:48; orig. 1690). The knowledge or the ideas with which the mind later comes to be filled are all acquired during the process of what we would call today enculturation. Although there are distinctly human, as opposed to animal, capacities, there are no innate ideas. This applies equally to such abstract logical principles as "It is impossible for the same thing to be and not to be," as to what Locke calls practical principles, or moral rules of conduct:

> Whether there be any such moral principles, wherein all men do agree, I appeal to any who have been but moderately conversant in the history of mankind, and looked abroad beyond the smoke of their own chimneys. Where is that practical truth that is universally received without doubt or question, as it must be if innate? Have there not been whole nations, and those of the most civilized people, amongst whom the exposing their children, and leaving them in the fields to perish by want or wild beasts has been the practice; as little condemned or scrupled as the begetting them? Do they not still, in some countries, put them into the same graves with their mothers, if they die in childbirth; or despatch them, if a pretended astrologer declares them to have unhappy stars? And are there not places where, at a certain age, they kill or expose their parents, without any remorse at all? In a part of Asia, the sick, when their case comes to be thought desperate, are carried out and laid on the earth before they are dead; and left there, exposed to wind and weather, to perish without assistance or pity. It is familiar among the Mingrelians, a people professing Christianity, to bury their children alive without scruple. There are places where they eat their own children. The Caribbees were wont to geld their children, on purpose to fat and eat them. And Garcilaso de la Vega tells us of a people in Peru which were wont to fat and eat the children they got on their female captives, whom they kept as concubines for that purpose, and when they were past breeding, the mothers themselves were killed too and eaten. The virtues whereby the Tououpinambas believed they merited paradise, were revenge, and eating abundance of their enemies [*ibid.*:66].

Locke was more concerned with the epistemological issue of how knowledge or ideas are established than specifically with how individuals and whole tribes and nations come to possess such (not always accurately reported) customs. However, since the prevailing view of the times regarded behavior as the consequence of knowledge, the answer which he supplied on the origin of understanding served equally as the answer for verbal and nonverbal behavior.

All of man's understandings Locke attributed to the perceptions conveyed through "sense impressions."

> Let us then suppose the mind to be, as we say, white paper, void of all characters, without any ideas:—How comes it to be furnished? Whence comes it by that vast store which the busy and boundless fancy of man has painted on it with an almost endless variety? Whence has it all the materials of reason and knowledge? To this I answer, in one word, from EXPERIENCE. In that all our knowledge is founded; and from that it ultimately derives itself [*ibid.*:122].

The inescapable consequence of this doctrine is that different *experiences*, or, in modern terms, differential environmental exposure, will produce both individual and national differences in behavior. The revolutionary sociopolitical implications of Locke's arid discussion should be evident: No social order is based upon innate truths; a change in the environment results in a change in behavior. In the words of Claude Helvetius, whose *On Man* (1772) was one of the most systematic developments of the radical implications of Locke's theories:

> . . . Locke and I say: The inequality of minds is the effect of a known cause, and that cause is the difference in education [HELVETIUS 1818:71; orig. 1772], . . . all then in us is acquisition . . . [HELVETIUS 1946:1019]. Our understanding, our talents, our vices and virtues, our prejudices and characters . . . are not therefore the effect of our several (hereditary) temperaments. Our passions themselves are not dependent on them [*ibid.*:1019] . . . I have proved that compassion is not either a moral sense, or an innate sentiment, but the pure effect of self-love. What follows? That it is this same love, differently modified, according to the different education we receive, and the circumstances, and situations in which chance has placed us, which renders us humane or obdurate: that man is not born compassionate, but that all may or will become so when the laws, the form of government and their education lead them to it [*ibid.*:1022].

TOLERATION VERSUS RELATIVISM

Perhaps the reason why anthropologists have been reluctant to trace the culture concept to Locke's *Essay* is that Locke, in company with all of the eighteenth century's formal and *de facto* students of culture, despite the power they attributed to experience to shape customs and beliefs, did not abandon the notion that there were universally valid moral beliefs and right and wrong rules and modes of conduct. It was not the concept of culture that was absent in 1750, but rather the moral indifference of cultural relativism. Neither Locke nor his followers cared to leap from the elusiveness of innate ideas to the abeyance of moral censure. And thus, during the next century and a half social science followed Locke in his conviction that despite differences in experience, reason, correctly applied, would eventually lead man, everywhere, to the same social institutions, moral beliefs, and scientific technical truths. Just as the information of the senses worked over by reason leads to an understanding of the laws of motion, so too would empirical inquiry eventually lead one to a knowledge of religious and moral verities. In the meantime, however, before these truths are demonstrated, the watchword is tolerance.

> For where is the man that has incontestable evidence of the truth of all that he holds, or of the falsehood of all he condemns . . .? The necessity of believing without knowledge, nay often upon very slight grounds, in this fleeting state of action and blindness we are in, should make us more busy and careful to inform ourselves than constrain others [LOCKE 1894, II:373; orig. 1690].

Toleration of alien ways is a characteristic attitude among Descartes, Vico, Voltaire, Diderot, Montesquieu, Turgot, Helvetius, and many other famous Enlightenment authors; but this toleration should not be confused with moral indifference or genuine cultural relativism. By the same token, moral commitment should not be equated with the lack of a culture concept.

TREASURE OF SIGNS

The very year for which Kroeber and Kluckhohn assert that there was no culture concept anywhere in existence is the year when the culture concept implicit in Locke's metaphysics was given its clearest and most enduring expression. This achievement, too long ignored by anthropologists, was the work of a twenty-five-year-old genius who later became one of France's most famous statesmen—Anne Robert

Jacques Turgot. It was in 1750 that Turgot conceived his *Plan for Two Discourses on Universal History,* a project that his duties as finance minister under Louis XV prevented him from completing, but which, even as a sketch, formulates several theories that are still essential to cultural anthropology. The subject matter of the universal history which Turgot planned corresponds precisely to what was in fact cultural anthropology's subject matter during the second half of the nineteenth century and to what perhaps has once again become its principal concern:

> Universal history embraces the consideration of the successive progress of humanity, and the detailed causes which have contributed to it: the earliest beginnings of man, the formation and mixture of nations; the origins and revolutions of government; the development of language; of morality, custom, arts and sciences; the revolutions which have brought about the succession of empires, nations, and religions [TURGOT 1844:627; orig. 1750].

This is followed by a statement that corresponds to one of the accepted modern definitions of culture:

> Possessor of a treasure of signs which he has the faculty of multiplying to infinity, he [man] is able to assure the retention of his acquired ideas, to communicate them to other men, and to transmit them to his successors as a constantly expanding heritage [*ibid.*].

At least two categories of definitions in Kroeber and Kluckhohn's compendium—"Emphasis on Social Heritage or Tradition" and "Emphasis on Symbols"—are clearly in debt to Turgot. Bronislaw Malinowski defined culture as follows: "This social heritage is the key concept of cultural anthropology. It is usually called culture" (KROEBER and KLUCKHOHN 1952:47). According to Leslie White, "The cultural category, or order, of phenomena is made up of certain events that are dependent upon a faculty peculiar to the human species, namely the ability to use symbols" (*ibid.*:69). Kroeber himself, in contrasting human with biological evolution, stressed the cumulative effects of culture or what Turgot calls a "constantly expanding heritage" (*cf.* KROEBER 1948a:5).

As in the case of Helvetius, the relationship of all these ideas to Locke is explicit in Turgot's explanation of how individuals come to display behavioral differences:

> A lucky arrangement of the fibers in the brain, a greater or lesser quickness of the blood, these are probably the only differences which nature establishes among men. Their spirits, or the power and capacity of their minds, display real inequality, the causes of

> which we shall never know and never be able to reason about. All the rest is the effect of education, and that education is the result of all our sense experience, of all the ideas we have been able to acquire from the cradle onward. All the objects which surround us contribute to that education; the instructions of our parents and teachers are only a small part of it [TURGOT 1844:645].

ENCULTURATION

It is clear that when "education" is equated with an individual's entire history of sense experience, a concept very similar to that of enculturation is being employed. This radical belief in the power of enculturation is one of the great themes of the Enlightenment. From it there issues the whole liberal as well as socialist tradition of class and racial democracy. One of its most important technical expressions is the doctrine of "psychic unity," the belief that in the study of sociocultural differences, hereditary (genetic) differences cancel each other out, leaving "experience" as the most significant variable. The origin of this doctrine has been associated quite erroneously with the writings of some of the mid- and late- nineteenth-century cultural evolutionists. Indeed, as I shall endeavor to show in subsequent chapters, the main nineteenth-century trend was to deny what the eighteenth century had established in this regard. As we shall see, the pristine fervor with which the idea of psychic unity was advanced by Turgot and his immediate successors, especially Helvetius, was not recaptured until the Boasian period. But by then, the consciousness of continuity with the Enlightenment had been thoroughly shattered. When Franz Boas wrote his *Mind of Primitive Man* in 1911, the only two eighteenth-century writers he deemed it relevant to mention were Boulainvilliers and Linnaeus, neither of whose ideas were especially representative of the Enlightenment (BOAS 1938c:19ff.). Yet, the following passage from Turgot would, except for style, serve as a summary of Boas' position:

> The primitive dispositions are equally active among barbarians and civilized peoples. They are probably the same in every place and time. Genius is spread throughout humankind somewhat like gold in a mine. The more ore you mine, the more metal you extract. The more men you have, the more great ones or ones fitting to become great. The chances of education and circumstances develop them or let them be buried in obscurity [TURGOT 1844:645].

One of the most intriguing by-products of Locke's environmentalism was the popular surmise that races of men might exist whose cultural exposure was so impoverished that they would be indistinguishable from animals. Jean Jacques Rousseau, in his *Discourse on the Origin and Foundation of Inequality among Men* (1751), implied that it was not beyond the power of education to accomplish the transition from ape to man. This possibility had its most ardent advocate in the Scotsman James Burnett, Lord Monboddo. In his *Of the Origin and Progress of Language* (1774), Monboddo argued that the great apes were really uncultured human beings. Monboddo's life-long belief that with proper conditioning apes could learn to talk, and his insistence that a race of men with tails would be found in Asia and Africa drew forth the scorn of many of his contemporaries (TINKER 1922:12ff.). Monboddo's flights of fancy, however, were grounded in a very solid appreciation of the power of enculturation and the plasticity and indefiniteness of human nature: the conviction that orangutans were wild men is merely an extreme instance of the popular faith in human perfectibility.

> It is . . . difficult to determine how far the natural capacities of the brutes may go with proper culture; but man, we know, may, by education and culture continued for many years, be transformed almost into an animal of another species. Thus with respect to his body, though he is undoubtedly by nature a terrestrial animal, yet he may be so accustomed to the water, as to become as perfectly amphibious as a seal or an otter.—And, with respect to the mind, it is impossible to say how far science and philosophy may carry it. The Stoics pretended, in that way, to make a *god* of a *man* [MONBODDO 1774:22-23].

ETHNOGRAPHY

As I have previously indicated, there is no compelling reason for insisting that the culture concept be made to include theories of psychic unity, dependence on learning, and extrasomatic heritage. Stripped of these factors, the culture concept comes down to behavior patterns associated with particular groups of peoples, that is, to "customs," or to a people's "way of life." In this sense, a *de facto* concept of culture is probably universal. Certainly, the practice of ethnography, the description of culture, is not dependent upon the theory that custom is a strictly extrasomatic heritage. It is doubtful that the great eighteenth-century Jesuit ethnographers, upon whom the *philosophes* were so dependent for their comparative information about primitive institutions, shared Locke's philosophy, despite their own educational mission and despite the papal dogma that the American Indian had a human soul and hence should be instructed in the sacraments. Nonetheless, it would be rather difficult to establish the point that these industrious ethnographers lacked a *de facto* notion of culture. For example, Martin Dobrizhoffer's *Account of the Abipones* is certainly not recommended for its secular scientism. Noting the diversity of Paraguayan languages, Dobrizhoffer comments:

> Truly admirable is their varied structure, of which no rational person can suppose these stupid savages to have been the architects and inventors. Led by this consideration, I have often affirmed that the variety and artful construction of languages should be reckoned amongst the other arguments to prove the existence of an eternal and omniscient God [1822, II:157].

Such views, however, did not prevent Dobrizhoffer from rendering a fairly accurate account of Abipone economy, material culture, wedding ceremonies, marriage, death and mourning ceremonies, warfare, and dozens of other standard ethnographic categories. The ethnographic coverage achieved by Joseph Lafitau in his influential account of the *Customs of American Savages Compared with Those of Earliest Times* (1724) should be considered in the same light. The table of contents of this book provides an interesting precedent for the universal pattern which Clark Wissler elaborated in 1926:

Lafitau's categories	*Wissler's categories*
Religion	Speech
Political government	Material traits
Marriage and education	Art
Occupations of men	Knowledge
Occupations of women	Religion
Warfare	Society
Commerce	Property
Games	Government
Death, burial, and mourning	War
Sickness and medicine	
Language	

The problem with Lafitau was not so much that he lacked a concept of culture, but that his view of American Indian cultural processes was completely trammeled by belief in the fall and the Biblical version of the dispersal of the tribes of Israel. This did not prevent him, as Sol Tax (1955b:445) has noted, from being the first European to describe a classificatory kinship terminology.

Probably the greatest ethnographer of the eighteenth century was the French scholar J. N. Demeunier. Although a stay-at-home himself, Demeunier rendered an invaluable service to his contemporaries by translating numerous ethnographic and travel reports. Demeunier and his works were widely cited before the close of the eighteenth century, but fell into an oblivion from which they were not rescued until Van Gennep found and bought *The Customs and Manners of*

Different Peoples (1776) on a Paris quai for a "ridiculous price" (VAN GENNEP 1910:23). Obscurity descended once again when Lowie neglected to mention Demeunier's name, much less accord him precedence as an ethnographer over C. Meiners. The latter's *Outline of the History of Mankind* (1785) is modeled after Turgot's and Voltaire's essays on "universal history" and contrasts sharply with Demeunier's essentially synchronic and ethnographic interests. Demeunier's working categories include: Food and Cookery, Women, Marriage, Birth and Education of Infants, Chiefs and Rulers, Distinction of Rank, Nobility, Warfare, Servitude and Slavery, Standards of Beauty, Modesty, Body Adornment and Disfigurement, Astrology, Magic, Society, Domestic Manners, Penal Codes, Trials, Punishment, Suicide, Homicide, Human Sacrifice, Sickness, Medicine, Death, Funerals, Sepulchres, and Burials. Dozens of non-European peoples are cited, including the Kalmucks, Mexicans, Ethiopians, Tartars, Hottentots, Tahitians, Ostyaks, Samoyeds, Auracanians, Yakuts, Tupinambás, Siamese, Chinese, Caribs, Dahomey, Jaggas, New Zealanders (Maori), Lapps, Maldive Islanders, Japanese, Kamchatkans, Gaunches (Canary Islanders), Omaguas, Moxes, Koryaks, Indian Fakirs, Illinois, Loango, Ambrym Islanders, Bukarians, Hurons, Iroquois, Javanese, Senegalese, Congo, Mandingo, Nayars, Tibetans, Mariana Islanders, Benin, Ceylonese, Natchez, Peruvians and Surinam Bush Negroes. Can one do this kind of comparative ethnography and not have a concept of culture? What Demeunier lacks, in company with other great ethnographers of his own and former times such as Herodotus, al Idrisi, Gabriel Soares de Souza, Cieza de Leon, Hans Staden, Bernal Dias, William Dampier, François Raynal, Cadwallader Colden, and François Xavier de Charlevois, is not a concept of culture, but rather the slightest clue as to how cultural differences might be scientifically explained. It was the philosopher Locke and his direct intellectual heirs, and not the ancient or modern ethnographers, who cleared the way to the scientific study of culture.

HUMAN BEHAVIOR AND NATURAL LAW

The possibility of creating a branch of learning that would do for human affairs what physics had done for inanimate nature—"discover" its laws—acted as a powerful stimulus upon the best minds of the Enlightenment. In its earliest stages, the search for this natural order was guided by Descartes's emphasis upon mathematico-deductive logic. In retrospect the results of Cartesian social science are scarcely more commendable than the medieval reckoning of the number of angels on a pinhead. But at least issues were joined and problems defined. Thus, Baruch Spinoza's attempt to apply Descartes's geometric method to human behavior has had no lasting influence upon the social sciences, but Spinoza's vision of nature, one and continuous, including man and his products, constituted a fundamental break with the past. Spinoza remarked in his *Ethics* (1632):

> Most writers on the emotions and on human conduct seem to be treating rather of matters outside nature than of natural phenomena following nature's general laws. They appear to conceive man to be situated in nature as a kingdom within a kingdom: for they believe that he disturbs rather than follows nature's order, that he has absolute control over his actions, and that he is determined solely by himself . . . [quoted in NAGEL 1948:272].

Spinoza flatly rejected such views:

> Nothing comes to pass in nature, which can be set down to a flaw therein; for nature is always the same, and everywhere one and the same in her efficacy and power of action; that is, nature's laws and ordinances, whereby all things come to pass and change from one form to another, are everywhere and always the same; so that there should be one and the same method of understanding the nature of all things whatsoever, namely, through nature's universal laws and rules [*ibid.*].

By "method of understanding," however, Spinoza meant the kind of Cartesian exercise which he had previously employed to furnish a geometric proof of God's existence. His science of man was to enjoy the same prospectus, as though human behavior were a matter of "lines, planes and solids" (*ibid.*).

More modern in its attitude toward sociocultural phenomena was the landmark magnum opus of Giambattista Vico: *The New Science* (1725). Vico specifically warned against "subjecting everything to the method of geometry" (GARDINER 1959:10). His new science was to be concerned with the empirical synchronic regularities of social life—"the perennial springs of the natural law of nations" (VICO 1948: 92; orig. 1725)—as well as with the regularities of history. This new "queen of the sciences" was in one of its two principal aspects "a history of human ideas, on which it seems the metaphysics of the human mind must proceed" (*ibid.*). The natural determinism, which Vico believed he had discovered, was so awe-inspiring that it required a divine providence to set it in motion; but once begun, history unfolded with unswerving regularity:

> The decisive sort of proof in our science is therefore this: that once these orders were established by divine providence, the course of the affairs of the nations had to be, must now be and will have to be such as our science demonstrates, even if infinite worlds were produced from time to time through eternity . . . [*ibid.*:92-93].

It is not for the mere notion of historical determinism that Vico and other eighteenth-century founders of social science command our attention. In Western theology, doctrines of national predestination are as old as the belief in a "chosen people," or a world running its downward course toward Armageddon and the second coming. The point is not merely that there is a direction or intelligibility to human history, but rather, that this orderliness is a consequence of natural rather than divine conditions. In actual practice, as we shall see, none of the eighteenth-century heralds of the "new science" was capable of sustained adherence to the emergent conception of undeviating orderliness. Throughout the period there runs a countercurrent that threatens to efface the mechanistic posture. This was the widely held belief that men in general at all times possessed the ability to change their social orders by exercising choice, rational or irrational, as the case might be. The paradox of a determined order in which the actors respond to unidentifiable causes, or willful inspirations, is beyond the capabilities of most of the *philosophes* to resolve. This difficulty helps to explain more precisely what Vico meant by his new science. It was Vico's belief that since man was the author of human history, he had a better chance of understanding cultural than physical events. "He believed that really to know the nature of something, it was necessary to have made it" (GARDINER 1959:10). Yet, paradoxically, the autonomous self-creativeness of man was to be reconciled with the fact that "law exists in nature" (VICO 1948:1).

A similar problem is evident in the work of Montesquieu, whose *The Spirit of Laws* (1748) is one of the most famous monuments of the age. In the preface, Montesquieu announces the orderliness he has discovered in the realm of sociocultural events:

> I have first of all considered mankind, and the result of my thoughts has been that amidst such an infinite diversity of laws and manners, they were not solely conducted by the caprice of fancy. I have laid down the first principles, and have found that the particular cases follow naturally from them; that the histories of all nations are only consequences of them; and that every particular law is connected with another law, or depends on some other of more general extent . . . [1949:lxvii; orig. 1748].

Montesquieu then proceeds to invoke material causative factors, most of which, as we shall see (p. 42), relate to climatic conditions. Nonetheless, neither his faith in universal law nor his essentially secular orientation prevents him from urging in effect that culture is, after all, inscrutable: "It is in the nature of human laws to be subject to all the accidents which can happen, and to vary in proportion as the will of man changes" (*ibid.*:58–59). The paradox of this position was expressed in Émile Durkheim's summary of Montesquieu's contribution to social science:

> He is convinced that this sphere of the universe is governed by laws, but his conception of them is confused. According to him, they do not tell us how the nature of a society gives rise to social institutions, but rather indicate the institutions that the nature of a society requires, as if their efficient cause were to be sought only in the will of the lawgiver [DURKHEIM 1960:63; orig. 1893].

Durkheim also correctly noted that since the time of Montesquieu "all social science has endeavored to dissipate this ambiguity." One can scarcely agree with Durkheim, however, that it was the nineteenth-century sociologist Auguste Comte who first "established that the laws of societies are no different from those governing the rest of nature" (*ibid.*). Moreover, Comte, whose faith in natural law was based on a dozen or more eighteenth-century predecessors, was no more successful in establishing the empirical vindication for such a belief, nor in resolving the paradox of cultural determinism and free will. Certainly, as we shall see, there were among Comte's contemporaries bolder approximations to the physicalist model.

The hesitancy with which eighteenth-century writers applied the Newtonian model to history is well illustrated in the work of Voltaire and Rousseau, two of the brightest luminaries of the age. Voltaire's *Essay on the Customs and Spirit of Nations* (1829; orig. 1745) is an important contribution to the development of modern historiography, especially in its attack on the then prevailing theological views of history. But Voltaire's fundamental orientation to the past is that time proclaims the omnipresence of stupidity. The author of the phantasmagoric travesty *Candide* (1759), despite his powerful influence in spreading the Newtonian gospel, did not take kindly to a science of culture. Similarly, Jean Jacques Rousseau, whose political doctrines were widely invoked by the Jacobins, contributed little, if anything, to the growth of this aspect of cultural theory. Rousseau's concern in *The Social Contract* (1762) with establishing the general or popular will as the legitimatizing force in political organization belongs, rather, with those romantic mystifications of history which replace the notion of natural law with unpredictable and ungovernable national or tribal collective souls. We shall meet again with this form of mystification in Chapter 8.

MATERIALIST MODELS

A fundamental influence in the expansion of the eighteenth century's natural-determinist outlook was exerted by J. O. de La Mettrie's *Man a Machine* (1748). La Mettrie was a practicing physician with medical experience. Thus, his concern with the man-machine idea had practical as well as philosophical motivation. Although Descartes's "animal machine" was an obvious forerunner, it is important to note that La Mettrie did not propose any comprehensive philosophical system, but, rather, that he regarded the man-machine as the best possible hypothesis to account for such recently discovered facts as the irritability of detached muscles and the peristalsis of the intestines (LA METTRIE 1912:129; orig. 1748). Experience and observation are the only guides he admits (*ibid.*:88). "The author of *L'Homme Machine* became the first to launch the medical sciences fatefully and creatively, as others had already done with mathematics, physics, and astronomy, onto the vast and brightly lit stage of Enlightenment thought" (VARTANIAN 1960:94). But it is as an argument for the continuity of man's behavioral capacities with those of infrahuman organisms and inert matter that the man-machine thesis made its mark upon the social sciences. The doctrine that "the transition from animal to man is not violent" (LA METTRIE 1912:103) is pregnant with consequences that are still unfolding in such fields as physiology, physical anthropology, and primatology. In the case of the social sciences, there is a well-charted path of intellectual awakening running from La Mettrie to D'Holbach and Diderot (*cf.* LANGE 1925, II:49ff.).

Perhaps the most uninhibited and systematic discussion of man's place in nature's determinate order came from the pen of Paul Henri Thiry, Baron d'Holbach. Written under the name of the dead academican M. Miraboud, and published under secret auspices, *The System of Nature, or The Laws of the Physical and Moral World* (1770) steadfastly embraced the full consequences of La Mettrie's materialism:

> Man is the work of nature; he exists within nature and is subject to nature's laws . . . [D'HOLBACH 1770, I:1]. There is neither accident nor chance in nature; in nature there is no effect without

> sufficient cause, and all causes act according to fixed laws . . . [*ibid.*:75]. Man is therefore not free for a single instant of his life . . . [*ibid.*:219].

Unlike La Mettrie, who was a deist and who simply did not think it was profitable to discuss the unknowable, D'Holbach intended to destroy every vestige of traditional religion, including prime movers, as well as souls, ghosts, and demons. "The universe," he declared, "consists of nothing but matter and motion" (*ibid.*:10). It is in this brusque abandonment of the skeptical mode that modern philosophical critiques of metaphysical materialism find most grist for their mill. For D'Holbach apparently accepted the forms in which the external world presents itself to human consciousness as ultimate reality. Matter was for him the literal universe of macro-objects; force the push-and-pull experience of human muscle.

As many twentieth-century philosophers of science have noted, modern physics itself is no longer committed to the kind of solidity which to philosophical materialists made matter seem more real than intangible thoughts. From the point of view of the social sciences, however, the literature of philosophical disputation concerned with proving the inadequacy of D'Holbach's metaphysical materialism is no more relevant than the somewhat lesser output concerned with preserving D'Holbach's metaphysical honor.

It would seem obvious that D'Holbach's materialism was intended to rid the scientific community of the debilitating effect of supernaturalism. That this is the only working assumption by which modern physical science proceeds remains as unassailable today as in the eighteenth century. That matter and energy are interchangeable is not expressed by a formula in which devils and angels constitute variables. Nor has the discovery that the orbits of individual electrons are unpredictable (in conformity with the Heisenberg principle) discouraged physicists from attempting to state the general determinate principles which govern all large samples of subatomic events. But I shall have more to say on this in subsequent chapters.

SOCIAL SCIENCE AND FREE WILL

The lingering disrepute of D'Holbach's uncompromising atheism still stands between him and a proper recognition of his influence upon behavioral science. In particular, the manner in which he avoided the paradox that Durkheim attributes to Montesquieu had an important effect on the theories of Marx. Since the behavior of the human organism is not exempted from the reign of universal law, it follows that the material influences impinging upon an individual, together with his innate physical character, are theoretically sufficient to account for his actions. What then accounts for the subjectively perceived impression of voluntary performance and choice? We do exercise choice, D'Holbach concedes; but it is a choice dictated by our wants and needs. Since we usually "want" what we choose, we experience the illusion of free choice. Actually, however, freedom is nothing more than the liberty to choose or act on behalf of wants that have been established by processes over which we have had no control (D'HOLBACH 1770:202ff.). The significance of this viewpoint for the development of the concept of culture has already been discussed. Here, let it suffice to say that most of the modern behavioral sciences have in large measure concerned themselves with untangling the conditions and processes which make an individual's or group's choice predictable, despite the apparent absence of material constraint in so much of what we do.

PREDICTABILITY

With the possible exception of D'Holbach and Helvetius (see pp. 43ff.) the *philosophes* invariably equated the orderliness of human history with the progressive perfection of mankind's rational decision-making policies. The expansion of science to include human affairs was, therefore, in itself the most important source of sociocultural change in the process by which humanity would eventually come to be endowed with "rational" social systems. According to some students of the Enlightenment, the consummate equation of natural law with right reason was achieved in Marquis de Condorcet's *Esquisse d'un Tableau Historique des Progrès de l'Esprit Humain* (*Outline of the Intellectual Progress of Mankind*) (1795). "No other volume produced in eighteenth-century France presents so faithfully the views of man and of the world held by the philosopher. Its attitude toward human society was inspired by the physics of Newton, in which the conception of uniform, universal, natural laws that governed the universe, was made to apply to social organization" (SHAPIRO 1934:259).

After sketching the advances achieved during the ninth epoch of world history, i.e., from the time of Descartes to the formation of the French Republic, Condorcet's faith in the uniformity of nature emboldens him to predict the main events of the next, or tenth, epoch. Why should it not be possible, he inquires, to foretell man's future? Since the only grounds for belief in the truth of the natural sciences is "that universal laws . . . which regulate the phenomena of the universe are necessary and constant" (CONDORCET 1822:262; orig. 1795), knowledge of the future should be as certain as that of the present and past: "If man is able to predict with almost complete certainty the phenomenon whose laws are known . . . why regard it as a chimerical enterprise to foretell the future destiny of the human species . . . ?" (*Ibid.*) There is a rather sad irony surrounding the circumstances under which Condorcet's *Outline*, called by Croce the "last will and testament" of the eighteenth century (SHAPIRO 1934:260), was composed. In 1793, Condorcet, urging lawfulness and moderation, stumbled into the crossfire between the anything but lawful and moderate leaders of the second phase of the French Revolution. Hunted by the Jacobins during the nine months of writing the *Outline*, he was finally caught in 1794 and died in jail, despite his stubborn faith in the power of reason to guide human behavior. He failed to see that Robespierre, who characterized Condorcet as a timid conspirator working "ceaselessly to darken the light of philosophy by means of the perfidious rubbish of his paid-for rhapsodies" (*ibid.*:97) was no less rational than he. Nature, at least, had sponsored both of them.

EARLY THEORIES OF SOCIOCULTURAL EVOLUTION

Evolution, taken to mean the change of one form into another, is a concept which few, if any, ideological traditions have failed to apply to sociocultural phenomena. That this understanding of evolution is the historically critical one in Western culture, despite its simplicity, is evidenced by the resistance with which the bare notion of biological transformation was greeted. The mere proposal that one biological species might have had its origin in another was regarded as a grave threat to Europe's traditional ideological order. This, however, was an oddity of the Judeo-Christian tradition. Nothing comparable occurred when theories were proposed concerning the transformation of institutions and customs.

Evolutionary doctrines were, after all, an essential part of the Biblical account of the origin of humanity. It will be recalled that according to the Old Testament, among the first men there was neither sex nor family nor economics, government, warfare, etc. Subsistence activities required practically no effort. This state of affairs was terminated by a foreign migration resulting in family life and onerous subsistence tasks. Economic specialization is announced shortly thereafter, with Cain the hunter and tiller of fields, and Abel the keeper of flocks. Then, the first crime occurred. This led, among Cain's descendants, to the development of urban life. Cities flourished until they were destroyed by a catastrophic flood. They sprang up again, however, with a high tower as safeguard against future inundations. This provoked a supernatural retribution, whereby the previous linguistic unity of the world was shattered, and men found themselves speaking mutually unintelligible languages. Polytheistic religions developed among the linguistically distinct tribes and nations. Later, monotheism was instituted among one of them by supernatural act. At the same time, new basic legal and moral principles were established.

Although the New Testament is not concerned with sociocultural evolution to the same extent, there is certainly no doctrinal negation of the possibility of fundamental changes in customs and institutions. In itself, the Christian Bible proclaims the orthodoxy of the notion that old religious patterns are subject to evolutionary change.

The novel contribution of the eighteenth century to historical perspective, therefore, cannot have been the mere notion of fundamental sociocultural change; much less was this the achievement of the nineteenth-century evolutionists. Rather, it was in the eighteenth century that a particular construal of the superorganic evolutionary process was achieved, which not only influenced all subsequent cultural evolutionary doctrines, but which also channeled the belated awakening in biology along special and quite inappropriate lines. The Enlightenment version of sociocultural evolution challenged the orthodox European outlook in two fundamental ways: The substance of the Biblical version of the origin of institutions, and the order in which they unfolded were systematically contradicted. Secondly, as I have already emphasized, the mechanisms responsible for sociocultural transformation were now regarded as purely natural expressions of cause and effect relations.

In effect, in the matter of sociocultural evolution, the Enlightenment merely restored an existing ancient doctrine to a position of intellectual respectability. Thus, all evolutionary thought during the Enlightenment betrays the influence of the great first-century-A.D. Roman materialist-poet-philosopher, Lucretius. In his *On the Nature of Things,* Lucretius, drawing upon still earlier evolutionary notions advanced by the Greek Epicurus, achieved a level of sociocultural and bio-evolutionary understanding that set him ahead of his times by at least eighteen centuries. For Lucretius' evolution was a cosmic process, responsible for the diversity of all levels of phenomena. A confluence of atoms formed the world. In the warm, damp soil of the young earth, vegetable life appeared. Later came the animals, including man. Spontaneous generation ceased and the earth no longer bore new life. Monstrous variations on existing forms appeared, but they did not survive. Early man started as a brute, hardier than modern man, larger-boned, stronger-sinewed, and less affected by climatic extremes. At first, men lived like beasts, without the plow and without iron tools with which to work the fields, plant, or cut down trees. These early men ate only what the sun and rain provided: they lacked clothing and built no permanent houses, but lived, instead, in caves and in brushwood shelters. Lacking the institution of marriage, they followed a career of sexual promiscuity. But their lot was not a happy one, for food was scarce and many died of hunger. Lucretius sought the beginnings of human speech in animal communication. Although he was unable to solve the problem (no one ever has), he surmised that language could not have been the invention of one man, but must, rather, have been the result of a long evolutionary process (LUCRETIUS 1910:197–215).

UNIVERSAL HISTORY

Enlightenment evolutionary reconstructions were concerned with a wide variety of evolutionary change. Voltaire's *Essay on the Customs and Spirit of Nations* (1745), for example, emphasized the development of Christianity in Europe, including the growth of the clergy and the origin of the Sacraments, the development of European feudal systems, and the growth of the French and English parliaments. Edward Gibbon's *Decline and Fall of the Roman Empire* (1776–78) also represents a mature product of this new approach to institutional history. Vico, on the other hand, was concerned more with recurring sociocultural transformations. Following precedents in Herodotus, he postulated that each nation evolves through three stages: the ages of the gods, heroes, and men—ages distinguished by the characteristic relationship between man and the supernatural and somewhat resembling Comte's theological, metaphysical, and positivist phases. Thus, "the first men among the gentiles, simple and crude, and under the powerful spell of most vigorous imaginations encumbered with frightful superstitions, actually believed they saw the gods on earth." As a result of the uniformity of ideas, "the Orientals, Egyptians, Greeks and Latins, each in ignorance of the others, afterwards raised the gods to the planets and the heroes to the fixed stars"; i.e., their religions made the supernatural increasingly more remote (VICO 1948:4).

Turgot's *Universal History* is an example of Lucretian evolutionary thought which provides many striking precedents from nineteenth- and twentieth-century formulations. According to Turgot, mankind had evolved through the stages of hunting, pastoralism, and farming.

> [The hunters,] without provisions, and in the middle of the forest, are only able to occupy themselves with subsistence. The foods which the earth produces without agriculture are very meagre; it is necessary to resort to hunting animals; the latter within a given area are very sparse and unable to supply nourishment for many men; as a result, the dispersal and diffusion of peoples is accelerated . . . families or nations are very far removed from each other because each requires a vast space to nourish itself—that is the state of the hunters. They have no fixed point of abode and they move about with extreme facility from one place to another. The difficulty of living; a quarrel; fear of an enemy is sufficient to separate the families of hunters from the rest of their nation [1844:629].

It is interesting to note the resemblance between Turgot's description of the hunting stage and Julian Steward's (1955:122–23) ecological interpretation of the patrilineal band, especially in view of the latter's insistence upon a rather sharp distinction between "universal" evolutionist and "multilinear" evolutionist approaches (see p. 642). It is clear that Turgot, with a universal stage in mind, nonetheless foreshadows Steward's ecological orientation:

> They follow where the hunt leads them, without fixed destination. If the hunt takes them in a given direction they continue to get further apart. It is this which accounts for the fact that peoples who speak the same languages are sometimes found separated by distances of over six hundred leagues, and are surrounded by people who don't understand them. This is common among the American savages, where one finds, for the same reason, nations of 15 to 20 men [TURGOT 1844:629].

Wherever there are domesticable species, men gradually find it more advantageous to gather animals into herds than to chase after them:

> The life of the pastoralist is before long introduced everywhere these animals are found; [but] the life of the hunting peoples is preserved in the parts of America where these species are absent.

> Only in Peru, where nature has provided a species of sheep called llamas, is pastoralism found. This is probably the reason why that part of America was more readily civilized [*ibid.*].

Evidently, Turgot's evolutionism also embraced a fairly modern notion of the relationship between economic surplus and social stratification: "Pastoral people, with their subsistence more abundant and secure, are more populous. They become more familiar with the spirit of property" (*ibid.*). This tendency is increased in the agricultural stage: "The earth was able to sustain many more men than were required to till it. Hence, to a greater extent than among pastoral peoples, men were free for other work: hence towns, commerce . . . a greater ability in war; the division of labor, the inequality of men, domestic slavery and precise ideas of government" (*ibid.*:631).

EVOLUTIONARY STAGES

A generation of anthropologists in the United States has been brought up to believe that the division of cultural history into the stages of savagery, barbarism, and civilization was the ill-advised late-nineteenth-century accomplishment of Lewis Henry Morgan. But this trisection had already been performed by Montesquieu who noted: "There is this difference between savage and barbarous nations: the former are dispersed clans, which . . . cannot be joined in a body; and the latter are commonly small nations, capable of being united. The savages are generally hunters; the barbarians are herdsmen and shepherds" (1949:176). In Turgot's writing, the hunting, pastoral, and agricultural phases are still more prominent, and a culmination of this trend occurred with the publication in 1767 of Adam Ferguson's *An Essay on the History of Civil Society.* Drawing upon Charlevoix, Colden, Lafitau, Dampier, Wafer, and classical Greek and Roman sources, Ferguson sought to improve upon the conjectural reconstructions of man's primeval "state of nature." Like Montesquieu, Ferguson was well aware of the dangers of ethnocentric distortions in accounts of primitive peoples:

> Our method . . . too frequently, is to rest the whole on conjecture; to impute every advantage of our nature to those arts which we ourselves possess; and to imagine, that a mere negation of all our virtues is a sufficient description of man in his original state. We are ourselves the supposed standards of politeness and civilization; and where our own features do not appear, we apprehend, that there is nothing which deserves to be known . . . [1819:138; orig. 1767].

Ferguson, unlike many of his contemporaries, refused to regard the savage either as a simpleton or a superman. He possessed a true anthropological vision in that he saw the primitive as a whole human being:

> Who would, from mere conjecture, suppose, that the naked savage would be a coxcomb and a gamester? That he would be proud or vain, without the distinction of title or fortune? And that his principal care would be to adorn his person, and to find an amusement . . . that he would thus share in our vices, and, in the midst of the forest, vie with the follies that are practised in the town . . . that he would likewise . . . excell us in talents and virtues; that he would have a penetration, a force of imagination and elocution, an ardour of mind, an affection and courage, which the arts, the discipline, and the policy of few nations would be able to improve. Yet these particulars are a part in the description which is delivered by those who have had opportunities of seeing mankind in their rudest condition [*ibid.*:138-39].

Ferguson, perhaps more clearly than any of his predecessors, correctly surmised the essential features of primitive economic and social organizations. Moreover, with greater certainty than Morgan, he correlated the principal evolutionary stages with economic and social organization and the "means of subsistence" (*ibid.*:175)—a phrase widely in use long before Marx made it unfashionable. Among the people of the world there are those who

> entrust their subsistence chiefly to hunting, fishing, or the natural produce of the soil. They have little attention to property, and scarcely any beginnings of subordination or government. Others, having possessed themselves of herbs, and depending for their provision on pasture, know what it is to be poor and rich. They know the relations of patron and client, of servant and master, and by the measures of fortune determine their station. This distinction must create a material difference of character, and may furnish two separate heads, under which to consider the history of mankind in their rudest state; that of the savage, who is not yet acquainted with property; and that of the barbarian, to whom it is, although not ascertained by laws, a principal object of care and desire [*ibid.*:149].

Ferguson, unlike many modern critics of the concept of primitive communism, did not confuse the communal ownership of strategic resources among hunters and gatherers with complete absence of private property. Arms, utensils, and clothing are not shared communally. Erroneously, however, he equated matrilineality and matrilocality with this most primitive stage. But his phrasing of the political characteristics of low-energy hunters and incipient farmers is remarkably modern:

> They have in fact no degree of subordination different from the distribution of function which follows the differences of age, talents, and dispositions. Personal qualities give an ascendant in the midst of occasions which require their exertion; but in times of relaxation, leave no vestige of power or prerogative. [*ibid.*:153].

Ferguson also saw, although only in barest outline, that the transition from primitive to state-organized social systems involved fundamental changes in the role of the family and kinship. Thus, prior to the formation of the state, among savages and barbarians, "Families, like so many separate tribes, are subject to no inspection or government from abroad; whatever passes at home, even bloodshed and murder, are only supposed to concern themselves" (*ibid.*:156).

EVOLUTION OF SOCIAL ORGANIZATION

Ferguson's analysis of the evolution of social organization was surpassed with the publication in 1771 of John Millar's *Observations Concerning the Distinction of Ranks in Society*. Millar attempted to trace the evolution of the family, including sex relations and marriage forms, as well as the development of class differences and political systems. This great Scottish jurist-philosopher was probably the first social scientist to stress the economic and educational (enculturative) functions of the family, over against sexual passions and romantic love: "The Savage is seldom or never determined to marry from the particular inclinations of sex; but commonly enters into that connection when he arrives at an age, and finds himself in circumstances which render the acquisition of a family expedient or necessary, in order to his comfortable subsistence" (MILLAR 1771:7). He notes the prevalence of premarital sexual license among primitives and properly emphasizes the frequent harsh punishment for postmarital infidelity (*ibid.*:10). He also identifies and discusses a surprisingly wide spectrum of primitive kinship and marital institutions, including wife-lending, polygyny, polyandry, brideprice, and matrilineality. In most of his interpretations and postulations of sequence, Millar is, in retrospect, quite wrong. He advances the incorrect opinion that the more primitive the group, the more degraded the women are in relation to men. From this there follows the further error, that brideprice is an expression of female servitude. Matrilineality is said to arise from the weakness of marital bonds (*ibid.*:30). Polyandry is supposed to result when women in matrilineal systems become powerful through having many sons, and these females then indulge their passions by retaining a number of male concubines. Millar's picture of the primitive father's relations with his children is also severely distorted. The father is presented as a callous, emotionally detached tyrant, and old men are erroneously reported as universally feared and respected. Just as the increasingly greater leisure made possible by improved means of subsistence supposedly leads to a softening of the relation between the sexes, so too the life and death powers of father over children are gradually relinquished (*ibid.*:102). More compatible with modern theories is Millar's contention that the advent of commerce and a heightened division of labor promoted the geographical mobility of the sons and thereby reduced their subordination to the patriarch. Like Turgot and Ferguson, Millar emphasized the lack of permanent extrafamilial centers of authority among hunting peoples, and more explicitly than his predecessors, he associated the beginning of political control with the accumulation of wealth and the establishment of hereditary private property during the agricultural and pastoral stages. As the amount of wealth increases the communal systems of production and distribution become unwieldy:

> They grow weary of acting in concert with each other, by which they are subject to continual disputes concerning the distribution and management of their common property; while everyone is desirous of employing his labor for his own advantage, and of having a separate possession, which he may enjoy according to his inclination. Thus, by a sort of tacit agreement, the different families of a village are led to cultivate their lands apart from each other . . . [*ibid.*:135].

Among the peoples with communal ownership, cultivated lands "fall of course under the management of the chief, who superintends their labor, and assumes the privilege of distributing the produce among the several members of the community" (*ibid.*:135–36). Millar, in other words, had come to an understanding of the relationship between social stratification and what we today call "redistribution" (see p. 313). Millar further suggests in effect that when private holdings develop, the power of the redistributor-chief is augmented by his ability to deprive individuals of access to strategic resources. Gradually, this power attracts to itself a religious aura, culminating in the deification of the god-king ruler (*ibid.*:140–41). Millar also went beyond his predecessors in grasping the essence of the relationship between kinship and the rise of the state:

> . . . the distinctions of families were soon extinguished and forgotten. The power of the chiefs, or nobility, which depended upon the attachment of their respective clans, was therefore quickly destroyed; and the monarch, who remained at the head of the nation without a rival to counterbalance his influence, had no difficulty in extending his authority over the whole of his dominions [*ibid.*:164].

Millar viewed feudalism as a recurrent political system, associated with the process by which smaller social units are linked together into larger communities. He expected to "find something of the same kind in every extensive kingdom that is formed by the association of many different tribes or families" and cites as examples the Congo, Loango, Benin, Angola, Laos, and Siam (*ibid.*:174–77).

Perhaps the most brilliant part of Millar's book is the last chapter in which the origin of servitude and slavery is discussed. His remarks on the relationship between slavery and the liberal creed of the English colonists are reserved for the final section of this chapter. In general, let it be said that Millar saw slavery as an ancient institution which was gradually modified and eliminated in Europe by the discovery that wage labor and cash rents are more lucrative institutions. His explanation of the absence of slavery among the most primitive societies is repeated by Hobhouse, Wheeler, and Ginsberg (1915) and remains essentially unchallenged today:

> There are indeed but few slaves among the greater part of the savages of America; because from the situation of that people, they have no opportunity of accumulating wealth for maintaining any number of servants. As, in ordinary cases, they find it burdensome to give subsistence to an enemy whom they have subdued, they are accustomed to indulge their natural ferocity by putting him to death, even in cold blood. If ever they behave with more humanity to their captives, it is when they have been greatly reduced by war, or by uncommon accidents; and as this rarely happens, the persons whose lives have been thus preserved, are not distinguished from the children of the family into which they are brought; but are formally adopted into the place of the deceased relations whose loss they are intended to supply [MILLAR 1771:198-99].

METHODOLOGY OF EVOLUTIONISM

Reference to one additional figure in the great Scottish Enlightenment, whose contribution to the rise of anthropological theory has only recently been pointed out, must suffice. We are indebted to E. Adamson Hoebel (1960:648) for the recognition that William

Robertson's *History of America* (1777) is "a significant landmark in the development of cultural anthropology." Robertson's evolutionary typology went from "savagery" to "barbarism" to "civilization," the evidence for this sequence being derived from both ethnology and archaeology. His presentation of an archaeological justification for this sequence does much to refute Hodgen's (1964:505ff.) charge that the Scottish historians had nothing to go on but logic and that they were all equally guilty of the vice of "speculative history":

> It is only by tradition, or by digging up some rude instruments of our forefathers, that we learn that mankind were originally unacquainted with the use of metals, and endeavored to supply the want of them by employing flints, shells, bones, and other hard substances, for the same purposes which metals serve among polished nations. Nature completes the formation of some metals. Gold, silver, and copper . . . were accordingly the first metals known, and first applied to use [quoted in HOEBEL 1960:649].

As we shall see in Chapter 6, further archaeological vindication of the eighteenth century's evolutionary hypotheses played a crucial role in establishing the so-called comparative method as the basic strategy of the nineteenth-century anthropologists. Ignorance of this aspect of anthropological research may account for Hodgen's (1964:511) astounding claim that when the concept of an evolutionary hierarchy entered "into the work of social scientists in the nineteenth and twentieth centuries, it lost none of its scholastic, philosophical, or conjectural characteristics."

Robertson's evolutionary views are also distinguished by a remarkably advanced discussion of the conditions under which cultural similarities in different parts of the world could be treated as evidence of independent evolution as opposed to some form of convergence or survival through diffusion or migration. In general, Robertson believed that similarities found on different continents argued for independent invention and parallel evolution:

> The character and occupations of the hunter in America must be little different from those of an Asiatic, who depends for subsistence on the chase. A tribe of savages on the banks of the Danube must nearly resemble one upon the plain washed by the Mississippi. Instead then of presuming from this similarity, that there is any affinity between them, we should only conclude, that the disposition and manners of men are formed by their situation, and arise from the state of society in which they live [*ibid.*:652].

But this rule cannot be applied where the traits in question do not reflect widespread determinate processes. Thus, provision must be made for "customs which, as they do not flow from any natural want or desire peculiar to their situation, may be denominated usages of arbitrary institution" (*ibid.*:652–53). The best way to account for such "arbitrary" or, as we might say today, "nonadaptive" traits, when they occur in widely dispersed areas, is to suppose, argued Robertson, that they resulted from previous contact.

No summary of Enlightenment evolutionary thought would be complete without mention of Condorcet's ten-stage scheme as included in the *Outline of the Intellectual Progress of Mankind* (orig. 1795). Although this work is regarded by many as an outstanding contribution to the literature of the social sciences (*cf.* SHAPIRO 1934:262), its method and content present little of specifically anthropological interest. Of the ten stages that Condorcet describes, the first three, during which mankind passes from tribal to pastoral to agricultural society, up to the invention of the alphabet, are precisely the ones that least interest him. In Condorcet's perspective, the more remote the age, the duller the mind, the less enlightened is man's social life. For the *Outline* is above all an intellectual history, concerned with the emancipation of man's reason from the shackles of superstition and ignorance. It exhibits none of the portents of sociological analysis which distinguish Ferguson's and Millar's work. Beyond the invention of the alphabet, Condorcet's "stages" become increasingly ethnocentric and confined to European history as follows:

- 4th The progress of the human mind in Greece up to the division of the sciences about the time of Alexander the Great.
- 5th The progress of the sciences from their division to their decline.
- 6th The decadence of knowledge to the restoration about the time of the Crusades.
- 7th The early progress of science from its revival in the West to the invention of printing.
- 8th From the invention of printing to the time when philosophy and the sciences shook off the yoke of authority.
- 9th From Descartes to the foundation of the French Republic.

This work, nonetheless, remains an important landmark in the social sciences. It will long be remembered for its role in provoking Malthus to write his *An Essay on the Principle of Population* (1798) and, hence, for its indirect effect upon Spencer and Darwin (see Chap. 4). The *Outline* is also justifiably regarded as the Enlightenment's culminating attempt to interpret sociocultural evolution in terms of increments in the rational content of thoughts, customs, and institutions. As such, its idealism is unmitigated; and, as we shall see in a moment, its notion of sociocultural causality, inadequate.

CONFOUNDING EVOLUTION WITH PROGRESS

The word evolution is rarely employed in the writings of the philosophers and their contemporaries. Yet, it is beyond dispute that it is sociocultural evolution that is the main subject of their historical concern. According to Peter Gay (1964:24), "Voltaire's histories are histories of the 'mind' of an age; they portray a network of institutions in which political forms, social ambitions, artistic productions, and foreign policy all act upon one another and are, collectively and separately, more important than details of battles, court intrigues, or the history of the Chosen People." This special kind of history is history in evolutionary perspective. Voltaire himself said that he wanted by his history to "know what were the steps by which men passed from barbarism to civilization" (as quoted in BUCKLE 1857:736). Indeed, so powerful is the evolutionary mode during the Enlightenment that the interest in fundamental sociocultural transformation threatens on occasion to violate the sanctuary into which biological thought had retreated. By 1774 the great compiler of the *Encyclopédie*, Denis Diderot, had begun to speculate that "the vegetable kingdom might well be and have been the first source of the animal kingdom, and have had its own source in the mineral kingdom; and the latter have originated from universal heterogeneous matter" (DIDEROT 1875-79, IX:265). The Enlightenment philosopher Immanuel Kant noted "the agreement of so many genera of animals in a common scheme which appears to be fundamental not only in the structure of their bodies but also in the disposition of their remaining parts . . . " (quoted in FOTHERGILL 1952:56). Kant proposed that "this analogy of forms, which with all their differences seem to have been produced according to a common original type, strengthen our suspicions of an actual relationship between them in their production from a common parent . . ." (*ibid.*) Kant's views on organic evolution were also subscribed to by Goethe. As Darwin himself came to appreciate, the eighteenth century ended with a veritable burst of evolutionary proposals: "It is rather a singular instance of the manner in which similar views arise at about the same time, that Goethe in Germany, Dr. Darwin, in England [Erasmus Darwin, Charles's grandfather] and Geoffroy Saint-Hilaire . . . in France, came to the same conclusion on the origin of species in the years 1794-5" (DARWIN 1958:18). With the first of Lamarck's publications in 1801, the consequences of the general evolutionary outlook irresistibly swept biological thought along toward its great nineteenth-century synthesis. But by that time, the notion of organic transformation had long since become hopelessly infected with the virus of "progress." Neither organic nor superorganic evolutionist formulations have yet recovered fully from this childhood affliction.

The word progress is an essential element in the vocabulary of the Enlightenment. It was employed by the *philosophes* to convey a sense of moral satisfaction with certain evolutionary trends. Thus, the emergence of representative parliaments was widely regarded as a progressive change; similarly, for Condorcet, Newton's laws represent a stage in the progress of the mind. On the other hand, the burning of Rousseau's books and the expansion of slave-systems in the New World were not examples of progress.

When presented in its most sophisticated form, the decision that a particular change is progressive requires two steps. First, a judgment must be rendered as to whether or not the change had modified the form in question in a particular direction as established by quantitative or qualitative measures. Thus, any change whose direction is defined, by whatever arbitrary criteria, is potentially a progressive change. Consider, for example, the changes involved in continental glaciations. As the glaciers retreat, the earth may be regarded as exhibiting progress toward a tropical climate; or with no less justification, the very same retreat may be regarded as a retrogression away from an arctic climate. By the same token, it is altogether a matter of no scientific consequence for us to describe the recent evolution of American agriculture as progress toward corporate monopolies or retrogression away from small family units. From a scientific point of view nothing is added or subtracted by calling a particular trend progressive or retrogressive. What counts is an adequate description and correct understanding of the direction of the change as defined by intersubjectively valid criteria. It is equally superfluous for us to decide that a particular instance of progress merits our moral or aesthetic endorsement. Usually, of course, progress is already cryptically identified with conditions which go from bad to better in terms of a cultural or idiosyncratic value system. Thus large farms usually represent progress only to those who approve of their social consequences, and this certainly was the way in which the term was used in its Enlightenment milieu. That is, not only was a direction of change specified, but progress in that direction was regarded as valuable and emotionally gratifying. The risk incurred through this dispensable procedure was that frequently enough there was a neglect of the first step, whereby the direction of change was only vaguely defined; the second step was then taken without loss of enthusiasm, and the result was a purely idiosyncratic expression of approval or disapproval for a particular historical event. Thus, the prevailing criterion of progress during the Enlightenment was change in the direction of greater rationality. The latter was a fairly serviceable measure of change, as long as one stuck to the evolution of physical or astronomical theory, but it was hopelessly vague when it came to judgments about institutions. Was the league of the Iroquois or the French Republic the more rational political system? Condorcet was convinced the French Revolution had produced the world's most rational and hence most progressive social order; but this judgment was not more (or should one say, not less?) than the ethnocentric prejudice of a revolutionary partisan. In the nineteenth century, as we shall see, reasonability ceased to be the measure of progressive change. Instead, with Marx, Spencer, and Darwin progress became somewhat less vague, centering, respectively, around the notions of the advance toward the communist millennium, organizational complexity, and efficiency in the struggle for survival. But the partisan involvement of these value judgments remained undiminished. Neither Spencer nor Darwin, two of the last century's greatest minds, could rise to the understanding of the fact that the moral order they perceived in history was the moral order that their society and not their science required them to see. Marx alone rendered his judgments of progress in full awareness of their culture-bound (class-bound) origins. But this made him, if anything, even more determined to uphold "progressive" change, and indeed, to fight for it.

EIGHTEENTH-CENTURY THEORIES OF SOCIOCULTURAL CAUSALITY

It was a conviction common to all of the advanced social philosophers of the Enlightenment that in a more or less remote past the world's peoples had enjoyed a social life which by its general simplicity and by the absence of certain specific institutions, such as private ownership of land, centralized government, sharp class differences, and priest-directed religions, contrasted markedly with Europe's modern social order. This early phase in cultural evolution was referred to as the "state of nature." Although considerable difference existed as to the specific characterization of this primitive condition, ranging from Hobbes's "war of all against all" to Rousseau's "noble savage," the explanation of how some men had terminated the state of nature and arrived at their present customs and institutions was approached in a fairly uniform fashion. In general it was accepted that the grand mover of history and the prime cause of continuing differences in manners and customs was variation in the effectiveness of ratiocination. Civilized man was supposed to have literally thought himself out of the state of nature by steadily inventing more and more clever and reasonable institutions, customs, and subsistence processes. It is on this account that the title of Condorcet's sketch contains the word *l'esprit,* which is translated as intellect or mind—*Outline of the Intellectual Progress of Mankind*—and that Voltaire had made it his objective to "know the history of the human mind" (quoted in BUCKLE 1857:736). From whence derives the unwarranted ease with which freshmen in college survey courses are taught to roll off phrases about the "mind of modern man" or the "mind of Europe."

THE FALLACY OF CULTURAL IDEALISM

A few preliminary comments concerning the problems that an emphasis upon "mind" and "reason" present to the theory-building endeavors of cultural anthropology are needed at this point. Let us agree that scientific explanations are statements of the conditions under which predicted or retrodicted events will occur. To explain sociocultural differences and similarities exclusively in terms of more or less reasonable thought and action is to omit any statement of conditions. In the view of many eighteenth-century social philosophers, the explanation of why the Iroquois did not behave like Frenchmen was the Indians' self-imposed failure to think their way far enough out of the state of nature. But under what conditions will a group think themselves into bilaterality rather than matrilineality, monogamy rather than polygamy, private property rather than communal ownership, etc.? Unless such conditions are specified, appeal to the effects of rational inventiveness serve merely to obscure an enduring ignorance of scientifically admissible explanations. Thus, to Immanuel Kant, the revolutionary times through which he was living were characterized by "man's emergence from his self-imposed nonage." All that was necessary for Europe's Enlightenment to modify social life radically was for the public to be given the freedom to think: "indeed, if it [the public] is only given freedom, enlightenment is almost inevitable. There will always be a few independent thinkers, even among the self-appointed guardians of the multitude. Once such men have thrown off the yoke of nonage, they will spread about them the spirit of a reasonable appreciation of man's value and of his duty to think for himself" (KANT 1946:1071-72).

The fatal potentialities of this approach are realized as soon as an attempt is made to explain customs which because they are totally unfamiliar appear to be totally irrational. It is like the case of the American psychiatrist of my acquaintance who asked his interpreter what a mental patient in a Bahian hospital had just said: "Nothing, doctor, it's too stupid to repeat," was the answer. That was precisely the quandary of Demeunier. For a brief moment, this great ethnographer stood, a hundred years before his time, on the threshold of the study of totemism. It was reported in many accounts that men believe they have animals as ancestors. But how can one take such ideas seriously? "It is not necessary to examine how some men and even whole nations are able to believe that they are descended from certain animals. . . . It is clear that this is nonsense, and one is not able to give a reason for nonsense" (DEMEUNIER 1776, II:105).

The approach to sociocultural differences through the unfolding of man's reasoning potential is best understood as a special variety of nondeterministic idealism. It should be noted once again for comparison with future developments, that for Condorcet, Voltaire, and Montesquieu it is rational human *mental* choice that directs history. As a consequence men are free to shape their social world any way they see fit. Why, then, is Condorcet able to predict the content of his tenth epoch? Because men tend eventually to choose what is more rational, or at least, that was what the *philosophes* hoped would happen. For as Peter Gay has pointed out, the notion that the Age of the Enlightenment preached the inevitability of progress is a myth:

> Locke, Montesquieu, Hume, Diderot had no theory of progress; Rousseau's thought stressed the fact of man's retrogression and the hope for man's regeneration; Voltaire saw human history as a long string of miseries broken by four happy ages. Only Kant, with his speculative world history, Turgot with his five stages, and Condorcet with his ten epochs, may be said to have held a theory of progress, and these three thinkers stood not at the center but at the bright end of the spectrum of enlightenment thought [1964:270-71].

It is obvious that the optimism so often erroneously attributed to the Enlightenment could only have been a sort of whistling in the dark. Unable to state the conditions under which men would opt for "progress," for peace over war, intelligence against superstition, democracy over tyranny, they could only hope for "progress" bereft of the deterministic comfort that Hegel, Marx, and the Social Darwinists later gave themselves. In this context, Malthus with his emphasis on the uncontrollable sexuality of human populations seems not atypical of the Enlightenment. If history proved anything about the exercise of the power of rational free choice, it was that man tended to make a fool of himself (at least in the Enlightenment's frame of reference) quite as often as not. This then was the grand paradox of the times: law governed the universe, determining the smallest motion of the least grain of sand, but men need not necessarily believe this to be true, and even if they do, they are free to ignore its consequences. On the other hand, no age which insisted that man was a part of nature and that nature was governed by immutable law could totally abandon history to the vagaries of the human will.

GEOGRAPHICAL DETERMINISM

There are many crosscurrents of material causation stirred up by the Enlightenment, some of which lead directly to the first full-scale material-determinist theories of sociocultural evolution. One of the best elaborated of the determinist positions is that of the influence of geographical conditions on sociocultural life. Theories of geographical causation were of course first advanced long before the Enlightenment. Hippocrates' treatise *On Airs, Waters, and Places* was regarded as an authoritative work well into the seventeenth century. Polybius, the Greek historian, asserted that "we mortals have an irresistible tendency to yield to climatic influences; and to this cause, and no other, may be traced the great distinctions that prevail among us in character, physical formation, complexion, as well as in most of our habits . . ." (quoted in F. THOMAS 1925:34). Among the Romans, the architect Marcus Vitruvius Pollio contributed one of the most extensive discussions, including such tidbits as, "Southern peoples have a keen intelligence, owing to the rarity of the atmosphere and the heat, while northern nations, being enveloped in a dense atmosphere, and chilled by moisture from the obstructing air, have but a sluggish intelligence" (*ibid.*:35). Eighteenth-century notions of geographical determinism were also indebted to the work of Arab geographers such as the twelfth-century al Idrisi and the fourteenth-century Ibn Khaldun. The latter believed that the inhabitants of the warm climates have passionate natures while those of the colder climates are stolid and lack vivacity. These contrasts arise from the differential effect of heat upon the animal spirits (*ibid.*:46). Much of the influence of these early sources was transmitted to the Enlightenment through the efforts of the sixteenth-century French political philosopher Jean Bodin. Working on the theory that for northerners the dominant life fluid was phlegm, while for southerners it was black bile, Bodin tried to explain why northern peoples were faithful, loyal to government, cruel, and sexually uninterested, and why southern peoples were malicious, crafty, wise, expert in science but ill-adapted to political activity (*ibid.*:52). Similar problems occupied John Arbuthnot, whose *An Essay Concerning the Effects of the Air on Human Bodies* (1733) was evidently an important source for Montesquieu's *The Spirit of Laws* (1748). Arbuthnot believed that languages as well as national temperaments were subject to climatological influences. Northern peoples have languages that abound in consonants because they are afraid to open their mouths and let in the cold air, while tropical peoples, who need the extra ventilation, specialize in vowels. The most sustained Enlightenment elaboration of geographical determinism was the contribution of Montesquieu. Northern peoples tend to be brave, vigorous, insensitive to pain, weakly sexed, intelligent and drunkards; southern peoples are the opposite. Since the women of warm countries mature early, they are much younger than their husbands and hence less wise; this gives them an inferior status, which, occurring together with a preponderance of female births and the cheapness of tropical living, stimulates the development of polygyny (THOMAS 1925:68).

But this point of view was not without its critics. Helvetius, as we shall see, derided Montesquieu's theories while D'Holbach would also have none of them: "Can it be claimed that the sun which once shone on the freedom loving Greeks or Romans is today shedding different rays upon their degenerate descendants?" (D'HOLBACH 1774, III:6). Yet it would be rather pointless to refute the determinism Montesquieu attributes to geographical factors. Neither *The Spirit of Laws* nor any of its antecedents amounts to a self-consistent exposition of cultural causation. Montesquieu's approach was essentially concerned with how legislators ought to adjust their laws to the condition of climate and soil. In company with all his contemporaries, Montesquieu was not capable of rising to a genuinely superorganic view of history. In the final analysis, the human social order was the product of actors who might or might not consent to what natural law suggested was the rational arrangement of a particular time and place. Ultimately it would be the will and sense of the legislator that would decide the course of history.

ON THE THRESHOLD OF CULTURAL MATERIALISM

The great luminaries of the eighteenth century struggled toward the concepts which unlock the secrets of superorganic causality only to be beaten back by their own implacable dedication to the power of individual rational choice. Turgot, elaborating his conception of universal history, urges us on to unveil the influence of general, necessary, and particular causes, but he cannot avoid adding at the same time, "and of the actions of great men" (1844:627). He believed: "One is forced to admit that if Corneille . . . had been brought up in a village and spent his life behind a plow, and that if Racine had been born in Canada among the Hurons or in Europe in the eleventh century, they would never have displayed their genius." But he also implies that if Newton had died at fifteen, or if Columbus had died in his youth, the transformations of the Enlightenment and of the age of discovery would have been substantially altered (*ibid.*:45–46).

The inability of the Enlightenment to generate a system of superorganic causality is especially striking in the case of D'Holbach, whose programmatic statements on behalf of materialist determinism have already been cited. In his *Système de la Nature*, D'Holbach argues in typical Enlightenment fashion that man is a product of his enculturation experience. "We are born without our consent, our ideas come to us involuntarily, our customs are controlled by those who stipulate them to us" (1770, I:202). And again in the *Système Social:* "It is in education that we should seek for the chief sources of the passions and virtues in man, of the errors or truths which fill his head, of the habits praiseworthy or demanding of censure . . ." (1774, I:15). But how does this social environment arise? D'Holbach's sociological imagination can only struggle back to another point on the treadmill: Human beings, individually and collectively, make decisions, and their decisions create institutions which constitute the cultural environment. G. V. Plekhanov's description of the circularity of this argument cannot be improved:

> Man is the product of social environment. The character of this environment is, by hypothesis, determined by the action of the "government." The actions of the government, for example legislative activity, belong to the sphere of conscious human activity. This conscious activity in its turn, depends on the "opinions" of the persons acting. . . . Unnoticed one of the sides of the antinomy has turned into its opposite. The difficulty is evidently set

> aside and the "philosopher" continues his "investigations" with quiet conscience. . . . The apparent solution of the antinomy is simply a complete break with materialism. The human brain, that "soft wax" which assumes different forms under the influence of impressions coming from the social environment, is finally transformed into the creator of this environment to which it was obliged for its impressions [1934:73-74].

D'Holbach's approach to superorganic causality was surpassed by his great contemporary Claude Helvetius. This frequently maligned figure ranks high among those who came closest to elaborating a set of principles capable of breaking through the mind-culture-mind tautology. Helvetius starts from the assumption that all customs and morality are ultimately the expression of physical sensations and the needs of hunger, thirst, and other bodily requirements. These physical drives establish in man characteristic interests, first of all ego-centered, but inevitably expanding to embrace social groupings by which the maximum pleasures and minimum pains per individual are guaranteed. The only significant variables affecting these interests which Helvetius admits are those resulting from experience. Although Helvetius does not categorically deny the possibility of inborn inequalities, he insists, in effect, that it is from education that all significant interpersonal differences arise. Not again until the twentieth century is there such a sustained and uncompromising denial of racial and hereditary influence upon individuals and societies. "The race theory of human history, the idea that different social classes correspond to different ability levels biologically transmitted forms the opposite extreme to the thoughts of Helvetius" (GROSSMAN 1926:172). Having mounted the sociocultural treadmill, Helvetius proceeds to kick away one of the previously most favored escape ladders—geography. Montesquieu does not fare well in *De l'Esprit:*

> If the different temperature of climates had such an influence on the need and its capacities, how comes it that the Romans so magnanimous, so brave, under a republican government, are now so dastardly and effeminate? How comes it that the Greeks and Romans, who were formerly so worthy of esteem for their wit and virtue, and were the admiration of the earth, are now dwindled into contempt? How comes it that those Asiatics, so brave under the name of Elamites, were so cowardly and base in the time of Alexander, under that of Persians; and yet under the name of Parthians became the terror of Rome, and that in an age when the Romans had lost none of their courage and discipline. How comes it that the Spartans, the most brave and virtuous of the Greeks, while they were religious observers of the laws of Lycurgus,

> lost their reputation for both, when, after the Peloponnesian war, they suffered gold and luxury to be introduced among them? . . . How comes it that the Jews, so often defeated by their enemies shewed under the conduct of the Maccabees a courage worthy of the most warlike nation? How comes it that the arts and sciences have been by turns cultivated and neglected by different nations, and have successively run through almost all climates? . . .
>
> Why did philosophy pass from Greece into Hesperia, from Hesperia to Constantinople and Arabia? and why, repassing Arabia into Italy, has it found an asylum in France, England, and even in the north of Europe? Why do we no longer find a Phocion at Athens, a Pelopidas at Thebes, and a Decius at Rome? The temperature of these climates is not changed [HELVETIUS 1810: 340-41].

Helvetius goes on to argue in a similar fashion against the geographical interpretation of the conquest of southern Europeans by northerners, and the apathy of Asiatic people before their despotic rulers (1810:350ff.). He does not skirt the question which must inevitably follow: What then is the cause of these changes in the arts, sciences, courage, virtue, and customs? His general answer is that we must look to "moral" causes; i.e., in modern terms, to sociocultural causes. Very good. Our appetite is whetted, but what precisely are these sociocultural causes? We are not destined to be satisfied. On Asiatic tyranny, for example, the solution offered is so peculiar in its inspiration that it deserves to be quoted in full:

> After having in vain exhausted physical causes for the foundation of the eastern despotism, it is proper to have recourse to moral causes, and consequently to history. This informs us that the nations, by becoming civilized, insensibly lost their courage, their virtue and even their love of liberty; that every society, immediately after its institution, according to the different circumstances in which it was placed, marched with a slower or more rapid pace towards slavery. Now the southern nations, being the first assembled in society, must consequently have been the first subject to despotic power; because to this every species of government tends, and it is a form which every state preserves till its entire destruction.
>
> But, say those who believe the world more ancient than we do, how does it happen that there are still republics upon earth? To this it may be replied, that if all societies, by being civilized, tend to despotism, all despotic power tends to depopulation. The climates subject to this power, after a certain number of ages becoming uncultivated and depopulated, are changed into deserts;

> the plains in which were cities of immense extent, or where sumptuous edifices were raised, became by little and little covered with forests, in which some families took refuge, who insensibly formed new nations of savages; and this succession must constantly preserve republics upon earth.
>
> I shall only add to what I have just said, that if the people of the south have been longer slaves, and if the nations of Europe, except the Muscovites, may be considered as free, it is because these nations have been more lately polished: because, in the time of Tacitus, the Germans and Gauls were still no more than a kind of savages, and that, unless a nation be at once driven to slavery by force of arms, this will not be accomplished till after a long succession of ages, and by insensible but continued attempts made by tyrants to extinguish in the hearts of their subjects that virtuous love which all mankind naturally have for liberty, and thus to debase the mind, so far as to make it bow to oppression and slavery [*ibid.*:351-52].

This strange sort of cyclical evolutionism does not, of course, explain why all nations should march implacably toward slavery. Elsewhere, in the explanation of why the age of Greek science has passed, Helvetius falls back into the familiar idealist circle:

> It is because the form of their government is changed; like water which assumes the shape of all the vessels into which it is poured, the character of nations is susceptible of all forms, and in every country the genius of the government constitutes the genius of the nation [*ibid.*:353].

(See p. 456 below for Helvetius' devastating and currently relevant critique of national character theories.)

Finally, the "government," vague to begin with, expands to fill the entire social universe:

> The inequality observable among men, therefore, depends on the government under which they live; on the greater or less happiness of the age in which they are born; on education; on their desire of improvement, and on the importance of the ideas that are the subject of their contemplations [*ibid.*:361].

In this fashion, the material "interests" surmised by Helvetius to lie at the root of sociocultural differences forever escape concrete formulation. Material interests become instead concrete desires; desires are specific products of the mind; the mind shapes its products through legislation, and we are back again to the central dilemma. The spectacle of Helvetius struggling against the limitations of his own culture is again depicted in a striking fashion by Plekhanov:

> The insuperable influence of government is a kind of *impasse* from which it is only possible to emerge by means of a miracle, that is by means of a government which shall suddenly decide to cure all the ills which it has brought on itself or which have been inflicted by previous governments [1934:160].

The irony of this recurrent retreat to cultural idealism is that several important fragments of cultural-materialist theory were already being employed with enduring results. Indeed, most of the essential ingredients of a cultural-materialist strategy were embodied in widely accepted proposals concerning the relationship between subsistence and social structure. Turgot, it will be recalled, subscribed to what may fairly be called an early version of a techno-environmental theory of social stratification. A similar kind of causal approach had even been ventured upon by Montesquieu when he noted:

> The people of Siberia cannot live in bodies, because they are unable to find subsistence; the Tartars may live in bodies for some time, because their herds and flocks may for a time be reassembled. [Among noncultivators,] people wander and disperse themselves in pasture grounds and forests. Marriage cannot there have the security it has amongst us, where it is fixed by habitation, and where the wife continues in one house; they may then more easily change their wives, possess many, and sometimes mix indifferently like brutes [1949:176–77].

The same theme was also touched on by Ferguson:

> A hoard, collected from the simple productions of nature, or a herd of cattle, are, in every rude nation, the first species of wealth. The circumstances of the soil, and the climate, determine whether the inhabitant shall apply himself chiefly to agriculture or pasture; whether he shall fix his residence, or be moving continually about with all his possessions [1819:177].

And Helvetius is no stranger to the idea. Indeed, in the case of the custom of killing off aged parents, Helvetius's method of explanation provides a tantalizingly clear demonstration of how a general solution to the problem of sociocultural differences and similarities might be achieved. It is not legislation out of a cloud which established the custom; rather, the custom results from the interaction between a social group, its subsistence equipment, and its natural habitat. To give the accepted modern formulation, perfectly anticipated by Helvetius, low-energy hunting societies frequently cannot support nonfood producers other than those destined to replace the adult generation:

> This is the cause of this disgusting custom; for this reason a nomad people which is kept by its hunting and lack of means of existence for six months in a year in impassable forests, sees itself, as it were, forced to this barbarity; in this way parent-murder in these countries arises out of, and is carried out on, the basis of the same principles of humanity which cause us to shudder at the perpetrators [HELVETIUS, quoted in PLEKHANOV 1934:141].

Here then were the specific "interests," spelled out not by mind in a vacuum, but by the whole human organism pitted against an array of natural forces which would admit only a limited spectrum of individual and social responses. But neither Montesquieu, Turgot, Ferguson, nor Helvetius really grasped the potentialities of this approach; instead, it appeared as one element among many, in a puzzle whose full dimensions had not yet dawned upon the consciousness of the times.

MILLAR'S CONTRIBUTION

There was, however, at least one tour de force achieved during the eighteenth century which in practice consistently employed the principles of techno-economic analysis. The work in question, previously mentioned, was John Millar's *Observations Concerning the Distinction of Ranks in Society* (1771). Millar's statement of the surplus theory is similar to that of his contemporaries:

> A savage who earns his food by hunting and fishing, or by gathering the spontaneous fruits of the earth, is incapable of attaining any considerable refinement in his pleasure. He finds so much difficulty and is exposed to so many hardships, in procuring the necessaries, that he has no leisure or encouragement to aim at the luxuries and conveniences of life. His wants are few, and in proportion to the narrowness of his circumstances. His great object is to be able to satisfy his hunger; and, after the utmost exertion of labour and activity, to enjoy the agreeable relief of idleness and repose [1771:2].

From differences in productive mode, Millar deduces not only differences in settlement pattern, degree of social stratification, and nature of political organization—all of which are sporadically treated in a similar fashion by one or another of his contemporaries—but he also goes on to handle family form, marriage patterns, sexuality, and patterns of labor utilization in an almost completely consistent fashion. As I have previously suggested, Millar's achievement in treating the development of slavery is particularly impressive. With the possible exception of Helvetius, the Enlightenment social philosophers tended to regard slavery as the outcome of depraved minds wallowing in a sea of irrational decisions. Millar, however, never loses sight of the material, social, and individual rewards and disadvantages which attend different labor systems under different techno-economic conditions. Millar implicitly appears to subscribe less than any of his contemporaries to the notion that "rational" decisions always result in institutions that are sanctioned by traditional European norms. It is implicit on every hand that the order in history arises from material and bodily conditions rather than from mental exercise:

> It is difficult to ascertain the degree of authority which, from the principles of justice and humanity, we are, in any situation, permitted to assume over our fellow creatures. But the fact admits of no question, that people have commonly been disposed to use their power in such a manner as appears most conducive to their interest, and most agreeable to their predominant passions. It is natural to suppose that the master would set no bounds to his prerogative over those unhappy persons who, from their circumstances, were under the necessity of yielding an implicit obedience to his commands. He forced them to labor as much, and gave them as little in return for it as possible [MILLAR 1771:196].

Millar accepts the possibility that "prejudices" and "the blind prepossession which is commonly acquired in favor of ancient usages" might prevent the abolition of slavery even "during the successive improvements of society in knowledge, arts, and manufacture" (1771:205-6), but he rejects the possibility that it was the advent of Christianity which brought an end to slavery in Europe. Instead of resorting to this common ideological *deus ex machina*, he attempts to trace, step by step, how slaves were replaced by serfs and serfs by rent-paying peasants, always in conformity with the previously discussed principle that the masters, lords, landlords, and employers never abandon their intent to get the maximum return for the least outlay:

> Thus, by degrees, the ancient villenage came to be entirely abolished. The peasants, who cultivated their farms at their own charges, and at their own hazard, were of course emancipated from the authority of their master, and could no longer be regarded as in the condition of servants. Their personal subjection was at an end. It was of no consequence to the landlord how they conducted themselves; and, provided they punctually paid his rent, nothing farther could be required of them. There was no reason to insist that they should remain in the farm longer than they pleased; for the profits it afforded made them, commonly,

> not more willing to leave it than the proprietor to put them away. When agriculture became so beneficial a trade, when the state of those who followed that profession was so much improved, no person had any difficulty to procure a sufficient number of tenants to labour his estate. It was, on the contrary, sometimes difficult for the farmer to obtain land sufficient for the exercise of his employment; and, after he had been at pains to improve the soil, he was in danger of being dispossessed by the proprietor, before he was indemnified for the trouble and expence which he had sustained [*ibid.*:220-21].

Millar also correctly drew attention to the special relationship between slavery and what we would today call "gang labor." He appreciated the fact that only certain kinds of productive tasks could employ a labor force that was obliged to work essentially without reward. Thus, the closest approximation to slavery in eighteenth-century Scotland was found at the coal and salt mines:

> In coal-work, as the different workmen are collected in one place, instead of being scattered, like the ordinary peasants, over an extensive territory, they were capable of being put under the care of an overseer, who might compel them to labour; and the master did not so immediately feel the necessity of resigning that authority over them with which he was invested [*ibid.*:230].

Millar was thus able correctly to identify (if somewhat sarcastically) one of the fundamental ecological bases of Negro slavery in the New World:

> It merits particular attention, that the chief circumstance which contributed to procure freedom to the slaves in Europe, had no place in our American plantations. From the manner of working the mines, a number of slaves are usually collected together and may therefore be placed under the command of a single person, who has it in his power to superintend their behaviour, and to punish their negligence. The same observation is applicable to the planting of sugar, and to the other occupations in our colonies, in which the negroes perform the same sort of work which in Europe is commonly performed by cattle, and in which, of consequence, many servants are kept upon the same plantation. As the slaves are continually under the lash of their master, he has not been forced to use the disagreeable expedient of rewarding their labour, and of improving their condition by those means which were found so necessary, and which were employed with so much emolument to encourage the industry of the peasants in Europe [MILLAR 1771 in W. C. LEHMANN 1960:315].

As long as the Enlightenment theoreticians stressed the factor of conscious rational choice as the key to the explanation of sociocultural differences, they remained cut off from genuine understanding of the systemic and adaptive nature of social organization. They could only see a collection of individuals more or less successfully controlling their passions under the halting influence of reason. They could not see a superorganic system interacting with the natural environment and responding with adaptive evolutionary transformations, which were neither comprehended nor consciously selected by the individual members of the society. Glimpses of such superorganicity are found here and there throughout the century. Ferguson, for one, had a perfectly clear conception of its importance:

> Like the winds that come we know not whence, and blow withersoever they list, the forms of society are derived from an obscure and distant origin; they arise long before the date of philosophy, from the instincts, not from the speculations of men. The crowd of mankind are directed in their establishments and measures, by the circumstances in which they are placed. . . . Every step and every movement of the multitude, even in what are termed enlightened ages, are made with equal blindness to the future; and nations stumble upon establishments which are indeed the result of human action, but not the execution of any human design. If Cromwell said, that a man never mounts higher than when he knows not whither he is going; it may with more reason be affirmed of communities, that they admit of the greatest revolutions where no change is intended, and that the most refined politicians do not always know whither they are leading the state by their projects [1819:222-23].

But Ferguson, whose faith in rational political solutions is nowhere exceeded among his contemporaries, scarcely maintained this point of view throughout his writings. Millar's efforts, on the other hand, bring forth specific instances of how the expressed intentions of men are seldom adequate guides to their ultimate performance. *Observations* concludes with a devastating critique of slavery in the English colonies which were just then beginning to send out their first cries for independence based on liberty and natural rights. In Millar's final paragraph there are lessons which since have been rediscovered as many times as they have been buried:

> . . . it offers a curious spectacle to observe, that the same people who talk in so high a strain of political liberty, and who consider the privilege of imposing their own taxes as one of the inalienable rights of mankind, should make no scruple of reducing a great

> proportion of the inhabitants into circumstances by which they are not only deprived of property, but almost of every right whatsoever. Fortune perhaps never produced a situation more calculated to ridicule a grave and even a liberal hypothesis, or to show how little the conduct of men is at bottom directed by any philosophical principles [1771:241-42].

It is thus possible to discern, scattered here and there in the writings of the eighteenth century, implicit in one instance, explicit in others, ordinarily strewn at random, among contrary and self-defeating convictions, but occasionally as part of a clear and definite system, the raw materials, the conceptual tools, and the first faltering practical experiences with the scientific explanation of sociocultural phenomena.

Reaction and Recovery: The Early Nineteenth Century

3

The French Revolution, the Napoleonic wars, the political restorations ushered in by the Congress of Vienna, and the rapid expansion of industrial manufacture and international trade did not crystallize any single line of approach to sociocultural studies. Although the political aftermath of the French Revolution was the occasion for a resurgence of some ideas which the *philosophes* thought had been permanently laughed out of educated discourse, the trend toward a natural-science approach to history and sociocultural differences was in no danger of being extinguished. Continuing advances in the applied physical and chemical sciences, vital to warfare, industry, and commerce, insured safe passage for the nascent social sciences through reactionary intervals. Moreover, the European bourgeoisie, which came increasingly to dominate political life in Europe, had not been so frightened by the radical phases of the French Revolution as to accept a full-scale return to the theological doctrines of the *ancien régime*. There is no doubt, however, that fear of the urban mobs committed influential segments of the bourgeoisie to the discouragement of materialistic interpretations of history.

The Napoleonic wars and their immediate aftermath slowed, but did not halt, the movement toward a science of man. During the first quarter of the century, the balance shifted against the heritage of the *philosophes*; but in the second quarter, scientism rallied, gathered new strengths, and prepared for the decisive battles of the Darwinian era. While religious revivalism, political conservatism, and romantic nationalism all tended to undermine the foundations of the nascent social sciences, these were offset by the advances in physics, chemistry, and engineering, which enhanced the economic importance and prestige of the scientific method.

In the perpetuation of the scientific approach, the theory of *laissez-faire* must be accorded an important role. It was early in this period that Jeremy Bentham, James Mill, David Ricardo, and John McCulloch worked out the classical principles of natural, self-regulating economic systems. Paradoxically, while serving as the scientific ideology of industrial capitalism, classical economic theory provided the basis and inspiration for socialist and communist attempts at social science. Thus, John Stuart Mill as well as Marx and Engels reared their interpretations of sociocultural phenomena on this common foundation. At the same time, the antiscientific forces found it increasingly difficult to contain the advances in biological and geological knowledge within the limits of the Judeo-Christian eschatology. As we shall see in subsequent chapters, the religious opposition to a science of man was shortly to be routed by the combined forces of Darwinian biology and Spencerian sociology.

The triumphs of Darwinism and Spencerism do not relieve us of the necessity of noting the special nature of the challenge embodied in the post-Napoleonic period of political and religious reaction. When the specifically anthropological expression of the science of man comes to be formulated by Edward Tylor, Lewis Henry Morgan, John Lubbock, and John McLennan, the frame of reference most vital to their arguments assumes the prior existence of the views of such reactionaries as Louis De Bonald, Joseph de Maistre, Richard Whately, and W. Cooke Taylor. This background is essential if we are to understand the special meaning associated with the distinction between early nineteenth-century theories of "degenerationism" and later nineteenth-century theories of evolutionism. Degenerationism—the belief that all contemporary primitives are descended from peoples who enjoyed civilization prior to the construction of the Tower of Babel—was, in its multifarious expressions, little more than an attempt to preserve the authority of Biblical history. It was not, in any strict sense, antievolutionary. That is, it did not deny for the cultural domain the transformation of types so vehemently opposed in biology. When the later nineteenth-century "evolutionists" argued for evolutionism, their rather vapid notions of a movement from simple to complex forms acquired intellectual significance only in relation to the prevailing Judeo-Christian ideology. In the context of the times, to assert that there had been a general movement from savagery to civilization was to avow that the Biblical account of the origin of institutions was wrong and that history could be understood without calling upon God as an active historical agent. It was this issue and not evolutionism per se which dominated the century.

THE THEOLOGICAL REACTION

The political reaction to the Napoleonic wars was especially favorable to the temporary resurgence of theological interpretations of history. Intense missionization abroad was accompanied by fundamentalist and pietistic revivalism at home. In England there was the "Christian Evidences" movement founded by William Paley, which aggressively sought to restore faith on the basis of the "argument from design" (i.e., the wonders of nature could have been made only by a Creative Intelligence). Later, in the 1830's, there was the "Oxford Movement," whose most famous member, John Henry Newman, urged the return of Anglicanism to Catholicism on the grounds that "Outside of the Catholic Church all things tend to atheism" (quoted in H. E. BARNES 1965, II:859). In France, comparable reassertions of orthodoxy were led by François René de Chateaubriand, who urged that it was more valuable to preserve the mysterious than to achieve enlightenment.

Some of those who won prominence as spokesmen of the theistic resurgence sought to discredit the total scientific-philosophical contribution of the previous four centuries. The influential Savoy count, Joseph de Maistre, for example, attacked the Enlightenment in every aspect, down to its Lockean foundations. Declaring the attempt to discover the origin of ideas "an enormous ridiculousness," he accused John Locke of being the enemy of all moral authority. "By his coarse system, Locke has unchained materialism" (quoted in MAZLISH 1955: 214).

De Maistre's know-nothing antiscientism sought to return to the pre-Lockean emphasis upon absolute knowledge imparted by unreasonable and unknowable processes. The directing hand of God works in all things: ". . . truth, whose name men pronounce so boldly, is nothing else, at least for us, than that which appears true to the conscience of the greatest number of people . . ." (*ibid.*:77). Science, the brazen upstart, corruptor of truth, ought to be put back in the place it had occupied during Medieval times:

> If we do not return to the old maxims, if education is not restored into the hands of the priests, and if science is not everywhere placed in the second rank, the evils which await us are incalculable: we shall become brutalized by science, and this is the lowest degree of brutality [*ibid.*:199].

De Maistre insisted that there was no disorder in the universe, since everything happened according to God's plan. God was not, however, incapable of miracles, and these happened frequently enough (and at the convenience of the observer) to suspend for all practical purposes belief in the watchmaker model. The "most perfidious temptation" of the human mind is "that of believing in invariable laws of nature" (*ibid.*:173). In the realm of sociocultural events, miracles were the order of the day. Indeed, De Maistre's explanation of the French Revolution itself is that it was a miracle caused by God's desire to punish and regenerate man. "It is because of the fall, owing to his evil nature, that man must suffer wars, famine, and earthquakes; the Revolution is of the same character as these other visitations" (*ibid.*:79). Belief in the fall opposed itself, of course, to the previous century's doctrine of a universal evolutionary sequence running from savagery to civilization. For De Maistre, there was no greater error than the postulation of this sequence: "We always start from the banal hypothesis that man has raised himself gradually from barbarism to knowledge and civilization. This is the favorite dream, the mother-error . . . of our century" (*ibid.*:90). Although De Maistre urges that "the moral order has its laws as well as the physical, and the investigation of these laws is altogether worthy of occupying the meditations of a true philosopher" (*ibid.*:196), it is clear that the overwhelming drift of his thought is toward the suppression of genuine social science.

The antiscientism of the counterrevolutionary social philosophers was not always as evident as in the case of De Maistre. In the writings of De Maistre's fellow royalist, Louis De Bonald, much lip service is paid to the importance of proper reasoning in sociocultural matters and to the need for a science of society. But De Bonald is not free of animistic flights whenever science might threaten to dislodge a Biblical prejudice. Thus, in his *Philosophical Reflections on the First Objects of Moral Understanding* (1826), De Bonald pursues at great length and with some erudition the question of the origin of language, only to conclude, along with Martin Dobrizhoffer (see p. 17) that God alone must have invented words and grammar—not only spoken language, but written language as well: "It is thus philosophically and morally impossible for man to have invented the art of speaking or the art of writing" (DE BONALD 1826:283). Both De Maistre and De Bonald devoted themselves to linking up a people's language with immutable national character and historical destiny. Their emphasis upon the mystical maturation of each nation's language, laws, and customs under the guidance of providence was echoed in the Romantic nationalism of Johann Gottlieb Fichte and Georg W. F. Hegel. The fundamentally antiscientific and obscurantist roots of all of these doctrines is perhaps best communicated by reference to De Bonald's ultimate political vindication, when in 1827 he became State Censor in the government of Charles X.

It has been inadequately appreciated that the extremist ideological counterattack represented by De Maistre and De Bonald was properly speaking antirational and antiscientific, but not antievolutionist, as far as cultural evolution is concerned. By their insistence upon the essential accuracy of the Biblical account of the origin and transformation of institutions, these reactionary figures were promulgating cultural evolutionary doctrines. Despite his opposition to the "banal hypothesis" that man had raised himself from barbarism to civilization, De Bonald was perfectly well acquainted with the evolutionary transformations that had occurred in the classical, medieval, and modern worlds. On the other hand, biological transformism, as presented by Jean Baptiste Lamarck, is for De Bonald and his counterrevolutionary colleagues, anathema, "a monstrous hypothesis":

> They have imagined myriads of centuries during which man . . . could have been born from the slime of the earth, warmed by the rays of the sun, at first imperceptibly animalcule, then insect, fish, biped or quadruped, finally man; and in this hypothesis it was as easy to make man the inventor of his language as to make the sun creator of man [MAZLISH 1955:199].

The companion heresy in the superorganic realm is not that cultural forms have evolved, one from the other, but rather that they have originated, endured, and/or changed without the design and intervention of members of the Judeo-Christian pantheon. As in the previous century, this heresy was promulgated principally by cultural idealists, who ranged from atheists to deists and pantheists. The immediate enemies of De Bonald and De Maistre were thus not Marx and Engels, but rather all those who had acquired from the Enlightenment the belief that human history was the *natural* product and embodiment of man's mental and spiritual life.

The theological issue of degeneration versus evolution should also not be confused with the question of progress and perfectibility. Nothing prevented the defenders of orthodox theology from viewing history as an unfolding of successively more perfect moral and physical states. After the "fall," in other words, humanity was seen as struggling to regain the perfection it had once possessed. W. Cooke Taylor's *Natural History of Society* (1840, II:341), a degenerationist milestone, was strongly devoted to the Enlightenment principle that "a capacity for improvement was the essential characteristic of man." Yet Taylor, under the inspiration of Richard Whately, the Archbishop of Dublin, insisted upon a literal sequence of fall, flood, Babel, and diaspora. Some groups thereafter degenerated into savagery, but others, aided by God, progressed toward new heights of civilization. Taylor's views are summarized in the following passage:

> We have seen that no savage nation ever emerged from barbarism by its own unaided exertions; and that the natural tendency of tribes in such a condition is to grow worse instead of better. Civilization could not have been an invention, for the inventive faculty proceeds from something already known. . . .
>
> This account of the origin of man, and of civilization, to which we have attained, by a long course of reasoning, is precisely that which is contained in the oldest book existing—the Book of Genesis. "God created man in his own image,"—gave him "dominion over the fish of the sea, and over the fowl of the air, and over every living thing that creepeth on the earth,"—and "he put him into the garden of Eden to dress it and to keep it,"—and "he saw that it was not good for man to be alone." Here we have it clearly stated, that man, instead of being placed upon the earth a helpless, untutored savage, was gifted with intelligence,—was taught the nature of the different beings by which he was surrounded,—was instructed in agriculture, one of the most important arts of life,—and was declared to be formed for society. To the truth of this statement, all the traditions of ancient nations, and all the investigations of modern science, bear concurrent testimony; they not only confirm the statement, but they deprive all other theories of the merit even of plausibility [*ibid.*, I:309-10].

In Archbishop Whately's own formulation of the issues, there is no mistaking the connection between degenerationism and the defense of Biblical authority:

> Divine instruction is proved to be necessary, not merely for an end which *we think desirable,* or which *we think* agreeable to Divine wisdom and goodness, but for an end which *we know has been attained.* That man could not have *made* himself, is appealed to as a proof of the agency of a Divine *Creator;* and that mankind could not in the first instance have civilized themselves, is a proof exactly of the same kind and of equal strength, of the agency of a Divine *Instructor* [quoted in TAYLOR 1840, I:329].

THE POSITIVIST COMPROMISE

Nineteenth-century anthropological theory was to become deeply involved in the rebuttal of this theological position. What was at stake in Whately's advice that "man could not have made himself" was really nothing less than the possibility of a science of man (*cf.* CHILDE 1951b). The reaffirmation of this possibility took shape under the tutelage of different philosophical and epistemological assumptions, many of which, from the standpoint of modern social science, constitute no great improvement over Whately's or De Maistre's bibliology. Most of the rebuttals exhibited evident signs of compromise with the regnant religious and political ideological establishments. The element of compromise was clearest and most debilitating in the case of the philosophical and cultural idealists—Claude Henri Saint-Simon, Auguste Comte, and Georg W. F. Hegel; others, like John S. Mill, Adolphe Quételet, and Henry Thomas Buckle, approached the physicalist model of science with less embarrassment; finally, but reserved for discussion in later chapters, are the radical expressions of scientism embodied in the works of Spencer and Marx.

The curious twisting effects of the intellectual reaction to the French Revolution and the Napoleonic wars are prominently displayed in the works of Claude Henri Saint-Simon and his one-time secretary and collaborator, Auguste Comte. While their scientific inspiration was clearly pre-Revolutionary, their major concern seems to have been to avoid being identified with political subversion. To prove themselves harmless, they adopted eccentricities of behavior and thought that greatly diminish their stature relative both to the Enlightenment and to many of their actual or near contemporaries. Like a score of Enlightenment predecessors, Saint-Simon and Comte argued for the creation of a new "science of man," which was to embrace human affairs with the objectivity that had won notable success in the inorganic and organic realms. In Saint-Simon's version, this new science was conceived as a branch of physiology and hence was called "social physiology" (MARKHAM 1952:xxi). It was Saint-Simon's hope that eventually a unifying principle, such as gravity, would be found applicable to all of the sciences. Comte, on the other hand, envisioned what he called, in the first volume of his *Cours de Philosophie Positive,* "social physics," a discipline which presupposed the existence of all the inorganic and organic sciences, but which could not be reduced to the terms or principles of any of them. When Adolphe Quételet began in 1835 to use the phrase "social physics," Comte, who was addicted to slogans, felt obliged to change the name of the new science to "sociology" (COMTE 1830–42, IV:7*n*). The innovation was not made until the appearance of the fourth volume of *Cours de Philosophie Positive* (*ibid.*:252*n*). This terminological quirk earned for him the reputation of being the "founder of sociology," a distinction which, if not more appropriate for any number of more original predecessors, is certainly better reserved for Quételet, and his quantified treatment of European institutions, to which we shall return in a moment.

Saint-Simon called his approach to phenomena "positive" to distinguish it from the critical or nonconstructive modes of thought he attributed to the *philosophes* (*cf.* MARCUSE 1960:327). Saint-Simon's "positivism" represents a phase of human intellectual growth that follows upon the previous polytheistic and theistic periods. In Comte's elaboration of Saint-Simon's program, positivism is defined as the dedication to the discovery of the "invariable relations among phenomena" as distinct from the search for causes (COMTE 1830–42, I:14). Preoccupation with unknowable causes was the principal defect of the earlier theological and metaphysical stages of intellectual evolution. It was Comte's belief that not only was he the first to suggest this intellectual series, but that it was universally valid, the most important of all sociological laws:

> I believe I have discovered a great fundamental law. This law is that each of our principle conceptions, each branch of our knowledge, passes through three different theoretical states: the theological or fictive state; the metaphysical or abstract; the scientific or positive state [*ibid.*].

Despite the fact that, as Émile Durkheim once observed, "the idea, the word, and even the outline of positivist philosophy are all found in Saint-Simon" (DURKHEIM 1962:142), Comte attempted to suppress all evidence of the influence exerted upon him by his master and went so far as to call him "a depraved charlatan" (MARKHAM 1952: xxxiii). Eccentricities of a messianic cast marred the contributions of both Saint-Simon and Comte, rendering neither of them very palatable as scientific paragons. Saint-Simon declared: "I am convinced that I am fulfilling a divine mission," and after his death his pronouncements on the need for a new ethically oriented religion in which scientists and artists were to be the priests actually led to the establishment of communistically oriented cults in France, with "missions" in England, Germany, and Belgium. Comte, who was initially disdainful of pandering to human emotions, underwent a conversion during a love affair, to emerge finally in his *Politique Positive* (1851-54), as the "pope" of positivism.

In his *Philosophie Positive,* Comte promised his readers that the empirical evidence for the great law he had discovered would be elaborated in subsequent publications. After his conversion, however, Comte had no time for such trifles. When *Politique Positive* was published, it contained none of the promised documentation; instead, Comte referred the reader back to the earlier volumes, as the best one could hope for under the circumstances. This kind of unfulfilled promise is, of course, not uncommon in the grandiose scholarly world of the nineteenth century. What is exceptional about Comte's case is the extraordinary rationalization he used as a license for his conjectural flights:

> The progress I have achieved has procured for me a certain authority; and my conceptions are now sufficiently matured. I am entitled, therefore, to proceed with the same freedom and rapidity as my principle ancestors, Aristotle, Descartes and Leibnitz, who confined themselves to a definite expression of their views, leaving the verification and development of them to the public [1875-77, III:xi; orig. 1851-54].

Comte's earlier writings nonetheless contain much that is of permanent value. He is at his best when discussing the abstract grounds and general strategies of sociocultural studies. Although he failed to translate his theoretical and programmatic statements into substantive products, more empirically oriented anthropologists and sociologists may still benefit from his methodological invocations. It remains true that many a hardheaded empiricist, supposedly dealing only in "facts," is just as far from a science of society as Saint-Simon, Comte, and other abstract system-builders. Comte's understanding of the relationship between theory and research was fundamentally correct: "No real observation of any kind of phenomena is possible which is not initially guided and finally interpreted by some theory" (1830-42, IV:418). His appreciation of the intellectual dangers inherent in a "fact"-oriented, micro-focused, piecemeal approach to history is certainly relevant to the fate of modern academic historiography and the modern historical and ethnolinguistic schools of cultural anthropology:

> The irrational spirit of specialization which has become ascendant in our times would have the final result of reducing history to a vain accumulation of unrelated monographs, where all idea of the real and simultaneous connection between diverse human events would inevitably be lost in the midst of the sterile encumbrance of these confused descriptions. In order to have a true scientific character, historical comparisons of the diverse ages of civilization must be viewed in relation to social evolution [*ibid.*:454–55].

Comte also merits our admiration for rendering explicit a number of basic assumptions about sociocultural systems which, although certainly not original with him, owe much of their modern formulation to his efforts. Especially striking is Comte's concern with what we would call today functional relations.

Anticipating Herbert Spencer, Émile Durkheim, A. R. Radcliffe-Brown, and the whole modern British functionalist school, Comte regarded the study of sociocultural phenomena as having two pragmatically justified divisions or aspects, the static and dynamic. An approach to phenomena through the static aspect leads to "the investigation of the laws of action and reaction of the different parts of the social system—apart, for the occasion, from the fundamental movement which is always gradually modifying them" (COMTE 1830–42, IV: 324). Social dynamics, on the other hand, are concerned with conceiving each of the

> consecutive social states as the necessary result of the preceding, and the indispensable mover of the following, according to the axiom of Leibnitz—*the present is big with the future.* In this view, the object of science is to discover the laws which govern this continuity and the aggregate of which determines the course of human development [*ibid.*:365-66].

It should be emphasized that, unlike many twentieth-century functionalists, Comte could not conceive of following a functional at the expense of a "dynamic" approach. On the contrary, social statics was of interest only to the extent that it revealed the structures with which the evolutionary process was involved.

The basic division into statics and dynamics was fitted into the moral mission of positivism, from which it emerged mystically transmuted into the highest slogan of the new secular religion: *Order and Progress.* This motto, with its implications of a smoothly running social organization gradually and smoothly undergoing beneficial transformations, readily garnered the sympathy of the bourgeoisie both at home and abroad. Its appearance as far away as on the flag of Brazil testified to the strong appeal that Comte's views exerted upon liberal politicians and intellectuals who believed that fundamental change was not incompatible with stability.

Comte employed an organismic analogy, the basis of most previous and succeeding functionalist positions, to elaborate his description of social statics. In this connection he introduced the terms "social anatomy," "social organism," and "social organization," and insisted upon the importance of emphasizing the concatenation of influences within the social system:

> This preliminary aspect of political science evidently thus presumes, contrary to present-day philosophical habits, that each of the numerous social elements ceases to be regarded in an absolute and independent manner and insists that they can only be known relative to all the others . . . [COMTE 1830-42, IV:325].

In *Politique Positive* Comte succumbed, as Spencer was to do a number of years later, to the temptation to render the biological analogy in terms of specific (and quite incomparable) structures. Written in an epoch before the cell had been identified as a fundamental unit of physiology, Comte's comparison of "elements," "tissues," and "organs" respectively to "family," "class," and "communities" is singularly unconvincing (COMTE 1875–77, II:240–42). But this was true of every attempt Comte made to "flesh out" the bones of theory.

Many cultural anthropologists have proposed that the distinctive feature of the anthropological approach is its holistic framework, that is, the point of view which attempts to describe the parts of a system by reference to the whole. Comte quite properly discusses this subject in the context of the organismic analogy. In studying the physiology of organisms, description of the whole must precede the analysis of the parts: "It is, therefore, uncontestable that holistic concepts and studies are alone proper for the establishment of positive sociology. . . . The study of the parts must always be dominated by the study of the system" (COMTE 1830–42, IV:355).

In actual practice, Comte never attempted the detailed analysis of any specific social system. Instead, he took over Condorcet's fatal invention, "the device of supposing a single nation to which we may refer all the consecutive social modifications actually witnessed among distinct peoples" (*ibid.*:364–65). This unfortunate decision deprived his historical law of substantive value. It resulted not only in a superficial treatment of the history of Western culture, but in the arbitrary exclusion of non-Western societies on the grounds that they were "non-progressive." Thus, in *Philosophie Positive,* Comte declared his intention of applying his theory of history only to the "most advanced nations, not allowing our attention to be drawn off to other centers of independent civilization which have, from any cause whatever, been arrested, and left in an imperfect state" (*ibid.*, V:3–4). In discussing the remote past, only the population ancestral to the Europeans (and Western Europeans at that) need be studied! Comte criticized "those who would produce their whole stock of erudition, and mix up with the review [of the past] such populations as those of India and China that have not aided the process of development . . ." (*ibid.*:5). This attitude seems to have been common among Comte's contemporaries. We shall meet with it in Hegel in a moment; and later, we shall detect its damaging influence in the writings of Marx and Engels. It is an attitude, of course, which runs counter to the basic strategy of any minimum definition of an anthropological approach to a science of culture. To exclude nine-tenths of the world's sociocultural systems from consideration can only result in an atrophied and culture-bound understanding of history. The argument that only "progressive" societies can yield an understanding of "progressive change" is totally specious, probably little more than a rationalization for the lack of knowledge about primitive and non-Western systems so conspicuous in the writings of Saint-Simon, Comte, Hegel, Marx, Engels, and many other early nineteenth-century figures who are reckoned among the founders of academic sociology.

Those who would have us regard Comte as the "father of sociology" burden that discipline with another debilitating heritage in the form of Comte's strong cultural-idealist commitment. Disdain of mysticism on the one hand and fear of the materialist bogey on the other account for the main thread of the positivist program. As we have already seen, Comte's "law" of history is couched in terms of dominant modes of thought. It remains to be made sufficiently clear that, for Comte and his followers, antimaterialism was a conscious and much esteemed part of the positivist system. It was their belief that "positivism . . . reconciles all that is tenable in the rival claims of both materialism and spiritualism: and having done this, it discards them both. It holds the one to be as dangerous to Order as the other to Progress" (COMTE 1875–77, I:41). But in casting out the spirits, Comte fell far short of reaching a neutral position between cultural materialism and its principal eighteenth-century idealist rivals. Turgot, Voltaire, Condorcet, etc., had all previously shrived themselves of animism, but they all, nonetheless, remained victims of the anthropocentric illusion that societies propelled themselves through history by thinking now one way, now another.

Why did the Greeks think up one set of social forms, e.g., the city-state, while the Persians thought themselves into oriental despotism and the Bushmen never thought themselves out of hunting bands? Comte never really faces the question. To him, it is self-evident that the analysis of all social change must begin with an examination of the ideas of the moment. The smugness of his position is memorable:

> It cannot be necessary to prove to anybody who reads this work that ideas govern or overthrow the world; in other words, that all social mechanism rests on opinions. They know above all that the great political and moral crises which present-day societies are experiencing arise in the final analysis from intellectual anarchy. Our worst problem resides in effect in that profound divergence which now exists among us relative to fundamental beliefs. . . . It is equally certain that, once agreement is reached, the appropriate institutions will unfold, without shock or resistance . . . [COMTE 1830-42, I:48-49].

If sociocultural systems take their form from the opinions of their participants, one might very well suppose, upon noting the variety of opinions among men, that endless diversity must characterize the superorganic universe, and that no observer could predict the content of the consensus achieved in any past or future exchange of ideas. Yet it is the ultimate irony of Comte's position that historical determinism has had no more staunch supporter:

> No enlightened man can doubt that in this long succession of efforts and discoveries the human mind has followed a precisely determined course, the exact preparatory knowledge of which would have enabled a sufficiently well-informed intelligence to predict, before their more or less distant occurrence, the progress characteristic of each epoch [*ibid.*, IV:372].

So great are the determining influences of history that, to echo Vico, given a plurality of worlds, they all must evolve in the same way: "This order of change is remarkably fixed; it leads to the exact comparison of parallel developments among distinct and independent populations" [*ibid.*:370]. Why should thought be thus constrained? If parallelism is so conspicuous a feature of cultural evolution, there must be powerful forces that direct human beings to accept certain kinds of "opinions" rather than others. What are these forces? Ask this question, and the whole Comtean edifice goes up in a puff of smoke. Something might be saved were it possible to invoke the defense that positivism is concerned only with the correlations of events or "their invariant relations," rather than with metaphysical causes. Thus, human ideas start at the theistic level with fetishism and associated institutions and evolve toward positivism and Comte's popehood. Why? Because they do, and let it go at that. Need one demand of Newton's formula why the earth and the moon attract each other? But Comte would be the last to be entitled to such a defense. It is he, first of all, who proposes that ideas (i.e., opinions) "govern" cultural evolution. That there is an equivalence between "govern" and "cause" is shown in Comte's explanation of the origin of agriculture. "It is usual," he argues, "to suppose that the condensation of numbers, as the race increased, would compel the tillage of the soil, as it had before compelled the keeping of flocks." But this is insufficient since "no social exigency will find satisfaction if Man is not already disposed to provide it . . . ," i.e., unless his ". . . intellectual and moral nature was duly prepared for it" (COMTE in MARTINEAU 1896, III:21). It is true that Comte occasionally manifests an interest in material conditions, as when among "the three general sources of social variation" he lists "race" and "climate." But the fatally muddled outlook from which he surveys these influences leads him to cite in familiar tautology "political action" as a third and possibly equal source. Moreover, he leaves no room for misinterpreting the relatively minor effect which "variations"—racial, climatological, or political—exert upon world history.

THE HEGELIAN COMPROMISE

In Germany, the role of adapting the idealist heritage of the Enlightenment to the post-Napoleonic milieu was taken up by the philosopher Georg W. F. Hegel. Although Comte regarded Hegel as an exemplar of the metaphysical phase of thought, the salient influence of both of these men was the strengthening of idealist versions of sociocultural determinism. In retrospect, Comte was not very much less metaphysical than Hegel. Both the positivists and the Hegelians viewed history as the unfolding of ideas that for unexplained reasons, in the one case, and unintelligible reasons, in the other, follow a predetermined course. But Hegel's notion of the role played by mental events in world history is at once more grandiose, obscure, and anthropocentric than Comte's.

"The History of the World," Hegel declared, "begins with its general aim—the realization of the Idea of Spirit [Mind]" (HEGEL 1956:25).

This means (roughly) that the potential everything called the World-Spirit (Mind) is bringing itself into "full existence," defined as the pure or abstract idea of mind. The World Mind is, thus, an evolutionary process, and all its emanations are, in turn, evolutionary processes. Like his Enlightenment predecessors, Hegel believed that these processes beget morally better states of existence in progressive succession, marked in human affairs by the greater and more perfect use of reason. Through reason not only man, but the World Mind achieves freedom. Thus "the history of the world is none other than the progress of the consciousness of freedom" (quoted in MARCUSE 1960:229).

Most of Hegel's philosophy is a worthless ruin, although it is still, in some quarters, an object of serious study. Among Marxists, Hegel's philosophy continues to be regarded as a hallowed steppingstone to dialectical materialism. This honor was, of course, bestowed by Marx and Engels, who described themselves as Hegelians who had stopped standing on their heads. It is regrettable that Marx, in company with the young German intellectuals of his generation, studied the Hegelian system and became habituated to its mental attitudes. Marx, the boldest and clearest of the nineteenth-century cultural materialists, never succeeded in throwing off the metaphysical notions upon which Hegel's fame rested. As we shall see in our discussion of Marx, everything that is scientifically sound in Marxism could just as well have derived from dozens of social philosophers other than Hegel, while all that is most conspicuously blighted with antiscientism betrays Hegel's influence.

Hegel, like his Enlightenment predecessors, conceived the world in terms of progressive evolutionary flux. To the pervasive evolutionism of his times, he added the peculiar notion that entities or events could be comprehended, or to say the same thing, exist, only by virtue of their opposite, contradiction or negation. This is the epistemological basis of Hegel's famous "dialectical" point of view.

The world consists of entities in "dialectical" relationship with their opposite, contradictory, or negative ideas. The tension between the opposites reflects the evolutionary working of the world mind. Out of the "negation of the negation" there evolves a new entity or state of existence which in turn is meaningful only in relationship to its contradictory ingredients. As explained by Herbert Marcuse:

> Dialectics is a process in a world where the mode of existence of men and things is made up of contradictory relations, so that any particular content can be unfolded only by passing through its opposite. The latter is an integral part of the former, and the

> whole content is the totality of all contradictory relations implied in it. . . . It exists, as Hegel puts it, in its "otherness" (*anderssein*) [1960:66-67].

As things pass through their opposites, they get progressively better, or closer to their ideal form. According to Hegel, it is a "necessity of nature" that:

> The logical, and—as still more prominent—the *dialectical* nature of the Idea in general, viz., that it is self-determined—that it assumes successive forms which it successively transcends, and by this very process of transcending its earlier stages, gains an affirmative, and, in fact, a richer and more concrete shape . . . [HEGEL 1956:63].

There is no empirical support for the assertion that the evolution of forms is constrained by the necessity of passing through a series of opposite or contradictory stages. Hegel's attempt to characterize the course of world evolution in terms of upward spiraling negations was the result of an infatuation with word and number magic. As Karl Eugen Dühring, the famous nineteenth-century critic of Marx's use of the dialectic, pointed out, "Hegel's first negation is the idea of the fall from grace, which is taken from the catechism, and his second is the idea of a higher unity leading to redemption. The logic of facts can hardly be based on this nonsensical analogy borrowed from the religious sphere" (quoted in ENGELS 1947:193; orig. 1888). Dühring might also have noted that Hegel's dialectic is another example of the cabalistic fixation upon the number three which is so conspicuous in Western culture. Thus the thesis, antithesis, and synthesis of the dialectic takes its place alongside such other holy trinities as the Catholic Father, Son, and Holy Ghost; the psychoanalysts' id, ego, and superego; the positivists' theological, metaphysical, and positivist stages; and the anthropologists' savagery, barbarism, and civilization.

If the world evolutionary process exemplifies the dialectic of negation, it does so simply by virtue of the absence of workable rules for distinguishing between negative and positive changes. Since evolution means transformation, or difference, it is always possible, in the absence of definite criteria, to declare that each and every evolutionary product is the negation of some earlier condition. In this manner, Engels sought to defend Marx and the Hegelian dialectic against Dühring's attack. "What is this fearful negation of the negation which makes life so bitter for Herr Dühring and fulfills the same role with him of the unpardonable crime as the sin against the Holy Ghost does in Christianity?" Engels asked himself. "A very simple process," he answered, "which is taking place everywhere and every day, which any child can understand, as soon as it is stripped of its veil of mystery in which it was wrapped by the old idealist philosophy . . ." (*ibid.*:201). Engels then proceeded to give some simple examples of the negation of the negation. Thus, grains of barley are "negated" when the seed germinates and the plant grows. Later on, the plant flowers and puts out more seeds. "As a result of this negation of the negation, we have once again the original grain of barley, but not as a single unit, but ten, twenty, or thirty fold." This quantitative change is also accompanied by qualitative changes, which are too slow to be perceived.

> But if we take an artificially cultivated ornamental plant, for example, a dahlia or an orchid, and if we treat the seed of the plant which grows from it as a gardener does, we get as a result of this negation of the negation not only more seeds, but also qualitatively better seeds, which produce more beautiful flowers, and each fresh repetition of this process, each repeated negation of the negation, increases the improvement [*ibid.*:201-2].

There follow similar remarks concerning negations of eggs, rock formations, and primitive communal land tenure.

In all of these examples, the description of the evolutionary processes involved as negations of negations adds nothing to our understanding of how the transformations have occurred. Moreover, it is mere poetic analogy which permits one to claim that what ensues during the development of an embryo or during natural selection is a "negation." What all evolutionary processes have in common is not the "negation" of earlier forms, but simply their transformation. In order for an evolutionary series to be identified as such, some link between the earlier and later forms must be preserved. Eventually, the end product of the series may bear no readily apparent similarity to the initial forms; however, there is no empirical justification for supposing that each evolutionary series must inevitably result in drastic changes regardless of how long the series continues. Certainly, for short-run series such as speciation in bio-evolution, emergent forms are scarcely "negations" of their predecessors. Of course, no one can prevent an Hegelian from calling Homo sapiens the negation of Homo neanderthalensis, but such a semantic maneuver will not further illuminate the conditions which were responsible for the evolution of modern human types. Similarly, nothing is gained but a kind of poetic thrill when Marx and Engels decide that the emergence of private land tenure is the negation of primitive communal tenure and that socialist communal tenure is the negation of the negation, thereby supposedly vindicating the genius of Hegel, who despite his idealistic shackles managed to grasp the dialectical nature of the universe.

The futility of Hegel's dialectical idealism is nowhere better exhibited than in his own attempts to interpret history. Like Comte, he evinced a splendidly ethnocentric disdain of all pre-state societies. Africa is dismissed from consideration because "it has no movement or development to exhibit" (HEGEL 1956:99). There is likewise no need to be concerned about the pre-Columbian America:

> Of America and its grade of civilization, especially in Mexico and Peru, we have information, but it imparts nothing more than that this culture was an entirely national one, which must expire as soon as Spirit approached it [*ibid.*:81].

Although Hegel deigns to consider China and India worthy of antiquarian interest, he is convinced that these countries have no further role to play in world affairs. For reasons known only to Spirit, "the history of the world travels from East to West, for Europe is absolutely the end of History, Asia the beginning" (*ibid.*:103). The general guide lines of this movement are provided by the development of the consciousness of freedom. Among the Orientals only one man had freedom; among the Greeks some had freedom; and now "the German world knows that all are free" (*ibid.*:103). The final irony of this formula is that Hegelian exegesists are unable to agree on what kind of German state was intended as the ultimate goal of history. But it does seem that Hegel believed the Prussian monarchy was the system under which "all are free" (*cf.* MARCUSE 1960:235ff.).

In deference to Marx, one is tempted to credit Hegel at least with a view of history in which the relationship between individual actors and impersonal sociocultural forces is clarified. Hegel did, of course, plausibly argue that personal greatness resided in the conjunction of individual genius and appropriate cultural developments, i.e., that the great man was the agent of history. But similar doctrines had been advanced by John Millar and Adam Ferguson (see p. 51) without metaphysical infestation. Similarly, it would scarcely be possible to defend Hegel on the grounds of his sociocultural evolutionism. In this matter, he had also not advanced beyond his eighteenth-century predecessors. The strict determinism of his scheme of course did represent an improvement over proposals which provided for God's frequent miraculous intervention, as in the cases of De Maistre and De Bonald. But the vagueness of the "World Spirit" is too great a price to pay for an end to miracles.

There is one aspect of the Hegelian dialectic that requires further comment. If we interpret the dialectic mode of thought as an hypothesis concerning human cognitive processes (as distinguished from world evolutionary processes), we may credit Hegel with a useful suggestion. There may, in fact, be a tendency for human beings to reason about themselves and their physical and cultural worlds in terms of binary oppositions, or dichotomies. Certainly in the history of Western thought, it frequently appears as if ideas present themselves in both a negative and positive form and that an advance is made by resolving the contradictions between the extremes. The resolution of the particulate and wave interpretations of light in quantum theory, or of the polygenist versus monogenist argument in Charles Darwin's *Origin of Species*, and the unresolved dichotomy of the "big bang" versus the "continuous creation of matter" theories in astrophysics might be cited as scientific examples. It may also be possible that many aspects of myth and ritual reflect this tendency. At least, in recent years, an elaborate interpretive literature based on some such assumption has been produced by Claude Lévi-Strauss and his followers (see Chap. 18). Additional cross-cultural research utilizing the techniques of modern social psychology is badly needed to shed light on this issue. In the meantime, however, we may note that if it is finally demonstrated that human cognitive processes are dominated by dialectic modes of thought, our understanding of *historical* processes—of sociocultural evolution—would remain unaffected. Thinking of the world in dialectic terms will not cause it to change dialectically, unless, of course, we believe in the omnipotence of thought.

CONTINUITY IN THE LIBERAL TRADITION: JOHN STUART MILL

In the winter of discontent, Saint-Simon, Comte, and Hegel nourished the hope of spring. The underground currents which flowed from the prerevolutionary epoch now rose to the surface. The voice of Locke was heard in the land. It was heard with especially great force and clarity in another prodigy of the liberal intellect, John Stuart Mill. It is true that Mill, like Comte, was concerned almost exclusively with the analysis of the Euro-American capitalist order. Yet in his *Principles of Political Economy* (1848) Mill reached out to the perennial central issues of anthropological inquiry. In the entire nineteenth century, his contribution to the development of a climate favorable to social science was surpassed only by that of Herbert Spencer.

Principles of Political Economy was Mill's attempt to write the sequel to Adam Smith's *Wealth of Nations*, summing up classical economic theory, but including an enlarged understanding of, and sympathy for, the underprivileged segments of the capitalist order. His eclectic approach, coupled with high standards of evidence and great logical acumen, exerted, if nothing else, an enormous influence on the definition of the proper liberal scholarly style.

In his "Preliminary Remarks," Mill provided an important summary of the evolution of productive systems, notable for its contribution to the surplus theory of social stratification. We find first the familiar Enlightenment scheme of the stage of hunting tribes giving way to pastoralism, during which "active and thrifty individuals" first come into possession of significant wealth differences. Inequality in wealth next gives rise to a group who are able "to divest themselves of all labor except that of government and superintendence." The greater security and leisure of this more productive system gives rise to "new wants . . . for better clothing, utensils, and implements." Next comes the stage of agriculture, brought about when "the growth of the population of men and cattle began in time to press upon the earth's capabilities of yielding natural pasture." At this point, however, Mill departs from the usual formula. Progress during the agricultural phase is not so rapid as one might suppose, because, except in unusually fertile areas, agriculture is less productive than herding. Furthermore, agricultural produce is more vulnerable to taxation:

> Agriculturists do not, unless in unusually advantageous circumstances of climate and soil, produce so great a surplus of food, beyond their necessary consumption, as to support any large class of laborers engaged in other departments of industry. The surplus, too, whether small or great, is usually torn from the producers, either by the government to which they are subject, or by individuals, who by superior force, or by availing themselves of religious or traditional feelings of subordination, have established themselves as lords of the soil [MILL 1923:12; orig. 1848].

Next there follows a discussion of the role of taxation in "the extensive monarchies which from a time beyond historical record have occupied the plains of Asia." Mentioning the role of Asiatic government in works of public utility—"tanks, wells, and canals for irrigation, without which in many tropical climates cultivation could hardly be carried on" (*ibid.*:13)—Mill proceeds to give a fair description of the basic ingredients of "Oriental Despotism." As Karl Wittfogel has indicated (1957: 372-73), this analysis was based upon precedents in the writings of the earlier classical economists, James Mill, Richard Jones, and Adam

Smith. Mill goes on to contrast the Oriental monarchies with the trajectory of development in Europe which is characterized by "small town-communities" or by "little communities" (MILL 1923:14-15). As a result of warfare, these evolve into larger units based on conquest and slavery, culminating with the Greco-Roman empires. Mill next describes the characteristics of feudalism and the transition of feudal Europe into "commercial and manufacturing Europe" (*ibid.*:18). Thus implicit in Mill's summary is a techno-environmental, techno-economic classification of culture into six types: (1) hunting; (2) pastoral; (3) Asiatic; (4) Greco-Roman; (5) feudal; and (6) capitalist.

Principles of Political Economy is also of special interest for its treatment of European and Indian peasant systems of agriculture. In this enterprise Mill systematically compared the productivity and well-being of peasant proprietors, renters, share-croppers and cottiers, in an attempt to disentangle the effects of the relations of production from those of climate, soil, race, and government. His analysis of the sources of poverty among the Irish is especially memorable for his clear stand against racism at a time when, as we shall see in the next chapter, the drift of the more narrowly anthropological literature was overwhelmingly toward the biologization of history:

> Is it not, then, a bitter satire on the mode in which opinions are formed on the most important problems of human nature and life, to find public instructors of the greatest pretension, imputing the backwardness of Irish industry, and the want of energy of the Irish people in improving their condition, to a peculiar indolence and *insouciance* in the Celtic race? Of all vulgar modes of escaping from the consideration of the effect of social and moral influences on the human mind, the most vulgar is that of attributing the diversities of conduct and character to inherent natural differences. What race would not be indolent and insouciant when things are so arranged, that they derive no advantage from forethought or exertion? . . . It speaks nothing against the capacities of industry in human beings, that they will not exert themselves without motive. No labourers work harder, in England or America, than the Irish; but not under a cottier system [*ibid.*:324].

SCIENTISM REAFFIRMED: QUÉTELET

The strength of the early nineteenth-century impulse toward social science is dramatically illustrated in the work of the amazing Belgian astronomer, meteorologist, and statistician Adolphe Quételet. As previously mentioned, it was Quételet's appropriation of "social physics" which drove Comte to invent the term "sociology." While employed in the task of developing actuarial tables for Brussels life-insurance companies, Quételet's attention was drawn to the regularities of sociocultural phenomena considered *en masse*. In 1828, he was greatly impressed by the regularities exhibited in criminological phenomena and quickly grasped their significance in relation to the problem of free will (*cf.* HANKIN 1908:17). The fact that year after year predictable numbers of crimes of predictable varieties would be committed by predictable proportions of the sexes at predictable ages convinced him that the individual's subjective experience of free will did not alter the determinate nature of the actions of large numbers of people considered in the aggregate.

> Society includes within itself the germs of all the crimes committed, and at the same time, the necessary facilities for their development. It is the social state, in some measure, which prepares these crimes, and the criminal is merely the instrument to execute them. Every social state supposes, then, a certain number and a certain order of crimes, these being merely the necessary consequences of its organization [QUÉTELET 1842:6; orig. 1835].

It would seem quite evident that Quételet's "social physics" involves an implicit concept of culture viewed as a superorganic domain of causal relations. The resemblance between his ideas of social causality and the concept of culture is embodied in the arguments for the predictability of behavior. Anticipating similar arguments propounded in Herbert Spencer's *The Study of Sociology* (1873), Quételet drew attention to the fact that social life is carried out on the assumption that even the behavior of specific individuals can be predicted. This expectation snares those who would argue that social science is not possible because of the volitional nature of human responses. Quételet was well-credentialed for the task of proving that the larger the number of individuals considered, the greater the confidence in one's predictions. This result can be achieved only if lawful principles govern the domain under study (if the phenomena were purely random, more cases should lead to diminishing confidence):

> When it is necessary to take the most simple resolve, we are under the domination of our habitudes, our wants, our social relations, and a host of causes which, all of them, draw us about in a hundred different ways. These influences are so powerful, that we have no difficulty in telling, even when referring to persons whom we are scarcely acquainted with, or even know not at all, what is the resolution to which they will lead such parties. Whence, then,

> this certainty of foresight, exemplified by you daily, if you were not convinced, at the outset, that it is extremely probable the empire of causes will carry it over free-will. In considering the moral world *a priori*, you give to this free-will the most entire latitude; and when you come to practice, when you speak of what passes around you, you constantly fall into contradiction with yourselves. [QUÉTELET 1842:vii-viii].

In this connection, it is historically of interest to note that suicide was one of the crimes studied by Quételet to show how statistical analysis could reveal unsuspected sociocultural uniformities. Quételet thus anticipated by more than sixty years the famous attempt by Émile Durkheim (see Chap. 18) to use suicide as proof of the existence of a supra-individual "group mind."

Quételet, like Mill and Comte, had to ward off the accusation of his critics that his theories led to fatalism and materialism. These pressures adversely affected his program for sociocultural research. His answer to the charge that he viewed man as a mere automaton was to separate synchronic from diachronic causality. Thus, he contended that while our actions are determined by social conditions, it is possible for man to change those social conditions:

> I have always comprehended with difficulty, moreover, how persons, pre-occupied doubtless by other ideas, have seen any tendency to materialism in the exposition of a series of facts deduced from statistical documents. In giving to my work the title of *Social Physics*, I have had no other aim than to collect, in a uniform order, the phenomena affecting man, nearly as physical science brings together the phenomena appertaining to the material world. If certain deplorable facts present themselves with an alarming regularity, to whom is blame to be ascribed? Ought charges of materialism to be brought against him who points out that regularity? . . .
>
> I repeat, that in a given state of society, resting under the influence of certain causes, regular effects are produced, which oscillate, as it were, around a fixed mean point, without undergoing any sensible alterations. Observe, that I have said *under the influence of the same causes*; if the causes were changed, the effects also would necessarily be modified. As laws and the principles of religion and morality are influencing causes, I have then not only the hope, but, what you have not, the positive conviction, that society may be ameliorated and reformed [*ibid.*:vii].

In thus escaping from the opprobrium attached to materialism, Quételet failed to take up the question of the lawful conditions which are in turn responsible for changing "law and the principles of religion and morality." The little attention which Quételet did bestow upon the question of the causes of sociocultural differences and similarities reveals him as hopelessly lost in the typical Enlightenment daydream of progress through reason. His misunderstanding of historical forces and his failure to make use of the comparative method, made him an execrable prophet of what the future had in store for Euro-American culture. I know of no more striking demonstration of how synchronic functionalism, carried out with the most meticulous attention to empirical data, can result in a fundamentally false picture of the sociocultural universe:

> The perfectibility of the human species results as a necessary consequence from all our researches. Defects and monstrosities disappear more and more from the physical world; the frequency and the severity of diseases are combated with more advantage by the progress of medical science; the moral qualities of man experience not less sensible improvements; and the farther we advance, the less are great politic overthrows and wars (the scourges of humanity) to be feared, either in their immediate effects or in their ultimate consequences [*ibid.*:108].

SCIENTISM REAFFIRMED: BUCKLE

By mid-century, the advance of industrial capitalism had created an ambience more receptive to social science than that of any previous epoch. With its technological wonders—its railroads, steamships, telegraph, and thousand-spindled factories—science had already emerged as the new miracle worker of Western culture. The wave of secularism and skepticism that had arisen during the Enlightenment grew once again to tidal proportions. It was this ambience of euphoric scientism in which anthropology would achieve disciplinary identity.

A final interesting example of the extent to which the pre-Darwinian assault on religious orthodoxy had advanced is to be found in the work of Henry Thomas Buckle. Although usually identified as an historian and neglected by anthropologists, Buckle's interests were cut from the cloth of Turgot's universal history. He was a vigorous advocate of a scientific approach to history. Buckle dismissed the theological resurgence of the twenties and thirties as superficial and temporary setbacks in the Enlightenment program. Indeed, his influential and comparative *History of Civilization in England* (1857) was devoted mainly toward documenting the struggle between scientism and politico-religious orthodoxy in postfeudal Europe. While admitting that "an immense majority of the clergy" were still "striving to check the progress of that scepticism which is now gathering in upon us from every quarter" (*ibid.*, I:257), he asserted that the "higher order of minds" among his contemporaries had already passed beyond that stage (*ibid.*:258). "The truth is, that the time for these things has gone by. Theological interests have long ceased to be supreme; and the affairs of nations are no longer regulated according to ecclesiastical views" (*ibid.*:256).

Buckle's convictions concerning the coming triumph of the scientific approach to history led him into a premature review of the ecological determinants of cultural differences on a broadly comparative world-wide scale, which included Asia, Africa, and the New World. Unfortunately, he lacked both the factual and theoretical basis for such a survey, and his efforts along these lines ended in one of the worst cases of naive geographical determinism on record. He attributed to soil, climate, and diet a direct influence on the quality of mind. Hence, he explained differences in religious and political behavior as manifestations of geographically determined propensities toward more or less imaginative or reasonable national characters. Despite his scientism and his emphasis on geographical factors, Buckle thus failed to achieve anything resembling a consistent cultural-materialist outlook. Indeed, one of his major points is that "mental law" is more important than "physical law" for an understanding of the history of Europe. But by mental law, Buckle intended nothing more than the familiar Enlightenment concept of progress through reason.

In the context of his times, the most notable quality of Buckle's approach was his rejection of racial determinism. Buckle was perfectly correct in his assessment of the strength of the movement to return history to science. He failed to realize, however, that the egalitarian environmentalism of his Enlightenment heroes would not accompany the coming renaissance in sociocultural theory. As we shall see in the next chapter, many of Buckle's contemporaries agreed that a science of history was now possible, but except for Marx and Engels, they increasingly supposed that the study of racial and hereditary factors would alone provide the basis for its major generalizations. Uncompromisingly environmentalist denials of the significance of racial differences, such as the following, were destined not to be heard again until the beginning of the Boasian period:

> Whatever, therefore, the moral and intellectual progress of men may be, it resolves itself not into a progress of natural capacity, but into a progress, if I may so say, of opportunity; that is, an

> improvement in the circumstances under which that capacity after birth comes into play. Here, then, lies the gist of the whole matter. The progress is one, not of internal power, but of external advantage. The child born in a civilized land, is not likely, as such, to be superior to one born among barbarians; and the difference which ensues between the acts of the two children will be caused, so far as we know, solely by the pressure of external circumstances; by which I mean the surrounding opinions, knowledge, associations, in a word, the entire mental atmosphere in which the two children are respectively nurtured [*ibid.*:128].

It is essential for an understanding of the history of anthropological theory that we appreciate the tension which existed between the racial egalitarianism of Mill and Buckle and the overarching racial determinism of every major mid-nineteenth-century figure who is customarily assigned a formative role in the development of anthropology as a distinctive discipline. The opprobrium attached to Enlightenment egalitarianism was still so great that Mill and Buckle were denounced by anthropologists as "materialists." Thus, according to James Hunt (1866b:115), Buckle and Mill were merely "the continuation of Helvetius and the French Encyclopedists, who were again but a far-off reverberation of Democritus and Epicurus."

> John Stuart Mill cannot help claiming the suffrage for the Negro —and the woman. Such conclusions are the inevitable result of the premises whence he started. And had he paused at such a *reductio ad absurdum*, his school would not. That school, as we have said, dates from the remotest antiquity. The omnipotence of circumstances and the natal equality of mankind are not new doctrines. They are simply materialism, and the philosophy of the external ultimated. He who starts from atoms, guided by chance, must end in absolute democracy, that is, in racial and individual equality. It is simply the completion of the circle, from chaos to chaos [*ibid.*:115-16].

Perhaps the explanation of why anthropologists have characteristically exhibited such a deep ignorance of the roots of their science is that the beginnings of disciplinary identity coincided with and are almost wholly attributable to the mid-century vogue of racialist scientism. As we shall see, anthropology was in no small measure responsible for blotting out the great surmise of the Enlightenment environmentalists concerning the power of enculturation. Although Buckle and Mill, as much as Marx and Engels, have hitherto been considered irrelevant to the rise of anthropological theory, their continued neglect leaves an inexplicable gap between the Boasian concept of culture and the sources of radical environmentalism in the eighteenth century. It is a great irony that when the Boasians came to reassert the importance of enculturation, it was as part of a reaction not only to racialism but to scientism as well. The issue we next confront, however, is how cultural theory in the nineteenth century came to be dominated by racism.

Rise of Racial Determinism

4

The declaration "all men are created equal" is one of the best known of John Locke's subversive effects. It was Thomas Jefferson who had insisted on the phrase, but apparently not without misgivings. His *Notes on the State of Virginia* (1786) gave voice to the suspicion "that the blacks, whether originally a distinct race, or made distinct by time and circumstances, are inferior to the whites in the endowment of body and mind" (quoted in GOSSETT 1963:42). Although Jefferson later modified this view, the question of racial differences increasingly conflicted with Locke's egalitarian concept of the mind as an "empty cabinet." On the crest of reaction to the French Revolution, educated opinion moved steadily to an opposite extreme: by the middle of the nineteenth century no "truth" had become more "self-evident" than that all men were created *unequal*. And no "truth" was to exert a more noxious influence upon the course of social science.

Racial determinism was the form taken by the advancing wave of the science of culture, as it broke upon the shores of industrial capitalism. It was in this guise that anthropology first achieved a positive role alongside of physics, chemistry, and the life sciences, in the support and spread of capitalist society. Certain Marxists (*cf.* COX 1948) insist that racism itself is confined to the capitalist epoch, but such a view can find no support in ethnographic facts. Folk racism, a popular system of prejudice and discrimination directed against one endogamous descent group by another, is probably as old as humanity. But the phenomenon with which this chapter deals is the elevation of these ancient ideas to pre-eminent scientific dignity. Prior to the nineteenth century, nations had never rewarded their wise men to prove that the supremacy of one people over another was the inevitable outcome of the biological laws of the universe.

According to the doctrine of scientific racism, the significant sociocultural differences and similarities among human populations are the dependent variables of group-restricted hereditary drives and attitudes. Racist explanations thus depend on the correlation of hereditary endowment and group behavioral specialties. It is in the difficulties associated with the identification of the hereditary components that the great weaknesses and temptation of the racist approach resides. Since it is impossible to observe the hereditary factors, their existence must be inferred from the behavioral traits which they are intended to explain. Racial determinism is a tempting substitute for genuine sociocultural theory because the hereditary components, being inaccessible to direct observation, can be shaped into whatever quantity or quality of influence is necessary in order to account for the specialties in question. If our task is to explain the horse complex among the Crow and Blackfoot, what is easier and more invulnerable to empirical challenge than to attribute their horsemanship to an "equestrian instinct"? How can one disprove the assertion that Gypsies keep on the move because they have a "wanderlust" in their "blood"? Or that American Negroes succeed as musicians because they have an "instinct for rhythm"? By a similar summoning of imaginary hereditary components, it would be possible to attribute every sociocultural phenomenon to an hereditary specialty. The basis for the existence of the social sciences, however, is that there are sociocultural explanations of such phenomena. While the possible effect of hereditary specialties is not denied, recourse to racial determinism is acceptable only after sociocultural theories have proven themselves inadequate to the task.

We should note that the rise of nineteenth-century racist theories did not obliterate the attempt to understand the sociocultural components in human behavior. Scientific racism enters the history of social sciences rather as a position along the nature-nurture continuum, with a considerable degree of natural and cultural environmental influence sometimes willingly conceded. Racist theoreticians have seldom attempted to establish a causal correlation between specific human hereditary components (instinct, drives, "blood," genes, etc.) and such familiar ethnographic specialties as cross-cousin marriage, bilateral descent, polyandry, monotheism, brideprice, private property in land, mother-in-law avoidance, shamanism, or thousands of other cultural entities of less than universal occurrence. (Lewis Henry Morgan provides a conspicuous exception.) In fact, the direct association between heredity and specific cultural traits is rather uncommon even among doctrinaire racists such as were spawned by the Nazi era. Examples such as the attribution of West African rhythm to Negro heredity or of phonemic differences between German and other European languages to "Aryan blood" are relatively rare. The kinds of associations brought forth have usually been more general in scope. Negroes are said to be libidinous; whites intelligent; Germans industrious; Japanese imitative; or Yankees mechanically ingenious. The generalized nature of these stereotypes is significant for an understanding of the durability of racist theories. If it were a question of hereditary control over something as specific as mother-in-law avoidance or circumcision, one would need only to point out instances of similar behavior in all of the major racial groupings to discredit the racist approach. But the development of racial determinism in the nineteenth century was rooted in the previous century's concern with progress, and this same preoccupation with broadly conceived aptitudes for creating, acquiring, or reaching "civilization" continues to characterize the popular racism of the mid-twentieth century.

RACISM IN THE EIGHTEENTH CENTURY

The evolutionism of the eighteenth century with its "state of nature" and belief in man's perfection through enlightenment focused attention on the degree to which the different branches of humanity had progressed toward the utopia of reason. Given the grandiose strategy of Turgot's universal history, it was inevitable that the nascent social sciences should center their attention on the explanation of why certain groups had advanced further than others. Perhaps it was also inevitable, given the ubiquitous occurrence of folk varieties of racism, that learned theories of racial determinism should be invoked to account at least for the more exotic associations of race and culture.

Yet, despite the evolutionary focus of eighteenth-century intellectual life, scientific racism remained a minority point of view until after the French Revolution. With a radical form of environmentalism as the guiding doctrine of the *philosophes*, permanent hereditary disabilities could not very well be conceived as the key to the understanding of history. If the misery and social inferiority of the sans-culottes arose from sociocultural deprivations, there was little inclination to attribute the misery or nobility of the American Indians or Tahitians largely to hereditary factors. Throughout the eighteenth century, the balance on the nature-nurture continuum remained well over on the nurture side.

One of the most impressive demonstrations of the eighteenth century's commitment to environmentally induced modifications was the interpretation of race itself as the product of environmental influences. Both Jean Jacques Rousseau's and Lord Monboddo's interest in orangutans, caudal appendages, and wild men reflected a belief that man's physical appearance as well as his behavior varied in conformity with his surroundings. For Monboddo, as the historian John Greene (1959:215ff.) has indicated, the most important part of the environment was the mental or sociocultural heritage. Unlike many of his contemporaries, however, Monboddo explicitly rejected the idea that the physical and cultural differences among the peoples of the world were primarily the result of climate, diet, and other noncultural environmental factors. Nonetheless, Monboddo did feel that the wild men who had been captured in the forests of Europe and the orangutan could learn to speak and were capable of arriving at intellect and science, if only they were accorded, to use Greene's words, "sufficient time and favorable circumstances" (*ibid.*:213).

THE DOCTRINE OF MONOGENESIS

Oddly enough, one of the principal sources of inspiration for the eighteenth century's belief in the modifiability of human nature was the Book of Genesis. In the Mosaic account of creation, all humanity shares a common ancestry with Adam and Eve. This was the doctrine of monogenesis; and all who adhered to it, either actively or in some inertial fashion, were automatically obliged to think of racial differences in terms of an evolutionary process involving more or less rapid environmental feedback. It was only by being an evolutionist and an environmentalist that one could accept the humanity of non-Europeans and at the same time account for their failure to conform to the European physical type. To be sure, the evolutionism of the monogenist stopped short of species transformation. But there is little doubt that Lamarck's use of the idea of acquired characteristics was merely an extension of the evolutionary mode of thought common to most of these monogenists. Lamarck's doctrine of the inheritance of acquired characteristics is identical with an environmentalism which proposes that the life experience of the human organism immediately and directly modifies our hereditary nature.

Possibly more than any other factor, it was the lingering influence of bibliotary which guaranteed that the most esteemed naturalists of the eighteenth century would be monogenists. The impulse to find the hand of God in human affairs existed side by side with a growing belief in natural law. As the eighteenth-century anatomist Petrus Camper expressed it:

> No man who contemplated the whole human race as it is now spread over the face of the earth, without a predilection for hypothesis, can doubt of its having descended from a single pair, that were formed by the immediate hand of God, long after the world itself had been created and had passed through numberless changes. From this pair all the habitable parts of the earth were gradually propagated [quoted in SLOTKIN 1965:198].

MONOGENESIS, ENVIRONMENTALISM, AND EVOLUTION

Although the monogenist position could be, and eventually was, reconciled with severe forms of folk racism, especially in the American Bible belt, full-fledged scientific racial determinism could not flourish as long as raciation was conceived in terms of the rapid acquisition of new hereditary characteristics. This is not to say that the prevailing doctrine of the origin of the races would have been reconcilable with the idiom of the modern civil-rights movement. On the contrary, the two outstanding scientific monogenists of the times, Johann Blumenbach in Germany and Georges Louis Leclerc, Comte de Buffon, in France, were in their own fashion white supremacists. Both believed that Adam and Eve had been white (God's image!). Both regarded the emergence of other types as a form of "degeneration." But unlike the racists of the nineteenth century and thereafter, both Blumenbach and Buffon believed that the degenerative course of raciation could be reversed and that under proper environmental control all the contemporary forms of man could be made to revert to the original. On the whole, raciation, they believed, was the result of exposure to the material conditions of the environment. For example, Negroid pigmentation arose as the result of exposure to the tropical sun; wind and cold produced the tawny color of the Samoieds, the Laplanders, and the Eskimo; the Chinese were fairer than the Tartars because they live in towns and protect themselves from the elements. Poor food, disease, and other pathogenic influences could also cause racial differences. In the standard biological text of the *philosophes,* Georges Buffon's *Histoire Naturelle* (1749–1804), there is even an environmental explanation for why poor Frenchmen are "ugly and ill made" (quoted in COUNT 1950:15). Buffon repeatedly emphasized the superficial quality of race differences and the unitary nature of the hominid type:

> Upon the whole, every circumstance concurs in proving, that mankind are not composed of species essentially different from each other; that on the contrary, there was originally but one species, who, after multiplying and spreading over the whole surface of the earth, have undergone various changes by the influence of climate, food, mode of living, epidemic diseases, and the mixture of dissimilar individuals; that, at first these changes were not so conspicuous, and produced only individual varieties; that these varieties become afterwards specific because they were rendered more general, more strongly marked, and more permanent, by the continual action of the same causes; that they are transmitted from generation to generation, as deformities or disease pass from parents to children; and that, lastly, as they were originally produced by a train of external and accidental causes, and have only been perpetuated by time and the constant operation of these causes, it is probable that they will gradually disappear, or, at least, that they will differ from what they are at present, if the causes which produced them should cease, or their operation be varied by other circumstances and combinations [*ibid.*].

In his *De generis humani varietate nativa* (1770), Johann Blumenbach argued for a similar set of factors—climate, diet, mode of life, hybridization, and disease—as the principal causes of "degeneration" from the "primitive" Caucasoid stock. To prove that Negroid and Caucasoid shared a common origin, the physician John Hunter (1865:372; orig. 1775) insisted that Negro children were white at birth: "Since all blacks are born white, and remain so for some little time, it is clear from this that the sun and the air are necessary agents in turning the skin to a black color." Hunter also pointed to the fact that blisters or burns on a Negro were likely to turn white as further evidence of the color of the Negro's ancestors (GOSSETT 1963:37).

As a result of their environmental interests, many of the eighteenth century's naturalists anticipated modern views of the adaptive nature of racial traits. For example, Immanuel Kant (quoted in COUNT 1950: 20) made special note of the "disproportion between the total body stature and the short legs of the northernmost peoples" in relation to the problem of heat conservation. In the next century, Carl Bergmann

(1848) was to consolidate information of this sort on mammalian varieties in general. "Bergmann's Rule" now constitutes an essential ingredient in Carlton Coon's (1962:59) view of hominid racial adaptations, a view, however, that is contested by other physical anthropologists (WASHBURN 1963; DOBZHANSKY and MONTAGU 1963).

In order to grasp the difference between eighteenth- and nineteenth-century doctrines of racial determinism, the all-important matter of time reckoning must be kept in mind. This is a crucial matter that arises as soon as hereditary features are interpreted as adaptive traits. How fast is the environment-heredity feedback? How long did it take for the adaptation to occur, and how permanent is the change? Compared with all mid-nineteenth-century racist theories, the eighteenth-century monogenists were inclined to regard racial specialties as recent acquisitions. This followed because the monogenists as a group tended to accept the Mosaic chronology. For the date of the origin of the earth they had a choice of 3700 B.C. according to Rabbinical sources; 5199 B.C. according to Pope Clement's edition of the Vulgate; or 4004 B.C. according to Archbishop Ussher's marginalia to the King James Authorized Version (HABER 1959:1). Although Buffon's *Epochs of Nature* (1778) proposed that geological time be extended to 75,000 years, he acquiesced in a date of only 6,000 or 8,000 years since Adam (HABER 1959:125). Relevant to so short a time span, it is difficult to conceive the distinction between hereditary and acquired characteristics as expressed in the modern notion of genotype and phenotype. It is not surprising therefore that among the monogenist environmentalists there should appear the belief that skin color differences were subject to change within a single lifetime, given the proper conditions of climate and diet.

In the United States, this ultimate pitch of environmentalism was achieved by the Reverend Samuel Stanhope Smith, seventh president of Princeton College. Smith's *Essay on the Causes of the Variety of Complexion and Figure in the Human Species* (1787) was one of the earliest anthropological essays in the United States (STANTON 1960:4). Sharing Hunter's views about the lightness of the Negro skin color at birth, Smith made much of the correlation between the relatively lighter complexion of Negroes in the northern states as compared with their slave ancestors in the South (an effect real enough, but produced by hybridization and manumission). According to Smith, Negro pigmentation was nothing more than a huge freckle that covered the whole body as a result of an oversupply of bile, which was in turn stimulated by the "putrid exhalations" of tropical climates. Negroid hair was also formed by climate since the tropical sun caused the skin to contract which in turn pulled the hair into tight whorls. In a later edition (1810) Smith was able to point to the case of Henry Moss, a famous ex-slave who had put himself on exhibition throughout the North after white patches began to appear on his body. In three years he had practically become white all over. This case was also reported by Dr. Benjamin Rush (1797) at a special meeting of the American Philosophical Society to prove that Negroid skin color was a disease, a mild form of leprosy in fact, from which Moss was said to be undergoing a spontaneous cure.

POLYGENESIS

Although evolutionary environmentalist interpretations of racial differences prevailed in biological and philosophical circles, the eighteenth century also produced its crop of polygenists—those who rejected the authenticity of the account in Genesis and attributed racial differences to acts of special creation. Their line of thought grew out of certain heretical Biblical exegeses of the preceding century. For example, Isaac La Peyrère's *Praeadamitae* (1655) took the position that Adam was the ancestor only of the Jews, while such ancient peoples as the Chaldeans, Egyptians, Chinese, and Mexicans had propagated from pre-Adamite ancestors. Since Biblical criticism was part of the rationalist attack on revealed religion, several of the *philosophes* were polygenists. Voltaire, for example, ridiculed the idea that the Jews, whom he regarded as an insignificant nation of desert tribesmen, should have been the ancestors of the entire human species. Other famous polygenists were David Hume, Henry Home, Lord Kames, Edward Long, and Charles White.

COMPARING POLYGENISTS AND MONOGENISTS ON THE RACE ISSUE

Although the correlation was not perfect, those who advocated the polygenist point of view tended to be racial determinists. Voltaire, for example, argued that the Negro's state of civilization was a result of their inferior intelligence:

> If their understanding is not of a different nature from ours, it is at least greatly inferior. They are not capable of any great application or association of ideas, and seemed formed neither for the advantages nor the abuses of philosophy [quoted in GOSSETT 1963:45].

Given David Hume's uncompromising skepticism, it is not unexpected that he should have shared Voltaire's opinion on both polygenesis and racial determinism:

> There never was a civilized nation of any other complexion than white, nor even any individual eminent either in action or speculation. No ingenious manufacturer among them, no arts, no sciences. . . . Such a uniform and constant difference could not happen, in so many countries and ages, if nature had not made an original distinction betwixt these breeds of men [quoted in CURTIN 1964:42].

Henry Home, Lord Kames, sought to compromise with Genesis by dating the creation of separate races to the events that followed the construction of the Tower of Babel. He argued that variation in "national character of courage or cowardice must depend upon a permanent and invariable cause" (1774:20). To explain the most obvious instances of physical adaptation to environmental extremes, he suggested that God had equipped each group of men at the time of dispersal from the Tower of Babel with special hereditary dispositions. These differences, however, do not appear to have included intelligence:

> The colour of the Negroes . . . affords a strong presumption of their being a different species from the Whites; and I once thought, that the presumption was supported by inferiority of understanding in the former. But it appears to me doubtful, upon second thoughts, whether that inferiority may not be occasioned by their condition. A man never ripens in judgment nor in prudence but by exercising these powers. At home, the Negroes have little occasion to exercise either . . . [*ibid.*:32].

In contrast, unequivocal declarations of racial equality were quite common among the monogenists. Hunter's (1865:342; orig. 1775) exposure of the weakness of accepting ethnocentric estimates of intelligence creates a strikingly modern effect:

> Travelers have exaggerated the mental varieties far beyond the truth, who have denied good qualities to the inhabitants of other countries, because their mode of life, manners, and customs have been excessively different from their own. For they have never considered that when the Tartar tames his horse, and the Indian erects his wigwam, he exhibits the same ingenuity which an European general does in manoeuvering his army, or Inigo Jones in building a palace. . . . There is nothing in which men differ so much as in their customs.

Johann Herder, another firm believer in the unity of the human species, also anticipated the Boasian argument against ethnocentrism, but in an idiom which verged on romantic adulation:

> It is but just when we proceed to the country of the blacks that we lay aside our proud prejudices, and consider the organization of this quarter of the globe with as much impartiality, as if there were no other. Since whiteness is a mark of degeneracy in many animals near the pole, the Negro has as much right to term his savage robbers albinoes and white devils, as we have to deem him the emblem of evil, and a descendant of Ham, branded by his father's curse. [Well] might he say, I, the black, am the original man. I have taken the deepest draughts of the force of life, the Sun: on me, and on everything around me, it has acted with the greatest energy and vivacity. Behold my country: How fertile in fruits, how rich in gold! Behold the height of my trees! the strength of my animals! . . . let us enter the country appropriate to him with modesty [HERDER 1803:260; orig. 1784].

POLYGENESIS, MONOGENESIS, AND THE ISSUE OF SLAVERY

Toward the end of the eighteenth century, the polygenist cause became entwined with the slavery question. Some of the most rabid defenders of slavery were doctrinal polygenists. Edward Long, a resident of the British West Indies, claimed in his *History of Jamaica* (1774) that European and Negroes belonged to different species. Long's opinion of Negroes reflected all of the bitter realities of plantation life and little of the restraint and tolerance characteristic of the age of reason. Africans in his opinion were "brutish, ignorant, idle, crafty, treacherous, bloody, thievish, mistrustful, and superstitious" (quoted in CURTIN 1964:43). Long's racist views were reprinted in the United States where they became a standard source for arguments in favor of slavery. They also served to influence the opinion of Charles White, a Manchester physician, who tried to prove on anatomical evidence that Europeans, Asians, Americans, and Africans constituted four separated species, in descending order of excellence. In his *An Account of the Regular Gradation in Man* (1799), White argued that Negroes occupied a place in the "great chain of being" closer to the apes than to Caucasians. Although he himself objected to slavery, his book incorporated the racist stereotypes of the West Indian planters and lent them a scientific aura that was ill-deserved. White's insistence that Negroes had smaller brains, larger sexual organs, an apelike odor, and an animal immunity to pain was repeated over and over again by the proslavery forces.

One might suppose that a firm correlation would exist between polygenesis and proslavery, and monogenesis and antislavery. The historian William Stanton (1960) has shown, however, that polygenesis, for all its attractions as a rationale for treating some human groups like animals of another species, never caught on as the ideology of slavocracy.

POLYGENESIS AND THE AMERICAN SCHOOL OF ANTHROPOLOGY

The failure of polygenesis to take hold in the antebellum South was certainly not due to any dearth of interest in the subject. A vigorous defense of polygenesis lay at the very heart of what was the first distinctive school of anthropology to flourish in the United States. Known widely and respectfully throughout Europe as the "American School," it was founded by the Philadelphia physician and professor of anatomy Samuel George Morton. The basis for Morton's conclusions was his collection of human crania, an interest he acquired about the year 1820. Morton's *Crania Americana* (1839) referred to thirteen separate measurements of 276 specimens representative of Caucasian, Malayan, American, and Ethiopian types. Each of these races, concluded Morton, had a separate phylogeny stretching back through at least several thousand years. Morton initially refrained from asserting that these races lacked a unitary origin; he implied rather, on the model Lord Kames's evasion, that there had been divine intervention after Adam to bring about racial differences. In this way Morton argued that there "was a primal difference among men" which cannot be effaced by climate or learning; at the same time he avoided direct conflict with prevailing theological dogma. By 1849, however, Morton was arguing that the races were separate species, despite their ability to produce fertile hybrids, and he had, in effect, embraced a full-fledged theory of divine polygenesis. One of the considerations in Morton's change of mind was the dawning appreciation of the antiquity of the Egyptian skeletal material brought about by the decipherment of the Rosetta stone in 1821. Morton's second book, *Crania Egyptica* (1844), made much of the fact that Negroid and Caucasoid types were depicted in Egyptian paintings dating back several thousand years. Too little time was left over between the creation and the early dynasties for these racial types to have evolved from a common ancestor.

After 1846, Morton's position was strongly supported by the prestigious figure of the Harvard naturalist Louis Agassiz, who found it "much more in harmony with the laws of nature" to admit that "in the beginning the Creator had designed different species of men, as he had done with all other animals, to occupy a particular geographical region." But Morton's two most devoted disciples were George R. Gliddon, who as vice-consul in Cairo had kept Morton supplied with Egyptian skulls, and Josiah Clark Nott, probably the first American scientist to state publicly a belief that God had made several different human species at the time of creation (*cf.* STANTON 1960:69). Nott and Gliddon (1854) collaborated on a voluminous study entitled *Types of Mankind* in which it was argued that the races of man were separately created species, and that each possessed a "constant and undeviating" physical and moral nature which could be changed only by interbreeding.

THE AMERICAN SCHOOL AND SLAVERY

Although Morton regarded the Negro race to be inferior to the Caucasoid, he denied any interest in contributing to the proslavery position. Nott and Gliddon, on the other hand, were openly committed to a defense of slavery on the grounds that for an inferior species, slavery was the most humane condition of life. Agassiz completed the spectrum of opinion among the polygenists of the American School by insisting that there was no justification for slavery in man's polygenetic origin since all the races share a common generic human nature. Privately, however, Agassiz did not conceal his contempt for the Negro type.

William Stanton's denial of a correlation between the polygenists and proslavery rests largely upon the fact that John Bachman (1850), the most effective opponent of Morton's school, was a dedicated supporter of the South's "peculiar institution." Bachman was both a collaborator of John Audubon and the minister of a Lutheran congregation in Charleston, South Carolina. He not only fought the doctrine of separate creations, but he also rejected the ancillary arguments that might have been useful for the slavocracy. For example, Bachman ridiculed the idea that Negro-white hybrids were infertile and that there was a natural sexual aversion between the races. Bachman's interest in opposing polygenesis was not to urge abolition, but rather to protect the prevailing Biblical justification of slavery. Holy Scripture tells how Noah blessed the descendants of Shem by making them "the parents of the Caucasian race—the progenitor of the Israelites and our Savior."

The Mongolians were the children of Japheth, and as the Bible predicted, many of them are still living in tents. Ham was the third of Noah's sons and the ancestor of the black "servant of servant" race. In slavery, the superior white race leads the inferior black race by the hand, protecting and improving them. Bachman's Biblical exegesis was the main intellectual pap from which the slavocrats drew their moral sustenance. Nott and Gliddon who also frankly professed the wisdom of slavery were apparently more interested in "skinning parsons" than in defending the South. Their polygenism threatened the ideological fabric of Christian civilization; it brought into question not only the origin of the races, but the authority of the Christian priesthood and the authenticity of the West's sacred writings. This was too high a price to pay, even for the defense of slavery.

> In 1854 the editor of the hotly secessionist Richmond *Enquirer* suspected that many readily accepted the "infidel" doctrine of diversity because it seemed to "favor the system of slavery." But the system could afford no such defenders as Nott and Gliddon if the Bible was to be "the price it must pay for them." The Bible, he pointed out with some acumen, was now "the grand object of attack from Abolitionists, because they know it is the bulwark of Southern principles. . . . Destroy the Bible, and you lay bare the very citadel of our strength to our foes. . . . Let us not then allow this shield of strength to be torn from us until we have something to put in its place." The Bible did lend considerable support to slavery, but so did science. Opting for the Bible was a mark of the South's already profound commitment to religion. Heretofore this had not necessarily been an anti-intellectual position. But when the issue was clearly drawn the South turned its back on the only intellectually respectable defense of slavery it could have taken up [STANTON 1960:194].

It was not true, of course, that the abolitionists had made the Bible "the grand object of attack." This was nothing but rhetoric. Both North and South appealed to the Bible for their main arguments; the question was whose interpretation was the correct one, not whether the Bible itself was reliable. In this connection, it is important to note that the abolitionists, unlike the slavocrats, would have been unable to turn to a scientific justification of their position, had they been so inclined. There was no school of anthropologists in the United States that opposed both Morton and slavery, nor was one to appear for another fifty years. Moral arguments gleaned from the New Testament were thus the principal weapons of the abolitionists. The importance of Biblical authority to both the pro- and antislavery forces provides a preview of the ideological storm that was about to break over Darwin's attempt to discredit the Bible in a more vigorous and sweeping fashion.

POLYGENESIS AND DARWINISM

Almost every major anthropological volume written in Europe and the United States between 1800 and 1859 concerned itself with the controversy between polygenesis and monogenesis. As James Hunt noted in 1863, many persons still believed "ethnology merely attempts to solve the question whether there was unity of origin for different races of man." It might be thought that with the publication of the *Origin of Species* in 1859, the dispute between the monogenists and the polygenists would come to an abrupt end. From the point of view of the new theory, both sides were in error. If mankind had a common ancestor, it was no longer Adam, but some sort of monkey. Why argue about whether it was the same kind of monkey for everybody? Indeed, Thomas Huxley took the position that Darwin's theory had had the effect of "reconciling and combining all that is good in the Monogenistic and Polygenistic schools" (quoted in HUNT 1866b: 320). The monogenists kept their common humanity and their progressivism; the polygenists were upheld in their Biblical criticism and their scientism. Actually, Darwin's reconciliation was not as decisive as Huxley had made it out to be. James Hunt, president of the Anthropological Society of London, was quick to accept Darwin's major points, but he accused Huxley of being a monogenist in disguise. According to Hunt, Darwin's theories merely made it more probable than ever that the contemporary races were actually different species. Moreover, some of them were doomed to meet their extinction at the hands of the others, just as in the struggle for survival among the members of the animal kingdom.

Although it gradually came to be accepted that all contemporary human groups belong to the same species, even this did not really put an end to the monogenist-polygenist controversy. The question still remained as to how long the races have maintained a separate phylogeny within the species. An unbroken tradition within physical anthropology connects James Hunt and the pre-Darwinian polygenists with such figures as Ernest Hooton and Carlton Coon in the twentieth century. For Hooton, the splitting off of the non-Caucasoids from the central hominid line (which he identified with Piltdown Man, later exposed as a hoax) occurred almost a million years ago. Indeed, according to Hooton, the Bushmanoid type had split off in the Pliocene, even earlier than the beginning of the specific difference between gorillas and chimpanzees. Coon (1962) preserves this tradition by arguing that the major racial types underwent parallel evolution throughout the transition from the australopithecine to the Homo sapiens "grade." It should be noted that all of these attempts to maintain a separate genealogy for the Caucasoids rest on pure speculation as soon as an antiquity in the order of tens of thousands of years is invoked. Fossils tell us nothing about skin color, hair form, nose and lip size, or epicanthic folds—precisely the features that provide the basis for traditional raciological constructs.

Despite twentieth-century polygenist survivals, there is much to be said for Huxley's view that Darwinism had saved all that was "good" in the rivalry between monogenism and polygenism. Only, we must be careful to confine our understanding of "good" to what was functional in the mid-century context in which Darwin and Huxley found themselves. Because Darwin's theory did not address itself directly to the polygenist or monogenist argument, it appears superficially to constitute a rather separate phase of intellectual history. Yet Darwin and the monogenists and polygenists were all being borne along by a fundamentally similar set of ideological needs. In a functional sense, the *Origin of Species* was the culmination of an uninterrupted series of attempts to satisfy these needs—a culmination toward which the monogenists and polygenists also tended, but which they were prevented from achieving due to their failure to break away sufficiently from the confines of Biblically inspired discourse.

THE INGREDIENTS OF THE DARWINIAN SYNTHESIS

What were these underlying ideological trends? First, there was increasing dissatisfaction among scientists with the Biblical version of creation. Another was mounting pressure to return to the doctrine of human progress, despite its connection with the French Revolution; and the third was an intensification of racist arrogance, of which the biologization of sociocultural theory was a symptom.

All three of these trends were embodied in the work of James Cowles Prichard, the most prominent English anthropologist of the first half of the nineteenth century. Prichard's influence, based on multiple editions of his *Researches into the Physical History of Man* (1813), overlapped the Darwinian period. According to J. A. Barnes (1960:373) it was Prichard rather than Darwin or Alfred Wallace whose writings provided the background for the discussion of race during the sixties. What is remarkable about Prichard's work is the extent to which his insistence on monogenetic orthodoxy led him down the path toward the heresy of bio-evolution. Where Buffon and Blumenbach had viewed the Negro as a product of degeneration from Adamic perfection, Prichard introduced the novel proposal that Adam had been a Negro. Under the influence of civilization, man had gradually turned white: ". . . it must be concluded that the process of Nature in the human species is the transmutation of the characters of the Negro into those of the European, or the evolution of white varieties in black races of man" (PRICHARD 1813, quoted in GREENE 1959:242). Prichard was convinced that the lower classes of civilized societies, and barbarians and savages, represented a continuum of darkening pigments. Anticipating Darwin's *Descent of Man*, he sought to explain this correlation in terms of a principle closely resembling sexual selection. Providence had implanted in original human nature an idea of physical beauty by which matings favor the lighter types. As the dark savages advance toward civilization, their perception of the ideal becomes intellectually clearer and they become physically lighter. Because of Prichard's firm belief in the *potential* equality of all the races, his scheme bears a benign resemblance to the synthesis Spencer was to achieve some years later. Given enough time, the inferior races will become civilized and then will even come to resemble their European conquerors. What was lacking to complete the picture was the utilization of the principle of struggle to explain why some races never "made it."

Despite Prichard's belief in the inferiority of the darker races, he was an outspoken critic of slavery and a staunch advocate of human rights. Like most of the humanitarians of the period, his scientific views were heavily dependent on Biblical inspiration. Religion was for him the chief distinguishing characteristic between man and beast. The very fact that Christianity could be preached and understood among so many different peoples proved that the races had psychological unity, which in turn proved that they must have had a common origin.

RACIAL DETERMINISM AND THE ROOTS OF DARWINISM

The importance of early nineteenth-century theories of racial determinism as a spawning ground for Darwin's synthesis is well demonstrated in the work of Prichard's contemporary, the Anglo-American physician William Charles Wells. On the basis of his examination of a white woman on whose body black patches had begun to appear, Wells (1818) concluded that climate was not the originating factor in racial differences. He took skin color to be a rather superficial aspect of these differences. To account for the color of human skin, Wells assumed that certain pigments happened to be correlated with resistance to disease. This led him to a theory of natural selection based on differential survival, a full thirty years before Darwin:

> Of the accidental varieties of man, which would occur among the first few scattered inhabitants of the middle region of Africa, some one would be better fitted than others to bear the diseases of the country. This race would consequently multiply, while the others would decrease, not only from their inability to sustain the attacks of disease, but from their incapacity of contending with their more vigorous neighbors. The colour of this race I take for granted, from what has been already said, would be dark. But the same disposition to form varieties still existing, a darker and darker race would in the course of time occur, and as the darkest would be the best fitted for the climate, this would at length become the most prevalent, if not the only race, in the particular country in which it had originated [quoted in GREENE 1959:245].

By a similar correlation between skin color and resistance to disease in the North, the Caucasoids came to dominate the temperate region. Although Darwin did not mention Wells in his original list of acknowledgments, James Prichard and Robert Knox (see p. 99) were influenced by him; and both of these evolutionists, in turn, did influence Darwin (CURTIN 1964:238; SHRYOCK 1944).

To the modern temper, racial determinism and humanitarian piety are not easily reconcilable. But in Darwin's century there was to be no limit to Christian charity on behalf of "inferior" races. Sir William Lawrence, perhaps the second-ranking British anthropologist of the early nineteenth century, was more outspoken than Prichard about the innate inferiority of the non-Caucasoids. Lawrence subscribed to Blumenbach's degeneration theory, but unlike the latter, he was not inclined to collect examples of Negroes who had gone to school and written books:

> The distinction of colour between the white and black races is not more striking than the pre-eminence of the former in moral feelings and in mental endowments. The latter, it is true, exhibit generally a great acuteness of the external senses, which in some instances is heightened by exercise to a degree nearly incredible. Yet they indulge, almost universally, in disgusting debauchery and sensuality, and display gross selfishness, indifference to the

> pains and pleasure of others, insensibility to beauty of form, order, and harmony, and an almost entire want of what we comprehend altogether under the expression of elevated sentiments, manly virtues, and moral feelings [quoted in CURTIN 1964: 232].

Lawrence, like Prichard, was an outspoken critic of slavery. Just as a monogenist like Bachman could support slavery on the grounds of paternalism, a monogenist like Lawrence could decry slavery, on the same grounds. Indeed, in British antislavery circles, the more childlike and savage the "inferior" races, the more they were regarded as needing the help of the civilized branches of humanity. According to Lawrence, the proslavery forces were

> . . . perverting what should constitute a claim to kindness and indulgence into justification or palliation of the revolting and anti-christian practice of traffic in human flesh. . . . Superior endowments, higher intellect, greater capacity for knowledge, arts and science, should be employed to extend the blessings of civilization and multiply the enjoyments of social life; not as a means of oppressing the weak and ignorant, or plunging those who are naturally low in the intellectual scale still more deeply into the abysses of barbarianism [*ibid.*:240].

As Phillip Curtin emphasizes, Lawrence here was expressing a pre-Darwinian version of "White-man's burden." The essential ingredients of this rationalization of empire were clearly not dependent upon Darwin's or even Spencer's genius. It was merely necessary to believe that the "inferior" races were retarded branches of humanity; to feel a strong sense of Christian charity; and to have an unlimited need for cheap labor and raw materials. All these ingredients were present long before Darwin and Spencer came on the scene. What remained to be added was the doctrine of the "survival of the fittest," by which it later became possible to relieve the white man of his sense of guilt for failing to shoulder enough of the weight of charity.

The years leading up to Darwin thus witnessed a steady increase in the degree of importance attached to racial differences. Few European or American men of science resisted the trend. More and more, it came to be accepted that the white race had an innate and almost permanent advantage over all the rest. The prima-facie case for these beliefs seemed overwhelming. Since the fifteenth century, Euro-Americans had met with countless peoples in Africa, America, Asia, and the Pacific Islands, not one of whom had been able effectively to ward off or retaliate against the advance of European military, economic, political, and religious institutions. As Samuel Morton put it to his anatomy class in 1840: "In Asia, in Africa, in America, in the torrid and in the frigid zones, have not all the other races of men yielded and given place to this one . . ." (quoted in STANTON 1960:41).

RACISM AND THE DOCTRINE OF PERFECTIBILITY

The men of the Enlightenment, Turgot and Condorcet for example, had also assumed the superiority of European civilization; and following Blumenbach and Buffon some had connected race with culture through a pre-Lamarckian version of the inheritance of acquired characteristics. The racism of the eighteenth century, however, remained a modest doctrine, circumscribed by environmentalism and plagued with doubts about the respective merits of the noble savages and their vice-ridden civilized conquerors (*cf.* FAIRCHILD 1928). Above all, the Enlightenment had qualified its racism with the doctrine of "perfectibility." Humanity, regardless of the present shape, color, or institution, could be led through unlimited stages of progress to earthly beatitude. Although this may have been more of a hope than a conviction among the *philosophes,* the opposite point of view was very much on the defensive. After the French Revolution both sides of the issue continued to be argued, but the balance seems to have shifted in favor of those who denied that all the races and classes of men could participate equally in the progress that one branch was achieving. Increasingly it came to be understood that mankind was engaged in a struggle that would eliminate the inferior and elevate the superior nations and races. As Curtin (1964:374) has remarked:

> The exterminated people were all of the colored races, while the exterminators always appeared to be European. It seemed obvious that some natural law of race relations was at work, that the extinction of the non-Europeans was part of the natural evolution of the world.

For Thomas Carlyle, as for many of those who took the side of the South in the slavery controversy, it could only be concluded that the darker races had been created inferior in order to serve the whites. Their status was fixed at that level for all time.

> That, you may depend on it, my obscure Black friends, is and always was the Law of the World, for you and for all men: to *be* servants, the more foolish of us to the more wise; and only sorrow, futility and disappointment will betide both, till both in some approximate degree get to conform to same [CARLYLE quoted in CURTIN 1964:380-81].

RACIOLOGY, PHRENOLOGY, AND THE CEPHALIC INDEX

One of the symptoms of the drift away from the principle of perfectibility was the increasing attention being paid to measuring the head. Through craniometry, anthropologists expressed their interest in the innate components of behavior—they were trying to find out what was inside the supposedly empty cabinet. Phrenology, founded by Joseph Gall (1825), was a manifestation of that interest. According to Gall, the human mind consisted of 37 different faculties, the strength or weakness of which could be detected by measuring the corresponding regions of the cranium. Although Gall himself refrained from applying phrenology to racial groups, his followers were quick to see its possibilities. It was Gall's disciple, George Combe (1819), who got Samuel Morton to start collecting skulls. While Morton himself turned to the measurement of cranial capacity through the use of pepper seed, his *Crania Americana* included an appendix by Combe in which the phrenological evidence for Caucasian superiority was set forth. William Lawrence (1819) also made use of phrenological concepts as did W. F. Edwards (1841), an English writer who was influenced by the French nationalist-racist, Augustin Thierry. Phrenological measurements were notoriously imprecise, and the entire system functioned as a kind of projective test in which the observer could match his prejudices to arbitrary eminences and ridges on his subject's head. The scientific interest in the skull as the bony container of the brain culminated with the establishment of the cephalic index, the ratio of head length to breadth, by Anders Retzius of Stockholm in 1840. With the use of calipers, the cephalic index can be obtained with considerable precision, and this measurement became the mainstay of anthropometry throughout the remainder of the century. Thought to be resistant to environmental influences, it was for long the favorite diagnostic of racial phylogeny, until Franz Boas' (1912) studies of immigrants to the United States showed that head form responded to environmental factors within the span of a single generation.

THE IMMINENCE OF DARWIN

In Britain the pre-Darwinian tendency to "biologize" history culminated in the theories of Robert Knox, an Edinburgh surgeon who made his living from lecturing on "transcendental anatomy" (1850:34–35). Knox believed that "race is everything; literature, science—in a word, civilization depends on it" (*ibid.*:7). Knox insisted that the Negroes were members of another species and presented (incorrect) evidence that successive generations of mulattoes became progressively infertile. No one can read Knox without sensing the imminence of Darwin, for Knox's interpretation of history involved a physical and cultural evolutionary progression, produced by a life and death struggle between the dark and light races of mankind. The dark races had evolved first, but the whites were destined to surpass them and to bring about their extinction. In this fashion Knox anticipated both Spencer and Darwin as far as natural selection applied to human evolution was concerned. Knox also proposed an evolutionary view of the origin of all other species, postulating an order of emergence through mollusks, fish, birds, quadrupeds, and man. But he failed to apply the concept of struggle and extinction to the process of speciation. His larger evolutionary model was based on embryology: new creatures emerged in their proper turn, just as the embryo goes through its phases of maturation.

THE RACIST AND ANTIRACIST SPECTRUM

Were there no countercurrents? During the 1860's Britain's rapidly growing community of anthropological scholars found itself sharply divided on the issue of race. Two factions had emerged out of the crisis produced by the American Civil War. One group carried on in the tradition of Prichard, favored the doctrine of perfectibility, was antislavery, and was associated with the Anthropological Society of London. The other group followed Knox, denied the doctrine of perfectability, was polygenist, pro-South, and proslavery. In 1862, the dissidents set up a new journal, the *Anthropological Review*, in which they attacked the older school. Under the influence of the syntheses achieved by Spencer and Darwin, the dispute was resolved toward the end of the decade and the achievement of unity formally celebrated in the founding of a new association, the Royal Anthropological Society of Great Britain and Ireland. It cannot be said, however, that Prichard's group was antiracist. Both factions during the sixties believed in the biocultural inferiority of non-Caucasoids, and both assumed that explanations of sociocultural differences and similarities necessarily involved racial factors. With the founding of the Royal Anthropological Society, the racist position remained dominant. It is a fact inadequately appreciated by modern anthropologists who are accustomed to viewing their image in the mirror of twentieth-century relativism that the professionalization of anthropology as a discipline coincided with, and was intimately associated with, the rise of raciology. By the sixties, anthropology and racial determinism had become almost synonyms. Within anthropology, the only issue was whether the "inferior" races could legitimately aspire to improvement.

To identify the antithesis of Knox and Hunt, one must look beyond the boundaries to which a tradition of exaggerated historicism has confined the formative place of anthropology. When professional anthropologists finally broke through to an antiracist environmentalism in the twentieth century, they often seemed convinced that such ideas had never been entertained before; and in fact, among those who had called themselves anthropologists during the preceding fifty years, no glimmer of egalitarianism could be found. But the tradition of Helvetius did not die during the nineteenth century, however much what was then the mainstream of anthropology was dedicated to destroying it. As we have seen, the greatest defender of racial egalitarianism during the first half of the eighteenth century was John Stuart Mill. Building on the social engineering tradition of the utilitarians under Jeremy Bentham, Mill advocated a form of political and economic liberalism that took into consideration the immediate dependence of human "nature" on the sociopolitical arrangements to which individuals and groups are exposed. It was Mill and the Benthamites, not James Prichard or Theodor Waitz, who were the objects of the most scathing attacks in the *Anthropological Review*.

One other source of opposition to the nineteenth-century racists must be mentioned. A shade to the political left of Mill began the specter of the socialist and communist reformers and revolutionists. Most of these figures were considered to be too disreputable to be mentioned in a learned journal. As in the case of Marx, the socialists adhered to the radical environmentalism that eventually became the central doctrine of twentieth-century anthropology. But we must defer our discussion of the relationship between socialist theory and anthropology to a subsequent chapter.

RACISM IN GERMANY

The rise of racial determinism on the Continent paralleled developments in Great Britain. Both Hegel and Comte included racial factors in their analysis of world history and were contemptuous of non-European peoples. In Germany, the main thread of Gustav Klemm's (1843) ten-volume culture-history of mankind was the division of humanity into "active" and "passive" races. The latter included Mongoloids, Negroids, Egyptians, Finns, Hindus, and the lower classes of Europe. The Germanic stock represented the highest form of the "active" races. Both the active and passive races were working their way in a kind of Hegelian process through the stages of savagery, "tameness," and freedom. According to Klemm, one race needs the other, much as men need women, but the highest attainments of each stage are reserved for the active race. Although both Robert Lowie (1938:14) and Phillip Curtin (1964:377) minimize the racist ingredient in Klemm, it is clear that he was deeply involved in biologizing history.

Lowie (1938:17) also attempts to place Klemm's contemporary, Theodor Waitz, in the same favorable light, asserting that he "deprecates rash verdicts on racial disabilities." He even proposes Waitz's *Anthropologie der Naturvölker* (1859–72) as a "worthy forerunner of Boas' *The Mind of Primitive Man*" (1911). It is true that Waitz, like Prichard, took exception to the more extreme conclusions of what he calls the "American School": "According to the teaching of the American School, the higher races are destined to replace the lower. . . . The pious manslayer thus enjoys the consolation that he acts according to the laws of nature which govern the rise of man" (WAITZ 1863:351). But Waitz, again like Prichard, never doubted that there were "higher" and "lower" races of man even though he believed, as did Prichard, that "the psychic endowment of the various races was most probably originally the same or nearly so" (*ibid.*). Waitz saw the differences in the rate of evolution from the primitive state as depending on "the natural and social conditions in which they were placed" (*ibid.*). Although he further believed that there was no proof that "the so-called lower races are condemned to remain in their present state" (*ibid.*:320), he nonetheless insisted that "the development of civilization is, with some few unimportant exceptions, limited chiefly to the Caucasian race" (*ibid.*:8). As a compendium of misinformation about the relationship between race and culture, Waitz's books hold their own with those of his contemporaries. It is difficult to understand how Lowie could have mistaken Waitz's rather standard monogenesism as a precedent for Boas' *Mind of Primitive Man*. Waitz was fighting a rear-guard action against the extreme racial determinists who sought to base all of history on racial differences. Some idea of how far Waitz stood from Boas may be obtained from Waitz's assertion that the people of "all uncultured nations possess, in comparison with civilized nations, a large mouth and somewhat thick lips" (*ibid.*:74). There is also Waitz's belief that "the voice of the Negro is low and hoarse in the males, but acute and shrieking among women" (*ibid.*:95). Among the mental characteristics of the inferior races,

Waitz included improvidence, a condition he supports by reference to the imagined fact that the "Caribs sell their hammocks cheaper in the morning than in the evening" (*ibid.*:295).

RACISM IN FRANCE

In France, pre-Darwinian racism culminates in the writing of Count J. A. de Gobineau. A bitter foe of the entire Enlightenment heritage, Gobineau's ideas were destined to survive into the twentieth century. They received their ultimate expression in the Nazi attempts at genocide. It is interesting to note that Pitirim Sorokin, a staunch supporter of the worst of the racial determinist fallacies, said of Gobineau's book (1928:229) that it was "written brilliantly, with the charm of an excellent stylist, the fascination of an original thinker, and marked by clearness and logicity of ideas, and finally by unusual erudition." It is easy to understand Gobineau, defender of French reaction and sorrower after lost nobility. But history, in anthropological perspective, must deal more harshly with Sorokin. Gobineau's self-appointed task was to rid the world of the idea that a better life could be achieved by a significant segment of mankind. Race, like original sin, chains humanity to misery and eternal failure. Even though all nations are doomed eventually to pass away without achieving their dreams, some are noble, others despicable and brutish. The differences can never be effaced:

> It is said . . . that all branches of the human family are endowed with intellectual capacities of the same nature, which, though in different stages of development, are all equally susceptible of improvement. This is not, perhaps, the precise language, but certainly the meaning. Thus, the Huron, by proper culture, might become the equal of the Englishman and Frenchman. Why, then, I would ask, did he never, in the course of centuries, invent the art of printing or apply the power of steam; why, among the warriors of his tribe, has there never arisen a Caesar or a Charlemagne, among his bards and medicine-men, a Homer or a Hippocrates [GOBINEAU 1856:176; orig. 1853]?

Gobineau rejected any significant role for the sociopolitical or geographical milieu. All is race. Each ethnic group has its own peculiar capabilities and destiny:

> This is what the whole course of history teaches us. Every race has its own modes of thinking: every race, capable of developing a civilization, develops one peculiar to itself, and which it cannot

> engraft upon any other, except by amalgamation of blood, and then in but a modified degree. The European cannot win the Asiatic to his modes of thinking; he cannot civilize the Australian, or the Negro; he can transmit but a portion of his intelligence to his halfbreed offspring of the inferior race; the progeny of that half-breed and the nobler branch of his ancestry, is but one degree nearer, but not equal to that branch in capacity: the proportions of blood are strictly preserved. . . . Are we not, then, authorized to conclude that the diversity observable among them is constitutional, innate, and not the result of accident or circumstances—that there is an absolute inequality in their intellectual endowments [*ibid.*:438].

Gobineau's opposition to the doctrine of perfectibility was reactionary to the point of denying the superiority of modern Europe over that of Greece and Rome. He admitted only that advances had been achieved in the technological sphere. In social and political affairs, there had been little progress, and it was vain to believe that one civilization could surpass the others in all realms of life. Nonetheless, the perfectibility of the Caucasians, especially of the Aryans, was greater than that of the inferior races.

As a devout Christian, Gobineau had to reconcile the evident ability of savages to accept Christianity with the assertion that the inferior races could not rise to the level of European civilization. Prichard, Waitz, and many others among the scientific racists of the period based their main arguments for perfectibility on the fact that all men were susceptible to religious conversion. Gobineau's exit from this dilemma was achieved by stressing Christianity's appeal to the "lowly and simple." "Intellect and learning are not necessary to salvation." The superiority of Christianity resides in the fact that it can be understood and accepted by the lowest of human types. But this does not mean that in other matters the lower branches of humanity can aspire to equality with Europeans:

> It is wrong therefore to consider the equal aptitudes of all races for the true religion, as proof of their intellectual equality. Though having embraced it, they will still display the same characteristic differences, and divergent or even opposite tendencies [*ibid.*:223].

Although Gobineau's biologization of history corresponded to one of the three main pre-Darwin trends, his theories were directly opposed to the other two. There was little use in the aggressive bourgeois ambience of mid-century for a doctrine of despair. It is not in the nature of either the entrepreneur or the soldier of fortune to doubt the idea of progress. In addition, Gobineau was disdainful of science and had little interest in associating his theories with a secular outlook. In a sense, Gobineau was far ahead of his time. It was not until Europe once again grew weary of reason and progress that his ideas were properly appreciated.

In the meantime the ideological currents, of which early nineteenth-century racial determinism was a manifestation, were moving toward a different climax. Competition, progress, perfection, expansion, struggle, conquest—these were the themes, dynamic and optimistic, which awaited a joining with the biological interpretation of history. The fusion of all of these diverse elements into one grand scientific theory was the achievement of Herbert Spencer and Charles Darwin. Yet the sociocultural need for this synthesis was so clear and the ideological ground so thoroughly prepared that in the absence of both of these geniuses, exact replicas of their theories would soon have arisen from parallel and convergent sources. Evidence in support of this statement will be presented in a moment.

THE SOCIOCULTURAL ROOTS OF SPENCER AND DARWIN

It is beyond the scope of the present volume to provide a panorama of the sociocultural milieu that nourished and rewarded the theories of Spencer and Darwin. Yet certain general aspects of the epoch cannot be neglected. The milieu in question was remarkable for the intensity and geographical expanse of its international wars, its internecine political struggles and class warfare, its uninhibited economic competitiveness, and its rapid pace of technological and scientific change. The gigantic national mobilizations achieved during the Napoleonic wars had raised the organizational efficiency of the European nation-state to unprecedented levels. At the same time technological advances had increased the geographic range of military conquest and commercial exploitation to encompass the entire earth. But the European nations were complex heterogeneous supersocieties in which control over the state apparatus lingered on the outcome of domestic struggles no less fierce than those waged abroad. Within the rapidly expanding populations sharp differences in wealth and access to strategic natural resources and productive equipment generated intensely divisive forces. Domestic revolutions or near revolutions alternated with foreign wars carried out on an ever-increasing scale.

It would seem undeniable that the wedding between racism and the doctrine of struggle was in part an excrescence of this class and national warfare. Racism could be invoked to overcome the class and ethnic diversities of the modern nation. The fiction of common descent enshrined in the metaphor of fatherland and motherland, and applied indiscriminately to the overwhelmingly hybrid populations of Europe, improved the tone of civil and military organization. The racial interpretation of nationhood imparted to the physical, cultural, and linguistic hodgepodges known as England, France, Germany, etc., a sense of community based on the illusion of a common origin and the mirage of a common destiny. In the mystique of racially inspired patriotism, nations made war with increased efficiency while blunting the divisive effects of class antagonism at home. Romanticism in art and literature was an essential aspect of this mystique. National destinies, uncontrolled and uncontrollable, welling up from the racial past, were stridently proclaimed as the fulfillment of art and life. Racism also had its uses as a justification for class and caste hierarchies; it was a splendid explanation of both national and class privilege. It helped to maintain slavery and serfdom; it smoothed the way for the rape of Africa and the slaughter of the American Indian; it steeled the nerves of the Manchester captains of industry as they lowered wages, lengthened the working day, and hired more women and children.

As the racial interpretation of history cast its spell over the Euro-American intelligentsia, there arose a parallel doctrine that spread with equal speed across the same territory. This was the ideology specific to industrial entrepreneurship, *laissez-faire*, the justification for economic competition, wage labor, profits, and capital accumulation. It was the ideology of an ascendant economic system whose prodigious energies derived from maximizing rewards and punishments for the outcome of endless numbers of competitive encounters. Under Adam Smith, the material welfare of each individual as well as of the total society had been shown to be dependent upon unfettered competition in the market place. Progress in material welfare arose only from this endless economic struggle. Any softening of its conditions in the name of Christian charity or political sovereignty would inevitably decrease the well being of the citizenry. For the economic order was governed by immutable laws; capitalism was a self-regulating machine whose mainspring was competition.

Prior to Spencer's and Darwin's influence, racism and classical economic theory unfolded along separate trajectories. Adam Smith, Ricardo, and Malthus in their own writings made no contribution to racist theories of history. On the other hand, Prichard, Lawrence, Klemm, Waitz, and the other pre-Darwinian racial determinists were uninterested in uniting their ideas with the theory of the industrial capitalism. What connection after all could exist between such diverse phenomena as warfare, raciation, and competition in the market place? It took the combined geniuses of Spencer and Darwin to find the common ingredient, to see the "struggle for survival" operating in every sphere of life, to subsume all change, whether inorganic, organic, or superorganic, under a single law of evolution, and thus to complete the biologization of history without surrendering the Enlightenment's dream of universal progress.

Spencerism 5

To propose that Herbert Spencer's and Charles Darwin's theories were an inevitable product of a certain phase of Western history is not to deny the contribution of cumulative scientific advances to the perfection of biological and sociocultural evolutionism. The very same forces that brought the themes of progress, race, and struggle to the forefront of Spencer's and Darwin's attention were also responsible for strengthening the authority and prestige of science. Laissez-faire individualism was related by positive feedback to the development of science. Economic and political liberalism, themselves a product of technological and scientific advance, exerted an immensely stimulating effect on all forms of scientific inquiry. The technological pay-off resulting from this inquiry was essential to the maintenance of capitalism. Although theological dogmas continued to be useful in the control and discipline of the masses, a veritable cornucopia of technological miracles forced the theological establishment into an essentially rear-guard action. Finally, in 1859, Darwin's materialist explanation of the origin of species broke the authority of the theologians in the domain of the life sciences.

5. Spencerism

Why did Charles Darwin succeed where Jean Baptiste Lamarck had failed? It seems unlikely that it was merely the more advanced phase of capitalism in which Darwin was privileged to operate. We must not discount the fact that in the interval between Lamarck and Darwin a great strengthening of the secular world view had been quietly going on under the stimulus of continuing scientific advance. Driven partly underground by the political counterrevolution, it awaited the first possible opportunity to burst forth and resume the task that Galileo had begun. J. C. Nott and G. R. Gliddon's passion for "parson skinning" is an indication of how far this trend had been able to progress even under the most adverse conditions. In addition to the erosion of theological authority as a general consequence of scientific advance, the way had been prepared for Darwin by a confrontation between theology and science on an issue of the greatest importance for the theory of bio-evolution. This issue was the age of the earth. It was here that Darwin's main advantage over Lamarck resided. For Lamarck had to contend with the theologians not only on the question of organic evolution, but on the question of geological evolution as well. Let us pause for a moment, therefore, to consider the new understanding of the earth's history.

GEOLOGY SHOWS THE WAY

During most of the eighteenth century, the nascent discipline of geology languished under the tutelage of scriptural authority. Except for modifications introduced by the flood, the earth was regarded as having preserved the form imparted to it at the beginning of the world. A considerable amount of research effort was dedicated to proving that Genesis and the earth's strata both told the same story. Alpine deposits bearing the remains of marine life were hailed as confirmation of the former presence of water deep enough to submerge the highest peaks. Fossils of extinct animals simply proved that not all of the antediluvian creatures had managed to reach the safety of the ark.

> When the history of the earth began to be considered geologically, it was simply assumed that a universal deluge must have wrought vast changes and that it had been a primary agent in forming the present surface of the globe. Its occurrence was evidence that the Lord was a governor as well as a creator [GILLISPIE 1951:42].

Among geologists, James Hutton's *Theory of the Earth* (1788), the foundation of the so-called Vulcanist school, marked the first sustained refutation of this viewpoint. Hutton's theories challenged the explanation of the earth's strata offered by the Neptunist school. The latter was represented in Great Britain by Robert Jameson, who was in turn a student of the founder of Neptunism, Gottlieb Werner, professor of mineralogy at Freiburg in Saxony. Inspired by the Biblical account, Werner and Jameson argued that all the earth's rocks had precipitated out of a briny solution in several well-defined stages, corresponding to the stages of creation, and had remained in place ever since in the form of the geological strata. Hutton on the other hand avoided the issue of creation altogether and attempted to interpret geomorphological features in terms of the cumulative effect of natural physical and chemical processes such as heat, pressure, and various forms of physical and chemical weathering. The implications of Hutton's interpretation for the age of the earth were heretical since relatively minute forces working over long periods of time now were responsible for the effects hitherto attributed to instantaneous cataclysms.

EIGHTEENTH-CENTURY PRECEDENTS

It is interesting to note that Hutton's ideas had been preceded in the eighteenth century by a number of more outspoken, but geologically less well-informed, proposals. Georges Buffon, stimulated by Gottfried Leibniz, had even carried out a series of experiments with heated iron balls in an attempt to date the earth. Assuming that the earth had originally been in a molten condition, Buffon sought to estimate the time that would have had to elapse for it to have cooled to its present temperature. In *Epochs of Nature* (1778) Buffon concluded that a minimum of 75,000 years had passed, but he deliberately restrained himself from longer estimates in deference to the scriptural account. Immanuel Kant was the proponent of a more audacious view. In the *Universal Natural History and Theory of the Heavens* he postulated an infinite universe where "millions and whole myriads of millions of centuries will flow on during which always new worlds and systems of worlds will be formed" (KANT, quoted in HABER 1959:153). There were many other stirrings of a similar sort, especially among *philosophes* like D'Holbach and Diderot. Indeed, Haber presents the Wernerian Neptunists as the counterattack against the anti-Mosaic trends of the mid-eighteenth century. But by the time Lamarck wrote his *Hydrogeology* (1802) there was no remaining effective challenge to the short chronology. Lamarck's proposal that the earth had existed for several billion years was greeted with even more contempt than his idea that men were descended from fish. He himself regarded the resistance to the chronology of billions of years as the main obstacle to the acceptance of his idea on organic evolution. He despaired of convincing his contemporaries of the errors in their Wernerian empiricism and their slavish adherence to the Mosaic account:

> These considerations, I know, having never been presented elsewhere than in my Hydrogeology, and not having obtained the serious examination that I believe they deserve, can only appear extraordinary even to the most enlightened persons.
>
> Indeed, man, who judges the greatness of duration only relative to himself and not to nature, will undoubtedly never actually find the slow mutations which I have just presented and consequently he will believe it necessary to reject without examination my opinion on these great subjects [LAMARCK, quoted in HABER 1959: 179].

The defenders of the Biblical chronology held the upper hand through the first two decades of the nineteenth century. Under Georges Cuvier (1811) and William Buckland (1823), as evidence of not one "flood" but of dozens accumulated, the doctrine of "catastrophism"—a series of miraculous destructions and creations—was brought in to salvage the Biblical story. It was not until 1820 that the Vulcanists' requirements for an expanded chronology became a respectable position among geologists. Even then, however, geology continued to maintain an extraordinarily conservative outlook with respect to the Mosaic version of the origin of man:

> The main positions of providential natural history were still secure. . . . No one denied the importance of the flood, nor its intimate connections with the history of the human species. No one had impugned the recentness of the creation of man. Mutability of other species was seldom if ever mentioned, and the Creator had still to be immediately responsible for the appearance of new forms of life. . . . Nearly everyone implicitly accepted . . . the distinction between the present order of causes and some former, more powerful ones [GILLISPIE 1951:96].

THE CONTRIBUTION OF CHARLES LYELL

The turning point, marked by the publication of Charles Lyell's *Principles of Geology*, did not occur until 1830. Building on Hutton's work, Lyell insisted that the processes observable in the present suffice to account for all geomorphological phenomena. It was Lyell's uncompromising "uniformitarianism" and the consequent lengthening out of time that converted Darwin from a middle-of-the-road respecter of scriptural authority to a resolutely independent scientist.

Lyell's book went with Darwin on the voyage of the *Beagle*. It gave Darwin that liberty with time that had been denied Lamarck. As Haber (1959:268) writes, "There can be little doubt that it was through Lyell's *Principles* that Darwin's mind was emancipated from the shackles of Biblical chronology. . . ." Darwin himself confided:

> I always feel as if my books came half out of Lyell's brain, and that I never acknowledged this sufficiently; nor do I know how I can without saying so in so many words—for I have always thought that the great merit of the *Principles* was that it altered the whole tone of one's mind [*ibid.*].

Despite Lyell's advanced ideas about geology, he remained highly conservative in the matter of biological evolution. Indeed, Lyell devoted a whole chapter of the *Principles of Geology* to a critical review of Lamarck's theory of bio-evolution. This chapter, as we shall see, was to have a profound effect on Herbert Spencer, but Lyell, himself, had no use for Lamarck's ideas. In discussing the origin of bioforms, Lyell adopted the very position that his uniformitarianism had destroyed in geology. He accounted for the observed distribution of bioforms in time and space by postulating a series of continuous creations by which new species were introduced to replace those that were continually becoming extinct. According to Lyell, each new species was pre-adapted by the Creator to endure within a particular range of environmental conditions associated with a particular time and region of the world. When environmental change destroyed these conditions, the species underwent extinction.

Thus despite his dependence on special creationism, Lyell's biological theories reflect the main trends leading up to Spencer and Darwin in more than just the new chronology. Among the changes that produce extinction Lyell stressed the modifications in the biotic community as having primary importance. That is, the introduction of new species was itself the prime cause of the extinction of old ones. Old and new species engaged in a struggle for survival. Indeed, it was Lyell's firm belief in the ubiquity of the struggle for survival that prevented him from accepting Lamarck's evolutionism. For he could not understand how a less fit species could survive in the presence of a better fit species long enough to accumulate the modifications that would have guaranteed its survival.

Thus Lyell, like Spencer and Darwin, was groping toward a synthesis of the themes of struggle and progress. And like both Spencer and Darwin, Lyell's model of struggle was derived mainly from the human condition. Here is a uniformitarianism (sociocultural) of which Lyell never dreamed: his preferred example of how the struggle for existence leads to extinction of less-favored types is none other than the conflict between Europeans and savages!

> It is idle to dispute about the abstract possibility of the conversion of one species into another, where there are known causes so much more active in their nature, which must always intervene and prevent the actual accomplishment of such conversions. A faint image of the certain doom of a species less fitted to struggle with some new condition in a region which it previously inhabited, and where it has to contend with a more vigorous species, is presented by the extirpation of savage tribes of men by the advancing colony of some civilized nation. In this case the contest is merely between two different *races*. . . . Yet few future events are more certain than the speedy extermination of the Indians of North America and the savages of New Holland in the course of a few centuries, when these tribes will be remembered only in poetry and tradition [LYELL 1850:678].

LYELL'S INFLUENCE ON SPENCER

One of the most extraordinary indications of the inevitability of Darwin's and Spencer's evolutionary synthesis is the fact that Lyell's book loomed as large in Spencer's formative years as in Darwin's. As Spencer wrote in his autobiography (1926:359), it was the reading of Lyell which convinced him that species evolved and which set him on the road toward the discovery that evolution was the great law of nature. Although he had previously given some thought to the idea that "the human race had been developed from some lower race," reading Lyell's criticism of Lamarck convinced him that Lamarck was right. Spencer's belief in bio-evolution "never afterwards wavered, much as I was, in after years, ridiculed for entertaining it" (*ibid.*).

Thus, Lyell's rejection of Lamarck made confirmed evolutionists out of both Darwin and Spencer! Pondering the question of "why Lyell's arguments produced the opposite effect to that intended," Spencer mentions his aversion to "supernaturalism, in whatever form" (*ibid.*). One must also suppose that Lyell's success in explaining the history of the earth without calling upon miracles brought home to both Darwin and Spencer the imminence of a similar triumph in biology.

But there was something else in Lyell's rejection of Lamarck, to which Spencer does not allude, but which returns our attention at once to the major ideological trends leading toward the biocultural evolutionary synthesis of progress and struggle. In rejecting Lamarck, Lyell was rejecting the ultimate expression of the eighteenth century's faith in the perfectibility of mankind. Nature, according to Lamarck, was constrained by immutable law to bring forth ever more perfect creatures. As Lyell put it, Lamarck's

> . . . speculations know no definite bounds; he gives the rein to conjecture, and fancies that the outward form, internal structure, instinctive faculties, nay, that reason itself, may have been gradually developed from some of the simplest states of existence,—that all animals, that man himself, and the irrational beings, may have had one common origin; that all may be parts of one continuous and progressive scheme of development from the most imperfect to the more complex; in fine, he renounces his belief in the high genealogy of his species, and looks forward, as if in compensation, to the future perfectibility of man in his physical, intellectual, and moral attributes [LYELL 1830, quoted in GREENE 1959:251].

What thus seemed most absurd to Lyell was about to appear as the central theme in Spencer's lifework: the demonstration that the universe exhibited "one continuous and progressive scheme of development" embracing all inorganic, organic, and superorganic phenomena.

THE CONTRIBUTION OF MALTHUS

It should be stressed that Lyell's rejection of Lamarck was consistent with Lyell's acceptance of the pessimistic theories of the greatest of all enemies of the doctrines of progress, Thomas Malthus. It was Malthus who was responsible for the concept of the struggle for survival, upon which the theories of Lyell, Darwin, Spencer, and Alfred Wallace depended. But Lyell alone in this group accepted Malthus's negative conclusions concerning the perfectibility of man, namely, that a large portion of mankind was forever doomed to misery by the imbalance between productive and reproductive capacities.

Malthus's role in the development of Darwin and Spencer's synthesis may even have been more important than that of Lyell.

Indeed, it is Malthus's negative attitude toward progress and perfectibility that explains why both Darwin and Spencer reacted so powerfully to Lyell's antievolutionism. Both Darwin and Spencer, each in his own way, were committed to proving that one part of Malthus's theory was correct, and the other part wrong. In the familiar history of the case, Malthus's contributions to Darwin's theories are presented in their positive form, while Malthus's contributions to Spencer's theories are usually neglected altogether. In both cases, however, the reaction against Malthus was decisive. Let us turn first to the relationship between Malthus and Darwin.

It is by now well known that Darwin attributed the "discovery" of the principle of natural selection to his reading of Malthus's *An Essay on the Principle of Population* (1798). "I came to the conclusion," wrote Darwin (1903, I:118), "that selection was the principle of change from the study of domesticated productions; and then, reading Malthus, I saw at once how to apply this principle." The reading in question was said by Darwin to have taken place in October, 1838. Now, Malthus's *Essay* was emphatically conceived as a refutation of the Enlightenment's faith in progress. Although it is today rightly regarded as the foundation of the science of demography, it achieved this eminence only as a by-product of Malthus's main intent. "My object," he wrote in the Preface to the enlarged 1803 edition, "was to apply it [the *Essay*] to the truth of those speculations on the perfectibility of man and society, which at that time excited a considerable portion of publick [*sic*] attention" (MALTHUS 1803: iii). Addressing himself directly to Marquis de Condorcet's *Outline of the Intellectual Progress of Mankind* (see p. 35), Malthus laid bare the influence of the French Revolution in bringing about his own disillusionment with the doctrine of perfectibility. To think of Condorcet writing about perfectibility while in jail "is a singular instance of the attachment of a man to principles which every day's experience was, so fatally for himself, contradicting" (*ibid.*:354). Malthus expressed his feelings on the French Revolution in rather strong terms:

> To see the human mind, in one of the most enlightened nations of the world, debased by such a fermentation of disgusting passions, of fear, cruelty, malice, revenge, ambition, madness and folly, as would have disgraced the most savage nations in the most barbarous age, must have been such a tremendous shock to his ideas of the necessary and inevitable progress of the human mind, that nothing but the firmest conviction of the truth of his principles, in spite of all appearances, could have withstood [*ibid.*].

It will be recalled that Condorcet's historical sketch had concluded with speculation concerning the possibility that cultural improvements might eventually result in changing man's physical nature. Malthus ridiculed this idea, basing his arguments on the fixed nature of species. Although it was true, he admitted, that proper breeding could change plants, animals, and men to an indefinable extent, it was nonsense to suppose that these changes were potentially unlimited. Sheep may be bred for small legs and small heads, but "the heads and legs of these sheep would never be so small as the head and legs of a rat" (*ibid.*:361). Ironically, Darwin's theories were to make such hypothetical sheep the least of evolutionary wonders.

In reading Malthus and deriving from him the principle of natural selection, Darwin could not have been unaware that once again, as in the case of Lyell, he was attributing part of his theory to a man with whom he was in considerable disagreement. But the remarkable appeal of Darwin's ideas lay precisely in the union of what had hitherto been regarded as opposites. By applying the struggle for existence to the explanation of the origin of species, the positions represented by Condorcet and Malthus could be brought into harmony! All kinds of additional irreconcilables were reconciled. Following Darwin, one could be both a racist, believing in the hereditary limits of a race or species, and at the same time, one could be an environmentalist, secure in the knowledge that there was no limit to the perfectibility of any species, including man. Where Malthus could see only perpetual misery resulting from the struggle for survival, Darwin could see perpetual progress. Where Lyell saw extinction, Darwin saw creation. On the other hand, while Condorcet attributed progress to the effect of a beneficent environment, Darwin attributed it to unremitting struggle; and while Lamarck explained progress as the accumulation of a benign striving for improvement, Darwin saw it as the product of "nature, red in fang and claw."

DARWIN'S CONTRIBUTION

Let us not forget that Darwin, standing on the shoulders of Lyell, Lamarck, and a host of other scholars, put together an argument for the evolution of species that was unprecedented in detail, accuracy, and scope. The *Origin of Species* abided by standards of evidence and logic that before 1859 had seldom been equaled and never surpassed. Yet these features would guarantee the book's success only within a small technically minded circle capable of appreciating the virtue of a monographic tour de force. They do not by themselves account for the passion with which such prestigious leaders of the scientific community as Sir Joseph Hooker, Thomas Huxley, and Charles Lyell rallied to Darwin's defense, nor for the enthusiasm of whole cohorts of younger scientists and intellectuals. *Origin* was much more than a scientific treatise; it was a great book precisely because of the diverse cultural themes it consolidated and expressed. It dramatized and legitimatized what many people from scientists to politicians had obscurely felt to be true without themselves being able to put it into words.

I should like to take note here of historian Gertrude Himmelfarb's (1959:373) assertion that Darwin was especially well suited to this task because he was "without the taint of ulterior ideology" (*ibid.*). One may readily admit that Darwin was without the "taint" but not that he was lacking in ulterior ideology. Having attributed the inspiration for his greatest idea to Malthus, he could not have been unaware of the larger implications of a "struggle for survival." Darwin's great book had a rather sharply focused philosophical message, namely the reaffirmation of the lawfulness of nature, the inevitability of progress, and the justice of the system of struggle without which progress cannot be achieved. According to Darwin, nature's laws are both beneficent and beautiful. Although we cannot control nature, we have nothing to fear from her.

> All that we can do, is to keep steadily in mind that each organic being is striving to increase in a geometrical ratio; that each at some period of its life, during some season of the year, during each generation or at intervals, has to struggle for life and to suffer great destruction. When we reflect on this struggle, we may console ourselves with the full belief that the war of nature is not incessant, that no fear is felt, that death is generally prompt, and that the vigorous, the healthy, and the happy survive and multiply [DARWIN 1958:86].

In the penultimate paragraph of the *Origin of Species*, Darwin elaborated on the same theme, implying that his theory supported the doctrine of perfectibility and that it was opposed to the pessimism of both Malthus and Lyell:

> As all the living forms of life are the lineal descendants of those which lived long before the Cambrian epoch, we may feel certain that the ordinary succession by generation has never once been broken, and that no cataclysm has desolated the whole world. Hence we may look with some confidence to a secure future of

> great length. And as natural selection works solely by and for the good of each being, all corporeal and mental endowments will tend to progress towards perfection [*ibid.*:449].

In the last lines of the book, the conversion of Malthus's nightmare into Divine Comedy summons forth the image of a "tangled bank" filled with marvelously complex arrangements of plants and animals, all products of the same natural law. The book ends with an up-beat that reverberated throughout the remainder of the century:

> Thus from the war of nature, from famine and death, the most exalted object of which we are capable of conceiving, namely the production of the higher animals, directly follows. There is grandeur in this view of life, with its several powers, having been originally breathed by the Creator into a few forms or into one; and that whilst this planet has gone cycling on according to the fixed law of gravity, from so simple a beginning endless forms most beautiful and most wonderful have been, and are being evolved [*ibid*:449].

It can be argued, of course, that Darwin was concerned here only with organic evolution and that his idea of perfection through struggle was neither embedded in nor directed toward a theory of sociocultural evolution. But in Darwin's first unpublished sketch of the theory of natural selection written in 1842, he was already convinced that this theory included all mammals without exception. As Gertrude Himmelfarb (1959:290) admits, Darwin did not take up the issue of human evolution in the *Origin of Species* "because he thought it would prevent his book from getting a fair hearing."

Twelve years were to elapse between the *Origin of Species* and the appearance of the *Descent of Man,* the book in which Darwin addresses himself specifically to the question of the relationship between natural selection and human evolution. But by 1871, the blending of sociocultural evolution with biological theory under Spencer's version of the "survival of the fittest" had already swept the field.

DARWIN'S RACISM

Was Darwin a racial determinist? Did he think of racial differences in terms of the "survival of the fittest"? It would be most extraordinary if Darwin, practically alone among his contemporaries, had been able to escape the thralldom of biologized history. Yet the issue is raised (*cf.* HIMMELFARB 1959:298) because in the *Descent of Man,* Darwin opposed the long-established belief going back to Blumenbach and Buffon that such traits as skin color and hair form were useful for survival. Thus he explicitly denied that such racial features could have been established primarily by natural selection. The principle he advanced to explain human racial differences was not natural selection but sexual selection:

> For my own part, I conclude that of all the causes which have led to the differences in external appearance between the races of man and to a certain extent between man and the lower animals, sexual selection has been by far the most efficient [DARWIN 1871, II:367].

It should be made clear, however, that Darwin did not conceive of sexual selection as being opposed to natural selection any more than he believed that natural selection ruled out the possibility of evolution through Lamarckian use and disuse. By introducing the principle of sexual selection, Darwin hoped to explain those features of organisms that seemed not to be useful in the struggle for survival. The stag's antlers and the peacock's feathers are the classic examples with which he concerned himself on the infrahuman level. Such features could elaborate themselves along diverse pathways as long as they did not tip the balance against survival, if they conferred an advantage in mating. The equivalent features in man, Darwin urged, were those aspects of racial differences—skin color, hair form, eye color, nose and lip shape—which everyone had for so long assumed must be connected with something vital in the functioning of the human organisms in different regions of the world. The stated objective of the *Descent of Man*, served by a multichapter digression into examples drawn from lower organisms, was to prove that sexual selection better accounted for the *external* racial differences among hominids than natural selection. This was a perfectly reputable position and one which continues to be supported by many physical anthropologists and biologists. But Darwin never for a moment doubted that there were important *internal* differences between the races and that these were established by natural selection. Noting that "not one of the external differences between the races of man are of any direct service to him," and that therefore they could not be acquired through natural selection, he specifically exempts all those racial features that are significant for the question of differential rates of progress toward civilization: "The intellectual and moral or social faculties must of course be excepted from this remark; but differences in these faculties can have had little or no influence on external characters" (DARWIN 1871, II:239).

DARWIN'S VERSION OF PROGRESS THROUGH STRUGGLE

The ideology of progress through struggle, of which Darwin was an exponent, received emphasis even when he resorted to the principle of sexual selection. The most efficacious form of sexual selection was that of struggle between males for a chance at mating with the most desirable females. But the other form of struggle—struggle for survival—is by no means neglected in deference to the struggle for sex. It is impossible to read the *Descent of Man* without being struck by its almost total advocacy of the struggle for survival as the means of understanding sociocultural evolution. It is a struggle for survival, moreover, that involves not so much man against nature, as man against man, in the most direct, Spencerian paradigm. Although Darwin frequently qualifies the importance of this struggle, as for example in accounting for altruism, he returns always to the underlying sanction of survival:

> It must not be forgotten that, although a high standard of morality gives but a slight or no advantage to each individual man and his children over the other men of the same tribe, yet that an advancement in the standard of morality and an increase in the number of well-endowed men will certainly give an immense advantage to one tribe over another. There can be no doubt that a tribe including many members who, from possessing in a high degree the spirit of patriotism, fidelity, obedience, courage, and sympathy, were always ready to give aid to each other and to sacrifice themselves for the common good, would be victorious over most other tribes; and this would be natural selection [*ibid.*:159-60].

This qualification must be understood to apply as well to the passage in which Darwin flatly asserts that factors other than natural selection account for "the highest part of man's nature":

> . . . important as the struggle for existence has been and even still is, yet as far as the highest part of man's nature is concerned there are other agencies more important. For the moral qualities are advanced, either directly or indirectly, much more through the effects of habit, the reasoning powers, instruction, religion, etc., than through natural selection; though to this latter agency the social instincts, which afforded the basis for the development of the moral sense, may be safely attributed [DARWIN 1871, II:386].

Darwin's murky reference to habits, reasoning powers, instruction, and religion as opposed to natural selection is perhaps an expression of uneasiness about too blatant an advocacy of struggle both within and between societies. It does not cancel out the main point of the first half of this same paragraph in which there is an appeal for maintenance of "open competition":

> Man, like every other animal, has no doubt advanced to his present high condition through a struggle for existence consequent on his rapid multiplication; and if he is to advance still higher he must remain subject to a severe struggle. Otherwise he would soon sink into indolence, and the more highly-gifted men would not be more successful in the battle of life than the less gifted. Hence our natural rate of increase, though leading to many and obvious evils, must not be greatly diminished by any means. There should be open competition for all men; and the most able should not be prevented by laws or customs from succeeding best and rearing the largest number of offspring [*ibid.*:385–86].

It also should be pointed out that Darwin separated the evolution of "moral qualities" from the evolution of what he called the "mental faculties." It is to the latter that "man mainly owes . . . his preeminent position in the world"; and it is the struggle for survival in which the faculty of intelligence is perfected in the individual, made hereditary, and passed on to succeeding generations:

> All that we know about savages, or may infer from their traditions and from old monuments, the history of which is quite forgotten by the present inhabitants, shows that from the remotest times successful tribes have supplanted other tribes. Relics of extinct or forgotten tribes have been discovered throughout the civilized regions of the earth, on the wild plains of America, and on the isolated islands in the Pacific Ocean. At the present day civilized nations are everywhere supplanting barbarous nations, excepting where the climate opposes a deadly barrier; and they succeed mainly, though not exclusively, through their arts, which are the products of the intellect. It is, therefore, highly probable that with mankind the intellectual faculties have been gradually perfected through natural selection [*ibid.*:154].

Like all of his contemporaries, Darwin was utterly incapable of separating changes in a group's learned repertory from hereditary modifications. The idea that contemporary savages might be as intelligent as civilized people was simply inconceivable. Taking the case of a newly invented snare weapon, he admits that mere imitation could induce others to accept it. But each technical innovation necessarily also contributes to the perfection of the intellect:

> The habitual practice of each new art must likewise in some slight degree strengthen the intellect. If the new invention were an important one, the tribe would increase in number, spread, and sup-

> plant other tribes. In a tribe thus rendered more numerous there would always be a rather better chance of the birth of other superior and inventive members. If each man left children to inherit their mental superiority, the chance of the birth of still more ingenious members would be somewhat better, and in a very small tribe decidedly better. Even if they left no children, the tribe would still include their blood-relations; and it has been ascertained by agriculturalists that by preserving and breeding from the family of an animal, which when slaughtered was found to be valuable, the desired character has been obtained [*ibid.*:155].

It would be idle to expect a logical resolution of all the conflicting statements in the *Descent of Man.* Darwin's position was hopelessly compromised by the prevailing confusion between inherited and learned traits. It can be said with certainty that he was a racial determinist; that he believed the preservation of the fit and the elimination of the unfit produced biocultural progress, and that he had a deep ideological commitment to *laissez-faire.* Ashley Montagu's estimate of Darwin's position in the *Descent of Man* thus appears to be preferable to that given by Gertrude Himmelfarb. Says Montagu (1952:46):

> The few passages in which Darwin mentions altruism, and co-operation come exclusively from *The Descent of Man,* where in a book of a thousand pages they are virtually crowded out by numerous statements that appear to stand in direct and unequivocal contradiction to them. Darwin was going to have the cake of natural selection, which he had baked, and eat it, too. The flavoring was mostly "struggle for existence," but here and there, there was a sprinkling of the thinnest kind of co-operation. . . . It was, however, far too thin to make any more than a fleeting impression upon the intellectual taste-buds of those who concentrated their attention upon the consumption of the main body of the cake. Darwin was, in fact, a struggle-for-survivor. . . .

THE MISNOMER OF SOCIAL DARWINISM

One of the obstacles to a proper understanding of the relationship between Darwin and the social sciences is that the doctrine of progress through struggle goes by the name of Social Darwinism. This phrase both expresses and reinforces the erroneous notion that after 1859 social scientists, led by Herbert Spencer, "applied the concepts developed by Darwin to the interpretation of the nature and functioning of society" (MONTAGU 1952:32–33). The fact that needs to be established here is that Darwin's principles were an application of social-science concepts to biology. The discussion of sociocultural progress and evolution among such social theorists as Monboddo, Turgot, Condorcet, Millar, Ferguson, Helvetius, and D'Holbach provided the matrix for the discussion of biological evolution by Geoffroy St.-Hilaire, Erasmus Darwin (Charles's grandfather), and Lamarck. On Darwin's own authority we may accept Malthus's discussion of the struggle for survival as the inspiration for natural selection. As Darwin put it, "This is the doctrine of Malthus, applied to the whole animal and vegetable kingdoms" (DARWIN 1958:29).

If there are any lingering doubts about the importance of this debt (*cf.* GREENE 1959:258), there is also the testimony of Alfred Wallace, joint author of the memoir presented to the members of the Linnaean Society in 1858, at which the discovery of the principle of natural selection was first announced. It was Wallace who inadvertently forced Darwin into publishing the *Origin of Species* by sending him a manuscript outlining the very theory on which Darwin had already been working for some twenty years. Wallace's theory was so close to Darwin's that the latter was moved to exclaim "Even his terms now stand as heads of my chapters" (quoted in HIMMELFARB 1959:200). It is less well known that the parallelism between Wallace and Darwin, a striking example of the "principle of the simultaneity of invention" (see p. 327), extended as well to the reading of Malthus. In 1855, while recuperating from an illness on the island of Ternate, near New Guinea, Wallace fell to thinking about the checks on population increase described in Malthus's *Essay on Population.* In his own words:

> Then it suddenly flashed upon me that this self-acting process would necessarily *improve the race,* because in every generation the inferior would inevitably be killed off and the superior would remain—that is the *fittest would survive.* . . . The more I thought over it the more I became convinced that I had at length found the long-sought-for law of nature that solved the problem of the origin of species [WALLACE 1905:362–63].

THE PRIORITY OF SPENCER

The phrase "Social Darwinism" not only obscures our understanding of the functional matrix that inspired Darwin but it also distorts the actual order of precedence between Spencer's and Darwin's specific contributions to evolutionary theory. In 1842, the very year in which Darwin completed his first unpublished sketch of the theory of natural selection, Spencer began to publish a series of formative essays entitled "The Proper Sphere of Government." Spencer's first book, *Social Statics* (1850), consolidated these essays and included most of the ideas he is supposed to have taken from Darwin. By 1850 Spencer was already well embarked upon his life work of describing the universal laws of development. Moreover, where Darwin had dealt with the question of human perfectibility as an extrapolation from his main theme, Spencer deliberately set out to settle that issue.

He consciously attempted to prove that human nature, like everything else in the universe, was an evolutionary product. The question of the mutability of "human nature" is, of course, merely another way of looking at the question of speciation. By arguing for the mutability of human nature, Spencer was in effect arguing for bioevolution. In *Social Statics* he insisted not only that human nature is modifiable, but that it has undergone and will continue to undergo drastic changes in conformity with a universal law of development:

> Nature in its infinite complexity is ever growing to a new development. Each successive result becomes the parent of an additional influence, destined in some degree to modify all future results. . . . As we turn over the leaves of the earth's primeval history—as we interpret the hieroglyphics in which are recorded the events of the unknown past, we find this same ever-beginning, never-ceasing change. We see it alike in the organic and the inorganic—in the decompositions and recombinations of matter, and in the constantly-varying forms of animal and vegetable life. . . . With an altering atmosphere, and a decreasing temperature, land and sea perpetually bring forth fresh races of insects, plants, and animals. All things are metamorphosed. . . .
>
> Strange indeed would it be, if, in the midst of this universal mutation, man alone were constant, unchangeable. But it is not so. He also obeys the law of indefinite variation. His circumstances are ever changing; and he is ever adapting himself to them [SPENCER 1883:45–46; orig. 1850].

Imperfection, said Spencer, in the same work, is "unfitness to the conditions of existence" (*ibid.*: 79). Man achieves a higher degree of fitness through the process of "adaptation." These changes constitute the definition of "progress," and "the belief in human perfectibility merely amounts to the belief, that in virtue of this process, man will eventually become completely suited to his mode of life" (*ibid.*: 78).

> Progress, therefore, is not an accident, but a necessity. Instead of civilization being artifact, it is part of nature; all of a piece with the development of the embryo or the unfolding of a flower. The

> modifications mankind have undergone, and are still undergoing, result from a law underlying the whole organic creation; and provided the human race continues, and the constitution of things remains the same, those modifications must end in completeness. . . . So surely must the things we call evil and immorality disappear; so surely must man become perfect [*ibid.*:80].

While the phrase "struggle for existence" occurs in *Social Statics* (*ibid.*: 252), the context is not relevant to the explanation of human progress. Nonetheless, Spencer argues at length concerning the need for a savage stage of human nature as a prelude to the stage of civilization. The idiom is pregnant with struggle-for-survivalism:

> Evidently the aboriginal man must have a constitution adapted to the work he has to perform, joined with a dormant capability of developing into the ultimate man when the conditions of existence permit. To the end that he may prepare the earth for its future inhabitants—his descendants, he must possess a character fitting him to clear it of races endangering his life, and races occupying the space required by mankind. Hence he must have a desire to kill. . . . He must further be devoid of sympathy, or must have but the germ of it, for he would otherwise be incapacitated for his destructive office. In other words, he must be what we call a savage, and must be left to acquire fitness for social life as fast as the conquest of the earth renders social life possible [*ibid.*:448–49].

SPENCER'S POLITICAL BELIEFS

In Spencer's earliest as well as in his most mature works, the discussion of evolution, struggle, and perfectibility takes place within an avowedly political framework. His open defense of economic liberalism and his condemnation of cooperativism, socialism, and communism again illustrate the futility of isolating the development of theories of culture from their sociocultural context. To appreciate Spencer's contribution, we must see him as the most effective scientific spokesman of early industrial capitalism, just as, to appreciate Marx's contribution, we must see him as the most effective scientific spokesman of revolutionary socialism. In both cases we must guard against letting the respective political involvements of these men interfere with our recognition and utilization of the scientifically valid aspects of their thought. Spencer's and Marx's politicization of theory need not be ours, however much, for both of them, social science and politics were inseparable.

Social Statics is overtly dedicated to the defense of private property and free enterprise, warning of the biocultural disasters that will befall mankind if government is permitted to intercede on behalf of the poor. There were exceedingly few areas of life in which Spencer was willing to grant the state legitimate authority. He was opposed to free public schools, libraries, and hospitals; compulsory sanitation; the licensing of doctors and nurses; compulsory smallpox vaccination; "poor laws" and public welfare systems of all sorts. He deemed such manifestations of state planning to be against the laws of nature and predicted that they would increase the suffering of the weak and the underprivileged. The insistence that socialism and communism were opposed to natural law was, of course, not original with Spencer. There was an established tradition leading back to Adam Smith which contended that the role of government must be restricted virtually to the protection of private property, enforcement of contracts, and defense of the state. Under the leadership of Thomas Malthus, Edward West, David Ricardo, and James Mill, the prevailing doctrines also embraced a definite prognosis on the question of poverty and human suffering. The "iron law of wages," the "law of diminishing returns," and Malthus's laws of population increase provided the basis for a pessimistic creed, a "dismal science," the well-known features of which were summed up by economist Joseph Schumpeter (1954:570) as follows:

> . . . pressure of population, present already but still more to be expected; nature's decreasing response to human effort to increase the supply of food; hence falling net returns to industry, more or less constant real wages, and ever-increasing (absolutely and relatively) rents of land.

SPENCER'S ANSWER TO THE DISMAL SCIENCE

Spencer's outlook, however, as we have just seen, was anything but dismal. By trusting social life to the laws of nature, Spencer held that human suffering would eventually be eliminated. In 1852, Spencer directly confronted the disparity between his own and Malthus's views on the perfectibility of man. Out of this confrontation, in the essay entitled "A Theory of Population," Spencer (1852a) achieved essentially the same sort of resolution that Darwin had arrived at in 1838, but kept to himself until 1858, and which Wallace was not to arrive at until 1855. Malthus, in other words, was the basis not for two, but for three, independent "discoveries" of the idea of progressive evolution resulting from the struggle for survival. To be sure, Spencer's "A Theory of Population" contained a number of highly original observations concerning the factors governing population increase, and was, moreover, concerned only with sociocultural and hominid evolution. But the issue before us is precisely that of the sources of "Social Darwinism" as it was applied to human society.

Spencer's exit from the Malthusian dilemma was the idea that intelligence and fertility were inversely related. Characteristically, he gave this relationship a physiological rather than a sociocultural interpretation: Mind cells and sex cells compete for the same materials. Excess of fertility stimulates greater mental activity because the more people there are, the more ingenuity is required to stay alive. The least intelligent individuals and races die off, and the level of intelligence gradually rises. But this increase in intelligence is achieved only by intensifying the competition between mind cells and sex cells. Consequently there is a progressive diminution in fertility. By this means, "in the end, pressure of population and its accompanying evils will entirely disappear . . ." (1852a:500). Although this is counter to Malthus and is optimistic far beyond Darwin's formulation, its utopian climax is reserved for an indefinitely remote future toward which humanity is making a steady and slow advance. In the meantime, the exigencies of the struggle for life produce progress through the diminution of the unfit and the preservation of the fit, just as Darwin was to describe it, six years later. According to Spencer:

> Those to whom this increasing difficulty of getting a living which excess of fertility entails, does not stimulate improvements in production—that is, to greater mental activity—are on the high road to extinction; and must ultimately be supplanted by those whom the pressure does so stimulate. . . . And here, indeed, without further illustration, it will be seen that premature death under all its forms, and from all its causes, cannot fail to work in the same direction. For as those prematurely carried off must, in the average of cases, be those in whom the power of self-preservation is the least, it unavoidably follows that those left behind to continue the race are those in whom the power of self-preservation is the greatest—are the select of their generation. So that, whether the dangers to existence be of the kind produced by excess of fertility, or of any other kind, it is clear, that by the ceaseless exercise of the faculties needed to contend with them, and by the death of all men who fail to contend with them successfully, there is ensured a constant progress towards a higher degree of skill, intelligence, and self-regulation—a better coordination of actions—a more complete life [1852a:459–60].

In all essentials this passage corresponds to a statement of the principle of the "survival of the fittest." In the same year, 1852, Spencer published an article in *The Leader* entitled "The Development Hypothesis" in which he attacked special creationism and set forth a Lamarckian view of the transformation of species. Oddly enough, Spencer did not apply the principle of the survival of the fittest to the origin of species. As he explained in his autobiography (1926, I:390), his failure to connect the two ideas arose from "the belief that the inheritance of functionally produced modifications suffices to explain the facts. Recognizing them as a sufficient cause for many orders of change in organisms, I concluded that it was a sufficient cause for all orders of changes." When the *Origin of Species* was published, Spencer accepted natural selection as one of the most important sources of bio-evolutionary change. He continued to place greater emphasis upon Lamarck's principle of use and disuse, but it should be remembered that Darwin also regarded the inheritance of acquired characteristics as a valid evolutionary principle. Thus, despite Spencer's failure to connect the concept of progress-through-struggle with speciation, it is clear that he had independently achieved the essential ingredients of Social Darwinism without Darwin's assistance.

SPENCER AND EVOLUTIONISM

Let us also take due note of the fact that it was Spencer and not Darwin who popularized the term "evolution," using it for the first time in an article entitled "The Ultimate Laws of Physiology" in 1857. It was also Spencer and not Darwin who introduced the phrase "survival of the fittest" (in his *Principles of Biology*, 1866:444; orig. 1864), a contribution which Darwin acknowledged by changing the title of the chapter on natural selection in the fifth edition of the *Origin of Species* to read "Natural Selection; or The Survival of the Fittest," giving the following explanation:

> I have called this principle, by which each slight variation, if useful, is preserved by the term Natural Selection, in order to mark its relation to man's power of selection. But the expression often used by Mr. Herbert Spencer of the Survival of the Fittest is more accurate, and is sometimes equally convenient [DARWIN 1958:74].

Furthermore, as Robert Carneiro (1967) has pointed out, from 1852 onward Spencer was a friend of Thomas Huxley's, Darwin's most effective champion, whose formidable polemical style earned him the sobriquet "Darwin's Bulldog." In his autobiography, Spencer describes the animated discussions during which he tried to convince Huxley of the truth of "progressive development." Finally, there is the esteem in which Darwin himself held Spencer, calling him "about a dozen times my superior" and insisting that "he will be looked at as by far the greatest living philosopher in England; perhaps equal to any that have lived" (DARWIN, quoted in CARNEIRO: ix). Taking all of these factors into consideration, it seems evident not only that the word "Spencerism" suffices for naming the biocultural theories that have come to be known as Social Darwinism, but that the term "Biological Spencerism" would be an appropriate label for that period of the history of biological theory in which Darwin's ideas gained their ascendancy.

SPENCER'S DUBIOUS DISTINCTION

I would not dwell on this point if it merely involved a matter of convenience of labels. But the issue is worthy of serious consideration in view of the subordinate role that is today habitually assigned to the social sciences whenever there is a question of one discipline having exerted an influence on another. It certainly is not unimportant to have it clearly understood that in the nineteenth century the trend toward biologization had nothing to do with the greater prestige of the biological disciplines. (Indeed, it may very well have been the other way around.) It was not a matter of one discipline aping another, but rather a parallel response by both disciplines to similar ideological needs. The biologization of sociocultural theory arose from the need for countering the politically subversive environmentalism of the eighteenth century. The conversion of biological theory to evolutionism was an outgrowth of the social scientists' interest in progress and perfectability, while the concept of natural selection itself arose from an interest in racial, national, and class forms of war and conflict. From the point of view of the history of theories of culture, it is Spencer and not Darwin who bears the greatest share of the onus of having crippled the explanatory power of cultural evolutionary theory by merging and mixing it with racial determinism. This is not to say that Spencer deserves the oblivion into which he has fallen. As we shall see in the following chapter, his contribution to the development of anthropological theory and method clearly equals, if it does not surpass, the contributions of the more highly regarded figures of Edward Tylor and Lewis Henry Morgan. Nor, as we shall see in a moment, do Tylor and Morgan avoid the worst effects of the racial determinist outlook. Indeed, no major figure in the social sciences between 1860 and 1890 escaped the influence of evolutionary racism. Within anthropology this thralldom was not broken until the advent of the Boasian movement; in adjacent disciplines, the struggle to achieve a correct statement of the relationship between the hereditary and learned components in sociocultural repertories has by no means been resolved.

THE FALLACY OF SPENCERISM

Spencer's fundamental error was that he drastically overemphasized the importance of hereditary factors as causal elements in the explanation of the behavioral specialties exhibited by Homo sapiens populations. In his *Principles of Sociology* (1876), Spencer divided the causes of what he called superorganic phenomena into "original extrinsic" and "original intrinsic" factors. The latter consist of the physical, emotional, and intellectual traits characteristic of the individual members of a given group. Taken together, these intrinsic traits defined what Spencer frequently called "the nature of the social units," that is, the hereditary disposition of the individuals in the group. The intrinsic factors interacted with the extrinsic factors—organic and inorganic conditions—to bring about sociocultural evolution. Each stage of sociocultural evolution thus tended to have its appropriate version of human nature, and in feedback fashion, the one could not change without affecting the other:

> Inevitably, with [the] forms of social organization and social action, there go the appropriate ideas and sentiments. To be stable, the arrangements of a community must be congruous with the natures of its members. If a fundamental change of circumstances produces change in the structure of the community or in the natures of its members, then the natures of its members or the structure of the community must presently undergo a corresponding change [SPENCER 1896, II:593; orig. 1876].

This concept of human nature combines and confounds two radically different aspects of human behavior; namely, on the one hand, biologically transmitted responses, drives, and capacities for reinforcement; and on the other, socially transmitted responses, drives, and capacities for reinforcement. The question of social determinism hinges on the extent of the relationship between the hereditary and socially transmitted components in human behavior. Spencer, Darwin, and every other scientist of consequence among their contemporaries who was interested in human behavior correctly concluded that bio-evolution and cultural evolution were intimately connected. That is, all the weight of modern anthropological opinion supports Spencer's belief that in the transition from hominoid to hominid status mutually reinforcing biological and sociocultural changes took place. Such distinctively hominid traits as upright posture, enlarged cranial capacity, and the capacity for learning elaborate symbol systems were undoubtedly developed in mutual association with an ever-increasing dependence upon learned cultural repertories as the basis for reproductive success. But the weight of modern opinion supports the conclusions, totally unrecognized by Spencer and his contemporaries, that this relationship between hereditary and learned repertory has itself undergone an evolution in which the modification of cultural forms has become less and less dependent upon concomitant genetic changes.

RACISM IN MODERN PERSPECTIVE

In the interest of avoiding any possible confusion concerning the significance of Spencer's racial determinism, let us pause to state the post-Boasian formulations of the race-culture paradigm. At the present stage of biological and cultural development, the following statement holds true for all known Homo sapiens populations: *the acquisition of the bulk of one group's learned repertory by another need not require a single genetic innovation.* Furthermore the modern consensus concerning the relationship between race and culture is that the rate and direction of culture change among the various infraspecies groupings of Homo sapiens are not at present significantly affected by genetic specialties. Both archaeological and paleontological evidence, none of which was available to Spencer, indicate that man has evolved through three grades—australopithecine, Homo erectus, and Homo sapiens. During the passage from one such grade to another, it may very well be the case that man's learning ability, his symbolizing skills, and his culture-bearing capacity were strengthened and expanded in conformity with the principle of natural selection. But the total chronology of this process extends back at least 1,750,000 years. The order of difference in human nature that Spencer had in mind when he contrasted "savages" with Englishmen might be relevant when we contrast contemporary Homo sapiens populations with a group of australopithecoids or sinanthropoids. But the specialties of human nature that have made it possible to achieve the dubious blessings of industrial society undoubtedly became the general property of the species Homo sapiens at least fifty thousand years ago. On this issue, Helvetius and Monboddo have been thoroughly vindicated, Darwin and Spencer discredited. If all other factors are held constant except race, similar enculturation processes will result in similar sociocultural repertories. Indeed, it cannot be doubted that if perfect control over the enculturative process could be maintained, only *one* generation would suffice to equip any number of different Homo sapiens groups with essentially similar repertories, regardless of their respective racial phylogenies. Thus if Hottentot babies were to be substituted at birth for English babies, their average cultural performance would not differ in any significant fashion from a control group, except in features that respond to enculturation processes. The evidence for this point of view cannot be reviewed here. Suffice it to say that it is overwhelming. Social groups and individuals drawn from every Homo sapiens race have shown themselves in countless instances to be susceptible to acculturation influences bearing upon every aspect of sociocultural behavior. American Indians brought up in Brazil show no hereditary resistance to learning African dance rhythms; Englishmen reared in China can learn to speak flawless Chinese; American Negroes who attend conservatories write symphonies in the classical European tradition; the Japanese display not the slightest hereditary disability in acquiring a knowledge of Western electronics; Jews brought up in Germany have German food preferences, while those brought up in Yemen acquire Yemenite tastes; under the influence of Western missionaries, the South Sea islanders learned to govern their sexual affairs in conformity with strict Protestant codes; everywhere the children of illiterate persons, exposed to the proper set of enculturative conditions, acquire within one lifetime the learning and lore contributed by hundreds of generations of men from all the races of the world. Although it is not possible to prove that all large divisions of Homo sapiens have equal learning ability for all kinds of responses, it is beyond dispute that the overwhelming bulk of the response repertory of any human population can be learned by any other human population. Moreover, if average differences in learning ability exist, they are demonstrably insufficient to account for the major cultural and subcultural contrasts that occupy the attention of the social sciences.

No one familiar with modern ethnography can doubt the preponderant role of enculturative conditioning in the establishment of the behavioral specialties. No plausible connection has ever even been proposed between specific human genes and such specialties as cross-cousin marriage, bilateral descent, polyandry, divine kinship, monotheism, brideprice, private property in land, or thousands of other small and large chains of less than universal human behavior. On the other hand, the inadequacy of racist explanations of sociocultural differences and similarities is further underscored by the growing success achieved by strictly cultural or cultural-ecological explanations of these phenomena. For other than a handful of hereditary pathological disabilities, there does not exist a single instance of apparent average differential hereditary learning ability for which numerous counter-hypotheses involving differential conditioning experiences are not readily available. Certainly this is the case wherever differential scores on so-called intelligence tests have been correlated with races. Such scores have been demonstrated over and over again to respond rapidly to number of years of schooling, quality of academic exposure, specific training for test situation, nuclear and extended family milieu, and an abundance of other nongenetic conditioning parameters (KLINEBERG 1935, 1951, 1963; COMAS 1961; I. C. BROWN 1960; DREGER and MILLER 1960).

THE USES OF SPENCERISM

The peculiar appeal of Spencerism was that it safeguarded Christian charity by combining Malthusian pessimism about the immediate present with Helvetian optimism about the distant future. Human nature was modifiable, but not immediately. Institutions were modifiable but not immediately. Evolution must run its course. The survival of the fittest would modify both, but not one without the other. There was little if anything that could be done to speed up the process; the best that could be hoped for was that obstacles would not be thrown in nature's path by well-intentioned but stupid reformers. In Spencer's own words:

> No adequate change of character can be produced in a year, or in a generation or in a century. All which teaching can do—all which may, perhaps, be done by a wider diffusion of principles of sociology, is the checking of retrograde action [DUNCAN 1908, II:77].

One of the most frequently heard criticisms of Spencer and his contemporaries was that, believing themselves to represent the advanced wave of civilization, they judged other peoples by their own standards. Yet in Spencer's case, this criticism is contrary to fact. From the existence of differences in human nature, it followed that each group had to be judged on its own terms and treated in a manner that was appropriate to its own stage of development. What was good for civilized men was not good for the "natives." Spencer, in other words, was an advocate of an early version of cultural relativism, an outlook usually associated only with the post-Boasian critique of evolutionism and unquestionably accepted as the only attitude befitting the modern fieldworker. In *Principles of Sociology,* Spencer wrote:

> Though it has become a common-place that the institutions under which one race prospers will not answer for another, the recognition of this truth is by no means adequate. Men who have lost faith in "paper constitutions," nevertheless advocate such conduct towards inferior races, as implies the belief that civilized social forms can with advantage be imposed on uncivilized peoples; that the arrangements which seem to us vicious are vicious for them; and that they would benefit by institutions—domestic, industrial, or political—akin to those which we find beneficial. But acceptance of the truth that the type of a society is determined by the natures of its units, forces on us the corollary that a *regime* intrinsically of the lowest, may yet be the best possible under primitive conditions [SPENCER 1896, I:232–33].

Since other people are so different from us, we must avoid thrusting our standards of conduct upon them. Our ethical ideas cannot be meaningful to them. Modern cultural relativists, especially those of us who are concerned with the preservation of the cultural integrity of so-called tribal peoples, will find an ominous note in Spencer's line of reasoning:

> And since preservation of the society takes precedence of individual preservation, as being a condition to it, we must, in considering social phenomena, interpret good and bad rather in their earlier senses than in their later senses; and so must regard as relatively good that which furthers survival of the society, great as may be the suffering inflicted on its members [*ibid.*:233].

SPENCERISM AND IMPERIALISM

The utility of this position for an empire or a corporation on which the sun never sets needs no special emphasis. Adumbrated in colonial policy, it was a perfect rationalization of the status quo of conquest. Missionaries, merchants, industrialists, and administrators, each in their own way, used the imagined biocultural specialties of the "inferior" races as the justification for inferior treatment. Some of the classic refrains, familiar to anyone who has ever experienced the reality of a colonial system, go as follows: the natives are lazy; they do not respond like civilized men to the offer of wages; they need to be taught the virtues of civilized forms of labor by means other than those appropriate to civilized man. They must be forced to work by limiting their tribal lands, by imposing head taxes, and by compulsory contracts. Unlike civilized man, the "inferior" races suffer moral and spiritual ills if they are educated beyond the primary level. They therefore should receive advanced training only in manual skills. Being more childlike than Europeans, it is dangerous for the natives to have free access to alcoholic drinks. Such people, if given a chance, prefer to walk rather than to ride; they like to sleep on the cold ground rather than on warm beds; they work in the rain without feeling wet, work in the sun without feeling hot, and carry loads on their heads without getting tired. Life is not so dear to these people as to Europeans; when their children die, they are not so deeply disturbed, and when they themselves suffer injury, it does not hurt as much as it does in the civilized man:

> According to Lichtenstein, the Bushmen do not "appear to have any feeling of even the most striking changes in the temperature of the atmosphere." Gardiner says the Zulus "are perfect salamanders"—arranging the burning faggots with their feet and dipping their hands into the boiling contents of the cooking-vessels. The Abipones, again, are "extremely tolerant of the inclemencies of the sky." So it is with the feelings caused by bodily injuries. Many travellers express surprise at the calmness with which men of inferior types undergo serious operations. Evidently the sufferings produced are much less than would be produced in men of higher types [SPENCER 1896, I:51].

Spencer certainly shared in the responsibilities for propagating these stereotypes of pre-industrial populations. It should not be concluded, however, that he was unable to identify the underlying motivation in the use of evolutionary racism by persons directly involved in late-nineteenth-century imperialism. He himself believed that with the advance of "industrial" types of society, a new kind of human nature, adapted to industrial rather than military competition, would emerge. It was the lingering on of the military types that was responsible for corrupting European contact with the "inferior" races and which led to the exploitation of helpless peoples in the name of a false civilization. The widely accepted picture of Spencer as a smug Victorian for whom the benevolence of European colonial dispensation went unquestioned does not measure his true stature. Spencer's sympathies were with the peaceable industrial types; he thought of himself, despite his opposition to government charities, as a true friend of the poor; he abhorred the wars and preparations for wars by the nations of Europe; and he was disgusted by the callousness and hypocrisy exhibited by the Europeans in their bloody quest for cheap labor and raw materials. From the following lengthy, but rewarding, commentary on events associated with the late-nineteenth-century scramble for Africa, it is clear that Spencer cannot be dismissed as a mere propagandist of industrial capitalism:

> What the social man, even of advanced race, is capable of, has been again shown while these lines are standing in type. To justify the destruction of two African towns in Batanga, we are told that their king, wishing to have a trading factory established, and disappointed with the promise of a sub-factory, boarded an English schooner, carried off Mr. Grovier, the mate, and refusing to release him when asked, "threatened to cut the man's head off": a strange mode, if true, of getting a trading factory established. Mr. Grovier afterwards escaped; not having been ill-treated during his detention. Anchoring the *Boadicea* and two gunboats off Kribby's Town ("King Jack's" residence) Commodore Richards demanded of the king that he should come on board and explain: promising him safety, and threatening serious consequences in case of refusal. Not trusting the promise, the king failed to come. Without ascertaining from the natives whether they had any reason for laying hands on Mr. Grovier, save this most improbable one alleged by our people, Commodore Richards proceeded, after some hours' notice, to clear the beach with shells, to burn the town of 300 houses, to cut down the natives' crops, and to destroy their canoes; and then, not satisfied with burning "King Jack's" town, went further south and burnt "King Long-Long's" town. These facts are published in the *Times* of September 10, 1880. In an article on them, this organ of English respectability regrets that "the punishment must seem, to the childish mind of the savage, wholly disproportionate to the offence:" implying that to the adult mind of the civilized it will not seem disproportionate. Further, this leading journal of ruling classes who hold that, in the absence of established theological dogmas, there would be no distinction between right and wrong, remarks that "if it were not for the dark shadow cast over it by the loss of life" [of two of our men], "the whole episode would be somewhat humorous." Doubtless, after the "childish mind of the savage" has accepted the "glad tidings" brought by missionaries of "the religion of love," there is humour, somewhat of the grimmest, perhaps, in showing him the practice of this religion by burning his house. Comments on Christian virtue, uttered by exploding shells, may fitly be accompanied by a Mephistophelian smile. Possibly the king, in declining to trust himself on board an English ship, was swayed by the common Negro belief that the devil is white [SPENCER 1896, II:239–40].

SPENCERISM AND THE DOCTRINE OF PSYCHIC UNITY

One of the least understood aspects of late-nineteenth-century racism is the relationship between the doctrine of psychic unity and the belief in inferior racial types. Psychic unity was the belief, extremely common among monogenists, that the human mind was everywhere essentially similar. In the formulation of Adolf Bastian, psychic unity was freely invoked to explain similarities of culture wherever they occurred. Since Bastian was the proponent of an especially pronounced version of cultural idealism, the fact that an idea was potentially common to all mankind was sufficient explanation for its occurrence in one or more places. Some form of psychic unity is also implied whenever there is an emphasis upon parallel evolution, for if the different peoples of the world advanced through similar sequences, it must be assumed that they all began with essentially similar psychological potentials. But this assumption bears no necessary relationship to the post-Boasian concept of racial equality. Indeed, the nineteenth century's ideas on psychic unity have little in common with either the eighteenth or twentieth century's understanding of the race-language-culture equation.

LEWIS HENRY MORGAN, RACIST

The nature of the confusion surrounding this issue is well illustrated by the famous passage in Lewis Henry Morgan's *Ancient Society*, which describes the uniformity of human experience:

> It may be remarked finally that the experience of mankind has run in nearly uniform channels; that human necessities in similar condition have been substantially the same; and that the operations of the mental principle have been uniform in virtue of the specific identity of the brain of all the races of mankind [MORGAN 1963:7].

On the basis of this and similar passages, Eleanor Leacock has sought to exempt Morgan from the prevailing racism of his time. Writes Leacock (1963:ix):

> Morgan was clearly at odds with the view that inequalities in technological development among different peoples were due to differences in innate ability. Perhaps because of his familiarity with and respect for American Indians, Morgan was beyond crude

> assumptions of white supremacy. White colonial policies of the time were being buttressed with adjurations of racial inequality and the superiority of northwestern Europeans. Morgan, like Waitz before him, maintained the unity of the human race.

Yet Leacock herself is obliged to note on the very next page, "In the light of Morgan's views, it is surprising to find him referring occasionally to the 'inferior' brain of various peoples" (*ibid.*:x). Neither this, nor any of the other numerous passages in Morgan's books that assert the innate mental and physical variability of different human groups, should cause surprise since Morgan was every bit as much a racial determinist as Spencer. Morgan believed firmly that race and culture were interdependent and that specific cultural traits including kinship terminologies and habits of dress were carried in the "blood."

> There are some customs of such a strikingly personal character that they may in a pre-eminent degree, be regarded as customs of the blood. When prevalent over wide areas and persistently maintained from generation to generation, they seem to possess some significance upon the question of the probable genetic connection of the peoples by whom they are practised. There are three distinct customs or usages of this character, apparently transmitted with the blood, which I have taken some pains to trace, and have found them to be substantially universal in the Ganowanian family. They may possess some value as corroborative evidence of the unity of origin of these nations. These are, first, the custom of saluting by kin; second, the usage of wearing the breech-cloth; and third, the usage of sleeping at night in a state of nudity, each person being wrapped in a separate covering [MORGAN 1870: 274].

Morgan, his respect for the virtues of barbarism notwithstanding, did not consider the American Indian the equal of the European. In his *League of the Iroquois* he indicates that the Indians lacked an essential passion, namely the desire for economic gain:

> This great passion of civilized man, in its use and abuse, his blessing and his curse, never roused the Indian mind. It was doubtless the great reason for his continuance in the hunter state, for the desire of gain is one of the earliest manifestations of progressive mind, and one of the most powerful passions of which the mind is susceptible. It clears the forests, rears the city, builds the merchantmen . . . in a word, it has civilized our race [1851:139].

Morgan's ideas concerning the effects of race mixture on temperament and behavior are the standard thoughts of the period, parallel in all respects with Spencer's views:

> The Indian and European are at opposite poles in their physiological conditions. In the former there is very little animal passion, while with the latter it is super-abundant. A pure-blooded Indian has very little animal passion, but in the half-blood it is sensibly augmented; and when the second generation is reached with a cross giving three-fourths white blood, it becomes excessive, and tends to indiscriminate licentiousness. If this be true in fact, it is a potent adverse element leading to demoralization and decay, which it will be extremely difficult to overmaster and finally escape. In his native state, the Indian is below the passion of love. It is entirely unknown among them, with the exception, to a limited extent, of the Village Indians. This fact is sufficiently proved by the universal prevalence of the custom of disposing of the females in marriage without their knowledge or participation in the arrangement [MORGAN 1870:207*n*].

Like a long line of Indianophiles stretching back to Bartolomé de las Casas, Morgan's life-long appreciation and defense of the American Indian was coupled with a strong prejudice against Negroes (*cf.* HARRIS 1964b). In the 1850's, as the historian Carl Resek (1960:63) tells us, Morgan espoused the cause of abolition in the hope that unprotected by slavery, the Negro race would disappear:

> During the debate in Congress over the Compromise of 1850, Morgan expressed the not uncommon sentiment of Negrophobia, based partially on the belief that the Negro was a separate species. He urged Seward to limit the expansion of slavery because "it is time to fix some limits to the reproduction of this black race among us. It is limited in the north by the traits of the whites. The black population has no independent vitality among us. In the south while the blacks are property, there can be no assignable limit to their reproduction. It is too thin a race intellectually to be fit to propagate and I am perfectly satisfied from reflection that the feeling towards this race is one of hostility throughout the north. We have no respect for them whatever."

What then is the meaning of the phrase the "specific identity of the brain of all the races of mankind"? Merely that in later years, as Resek points out, Morgan rejected the notion of polygenesis and became a firmly convinced monogenist. This position, however, was not, as we have seen, incompatible with racial determinism. Like all monogenists, Morgan had to be something of an evolutionist even before he began to feel the influence of Darwin and Spencer. As the races evolve, they pass through similar biocultural stages. At any particular stage, the innate mental condition of the descendants of any branch of the human species tends to be essentially similar. They thus tend to react to similar conditions in similar ways and to move in parallel fashion from savagery to civilization. However, they certainly do not move in tandem, all at the same time. Hence, at the present moment in history, there are men who are bioculturally representative of all phases of evolution; there are, in other words, "superior" and "inferior" races.

EDWARD BURNETT TYLOR, RACIST

Precisely the same interpretation must be rendered of Edward Tylor's position. In *Primitive Culture* (1958; I:7; orig. 1871) Tylor seems to be taking an extremely advanced view when he proposes to "eliminate considerations of hereditary varieties or races of man, and to treat mankind as homogeneous in nature, though placed in different grades of civilization. . . ." Yet in his *Anthropology* (1899), the first textbook in the field, Tylor displays little understanding of the difference between racial and cultural capacities. Noting the "unlikeness between the melancholy Russian peasant and the vivacious Italian," he insists that the difference "can hardly depend altogether on climate and food and government." Similarly, civilization can hardly be explained by such extrinsic factors.

> There seems to be in mankind inbred temperament and inbred capacity of mind. History points the great lesson that some races have marched on in civilization while others have stood still or fallen back, and we should partly look for an explanation of this in differences of intellectual and moral powers between such tribes as the native Americans and Africans, and the Old World nations who overmatch and subdue them [TYLOR 1899:74].

Although Tylor is certainly more restrained than many of his contemporaries, rarely invoking racial determinants, he appears in this to be influenced by a sense of politeness as well as by scientific acumen. Nonetheless, the chapter "Races of Mankind" concludes with an attempt to explain why the white race is the best endowed for leading a civilized existence. Assuming that man's first appearance was in the tropics, the more primitive forms of man were least in need of civilized arts. Spreading to cooler climates, man then evolved the specialties better suited to civilized life:

> It may perhaps be reasonable to imagine as last formed the white race of the temperate region, least able to bear extreme heat or live without the appliances of culture, but gifted with the powers of knowing and ruling which gave them sway over the world [*ibid.*:113].

In this fashion, the greatest figures of late-nineteenth-century anthropology fell under the spell of racial determinism. Even when the racial factor simply hovered over a discussion without actually coming to roost, it crippled the attempt to apply scientific methods to sociocultural phenomena. Aside from its own inherent errors, it gave the theorists of this period a false sense of accomplishment with respect to the nonracial aspects of their ideas about sociocultural processes. When a sociocultural theory, such as Morgan's, left huge chunks of unexplained debris strewn about, one could always count on the racial broom to sweep them out of sight. Despite their panoramic grandeur, the theories of Spencer, Morgan, and Tylor lack the overall coherence which one might suppose would have been insisted upon by men so deeply convinced of the dominion of natural law. As we shall see in the next chapter, Spencerism in practice meant eclecticism. Despite their biological reductionism, and hence their materialism, neither Spencer, Tylor, nor Morgan experienced the need to explore a consistent cultural-materialist strategy. They were greatly to advance our picture of the evolution of sociocultural phenomena in terms of typical sequences; but their understanding of sociocultural causality was blinded by the sands of racism.

Evolutionism: Methods

6

It has been said of the period between 1860 and 1890 that in these thirty years cultural anthropology had "grown from nothing to maturity" (TAX 1955b:466). While agreeing with Sol Tax's estimate of the great formative influences of Tylor, Morgan, Spencer, and their lesser contemporaries, we must resist the cliché that anthropology was "nothing" before 1860. We have seen how evolutionism and racial determinism flourished among Darwin's predecessors and how the *Origin of Species* arose from this general matrix. The burst of activity in "cultural" anthropology after 1860 was not triggered by Darwin's book, but rather accompanied it, as a product of the same generative influences. Tax himself draws attention to Prichard, Waitz, and a number of amateur ethnologists reaching back to Lafitau whose work provided the foundation for the period under discussion. But Tax, in company with Lowie, Kroeber, and Kluckhohn, underestimates the degree of continuity between the favorite anthropological fathers and the earlier formulators of the principles of sociocultural evolution. The "historical evolutionary school," which according to Tax "had run its course" in thirty years, was an integral part of a tradition that had its roots firmly and widely planted in the eighteenth century. As we have seen, the continuity between the biocultural evolutionism of the 1860's and the belief in progress and perfectability of the 1760's was unbroken. This continuity appears more pronounced if we reject the self-constituted disciplinary boundaries which propound the novelty of anthropological evolutionism in the 1860's while ignoring the existence of Saint-Simon, Comte, and Hegel in the 1820's and 1830's. What the period commencing with 1860 produced was simply a large number of better-documented and more specialized versions of Turgot's "universal history of mankind."

That Darwin's theories were not the trigger for the surge in evolutionary formulations commencing shortly after the publication of *Origin* is clear from the first two classic products of the period, both published in 1861: Johann J. Bachofen's *Das Mutterrecht* (*Mother Right*) and Henry Maine's *Ancient Law*. Concerned with the evolution of the family, political organization, and law, neither of these treatises suggests the need for any acknowledgment of Darwin's influence. Bachofen's *Mother Right* was first presented as a series of lectures in Stuttgart in 1856, three years before Darwin's book was published (HAYS 1958:35), and was based almost entirely on Greek and Roman sources, while Maine's *Ancient Law* was a lawyer's attempt to explain the origins of different legal concepts in the tradition of Adam Ferguson and Montesquieu. It was also based on ancient Roman sources, supplemented by a personal knowledge of India's traditional communities and legal systems. Both Maine and Bachofen produced evidence to show that the modern European family was the resultant of evolutionary modifications wrought on ancient kinship forms. These were matriarchy and matrilineal descent in Bachofen's theories, and patriarchy and patrilineal descent in Maine's theories. It should be noted that Maine hedged on the question of the universality of the patriarchal "stage," regarding the transition from the Roman to modern English family as a characteristic of "progressive" societies. Bachofen, on the other hand, was convinced of the prior existence of a matrilineal stage everywhere on earth. But we shall return to a comparison of the principal features of these and other evolutionary sequences in the next chapter.

CONTINUITY IN ETHNOGRAPHY

There is also continuity between the 1860's and the earlier decades of the nineteenth century in the matter of ethnographic sources. Turgot, Meiners, Klemm, Prichard, Waitz, Spencer, Morgan, and Tylor represent so many points along a continuum of gradually rising ethnographic standards. At the same time there occurred a steady expansion in the number of different societies, knowledge of which could be utilized in systematic comparisons. Although these materials were for the most part contributed by poorly qualified travelers or missionaries, there was some accumulation of data based on the work of trained and skilled observers, among whom were illustrious figures like Henry Schoolcraft, Alexander von Humboldt, Johann von Spix and Karl von Martius, and Lewis and Clark.

It seems essential for a proper understanding of the rise of anthropological theory not to posit at any point between 1750 and the present a sharp break in the quality and quantity of ethnographic knowledge. In subsequent chapters we shall examine the claim that the Boasians and the British social anthropologists abruptly introduced radically improved ethnographic standards. And we shall have occasion to remark on the manifest shortcomings that still remain despite the expansion of systematic fieldwork by anthropologically trained ethnographers. This is not to deny the great advance in quantity and quality of ethnographic information available to the twentieth-century theoretician. Rather, it is to affirm the fact that such improvements accumulated all during the nineteenth century and that the past and present centuries belong on the same curve of rising standards. This point is important because it may help to disabuse certain critics of social science of the notion that the progressive accumulation and refinement of data and theory are somehow an exclusive property of the biological and physical sciences.

To estimate the quantity and quality of ethnographic materials available at the beginning of the period 1860–90, a brief analysis of the sources in one of the era's evolutionary monographs may prove instructive. Edward Tylor's *Researches into the Early History of Mankind* (1865) can be taken as representative of the higher scholarly standards of these times. Concerned with the question of general evolutionary directions and the origin of language, writing, naming, tools, marriage, fire, and myths, *Researches* contains in embryonic form most of the themes developed in Tylor's more mature writings. One notes first of all extensive utilization of the ethnographic compilations of Gustav Klemm (1843). References to smaller compendia such as those of J. G. Wood (1874–80), W. Cooke Taylor (1840), and R. G. Latham (1859) are also conspicuous. Next in prominence are the sources that were used extensively by Tylor's Enlightenment predecessors but which still yielded (then as well as today) valuable and otherwise unobtainable information about exotic peoples in early stages of contact: (1) the ancients, such as Herodotus, Strabo, and Lucretius; (2) the Spanish Chroniclers, such as Oviedo, Garcilaso de la Vega, and Sarmiento; (3) the early Jesuit "relations" and missionary reports, such as those of Charlevoix, Colden, Lafitau, and Dobrizhoffer; and (4) the narratives of great explorers, such as those of Columbus, Cook, and many others available in the publications of the Hakluyt Society. In addition to pre-nineteenth-century sources of this nature, Tylor used the writings of many nineteenth-century travelers, missionaries, and scientists. Thus for the ethnography of Oceania he had the United States Government-commissioned reports of the explorations of Hale and Wilkes. There was Mariner on Tonga; St. John on the Dyaks; T. H. Williams on Fiji; G. Grey and W. Ellis on Polynesia; R. Taylor and J. S. Polack on the Maori; and G. Grey, J. E. Eyre, and J. Backhouse on Australia. For his African ethnography Tylor drew on Adolf Bastian, D. Livingstone, W. H. I. Bleek, Sir Richard F. Burton, J. S. Moffat, Du Chaillu, E. W. Lane, J. I. Krapf, and A. Casalis. For Asia there was Sir John Bowring on Siam; Mouat on the Andamanese; and Sir James E. Tennent, F. Ward, and Logan on India. The richest materials were those pertaining to the New World. For South America, Tylor drew on Darwin, Alexander von Humboldt, Spix and Martius, and Alfred Wallace. For Central America and Mexico, he had his own travels to fall back on as published in his *Anahuac* (1861), while for North America he used the rich firsthand accounts of Lewis and Clark, H. R. Schoolcraft, and George Catlin. (Unaccountably Morgan's study of the Iroquois is not cited.) All of these sources predate 1860.

THE IMPORTANCE OF ARCHAEOLOGY

The burst of anthropological theorizing after 1860 is not to be understood only in relationship to the accumulation of *ethnographic* knowledge. Perhaps even more important was the steady increase in data derived from archaeological research. The first half of the nineteenth century was a period of great archaeological discoveries. These discoveries essentially confirmed the stages of history that the eighteenth-century social philosophers had argued must have existed on the basis of logic and their meager knowledge of contemporary primitive peoples. By 1860, the speculation that Europeans must formerly have been savages had already been confirmed by unimpeachable evidence brought out of the earth. Without keeping this triumphant vindication in mind, we cannot appreciate the strength of the conviction among the evolutionists of the period 1860–90 that contemporary primitives could provide valid information about the ancient condition of humanity.

STONE, BRONZE, IRON

One of the most significant accomplishments of nineteenth-century archaeology was the demonstration that the first Europeans had lacked a knowledge of metallurgy. During the previous century, the absence of metals among many contemporary primitive groups was widely noted, and many scholars assumed that such a condition must also have been generally characteristic of ancient times. Antoine Goguet (1758), for example, had remarked that "the savages set before us a striking picture of the ignorance of the ancient world, and the practices of primitive times. They have no idea of metals and supply the want of them by [stones and flints]" (quoted in HEIZER, 1962: 263). Many other eighteenth-century writers, basing themselves mainly on ancient Greek and Roman sources, believed in the "three-age system," a stone-bronze-iron sequence of technology. It was not until the beginning of the nineteenth century, however, that systematic evidence for this view began to be produced. In 1806, extensive government-sponsored excavations of Denmark's shell middens and dolmens were begun. These excavations, under the supervision of R. Nyerup, brought to light stone implements that predated the earliest cultures referred to in the Danish sagas. The collections from these sites were placed in the Museum of Northern Antiquities in Copenhagen where C. J. Thomsen (1848; orig. 1836) used them to establish the first archaeologically validated sequences of the Stone, Bronze, and Iron ages (PENNIMAN 1965:55–56). The sequence was confirmed in the 1850's by stratigraphic techniques applied by Thomsen's student J. J. A. Worsaae, to Danish peat-moss sites. In the meantime, under the influence of the Danish historian Vedel-Simonsen, the three-age formulation had been taken up in Sweden by M. Bruzelius in 1816 and Sven Nilsson in 1838.

THE DISCOVERY OF THE NEOLITHIC AND PALEOLITHIC

Another set of influential archaeological discoveries involved neolithic lake sites. The Irish bogs were reported on first by W. Wilde in 1840, followed by F. Keller's studies of pile dwellings near Zurich in the mid 1850's. Further corroboration of the evolutionist position came from the discovery of flint implements recognized as even older than the Danish stone age. Grappling with the problem of the Mosaic chronology, John Frere (1800) had already suggested that certain buried implements dated from a time "even more remote than the present world." In France in the late 1820's, Mme. de Chistol, Marcel du Serres, and M. Tournal (1833) presented evidence of the contemporaneity of man and extinct Pleistocene fauna. This was followed in 1836 by Boucher de Perthes' studies of paleolithic tools and fauna at Abbeville. One of Boucher de Perthes' principal antagonists, Dr. Rigollot, was converted to the new chronology by his own discoveries at St. Acheul in 1855. By 1860, additional work by Falconer, Prestwick, Lartet, and Lyell placed man's earliest beginnings well back into the Pleistocene. Nonetheless, the belief that man's antiquity did not exceed 6,000 years remained a respectable opinion until the beginning of the Darwinian period. This belief somewhat diluted the archaeological evidence of progressive evolution, since it remained possible within the compressed chronology that the earliest stone-age periods of Europe were merely degraded epilogues to a higher "golden age" represented by the Egyptian and Babylonian civilizations.

LYELL'S INTERPRETATION OF THE PALEOLITHIC

The most decisive event in the defeat of this objection was the publication of Charles Lyell's *Antiquity of Man* (1863), a book whose contributions to the foundation of modern anthropological theory cannot be overestimated. Lyell, confronting the issues that Darwin had assiduously avoided, put together the available geological, archaeological, linguistic, and ethnological evidence in proof of the contemporaneity of artifacts and extinct animals, whose evolution into modern types, on the hypothesis of transformism, would have required tens of thousands of years. The men who made these artifacts, Lyell concluded, must have been drastically inferior in mental constitution to modern man. Otherwise, so great was the time represented at the St. Acheul gravel pits and the Liège caves that we should expect to find the earth full of the remains of all sorts of civilized achievements, long antedating our own. If the earliest men had been as intelligent as modern Englishmen, we should now be finding:

> . . . lines of buried railways or electric telegraphs, from which the best engineers of our day might gain invaluable hints; astronomical instruments and microscopes of more advanced construction

> than any known in Europe, and other indications of perfection in the arts and sciences, such as the nineteenth century has not yet witnessed. . . . Vainly should we be straining our imaginations to guess the possible uses and meaning of such relics,—machines, perhaps, for navigating the air or exploring the depths of the ocean, or for calculating arithmetical problems, beyond the wants or even the conception of living mathematicians [LYELL 1863: 379].

Thus, in Lyell's new perspective on man's place in geological time, there was little room for the claim that the ancient civilizations in Egypt and Mesopotamia marked a high point from which the stone-age peoples and contemporary primitives had degenerated. Compared to the Abbevillian hand axes and the extinct animal species with which they were associated, the age of the Egyptian monuments faded into insignificance:

> Nevertheless, geologically speaking, and in reference to the date of the first age of stone, these records of the valley of the Nile may be called extremely modern. Wherever excavations have been made into the Nile mud underlying the foundations of Egyptian cities, as, for example, sixty feet below the peristyle of the obelisk of Heliopolis, and generally in the alluvial plains of the Nile, the bones met with belong to living species of quadrupeds, such as the camel, dromedary, dog, ox, and pig, without, as yet, the association in any single instance of the teeth or bone of a lost species [*ibid.*:383].

For an understanding of the continuity between the evolutionary formulations of the second and first halves of the century, we must note the fact that Lyell himself had visited the pits at St. Acheul in 1859. Witnessing the excavation of a flint tool, he returned at once to express his opinion in favor of the antiquity of the Acheulian artifacts at the meeting of the British Association at Aberdeen (*ibid.*:104).

TYLOR'S DEPENDENCE ON ARCHAEOLOGICAL DATA

Edward Tylor's *Researches into the Early History of Mankind* may once again serve to demonstrate the importance of pre-Darwinian archaeological achievements for the theories of the period 1860–90. It may be said without exaggeration that archaeological evidence is at least as important as ethnographic evidence for Tylor's conclusions concerning the overall uniformity of evolutionary change. The "three-age" classification is employed throughout the book, as well as a modification that had recently been introduced whereby the "Stone Age" was divided into "Ground" and "Unground" phases. In addition to the ethnographic sources previously discussed, Tylor cites Lyell, Christie, Lartet, Prestwick, Wilde, Wilson, and Goguet. The scope and importance of archaeological evidence in Tylor's evolutionism is set forth in the following passage:

> These combined characters of rudeness and the absence of grinding give the remains of the Unground Stone Age an extremely important bearing on the history of Çivilization, from the way in which they bring together evidence of great rudeness and great antiquity. The antiquity of the Drift implements is, as has been said, proved by direct geological evidence. The Cave implements, even of the reindeer period, are proved by their fauna to be earlier, as they are seen at a glance to be ruder, than those of the cromlech period and of the earliest lake-dwellings of Switzerland, both belonging to the Ground Stone Age. To the student who views Human Civilization as in the main an upward development, a more fitting starting point could scarcely be offered than this wide and well-marked progress from an earlier and lower, to a later and higher, stage of the history of human art [1871:198].

Later, in his article on "Anthropology" in the ninth edition of the *Encyclopaedia Britannica,* Tylor (1878) again acknowledged the debt that the evolutionists owed to archaeological discoveries:

> It has been especially the evidence of prehistoric archaeology which, within the last few years, has given to the natural development theory of civilisation a predominance hardly disputed on anthropological grounds. . . . The finding of ancient stone implements buried in the ground in almost every habitable district of the world, including the seats of the great ancient civilisations, such as Egypt, Assyria, India, China, Greece, etc., may be adduced to show that the inhabitants of these regions had at some time belonged to the stone age [TYLOR quoted in OPLER 1964a:132].

THE LIMITATIONS OF ARCHAEOLOGY

To a substantial degree, the contributions of Tylor and his evolutionistic contemporaries were an attempt to flesh out the archaeologically revealed seriation of artifacts with the stages of social and ideational growth, especially of kinship, political, and religious institutions. It was recognized that archaeology had relatively little to contribute on its own in these matters. It was impossible from archaeological evidence to decide whether the Ground Stone Age peoples practiced monogamy, were patrilineal or matrilineal, or believed in one god or many.

The intent of supplementing archaeological evidence by utilizing ethnographic and historical data is quite explicit throughout the period. Morgan (1877:8), for example, established his definition of "ethnical periods" in terms of savagery, barbarism, and civilization, only after duly noting the usefulness of the Danish archaeologists' terms "Age of Stone, of Bronze and of Iron" for the "classification of objects of ancient art." Morgan's testy adversary, John McLennan, spelled out the limitations of archaeological materials in the following terms:

> The geological record, of course, exhibits races as rude as any now living, some perhaps even more so, but then it goes no farther than to inform us what food they ate, what weapons they used, and what was the character of their ornaments. More than this was not to be expected from that record, for it was not in its nature to preserve any memorials of those aspects of human life in which the philosopher is chiefly interested—of the family or tribal groupings, the domestic and political organisation [MC LENNAN 1865:6].

THE COMPARATIVE METHOD

All theorists of the latter half of the nineteenth century proposed to fill the gaps in the available knowledge of universal history largely by means of a special and much-debated procedure known as the "comparative method." The basis for this method was the belief that sociocultural systems observable in the present bear differential degrees of resemblance to extinct cultures. The life of certain contemporary societies closely resembles what life must have been like during the paleolithic; other groups resemble typical neolithic culture; and others resemble the earliest state-organized societies. Morgan's (1870:7) view of this prolongation of the past into the present is characteristic:

> . . . the domestic institutions of the barbarous, and even of the savage ancestors of mankind, are still exemplified in portions of the human family with such completeness that, with the exception of the strictly primitive period, the several stages of this progress are tolerably well preserved. They are seen in the organization of society upon the basis of sex, then upon the basis of kin, and finally upon the basis of territory; through the successive forms of marriage and of the family, with the systems of consanguinity thereby created; through house life and architecture; and through progress in usages with respect to the ownership and inheritance of property.

A similar viewpoint on the relevance of contemporary primitives to the interpretation of prehistory formed the essential premise of A. Lane-Fox Pitt-Rivers, founder of the Pitt-Rivers Museum at Oxford:

> . . . the existing races, in their respective stages of progression, may be taken as the bona fide representatives of the races of antiquity. . . . They thus afford us living illustrations of the social customs, the forms of government, laws, and warlike practices, which belong to the ancient races from which they remotely sprang, whose implements, resembling with but little difference, their own, are now found low down in the soil . . . [PITT-RIVERS 1906:53].

To apply the comparative method, the varieties of contemporary institutions are arranged in a sequence of increasing antiquity. This is achieved through an essentially logical, deductive operation. The implicit assumption is that the older forms are the simpler ones, but in practice many different kinds of logical assumptions are involved, a matter to which we turn in a later section.

THE ORIGIN OF THE COMPARATIVE METHOD

What justification existed for this extrapolation from contemporary primitives to ancient society? It has commonly been assumed on Lowie's (1937:19-29) authority that the main stimulus for this practice came out of biology where zoological and botanical knowledge of extant organisms was routinely applied to the interpretation of the structure and function of extinct fossil forms. No doubt there were several late-nineteenth-century anthropological applications of this principle which explicitly referred to biological precedent. In the 1860's, however, it was the paleontology of Lyell, rather than of Darwin, that was involved. Thus, the greatest of the British prehistorians, John Lubbock (1865), justified his attempt to "illustrate" the life of prehistoric times in terms of an explicit analogy with geological practices:

> . . . the archaeologist is free to follow the methods which have been so successfully pursued in geology—the rude bone and stone implements of bygone ages being to the one what the remains of extinct animals are to the other. The analogy may be pursued even further than this. Many mammalia which are extinct in Europe have representatives still living in other countries. Our fossil pachyderms, for instance, would be almost unintelligible but for the species which still inhabit some parts of Asia and Africa; the secondary marsupials are illustrated by their existing

> representatives in Australia and South America; and in the same manner, if we wish clearly to understand the antiquities of Europe, we must compare them with the rude implements and weapons still, or until lately, used by the savage races in other parts of the world. In fact, the Van Diemaner and South American are to the antiquary what the opossum and the sloth are to the geologist [LUBBOCK 1865:416].

But Lubbock was here simply employing a stylish rationale for a sociocultural method that antedated both Darwin and Lyell. The roots of the comparative method go back into the eighteenth century. Indeed, the Cambridge historian J. W. Burrow has attempted to isolate the origin of the practice among the "philosophic historians of the Scottish Enlightenment." Thus he points out that Adam Ferguson (1767) believed that in the present conditions of the American Indian, "we behold, as in a mirror, the features of our own progenitors." Sir James Mackintosh (1798) referred specifically to the preservation of barbarous phases of culture side by side with civilization: "We can [now] examine almost every variety of character, manners, opinions and feelings and prejudices of mankind into which they can be thrown either by rudeness of barbarism or by the capricious corruption of refinement" (quoted in BURROW 1966:11–12). There is no reason, however, to confine the roots of the comparative method to the Scots. The idea is actually an integral part of the Enlightenment's notion of "progress" and was shared in embryonic form at least by every eighteenth-century social philosopher who believed that European civilization represented an advance over an earlier and "ruder" condition. For how could one speak of such progress if there were not some base line for comparison? Almost simultaneously with the introduction of the concept of the "state of nature," "savages" viewed alternatively as miserable, innocent, or noble were used to "illustrate" the condition out of which European society was presumed to have arisen.

It is true that zoologists were making use of the comparative method as early as the eighteenth century. Indeed, as soon as the extinct fossil forms of life came to the attention of geologists and biologists, the comparative method was applied in an attempt to understand what kinds of organisms they had been and to assign them a place in the Linnaean taxonomy. It is important to remember, however, that these early manifestations of the comparative method in paleontology were not part of a theory of bio-evolution. In biology the method was first applied to guide the assignment of fossil missing links to positions in the "great chain of being."

Another eighteenth-century manifestation of the comparative

method is associated with the establishment of linguistic science. When William Jones in 1786 first proposed that Greek, Latin, Gothic, Celtic, and Sanskrit had a common origin, he was in effect asserting that the comparison of contemporary languages could yield reliable information concerning the nature of languages spoken by chronologically remote peoples. Jones's suggestions were systematically pursued by Friedrich von Schlegel (1808) and Franz Bopp (1816). In 1837 Jacob Grimm's formulations of the regularities of vowel changes in the Indo-European languages provided a fresh confirmation of the validity of the comparative method applied to linguistic phenomena. By the 1860's the triumphs of "philology" in outlining the steps in the evolution of Indo-European phonology, grammar, and semantics served along with paleontology and archaeology to remind anthropologists of the validity of the comparative approach.

Although not named as such, we might also note here that the introduction of the principle of uniformitarianism by Hutton and Lyell into geology was actually another example of the same general method: it was this principle which made it possible to connect varieties of contemporary and ancient geomorphological phenomena in a logical sequence based upon processes demonstrable for the present, but only inferential for the past.

Finally we may note that it is merely another version of the comparative method which permits astronomers to inspect populations of recent (close) and "fossil" (distant) stars and galaxies, and to arrange them in probable evolutionary sequences, without ever hoping to be able to observe any of the postulated transformations. It is clear, therefore, that the comparative method is closely related to the rise of scientific theory in many different disciplines.

THE VALUE OF THE COMPARATIVE METHOD

Placing the origin of the comparative method in the Enlightenment prepares us to evaluate the evolutionists of 1860-90 from a more generous perspective than has hitherto been fashionable. We see that when a great prehistorian like Lubbock made an attempt to illustrate the life of the "paleolithic" and "neolithic" peoples (Lubbock's terms) by reference to contemporary primitives, it was at the end of a period of archaeological discoveries that had vindicated the use to which the comparative method had been put by the social philosophers of the preceding century. This point is grudgingly conceded by Lowie (1937:22) who notes that

> prehistory proved evolution by the rigorous techniques of geological stratigraphy at a time when ethnographers were still groping for proper methods of investigating living aborigines. No wonder that ethnographers leaned heavily on the staff of archaeology.

But for Lowie, as for all of the Boasians, the use of the comparative method was the cardinal error of the evolutionist school. According to Lowie, the evolutionists as a class failed to see "the limited range of cultural facts for which progress could be directly demonstrated. . . . Prehistory," he continued, "had nothing whatsoever to offer on the growth of supernaturalism and social organization" (*ibid.*:23). "A fatal fallacy of all this reasoning lay in its naive equation of modern primitive groups with the primeval savage. . . " (*ibid.*:24).

> The resemblance of modern savages to a primeval ape-man is so important a tenet that we must explicitly expose the error. It lies in failing to understand that even the simplest recent group has a prolonged past, during which it has progressed very far indeed from the hypothetical stage [*ibid.*:25].

These abuses of the comparative method must be dissociated from the general principle at issue. Some of them, as Lowie himself points out, were avoided by the "greatest of the evolutionists." Morgan, for example, was perfectly well aware that none of the contemporary groups of primitives could be equated with "primeval ape-man." His "Lower Status of Savagery" which "commenced with the infancy of the human race" was a purely deductive condition not represented by any contemporary primitive group: "No exemplification of tribes by mankind in this condition remained to the historic period" (Morgan 1877:10). As for an awareness of the particular historical careers of primitive cultures, all the great evolutionists conceded the necessity of accounting for specialties of each group in terms of the natural and cultural features of local environments.

What we must consider in Lowie's criticism is not the abuse of the comparative method, but the question of its general validity as a means of understanding the evolution of culture. The issue to be confronted is whether the cultures of contemporary primitive groups can be used to orient our understanding of chronologically earlier sociocultural arrangements. Are there such things as surviving stone-age cultures? The answer, as undeniable today as it was in 1860, is yes. This does not mean, of course, that each and every marginal band-organized society may be taken as equally representative of a particular stage of sociocultural evolution. Throughout prehistory, as throughout the contemporary primitive world, many different varieties of culture flourished in adaptation to varieties of specific cultural and ecological conditions. The late-nineteenth-century evolutionists, as we shall see in a moment, tended to underestimate the amount of diversity characteristic of both contemporary and paleolithic groups. Ludicrous errors were committed, for example, on the assumption that peoples who lacked metallurgy necessarily also lacked social stratification or that there must have been a universal stage of matrilineality preceding patrilineality. On the other hand, equally ludicrous errors were committed by the Boasians in their attempt to discredit the comparative method. For example, many "historical particularists" argued that sociocultural evolution had taken so many diverse paths that the simplest sorts of technologies could be found in association with the most "complex" forms of social organization. The Australian "section" system was a favorite example of this alleged disparity between techno-economic and social-organizational levels. Similarly, the Boasian critics of the comparative method attempted to show that such institutions as slavery, private property, and state government were capriciously associated with a great variety of additional sociocultural features. Several of these examples of apparently quixotic and fortuitous associations will be examined at length in the chapters devoted to Boas and his pupils. For the moment it must suffice to state that there is no specific abuse of the comparative method which could justify the denial of the relevance of our ethnographic knowledge of contemporary pre-state societies to the task of unraveling the course of sociocultural evolution. It is unquestionable that contemporary primitives exhibit techno-environmental, techno-economic, social-organizational, and ideological adaptations which are both structurally and chronologically distinctive of preliterate and pre-state societies. A list of primitive features would include: egalitarian unilineal descent groups, age grades, classificatory kinship terminologies, men's cults, low-density settlements, erratic labor schedules, communal ownership of strategic resources, absence of internal political sanctions, egalitarian redistribution systems, and relative impermanence of settlements, to mention only a few. These features can be given a causal nomothetic explanation only to the extent that we assume similar institutional complexes existed during the paleolithic and were and are everywhere displaced by the evolution of state-organized societies.

In principle, that is, ignoring abuses which can arise from the overly mechanical application of any good idea, there is no less justification for the comparative method in anthropology than in biology. Indeed, it could very well be argued that there is a much firmer basis for the extrapolation from contemporary primitives to paleolithic societies than from contemporary bioforms to extinct species. This contention rests on the fact that cultural evolution may be said to involve fewer major types of adaptations at any single instant than is true of biology. Such a judgment is rendered plausible because of the absence of any process among cultural forms analogous to that of speciation among bioforms. Since cultural innovations diffuse, even between radically different sociocultural systems, rapid rates of evolution do not eventuate in a multiplicity of new types (see pp. 173ff.).

THE LIMITATIONS OF THE COMPARATIVE METHOD

Of course, in practice, the comparative method can yield results which are only as good as the archaeology and the ethnography from which its data derives. If the ethnography itself presents a false picture of contemporary primitive life, it is scarcely worth transferring to temporally remote cultures. In order for ethnography to be applied to the interpretation of prehistory, systematic comparisons of many different cultures of a similar basic techno-environmental and techno-economic type are needed. From such a comparison, it is possible to identify which elements in any given case are the result of contact with more complex societies, which are a result of local environmental circumstances, and which are statistically associated with the type itself. It is a serious error, for example, to suppose that contemporary band-organized hunting and gathering societies are representative of the great bulk of paleolithic hunting and gathering groups. Almost all of the ethnographically classic cases of band-organized hunters and gatherers are marginal or refugee peoples driven into, or confined to, unfavorable environments by surrounding groups of more advanced societies. Many evolutionary anomalies in social organization are traceable to contacts between low density band- or village-organized groups and complex state societies resulting in special colonial or minority status.

There is no denying that the late-nineteenth-century applications of the comparative method were based on grossly inadequate ethnographic data. But many of the evolutionists, especially Morgan, Tylor, and Spencer, attempted to overcome these deficiencies by a strategy which has numerous votaries among the statistical schools of modern anthropology. Unable to vouch for the accuracy of any given instance, each of these evolutionists turned to the amassment of large numbers of cases. As we shall see in Chapter 21, there is much to be said in favor of the claim that ethnographic errors can be balanced out when large samples are employed. Of course, in the nineteenth century the basis of selection of cases tended to be rather crude, exposing the evolutionists to the charge of selecting only the cases which confirmed a particular hypothesis. Nonetheless, the practice of amassing large numbers of cases must be considered in relation to the stereotyped version of ethnographic irresponsibility that was imposed upon the evolutionists during the Boasian critique of the comparative method.

TYLOR'S USE OF THE COMPARATIVE METHOD

Tylor's (1958, I:9-10) account of this aspect of the comparative method is especially noteworthy. He was asked by an historian to explain how a "statement as to customs, myths, beliefs, etc., of a savage tribe" could "be treated as evidence where it depends on the testimony of some traveler or missionary, who may be a superficial observer, more or less ignorant of the native language, a careless retailer of unsifted talk, a man prejudiced or even willfully deceitful" (*ibid.*)?

> This question is, indeed, one which every ethnographer ought to keep clearly and constantly before his mind. Of course he is bound to use his best judgment as to the trustworthiness of all authors he quotes, and if possible to obtain several accounts to certify each point in each locality. But it is over and above these measures of precaution that the test of recurrence comes in. If two independent visitors to different countries, say a medieval Mohammedan in Tartary and a modern Englishman in Dahome, or a Jesuit missionary in Brazil and a Wesleyan in the Fiji Islands, agree in describing some analogous art or rite or myth among the people they have visited, it becomes difficult or impossible to set down such correspondence to accident or wilful fraud. A story by a bushranger in Australia may, perhaps, be objected to as a mistake or an invention, but did a Methodist minister in Guinea conspire with him to cheat the public by telling the same story there? The possibility of intentional or unintentional mystification is often barred by such a state of things as that a similar statement is made in two remote lands, by two witnesses, of whom A lived a century before B, and B appears never to have heard of A. How distant are the countries, how wide apart the dates, how different the creeds and characters of the observers, in the catalogue of facts of civilization needs no farther showing to any one who will

> even glance at the footnotes of the present work. And the more odd the statement, the less likely that several people in several places should have made it wrongly. This being so, it seems reasonable to judge that the statements are in the main truly given, and that their close and regular coincidence is due to the cropping up of similar facts in various districts of culture. Now the most important facts of ethnography are vouched for in this way [*ibid.*:9–10].

MORGAN'S STRATEGY

The same basic strategy may be found in the approach which Lewis Henry Morgan developed in his comparative study of kinship structures. Having discovered in 1858 that the Ojibwa in Wisconsin had essentially the same kinship terminology as the Iroquois, Morgan at once prepared a questionnaire to secure information from Indian agents and missionaries all over the country. Encouraged by the responses, he himself went on expeditions between 1859 and 1862 through Kansas and Nebraska, up the Missouri, to Hudson's Bay and to the Rocky Mountains. In 1859, he discovered that the same terminology occurred in India and obtained the support of the Smithsonian Institution to mail out hundreds of his questionnaires to United States consular officials and representatives throughout the world. Forty-eight completed schedules formed the factual basis for *Systems of Consanguinity and Affinity* (1870).

THE ORIGIN OF THE STATISTICAL COMPARATIVE METHOD

Perhaps the greatest anthropological paper of the nineteenth century was Edward Tylor's "On a Method of Investigating the Development of Institutions, Applied to Laws of Marriage and Descent" (1889). Using a sample of between 300 and 400 societies, Tylor placed the comparative method on a statistical basis. He calculated percentages of probabilities of association ("adhesions" is his word) between postmarital residence, descent, teknonymy, and couvade and thereby advanced toward an understanding of exogamy, endogamy, and the origin of cross-cousin marriage and incest prohibitions. With this contribution, Tylor may be considered to have founded the modern statistical cross-cultural approach as represented in the work of George P. Murdock and the Human Relations Area Files (see Chap. 21). Characteristically, Tylor's article ends with a plea for better ethnographic data.

SPENCER'S STRATEGY

Herbert Spencer must also be credited with an ambitious attempt to improve the ethnographic basis of the comparative method. This took the form of a multivolume series of tables and citations published in huge folios under the title *Descriptive Sociology* (1873-1934). Each volume had two main parts. First the tables, consisting of condensed statements arranged in a uniform manner and intending, in Spencer's words, to give a summary view of each society's "morphology, its physiology and (if a society having a known history) its development." Second, each volume contained the relevant extracts from cited works that provided the basis for the tabular summaries. Spencer projected a third part of *Descriptive Sociology*, in which the extracts under one heading, such as Political, Ecclesiastical, or Ceremonial institutions, would be brought together; but this aspect of the work was never completed. The entire project was conceived by Spencer to be a necessary prelude to the writing of his *Principles of Sociology* (1876), which was in turn conceived as the capstone to his lifework as embodied in the various volumes of his "synthetic philosophy". The plan for *Descriptive Sociology* was laid down as early as 1859 in an article in the *Westminster Review*, entitled "What Knowledge Is of Most Worth?" In this article, Spencer urged that the biographical approach to history be superseded by the collection of information bearing upon "the natural history of society." It is clear that in Spencer's view the amassment of sociocultural data was inseparable from the task of describing the stages of sociocultural evolution, or in other words, that the comparative method was an integral part of social science. I shall quote at length from this original conception since, as a guide to the collection of ethnographic information, it foreshadows the instructions embodied in the Royal Anthropological Institute's *Notes and Queries* as well as those in George P. Murdock's list of cultural universals—the organizing frame for the Cross Cultural Survey and Human Relations Area Files (see p. 613).

> The thing it really concerns us to know is, the natural history of society. We want all facts which help us to understand how a nation has grown and organized itself. Among these, let us of course have an account of its government; with as little as may be of gossip about the men who officered it, and as much as possible about the structure, principles, methods, prejudices, corruptions, etc., which it exhibited; and let this account include not only the nature and actions of the central government, but also those of

> local governments, down to their minutest ramifications. Let us of course also have a parallel description of the ecclesiastical government—its organization, its conduct, its power, its relations to the state; and accompanying this, the ceremonial, creed, and religious ideas—not only those nominally believed, but those really believed and acted upon. Let us at the same time be informed of the control exercised by class over class, as displayed in social observances—in titles, salutations, and forms of address. Let us know, too, what were all the other customs which regulated the popular life out-of-doors and in-doors, including those concerning the relations of the sexes, and the relations of parents to children. The superstitions, also, from the more important myths down to the charms in common use, should be indicated. Next should come a delineation of the industrial system: showing to what extent the division of labor was carried; how tribes were regulated, whether by caste, guilds, or otherwise; what was the connection between employers and employed; what were the agencies for distributing commodities; what were the means of communication; what was the circulating medium. Accompanying all of which should be given an account of the industrial arts technically considered; stating the processes in use, and the quality of the products. Further, the intellectual condition of the nation in its various grades should be depicted; not only with respect to the kind and amount of education, but with respect to the progress made in science, and the prevailing manner of thinking. The degree of aesthetic culture, as displayed in architecture, sculpture, painting, dress, music, poetry, and fiction, should be described. Nor should there be omitted a sketch of the daily lives of the people—their food, their homes, and their amusements. And, lastly, to connect the whole, should be exhibited the morals, theoretical and practical, of all classes, as indicated in their laws, habits, proverbs, deeds. These facts, given with as much brevity as consistent with clearness and accuracy, should be so grouped and arranged that they may be comprehended in their *ensemble*, and contemplated as mutually-dependent parts of one great whole. . . the highest office which the historian can discharge is that of so narrating the lives of nations as to furnish materials for a Comparative Sociology, and for the subsequent determination of the ultimate laws to which social phenomena conform [SPENCER 1859, quoted in SPENCER 1875:iv-vi].

In 1870 Spencer hired three assistants to begin the work of compiling the materials for *Descriptive Sociology*. The first volume appeared in 1873, and additional installments continued to be issued after Spencer's death, until 1934, under the provisions of his will. They are as follows: I. *English* (1873); II. *Ancient Mexicans, Central Americans, Chibchans, Ancient Peruvians* (1874); III. *Types of Lowest Races, Negritto, and Malayo-Polynesian Races* (1874); IV. *African Races* (1875); V. *Asiatic Races* (1876); VI. *North and South American Races* (1878); VII. *Hebrews and Phoenicians* (1880); VIII. *French* (1881); IX. *Chinese* (1910); X. *Hellenic Greeks* (1910); XI. *Ancient Egyptians* (1925); XII. *Hellenistic Greeks* (1928); XIII. *Mesopotamia* (1929); XIV. *African Races* (1930); and XV. *Ancient Romans* (1934).

Spencer's intense concern with ethnographic data casts a curious shadow over Lowie's *History of Ethnological Theory*, from whose index Spencer's name is absent. Evidently Spencer's use of the term "sociology" in his titles reassures many anthropologists that Spencer can safely be ignored by a discipline that emphasizes primitive and peasant sociocultural systems as opposed to modern Euro-American societies. What then are we to make of the complaint by J. Rumney (1934:22), Spencer's scientific executor, that *Principles of Sociology* was too much involved with primitive ethnography to qualify as sociology?

> Spencer stressed too much what is now called cultural anthropology, which is only a division of general sociology, . . . Spencer was far too interested in the origin of institutions, primitive habits and the survival of ancient customs. . . .

THE ABUSE OF THE COMPARATIVE METHOD

Despite the great labor expended by the late-nineteenth-century anthropologists on behalf of improving ethnographic competence, it cannot be denied that the evolutionists were perpetrators and victims of massive ethnographic errors which, far from being canceled out by appeal to a large number of cases, became that much more entrenched by reiteration. We shall have occasion to discuss some of the worst of these in connection with the evolutionary schemes of Morgan and McLennan. The errors of the ethnographically less well-informed theoreticians are highly offensive to the modern reader. John Lubbock, despite his fine grasp of the evidence for the European prehistoric sequences, is the classic example. His *Pre-Historic Times* is replete with tables, charts, and diagrams setting forth in minutest detail the quantitative and qualitative aspects of the major European archaeological sites and museum collections. Lubbock, himself, systematically combed Europe for traces of prehistoric cultures, visiting a half-dozen lake sites in Switzerland, shell mounds in Denmark and Scotland, and the bone caves of the Dordogne. He claimed to have personally examined "almost every gravel pit and section from Amiens down to the sea" (1865:vii). But when Lubbock turned in his final chapter to the evidence from ethnography, he exhibited an atrocious indifference to the reliability of his sources; and Lowie justly upbraids him for certain extravagances:

> The Andamanese have "no sense of shame"; "many of their habits are like those of beasts." The Greenlanders have no religion, no worship, no ceremonies. The Iroquois have no religion, no word for God, Fuegians not the least spark of religion. ". . . there can be no doubt that, as an almost universal rule, savages are cruel" [LOWIE 1937:24].

But Lowie permits his indignation over these errors to carry over into a critique of the principle of the comparative method. He blames the "naïve equation of modern primitive groups with the primeval savage" for leading "serious writers" like Lubbock "into absurd underestimation of recent tribes and uncritical acceptance of tourists' tales" (*ibid.*). It should be apparent that this line of disparagement of the comparative method is a *non sequitur*. Lubbock's low level of ethnographic understanding was not induced by the comparative method; rather his use of the comparative method was rendered unsatisfactory by his meager understanding of contemporary primitive societies. The origin of Lubbock's mistakes rested in the thralldom of racial determinism which lay over Lubbock and all his contemporaries. Since they believed that primitive peoples represented biologically inferior grades of humanity, or even different species, they were prone to accept reports exaggerating the difference between European and primitive bio-psychological dispositions and capacities. This leads us to the next step in Lowie's critique of the comparative method—what he calls "the complete abandonment of objective criteria":

> Sir John's writings teem with subjective judgments, naïvely passed on the basis of resemblance to or deviation from European standards. The Hottentots are "disgusting," the Australians "miserable" savages . . . he is himself constantly mortified, shocked, horrified, by the savage scene [*ibid.*].

Once again it is obvious that the peculiarly obnoxious character of Lubbock's judgments results not from the comparative method but from the prevailing conviction that Europeans are racially superior and that their institutions are justified by that superiority.

THE RELATIVIST CRITIQUE

Lowie goes on to say that, in contrast to Lubbock's ethnocentrism, "the modern scientific procedure is to refrain from *all* subjective judgments" (*ibid.*:25, Lowie's italics). This certainly was the self-image developed by the Boasians and others who insisted that ethnography be founded upon complete moral and ethical relativism. But we shall examine evidence in subsequent chapters which indicates that the relativists were unable to achieve the semblance of political neutrality with respect to the destinies of primitive peoples. Modern anthropologists can criticize Lubbock for his ethnocentric judgments only at the risk of hypocrisy if the objection be that he had strong convictions concerning the relative values of primitive and civilized institutions. During the period of reaction to the nineteenth-century evolutionists, it was considered the worst of anthropological manners to evaluate the relative merits of different cultural practices, especially if primitive patterns were compared unfavorably to Euro-American ones. But contributions to the political expression of particular value positions consist of both action and inaction. Merely to refrain from opinion is not therefore to avoid the expression of opinion. Thus, as we shall see, the selection of subjects about which one will *not* carry on research, teach, or publish represents as much of a commitment as the reverse. This being the case, then cultural relativism, at its best, would represent a state of moral and ethical confusion characterized by contradictory, weak, unconscious, or disguised value judgments. In ethnography, it is not at all clear that a cryptic or confused moral and ethical stance is preferable to an openly avowed one. According to Lowie, while "an anthropologist as an individual cannot but respond to alien manifestations in accordance with his national and individual norms," no carry-over of these reactions can be tolerated in his ethnographic work: ". . . as a scientist, however, he merely registers cannibalism or infanticide, understands, and if possible explains such customs" (*ibid.*:25). The preposterous assumption here is that reliable descriptions of cannibalism and infanticide cannot be achieved by ethnographers who openly oppose these practices. But the two functions are not at all necessarily incompatible. We must presume at least that reliable descriptions have been submitted by ethnographers who openly expressed their distaste for cannibalism. Moreover, in an age where so much anthropological teaching and research is supported by organizations with definite value commitments—such as the National Institutes of Health, the Ford Foundation, and the United

States Agency for International Development—it will become increasingly difficult to convince anyone that descriptions of poverty, exploitation, disease, and malnutrition are admissible only to the extent that they lack "subjective pronouncements." Thus to return to Lubbock and his ethnocentric contemporaries, we condemn them not because they expressed value judgments, but because their judgments were based on false facts and theories. Their arrogance with respect to contemporary primitives and preliterate societies is intolerable first because they assumed that had they themselves been brought up among London's poor or among the Hottentots they would nonetheless have behaved like Victorian gentlemen; and second, because in expressing shock over cannibalism, infanticide, and head-hunting, they naïvely assumed that comparable practices had already been, or were shortly about to be, extirpated from the repertories of their own civilized communities.

SURVIVALS AND THE COMPARATIVE METHOD

Another aspect of the comparative method which became the object of intense but unmerited criticism during the twentieth century was the concept of "survivals." Once again, we must guard against an overemphasis of the precedent of biological models. The essence of the concept of survivals is that phenomena originating under a set of causal conditions of a former era perpetuate themselves into a period during which the original conditions no longer exist.

The term itself was first employed by Tylor in *Primitive Culture,* where he emphasized the value of survivals for the reconstruction of history by means of the comparative method.

> These are processes, customs, opinions, and so forth which have been carried on by force of habit into a new state of society different from that in which they had their original home, and they thus remain as proofs and examples of an older condition of culture out of which a newer has been evolved [TYLOR 1958:16; orig. 1871].

The historian Margaret Hodgen (1936:89-90) has expended a whole volume on the attempt to prove that Tylor's concept of survival was restricted to "irrational customs maintained by civilized peoples and remarked for their non-conformity with the existing pattern of advanced culture." Hodgen's principal interest seems to have been to degrade the earlier attempts by Morgan, Maine, and McLennan to use survivals to reconstruct antecedent institutions among primitives. I shall take it as requiring no extended justification that the idea of survivals was an integral part of the comparative method, and that in one form or another it came into use more or less simultaneously in the writings of the great evolutionists. Maine (1873:304; orig. 1861), for example, was clearly dealing with survivals when he attempted to explain anomalous features of both Roman and Modern English jurisprudence as remnants of earlier systems:

> The old general conception is not obliterated, but it has ceased to cover more than one or a few of the notions which it first included. So too the old technical name remains, but it discharges only one of the functions which it once performed.

Similarly, Morgan's use of Hawaiian terminology in *Systems of Consanguinity and Affinity* to prove the existence of a prior stage of group marriage and his use of "relics," "traces," "outcrops," and "remains" to prove the existence of matrilineal descent among the Barbarian forebears of the ancient Greeks and Romans constitute typical applications of the doctrine of survivals. Finally, we may note the similarity between survivals and what McLennan called "symbols." The latter, said to reflect an earlier actuality, provided the main source of evidence in *Primitive Marriage* (1865). It was through the widespread occurrence of symbolic nuptials involving mock battles, pretended flight, and chase that McLennan arrived at his theory of marriage-by-capture as a stage in the evolution of domestic institutions (see p. 193).

USEFUL AND USELESS SURVIVALS

Emphasis upon "survivals" or equivalent concepts early in the 1860's once again impresses upon us the gratuitous nature of the attempt to regard biology as the source of evolutionary doctrines in the social sciences. Lowie's (1937:25) equation of "survivals" with "rudimentary organs of social groups" or with "useless organs" (*ibid.*: 26) ill prepares us for an understanding of the historical significance of this concept. It may be true, as Hodgen insists, that for Tylor the bulk of survivals were relatively useless items. But it is clear that for others who employed the concept or its equivalents, survivals might very well have had a use, however impaired or transmuted. Indeed, the first example of a survival given by Tylor is that of an old woman operating a loom by throwing the shuttle from one hand to the other—clearly not an entirely useless activity. Moreover, Maine certainly did not hold that legal fiction was useless, nor did Morgan imply that kinship terminologies that reflected past rather than present marriage forms were not therefore useful for designating classes of relatives. The fact is that in both biological and sociocultural survivals, there is a spectrum of utility rather than a dichotomy of useful and useless.

At one extreme, consider the wing of a bat, the result of modification of a primitive mammalian pentadactyl forelimb, which is eminently functional in all of its aspects. The pentadactyl pattern, however, cannot be explained by reference to the conditions of contemporary bat existence and hence is a "survival" in the previously defined sense. At the other extreme there is the true vestigial organ, like the human appendix, which lacks positive functions altogether. Similarly, there are a small number of sociocultural "survivals" which appear to be almost devoid of utility. The buttons on a man's coat sleeves or the bow on the band inside of a man's hat are frequently cited examples. Most sociocultural survivals, however, involve some degree of continuing utility. Tylor's numerous cases of survivals in sports, games, and popular sayings clearly fall into this latter category.

THE FUNCTIONALIST CRITIQUE OF SURVIVALS

This point is essential in view of the twentieth-century British functionalists' attack on survivals, which was in turn, a part of the reaction to evolutionary formulation in general. Examination of Bronislaw Malinowski's famous tirades against survivals reveals that the concept he attacked was itself lifted bodily from the functional context in which it had first been proposed. He employs a definition of survival offered by Alexander Goldenweiser rather than Tylor whereby, "A survival is 'a cultural feature which does not fit in with its cultural medium. It persists rather than functions, or its function somehow does not harmonize with the surrounding culture' " (MALINOWSKI 1944b: 28). With this definition to go on, it becomes child's play to show that survivals are nonexistent. Does a horse-drawn hansom cab in automobile-age New York fail to "fit" in with its cultural medium? "Obviously not. Such an antiquated means of locomotion is used for retrospective sentiment . . . it moves where the fare is slightly intoxicated or else romantically inclined" (*ibid.*:28-29). But the implication that Tylor or Morgan would deny such an interpretation is wholly gratuitous. Tylor's works are filled with examples of items which in surviving to the present have had their utility transformed to recreational or to aesthetic functions. When he explains the relationship of Victorian evening dress to older "practical coats in which a man rode and worked"

(TYLOR 1899:15; orig. 1881), it is not to assert that a Victorian gentleman has no use for evening wear! When he shows that the widespread custom of invoking supernatural assistance when a man sneezes (God bless you!) derives from an earlier fear that the soul was in danger of being expelled from the body, it is not to deny the importance of displaying solicitude to a potential or actual victim of a cold (TYLOR 1958, I:97ff.). When he notes that the bow and arrow of archery contests and children's games is "a mere sportive survival" of a "formerly serious practice," it is not to deny the pleasure that human beings derive from sports and games (*ibid.*:73). Malinowski's concept of survivals is thus as much filled with straw as his concept of economic man (see p. 564). Tylor and Morgan were not interested in denying utility to this trait and lack of utility to that one. They were concerned rather with the task of reconstructing the general history of institutions.

THE IMPORTANCE OF HISTORY

Tylor and Morgan believed present-day institutions could not be understood without reconstructing evolutionary antecedents. Survivals were "traces" which helped in the task of reconstruction, and they were at the same time conspicuous warnings that a synchronic method (which the British functionalists actually later adopted) could never suffice to explain sociocultural differences and similarities. In pointing to hansom cabs in New York, the evolutionists were demonstrating that the present cannot be explained solely in terms of the present. Given only Malinowski's factors of nostalgia, inebriation, and courtship, it would be impossible to predict the existence of hansoms, present, past, or future. The context out of which Malinowski wrenched the concept of survivals was that which insisted that the reconstruction of the earlier forms is essential for an understanding of later ones. Tylor makes this context abundantly clear by citing Auguste Comte's strictures concerning the necessity for evolutionary perspective (see p. 62).

> They who wish to understand their own lives ought to know the stages through which their opinions and habits have become what they are. Auguste Comte scarcely overstated the necessity of this study of development when he declared at the beginning of his "Positive Philosophy" that "no conception can be understood except through its history," and his phrase will bear extension to culture at large. To expect to look modern life in the face and comprehend it by mere inspection, is a philosophy whose weak-

> ness can easily be tested. Imagine any one explaining the trivial saying, "a little bird told me," without knowing of the old belief in the language of birds and beasts. . . . It is always unsafe to detach a custom from its hold on past events, treating it as an isolated fact to be simply disposed of by some plausible explanation [TYLOR 1958:19–20].

In this broader context, it is clear that the question of the importance of diachronic data takes precedence over that of useful and useless "survivals." In a sense, every historical explanation is an explanation which makes use of "survivals," regardless of whether the survivals are useful or useless.

STUPID CUSTOMS

It cannot be denied that Tylor derived a special delight in ridiculing what he regarded to be silly and irrational customs which had survived extensive formal and functional modification. Explaining why he devoted so much of *Primitive Culture* to traits that are "worn out, worthless, or even bad with downright harmful folly" (*ibid.*:156), he rejoices that "in such inquiries we have continual reason to be thankful to fools." That is, "ethnographers, not without a certain grim satisfaction, may at times find means to make stupid and evil superstitions bear witness against themselves" by revealing their origins in barbaric and savage stages of culture (*ibid.*:156-57).

> It is quite wonderful, even if we hardly go below the surface of the subject, to see how large a share stupidity and unpractical conservatism and dogged superstition have had in preserving for us traces of the history of our race, which practical utilitarianism would have remorselessly swept away [*ibid.*:156].

Under the combined influence of cultural relativism, historical particularism, and synchronic functionalism, it has become bad form for anthropologists to make public judgments concerning the relative "stupidity" of various primitive and civilized customs. Once we take care to emend Tylor's maxim to embrace traits which Tylor ascribed to "practical utilitarianism," there is no reason why future generations of anthropologists should deny themselves that "grim satisfaction" with which the history of human folly has always repaid its serious students. When Tylor's "practical utilitarianism" gave birth to a war in which practical machines enabled 30 million people to be killed, it seems that many anthropologists suffered a loss of critical verve. Instead of declaring these machines and the social arrangements that dictated their use "stupid," they went about adding witchcraft and circumcision to the list of man's great achievements (see p. 534). It has yet to be demonstrated, however, that our understanding of cultural evolution is enhanced by an attitude of equal respect for all of its products.

FIELDWORK

Malinowski (1944b:30-31) blamed the doctrine of survivals for one additional failing of the evolutionists:

> The real harm done by this concept was to retard effective fieldwork. Instead of searching for the present-day function of any cultural fact, the observer was merely satisfied in reaching a rigid, self-contained entity.

It is perfectly true that the evolutionists did not carry out ethnographic research which could be likened to Malinowski's own experience. Moreover, neither Morgan, Tylor, nor Spencer initiated programs of intensive fieldwork. Of these three, only Morgan achieved a firsthand knowledge of the cultures of primitive groups. But even Morgan's work with the Iroquois would not be considered a bona fide field experience by modern standards, since it did not involve continuous or prolonged contact with the daily routine of a given local community. Tylor, while an avid traveler and keen observer, lacked research which could even be compared with fieldwork in the modern sense, while Spencer was not even a good traveler. It is questionable, however, that the concept of survivals per se had anything to do with this aspect of the evolutionists' program. At the heart of the matter there lies a much more general situation. Anthropology achieved its professional identity under the guiding influence of eighteenth-century proposals for a science of universal history. Morgan, Tylor, and Spencer were universal historians who made use of the comparative method in order to achieve a more detailed and, on the whole, more accurate rendering of the sequence of cultural change which had led from the paleolithic hunters to industrial civilization. They were convinced that evolutionary changes had been regular enough to permit the recovery of missing historical data through comparison and the logical construction of intermediate and transitional types. Although they were aware of the inadequacy of much of the ethnographic literature, they expected that the regularities of evolutionary change would be identified when a sufficiently large number of cases were assembled. Two general considerations inclined the evolutionists to this optimistic view of the reconstructive powers of the comparative method. As previously stressed, in assessing their contributions to the rise of anthropological theory, we must bear in mind that the basic principles of the comparative method had already been vindicated by the findings of archaeology and that a similar strategy had achieved great success in philology. In addition, it must also be remembered that all of the mid-nineteenth-century sciences were dominated by a euphoria, arising from the widespread belief that the mechanical model in physics was on the verge of achieving a perfect description of the laws of matter and energy. Anthropologists were not the only scientists who grossly underestimated the complexity of the lawful relations governing the unfolding of phenomena in their field of inquiry. And to that extent, there is a certain amount of parallelism between the reactions in physics and cultural anthropology to the discovery that Newtonian-type regularities did not pertain on all levels of physical and sociocultural phenomena. There is much to be said therefore on behalf of the view that the evolutionists, in attending to the comparative method and to the data of unreliable but abundant ethnographic reports, rather than to intensive fieldwork with individual groups, were, for the times, following an essentially correct strategy. Given the new evidential basis for the predicted stages of progress from a "state of nature" through savagery, barbarism, and civilization, it was the strategically correct next step to seek for greater precision in the definition of the relevant institutional transformations without assuming that such refinements could be obtained only by abandoning the notion of universally valid stages. That this assumption ultimately proved necessary was a theoretical advance which could not have been achieved without the formulation and testing of the nineteenth-century evolutionary schemes. Indeed, it is a matter of historical record that the turn to intensive fieldwork did not by itself automatically result in a more sophisticated application of the comparative method. On the contrary, what happened was that the comparative method was virtually abandoned. Instead of refining the evolutionary sequences, the concentration on fieldwork even resulted in the abandonment of all diachronic interests. Instead of perfecting the science of universal history, the "cult" of fieldwork temporarily effaced the heritage of Enlightenment scientism and gave rise to frankly idiographic or humanistic varieties of anthropological descriptions. Noting that Boas failed to produce a description of Kwakiutl social organization adequate for modern applications of the comparative method (see p. 314), one may reasonably doubt that much was to be gained from similar performances by Morgan and Tylor. One or two cases were not going to settle any of the issues of sequence in which the evolutionists were interested; they were concerned not with exceptions, but with general trends.

THE MYTH OF UNILINEAR EVOLUTIONISM

This brings us to another of the important issues on which the evolutionists have been systematically misrepresented. It is commonly believed that the evolutionary stages revealed by the comparative method were regarded as fixed sequences, every step of which had to be gone through by all cultures. This misunderstanding has been consolidated by the label "unilinear evolutionism," which Julian Steward (1955:14) has assigned to the "classical evolutionary formulation" which "dealt with particular cultures, placing them in stages of a universal sequence" (*cf.* LOWIE 1937:190). There is no support for the contention, however, that the "classical evolutionary formulation" denied that specific cultures could skip certain steps in a sequence or evolve in a divergent fashion. It was Morgan's (1877:8) view that "the experience of mankind has run in *nearly* uniform channels; that human necessities in similar conditions have been *substantially* the same" (italics added). These qualifiers deserve to be emphasized because it is quite obvious that Morgan remained uncertain concerning just how much uniformity there had been. He was aware that "differences in the culture of the same period in the Eastern and Western hemisphere undoubtedly existed . . ." and he attributed these differences to "the unequal endowments of the continents" (*ibid.*). On the one hand we find him asserting:

> So essentially identical are the arts, institutions and mode of life in the same status upon all the continents, that the archaic form of the principal domestic institutions of the Greeks and Romans might even now be sought in the corresponding institutions of the American aborigines . . . [*ibid.*].

But on the other hand he warns us that his "ethnical periods" cannot be regarded as absolute in their application and that there are exceptions. What we must bear in mind is that to Morgan and his contemporaries the most interesting features of history were the similarities rather than the differences. For it was upon the similarities that a science of universal history depended. A modicum of sympathy for the attempt to found such a science will suffice to justify Morgan's strategy. The first step in the development of any science must be the assumption that the phenomena to be studied are related in an orderly fashion. It does less harm to begin with a picture of maximum than with minimum order, for the exceptions will soon enough make their claim to attention. Surely, neither a science of universal history nor of anything else could begin with the exceptions! Morgan readily acknowledged the existence of such exceptions, but in the context of his task, he could scarcely be expected to make them his central concern:

> It is difficult, if not impossible, to find such tests of progress to mark the commencement of these several periods as will be found absolute in their application, and without exceptions upon all the continents. Neither is it necessary, for the purpose in hand, that exceptions should not exist. It will be sufficient if the principal tribes of mankind can be classified, according to the degree of their relative progress, into conditions which can be recognized as distinct [*ibid.*].

A further discussion of Morgan's position will be given below in conjunction with the issue of parallel versus convergent evolution. But if Morgan is exempt from the charge of unilinear evolutionism, it is obvious that Tylor's evolutionism must also be exempted. In his great article on the statistical interpretation of marriage and locality rules, Tylor (1889:269) argues for historical uniformities in terms that are indistinguishable from Morgan's:

> The institutions of men are as distinctly stratified as the earth on which he lives. They succeed each other in series substantially uniform over the globe, independent of what seem the comparatively superficial differences of race and language, but shaped by similar human nature acting through successively changed conditions in savage, barbaric, and civilized life.

Yet, what is the meaning of the statistical version of the comparative method, if not precisely that "substantially uniform" is not equivalent to "unilinear"? In *Primitive Culture*, Tylor declares that few "would dispute that the following races are arranged rightly in order of culture: Australian, Tahitian, Aztec, Chinese, Italian" (1958, I:27). He promptly follows this up, however, with the warning that "even those students who hold most strongly that the general course of civilization, as measured along the scale of races from savages to ourselves, is progress toward the benefit of mankind [must] admit many and manifold exceptions. Industrial and intellectual culture by no means advances uniformly in all of its branches . . ." (*ibid.*).

When we turn to Spencer, there is not the remotest resemblance between his view of evolution and the unilinear stereotype. Indeed, despite Spencer's strong conviction concerning the lawfulness of sociocultural change, he was actually more "multilinear" than either Julian Steward or Karl Wittfogel (see Chap. 23).

> As with organic evolution, so with super-organic evolution. Though, taking the entire assemblage of societies, evolution may be held inevitable . . . yet it cannot be held inevitable in each particular society, or even probable [SPENCER 1896, I:96].

> While the current degradation theory is untenable, the theory of progression, in its ordinary form, seems to me untenable also. . . . It is possible, and, I believe, probable, that retrogression has been as frequent as progression [*ibid.*:95].

> . . . social progress is not linear but divergent and re-divergent. Each differentiated product gives origin to a new set of differentiated products. While spreading over the Earth mankind have found environments of various characters, and in each case the social life fallen into, partly determined by the social life previously led, has been partly determined by the influences of the new environment; so that the multiplying groups have tended ever to acquire differences, now major, and now minor: there have arisen genera and species of societies [*ibid.*, II:331].

As Robert Carneiro (1967:43) concludes: "Thus Spencer was not only not a unilinear evolutionist, he was not even a *linear* evolutionist . . . he saw evolution as a process of successive branchings in which increased heterogeneity goes hand in hand with increased complexity."

THE MYTH OF THE DENIAL OF DIFFUSION

Closely related to the misconception surrounding the evolutionists' commitment to unilinear models is the equally misunderstood issue of diffusion versus independent invention. Under the influence of the historical particularists and the German and British diffusionist schools, the myth has grown up that the nineteenth-century evolutionists denied the importance of diffusion. The diffusionists identified themselves with the point of view that man was essentially "uninventive," while the evolutionists were portrayed as believing the direct opposite. The diffusionists not only set up the dichotomy between "borrowing" and "invention," but they dogmatically denied that similar invention could account for worldwide similarities. The historical particularists, on the other hand, followed a middle course, rejecting both the "overinventiveness" of Adolf Bastian and the "underinventiveness" of Wilhelm Schmidt and Fritz Graebner (see Chap. 14). But they subscribed to, and helped to perpetuate, the false dichotomy between independent invention and diffusion.

This dichotomy is false in two senses. First, it does not accurately reflect the position of the evolutionists, none of whom proposed, as a matter of principle, that similarities had developed more frequently from independent invention than from diffusion. And the dichotomy is also logically and empirically false, because it rests on the unsupportable notion that independent invention and diffusion are fundamentally different *processes*.

Lowie's entanglement in both of these fallacies impeded his ability to interpret the respective contribution of the evolutionists and diffusionists. He was perfectly aware, of course, that Tylor maintained a lively interest in tracing diffused traits side by side with a deep conviction that there had been a general uniformity in evolutionary stages. Indeed, Lowie's highest accolades are reserved for Tylor's "serene willingness to weigh evidence" for and against diffusion in the following cases: Pan-European paleolithic tools; the piston bellows of Madagascar and Indonesia; North American and Old World pottery; the Old and New World bow and arrow; the Australian, African, and American theory that disease is caused by an intrusive stone or bone; the game of parcheesi as played in Mexico and India; and various myths found in both the Old and New Worlds. Tylor, according to Lowie (1937:74), was the "very antithesis of a strict parallelist . . . he was thoroughly convinced of the force of borrowing in human history and expressed this faith both abstractly and with respect to special cases." And Lowie quotes Tylor's own words to the effect (1958, I:53): "Civilization is a plant much more often propagated than developed." But Lowie (1937:60) was also of the opinion that "diffusion plays havoc with any universal law of sequence." How, then, could Tylor's evolutionism be combined with so large a dose of diffusion? One gathers from Lowie's stress on the association between evolutionism and independent invention on the one hand and historicism and diffusion on the other, that Tylor was simply confused. But the confusion rests with Lowie, since it is evident that Tylor did not accept the diffusionist dogma that "diffusion plays havoc with any universal law of sequence." Tylor evidently did not even feel that the fact of diffusion obliged one in the slightest to alter his conception of evolutionary sequences. Indeed, independent inventions were of interest to Tylor for reasons that eluded Lowie.

To most of the evolutionists, independent inventions were of interest not for demonstrating parallel evolution, but for demonstrating psychic unity. From Tylor's point of view, the demonstration that similar stages of culture had succeeded each other in substantially uniform fashion did not require the separation of independently invented traits from borrowed ones. Whether the uniformity of a particular stage had resulted from borrowing or independent invention was unimportant for proving that there was a general movement to history. The demonstration of evolutionary uniformity resided in the worldwide, almost monotonous sameness of institutions which could be arranged in a single chronological and structural sequence.

That Tylor regarded independent inventions as a strong argument for psychic unity does not mean that he regarded diffusion as a strong argument *against* psychic unity. It will be recalled that one of the main points raised by the monogenists was the fact that Christianity was apparently capable of being learned by all human groups. Diffusion may very well be regarded therefore as providing additional evidence of the essential similarity of the human mind, although the evidence from independent invention would seem to be somewhat stronger and more direct. It was in precisely this frame of reference that Tylor (1865:378–79) summed up his discussion of diffusion and independent invention in his *Researches into the Early History of Mankind:*

> In the first place, the facts collected seem to favour the view that the wide differences in the civilization and mental state of the various races of mankind are rather differences of development than of origin, rather of degree than of kind . . . wherever the occurrence of any art or knowledge in two places can be confidently ascribed to independent invention, as, for instance, when we find the dwellers in the ancient lake-habitations of Switzerland, and the Modern New Zealanders, adopting a like construction in their curious fabrics of tied bundles of fibre, the similar step thus made in different times and places tends to prove the similarity of the minds that made it. Moreover, to take a somewhat weaker line of argument, the uniformity with which like stages in the development of art and science are found among the most unlike races, may be adduced as evidence on the same side, in spite of the constant difficulty in deciding whether any particular development is due to independent invention, or to transmission from some other people to those among whom it is found. For if the similar thing has been produced in two places by independent invention, then, as has just been said, it is direct evidence of similarity of mind. And on the other hand, if it was carried from the one place to the other, or from a third to

> both, by mere transmission from people to people, then the smallness of the change it has suffered in transplanting is still evidence of the like nature of the soil wherever it is found.

It is interesting to note the similarity between Tylor's comments on the compatability of diffusion and independent invention in terms of psychic unity and the critique which was eventually advanced denying that independent invention and diffusion represented fundamentally different evolutionary processes (see pp. 615–16).

Lowie's (1938:77) insistence that diffusion *explains* resemblances more satisfactorily than independent invention is totally unsubstantiable. Neither the one nor the other explains anything; both are mere labels for a single process of change. The lawful conditions of this process remain unstated in Lowie's formulation as much as in Bastian's. What have we achieved when we tell ourselves that two cultures are similar because they are or have been in contact? Since all cultures are in contact directly or indirectly with all others, all cultures should be the same. Since they are not, similarity is obviously not a simple function of contact. Nor is it a matter of frequency or intensity of contact measured in terms of distance or interaction, since adjacent cultures in continuous contact frequently manifest sharp cultural differences (e.g., Ituri pygmies and Bantu villagers; Southwest Pueblos and Navajos; Vedda and Ceylonese). But we must postpone further discussion of this issue to a later chapter (see p. 377).

PARALLEL AND CONVERGENT CONTRIBUTIONS TO EVOLUTIONARY UNIFORMITY

The unilinear-multilinear and the independent invention-diffusion dichotomies should be seen in relationship to a third misleading distinction: that between parallel and convergent evolution. In parallel evolution, cultures evolve from and to similar conditions step by step in tandem. In convergent evolution, cultures evolve toward a similar condition through dissimilar steps. The Boasians made much of this distinction because they were obliged to accept convergent evolution as a common phenomenon. The reason for this is that every case of diffusion is a case of convergence. Parallel evolution, however, was regarded as extremely rare and exclusively identified with the alleged unilinear evolutionism of Tylor, Morgan, and Spencer. The demonstration of convergent evolution brought about by diffusion or by any other series of different steps was regarded by the Boasians as constituting a disproof of the entire evolutionist position. As we shall see (p. 258), both Boas and Lowie attacked the evolutionists through repeated demonstrations that in the sociocultural realm "like effects" could be produced by "unlike causes." But, once again, we are dealing with a distinction that was not essential to the evolutionists; their main concern was with the general uniformity created by both convergent and parallel processes and not with a step by step concatenation of "identical" causes (*cf.* Lowie). As Tylor (1865:373) made clear: "The state of things which is found is not indeed that one race does or knows exactly what another race does or knows, but that similar stages of development recur in different times and places."

Indifference to the questions of independent invention versus diffusion and to parallel as distinguished from convergent evolution is also characteristic of Morgan's approach. Morgan (1877:39) explicitly includes diffusion as one of the mechanisms by which the *substantial* uniformity of sociocultural evolution was made possible:

LEWIS HENRY MORGAN, DIFFUSIONIST

> The most advanced portion of the human race were halted, so to express it, at certain stages of progress, until some great invention or discovery, such as the domestication of animals or the smelting of iron ore, gave a new and powerful impulse forward. While thus restrained, the ruder tribes, continually advancing, approached in different degrees of nearness to the same status; for *wherever a continental connection existed, all the tribes must have shared in some measure in each other's progress.* All great inventions and discoveries propagate themselves; but the inferior tribes must have appreciated their value before they could appropriate them. In the continental areas certain tribes would lead; but the leadership would be apt to shift a number of times in the course of an ethnical period [italics added].

In discussing the transition from the lower to middle status of barbarism, Morgan again makes explicit provision for borrowing without acknowledging any serious challenge to his overall scheme:

> Some of these inventions were borrowed, not unlikely, from tribes in the Middle Status; for it was by this process constantly repeated that the more advanced tribes lifted up those below them, as fast as the latter were able to appreciate and to appropriate the means of progress [*ibid.*:540].

As Lowie (1937:59) himself points out, "Morgan was not unduly disturbed by cultural loans, though he freely admits them." And Lowie (*ibid.*:60) was also perfectly aware that Morgan had explicitly rejected the possibility that the major types of kinship system had arisen independently and evolved in a parallel fashion. Indeed, Morgan's opinion of the Boasian stereotype of parallel evolution was that it would require "miracles" to occur:

> If it is assumed then that the Turanian and the Ganowanian [terminologies] . . . were created independently in Asia and America, would each by imperative necessity have passed through the same experience, have developed the same sequence of customs and institutions, and, as a final result, have produced the same identical system of relationship? The statement of the proposition seems to work its refutation on the grounds of its excessive improbability. . . . If the two families commenced on separate continents in a state of promiscuous intercourse, . . . *it would be little less than a miracle* if both should develop the same ultimate system of relationship. Upon the doctrine of chances it is not supposable that each would pass through the same experience, develop the same series of customs and institutions and finally produce for themselves the same system of consanguinity, which would be found, on comparison, to be identical in radical characteristics as well as coincident in minute details . . . [MORGAN 1870:504–5].

As we have already seen, it was at this point that Morgan's racism intruded and he was led to the absurd conclusion that Iroquois terminology was "carried in the blood," thereby proving that the American Indians were descended from Asian progenitors. The irony of this aspect of Morgan's denial of strict parallel evolution is that on this issue Lowie later came to champion precisely the point of view which Morgan had rejected, namely that in the presence of exogamous unilinear descent groups, Iroquois kinship terminology had been invented over and over again! The respective positions of Morgan and Lowie on the origin of unilinear descent groups constitute an equally spectacular reversal of stereotypes. Morgan, as Lowie well knew, argued at great length against the possibility of the independent invention of the gens (matriclan). According to Morgan (1877:388-89), the establishment of exogamic prescriptions along unilineal lines

> . . . was too remarkable and too improbable . . . to be repeated many different times, and in widely different areas. . . . Instead of a natural and obvious conception, the gens was essentially abstruse . . . a product of high intelligence for the times in

> which it originated. . . . Its propagation is more easily explained than its institution. These considerations tend to show the improbability of its repeated reproduction in disconnected areas.

Yet Lowie later came to argue that the clan had been independently re-invented four times in North America alone (see p. 349)!

It is clear that the classic image of the nineteenth-century evolutionist as a remorseless parallelist who insisted on identical evolutionary stages for all cultures is nothing but a convenient substitute for an embarrassing reality. In insisting upon the orderliness of sociocultural evolution, neither Tylor nor Morgan asserted that the history of all cultures consisted of an identical series of transformations. Divergent paths of evolution were also recognized, but both Morgan and Tylor believed that in the long run, parallelism *and* convergence acted to insure a substantial degree of global uniformity. On the other hand, Lowie (1937:59), identifying himself with "historians of culture," protested that culture "is far too complex to be reduced to chronological formulae; its development is mainly divergent, not parallel." But the opposite of "parallel" can be "mainly divergent" only when "convergent" and "divergent" evolution are lumped together to form an historically meaningless dichotomy over and against parallel evolution. The only historically applicable dichotomy is that which separates science from nonscience, namely one in which convergence and parallelism act frequently enough to produce substantial uniformities. The evolutionists, in brief, simply denied that history had been "mainly divergent"; the equation of that position with one which insists that evolution had consisted mainly of parallel development is an artifact of a highly biased understanding of the history of anthropological theory. In ringing up the balance between the historical particularists and the evolutionists, we must reckon therefore with an exaggeration by the historical particularists of the amount of disorder in history, which is as least as much in error as the exaggerated orderliness discerned by some but not all of the evolutionists. The errors of the evolutionists were committed on behalf of pushing a science of culture to (and beyond) its evidential limits; the errors of the historical particularists—with which we deal in later chapters—were committed out of a spirit of scientific nihilism, which denied that a science of history was possible.

The Evolutionists: Results

7

To affirm the strategy of the comparative method as practiced by Morgan, Tylor, Spencer, and their contemporaries is not necessarily to endorse any of the evolutionary schemes which they advanced for consideration. The important thing is that these schemes contained hypotheses which even today can fruitfully orient research and which can be corrected in the light of new evidence, without being utterly destroyed in the process. It so happens, however, that many of the evolutionists' sequences actually have endured the test of additional research and stand today as indestructible memorials to their faith in the scientific method. But both the successes and the failures must be considered if we are properly to evaluate either the evolutionists or their twentieth-century critics.

MORGAN'S SCHEME

Since Lewis Henry Morgan's developmental scheme is the most elaborate, embracing the widest spectrum of institutions in a single frame, we may profitably employ it as a focus of discussion and of comparison with competitive theories. Morgan envisioned human history as consisting of three major "ethnical periods"—Savagery, Barbarism, and Civilization—of which the first two were divided into subperiods denoted Lower, Middle, and Upper. These ethnical periods and their subdivisions were defined by the following sequence of technological innovations:

LOWER SAVAGERY	fruit and nut subsistence
MIDDLE SAVAGERY	fish subsistence and fire
UPPER SAVAGERY	bow and arrow
LOWER BARBARISM	pottery
MIDDLE BARBARISM	domestication of animals (Old World), cultivation of maize, irrigation, adobe and stone architecture (New World)
UPPER BARBARISM	iron tools
CIVILIZATION	phonetic alphabet and writing

In the domain of the family Morgan recognized five successive forms: (1) The *consanguine*, based on group marriage within the same generation (marriage of "brothers and sisters"); (2) the *punaluan*, based on a form of group marriage in which brothers were forbidden to marry sisters; (3) the *syndyasmian*, or *pairing*, family, a transitional form between group marriage and monogamy, in which husband or wife could end the marriage at will as often as he or she wished; (4) the *patriarchical*, a short-lived variety, mainly associated with the Hebrews and early Romans, in which supreme authority was vested in the male head (polygyny was a secondary feature, present among Hebrews, absent among Romans); and (5) the *monogamian*, based on monogamy and female equality, and progressively resembling the modern nuclear unit.

Morgan recognized the following sequence of kinship terminologies: (1) Malayan; (2) Turanian-Ganowanian; and (3) Aryan-Semitic-Uralian. In modern classifications these correspond respectively to the Hawaiian, Iroquois, and Eskimo types.

In the realm of sociopolitical organization, the sequence begins with the first two stages of the family: a promiscuous horde, succeeded by one organized into several intermarrying sets of male siblings and female siblings, corresponding to the punaluan phase of the family and exemplified for Morgan in the so-called Australian marriage classes (section and subsections in modern terms). The next phase is dominated by the matrisib. Matrisibs combine to form phratries; phratries combine to form tribes; tribes combine to form confederacies. All of these organizations, from the promiscuous horde to the confederacy, were founded upon what Morgan called "personal relations," i.e., upon sex and kinship. All such arrangements were to be distinguished from true political organization, which followed next, and which was based upon the reckoning of rights and obligations in terms of territorial identity and property relations. The true political units were the township, the county, and the state.

Morgan's approach to these sequences involved him in a remarkable attempt to coordinate and link the stages of each with all the rest. The overall effect therefore is of a diachronic and synchronic system of unprecedented structural and chronological scope. The overall movement from systems based on sex and kinship to those based on territoriality and property was connected by a series of negative and positive feedbacks to family form, kinship terminology, and the technological criteria of the ethnical periods.

To begin with the institutions of Lowest Savagery: Morgan's explanation for the Malayan terminology was that under group marriage it would be impossible to discover which male on the first ascending generation was one's father, hence all potential fathers were called by the same term. Similarly, since all women on the first ascending generation were either actual mother or potential "stepmothers," they were also designated by a single term. The connection with the technological criteria was more vague, being based on the assumption that only a stunted form of mentality could sanction such brutish arrangements as promiscuity and brother-sister incest. This low form of savagery was in turn reflected in, and reinforced by, the rudimentary technological level characteristic of a period in which the use of fire was unknown. With the introduction of the prohibition on brother-sister marriage—resulting in Morgan's "punaluan" form of group marriage—the kinship terminology underwent its first major transformation. Since brothers and sisters were no longer actual, or potential, mates, the children of brothers and sisters could no longer be "brothers" and "sisters." On the other hand, since brothers belonged to a single marriage group and since sisters all belonged to another marriage group, children of brothers continued to be "brother" and "sister," as did children of sisters. This then was the origin of the cross-sex and parallel-sex uncle and cousin terms of Iroquois terminology. At this point the whole organization of society is thus based on "sexual" distinctions. At the same time, improvements in technology are brought about by an increased intellectual capacity, one of the benefits of eliminating brother-sister incest. Indeed, Morgan

(1877:434) described this process as "a good illustration of the operation of the principles of natural selection." Heightened intelligence now prepares the way for the invention of the matrisib, a device that consolidates the gain of the punaluan system and further widens the scope of incest prohibitions to include all persons with common ancestry through females. The clan would be matrilineal at first because when it came into existence the family had not yet reached syndyasmian, or pairing, form. Since paternity was uncertain, descent could not be traced through males. One's mother, however, is never in doubt; hence, descent was traced exclusively through females. Arising in Savagery, the matriclan gradually became the central feature of primitive social organization. It lasts all through Barbarism until the beginning of political society and into the early stages of Civilization. Its undoing is brought about by the same force that brings in the monogamian family, patrilineality, and political society, namely the growth of property. The latter, in turn, is a result of the gradual improvement in the "arts of subsistence." The clan and the monogamian family are opposed in principle. One stands for the merging of the nuclear family in the clan collective, the other for independent family units. Similarly, the organization on the basis of territory is opposed to organization on the basis of kin. Large populations in dense aggregates cannot be organized on a kin basis. Propertied classes put an end to the democracy of clan life. But the inheritance of property promotes the stability of the male within the family (he "wants" heirs); thus in its last phases the descent rule of the clan shifts from matrilineality to patrilineality. But this is a short-lived form because the increase in property-mediated relations at the same time acts to destroy the clan and to usher in the era of political society. Finally, with the establishment of the monogamian family, the Iroquois terminology, last of the classificatory systems, gives way to the more highly descriptive categories of the Aryan system.

WEAKNESSES OF MORGAN'S SCHEME

It should be pointed out at once that the interconnectedness of the several sequences is far from perfect. The scheme outlined above permits several major institutional transformations to occur without corresponding modifications in related domains. Thus, for Morgan, neither the syndyasmian family nor the patrisib have an effect on the kinship terminology, yet it is now generally agreed that there is an important correlation between patrilineality and Omaha systems and between matrilineality and Crow systems.[1] According to Morgan, Iroquois terminology was introduced before clans came on the scene, and it continued unmodified during the long period of the clan's ascendancy. The most important lapses to which attention should be drawn, however, are those involving Morgan's evident failure to discover a systematic relationship between techno-economic and social structural parameters. All of the prepolitical structural arrangements of family, terminology, and clan relate to subsistence only through the vague intermediation of a biocultural principle of natural selection. That is, none of the specific differences and similarities of primitive social structure are related to specific innovations in the techno-environmental or techno-economic variables. It is only at the point of transition from kinship-organized to politically organized society that Morgan's scheme achieves anything resembling full internal coherence. This circumstance will be recalled when we turn to the question of whether Morgan can be credited, as Marx and Engels claimed, with an independent discovery of the materialist interpretation of history. For the moment let it suffice to say that it is doubtful that such an interpretation can be sustained even with respect to Morgan's transition from social to political organization. One may be certain, however, that it does not apply to the changes that precede the emergence of the state, since, as we have just seen, the several domains of the primitive sociocultural system are not closely interdetermined.

In the light of almost a century of additional research and theory, most of Morgan's sequences must be discarded as either false or inadequate. Even his technological sequence contains drastic errors. To begin with the "nuts and fruits" of Lower Savagery, it is now known that man has been a hunter for a million years or more. "Fish subsistence" is pre-eminently a matter of local adaptation and cannot be assigned a definite chronological position with respect to hunting. The introduction of the bow and arrow did not necessarily entail decisive shifts in the "ratio of technological efficiency": food calories output/ food calories input. Paleolithic groups which depended on spearing, bola-throwing, surrounds, and simple gathering were probably already

[1] Crow and Omaha terminologies tend to reflect a sociological emphasis upon membership in unilineal descent groups. The classifying principle of lineality overrides that of generation. Thus in Crow, a woman and all of her descendants through females are referred to by a single term, while in Omaha, a man and all of his descendants through males are referred to by a single term, regardless of how many generations are involved. For example, in Crow, father's sister, father's sister's daughter and father's sister's daughter's daughter, etc., are classed together.

capable of reaching a population size which was determined largely by the rate of reproduction of the natural biota rather than by a particular hunting and gathering technology. One of Morgan's worst ethnographic errors was the assignment of the proto-state agricultural Hawaiians to Middle Savagery because they lacked the bow and arrow. Pottery also turned out to be a poor choice as the diagnostic of the transition between Savagery and Barbarism. By emphasizing pottery, Morgan failed to give sufficient credit to the revolutionary significance of the introduction of agriculture—control over the rate of reproduction of the natural biota—and its consequent new possibilities for human life. The use of the domestication of animals as the criterion of Middle Barbarism was also ill-fated. It is simply contrary to archaeological evidence to posit a significant time interval between the domestication of plants and the domestication of animals—both occur in the earliest levels of the Near and Middle Eastern Neolithic. The emphasis upon iron tools for Upper Barbarism was responsible for another of Morgan's great disasters: the assignment of the Aztec to the same "ethnical period" as the Iroquois. In addition, Civilizations were attained in both the Old and New Worlds long before the introduction of iron. And the same may be said of Morgan's last criterion—the phonetic alphabet. The Incas managed an empire without using any kind of writing system.

Despite these inadequacies, it cannot be said that Morgan's technological series is today without research significance. Certainly, its historical contribution cannot be challenged, since it served to stimulate the search for better ways of identifying and conceptualizing the innovations responsible for major increments in food production, population density, and population size. Morgan's emphasis upon techno-economic factors for demarcating major evolutionary trends remains viable as a strategy. His "ethnical periods," shorn of their biological significance and equipped with nonpejorative labels, are probably accepted by the majority of contemporary American anthropologists as a valid, if overgeneralized, taxonomy of cultural types. As Eleanor Leacock (1963:lxi) has noted:

> In spite of the disfavor into which Morgan's work fell, his general sequence of stages has been written into our understanding of prehistory and interpretation of archaeological remains, as a glance at any introductory anthropology text will indicate.

Thus Morgan's Savagery is roughly equivalent to what are frequently called hunting and gathering societies, while Barbarism is more or less what most anthropologists have in mind when they discuss horticultural, "tribal," and pre- or proto-state societies. Finally, Civilization as defined by a stratified, state-level organization is very much in current use. Of course, it is another question, not faced by Leacock and other Morganists, whether in this attenuated form, Morgan's scheme was notably more advanced than its eighteenth-century antecedents.

The least satisfactory of Morgan's institutional sequences is that which is concerned with the family and kinship terminology. Speculations concerning a period of promiscuity have been deprived of all the inferential bits of evidence to which Morgan was able to appeal. No one today, despite numerous field studies of monkey and great ape mating patterns would seriously venture to suggest what kind of mating preferences were characteristic of the transitional hominids. Morgan's reconstruction of a stage of promiscuity rested on what he took to be evidence of forms of group marriage among the Hawaiians and the Australian aborigines. This evidence was spurious, and all other ethnographic cases in support of group marriage or the consanguine family have been conclusively disproved. In its place, the universality of pairing arrangements accompanied by incest prohibitions within the nuclear family—cohabiting adult male and female and adult female's children—have been established. Morgan's explanation for Hawaiian terminology as an adaptation to the consanguine family is thus totally devoid of evidential substance. The rout suffered by this explanation was all the more humiliating because of Morgan's assignment of the highly stratified Hawaiians to the status of Middle Savagery, far below the egalitarian Iroquois. The picture of monogamy as a condition reached only after numberless generations of the struggle to perfect the balance between the sexes is contradicted by the (serial) monogamic bliss enjoyed by the majority of the members of every known human society. Morgan's explanation of Iroquois terminology was also adversely affected by the rout of the consanguine family since the prohibition on brother-sister marriage obviously long antedated the development of the cross-parallel distinction. The repercussions extend still further to take in the explanation of the matriclan, whose invention and spread were linked by Morgan to alleged biological advantages of exogamy. Here, even if we grant the highly dubious hypothesis that local exogamy conferred direct biological advantages, it still remains difficult to see how clan exogamy, which affects parallel cousins but not cross-cousins, would be much of an improvement over the earlier nuclear family taboos.

The most bedeviled part of Morgan's kinship sequences was his insistence that the matriclan was chronologically prior to the patriclan. Here Morgan was a participant in one of the most heated and useless discussions in the history of the social sciences. He and his supporters were opposed by an equally numerous group, who argued for the reverse priority. Both groups were wrong, constituting one of those rare cases of diametrically opposed positions about which it is impossible to say that either contained a grain of truth. Descent rules, as they have come to be understood, reflect residence patterns; and residence patterns are primarily a matter of local techno-environmental and techno-economic conditions. Groups with similar ratios of technological efficiency and similar overall quanta of production may thus very well exhibit contrasting descent rules. The occurrence of matrilineal descent has no bearing on the status of women, since mother's brother rather than mother is generally the head of the descent group. Furthermore, the idea that matrilineality is a result of confusion concerning paternity is wholly confounded by the numerous cases of primitive peoples who deny that the male is necessary for conception but who regard themselves as descended from a line of males, and by the universal recognition of some degree of kinship with both maternal and paternal relatives, regardless of the nature of the unilineal rule.

ENDURING ASPECTS OF MORGAN'S SCHEME

Despite this profusion of errors, there remain several valuable suggestions in Morgan's approach to the evolution of the family, kinship terminology, and kinship groups. As we shall see, Morgan's basic and original contention that kinship terminology was produced by different forms of the family and of group organization has been vindicated and constitutes to this day the basic premise of innumerable books and articles. Furthermore, Morgan's description of the egalitarian clan marks the beginning of the serious study of unilinear descent groups.

A much more valuable contribution is to be found in Morgan's treatment of the emergence of stratified and state-organized societies. The pervasiveness of kinship statuses on the pre-state level; the withering away of egalitarian unilinear groups and the rise of endogamous castes, classes, and minorities; and the role of property in the development of stratified groups are all foreshadowed in Morgan's scheme. Once again, however, there were numerous deficiencies brought about by faulty data and by an overly mechanical pursuit of the contrast between social and political principles. It is clear that kinship as an ideology of identity is not incompatible with the formation of the state. It is rather to be said that with the development of marked inequalities of access to strategic resources, the ancient principles of kinship (affinity through marriage and descent) are pressed into serving functions which hitherto were inimical to sociocultural survival. In other words, stratified forms of kinship groupings take the place of egalitarian ones. In a similar vein, it should be noted that the principle of territoriality is also present on both state and pre-state levels, but its functions are transfigured in the change from one to the other. Citizenship in the modern nation state, for example, depends on a mixture of territorial and kinship principles. It is true that children of New Yorkers living in California are not entitled to special privileges when they visit New York. Yet the child of a United States citizen is a United States citizen wherever he is born. And of course kinship still determines the basic pattern of the inheritance of property.

Much fruitful historical research was stimulated by Morgan's suggestion that unilinear descent groups had existed among the Greek and Roman proto-states. While Morgan's Greek and Roman evidence is probably best regarded as indicating some form of nonunilinear grouping, the fact that scholars began to think of the predecessors of the Greeks as being something like the Iroquois had an immensely salutary effect upon culture-bound Euro-American historiography.

It will not be possible here to review all the schemes of universal history produced during the period 1860-90. The kinds of errors upon which they were based are well illustrated in Morgan's case, and little beyond an antiquarian curiousity would be served by providing their details. A brief exposition of some additional sequences, however, will be found useful as a preliminary to the next matter to be considered, namely the nature of the causal processes to which the evolutionists attributed their developmental panoramas.

BACHOFEN'S SCHEME

One of the wildest schemes from the point of view of causality is that of J. J. Bachofen. Social life begins with a period of sexual promiscuity identified by Bachofen as "hetairism." This was the time when the lawless materialist principle governed mankind. Only material motherhood can be ascertained, and women are exposed to the lust and sexual tyranny of men. The women now struggle to liberate themselves. By virtue of their religiosity, the weaker sex is able to subdue the stronger one, for Bachofen believed: "Religion is the only efficient lever of all civilization. Each elevation and depression of human life has its origin in a movement which begins in this supreme department" (BACHOFEN 1861:xiv, quoted in HOWARD 1904:42).

Mother-right or gynocracy now reigns. Female deities preside, the left is favored over the right, the earth over the sky, moon over sun, the youngest over the oldest. Women establish the family, oblige men to marry, and progressively take on more Amazonian qualities. But the reign of the gynocrats is founded on an inferior religious principle—the material tie between mother and child symbolized in the Earth-Mother deity. The men now seek to reverse the balance. At first they merely seek to assert themselves by pretending they are mothers. Hence, the origin of the couvade. Soon they rise to a new and higher principle of religion, ushering in the third epoch, that of spirit. This highest principle of life is based upon fatherhood as opposed to motherhood.

> It was the assertion of fatherhood which delivered the mind from natural appearances, and when this was successfully achieved, human existence was raised above the laws of material life. The principle of motherhood is common to all species of animal life, but man goes beyond this tie in giving the pre-eminence to the power of procreation, and thus becomes conscious of his higher vocation. . . . In the paternal and spiritual principle he breaks through the bonds of tellurism and looks upward to the higher regions of the cosmos. Victorious fatherhood thus becomes as distinctly connected with the heavenly light as prolific motherhood is with the teeming earth [BACHOFEN 1861:xxvii, quoted in HOWARD 1904:43].

Morgan and Bachofen exerted a reciprocal influence on each other. Bachofen's ideas concerning the priority of matrilineal descent and gynocracy are incorporated in *Ancient Society*. Bachofen benefited from the comparison of the classical matriclan with the Iroquois, and he expressed his gratitude by dedicating a book of essays (Bachofen 1966; orig. 1880) to Morgan.

MAINE'S SCHEME

It was symptomatic of the whole mother-right, father-right controversy that in the very year that Bachofen's *Mother Right* was published, Sir Henry Maine's *Ancient Law* also appeared, setting forth the proposal that in its original form, the family was patrilineal and patriarchical. Lowie (1937:51–52) has championed the view that Maine's evolutionary sequences, unlike those of Bachofen, Morgan, and McLennan and Lubbock, were not intended to embrace a universally valid scheme, and that his words of homage "to continuous sequence, inflexible order, and eternal law in history" were nothing but a "sop to regnant fashion." While it is true that Maine explicitly rejected the idea "that human society went everywhere through the same series of changes," similar explicit denials have already been demonstrated for the other so-called unilinear evolutionists. On this issue J. W. Burrow's (1966:164) analysis is to be preferred:

> Because Maine was not a systematic thinker, and because he never fully recognized the conflict between the historical and scientific elements in his intellectual equipment, it would be possible, by selective quotation, to make out a convincing case for either view of him—that he was a legal historian with perhaps too great a fondness for cross-comparison and "brilliant" generalization, or that he was a rigid evolutionary determinist. The only way to give a picture of his work that approaches accuracy is to try to give due weight to both aspects without pretending that they are wholly compatible.

Part of the confusion arises from Maine's original lack of interest in what he regarded as the backward races of mankind. While he was no less interested in the overall direction of history than was Morgan, he resembled Hegel, Comte, and Condorcet in believing that a knowledge of the history of the "progressive" nations would suffice to discern the "laws of history." Maine's (1883:284) interest focused on "the communities which were destined to civilization." In *Ancient Law* (1861:23) he says, "I confine myself in what follows to the progressive societies." These societies consisted exclusively of "Aryan" peoples, for "civilization is nothing more than a name for the old order of the Aryan world, . . ." (MAINE 1887:231). At the time of his original formulation of the patriarchal theory, Maine simply took it for granted that there was no need to discuss the origin of institutions in a framework larger than that of the Aryans; he could thus propound a theory manifestly restricted to Europe and India and at the same time make it sound as if he were referring to all of humanity. How else explain the statement also found in *Ancient Law*: "The effect of the evidence derived from comparative jurisprudence is to establish the view of the primeval condition of the human race which is known as the Patriarchal Theory" (*ibid.*: 118). Regardless of whether Maine initially intended to restrict this patriarchal theory to the "Aryans," his contemporaries certainly reacted as if that was not the case. McLennan (1865:115), for example, attacked Maine as one who "has been unable to conceive how human beings could be grouped on any principle more primitive than that of the patriarchal system. . . ." Maine's response to this was not to say that his work dealt only with a restricted portion of mankind and that he was unable to conceive of matrilineality in the history of the "Aryan" peoples. Instead, he chose to counterattack by casting doubt upon the matriarchal theory, suggesting that the institutions which McLennan and Lubbock had attributed to ancient man were either falsely described or the result of recent changes.

> Sir John Lubbock and Mr. McLennan conceive themselves to have shown that the first steps of mankind towards civilisation were taken from a condition in which assemblages of men followed practices which are not found to occur universally even in animal nature. Here I have only to observe that many of the phenomena of barbarism adverted to by these writers are found in India. The usages appealed to are the usages of . . . wild tribes . . . now for many years . . . under British observation, . . . The evidence, therefore, [from India] . . . is very superior indeed to the slippery testimony concerning savages which is gathered from travellers' tales. . . . Much which I have personally heard in India bears out the caution which I gave as to the reserve with which all speculations on the antiquity of human usage should be received. Practices represented as of immemorial antiquity, and universally characteristic of the infancy of mankind, have been described to me as having been for the first time resorted to in our own days through the mere pressure of external circumstances or novel temptations [MAINE 1887:16–17].

It seems literally to have been the case that Maine was unable to conceive how matriclans could constitute a viable form of social organization. Thus in a letter to Morgan, commenting on *Ancient Society*, Maine laments that he has been unable to find a copy of Morgan's *The League of Iroquois* and takes the opportunity to ask a number of questions centering on his "difficulty in conceiving ['female' gentes] as localized or combattant bodies" (MAINE, quoted in STERN 1931:141–42). There is good reason to suspect, therefore, that the sophisticated historical approach with which Lowie credits Maine is more a result of ethnographic naïveté than of methodological rigor.

Maine's most important contribution lies in his suggestion that kinship had provided the basic principle of organization of primitive society. The primeval groups are families such as Homer attributed to the Cyclops in which a despotic father exercises absolute power over his wives and children. These families aggregated through legal fictions to form larger groups without surrendering their autonomy. Hence, "the unit of an ancient society was the Family, of a modern society the Individual" (1861:121). Thenceforth, "the movement of the progressive societies has been uniform" with respect "to the gradual dissolution of family dependency and the growth of individual obligation in its place" (*ibid.*:163). This movement is examined by Maine with respect to a number of related transitions expressed in terms of useful dichotomies: Family-organized society is fixed-status society; individualized society is free-contract society. The movement is from status to contract. Family-organized society owns property in common; individual-organized society embodies the growth of private ownership. In the most primitive stage of law, all injuries may be compensated by agreement of the families involved, and civil and criminal law are confounded; later, certain injuries involve only individuals while others are crimes against the whole society.

CONVERGENCE TOWARD THE FOLK-URBAN CONTINUUM

Maine's emphasis on the progressive individualization of society preceded Morgan's treatment of the rise of the state in terms of the contrast between relations through persons and relations through territory; and there probably was some influence which flowed from the former to the latter. But judging from the almost simultaneous appearance of several similar formulations, the idea must have been very much "in the air." Thus in 1887, Ferdinand Tönnies published his *Gemeinschaft und Gesellschaft,* in which the transition from feudal to capitalist society was described in terms of the following kinds of contrasts: confident, intimate personal relations versus relations between strangers; moral, collective, cooperative, joint bonds versus independent, depersonalized bonds; reciprocities, barter, and exchange versus purchase and contract; and divine sanction versus secular sanctions. In the next decade, essentially the same theme was elaborated by Émile Durkheim under the rubrics "mechanical" versus "organic" solidarity (see p. 466).

During the Boasian period, when the terms "primitive" and "civilized" were regarded as offensive to the principle of cultural relativism, interest in the *gemeinschaft-gesellschaft* distinction waned among anthropologists. Among sociologists influenced by Durkheim and Max Weber, however, this dichotomy was kept alive, at least as far as synchronic comparisons were concerned. In the 1940's the idea finally circled back into anthropology in the form of Robert Redfield's (1947) folk-urban dichotomy, the vaguely evolutionistic contrast between preliterate, homogeneous, religious, familial, personalized primitive and peasant communities and the literate, heterogeneous, secular, individualized, depersonalized urban society. It is interesting to note that Redfield, while acknowledging his debt to Maine, Tönnies, and Durkheim, makes no reference to Morgan. Yet Morgan's treatment of the transition from the personal to impersonal, kinship to political organization is not inferior to those which are acknowledged. Herbert Spencer's conception of the transition from the military to industrial types of society, with the increase in heterogeneity that for Spencer marked all evolutionary processes, probably also belongs in this same set of proposals. Finally, it should be noted that none of the aforementioned folk-urban theorists seem to have been aware of the fact that Marx had anticipated their formulations as early as the 1848 *Communist Manifesto* (see p. 226).

MC LENNAN'S SCHEME

The scheme that most rivaled Morgan's was that proposed by the Edinburgh lawyer John McLennan. McLennan's sequences, like Morgan's, began with a horde living, if not in strict promiscuity, at least in a state of indifference concerning marriage rules. The members of the horde, speculating on their origin, decided that they were all descended from an animal ancestor. This was the origin of "totemism."

The primal human population lived under harsh conditions and were subjected to an intense struggle for existence both within and between groups. In McLennan's (1865:165) scheme, the foremost effect of this "struggle for food and security" was an alleged prevalence of female infanticide:

> As braves and hunters were required and valued, it would be the interest of every horde to rear, when possible, its healthy male children. It would be less its interest to rear females, as they would be less capable of self-support, and of contributing, by their exertions to the common good. In this lies the only explanation which can be accepted of the origin of those systems of female infanticide still existing, the discovery of which from time to time, in out of the way places, so shocks our humanity.

The shortage of women within the group now led to the sharing of one female among several males (the origin of polyandry). At the same time an effort was made to compensate for the paucity of adult women by capturing those who remained in neighboring hordes. This practice was, so to speak, habit-forming; it eventually was regarded as a necessity that women be taken from other groups: "In time it came to be considered improper, because it was unusual, for a man to marry a woman of his own group" (*ibid.*:289). This was the origin of "exogamy," a term first coined by McLennan, as was its opposite "endogamy." Among the wife-sharing group of men, paternity could not be determined. Hence, when descent first came to be reckoned, it was necessarily in the female line.

In later versions, McLennan (1876:57ff.) shifted his ground and postulated that female descent originated before wife-capture and exogamy. He saw endogamous groups crystallizing around "primitive mothers." These broke up into separate "bands," which maintained their totem identity even while dispersed. Now began the period of infanticide and wife-stealing. But the bands with the same totem regarded it as a sacred obligation to refrain from stealing each other's women. They were thus "obliged to obtain them by capture from groups of a stock different from their own." McLennan recognized that there was something wrong with jumping immediately to exogamy because marrying out became a habit. But his attempt to improve the causal linkage added to the overburdened hypotheses. As the capture of women became more and more prevalent, the concept of marriage took on the meaning of cohabitation with a captured woman. This happened because cohabitation with a woman of one's own group came to be regarded as something other than marriage, namely, as a sin, equivalent to the theft and capture of one of the females who, while of another local group, was descended from the same totem:

> If, then, we conceive that . . . the name of "wife" came to be synonymous with a subject and enslaved woman in the power of her captor or captors, and the name of marriage to be applied to a man's relation to such a woman as possessor of her, the origin of exogamy becomes apparent. Since a subject and enslaved wife would, in the circumstances of the time, be attainable only by capture, marriage would be possible only through capture, and the prohibition which, as we have seen, would apply to capture, would apply to marriage. Marriage with a woman of the same stock would be a crime and a sin. It would be incest [*ibid.*:65].

Wife-capture now led to a transition from polyandry to polygyny, since men who were successful in their raiding activity started to accumulate harems. At first the captured wives were shared with one's brothers. Later the only sharing tolerated was after death; hence the origin of the levirate. The local bands now began to fill up with marriageable female descendants of "foreign" women. This permitted exogamic marriages to be arranged within the group by purchase and mock capture. At the same time the end of polyandry meant that paternity could be reckoned. Thus, with the growth of property, patrilineal descent replaced matrilineal descent. This once again made all the women and men in the group members of the same descent line. Some groups now proceeded to a patrilineal phase of exogamy—of marriage by capture all over again—while others became endogamous. McLennan's scheme also briefly encompassed the origin of the state. Like Maine and Morgan, he held that the continued growth of the importance of private property brought about a reduction of kinship relations outside of the nuclear family. Hence, the rise of the state was accompanied by the decay of the tribe and other kinship groupings.

THE MORGAN-MC LENNAN CONTROVERSY

Despite their agreement, reached independently, on the stage of promiscuity and the priority of matrilineal over patrilineal descent, McLennan and Morgan became embroiled in a bitter controversy. McLennan sought to destroy Morgan's scheme by belittling the significance of kin terminological systems. He denied their sociological significance, much as Kroeber was to do years later, asserting that they were mere modes of addressing persons that had no bearing on family or descent. McLennan displayed remarkable "cool" for a man who had never seen an Indian. Morgan responded with a long note in *Ancient Society* dedicated to a critique of McLennan's entire scheme. He successfully exposed McLennan's confusion concerning the nature of the exogamous groupings which were supposed to have taken wives from each other. Exogamy and endogamy, Morgan pointed out, could very well exist side by side. The clan was exogamous, but the tribe as a whole could be endogamous. Although Morgan sought to obliterate the two terms, his critique helped to assure their survival.

One of the most interesting points made by Morgan was that McLennan had erroneously construed matrilineal descent, a mode of reckoning clan affiliation, as the entire realm of kinship. Morgan correctly insisted that his systems of consanguinity and affinity proved the existence of bilateral reckoning of kinship regardless of the nature of the descent rule employed.

The great heyday of evolutionary schemes was like that; many valuable suggestions mixed indiscriminately with an equally large number of worthless ones. The materials of criticism were easy to come by; everyone could see logical and empirical flaws in his rival's arguments. The ingenious reformulations poured out in endless torrents. It was an inefficient method; but the procedure was not hopeless. The most absurd sequences were gradually eliminated as the issues subject to continuous controversy came into sharper focus.

MATRIARCHY, POLYANDRY, TOTEMISM

Consider, for example, the advances made with respect to the concept of matriarchy. Bachofen's formulations of mother-right had assumed that matrilineal descent was merely a concomitant of the more fundamental fact of gynocracy. Thus, Bachofen and his follower J. Lippert (1884) accepted the myth of the Amazons as a literal truth. But many writers who accepted a strengthened role for women within the family under matrilineal descent rejected the idea of a political and military gynocracy. Tylor (1889), Charles Letourneau (1888), and Ernst Grosse (1896) all made this point. It was also, of course, implied in Morgan's treatment of the Iroquois clan. L. Dargun (1883), Carl Starcke (1889), and Edward Westermarck (1891) went further and insisted that male domination of the family as well as of political life was compatible with matrilineal descent. According to Dargun, the distinction between power and kinship was an indispensable key to the evolution of the family. Thus, G. E. Howard (1904:46), without assistance from the Boasians, could conclude:

> In short, if among many peoples at some stage of progress research has clearly demonstrated the existence of mother-right, it has just as clearly shown that the notion of gynocracy, of a period of female supremacy, is without historical foundation.

None of Bachofen's critics, with the exception perhaps of Morgan, understood that the locus of authority under matrilineal descent was vested in mother's brother rather than in father. This understanding was not definitively achieved until Malinowski's Trobriand studies. Yet, it cannot be said that the evolutionists had made no headway as a result of their armchair deliberations.

To take another example, McLennan's fanciful notions concerning polyandry had also receded almost to oblivion by the end of the century. Both Spencer (1896, I) and Morgan (1877) adduced empirical evidence indicating that polyandry was a rare form of marriage, associated with highly localized conditions. Later, these objections were elaborated by Starcke and Westermarck.

McLennan's most effective disciple was the Cambridge orientalist W. Robertson Smith, who employed McLennan's scheme to interpret the sociological history of kinship and marriage among the Arabs and Hebrews. With their strong patriarchal, monotheistic, and polygamist traditions, no cultures would have seemed, on the face of things, less propitious for a theory that emphasized matrilineality, polyandry, and totemism. Yet Smith (1903, orig. 1885) managed to find circumstantial evidence to show that all of these unlikely institutions had actually existed among the "Semites." Regardless of the value of Smith's reconstruction of the primordial phases of Semitic history, his description of the social structure of classical Islam benefited greatly from McLennan's sociological arguments and concepts. Smith's greatest achievements, however, lay in the realm of comparative religious institutions (see p. 207). Thus, even McLennan's explanation of exogamy as a remnant of wife-capture had its positive aspects. Indeed, Napoleon Chagnon's (1966) recent study of the relationship between exogamy, marriage, and warfare among the Indians of the Brazil-Venezuela border promises to lend new dignity to McLennan's more lurid speculations.

THE ORIGIN OF INCEST TABOOS

It should be remembered that McLennan's analysis of exogamy and endogamy initiated the discussion of the origin of the universal incest prohibitions within the nuclear family. This problem quite legitimately continues to occupy the attention of modern anthropology, and no amount of doctrinal particularism will suffice to quiet our urge to understand why these taboos are so powerful and ubiquitous.

Despite the support of McLennan's theory of wife-capture by Robertson Smith, Lubbock, and Spencer, rival explanations of exogamic taboos had won the field by the end of the century. Morgan's approach was more influential. It was premised on the alleged biologically deleterious results of close inbreeding. According to Morgan, the brother-sister taboo arose from a realization that inbreeding was biologically unsound. The exogamy of the clan arose shortly afterward and represented a continuation of the same "reformatory movement." Clan exogamy and the brother-sister taboo then spread as a result of migration and natural selection. The trouble with this view is that clan exogamy is correlated with preferential cross-cousin marriage, a rule that promotes rather than hinders in-breeding within a small group. Another difficulty with Morgan's explanation is how to account for the taboos separating father from daughter and mother from son. Nonetheless, Morgan's focus upon the biological consequences of inbreeding remains a respectable minority position. It is not inconceivable that the nuclear family taboos arose from a combination of biological and cultural advantages consequent upon the introduction of incest prohibitions within the nuclear family, while descent group exogamy arose from separate and primarily cultural advantages (which in turn had biological consequences).

It was Tylor who pointed the way toward an understanding of these additional cultural advantages. For Tylor (1889:267–68) exogamy is the primitive mode of "alliance" and of "political self-preservation." "Among tribes of low culture there is but one means known of keeping up permanent alliance, and that means is inter-marriage." In this form, Tylor's theory underlies, or is convergent with, the vast field of kinship studies which stress marriage alliances between groups as the key to primitive social structure. Thus, great weight has been placed upon the alliance function of marriage by Lévi-Strauss and his followers (see pp. 499ff.). Unlike the latter, however, Tylor stressed the survival value of the exchange of women. The alternative has been between "marrying-out" or "being killed out":

> Exogamy . . . enabling a growing tribe to keep itself compact by constant union between its spreading clans, enables it to overmatch any number of small, intermarrying groups, isolated and helpless. Again and again in the world's history, savage tribes must have had plainly before their minds the simple practical alternative between marrying-out and being killed out [*ibid.*:267].

Leslie White (1949a:316ff.) has made Tylor's ideas the basis of his own theory of incest prohibition by applying Tylor's formula to the family as a basic unit, independent of, and prior to, the clan. "A way [exogamy] was found to unite families with one another, and social evolution as a human affair was launched upon its career" (*ibid.*).

Another important line of inquiry bearing on the explanation of exogamy and the incest taboos started with the nuclear family as a primordial given and went on to stress the disruptive effect of endogamy. This line was explored first by Carl N. Starcke (1901; orig. 1889), who contended that marriage between son and mother or brother and sister would endanger the father's authority. This suggestion figures in the modern incest theories of Malinowski and Murdock. New and important psychological dimensions to the problem were contributed by Edward Westermarck (1891), foremost opponent of the Morgan-McLennan-Tylor-Lubbock theory of original promiscuity. Westermarck followed Darwin, Charles S. Wake, and Starcke in arguing that some form of pairing must have been primordial in the human species since it occurs among the primates and even among lower organisms. According to Westermarck, there is a universal dread of incest based upon an instinctual human disgust for sexual relations with individuals who have been reared together at close quarters. This instinctual repulsion in turn was established within the species as a result of natural selection conferring adaptive advantages on outbreeding families.

> Through natural selection an instinct must have been developed, powerful enough, as a rule, to prevent injurious unions. This instinct displays itself simply as an aversion on the part of individuals to union with others with whom they have lived, but as these are for the most part blood-relations the result is the survival of the fittest [WESTERMARCK 1894:546].

Westermarck's espousal of natural selection greatly narrows the gap between him and Morgan. Although Morgan does not refer to an instinctual dread of incest, the advantages of the punaluan family are "carried in the blood" like all of man's other great innovations. For both Westermarck and Morgan, the incest regulations in the clan and community are outward extensions of the brother-sister prohibition. Westermarck's suggestion that there is a biopsychological component in the nuclear-family taboos cannot be dismissed. Some form of imprinting may be involved or, as Arthur Wolf (1966) has suggested, there may be something in the socialization process itself which supports Westermarck's view of the inability of persons reared together to enjoy sexual communion.

THE EVOLUTION OF RELIGION

Morgan's grand scheme of institutional evolution, so profoundly optimistic with respect to the potency of the comparative method, systematically avoided the reconstruction of the sequences connected with the evolution of religion. Morgan's reasons for not treating magico-religious phenomena are highly instructive with regard to the nature of his overall concept of sociocultural causality, to which we turn in a moment. Religion, said Morgan, is just too irrational to be understood by scientific means:

> The growth of religious ideas is environed with such intrinsic difficulties that it may never receive a perfectly satisfactory exposition. Religion deals so largely with the imaginative and emotional nature, and consequently with such uncertain elements of knowledge, that all primitive religions are grotesque and to some extent unintelligible. This subject also falls without the plan of this work excepting as it may prompt incidental suggestions [MORGAN 1877:5].

The attempt to describe evolutionary sequences for religion, far from being avoided, was actually given priority by most of the other evolutionists. There was ample precedent for this attempt in the Enlightenment doctrine that man's systems of belief were steadily moving toward higher forms of rationality which implied agnosticism if not atheism as an end state. Comte's theological, metaphysical, and scientific stages of thought continued this tradition into the nineteenth century. The theory that religious belief and institutions had undergone a natural evolution might be thought subversive with respect to revealed religion. Yet many of the late-nineteenth-century theorists not only clung to their childhood faiths but derived from them the added satisfaction that came from being convinced that their beliefs were demonstrably the highest form of religion. It was only among the Marxists that the evolution of religion was once again taken unambiguously to the end point postulated by D'Holbach, Helvetius, and Diderot.

Bachofen's scheme, it will be recalled, included not only the evolution of social organization, but also a parallel and functionally related evolution of religious ideas. Indeed for Bachofen it was a series of religious reforms that set the direction of history. Turning to McLennan, we may note that his treatment of religion was quite thin, despite the fact that his use of the concept of totemism led to an extraordinary outpouring of anthropological treatises. McLennan, it will be recalled, regarded the invention of totemism as an essential part of the explanation of the origin of exogamy. This is the aspect of McLennan's scheme that best exhibits the muddled views of sociocultural causality with which he and the other evolutionists were content to operate.

After Bachofen, a sustained treatment of the evolution of religion was first undertaken by a most unlikely member of the evolutionary school, John Lubbock. Two thirds of *The Origin of Civilization* (1870) is dedicated to a sketch of the stages of religious belief. Reaffirming his earlier view that the most primitive savages lack anything which could be called religion, Lubbock displays an infuriating certainty concerning the doctrinal superiority of his own brand of superstition. It is important to realize that men like Lubbock were under constant pressure to disclaim any proclivity toward atheism. We understand therefore why Lubbock insists that the savages lacked religion. Atheism and materialism are inferior conditions of belief; man only gradually acquires higher spiritual concepts. If there is "one fact more certain than another," he proclaims, it is "the gradual diffusion of religious light, and of nobler conceptions as to the nature of God" (1870:349). Lubbock even went so far as to call the first stage of religion "Atheism"! His scheme follows verbatim:

> *Atheism;* understanding by this term not a denial of the existence of a Deity, but an absence of any definite ideas on the subject.

> *Fetichism*; the stage in which man supposes he can force the Deity to comply with his desires.
>
> *Nature-worship*, or *Totemism;* in which natural objects, trees, lakes, stones, animals, &c. are worshipped.
>
> *Shamanism*; in which the superior deities are far more powerful than man, and of a different nature. Their place of abode also is far away, and accessible only to Shamans.
>
> *Idolatry*, or Anthropomorphism; in which the gods take still more completely the nature of men, being, however, more powerful. They are still amenable to persuasion; they are a part of nature, and not creators. They are represented by images or idols.
>
> In the next stage the Deity is regarded as the author, not merely a part, of nature. He becomes for the first time a really supernatural being.
>
> The last stage to which I will refer is that in which morality is associated with religion [*ibid.*:119].

Lubbock had equally definite ideas about the evolution of social structure. He believed for example that the primitive stage of promiscuity was followed by a period in which descent is first uniformly within the tribe, then through the mother, then through the father, and "lastly and lastly only," through both (*ibid.*: 113). But the coordination of the religion sequence with the evolution of the family and state is scarcely attempted. The casual nexus with which Lubbock operates is a tangle of evolving ideas, pushing themselves on to perfection: "the human mind, in its onward progress, everywhere passes through the same or very similar phases" (*ibid.*:192). Underlying the whole process is the perfection of man's physical nature. Advanced ideas are "entirely beyond the mental range of the lower savages, whose extreme mental inferiority we have much difficulty in realizing" (*ibid.*:5). The only functional connection between religion and social structure noted by Lubbock is that between the "increasing power of chiefs and priests" and the stage of Idolatry "with its sacrifices, temples, and priests etc." This analysis, however, he attributes to Solomon (Wisd. of Sol. 14:17).

TYLOR AND THE EVOLUTION OF RELIGION

Against Lubbock's dreary performance, Tylor's *Primitive Culture* (1871) stands out as a respectable contribution to anthropological theory. This work at once demonstrates that the comparative method, applied to dubious but abundant ethnographic material under the guidance of a sufficiently critical intelligence, was capable of producing enduring results. The central theme in *Primitive Culture* is the evolution of the concept of Animism, Tylor's minimum definition of religion. Animism exists wherever there is a belief in souls, ghosts, demons, devils, gods, or similar categories of phenomena. The root of all these concepts is traced by Tylor to the belief in the human soul. This belief, which is found in almost every culture, results from the universal subjective experience of dreams and visions. In dreams and visions one sees phantom people, doubles, who detach themselves from their bodies and move about independently of material conditions: one sees "a thin unsubstantial human image, in its nature a sort of vapour, film or shadow" (1958 II:12; orig. 1871). The immense utility of this concept lies in its power to account for another series of universal experiences of the greatest significance to man: the difference between life and death, health and sickness, wakefulness and sleep, trance and ordinary consciousness. It is the evolution of this belief in the human personal soul through vast extrapolations and embroideries which forms the subject matter of Tylor's great work:

> . . . the conception of human soul once attained to by man, served as a type or model on which he framed not only his ideas of other souls of lower grade, but also his ideas of spiritual beings in general, from the tiniest elf that sports in the long grass up to the heavenly Creator and Ruler of the world, the Great Spirit [*ibid.*:196].

Tylor refrained from attempting to set forth a rigid sequence; many different kinds of animistic beings come into existence at approximately the same stage, and they endure over long periods as survivals among peasant and illiterate members of modern societies. In general, however, there is a gradual movement toward monotheism and the removal of the pantheon of high gods from direct human appeal. "Lower animism" tends to be amoral; the soul is continued after death in a condition which does not depend on its deeds during life. "Higher animism" takes on the "retribution doctrine"—there are rewards and punishments for the soul, depending on its lifetime performance.

THE LIMITATIONS OF TYLOR'S APPROACH

Despite its vast erudition, its high standards of evidence, and its lordly pace, *Primitive Culture* is a curiously one-sided book. If *Ancient Society* suffers from a neglect of ideology, *Primitive Culture* suffers even more from its neglect of social organization and economics.

Once we have grown accustomed to the proposition that the doctrines of contemporary Christianity had their origins in the lower animism of savagery, there is little else of theoretical significance to be gained from the piling of additional case upon case. Even as a treatment of religion, *Primitive Culture* had its glaring limitations, since it is devoted almost exclusively to the cognitive as distinct from the institutional components of religion. As for the causal explanation of the evolution of animistic beliefs, the basic point of *Primitive Culture* seems to be that the human mind has the ability to perfect itself by thinking more clearly. The explanation by which Tylor connects ideology with social structure corresponds exactly to Lubbock's (and Solomon's): Men model their spirit pantheons after their own governments:

> Among nation after nation it is still clear how, man being the type of deity, human society and government became the model on which divine society and government were shaped. As chiefs and kings are among men, so are the great gods among the lesser spirits. They differ from the souls and minor spiritual beings which we have as yet chiefly considered, but the difference is rather of rank than of nature. They are personal spirits, reigning over personal spirits. Above the disembodied souls and manes, the local genii of rocks and fountains and trees, the host of good and evil demons, and the rest of the spiritual commonality, stand these mightier deities, whose influence is less confined to local or individual interests, and who, as it pleases them, can act directly within their vast domain, or control and operate through the lower beings of their kind, their servants, agents, or mediators [*ibid.*:334].

The issue of why such correspondences should exist between political structure and "projective systems" seems almost entirely to have escaped Tylor's comprehension. We find only the barest hint of the possibility that religion might have functions more complex and subtle than that of providing explanations for puzzling and distressing phenomena. "In the course of history," Tylor remarks in passing, "religion has in various ways attached to itself matters small and great outside its central scheme, such as prohibition of special meats, observance of special days, regulation of marriage or kinship, division of society into castes, ordinance of social law and civil government" (*ibid.*: 447). From this juxtaposition of such very small and very great matters, we derive some measure of Tylor's preoccupation with narrow, rather disembodied cognitive issues.

An emphasis on the relative parochialism of *Primitive Culture* seems justified in relation to Tylor's famous claim in his conclusion that "the science of culture is essentially a reformer's science" (*ibid.*:539) which will contribute to the "advancement of civilization." It is in this context painfully obvious that Tylor's "science of culture" could not be a "reformer's science" as long as it propagated the view that social change emanates from the "exposure of crude old culture" to the light of intellect. It is true of course that Tylor's interests did extend to social organization and that his contribution to the study of kinship in "On a Method of Investigating the Development of Institutions" surpasses Morgan's best sociological effort. Yet Tylor was unable to bring the religion sequence and the analysis of social organization into mutual conformity. In other words, he failed to achieve an understanding of sociocultural phenomena as a functional-causal *system*. Hence his sought-after "laws of evolution" merely described the unfolding of separate developmental sequences, each of which independently derived its main motive power from the force of reason.

Tylor's emphasis on the ideological content of religion stimulated a distinguished but monotonously idealist series of cultural studies. Under James Frazer, the preoccupation with the evolution of religious ideas lapsed into a frankly literary endeavor. Under Andrew Lang, it denied its natural science heritage and returned to mysticism.

FRAZER AND THE EVOLUTION OF RELIGION

Sir James Frazer's writings have been assigned by Edmund Leach (1966:562) to six categories: (1) translations and editions of the classics; (2) writings about primitive concepts of the soul; (3) writings about totemism; (4) writings about folklore in the Old Testament; (5) passages of the Bible; and (6) *The Golden Bough*. As Leach points out, Frazer was thus wholly occupied with "mental anthropology," while the "more sociological emphasis" lay quite outside his range of interest (*ibid.*:564). According to Leach (*ibid.*: 561), Frazer explicitly thought of himself "as making a contribution to literature rather than to science. . . ."

Frazer's application of the comparative method in *The Golden Bough*, which by 1914 required an edition consisting of twelve volumes, is the most grandiose ever undertaken by a single author. The theoretical product of Frazer's monumental effort, however, is quite feeble and certainly out of all proportion to the size of the undertaking. Chiefly, it consists in a further confirmation of the Tylorian view of modern religion as a natural growth from primitive antecedents. One theme is concerned with the relationships between the sacrifices of divine kings; the preservation of fertility; and by implication, the story of the Crucifixion. Another deals with the prevalence of survivals. Perhaps the most influential contribution is the distinction between religion and magic, a subject that Tylor had neglected. Thus Frazer sees magic as an early expression of science based on a false notion of the regularity of cause and effect processes. Religion is a higher achievement, substituting uncertainty and prayerful conciliation for misguided notions of causality. Science arises next, returning mankind to the principles of cause and effect, but on a basis of true correlations. Frazer's scheme, however, remains wholly alien to a science of society. The whole process of the alleged transition from magic through religion to science depends on nothing but an inherent tendency of thought to perfect itself: "In the last analysis magic, religion, and science are nothing but theories of thought" (*ibid.*:826) . . . thoughts of thought, . . . ideas about ideas.

With the publication of the 1922 abridgment of *The Golden Bough* and the flood of public honors that accompanied it, Frazer emerged as *the* anthropologist, whose books every educated man was supposed to have read. I shall not join Edmund Leach in begrudging Frazer his great success as an emissary to the educated masses. As literature, *The Golden Bough* does have its charms. The problem seems rather to have been that too many anthropologists, including Leach himself (see p. 544), never quite managed to throw off the habit of regarding culture as nothing more than a pack of ideas swarming around inside of people's heads.

MORE MENTALISM

The mentalistic emphasis in Tylor's treatment of religion was also furthered by Robert R. Marett, Tylor's successor at Oxford. Marett (1909) attempted to correct for the overintellectualized approach of Tylor and Frazer by insisting (without benefit of fieldwork) that primitives distinguished emotionally between supernatural and ordinary phenomena. Thus magic and religion should not be separated, since their cognitive essence lies in a sense of mystery. "Supernaturalism," Marett insisted, should embrace both magic and religion. Marett also criticized Tylor's concept of religion as failing to make provision for the personification of inanimate objects that did not involve a soul concept. To denote this kind of religious belief, Marett introduced the term "animatism." Like Frazer, Marett stands on the boundary between the scientist and man of letters. Indeed, Lowie (1937:111) calls him "a philosophical humanist."

RETURN TO MYSTICISM: ANDREW LANG

The culmination of the line of Tylor's philosophical humanist students lies with Andrew Lang. Unfortunately Lang and Lang's relationship to Tylor have been misinterpreted to the present generation of anthropologists through an error in Lowie's account (*cf.* WALLACE 1966:7; PENNIMAN 1965:140). According to Lowie (1937:82) "Tylor's *Primitive Culture* . . . denied high gods to the simpler peoples," and "on the subject Tylor was challenged by Andrew Lang." Tylor, however, never denied high gods to simpler peoples, and Lang never held that Tylor had made such a denial. Tylor's view is quite clear:

> Thus, then, it appears that the theology of the lower races already reaches its climax in conceptions of a highest of the gods, and that these conceptions in the savage and barbaric world are no copies stamped from one common type, but outlines widely varying among mankind. The degeneration-theory, in some instances no doubt with justice, may claim such beliefs as mutilated and perverted remnants of higher religions. Yet for the most part, the development-theory is competent to account for them without seeking their origin in grades of culture higher than those in which they are found existing. Looked upon as products of natural religion, such doctrines of divine supremacy seem in no way to transcend the powers of the low-cultured mind to reason out, nor the low-cultured imagination to deck with mythic fancy. There have existed in times past, and do still exist, savage or barbaric peoples who hold such views of a highest god as they may have attained to of themselves, without the aid of more cultured nations. Among these races, Animism has its distinct and consistent outcome, and Polytheism its distinct and consistent completion, in the doctrine of a Supreme Deity [TYLOR 1958, II:422].

It is true that Tylor was vigorously attacked by Lang, but Lang's stated motivation is not mentioned by Lowie. What Lang came to resent, after an initial period of enthusiasm for the genre of naturalistic evolutionary studies of religious thought, was first, the premise that animism has been based on an essentially false set of ideas. In his *The Making of Religion* (1898), Lang criticized Tylor for supposing that primitive man did not actually possess many of the powers which he attributed to souls and that all such manifestations of souls among contemporary Englishmen were necessarily "survivals."

> We hold that very probably there exist human faculties of unknown scope; that these conceivably were more powerful and prevalent among our very remote ancestors who founded religion; that they may still exist in savage as in civilized races, and that they may have conformed, if they did not originate, the doctrine of separable souls. If they *do* exist, the circumstance is important, in view of the fact that modern ideas rest on a denial of their existence [*ibid.*:66–67].

Second, Lang insisted that Tylor's animism could not explain the high gods in whom the simpler peoples believed. Tylor had underestimated the extent to which these high gods exercised a moral influence over primitive peoples. "The moral, heart-reading, friendly, creative being of low savage faith, whence was he evolved?" inquires Lang. His answer: "It is as easy, almost, for me to believe that they 'were not left without a witness,' as to believe that this God of theirs was evolved out of the maleficent ghost of a dirty mischievous medicineman" (*ibid.*:185). In other words, Lang toyed with a return to the degeneration theory and to the doctrine that monotheism was the gift of God to man.

STRUCTURAL APPROACHES TO RELIGION

The analysis of religion as part of a larger social system was initiated by evolutionists outside of Tylor's orbit. Two figures require our attention, W. Robertson Smith and Herbert Spencer.

Smith was a disciple of McLennan's, who found McLennan's developmental sequences applicable to the history of the Semitic peoples. His *Religion of the Semites* (1889) stands out among all of the contemporary evolutionist treatments of religion because of its focus on what is essentially a single cultural tradition and by its extraordinarily detailed treatment of certain relationships between social organization, ritual, and belief. Smith cannot be said to have systematically explored the entire range of structural relationships between social organization and religion, nor did he manage always to rise above the kind of projective or imitative view that was current among the Tylorians. Yet the relatively restricted ethnographic compass within which he confined himself guaranteed a result that was closer to modern structural-functionalist standards than anything produced up to that time. His treatment of the social functions of feasting, ritual communion, and sacrifice with its emphasis upon the maintenance of a sense of social solidarity constitutes an important if imperfectly acknowledged influence on British social anthropology. Smith's (1956:21) cardinal hypothesis was that religious and political institutions are "parts of one whole of social custom." Myth and doctrine—the essence of religion for Frazer—were thus something of an epiphenomenon. Not that Smith relished ideological details less keenly than Frazer, but he regarded the institutional matrix as the source of religious ideas.

> When we study the political structures of early society, we do not begin by asking what is recorded of the first legislators, or what theory man advanced as to the reason of their institutions; we try to understand what the institutions were, and how they shaped men's lives. In like manner, in the study of Semitic religion, we must not begin by asking what was told about the gods, but what the working religious institutions were, and how they shaped the lives of the worshippers [*ibid.*].

SPENCER'S SCHEME

It is quite likely that Smith here reflected the influence of Spencer. For of all the evolutionists, it was Spencer who approached most closely to the understanding of sociocultural phenomena in terms of evolving systems, each of whose parts contributed to each other and to the continuity and change of the whole. Unfortunately, the value and historical effectiveness of Spencer's synthesizing genius was not matched by his ability to handle ethnographic data. He seems to have lacked the critical flair which came so easily to Tylor. The result is an embarrassing mixture of a highly sophisticated methodology based on abundant but inappropriate or fanciful examples that give rise to improbable or overly mechanical evolutionary sequences. In his *Principles of Sociology* Spencer undertook to sketch developmental sequences for all the major branches of culture. His guiding principle was the "law of evolution"; namely, that in all spheres of the universe, there is

> an integration of matter and concomitant dissipation of motion; during which the matter passes from an indefinite incoherent homogeneity to a definite coherent heterogeneity; and during which the retained motion undergoes a parallel transformation [1912:367; orig. 1864].

Thus, in the evolution of the family, the "incoherent homogeneity" of promiscuity yields the progressively greater "definiteness" of matrilineal and then patrilineal descent; marriage moves to higher levels of order through polyandry, polygamy, and monogamy; the social system as a whole moves from the military type to the industrial type involving increasing degrees of individuation and the multiplication of specialized parts.

It is to the domain of religion, however, that I must now limit my remarks. Here we find Spencer dealing first of all with a sequence of beliefs which are markedly parallel to Tylor's. Indeed, both Tylor and Spencer virtually accused each other of plagiarism in deciding who had been the first to trace the concept of a monotheistic god back to the ghosts and dreams of primitive men (*cf.* HAYS 1958:80). Spencer's sequence is typically more rigid and mechanical than Tylor's. In compensation, however, Spencer addresses himself to more stimulating and historically important questions. He proceeds to his analysis only after observing that "there can be no true conception of a structure without a true conception of its function" (SPENCER 1896, II:671). The functions of various stages of religions are then viewed in relationship to political control, social cohesion, military activities, and ecclesiastical bureaucracies. His conclusions have a distinctly modern ring to them in their emphasis upon "cohesion" and "social continuity":

> Thus, looking at it generally, we may say that ecclesiasticism stands for the principle of social continuity. Above all other agencies it is that which conduced to cohesion; not only between the coexisting parts of a nation, but also between its present generation and its past generations. In both ways it helps to maintain the individuality of the society. Or, changing somewhat the point of view, we may say that ecclesiasticism, embodying in its primitive form the rule of the dead over the living and sanctifying in its more advanced forms the authority of the past over the present, has for its function to preserve in force the organized product of earlier experiences *versus* the modifying effects of more recent experiences. Evidently this organized product of past experiences is not without credentials. The life of the society has, up to the time being, been maintained under it; and hence a perennial reason for resistance to deviation [*ibid.*:773].

Again:

> As furnishing a principle of cohesion by maintaining a common propitiation of a deceased ruler's spirit, and by implication checking the tendencies to internal warfare, priesthoods have furthered social growth and development. They have simultaneously done this in sundry other ways: by fostering that spirit of conservatism which maintains continuity in social arrangements;

> by forming a supplementary regulative system which cooperates with the political one; by insisting on obedience, primarily to gods and secondarily to kings, by countenancing the coercion under which has been cultivated the power of application; and by strengthening the habit of self-restraint [*ibid.*:817].

EVOLUTIONISM, A SCIENTIFIC ADVANCE

Enough has now been said to demonstrate the powerful forward motion generated during the period 1860–90 as far as the main task of the comparative method was concerned. It cannot be denied that a better knowledge of the most general directions of sociocultural evolution was achieved. Nor can it be denied that in the very process of reproducing the possible lines of development, false hypotheses came to enjoy an orthodoxy which diminished the luster of the equally numerous correct and productive ones. In balance, however, this period must be reckoned as one of the great epochs in the enlargement of Western man's comprehension of his place in nature. Under the impact of relativism, we are much too prone to emphasize the snobbery of the Victorian anthropologists and their irritating conviction that all men would ultimately aspire to live and look like middle-class Englishmen. We must not forget that there is an aspect to the evolutionism of the period which stands opposed to the ethnocentric naïveté of men like Lubbock and McLennan. In *their* culture, evolutionism was a daring admission that the sacred institutions of family, church, property, and state had an ancestry, as Lang put it, of maleficent ghosts and dirty mischievous medicinemen. Admittedly it was a source of comfort to know that nature had equipped modern Euro-America with the best institutions which "the survival of the fittest" could provide. But this rationalization of contemporary mores, institutions, and beliefs involved turning away from the much more convincing and satisfying rationales of divine revelation and divine commandments. The enduring significance of the late-nineteenth-century use of the comparative method was that it completed the demonstration, begun in the previous century, that Western man's institutions from Christianity to motherhood had a natural and not a divine origin. This achievement may not impress a generation whose theologians, driven to despair by the crimes of man, hint that "God is dead." But educated opinion in the Victorian era found it hard to believe that conjugal fidelity, filial respect, and love of God were nothing more than human artifices, slowly evolved by trial and error, and destined to be replaced by as yet unknown but equally mundane arrangements. What the evolutionists faced were learned men, like the Archbishop of Dublin, Richard Whately:

> We have no reason to believe that any community ever did, or ever can emerge, unassisted by external helps, from a state of utter barbarism unto anything that can be called civilisation. Man has not emerged from the savage state; the progress of any community in civilisation by its own internal means, must always have begun from a condition removed from that of complete barbarism, out of which it does not appear that men ever did or can raise themselves [WHATELY quoted in LUBBOCK 1870:326].

In this context, when Lubbock insists that primeval man was an atheist (thereby protecting himself from being called the same), we must not conclude that his main interest lay in maligning the Tasmanians and Fuegians in order to praise Englishmen. It rather seems to have been his intent to emphasize the "utter barbarism" of the earliest men in order to confound Whately and other "degenerationists" who refused to surrender the comforting illusion that it was God who had made Englishmen monogamists and monotheists.

If I seem to lay insufficient stress on the absurdly false sequences for which Morgan, Spencer, Lubbock, McLennan, and even Robertson Smith were responsible, it is not because the distortions of history in the name of science are ever to be taken lightly. Rather, it seems that in condemning the method responsible for these aberrations, many contemporary anthropologists have lost their own sense of historical perspective.

THE ABSENCE OF CULTURAL MATERIALISM

While the historical errors and sequential flim-flammery of the evolutionists have been the subject of abundant critical appraisal, there is another aspect of their work which has gone virtually without serious discussion. The aspect in question is the nature of the causal process which the evolutionists substituted for the "hand of God"—the processes which had brought about that degree of parallelism and convergence without which the comparative method could not have been utilized. It should be apparent that without exception, none of the evolutionists were cultural materialists. By thus saying at once what they were *not*, we shall spare ourselves the confusion which results if we attempt to say precisely what they were in positive terms. Thus Opler (1964a:123) attempts to refute White's (1949b:364) assertion that Tylor expressed "the materialist interpretation of culture." Stocking (1965c:136), on the other hand, attempts to prove that Opler's label "philosophical idealist" is equally inappropriate. The truth is that Tylor was a philosophical and cultural eclectic. He had no consistent theory of cultural causation. On the one hand, like all of his contemporaries, he believed that the direction of history was governed by a process of natural selection in which the survival of the fittest men and institutions was assured: "institutions which can best hold their own in the world gradually supersede the less fit ones, their incessant conflict determines the general resultant course of culture" (TYLOR 1958, I:69). On the other hand, again, like all of his contemporaries, Tylor also fervently embraced the cultural-idealist heritage of the Enlightenment. While Tylor emphasized the importance of material culture in the evolutionary process, the ultimate pre-eminence of mind in shaping the direction of material progress remains unquestioned. Our previous discussion of the independent nature of Tylor's religion sequence should have made this sufficiently clear. Opler's remarks on the subject may nonetheless be cited to remove any lingering doubt:

> Of man's "brain-organization" and his ability to use symbols he [Tylor] says: "Man's power of using a word, or even a gesture, as the symbol of a thought and the means of conversing about it, is one of the points where we most plainly see him parting company with all lower species, *and starting on his career of conquest through higher intellectual regions*". . . . In another place he [Tylor] declares: "Man's power of accommodating himself to the world he lives in, and even of controlling it, *is largely due to his faculty of gaining new knowledge*". . . . "History," he [Tylor] tells us, "is an agent powerful and becoming more powerful, in shaping men's minds, and *through their minds their actions in the world* . . . ." The key to man's achievements, as Tylor saw it, lay in his "power of coordinating the impression of his senses, which enables him to understand the world he lives in, and *by understanding* to use, resist, and even in a measure rule it" . . . [OPLER 1964a:138–39].

It is interesting to note that while Opler himself argues at length (in order to refute White) that Tylor was a Social Darwinist, he nonetheless flatly concludes, "The central place of the evolution of the mind in Tylor's theory stamps him as a philosophical idealist and invalidates any attempt to select passages to prove him a materialist" (*ibid.*:143). But to be a Social Darwinist, as we have seen, is to be a racial determinist, a biological reductionist. Indeed, Opler even quotes at length from Tylor's racist statements. But how could a philosophical idealist propose that mind is determined by the material conditions of the struggle for existence? After all, what was the fuss about, if Darwin's theory was not viewed as the very essence (so to speak) of the incarnation of materialism? Thus if Tylor is to be called a "philosophical idealist," it can only be with the proviso that he was more confused than philosophical.

MORGAN NOT A CULTURAL MATERIALIST

Exactly the same observation is required in the case of Morgan. The precedent for regarding Morgan as a materialist was, of course, set by Marx and Engels; and in the next chapter, we shall inquire into the reasons for this unfortunate error. In the meantime attention should be drawn to the extraordinary exchange between Opler, Harding, and Leacock (in OPLER 1964b), in which one side demonstrates conclusively that Morgan was a materialist, while the other demonstrates equally well that Morgan was not a materialist. On the materialist side, Harding quotes the following chapter and verse from Morgan's *Ancient Society* (1877:9):

> It is probable that the successive arts of subsistence which arose at long intervals will ultimately, from the *great influence* they must have exercised upon the condition of mankind, afford the most satisfactory bases for these divisions [the "ethical periods" and subdivisions of Savagery, Barbarism, and Civilization].

On the same side, Leacock's favorite passages are as follows:

> The most advanced portion of the human race were halted, so to express it, at certain stages of progress, until some great invention or discovery, such as the domestication of animals or the smelting of iron ore, gave a new and powerful impulse forward . . . [MORGAN 1963:39].

Or

> . . . improvement in subsistence, which followed the cultivation of maize and plants among the American aborigines, must have favored the general advancement of the family. It led to localization, to the use of additional arts, to an improved house architecture, and to a more intelligent life. . . . The great advancement of society indicated by the transition from savagery

> into the Lower Status of barbarism, would carry with it a corresponding improvement in the condition of the family . . . [*ibid.*:469].
>
> Cities . . . imply the existence of a stable and developed field agriculture, the possession of domestic animals in flocks and herds, of merchandise in masses and of property in houses and lands. The city brought with it new demands in the art of government by creating a changed condition of society [*ibid.*:264].

Convincing as this might seem, Opler has citations to prove that *Ancient Society* was actually a study of cultural evolution from the point of view of the mental and moral development of certain fundamental "germ" ideas. Opler's favorite chapter and verse appears to be the following:

> Out of a few germs of thought, conceived in the early ages, have been evolved all the principal institutions of mankind. Beginning their growth in the period of savagery, fermenting through the period of barbarism, they have continued their advancement through the period of civilization. The evolution of these germs of thought has been guided by a natural logic which formed an essential attribute of the brain itself. So unerringly has this principle performed its functions in all conditions of experience and in all periods of time, that its results are uniform, coherent and traceable in their courses. These results alone will in time yield convincing proofs of the unity of origin of mankind. The mental history of the human race, which is revealed in institutions, inventions and discoveries, is presumptively the history of a single species, perpetuated through individuals, and developed through experience. Among the original germs of thought, which have exercised the most powerful influence upon the human mind, and upon human destiny, are these which relate to government, to the family, to language, to religion, and to property. They had a definite beginning far back in savagery, and a logical progress, but can have no final consummation, because they are still progressing, and must ever continue to progress [MORGAN 1877:59–60].

Opler again weakens his own case by drawing attention to Morgan's "Cultural Darwinism" (*ibid.*:112). But the "materialists" on the other side fail to exploit this lapse since *that kind of materialism* with its racist taint, is as embarrassing to their image of Morgan as is the notion of philosophical idealism. For Opler, however, the implication of biological reductionism is not quite as devastating as in the case of Tylor, since his point is to prove not that Morgan was a "philosophical idealist" but that he was a "dualist": materialist for material culture and idealist for everything else. Thus the point here under consideration—the confused eclecticism of the evolutionist—is actually conceded by Opler.

SPENCER NOT A CULTURAL MATERIALIST

The best case for philosophical materialism (not cultural materialism) is furnished by Herbert Spencer. As the staunchest and most consistent of the biological reductionists, Spencer's materialism seems unquestionable. Moreover as Carneiro (1967:xxxv) has pointed out, for Spencer the universe was composed exclusively of matter and energy, and the entire course of evolution was at bottom a physical process. Furthermore, in cultural matters, Spencer frequently stressed the importance of subsistence, energy systems, warfare, and impersonal social forces. According to Carneiro (*ibid.*:xxvi): "He denied that recognition of 'advantages or disadvantages of this or that arrangement furnished motives for establishing or maintaining' a form of government, and argued instead that 'conditions and not intentions determine.' Correspondingly, he saw the values and attitudes of a society, not as shaping, but as reflecting the society: '. . . for every society, and for each stage in its evolution, there is an appropriate mode of feeling and thinking . . . [which] is a function of the social structure. . . .'" Fortunately we need not concern ourselves with the philosophical significance of the fact that, despite all this, Spencer himself frequently denied that he was a materialist. The question is, whether he was a *cultural* materialist, that is, whether he systematically elaborated a theory which accounted for cultural differences and similarities in terms of techno-economic and techno-environmental conditions. Although Spencer came closer than Morgan to such a viewpoint, he failed ultimately to achieve it because at each approach, the principle of biological reductionism interceded, providing a direct feedback between social structure and ideology and the stage reached in the progress of man's biological and psychological nature. Thus, while Spencer held that each successive stage in the sequence of the family or in the ideology of ghosts is a result of a materialist process of selection, the selective factors do not necessarily or preponderantly act through the techno-economic, techno-environmental parameters. To take one example, we may note how in explaining the functional relationship between ecclesiastical and political hierarchies, Spencer so readily lapses into the familiar cultural-idealist frame, lured by the seductive gossamers of the state of "human nature":

> Examination discloses a relation between ecclesiastical and political governments in respect of degree. Where there is but little of the one there is but little of the other; and in societies which have developed a highly coercive secular rule there habitually exists a highly coercive religious rule.
>
> It has been shown that growing from a common root, and having their structures slightly differentiated in early societies, the political and ecclesiastical organizations long continue to be distinguished very imperfectly.
>
> This intimate relationship between the two forms of regulation, alike in their instrumentalities and in their extents, has a moral origin. Extreme submissiveness of nature fosters an extreme development of both the political and religious controls. Contrariwise the growth of the agencies effecting such controls, is kept in check by the sentiment of independence; which while it resists the despotism of living rulers is unfavourable to extreme self-abasement in propitiation of deities [SPENCER 1896, II:671].

The confusion among evolutionists on the question of philosophical idealism versus philosophical materialism has been discussed at length by the historian George Stocking. From the fact that this muddle existed and from the manifest emphasis which the evolutionists place upon the task of reconstructing the stages of history, Stocking reaches the conclusion that the philosophical categories, idealism and materialism, do not provide the proper frame for a discussion of nineteenth-century anthropology. Anthropologists who seek to understand the history of their discipline are warned by Stocking that "the present day polemical point obfuscates historical understanding" (1965c:142). To this we must at once reply, on the contrary, present-day polemical point alone makes historical understanding possible. The fact that none of the classical evolutionists proposed a cultural-materialist explanation of sociocultural evolution was indeed of no significance to Morgan, Tylor, or Spencer. In retrospect, however, there is no fact of greater significance for the present-day anthropologist who seeks a knowledge of the foundations of contemporary theory.

Dialectical Materialism

8

"As Darwin discovered the law of evolution in organic nature so Marx discovered the law of evolution in human history. . . ." Thus spoke Friedrich Engels (quoted in MEHRING 1935:555) at the grave of his lifetime friend and collaborator. Needless to say, few non-Marxist social scientists have subscribed to Engels's estimate. On the other hand, the attempt on the part of a minority of Western social scientists to diminish Karl Marx's stature in relation to his contemporaries—to Comte, Spencer, or J. S. Mill—has met with little success. One may reasonably object to regarding Marx as the historical equal of Darwin. Marx's theories are surrounded by a polemic which in Darwin's case no longer exists. But the continuation of this polemic itself testifies to the power of Marx's ideas as compared with those of other nineteenth-century social scientists.

This polemic has produced a vast critical literature, especially in economics, political science, and sociology. It also has produced a sustained critique of even greater magnitude, in which the author's point cannot be understood except as an implicit rejection of Marxist principles. Frequently enough, the reaffirmation of non-Marxist positions takes the form of rote or unconscious acceptance of principles which have been elaborated in response to the Marxist challenge. These visceral "critiques" of Marxism have their counterpart in the degraded Marxist catechisms and "Manuals" directed against "bourgeois" social science. To the bourgeois and Marxist ideologues, a new generation says, a plague on both your houses.

MARX'S INFLUENCE

Many have argued that Marx was wrong; few have argued that his ideas can or should be ignored. Pitirim Sorokin's (1928:522) contention that one Georg Wilhelm von Raumer anticipated Marx's "economic conception of history" has succeeded neither in detracting attention from Marx nor in rescuing von Raumer from obscurity. Sorokin is one of the few who have claimed that Marx and Engels were so far from being "Darwins or Galileos" that "There is no reason even for regarding their scientific contribution as something above the average" (*ibid.*:545). But the lifework of the most esteemed figures of non-Marxist twentieth-century sociology weighs against this pique. Almost the entire galaxy of great figures in early twentieth-century sociology were, as the non-Marxist sociologist T. B. Bottomore (1965: 11ff.) maintains, "discussants of Marx." One simply cannot understand Max Weber, Émile Durkheim, Georges Sorel, Vilfredo Pareto, or George Simmel without taking into consideration the fact that they come after Marx. The same is true of Thorstein Veblen, Werner Sombart, Karl Mannheim, Lester Ward, and Alfred Keller.

Even to understand Sorokin, one must consider first and foremost his hatred of Bolshevism. It is historically indisputable that no nineteenth-century figure has exerted an influence upon non-Marxist twentieth-century sociology which in any significant respect approaches that of Marx and Engels. Nor can it be denied that this prominence is deserved regardless of political issues. It is one thing to compare Marx with Max Weber, his greatest twentieth-century critic, but quite another to compare Marx with his floundering contemporaries. The historically informed non-Marxist who is aware of Marx's errors of fact and theory is also aware of the blunders and inanities of Comte, J. S. Mill, and Spencer. In the final analysis, Engels's graveside claim boils down to this: either Marx (with Engels's help) was the Darwin of the social sciences, or nobody was. To quote from another prominent avowedly non-Marxist sociologist, C. Wright Mills (1962:35), Karl Marx "was *the* social and political thinker of the nineteenth century." It remains to be shown, however, that this eminence adds up to a scientific contribution analogous to that which is generally attributed to Darwin. Most non-Marxist social scientists seem to believe that their Darwin has yet to be born.

DID MARX DISCOVER THE LAW OF CULTURAL EVOLUTION?

In my opinion, Engels was correct when he attributed to Marx the "discovery of the law of evolution in human history." Yet it is possible to hold this view and to deny that Marx's role in the development of social science was like that of Darwin in the development of biology. Marx formulated a scientific principle at least as powerful as Darwin's natural selection—a general principle that showed how a science of human history might be constructed. Yet Marx glimpsed this principle only after a long journey through the thicket of Hegelian philosophy and in the midst of a political career predicated on an imminent proletarian revolution. Both of these circumstances had a corrosive effect on Marx's ability to found a true science of history. In order to apply Marx's "law of history," the non-Marxist social scientist must strip away the Hegelian and political accretions, the one with its ponderous double-talk, the other with its unrequited debt to nineteenth-century communism. What remains will scarcely satisfy the doctrinaire Marxist, for it is no longer mainly a theory of proletarian revolution in Euro-American capitalist society. Stripped of the burden of the dialectic and of the necessity for providing not only a theory but also the ideology of revolution, Marx's sociology will strike the faithful as singularly uninteresting. But even a de-Hegelianized, de-proletarianized Marx subsumes several of the major trends in contemporary anthropological theory and challenges the remainder.

THE DOCTRINE OF THE UNITY OF THEORY AND PRACTICE

To rescue Marx's "law of history" for non-Marxist applications, we must break the grip which political activism holds on the scientific aspects of his contribution. It was Marx himself, of course, who insisted that social science and political action were inseparable. This scientifically unacceptable proposition was first enunciated by Marx in his critique of the philosopher Ludwig Feuerbach: "The philosophers have *interpreted* the world in various ways: the point however is to *change* it" (1941:82). In this view, only a theory of history which enables men to make history is worth the effort. Thus, the only effective answer to the challenge presented by alternative interpretations is to prove them wrong by helping to bring about the predictions of one's own theory.

There is a superficial resemblance between the test of "changing the world" and the fulfillment of prediction in conformity with the rules of the scientific method. Thus, engineers do prove that their interpretations of the laws of aerodynamics and hydraulics are correct when the airplanes they design and help to build fly, or when the dams they design and help to build hold back the river. But the so-called unity of theory and practice cannot be applied in most of the nonlaboratory sciences. No one insists that geologists must justify their respective models of the ice ages by producing new advances of the continental glaciers. Nor do we expect that alternative explanations of meteorological phenomena require made-to-order hurricanes, tornadoes, and thunderstorms.

In the historical sciences, the doctrine of the unity of theory and practice is rendered superfluous by the possibility of subjecting one's predictions to the test not of future, but of past events. That is, there is no reason why the social sciences cannot accept retrodiction as the test of theory. Thus, the retrodiction of irrigation agriculture in the highland meso-American formative period, does not require an archaeologist to establish the truth by digging irrigation ditches. It suffices that the archaeologist find the evidence that the ditches once existed. Similarly, if one suspects a correlation between patrilineal descent and Omaha kinship terminology, the evidence from extinct cases is as acceptable as that from present or future cases, while the question of helping to build an Omaha terminology is obviously irrelevant.

THE THREAT OF POLITICS

The Marxist stress on the unity of theory and practice contains an implicit threat to the most fundamental rule of the scientific method, namely, the obligation to report data honestly. Marx himself took pains to elevate scientific responsibility over class interests. Thus, according to Karl Wittfogel (1953:355), Marx demanded that scholars:

> be oriented toward the interests of mankind as a whole and seek the truth in accordance with the immanent needs of science, no matter how this affected the fate of any particular class, capitalists, landowners, or workers. Marx praised Ricardo for taking this

> attitude, which he called "not only scientifically honest but also scientifically required." For the same reason, he condemned as "mean" a person who subordinated scientific objectivity to extraneous purposes: ". . . a man who tries to accommodate science to a standpoint which is not derived from its [the science's] own interests, however erroneous, but from outside, alien, and extraneous interests, [such a man] I call 'mean' (*gemein*)."

But Wittfogel goes on to accuse Marx of "violating his own scientific principles" (*ibid.*:359) in his persistent refusal to acknowledge that in the Oriental state it was the bureaucracy that constituted the ruling class (see page 671). Regardless of Marx's intentions, it is clear that a science which is explicitly bound to a political program is dangerously exposed to the possibility that the values of that program will gain the ascendancy over the values of science. It is a matter of historical record that Lenin and Stalin were fully prepared to corrupt scientific standards in order to prove by practice what their theories predicted. As Wittfogel (*ibid.*:355) has stated:

> Starting from Lenin's thesis that all socialist literature must be party literature, which must "merge with the movement of the really most progressive and consistently revolutionary class," they scorn objectivity and exalt in its stead the "partisanship" (*partiinost*) of science.

The admission that a particular proletarian movement lacks the conditions for the growth of class consciousness necessarily weakens that movement's revolutionary potential. If the point is to change the world, rather than to interpret it, the Marxist sociologist ought not to hesitate to falsify data in order to make it more useful. When the ethics of social science are derived primarily from the class struggle, information, as in any war, is an important weapon. Thus the Marxist sociologist would seem to enjoy a mandate to change data in order to make it more useful in changing the world, subject only to the usual limitations imposed upon wartime propaganda: on the one hand, repeated falsification diminishes credibility and runs the risk of self-defeat; on the other, acceptance of one's own propaganda may eventually destroy the objective basis of action. Under Stalin, the consistent errors in the interpretation of the class structure of the United States by Communist observers no doubt reflected in part this aspect of the unity of theory and practice. The failure among Marxist theoreticians to expose Morgan's principal blunders likewise reflects the tendency of politicized social science to harden into dogma. Wittfogel (1957:369ff.) has shown how the ideologues of the Soviet

Communist Party even succeeded in repressing Marx's concept of an oriental mode of production in an attempt to prepare the way for the spread of Communism to China.

Of course, Marxists are not the only ones whose facts and theories are vulnerable to political currents. Many non-Marxists consciously or unconsciously accept the view that political goals must take precedence over scientific ones and consciously or unconsciously suppress or distort findings which support the Marxist interpretation of history. As I have previously had occasion to stress, ethical and political neutrality in the realm of social-science research is a limiting condition which cannot be approached by a posture of indifference. Neither the researcher who preaches the partisanship of science, nor he who professes complete political apathy, is to be trusted. Naturally, we demand that the scientific ethic—fidelity to data—must be the foundation of all research. But we must also demand that scientific research be oriented by explicit hypotheses, whose political and moral consequences in both an active and passive sense are understood and rendered explicit by the researcher.

MARX AS AN EVOLUTIONIST

In explaining Marx's theories from the perspective of the development of anthropology, it is appropriate first of all to emphasize the many parallels that link Marx, along with Darwin, Morgan, Spencer, and Tylor, to a common heritage of eighteenth-century doctrines. Marx's belief in the generally progressive nature of history is distinctive only in the strength of its apocalyptic emphasis. Poverty and exploitation in all its forms are destined by the workings of natural law to be eliminated as a result of the proletarian revolution. The strong utopian ingredient in Marx's vision of progress is illustrated in the distinctive motto of ultimate communism: "from each according to his abilities, to each according to his needs." However, the ultimate stages of Spencer's industrial society do not lack for similar manifestations of spontaneous altruism. As Marxism predicted the end of exploitation in the communist millennium, Spencerism predicted a future society in which the desires of each individual would be in adaptive equilibrium with the desires of all others and with the means of satisfying them (*cf.* HIMMELFARB 1959:347).

Marx shared with Darwin and Spencer that curious nineteenth-century faith in the ability of violence and struggle to bring about unlimited social improvement. The publication of Darwin's *Origin of Species* at once found Marx and Engels clucking happily over what they took to be the natural-history analogue to their own materialist interpretation of nature. Marx declared, upon first reading the *Origin of Species,* that it provided "a basis in natural science for the class struggle in history"; recommending it to Lasalle, he wrote, "Despite all deficiencies, not only is a death-blow dealt here for the first time to teleology in the natural sciences, but their rational meaning is empirically examined" (MARX, quoted in HIMMELFARB 1959:347). Within a month of the publication of Darwin's book, Engels wrote to Marx (December 12, 1859): "Darwin, whom I am first now reading, is splendid" (quoted in ZIRKLE 1959:85).

THE CONVERGENCE OF MARX AND SPENCER

Although Marx and Engels thought it highly amusing that Darwin had been able to understand the animal kingdom by an analogy with the animal-like behavior of British capitalist society, and although they detested Malthus, they were not beyond having their own principle of the survival of the fittest. Indeed, both Spencer and Marx warned against the deleterious effect of diminished competition. The only difference was that for Spencer, the danger lay in the possibility that individuals would somehow manage to avoid natural selection because of misguided altruism; while in Marx's version of progress-through-struggle, the danger lay in the failure of one class to perceive another as its enemy. Spencer's fetishistic veneration of competition as expressed in the phrase "survival of the fittest," has its counterpart in Marx's Hegelian infatuation with "contradictions." The class struggle is simply an expression of irreconcilable competition between proletarians and bourgeoisie for control of the means of production.

Even in regard to the relationship with Malthus, there is much that unites the Spencerians and Marxists. This commonality is obscured by the fact that Darwin gratefully attributed his main inspiration to Malthus's theory of population. Marx, on the other hand, had nothing but contempt for Malthus and called him "the mountebank parson . . . a bought advocate" and "a shameless sycophant of the ruling classes" (quoted in ZIRKLE 1959:66–67). What Marx objected to in Malthus was the assumption that the "struggle-for-life" characteristic of capitalism was equally prevalent in all forms of society. Instead of seeing the struggle for survival in nature as the justification for a similar struggle in society, Marx regarded the similarity between the animal and human condition as an indictment of capitalism:

"nothing discredits modern bourgeois development so much as the fact that it has not succeeded in getting beyond the economic forms of the animal world . . ." (*ibid.*:90). But the main thrust of Spencerism is precisely that man must overcome the animal propensity to destructive competition. This change in human nature will take place in Spencer's scheme only if industrial society is permitted to evolve unhampered by state interference. As we have already seen, Spencerism rose to ideological pre-eminence not because it confirmed but because it denied Malthus's dire predictions. Marx, of course, regarded the Spencerian advocacy of progress through struggle as a mere bourgeois maneuver calculated to appease the conscience of the capitalist exploiters. Thus the concrete brutality of the present was to be justified by an illusory future. But Marx's scheme also had its brutal interlude. To overcome Malthus's predictions, it too urged the continuation of an animal-like struggle out of which alone would come a future better life (see p. 468).

MARX'S EVOLUTIONARY SCHEME

Like all the other mid-nineteenth-century cultural evolutionists, Marx and Engels had their scheme of world historical stages. By means of these stages, the degree of progress toward communist perfection could be measured. Distinctively, their periodization of universal history was based on the forms of property associated with various modes of production. Several different versions were offered, each of which contained baffling ambiguities, which to this day are the bane of Marxist exegesists.

In Marx and Engels's "The German Ideology" (1965; orig. ms. 1846), the first stage was described as based on "tribal ownership" and was associated with the "undeveloped stage of production at which a people lives by hunting and fishing, by the rearing of beasts or, in the highest stage, agriculture." (*ibid.*:122). The main feature of social structure at this stage is the family and its extensions. With increase in population, families develop distinctions between commoners and chieftains and slavery begins to develop. The second stage is based upon "ancient communal and state ownership" (*ibid.*:123) and is accompanied by the formation of cities through voluntary tribal merger and conquest. Land and slaves are at first held in common, but private ownership of immovable property soon begins to assert itself. With the growth of private property in land, the tribal collective decays. The development of the ancient city-state, of which Roman society was the ultimate expression, marks the culmination of these trends. The third stage is based on "feudal or estate property" (*ibid.*:125). Feudal lords collectively own the land which is worked not by slaves but by serfs. During this same period, there is an analogous organization in the towns, whereby guilds of master craftsmen and merchants control the work of apprentices and journeymen.

In this scheme, the relationship between the ancient city-state and feudalism is difficult to decipher. There appears to be no necessary relationship between one and the other. Indeed, Eric Hobsbawm (1965:28) argues that feudalism appears to be an *alternative* evolutionary path out of "primitive communalism" under conditions of low regional population density and no large cities. Yet it is clear that Marx and Engels treat only that feudalism which followed on the collapse of the Roman Empire—the feudalism which "is prepared by the Roman conquests and the spread of agriculture connected with these." There is no doubt, however, that the next stage, capitalism, arises only on the basis of feudalism, with the emergence of the burgher classes dedicated to trade and manufacture.

In the brief historical sections of their 1848 *Communist Manifesto*, Marx and Engels described an evolutionary sequence of class society, consisting of the slave society of antiquity, feudalism, and capitalism. No treatment is accorded the prehistoric, classless societies. Once again, the question of a necessary connection between slave society and feudalism is left in doubt.

MARX NOT A UNILINEAR EVOLUTIONIST

Up until 1941, the definitive listing of the evolutionary stages of class society was regarded as those given in Marx's "Preface" to *The Critique of Political Economy* (1904; orig. 1859), namely, the "Asiatic, ancient, feudal, and modern bourgeoisie." However, in 1939–41 a manuscript written by Marx in preparation for *The Critique of Political Economy* was published under the title *Grundrisse der Kritik der politischen Ökonomie (Outlines of a Critique of Political Economy).* This work, composed in 1857–58, contained a section, entitled "Formen," dealing with precapitalist economic formations which has now become the most important source of information concerning Marx's evolutionary periodization.

In the "Formen," the transition from the stage of tribal economic types is definitely presented as following a number of different routes, apparently dictated by local conditions, the nature of which remains disappointingly obscure. Specifically identified are the oriental, with a Slavonic-Rumanian variant, the ancient, and the Germanic. Marx makes it clear that all of these forms of property and production may progress into feudalism, although with different probabilities. Thus the stereotyped interpretation of Marx as a unilinear evolutionist is as defective as the common stereotype of unilinear evolution applied by the Boasians to the anthropological evolutionists.

MARX ANTICIPATES MAINE

Marx's interest in the precapitalist economic forms is totally marginal to his consideration of the feudalism-capitalism transition, which in turn is marginal to his major concern, the analysis of capitalist society. The step from tribal communities to the oriental, ancient, and Germanic levels receives cursory if not sloppy treatment. Apparently, the guiding thread in Marx's periodization is the progressive and gradual emergence of alienated men conditioned to sell their only possession—their labor, which they cease to regard as a part of themselves. Thus, the ancient slave societies are more "progressive" than the Asiatic type, because they allow for considerable private holdings in land and slaves and a complex individualized monetary economy (MARX 1965:83).

In the Asiatic type, communalism "survives longest and most stubbornly" (*ibid.*).

> This is due to the fundamental principle on which it is based, that is, that the individual does not become independent of the community; that the circle of production *is* [a] self-sustaining unity of agriculture and craft manufacture, etc. [*ibid.*].

In the ancient slave societies, however, the city rather than the land is the basis of the lingering communalism:

> The *community* is here also the first precondition, but unlike our first case, it is not here the substance of which the individuals are mere accidents or of which they form mere spontaneously natural parts. The basis here is not the land, but the city as already created seat (center) of the rural population (landowners). The cultivated area appears as the territory of the city; not, as in the other case, the village as a mere appendage to the land [*ibid.*:71].

In describing the influence of communalism in the ancient states, Marx anticipated major points in the analyses of Maine and Morgan, by giving emphasis to emerging tribal and kinship relations: "The tribes of the ancient states were constituted in one of two ways, either by *kinship* or by *locality*. *Kinship tribes* historically precede locality tribes and are almost everywhere displaced by them" (*ibid.*: 76). The new manuscripts of 1857–58 therefore lend support to Engels's (1954a:132; orig. 1884) claim that he and Marx had set forth Henry Maine's ideas about the transition from "status to contract" as far back as 1848.

> H. S. Maine, the English jurist, believed that he had made a colossal discovery when he said that our entire progress in comparison with previous epochs consists in our having evolved from status to contract, from an inherited state of affairs to one voluntarily contracted—a statement which in so far as it is correct, was contained long ago in the *Communist Manifesto*.

Actually, of course, Ferguson and Millar were responsible for a still earlier formulation of the same trend of thought.

MARX'S IGNORANCE OF PRIMITIVES

Despite occasional insights, Marx's treatment of prefeudal society is highly schematic, superficial, and disorganized. The ancient type includes varieties which evolved over thousands of years from tiny city-states to the Roman Empire. Asiatic society includes independent village communities and gigantic Oriental despotisms: societies as diverse as those of peasant Russia, Mexico, Peru, "the ancient Celts and some tribes of India" (MARX 1965:70; orig. 1857–58). As for the stage of primitive communalism, it is obvious that Marx's knowledge of ethnography had still not advanced much beyond that of Turgot or Rousseau. As in "The German Ideology," pastoral, agricultural, and hunting modes of existence are indiscriminately associated with "tribal community, the natural common body" (*ibid.*:68). Hobsbawm, who attempts to defend Marx and Engels's understanding of Greco-Roman history and of India (although Henry Maine clearly surpassed them in both areas) frankly admits the poverty of their knowledge of primitive societies:

> At the time the *Formen* (1857–8) were written, Marx's and Engels' knowledge of primitive society was . . . not based on any serious knowledge of tribal societies, for modern anthropology was in its infancy . . . [HOBSBAWM 1965:25].

The ignorance of Marx and Engels with respect to nine-tenths of human history does not appear quite as natural to the anthropologist as to the Marxist philosopher. Granted that anthropology was in its infancy when Marx wrote *The Critique of Political Economy* (1859), it does not follow that the failure to use ethnographic data was primarily a reflection of that circumstance. Rather we must consider the fact that almost all of the sources employed by Tylor in his *Researches into the Early History of Mankind* were already available. Instead of the infancy of anthropology, one suspects the dead hand of Hegel, with the latter's contempt for knowledge of the "unprogressive" parts of mankind. When Marx and Engels declared in the very first line of the *Communist Manifesto,* "The history of all hitherto existing society is the history of class struggles," the immense residual category, "prehistory," during which there are no classes, is banished from view, not simply because it deals with classless societies, but because such societies were conventionally regarded as uninteresting and unilluminating.

No prejudice is more calculated to arouse bitter feelings among anthropologists than that of the European historian who feels he has nothing to learn from the history of savages, because savages cannot "contribute to history." This bitterness arises not only from the sentiment that primitives are human too, but from a practical conviction that ethnographic data are indispensable for a science of culture. In this context it might seem that the profound neglect of Marx by anthropology is merely the reciprocal of Marx's neglect of primitives. It would at least seem the better part of charity to attribute the anthropologist's ignorance of Marx, in contrast to his knowledge of such third-order luminaries as Gustav Klemm and Adolf Bastian, to this *quid pro quo.* But other circumstances intervene and compel us toward different conclusions.

MARX AND ANTHROPOLOGY

There is no doubt that a consensus exists among contemporary anthropologists that Marx and Engels are irrelevant to the history of anthropological theory. Robert Lowie did not even permit these names to appear in his index; while T. K. Penniman (1965:52–53) allots Marx a few disjointed lines, and A. I. Hallowell (1960) mentions Comte and Buckle but not Marx. According to Alfred Meyer (1954:22), cultural anthropology "developed entirely independently from Marxism." This neglect, if true, was surely undeserved. There are additional aspects of Marx and Engels's approach to cultural evolution which demand that their work be placed in the mainstream of the history of anthropological theory. First, despite Marx and Engels's initial neglect of ethnographic data, their formulation of the principles of cultural evolution was intended as a contribution to the explanation of cultural differences and similarities with respect to all cultural types. It is in this regard that their contribution was strictly analogous to Darwin's principle of "natural selection"—as an explanatory principle, applicable not just to one phylum or genus, but to the evolution of all life forms. Second, toward the end of his life, Marx seized upon the opportunity furnished by the publication of Morgan's *Ancient Society* to redress his neglect of the primitive world. His notes furnished the inspiration for Engels's *The Origin of the Family, Private Property and the State,* an event which, as we shall see, destroys Meyer's claims about the lack of relationship between Marxism and the development of cultural anthropology. But first we must attend to the nature of these theories themselves.

MARX'S PRINCIPLE OF CULTURAL SELECTION

In the "Preface" to *The Critique of Political Economy* (not included in the original 1859 edition), Marx summed up his strategy for achieving an explanation of cultural evolution, in what is undoubtedly the closest equivalent in the social sciences to Darwin's principle of natural selection:

> In the social production which men carry on they enter into definite relations that are indispensable and independent of their will; these relations of production correspond to a definite stage of development of their material powers of production. The sum total of these relations of production constitutes the economic structure of society—the real foundation, on which rise legal and political superstructures and to which correspond definite forms of social consciousness. The mode of production in material life determines the general character of the social, political and spiritual processes of life. It is not the consciousness of men that determines their existence, but, on the contrary, their social existence determines their consciousness [1904:11–12].

Beyond this point, Marx's exposition, while no less lucid, refers not to social life in general, but rather to class society. Thus, we learn that the "material forces of production . . . come in conflict with the existing relations of production," and that thence commences "the period of social revolution" when "the entire immense superstructure is more or less rapidly transformed." Here the Hegelian and revolutionary activist ingredients in Marx would come forward to overwhelm the more general strategy.

THE HEGELIAN MONKEY

If we grant the relevance of Marx's analysis of the "inner contradictions" of nineteenth-century capitalism, there remains considerable doubt concerning the relevance of the same analysis with respect to the modified capitalism of the modern industrially advanced Euro-American nations. In some cases at least—as in the mixed economies of the Scandinavian democracies—capitalism's "internal contradictions" seem to have been solved by multiple compromises, by the dreaded "revisionism," rather than by the "negation of the negation." The dialectic, however, grows less useful as its principles of analysis are applied to situations increasingly remote from the social system which inspired its founders. Marx's attempt to identify the inner Hegelian logic of the breakdown of the Greco-Roman world into feudalism was singularly unsuccessful. His treatment of the Asiatic type was even less rewarding. If the great oriental despotisms of Egypt and Babylonia contained the seeds of their own destruction, they remained dormant for remarkably long epochs. When we get to the domain of pre-state societies, however, the dialectic is clearly just so much excess baggage. Morgan, of course, pictured progress from Savagery to Civilization as a smooth unfolding of germ ideas under the tutelage of natural selection. As we shall see, when Engels attempted to assimilate Morgan's scheme to a materialist view of world history, his vague dialectical excursions become wholly superfluous and inconsequential. It seems impossible not to conclude, therefore, that if dialectical materialism is a useful guide to sociocultural analysis, it is as a special case of a more general materialist strategy. As a local mode of analysis, which arose at the juncture of romanticism and industrialism, it is ill suited for the general history of mankind. It is a romanticized, mysticized, partisan materialism, appropriate to men who wish to foment a revolution based on mid-nineteenth-century European class structure and ideology. It is Marx's more general materialist formulation that deserves our closest scrutiny.

MARX AND ENGELS: CULTURAL MATERIALISTS

Despite the Hegelian monkey on their back, Marx and Engels must be credited with an important "breakthrough." There were many predecessors and contemporaries who were convinced that natural law governed the realm of sociocultural phenomena. But

Marx and Engels were the first to show how the problem of consciousness and the subjective experience of the importance of ideas for behavior could be reconciled with causation on the physicalist model. If there had been an orderliness in human history, it cannot, as the Enlightenment philosophers supposed, have originated from the orderliness of men's thoughts. Men do not think their way into matrilineality, the couvade, or Iroquois cousin terminology. In the abstract, can a good reason be found why anyone should bother to think such apparently improbable thoughts? And if one man had thought of them, whence arose the compulsion and the power to convince others of their propriety? For surely it could not be that these improbable ideas construed as mere spontaneous products of fancy occur simultaneously to dozens of people at a time. Obviously, therefore, thoughts must be subject to constraints; that is, they have causes and are made more or less probable in individuals and groups of individuals by prior conditions.

It is tempting to suppose that these prior conditions are prior thoughts, and that, as in the Enlightenment model, one idea leads to another. The development of mathematics and the physical sciences might be described fairly successfully in this manner, but the same track takes us nowhere if we seek to explain matrilineality or the couvade. There is no purely logical progression which unites these practices with prior or subsequent practices. Indeed, as we have seen, one of the main sources of error of late-nineteenth-century attempts to reconstruct world history was the assumption that logic alone would suffice to unravel the relationship between matrilineality and patrilineality, exogamy and endogamy, and all the other aspects of cultural evolution.

We are led inexorably to conclude that thoughts about institutions are constrained by the institutions under which men do their thinking. Now there arises the question, whence come the institutions? Marx attempted to answer this question by giving separate consideration to different varieties of institutions. He split the nonideological aspects of sociocultural life into two parts: the economic structure ("the real foundation") and the "legal and political superstructure." He came to distinguish, therefore, three major sociocultural segments: (1) the economic base; (2) the legal-political arrangements, which in modern terms correspond to social structure, or social organization; and (3) "social consciousness" or ideology. Marx and Engels then boldly proclaimed that it was in the economic base that the explanation for both parts of the superstructure—social organization and ideology—were to be found.

Why was it not the other way round? Why not the dominance of social organization over economics? The answer here is contained in the phrase which associates "relations of production" with "a definite stage of development" of man's "material powers of production." It is the stage of development of the material powers of production which renders the "relations of production" *independent* of man's will. For no group of men can will into existence whenever and wherever they choose, the apparatus of production—*coup de poing,* plows, or Bessemer converters—*except in a definite order of progression.* That order of progression corresponds precisely to what the combined efforts of archaeologists and ethnographers have revealed it to be. The unbroken chain of technological innovations which connects digital computers with Oldowan choppers does not admit of deviations or leaps (although the rate of change might conceivably vary rather widely). Stone tools *had* to come before metal tools; spears *had* to come before bows and arrows; hunting and gathering *had* to precede pastoralism and agriculture; the digging stick *had* to precede the plow; the flint strike-a-light *had* to be invented before the safety match; oars and sails *had* to precede the steamboat; and handicrafts *had* to precede industrial manufacture. Indeed, none of the major opponents of cultural materialism has ever seriously questioned these facts.

The Boasians, for example, frequently pointed out that technology is cumulative and that objective measures of progress are possible in this realm. Thus, the only point at issue (aside from details concerning the order of emergence of certain innovations) is whether "the mode of production in material life determines the general character of the social, political and spiritual" aspects of sociocultural life. This, it will be seen at once, is an eminently empirical issue, not to be answered by logic alone.

THE MEANING OF "MODE OF PRODUCTION"

Unfortunately, the formulation of the empirical tests of the cultural-materialist strategy has been impaired by ambiguities inherent in Marx and Engels's definition of "base." A large literature has accumulated concerning whether or not Marx and Engels intended to give the technological factors equal weight with the "relations" or organization of production (cf. BOBER 1927). One of the principal sources of this confusion resides in the fact that Marx and Engels did not relate the transformation of feudalism into capitalism to changes in the technology of production. Instead, the transition to capitalism is supposed to occur as a result of the organization of the craft and merchant guilds. Capitalism was in existence for two hundred years before innovations in the technology of production become important in Marx's analysis. Here we may venture to express our disinterest in the attempt to find out precisely what Marx and Engels intended by the phrase "mode of production." It is as evident as it is understandable that an operationalized metataxonomy of sociocultural entities was not achieved by Marx and Engels any more than it has been achieved by the entire combined effort of twentieth-century social science. For most social scientists, the boundary between economics and technology remains as hazy today as it was a hundred years ago. The same may be said with respect to another evident fault in Marx's threefold sectioning of sociocultural systems, namely, the failure to consider the modifying effect of environment upon the quantitative and qualitative characteristics of a "definite stage of production." Moving toward the other end of the economic sector, we may also note the continued vagueness of the line which separates the organization of work from the organization of law and order and social interaction. Indeed, there is no more widely misunderstood term than "work" itself. Since all behavior produces some environmental effect, what portion is not "production"? Finally, we may take brief notice of the failure of social science to ground its categories in definite etic operations, with the result that mentalistic, subjective, and idealist—i.e., "emic"—entities contaminate even the most devotedly materialist analyses (see Chap. 20). We may take it as axiomatic that precise demarcation of the sectors of sociocultural systems is not possible without the prior establishment of an etic data language.

THE GREAT UP-ENDING

Despite the shadowy fringes on the concept "mode of production," there never has been any confusion concerning the *general* nature of the factors to which Marx pointed as the key to the understanding of sociocultural causality. It was not merely Hegel whom Marx "found standing on his head," but the entire body of Enlightenment social philosophy. Before Marx, the analysis of "mind" was regarded as the only conceivable understanding to which man, the "rational animal," could aspire. It is a pity that Marx's dialectical fixation has deprived so many social scientists of the enjoyment of that great up-ending of "heaven and earth."

> In direct contrast to German philosophy, which descends from heaven to earth, here we ascend from earth to heaven. That is to say, we do not set out from what men say, imagine, or conceive, nor from what has been said, thought, imagined, or conceived of men, in order to arrive at men in the flesh. We begin with real, active men, and from their real life-process show the development of the ideological reflexes and echoes of this life-process . . . [MARX and ENGELS in BOTTOMORE 1956:75].

Let us take note at this juncture of a second enduring theme in Marx and Engels's materialist program, the distinction between what men "say, imagine and conceive" about themselves and their social life and the actual or "real" nature of that life—their "real life-processes." To be sure, this theme is not specific to cultural materialism; it has already been encountered in the works of Ferguson and Millar (see p. 51); and it will recur in the discussions of Durkheim, British social anthropology, Freudian psychological anthropology, and French structuralism. All of these approaches are predicated upon the assumption that the actual participants in social life are incapable of an objective description of their own behavior or of a scientifically valid explanation of that behavior. All of these approaches thus share in common a commitment to clearing away the errors of autoanalysis, the façade of ideology, the rationalized appearances of things, in order to penetrate into the deeper levels of both thought and action. In several instances, however, as in the culture and personality and French schools, the penetration beneath the surface aims at a deeper understanding of what the actor thinks or feels, rather than at an explanation of the sociocultural factors which constrain and direct his thoughts and feelings. In other instances, most notably in Durkheim and the British social anthropologists, the focus more closely resembles that of cultural materialism. The announced goal at least is to explain social facts in terms of social facts, rather than ideas in terms of other ideas. But the structural-functionalists, as we shall see, do not even pretend to be able to explain sociocultural differences and similarities. Their insistence upon rendering psychological facts in a "structural" idiom is thus itself a most remarkable sociocultural phenomenon, calling for an extensive application of the principle that manifest content and autoanalysis are not to be trusted. In contrast, the relationship of the priority of observer-orientation over actor-orientation is an integral part of the cultural-materialist program. The hypothesis that causal explanations reside in the material conditions of life enjoins an attitude of extreme skepticism toward the relevance of the manifest meanings of all verbal events. This is beautifully expressed in Marx's critique of Feuerbach: "Social life is essentially *practical.* All mysteries which mislead theory to mysticism find their rational solution in human practice and in the comprehension of this practice" (MARX 1941:82).

DIACHRONIC CAUSAL FUNCTIONALISM

Although many readers will regard it as self-evident, we should also note that Marx and Engels depended upon a "functionalist" model of sociocultural life. This in itself was not remarkable, since Comte, Spencer, and Morgan were also functionalists, long before the German diffusionists and the Boasians gave Bronislaw Malinowski the pretext for supposing that there was some novelty attached to the idea that the parts of culture are interrelated. Moreover, Marx and Engels shared with Comte, Spencer, and Morgan a functionalism which was fully compatible, indeed was deliberately subordinate to an interest in change, in contrast to the twentieth-century functionalists who were capable only of synchronic analysis. But there is one respect in which the functionalism of Marx and Engels merits special comment. As a causal, as well as diachronic and synchronic model, the economic-structural-ideological concatenation provides the basis for stipulating the more or less durable and influential parts of the system. This provides, in theory at least, some prospect of being able to discern degrees of functional effectiveness or "fit," as between an innovation and an older element in the system. The measurement of degrees of functional effectiveness is essential to diachronic functionalism, if one intends eventually to account for the fact that the path of evolution is littered with extinct forms whose parts were once eminently functional. It is thus the cause-effect relationship between base and superstructure which provides "the strain toward consistency," a feature which gets introduced into non-causal functional models as a mysterious "essence" or "propensity" of social systems.

Thus, the Marxian functionalist model escapes the ultimate vapidity of the modern synchronic functionalist schools, by explicitly denying that all the features of a sociocultural system contribute equally to its maintenance. Indeed, as a result of the dialectic aspects of Marx's scheme, dysfunctional ingredients are not only accommodated, but assigned a central role as system-changing variables. Such variables are functional in a diachronic sense, since they are responsible for the emergence of a new adaptive system out of the old.

It cannot be denied that the Hegelian heritage has its merits at this juncture, since it is wholly concerned with the problem of how conflict leads to "higher" unity. We shall in a later chapter have occasion to observe the antics of the synchronic functionalists as they attempt to interpret hate, witchcraft, and violence as functional, system-maintaining variables. On the other hand, it is not necessary to concede to the dialectic a monopoly on functional models capable of handling conflict. The decisive advantage of the Marxian model is that it is diachronic and evolutionary, not that it is dialectic. Any diachronic model is capable of accommodating the fact that strains may accumulate until consistency on the old basis is no longer feasible, and there is a violent collapse in the whole system. But there is another kind of accumulation of dysfunctional strains which defeats the Hegelian dialectic: evolution through the slow accumulation of minor changes wrought by minor adjustments to minor stresses. What is needed is a causal-functional model which can explain all varieties of evolutionary processes.

WERE MARX AND ENGELS RACISTS?

The Marxian strategy was remarkably free of the endemic racism of the nineteenth century. Marx explicitly conceived it as his historical mission to link Hegelianism with eighteenth-century materialism. As materialists, Marx and Engels considered themselves the heirs of D'Holbach and Helvetius, whom they traced to Locke through the French philosopher Étienne Bonnot de Condillac. In *The Holy Family* (1845), they wrote:

> [Condillac] expounded Locke's ideas and proved that not only the soul, but the senses too, not only the art of creating ideas, but also the art of sensuous perception are matters of experience and habit. The whole development of man therefore depends on education and environment [quoted in SELSAM and MARTEL 1963: 58–59].

It is clear that Marx and Engels's political program was predicated on the same radical emphasis upon experience that had served as the ideology of the French Revolution. They believed in the "omnipotence of education" and regarded socialism and communism as virtually synonymous with radical environmentalism:

> There is no need of any great penetration to see from the teaching of materialism on the original goodness and equal intellectual endowment of man, the omnipotence of experience, habit, and

> education, and the influence of environment on man, the great significance of industry, the justification of enjoyment, etc., how necessarily materialism is connected with communism and socialism [*ibid.*:60].

This does not mean that Marx and Engels achieved a modern understanding of the relationship between heredity and enculturation. Their environmentalism, like that of Monboddo, Condorcet, William Stanhope Smith, and Lamarck, provided for a rapid, direct feedback between race and culture. The inheritance of acquired characteristics was for them the main vehicle of bio-evolutionary change. For example, Engels's explanation of the "transition from ape to man" invoked a process of increasing manual dexterity passed on by heredity from one generation to the next:

> . . . But the decisive step was taken: *the hand became free* and could henceforth attain ever greater dexterity and skill, and the greater flexibility thus acquired was inherited and increased from generation to generation.
>
> Thus the hand is not only the organ of labour, *it is also the product of labour*. Only by labour, by adaptation to ever new operations, by inheritance of the resulting special development of muscles, ligaments, and, over longer periods of time, bones as well, and by the ever renewed employment of these inherited improvements in new, more and more complicated operations, has the human hand attained the high degree of perfection that has enabled it to conjure into being the pictures of Raphael, the statues of Thorwaldsen, the music of Paganini [1954b:230; orig. 1876; quoted in ZIRKLE 1959:107].

It was this strong Lamarckian theme which laid the foundation for the twentieth-century disaster of Soviet genetics. Under Lysenko, it became a Stalinist dogma that the direct feedback between cytoplasm and environment, rather than the indirect feedback mediated by Mendelian genetic processes, was responsible for bio-evolutionary novelty. The magnitude of this error cannot be overemphasized. But the attempt on the part of certain biologists to compound the disrepute of Lysenko by linking Lamarckianism to racism is an equally grave disservice to science (to social science). Thus, H. J. Muller gave as one of his reasons for resigning from the U.S.S.R. Academy of Science the fact that

> . . . the inheritance of acquired characters must lead inevitably, and indeed by the admission of some of its adherents, to the same dangerous Fascistic conclusions as that of the Nazis; that the

> economically less advanced peoples and classes of the world have become actually inferior in their heredity. The Nazis would have the allegedly lower genetic status, a cause, while the Lysenkoists would have it an effect of the lower opportunity of the less fortunate groups for mental and physical development [quoted in ZIRKLE 1959:109].

Zirkle goes on to indict both Engels and Marx with racist propensities, as evidenced by their obvious lack of sensitivity to the feelings of Negroes and Jews. Engels, extolling the importance of "the principle of the origin of all thought content from experience" (i.e., Locke's principle), attempts to show how the same principle can be applied to the social group as a whole:

> By recognizing the inheritance of acquired characters . . . individual experience can be replaced to a certain extent by the results of the experiences of a number of its ancestors. If, for instance, among us the mathematical axioms seem self-evident to every eight-year-old child, and in no need of proof from experience, this is solely the result of "accumulated inheritance." It would be difficult to teach them by a proof to a bushman or Australian negro [1954b:353].

Zirkle goes on to insist that Marx "also esteemed the different races very differently" and that "toward some of them, he was openly contemptuous." He then quotes Marx's letter of July 30, 1862, addressed to Engels, on the subject of Ferdinand Lassalle's failure to provide him with a loan:

> The Jewish nigger Lassalle, who fortunately left at the end of the week, has, again fortunately, lost 5000 Thaler in a bad speculation. . . . Now it is completely clear to me that, as his head shape and hair growth prove, he is descended from the Negroes who joined Moses on the journey out of Egypt (if not, his mother or grandmother on his father's side crossed with a nigger). Now this combination of Judaism and Teutonism with a negroid ground substance must produce a wonderful product. The obtrusiveness of the fellow is indeed negroid. . . . One of the great discoveries of our nigger—which he shared with me as a "most trusted friend"—is that the Pelagians stemmed from the Semites . . . [quoted in ZIRKLE 1959:111].

Despite this display of bad taste, directed as much against his own ancestry as against Lassalle's, Marx simply will not fit the mold of the racial determinist. Nor does the history of the principle of acquired characteristics admit of a close association with racism. Both William

Stanhope Smith and Herbert Spencer believed in the inheritance of acquired characteristics. For the one, this meant that physical and psychological racial differences were as evanescent as sicknesses; for the other, it meant that no fundamental social change could occur until human nature slowly evolved to a higher plane.

The crucial question concerning race at mid-century was not whether there were biological differences, nor whether these were subject to environmental modification, but rather how long it would take to change them. The answer of Marx and Engels was contrary to the prevailing view: they predicted great changes in their own lifetime. Although Marx believed that there were individual differences in intellectual and physical aptitudes, he clearly saw these as subordinate to the effects of societal, class, and individual learning experiences: "In principle a porter differs less from a philosopher than a mastiff from a greyhound. It is the division of labor which has set a gulf between them" (MARX 1963:129; orig. 1847). Marx declared in his critique of Proudhon, "all history is nothing but a continuous transformation of human nature" (*ibid.*:147). Now while this was a position to which the Spencerians also wholeheartedly subscribed, there was a fundamental difference. Marx was a revolutionary who devoted his life to the assumption that radical political changes, involving the up-ending of the social order on a global scale, could be accomplished within one or two generations. The Spencerians, on the other hand, while equally devoted to their own brand of "progress," warned that human nature could be changed only at a rate commensurate with the workings of natural selection. The differential consequences of the biological feedback in Marx's and Spencer's theories are well understood in the political implications of the vernacular contrast between "revolution" and "evolution" (a distinction which, in another sense, is technically incorrect, since revolution is a form of evolution). Thus while Marx shared with Spencer the prevailing and erroneous notion of a Lamarckian feedback between behavior and heredity, his conclusions concerning the human potentiality for rapid change correspond to the modern post-Boasian understanding of the relative strengths of enculturation and racial variables.

The same must be said of Engels, who explicitly associated his view about the mathematical capacities of various races with Spencer's belief that the sense of mathematical proof is acquired and transmitted through heredity: "Spencer is right in as much as what thus appears to us to be the *self-evidence* of these axioms is *inherited*" (ENGELS 1954b:340). The implications of these views, however, are almost totally at variance with their usual significance among nineteenth-century Spencerians. For Engels, the hereditary Euclidean incapacities of bushmen were evanescent effects brought on by the same sort of deprivations which kept Monboddo's chimpanzees from learned discourse with the *philosophes.* Thus Engels, in *Origin of the Family, Private Property and the State,* shared with Gobineau and the entire corps of mid-century anthropologists, including Tylor, Morgan and Spencer, the belief that the Germans were "a highly gifted Aryan tribe" (1954a:254). But he went out of his way to give a sociocultural, rather than a racist, explanation for this stereotype. "What was the mysterious charm with which the Germans infused new vitality into dying Europe? Was it the innate power of the German race, as our jingo historians would have it?" (*ibid.*).

> By no means . . . their personal efficiency and bravery, their love of liberty, and their democratic instinct, which regarded all public affairs as its own affairs, in short, all these qualities which the Romans had lost and which were alone capable of forming new states and of raising new nationalities out of the muck of the Roman world—what were they but the characteristic features of barbarians in the upper stage, fruits of their gentile constitution [i.e., their clan organization] [*ibid.*:254–55]?

THE STRATEGY OF CULTURAL MATERIALISM

It should be obvious to all scholars who are genuinely concerned with the scientific study of human history, that despite their Hegelian and revolutionary political environments, Marx and Engels had succeeded in going further than any of their contemporaries toward the formulation of a "law" of cultural evolution. The major ingredients in this "law" in retrospect may be seen as: (1) the trisection of sociocultural systems into techno-economic base, social organization, and ideology; (2) the explanation of ideology and social organization as adaptive responses to techno-economic conditions; (3) the formulation of a functionalist model providing for interactive effects between all parts of the system; (4) the provision for analysis of both system-maintaining and system-destroying variables; and, (5) the pre-eminence of culture over race.

The greatest caution is required if we are to comprehend the sense in which it is legitimate to ascribe to this unprecedented ensemble of proposals a status equivalent to Darwin's discovery of the "law of evolution." It must be established with uncompromising clarity that Darwin's so-called "law of evolution" was not a "law" but a *strategy:* a master research design for explaining the course of bio-evolution. This strategy was introduced by Darwin in the guise of what he called "the principle of natural selection." The latter purports to explain *all* biotransformation; yet in actuality, it explains *none*. Its value resides exclusively in the general directions it imparts to the researcher, who seeks an understanding in nomothetic terms of the trajectory of phylogenetic modifications. It does not matter whether the researcher is interested in amphibia or mammals, worms or fish, the strategy is the same: the explanation of biological transformations is to be found in the adaptative advantages (measured in terms of reproductive success), which particular innovations confer upon the organism and its lineage. The statement of this strategy per se yields no specific information concerning the quantitative or qualitative nature of the advantages in question. We are not told whether it is resistance to stress, avoidance of predators, improvement in thermal efficiency, invasion of new ecological zones, better care of young, etc. Each application of the principle of natural selection results in a separate theory, the confirmation or rejection of which is dependent upon logical and empirical operations whose specific terms and instruments cannot be deduced from the general statement.

The admissible sense in which one may propose Marx as the discoverer of a "law of cultural evolution" is that which separates the specific application of the cultural-materialist program on behalf of explaining capitalism from the general strategy set forth in the "Preface" to *The Critique of Political Economy*. This strategy states that the explanation for cultural differences and similarities is to be found in the techno-economic processes responsible for the production of the material requirements of biosocial survival. It states that the techno-economic parameters of sociocultural systems exert selective pressures in favor of certain types of organizational structures and upon the survival and spread of definite types of ideological complexes. It states that in principle, all of the major problems of sociocultural differences and similarities can be solved by identifying the precise nature of these selective parameters; yet as a general principle, it does not commit itself to the explanation of any specific sociocultural type or any specific set of institutions. It is possible, in other words, to accept Marx's research strategy without accepting any of his analyses of the specific phenomena of capitalist and feudal societies. This is not to suggest that Marx's analysis of nineteenth-century capitalism, the French Revolution, or of feudalism can be demeaned or ignored, but simply that in anthropological perspective, a strategy purportedly applicable to the study of three thousand sociocultural systems is an event of far greater significance than the application of that strategy to one or two of them.

THE MYTH OF THE MONADIC EXPLANATION

Before discussing the application of Marx and Engels's proposal to ethnographic data, we must take note of what is probably the most frequently misunderstood and misrepresented aspect of the cultural-materialist strategy. It is repeated *ad nauseam* by persons unfamiliar with the research and data-processing requirements of cultural hypotheses, that sociocultural phenomena are "too complex to be explained by any one factor." We hear over and over again the refrain that economic explanations of phenomena are "single-factor explanations" and that economic explanations are therefore invariably "simplistic explanations." For example, the historical particularist Melville Herskovits (1953:118) lauded Franz Boas for his lack of economic, geographical, and racial determinism, with the following "simplistic" reference: "He was obviously no Marxist—we have seen how vigorously he rejected any simplistic explanation of social phenomena, whose complexity none realized better than he." One does not know to which "Marxists" Herskovits was referring, but there are at least two who are not easily associated with simplemindedness, namely, Marx and Engels. One more typical instance of the simplistic single-factor myth can be seen in the following passage from the historian Frederick Teggart (1941:233):

> This theory, then, . . . is unacceptable as an explanation of how man has come to be as he is, for . . . it is based upon a limited view of the facts, and represents a projection of a single factor upon the complexity of human experience.

The purely customary status of this argument is exposed as soon as one actually begins to work on a specific problem from a cultural-materialist point of view.

Consider for example what is involved in a cultural-materialist explanation of the difference between race relations in Brazil and the United States. The prevailing idealist explanations stress Portuguese national character and Catholicism versus Anglo-Saxon racism and Protestantism. The materialist explanation starts with the ecological potential of colonial Brazil as compared with colonial North America, differences reflected in sugarcane plantations, as opposed to tobacco and cotton plantations. Next the differences in migratory patterns must be observed: large numbers of homesteaders and yeomen from overpopulated England, landowners and adventurers from underpopulated

Portugal. There is a more nearly balanced sex ratio among the English colonists; a markedly unbalanced one among the Portuguese. It is noted that miscegenation with African slaves occurs in both cases but with different treatment of the mulatto offspring. The Brazilians, lacking homesteaders ("poor whites"), assign the mixed types to cattle herding, local nonexport agriculture, and other services and productive tasks essential to the support of the sugar plantations; the Americans fill the analogous roles with the marginal whites, with the consequence that the mulatto in the South is either kept in slavery or expelled northward; in Brazil, the mulatto and freed slave colonize the interior; moreover, the demographic balance between the races works for the Negro and mulatto in Brazil, and against them in the United States: 3 to 1 versus 1 to 3 in 1820. Sugarcane, the basis of slavery in Brazil, experienced a long decline in the world market; cotton, the basis of the nineteenth-century slave system in the United States, was the world's most lucrative export crop when the northern industrial interests challenged the political hegemony of the southern slavocracy. The United States slaves were declared free (and only in the enemy slave states!) during the height of the most ferocious war in history. This was done in order to encourage uprisings in the South and to gain conscripts for the Union Army. Brazil's slaves were freed by an Imperial decree at a moment when the entire slave economy was in its senility and when there were millions of ex-slaves and racially mixed persons scattered throughout the interior. In the United States, the freed slaves faced an implacable white majority, with whom they had to compete for land and jobs (in a nascent industrial economy). The United States whites invoked a rule of descent whereby mixed types were jammed into the Negro category, while Brazil had already evolved a system for establishing racial identity which did not depend on a descent rule. Hence, the United States acquired the conflict-ridden two-caste system in contrast to the continuous color spectrum of Brazilian multiracialism (*cf.* HARRIS 1964b).

This sketch, of course, fails to mention many additional variables which would also have to be considered were we actually to attempt a full-scale analysis. It should be obvious, however, that there is nothing simplistic about the economic, demographic, ecological, political, military, and cognitive data which would be necessary to confirm the hypotheses generated by the assumption that the pattern of inter-racial conflict in the United States is rooted in material conditions, rather than in Anglo-Saxon national character.

MARX AND ENGELS WARN AGAINST OVERSIMPLIFICATION

Some may object that Marx and Engels had no such complicated skein of interrelated phenomena in mind when they sought to reduce history to the question of the ownership of the means of production. But such an objection could only be sustained by ignorance of Marx's analyses of specific events, such as the French Revolution, or the American Civil War. It was no less an economic determinist than Engels who pointed out that there was a danger in forgetting the difference between the main principle of a strategy and its actual application to concrete cases. In a letter to Joseph Bloch, written in 1890, Engels said:

> Marx and I are ourselves partly to blame for the fact that younger writers sometimes lay more stress on the economic side than is due to it. We had to emphasize this main principle in opposition to our adversaries, who denied it, and we had not always the time, the place or the opportunity to allow the other elements involved in the interaction to come into their rights. But when it was a case of presenting a section of history, that is, of a practical application, the thing was different and there no error was possible. Unfortunately, however, it happens only too often that people think they have fully understood a theory and can apply it without more ado from the moment they have mastered its main principles, and those even not always correctly. And I cannot exempt many of the more recent "Marxists" from this reproach, for the most wonderful rubbish has been produced from this quarter too, [ENGELS in SELSAM and MARTEL 1963:205–6].

Far from propounding "simplistic" explanations in terms of a single factor, Marx and Engels repeatedly emphasized the need for considering the interaction between base and superstructure in accounting for any particular historical situation. They made it perfectly clear that the determinism which they saw extending from base to superstructure was not an absolute one-to-one effect. Engels used the term "ultimately" to qualify the selective influence of the mode of production on ideology, much as we would today seek to qualify any deterministic statement in probabilistic terms, *given a sufficient number of cases and in the long run:*

> According to the materialist conception of history the determining element in history is *ultimately* the production and reproduction in real life. More than this neither Marx nor I have ever asserted.

> If therefore somebody twists this into the statement that the economic element is the *only* determining one, he transforms it into a meaningless, abstract and absurd phrase. The economic situation is the basis, but the various elements of the superstructure—political forms of the class struggle and its consequences, constitutions established by the victorious class after a successful battle, etc.—forms of law—and then even the reflexes of all these actual struggles in the brains of the combatants: political, legal, philosophical theories, religious ideas and their further development into systems of dogma—also exercise their influence upon the course of the historical struggles and in many cases preponderate in determining their *form* [*ibid.*:204].

DID ANTHROPOLOGY DEVELOP INDEPENDENTLY OF MARXISM?

In assessing the historical significance of Marx' and Engels's materialist proposals, it will not suffice merely to enumerate and explicate the merits of the strategy against some absolute set of standards, such as logical coherence, ability to generate causal hypotheses, compatibility with scientific canons of intersubjectivity, verifiability, and operationalism. The merit of a strategy such as Darwin's principle of natural selection resides not merely in its record of more or less successful applications to specific problems, but rather in its promise and its performance relative to the promises and performances of rival strategies. In like manner, we must compare the cultural-materialist strategy with its nearest rivals. Such a comparison, while taking note of the peculiar liabilities of the dialectical version of cultural materialism, cannot fail to recognize the predicament in which Hegel, Comte, Bastian, Bachofen, and the other idealists were wallowing. Spencerism alone appeared a worthy alternative to the cultural-materialist strategy. But it is unnecessary for the purpose on hand to pursue the comparison of Spencerism and Marxism. I shall leave it to the reader to trade the reductionism of the one against the dialecticism of the other, the tautology of the "survival of the fittest" against the ambiguities of the "mode of production." It should require no further discussion, however, to establish the point that the strategy which Marx and Engels proposed was one which the emergent science of culture could ill afford to judge inferior or to discard without first putting to the test of ethnography and the comparative method. Yet we have seen how Lowie could omit the very name of Marx from the *History of Ethnological Theory*, while Alfred Meyer claims that cultural anthropology developed "entirely independent of Marxism." Was it possible that the European focus of Marx and Engels's writing offended or bored the late nineteenth- and early twentieth-century anthropologists by its failure to discuss primitive cultures? Was that the reason why anthropology could develop so gloriously free of Marxist problems? We might almost suppose the truth lay in this direction were it not for one awkward fact. This fact is called *Origin of the Family, Private Property and the State.*

MORGAN'S EFFECT ON MARX AND ENGELS

Marx and Engels read omnivorously over a vast field. Their attention was drawn to Morgan's *Ancient Society* shortly after its publication, and Marx at once recognized the need of revising his own description of prehistoric evolution in the light of Morgan's superior knowledge of primitive institutions. While making an extensive abstract of Morgan's work, Marx expressed the intention of relating Morgan's discoveries to the materialist interpretation of history. He did not live to complete this task, but Engels, working from Marx's notes, brought it to completion in 1884.

Ancient Society was a work of supreme importance to Marx and Engels because it opened their eyes to the complexity of primitive cultures and to the inadequacies of their own dabbling in this area. Morgan, with his firsthand experience of American Indian tribes, was obviously better qualified than any of his European rivals. Indeed, Engels (1954a:47) appears, like many other library scholars, to have been somewhat overawed by anthropological fieldwork, apparently believing that Morgan "had spent the greater part of his life among the Iroquois." Engels's opening sentence declares: "Morgan was the first person with expert knowledge to attempt to introduce a definite order into the prehistory of man." Well over half of Engels's book consists of a summary paraphrase of *Ancient Society.* Such new materials as occur are based on Engels's own well-credentialed knowledge of Greco-Roman and European history. The important point here is that as far as primitive culture is concerned, Marx and Engels bought Morgan lock, stock, and barrel. Morgan's scheme, its tri-part periodization, its evolution from sexual communism to monogamy, from gens to state, from matrilineality to patrilineality, became the standard source of ethnological enlightenment for Marxists and communists throughout the world—a state of affairs which lasted well into the second quarter of the present century (*cf.* TOLSTOY 1952).

Morgan's effect on Engels was perhaps greater than Marx had intended. It appeared much later, to Stalinist theoreticians at least, that Engels had compromised Marxism by the attempt to reconcile Morgan's prehistoric scheme with the principle that the mode of production determines history. For in his "Preface," Engels declared that "according to the materialistic conception, the determining factor in history is the production and reproduction of immediate life," a twofold process consisting of the "production of the means of subsistence, of food, clothing and shelter and the tools requisite therefore" and of "the production of human beings themselves, the propagation of the species" (1954a:8). The reason for this startling innovation is to be found in the previously discussed nonconformities between Morgan's main techno-economic sequence and the evolution of the family and gens. Thus Engels was able to provide a cultural-materialist explanation of the origin of the nuclear family, incest taboos, and clan exogamy, only by subscribing to Morgan's Darwinian hypothesis concerning the deleterious effects of inbreeding. On this point Engels quoted directly from *Ancient Society:*

> In this ever widening exclusion of blood relatives from marriage, natural selection also continues to have its effect. In Morgan's words, marriage between non-consanguineous gentes "tended to create a more vigorous stock physically and mentally. When two advancing tribes are blended into one people . . . the new skull and brain would widen and lengthen to the sum of the capabilities of both" [*ibid.*:78].

Even more indicative of Engels's difficulty in providing a consistent cultural-materialist version of prehistory is his adoption of Morgan and Bachofen's explanation of the origin of monogamy. In a passage which proves that even the world's number two Marxist could have bourgeois prejudices about sex, Engels decides that primitive sexual communism came to an end because in effect the women enjoyed it less than the men:

> Bachofen is again absolutely right when he contends throughout that the transition from what he terms "hetaerism" or "*Sumpfzeugung*" to monogamy was brought about essentially by the women. The more the old traditional sexual relations lost their naive, primitive jungle character, as a result of the development of the economic conditions of life, that is, with the undermining of the old Communism and the growing density of the population, the more degrading and oppressive must they have appeared to the women; the more fervently must they have longed for the right to chastity, to temporary or permanent marriage with one

> man only, as a deliverance. This advance could not have originated from the men, if only for the reason that they have never—not even to the present day—dreamed of renouncing the pleasures of actual group marriage. Only after the transition to pairing marriage had been effected by the women could the men introduce strict monogamy—for the women only, of course [*ibid.*:87-88].

THE EFFECT OF MARX AND ENGELS ON THE INTERPRETATION OF MORGAN

But Marx and Engels were determined to find in Morgan independent corroboration of the materialist interpretation of history. Engels described Morgan as the man who

> rediscovered in America, in his own way, the materialist conception of history that had been discovered by Marx forty years ago, and in his comparison of barbarism and civilization was led by this conception to the same conclusions, in the main points, as Marx had arrived at [*ibid.*:7].

The substantial obstacles to such a conclusion have been discussed in the previous chapter. By omitting all reference to "germ thoughts" and by skillful editing, Engels succeeded in bringing forth a suitably materialistic Morgan. But it is Engels and not Morgan who presents the first clear-cut periodization of prehistory, based on the mode of production:

> Savagery—the period in which the appropriation of natural products, ready for use, predominated; the things produced by man were, in the main, instruments that facilitated this appropriation. Barbarism—the period in which knowledge of cattle breeding and land cultivation was acquired, in which methods of increasing the productivity of nature through human activity were learnt. Civilization—the period in which knowledge of the further working-up of natural products, of industry proper, and of art was acquired [*ibid.*:46].

The moral of this part of our story is not that Engels at Marx's instigation distorted Morgan's view of history. That is probably true, but it is insignificant. Moreover, the modifications which Engels introduced were on the whole quite sound and imparted to Morgan's scheme a logical coherence that it lacked in the original. The significant thing is that the cultural-materialist strategy had now, much for the worse rather than for the better, become wedded to an interpretation of primitive culture which was a by-product of a definitely non-materialist research strategy. For anthropologists, the viability of that strategy now became identified with the future of Morgan's scheme. With Morgan's scheme incorporated into Communist doctrine, the struggling science of anthropology crossed the threshold of the twentieth century with a clear mandate for its own survival and well-being: expose Morgan's scheme and destroy the method on which it was based. The anthropological attack against Morgan was to have these consequences: (1) the abandonment of the comparative method; (2) the rejection of the attempt to view history from a nomothetic standpoint; (3) postponement of actual tests of the cultural-materialist strategy during a forty-year interlude. Meyers would have been closer to the truth had he stated that cultural anthropology developed entirely in *reaction* to, instead of independently of, Marxism.

Historical Particularism: Boas

9

During the first half of the twentieth century, anthropology in the United States was characterized by a programmatic avoidance of theoretical syntheses. The basic research strategy for this period was formulated by Franz Boas, one of the most influential figures in the history of the social sciences. Boas was guided by a distinctive sense of inductive purity, which he transmitted to a generation of followers. It was a creed, however, which paradoxically denied its own existence. His students would admit only that Boas had trained them to pursue their varied interests mindful of the data, free of prejudice, and distrustful of all schemes. They explicitly denied that Boas was the center of a "school." His mission had been to rid anthropology of its amateurs and armchair specialists by making ethnographic research in the field the central experience and minimum attribute of professional status. With the passage of time, however, a definite central theme suggested in the label *historical particularism* has come to be associated with the Boasian period.

The perspective which we enjoy in these matters in no way diminishes the importance of Boas' contribution to the development of anthropology or of anthropological theory. It is true that the strategy of historical particularism required an almost total suspension of the normal dialectic between fact and theory. The causal processes, the trends, the long-range parallels were buried by an avalanche of negative cases. It is also true that the attempt to harden the fiber of ethnographic inquiry with higher standards of proof met with only limited success, and we shall have to take into account the notable instances in which Boas and his students abused the facts as others before and after have done. But the standards he proposed remain a permanent legacy.

Those who aver that Boas retarded the progress of anthropology as a science make improper allowance for the cultural forces that lay behind the historical particularist reform. There were culturally determined ideological limits within which anthropological theory was largely constrained. Transgressors left no heritage within anthropology of which we are today aware. Boas and his first generation of students were obliged to build professional, university-based anthropology practically from the ground up. They were remarkably successful despite the many obstacles to be overcome. The culturally prescribed limits were not so narrow and well-defined that options did not exist. We have merely to consider the fate of anthropology within the Soviet Union, Germany, and Italy during the same period to realize that if historical particularism was essentially negative and theoretically sterile, it nonetheless avoided the worst pitfalls of its times.

The list of famous and influential anthropologists who were trained by Boas testifies to his central importance in the establishment of the discipline: Alfred Kroeber, Robert Lowie, Fay-Cooper Cole, Edwin Sapir, Melville Herskovits, Alexander Goldenweiser, Alexander Lesser, Paul Radin, Clark Wissler, Leslie Spier, J. Alden Mason, E. Adamson Hoebel, Ruth Benedict, Margaret Mead, Ruth Bunzel, Jules Henry, M. F. Ashley Montagu, Frank Speck. These students in turn set forth the main lines of development of anthropological research and instruction at crucial installations throughout the country. For example, Kroeber and Lowie at Berkeley; Cole and Sapir at Chicago; and Herskovits at Northwestern. Boas himself maintained a patriarch's control over anthropology at Columbia from 1896 to his death in 1941. In addition, he was at the center of critical formative events, such as the modernizing of the *American Anthropologist* in 1898, the founding of the American Anthropological Association in 1900, the revitalization of the American Ethnological Society in the same year, and the founding of the American Folk-Lore Society in 1888.

Boas' accomplishments as a teacher, administrator, researcher, founder and president of societies, editor, lecturer, and traveler are exhausting to behold. To anyone who has ever worried about publishing or perishing, the fact that all of this activity was accompanied by the publication of a torrent of books and articles is well-nigh terrifying. In addition to half a dozen books, Boas published over 700 articles (LESSER 1968:26). Boas' stature increases with each passing year, as we find in his work the measure of our own shortcomings. Yet in order to achieve an understanding of twentieth-century anthropology, we must set aside the image of Boas as father, hero, and "guru" and turn our attention to the task of locating his contribution to theory within the patterns of an age. That is, we must rise above personalities and adopt a cultural perspective. In so doing, we render homage through objective criticism even more than through eulogies, which impair our understanding of Boas and of ourselves as well.

BOAS' IMAGE

Margaret Mead (1959b:31) has said, "Characteristically, there are no methods named after Boas, just as there is no Boas school. . . ." During an exchange with the South African critic A. W. Hoérnle (1933), Kroeber (1935:540) also expressed his belief that "there is no 'Boas school' and never has been." Many of Boas' students seem to have shared this view of themselves; and in some ways this belief in itself constituted the central feature of the Boasian position. According to Kroeber, partisan and propagandistic programs in the social sciences were a sign of immaturity. There were no schools in physics, he argued, only physicists doing their job with every available scientific technique. With Boas, anthropology had come of age; under his influence there was no "singling out of any one method—psychologic, sociologic, diffusionist, functional, or Kulturkreis—as constituting a king's highway superior to others" (*ibid.*). For Margaret Mead, Boas was "the man who made anthropology into a science" (1959b: 35).

The image of Boas which had the greatest appeal to his students was that of a professional scientist who had raised anthropological research methods and standards of proof to a level with which even a physicist would feel comfortable. In this regard, the special nature of Boas' doctorate has been emphasized repeatedly by his students. His principal thesis was submitted at the University of Kiel in 1881, and it was concerned with the color of sea water. Previously he had studied physics and geography at Heidelberg and Bonn, and he was also well trained in mathematics. For Kroeber, this background provides the key to the understanding of Boas' role:

> From physics Boas brought into anthropology a sense of definiteness of problem, of exact rigor of method, and of highly critical objectivity. These qualities have remained with him unimpaired, and his imparting them to anthropology remains his fundamental and unshakable contribution to our discipline [KROEBER 1935:540].

For Goldenweiser, Boas was anthropology's "culture-hero." Like the heroes of primitive myths who give the essentials of life to man, it was Boas who bestowed the gift of science upon anthropology:

> Indian mythologies tell of culture-heroes, supernatural animals or birds who bestow culture upon man, teach him the arts and crafts, introduce songs and ceremonies. To anthropology in this country Franz Boas, the "Man," came as such a culture-hero. Brought up in the atmosphere and methods of the natural sciences and steeped in the scholarly ideals of pre-war Germany, he bestowed upon American anthropology that clarification of issues and stiffening of scientific fiber which it stood so sorely in need of [GOLDENWEISER 1941:153].

According to Ruth Benedict (1943:61), "Boas found anthropology a collection of wild guesses and a happy hunting ground for the romantic lover of primitive things; he left it a discipline in which theories could be tested" (quoted in WHITE 1963:67). Lowie, as we shall see in greater detail later on, identified Boas with physicist-philosopher Ernst Mach and associated both of them with the development of "higher standards of proof" and the perfection of the scientific method.

THE STANDARDS OF BOAS' CONTEMPORARIES

There is considerable truth in this portrait. Boas was a veritable fortress of scientific sobriety in comparison with most of his contemporaries. Although his cautious approach to generalization appears in retrospect overdone and self-defeating, there was nothing illusory about the shoddy standards of his contemporaries. Lacking a firm foundation in the universities, anthropological subjects were still an easy prey for imaginative amateurs. Consider, for example, this 1893 description of chimpanzee behavior from the pages of the *American Anthropologist:*

> The cleared spaces . . . are used by the chimpanzees to build immense bonfires of dried wood. . . . When the pile is completed one of the chimpanzees begins to blow at the pile as if blowing the fire. He is immediately joined by others, and, eventually by the whole company, and the blowing is kept up until their tongues hang from their mouths, when they sit around on their haunches with their elbows on their knees and holding up their hands to the imaginary blaze. In wet weather they frequently sit in this way for hours together [BUTTEKOFER 1893:337].

It must be kept in mind that many of Boas' contemporaries were temperamentally unsuited to scientific discipline. It was an age in which the license to generalize on the basis of fragmentary evidence was claimed by second- and third-rate people. Lester Ward, one of the founders of American sociology, is a case in point. Reviewing a book on the origin of life, he could let himself go in the following manner, seemingly without qualms:

> The book is purely theoretical, and no facts whatever are adduced. This is not a criticism of the book. In fact it is one of the beauties of it. Anyone who reads the book can see that the author's head is full of facts and that all he was trying to do was to reason from a store of facts to certain conclusions. Those who speak disrespectfully of this method are often unable to make any use of their facts, however many they possess [WARD 1904:151].

Since cultural theory in the United States was dominated by a mixture of Spencer's and Morgan's evolutionism, it was to be expected that the prevalent debauchery of method frequently involved sins committed in the name of evolutionary reconstruction. William McGee, for example, first president of the American Anthropological Association, was often guilty of naïve stage-scheming replete with jingoistic Spencerian celebrations of America's evolutionary success:

> Just as patriarchy gives way to hierarchy, and hierarchy to absolute monarchy, so limited monarchy is giving way to democracy or republicanism; already the foremost nation of the earth is a republic, and all other civilized nations are either republican or undergoing changes in the direction of republicanism. So according to the experience of the ages, the best nation is a republican one, and the best citizen is the individual adapted to life under republican conditions [MC GEE 1894:353].

McGee was an inexhaustible mine of every error of substance and theory that it was possible to commit on the basis of the most vulgar prejudices masquerading as scientific expertise. In seeking to understand Boas' renaissancelike involvement with all four fields of anthropology, we must bear in mind that people of McGee's ilk had opinions about everything, most of them so blatantly wrong as to create a virtual vacuum once they were challenged and assigned to their proper oblivion. McGee's thoughts on the connection between race and language are sobering in the extreme. Here he seeks to explain "the ascendancy of the simple, tangible, and definite tongue and writing of the Anglo-Saxon":

> Possibly the Anglo-Saxon blood is more potent than that of other races; but it is to be remembered that the Anglo-Saxon language is the simplest, the most perfectly and simply symbolic that the world has ever seen; and that by means of it the Anglo-Saxon saves his vitality for conquest instead of wasting it under the Juggernaut of a cumbrous mechanism for conveyance of thought [MC GEE 1895a:281].

McGee's confusion of race, language, and culture was representative of learned opinion both within anthropology and in Western society in general. The debasement of contemporary primitive peoples to the level of Anthropoidea was, as we have seen, an important expression of Euro-American imperialism. McGee's version is especially obnoxious: "The savage stands strikingly close to sub-human species in every aspect of mentality as well as in bodily habits and bodily structure" (MC GEE 1901:13). John W. Powell, the founder of the American Bureau of Ethnology (in 1879), was another influential but distressingly undisciplined dabbler in anthropological evolutionism. Like many of his contemporaries, Powell could dash off a presidential address on the history of mankind with a comprehensive finality that even Turgot and Condorcet could not have surpassed. In one colossal synthesis, he arranged the stages of evolution into four grades: savagery, barbarism, monarchy, and democracy. Then to each of these grades he assigned specific social institutions, such as the family to savagery, the gentes to barbarism, and so forth. In music, the stages were rhythm, melody, harmony, symphony; in aesthetics: dance, sacrifice, ceremony, histrionic art; in technology: hunting, agriculture, artisanry, machinery (POWELL 1899).

One of the most influential anthropologists among Boas' contemporaries was Daniel G. Brinton. In his presidential address before the American Association for the Advancement of Science, Brinton (1896:12) reaffirmed the standard Spencerian position: "The black, the brown and the red races differ anatomically so much from the white, especially in their splanchnic organs, that even with equal cerebral capacity, they could never rival its results by equal efforts."

Brinton is especially important for an understanding of Boas' (1896b) famous critique of the comparative method. It was Brinton more than Morgan or Tylor who was closest to mind when Boas pointed out that insufficient caution was being exercised in the reconstruction of universal parallel sequences. For Brinton had spoken of "the nigh absolute uniformity of man's thoughts and actions, his aims and methods, when in the same degree of development, no matter where he is or in what epoch" (BRINTON 1896:12).

It is interesting to note that Leslie White (1963:43) has misrepresented Boas' reaction to Brinton by associating Brinton's use of the comparative method with that of Morgan and Tylor. Brinton, however, was prepared to go far beyond Morgan and Tylor in regarding "the modes of thought and feeling" of contemporary nations of "low culture" as representative of extinct tribes at "about the same stage of culture." Indeed, in his presidential address to the American Association for the Advancement of Science, Brinton attacked Morgan and Tylor for placing too great an emphasis upon diffusion as the explanation of transcultural similarities. Instead of identifying the target of Brinton's remarks as Morgan and Tylor, White has Brinton criticizing some vaguely defined group of "comparative mythologists and folk-lorists of the old school" who had not "caught up with the development of ethnologic science" (WHITE 1963:43). Although Brinton did not refer to Morgan and Tylor by name, it is quite clear that they are the intended targets:

> The anthropologist of today who, like a late-distinguished scholar among ourselves, would claim that because the rather complex social system of the Iroquois had a close parallel among the Munda tribes of the Punjab, therefore, the ancestors of each must have come from a common culture center; or, who, like an eminent living English ethnologist, sees a proof of Asiatic relations in American culture because the Aztec game of *patolli* is like the East Indian game of *parchesi*,—such an anthropologist, I say, may have contributed ably to his science in the past, but he does not know where it stands today [BRINTON 1896:9].

That is, Morgan and Tylor were accused of being overly conservative with respect to parallelisms, and Boas, in responding to Brinton, was implicitly defending Morgan and Tylor against an application of the comparative method which they, too, would have found unacceptable. Since this obviously would not be compatible with the picture of Boas as an archreactionary, White fails to mention who it is that Brinton considers to be out of date.

In contrast with many of his American colleagues at the turn of the century, Boas casts an heroic shadow. His natural gifts, superior education, and European cosmopolitan advantages make people such as McGee, Brinton, and even Powell look like hayseeds and bumpkins. But it is misleading to picture him as the high god-creator of scientific anthropology. There were many before him who urged and achieved field research as the basis for ethnology. The scientific description of American Indian cultures was certainly already well advanced when Boas arrived at the scene. As far back as the 1830's, Henry Schoolcraft, one of the founders of the American Ethnological Society, had begun the task of sympathetically recording the mental realities of Indian groups based on extensive firsthand exposure. (His wife was of Ojibwa descent.) Morgan's contact with the Iroquois and his subsequent westward journeys obviously removed him from his armchair for respectably prolonged periods. Both W. H. Holmes and Otis T. Mason acquired an excellent firsthand knowledge of aboriginal technology, and Alice Fletcher and James Mooney were pioneer ethnographers of high competence (*cf.* HELM 1966). What was unique in Boas' case was not the emphasis on field research and collection of facts, but his insistence that these activities were more critical, more prestigious, and more scientific than theory-making on any scale, grand or small.

Unprecedented also was the precise quality of Boas' devotion to the collection of facts. There is a strong puritan element in his outlook. For him, science was very much a sacred enterprise. Those who rushed to conclusions without proper attention to facts were in effect desecrating a temple. His eulogy of physiologist Rudolf Virchow, another product of nineteenth-century German empiricism, may be taken as representative of his own outlook:

> The sound progress of science requires of us to be clear at every moment, what elements in the system of science are hypothetical and what are the limits of that knowledge which is obtained by exact observation . . . many an impetuous student has felt his [Virchow's] quiet and cautious criticism as an obstacle to progress. On this account he has suffered many hostile attacks—until generally the progress of research showed that the cautious master was right in rejecting the far-reaching conclusion based on imperfect evidence. There are but few students who possess that cold

> enthusiasm for truth that enables them to be always clearly conscious of the sharp line between attractive theory and the observation that has been secured by hard and earnest work [BOAS 1902:443, quoted in KLUCKHOHN and PRUFER 1959:23].

CRITIQUE OF THE COMPARATIVE METHOD

What then was Boas' reaction to the widespread conviction concerning the uniformity, even "monotony," of evolutionary change? The fundamental issue to which he addressed himself in "The Limitations of the Comparative Method" was the problem of separating instances of convergent from instances of parallel evolution. He did not doubt that there were many remarkable resemblances of culture traits that could *not* be explained by diffusion. But the fact that such phenomena as shamanism, the concept of a future life, the use of the bow, geometric designs, masks, and many other items are widely distributed does not establish the uniformity of history. Conclusions concerning whether evolutionary uniformities, that is, parallel evolutionary sequences, have occurred or not must be held in abeyance until data of a certain sort are collected. The data in question are the facts of the historical sequences by which in particular local areas the observed phenomena have come into existence:

> The fact that many fundamental features of culture are universal, or at least occur in many isolated places, interpreted by the assumption that the same features must always have developed from the same causes, leads to the conclusion that there is one grand system according to which mankind has developed everywhere; that all the occurring variations are no more than minor details in this grand uniform evolution. It is clear that this theory has for its logical basis the assumption that the same phenomena are always due to the same causes [BOAS 1948:275; orig. 1896b].

This assumption, however, argues Boas, is patently false in a large number of concrete instances. Clans, for example, seem to have arisen among the Navaho by the fusion of separate groups, but among the Northwest tribes, they resulted from village fission. Geometric designs did not necessarily result, as Hjalmar Stolpe (1891) and Alfred Haddon (1895) had proposed, from gradual conventionalization of realistic representations, but rather from any of "four different lines of development and from an infinite number of starting points." Again, masks are sometimes used as disguises, so that harmful spirits will not recognize the wearer; elsewhere they are worn to frighten off people and spirits, and in still other contexts, they are worn to commemorate a deceased relative. It seems unlikely, therefore, that the same causal sequence can have accounted everywhere for the development of these phenomena.

> Therefore we must also consider all the ingenious attempts at constructions of a grand system of the evolution of society as of very doubtful value, unless at the same time proof is given that the same phenomena must always have had the same origin. Until this is done, the presumption is always in favor of a variety of courses which historical growth may have taken [BOAS 1948:275].

In emphasizing the variety of history, Boas had obviously taken a position against evolutionary schemes which embraced all of mankind in a single developmental formula. But a contempt for the vogue of logically fabricated worldwide parallelisms was fully merited in the context of the age. This does not mean that Boas had consciously set himself the task of championing the proposition that there were no regularities in history, but rather that he felt that the amount of regularity had been grossly overestimated. Appalled by the free-floating speculation, which his contemporaries had assumed to be their professional prerogative, Boas struggled to improve the balance. In the long run, there was a need for both the particularist and generalist approaches. But priority for the moment must be given to the study of specific sequences in delimited areas.

> The comparative method and the historical method, if I may use these terms, have been struggling for supremacy for a long time, but we may hope that each will soon find its appropriate place and function. . . . The comparative method, notwithstanding all that has been said and written in its praise, has been remarkably barren of definite results, and I believe it will not become fruitful until we renounce the vain endeavor to construct a uniform systematic history of the evolution of culture, and until we begin to make our comparisons on the broader and sounder basis which I ventured to outline. Up to this time we have too much reveled in more or less ingenious vagaries. The solid work is still all before us [*ibid.*:280].

WAS BOAS AN ANTIEVOLUTIONIST?

It was to be expected that the abuse of scholarly standards would be found among those whose ignorance and incompetence were buoyed up by the prevailing ideological dogma, which happened to be Spencerian evolutionism. When alternative schemes came to the fore, equally ambitious in scope and vapid in content but having nothing to do with evolutionism, Boas reacted with comparable vigor.

Boas' early interest in mythology and folklore was based upon the conviction that these materials would be useful in the attempt to distinguish independently invented from diffused items. Thus, his study of the diffusion of the North American raven myth provided the occasion for a critique of facile assumptions about parallel evolution. Yet Boas made it clear that he was not about to take up the cause of dogmatic "antievolutionism." His paramount interest was the achievement of high standards of scholarship:

> If we want to make progress on the desired line, we must insist upon critical methods, based not on generalities but on each individual case. In many cases, the final decision will be in favor of independent origin; in others in favor of dissemination [*ibid.*:435; orig. 1896a].

Boas tried to steer this middle course throughout his career. When he reviewed Leo Frobenius, one of the forerunners of the German diffusionist school, he commented: "By following the methods presented in this book, anything and everything can be proved. It is fiction, not science" (BOAS 1899b:755). To Fritz Graebner, chief architect of the German diffusionist methodology, he was more respectful, but no less critical. Independent invention, parallel evolution, and convergence are all upheld as commonplace facts of culture. Although Boas agreed with Graebner that diffusion is more common than independent invention, this was no license for assigning diffusionary explanations in the absence of practical geographical connections. Premature generalization is once again the worst error:

> I rather repeat once more the warning that I have given again and again for twenty years: rather to be overcautious in admitting transmission as the cause of analogies in cases of the sporadic occurrence of similar phenomena, than to operate with the concept of lost links of a chain of cultural intercourse [1948:303; orig. 1911].

METHODOLOGICAL PURITANISM

Boas seldom permitted himself the luxury of assuming that he himself had been able to meet his own standards. It was if the orgy of evolutionary and diffusionist speculation had nauseated him so that he could never again feel at ease in the presence of a generalization. This facet of Boas' outlook deserves the emphasis which Kroeber, Lowie, Sapir, Bunzel, and many others have insisted on giving it, despite the compilation by Leslie White (1963:41ff.) of a number of instances in which Boas himself reached speculative conclusions. There is no doubt that Boas' attempts to reconstruct the history of various American Indian groups are frequently based on thin evidence. Some of these speculative conclusions must be reckoned with in assessing Boas' influence upon the development of theory, and we shall consider them later on. But it seems to me that White overemphasizes these lapses. After all, as White and many other critics have pointed out, the chief objection to Boas' approach is that it led to a vast collection of primary materials—texts and descriptions in which practically no attempt was made to orient the reader with respect to even short-range and tentative generalizations. According to Helen Codere (1959:61), Boas published more than 10,000 pages on the Northwest Coast alone; and, as White has taken pains to point out, most of this went "without commentary, without the bare information that would be needed to render it intelligible to the reader" (WHITE 1963:55). In this ocean of facts, the speculations to which White objects are mere outcroppings, whose disappearance Boas would probably have accepted with perfect equanimity.

In comparison with his contemporaries, Boas was faithful to his inductive principles. That he did not inaugurate the reign of absolute truth goes without saying. But he surpassed most anthropologists before or since in his concern to present to others the evidence from which ethnographic statements could be constructed. Let us admit that Boas' empiricism involved standards which even he could not maintain. Certainly his students were destined to fall even shorter of the mark and, in some instances, to restore a debauchery of method comparable to that of Brinton, Powell, and McGee. Let us also admit, for reasons which I shall make plain in a moment, that Boas' basic philosophy of science involved errors which are in the long run inimical to the progress of social science. There still results no basis for the assertion that Boas retarded the development of anthropology by fifty years (*cf.* RAY 1955:140). Given the condition of anthropology at the end of the nineteenth century, the one great reformatory movement that was necessary (but not sufficient) to the further progress of the science of culture was precisely that which Boas initiated.

REJECTION OF PHYSICALISM

Recognition of Boas' salutary effect in clearing out the amateurs and charlatans, with their snake-oil evolutionary formula, in no way obliges us to overlook the negative influences that emanated from other facets of his approach. From the outset, Boas was involved in a philosophical paradox from which he never escaped, but which in the history of anthropology is of far greater significance than his methodological puritanism. The nub of this dilemma was that Boas believed that the patient accumulation of historical data would lead automatically to the improvement of anthropological theory. Although by his own admission he was temperamentally much more in sympathy with the collection of historical facts, he succeeded in convincing himself and his students that generalizing interests could not possibly suffer from a program of historical reconstruction. He never conceded that a choice must be made between history and science; rather he conceived of science as having historical and generalizing components, formally disallowing any invidious comparison between them. Regardless of his attempt to maintain an interest in the problem of formulating lawful principles, it is obvious from the research strategy he followed throughout his career that he was perfectly content to continue his particularist studies in complete independence of their nomothetic payoff. It is thus historically more correct to reverse the emphasis that his students give to his background in physics. Far from applying a physicalistic model to the study of sociocultural phenomena, Boas reacted against such a model and was much more concerned with showing how it needed to be supplemented in the special circumstances of the so-called *Geisteswissenschaften* or human sciences.

The published evidence for this reaction dates back to 1887. Having returned from a field trip among the Eskimo, which he undertook as a geographer, Boas sought to define the special qualities of geography as a discipline. "If we would maintain [geography's] independence," he argued, "we must prove that there exists another object for science besides the deduction (*sic*) of laws from phenomena" (1948:641; orig. 1887a). This other aim, argues Boas, is that which characterizes the difference between the descriptive or historical and physicalist methods. In the descriptive sciences, the single fact, the single phenomenon, is sufficiently compelling in itself.

"The object of the historian is . . . the study of the facts . . . [he] dwells admiringly on the character of his heroes. He takes the most lively interest in the persons and nations he treats of, but is unwilling to consider them as subject to stringent laws" (*ibid.*:642). Although the physicalists do not deny the importance of every phenomenon, "they do not consider it worthy of study for its own sake." The descriptive scientist, on the other hand, holds to the phenomenon which is the object of his study, may it occupy a high or a low rank in the system of physical sciences, and lovingly tries to penetrate into its secrets until every feature is plain and clear. This occupation with the object of his affection affords him a delight not inferior to that which the physicist enjoys in his systematical arrangement of the world [*ibid.*:645].

REJECTION OF MATERIALISM

It has now been established that this attempt to define the difference between an historical and a physicalist approach to knowledge expressed a fundamental shift in Boas' *Weltanschauung* and was part of the process which led him away from physics to anthropology. This shift took place during the decade 1878–88, or from his twentieth to his thirtieth year. During this period Boas gradually gave up the philosophical premises associated with the mechanistic syntheses of mid-century physics, chemistry, and biology. Under the influence of a widespread neo-Kantian idealist movement, Boas turned away from the materialism with which he had approached his earlier study of physics. The trajectory of his intellectual growth moved him steadily along the path from physics to geography to ethnography. Thanks to George Stocking's research on Boas' correspondence, we may now learn about this transition in Boas' own words, addressed to his American uncle, Abraham Jacobi, on April 10, 1882:

> The objectives of my studies shifted quite a bit during my university years. While in the beginning my intention was to regard mathematics and physics as the final goal, I was led through the study of the natural sciences to other questions which prompted me also to take up geography, and this subject captured my interest to such an extent that I finally chose it as my major study. However, the direction of my work and study was strongly influenced by my training in natural sciences, especially physics. In the course of time I became convinced that my previous materialistic *Weltanschauung*—for a physicist a very understandable one—was untenable, and I gained thus a new standpoint which revealed to me the importance of studying the interaction between the organic and the inorganic, above all between the life of a people and their physical environment [quoted in STOCKING 1965a:55].

From this awakening, Boas goes on to say, came the definition of what he wished to do for the rest of his life:

> Thus arose my plan to regard as my life's task the [following] investigation: How far may we consider the phenomena of organic

> life, and especially those of the psychic life, from a mechanistic point of view, and what conclusions can be drawn from such a consideration [*ibid.*]?

GEOGRAPHICAL AND PSYCHOLOGICAL INTERESTS COMBINED

Upon the threshold of his voyage to Baffin Island to study the Eskimo, Boas confided that the discipline to which he intended to devote himself was not geography, but rather "psychophysics." During the year of his military service (1882–83), he published six programmatic articles on this subject. But in order to receive sponsorship for his Baffin Island expedition, he felt it was necessary to restrict his research to physical and human geography. He therefore busied himself with the orthodox geographical proposal of "studying the dependence of the migration of present-day Eskimo on the configuration and physical conditions of the land" (*ibid.*:57). In the following year, just before his departure for Baffin Island, he repeated his interest in "physiological and psychological mechanisms" and lamented his inability to go at once to the heart of his life plan:

> From the pure scientific standpoint, I would begin the matter with psychophysics, and I have today the exact outline of a book on the subject which (I hope!) I may write sometime later. . . . But from the practical viewpoint I must willy-nilly begin with geography, since that is the science that I have thoroughly learned [*ibid.*:55].

Boas did his best to work out a compromise between the geographical and the psychophysical. This compromise was embodied in the proposal to study "the dependence of the knowledge of the land area of wandering of the peoples on the configuration of the land," that is, in modern idiom, the relationship between a people's understanding of their habitat's geography and their patterns of movement across the land.

> I am going now primarily to collect material that will give me points of view for more general studies. The general study will be about the knowledge peoples have of the local geography, which will be followed by a psychological study about the causes for the limitation of the spreading of peoples. From here I wish to gain the starting point for the general questions which psychophysics will give me possibly more rapidly and just as surely. Of course on my trip I must pursue many other goals, make geographical maps,

> found botanical and zoological collections, make ethnographical and anthropological investigations, etc., but I shall keep my chief aim always in mind [*ibid.*].

It should be noted that Boas actually did devote a portion of his work among the Eskimo to the comparison of the Eskimo's knowledge of the area with cartographic realities. The latter, being unknown, involved him in thousands of miles of mapping expeditions. To obtain an understanding of the Eskimo's point of view, he solicited numerous drawings, which are of continuing interest.

REJECTION OF GEOGRAPHICAL DETERMINISM

During the year 1882–83, Boas made the acquaintance of Adolf Bastian and Rudolf Virchow, upon whom his hopes for an appointment at the University of Berlin were pinned (HERSKOVITS 1957:114). Both of them, Bastian with his belief in universal germ thoughts and Virchow with his strong physiological interests, were concerned with regularities and processes. Earlier, at the University of Kiel, it had been the geographer Theobald Fischer with whom Boas had worked most intimately. (It is even possible that when Boas went from Bonn to Kiel, it was to accompany Fischer, who was making the same move [KLUCKHOHN and PRUFER 1959:9].) Fischer, in turn, was a disciple of the geographer Karl Ritter, who was explicitly devoted to the task of formulating the laws of migrations and cultural evolution. In a letter from Fischer to Boas, we learn that Boas has been reading Buckle, the archexponent of geographical determinism, and that, with some cautions, this was all to the good: "That you occupy yourself with Buckle is very desirable, but you must not be taken completely into his tow; he has been called, not unjustly, an 'ultra-Ritterian'" (*ibid.*:57). Although Fischer was somewhat less committed than Ritter to a geographical-determinist position, there can be no doubt that Boas planned his trip to Baffin Island in conformity with a strong presumption in favor of the primacy of geographical factors in the life of the Eskimo. In an earlier letter to his uncle, explaining his plans for the expedition, Boas described himself as having

> in mind a geographical investigation which, though it does not fit into my program of study, should give me materials for a thesis when I try for the post of University lecturer. That is, I am making

> studies of the Eskimo and their knowledge of the land they inhabit, as well as of the entire region, in the hope of demonstrating a certain relationship between the number of people in a tribe, the distribution of food, and the . . . [quoted in HERSKOVITS 1957:113. Complete sentence could not be deciphered].

The principal publication resulting from Boas' expedition to Baffin Island was *The Central Eskimo* (1888), a lucid account of life in the arctic which stressed the interrelationship between geographical and cultural factors. Henceforth, however, Boas never again gave prominence to a culture's geographic milieu. As Kroeber (1935:543) observed, the Eskimo study was "the only one in which the geographic setting is given other than perfunctory or minimal consideration." It is thus clear that in shifting over from geography to ethnography, Boas was moving away from a belief in geographical determinism. The Eskimo experience appears to have been critical in this conversion. According to Gladys Reichard (quoted in HERSKOVITS 1957: 115):

> His life with the Eskimo made him change radically his predisposition to assign geographic influence as primary to the development of culture which he went with after Ratzel's influence. In other words, he was taught to realize the significance of culture by the Eskimo, and the environment seemed to him to be at least secondary. He concluded that they did things in spite of rather than because of the environment. . . .

George Stocking (1965a:64) has recently attempted to refute the notion that Boas' first field trip was such a "conversion experience." This may be true as far as the overall drift of Boas toward mentalism and neo-Kantianism is concerned, but Boas himself seemed to believe that the Eskimo trip was decisive for his rejection of geographical determinism.

> If in later writings I did not stress geographical conditions the reason must be sought in an exaggerated belief in the importance of geographical determinants with which I started on my expedition in 1883–84 and the thorough disillusionment in regard to their significance as creative elements in cultural life. I shall always continue to consider them as relevant in limiting and modifying existing cultures, but it so happened that in my later field work this question has never come to the fore as particularly enlightening [BOAS 1948:306; orig. 1935].

Despite this reaction, Boas' initial publications on the Eskimo (BOAS 1884–85) were couched in the idiom of geographical determinism. According to Stocking, this proves the tendency of Boas' epigoni to exaggerate the importance of the Eskimo experience "as the unconscious archetype of their own ritual initiations into the culture of anthropology" (1965a:58). Ruth Benedict, Melville Herskovits, and Gladys Reichard were obviously wrong about what the conversion was all about, but something quite drastic certainly did happen on that trip. To overlook it or minimize it leads to a wholly false view of the main thrust of the Boasian program. It would take nothing short of a conversion experience for Boas to have regarded "geographical" issues as relatively unimportant in his Northwest Coast studies. As for the delayed effect in terms of publication, it is probably related to the fact that he was looking for a job back in Berlin as a geographer.

THE INFLUENCE OF THE NEO-KANTIAN MOVEMENT

It is impossible to understand the the significance of Boas' progress through the stages of physics, geography, and psychophysics to ethnology without some reference, however brief, to the main philosophical currents in nineteenth-century Germany. In an age characterized by great advances in the laboratory sciences, the grandiose speculative metaphysics propounded by Hegel and his followers fell into disrepute. As an alternative to materialism, a return was made to the teachings of Kant. The philosophy of Kant was congenial to the times precisely because it embodied a compromise between idealism and materialism. The essence of external "things-in-themselves" was neither mind nor matter, but simply unknowable. To the extent that knowledge is at all possible, it must depend on sense impressions. These, however, are constrained by the fundamental a priori categories of mind, such as a moral sense and concepts of space and time. Knowledge is thus an interactive product in which mind and reality collaborate. It is possible to construe this formula two ways: first, as a justification for a strong empiricist approach through sense data; or, second, as the justification for emphasizing the contribution that the observing mind makes to the perception of the data. Initially the neo-Kantian movement stressed the former; by the end of the century, however, it was the influence of mind that was being stressed, and in effect, the same path that had led from Kant to Hegel had to be trod once again. The various stages of Boas' progress toward anthropology mirror this trend of Kantian styles. Fechner's psychophysics, which Boas at one point saw as his lifework, was itself nothing more than an attempt to provide a laboratory basis for Kant's ideas. As Wolfgang Metzger (1965:111) notes, "Fechner's original aim was to prove scientifically some assumption about the relations between body and soul that he had derived from [Kant's] philosophy."

Boas' involvement with the neo-Kantian movement dates at least from his last four semesters at Kiel when he studied philosophy under Benno Erdmann, a leading contemporary authority on Kant. Another prominent neo-Kantian was Rudolf Lehman, with whom Boas corresponded on the eve of his arctic expedition. And amazing as it may seem, during his first field trip to the arctic, Boas spent long evenings, with the temperature outside at minus forty degrees centigrade, reading a copy of Kant "so that I shall not be completely uneducated when I return" (STOCKING 1965a:58).

WILHELM DILTHEY

For a number of circumstantial reasons it seems appropriate to look for the specific influence of the neo-Kantian philosopher Wilhelm Dilthey. Boas' 1888 defense of geography bears a striking resemblance to Dilthey's treatment of the distinction between the *Naturwissenschaften* (natural sciences) and *Geisteswissenschaften* (human sciences), first published in 1883. It is especially instructive to compare Boas' description of the historian's approach to a phenomenon—he "lovingly tries to penetrate . . . into its secrets" (see above, p. 263)—with Dilthey's own version of the same:

> The secret of the individual draws us, for its own sake, into ever new and more profound attempts to understand it, and it is in such understanding that the individual and mankind in general and its creations are revealed to us [DILTHEY 1959:219; orig. 1883].

Although Boas makes no specific mention of Dilthey until 1907 (*cf.* STOCKING 1965a:64), he could not possibly have escaped Dilthey's influence.

> Within the German area, including Switzerland, no school of psychology has ever been so generally accepted, so highly estimated and so predominant among educated people in general and particularly among the members of the university staffs as the "geisteswissenschaftliche Psychologie" of Wilhelm Dilthey. This public opinion has been so effective that even at present it is hard for the representatives of scientific psychology to carry through those measures as are necessary to keep up with the international development [W. METZGER 1965:112].

For Dilthey, the crucial difference between the human and the natural sciences resided in the special attributes of mind as distinct from other phenomena: "we do not know the inner nature of physical things and processes and have to read causal order into them by hypothesis, whereas in the world of mind we know directly what we are dealing with" (HODGES 1952:230). This emphasis upon knowing from within—foreshadowed as far back as Vico—constitutes one of the central themes of the Boasian program. It is unlikely that Boas would have articulated the reasons for this emphasis in conformity with Dilthey's technical elaboration, but it is clear from the trajectory of his career and from the kind of research he carried out and inspired others to carry out, that a similar stress on the "inner life" was a fundamental element in his approach to culture.

There is much in Dilthey that is also preparatory to the more general intention among post-Boasian cognitive specialists in the United States to "get inside of other peoples' heads" (see Chap. 20).

> Wherever there is cognitive activity, wherever values are appreciated or ends pursued, wherever in the midst of the processes of nature a free agent appears, there is matter for the Geisteswissenschaften. . . . It is true . . . that they also deal with many physical facts; but they deal with them only in so far as they are related to an inner life, having value for a subject or conditioning the execution of his purpose [HODGES 1952:228-29].

Like the Boasians, but very unlike the modern "ethnosemanticists," Dilthey combined this stress on "emics" with an equally important emphasis upon history. That is, the path to the understanding of the inner life lies through the study of an individual's history. It was partly as a result of this belief that Dilthey came to oppose the development of experimental psychology, in favor of "lived experience" and "understanding." According to Metzger (1965:111), Dilthey's effect upon the development of psychology in Germany was disastrous:

> Dilthey's combat against experimentation in psychology originated in another inheritance of German romanticism that lasted through the whole nineteenth century and in some disciplines, e.g., in education, has not yet been abandoned in our time. The pivotal idea of this doctrine of historicism is the assumption that you know all about a person or a fact, or even of an art, if you know its history. (E. g., German high school teachers are prepared for their educational duties by lectures and examinations in history of education.)

THE INFLUENCE OF RICKERT AND WINDELBAND

Lowie (1956b:1006) has been one of the few anthropologists to draw attention to the "Southwest German" school of philosophy—to Heinrich Rickert and Wilhelm Windelband, who were neo-Kantians based at Baden and who formulated the difference between human and natural sciences in terms of the concepts of "idiographic" and "nomothetic" studies. Lowie correctly associates this point of view with Boas' 1887 discussion of geography, but he fails to mention Dilthey, with whom the Baden group was closely involved, but who differed from them in certain historically important respects. In its original presentation by Windelband in 1894, the nomothetic/idiographic distinction sharply divided the sciences into generalizing and particularizing disciplines. The study of history could not and should not be made to yield generalizations. Although Windelband and Rickert eventually retreated from this position, it was in its original extreme form that this dichotomization influenced Boas' students. Lowie points to eight references to Windelband's follower, Rickert, in Kroeber's collected essays. Most of these are subsequent to Sapir's urgings in his critique of Kroeber's "Superorganic" that all anthropologists and social scientists interested in method ought to read Rickert, to whom he expressed his own great debt. Lowie emphasized the fact that "The reader of Windelband or Rickert might certainly conclude that the historical disciplines not only failed to demonstrate laws, but most emphatically did not wish to find any" (*ibid.*: 1007). Dilthey on the one hand and Windelband and Rickert on the other carried out a long controversy in which the sharpness of the separation between the particularizing and generalizing sciences was one of the main issues. In his rejoinders to Windelband, Dilthey insisted that both idiographic and nomothetic interests were legitimate within the human sciences. There is a matter of method, however; the natural sciences systematize their data by moving toward the abstract, seeking the kind of relation that can be put into an equation. "The human studies systematize by seeing the particular fact more and more fully in its context among other facts structurally related to it" (HODGES 1952:230). The human studies do indeed take an interest in the individual

> for his own sake, just as he is, apart from all thought of his relation to laws and determining conditions, and without any attempt to explain him at all. The human studies, therefore, contain an ele-

> ment of pure description, a "loving understanding (Verständnis) of the personal, a reliving of the inexhaustible totalities," which is seen at its simplest in biography [*ibid.*:231].

However, this does not mean that lawful generalizations cannot be sought in the sphere of human sciences. The line of division between the two spheres is not rigid, and provision must be made for inquiries which have a footing in both realms (*ibid.*:169). In Dilthey's view, human studies actually have three objectives: the description of historical facts, the discovery of laws and regularities, and the formulation of standards of value (*ibid.*:169–70).

THE ATTACK AGAINST MATERIALISM AND SCIENTISM

The controversy between Dilthey and Windelband was only a small eddy in a huge Euro-American ideological whirlpool. It seems likely that the motive power of this vortex derived from the menace of materialism.

> The first indication of the awakening of the mind from the extremely negative attitude of the materialists may be seen in the return to the teaching of Kant; the activity of the subject in the elaboration of science, which had been for long ignored, and had been thrust into the background by the triumphs so easily achieved by the mechanical method, asserts its right once more and inaugurates the fruitful work of salutary criticism [ALIOTTA 1914:13].

It scarcely seems necessary to elaborate on the connection between philosophical materialism and the rise of radical political movements, especially Marxism. Toward the end of the last century, the social structures of Europe and America had become vulnerable to communist and socialist subversion. As the political struggle for the control of the bourgeois state intensified, learning and lore were swept up into the battle. Conscious as well as unconscious attempts were made on a wide front covering all intellectual media to annihilate the subversive doctrines. In the rapidly expanding and highly competitive subcommunity of professional intelligentsia, prestige and emolument closely adhered to the contribution which one made to the rout of the materialists. Science itself became the object of suspicion. Contrary to all the experience of the past four hundred years, science was declared incompetent to judge or modify religious doctrine. This peculiar belief, unique to Western civilization, saved theology from any repetition of the severe mauling it had received at the hands of the Darwinists. The floodgates of science were lifted. Out poured countless varieties of idealist, vitalist, pragmatist, and historicist fads and philosophies. Looking at this advancing tide from the vantage point of a rationalist, the philosopher Morris Raphael Cohen prophetically grasped its ultimate significance for the twentieth century in an essay entitled, "The Insurgence against Reason."

> There can be little doubt that this distrust of reasoning and intellect has its roots deep in the temper of our age. The art, literature, and politics of Europe and of our own country show an ever-growing contempt for ideas and form. The popular philosophies of the day, those which emanate from James, Bergson, Croce, Nietzsche, Freud, Chamberlain, Spengler and others, are certainly at one with the recent novel, drama, music, painting, and sculpture in attaching greater value to novel impressions and vehement expression than to coherency and order. The romantic or "Dionysiac" contempt for prudence and deliberative (so-called bourgeois) morality is simply a more intense, if not more crude, expression of the reaction against scientific or rigorous intellectual procedure, a reaction which makes our modern illuminati like Bergson and Croce dismiss physical science as devoid of any genuine knowledge, or as at best a merely practical device for manipulating dead things [1925:113].

Darwinism of course was one of the chief objects of this onslaught. Everywhere voices were raised arguing for the return of life to mystery. Among the intelligentsia there were many who accepted the facts of evolutionary transformation, but all kinds of reasons were brought forth to cast doubt on the adequacy of natural selection to explain the evolutionary panorama. Under the skirts of Darwin's qualified detractors, mystics and metaphysicians flourished. The tide against Spencer was no less powerful, not against his racism, but rather for his having dared to encapsulate history in the materialist principle of the survival of the fittest. Actually, one aspect of the emphasis upon the idiographic was the escalation of the rhetoric of nationalism. Neo-Hegelian racist visions of national souls working their way toward ineffable glories were expressed in the writings of men like Houston Stewart Chamberlain, Oswald Spengler, Ernst Troeltsch, Othmar Spann, and other harbingers of fascism.

IDIOGRAPHIC IDEALISM

Boas' turn toward psychophysics; his questioning of the materialism which had seemed congenial at the outset of his university studies; his defense of geography in the idiom of the *Geistes-*

wissenschaften; and his ultimate vision of anthropology must all be seen in relationship to this huge cultural tide. It is clear that although Boas was borne along, he remained far behind the advancing crest. In others, the idiographic option was seized upon to deprive science virtually of all claim to knowledge in human affairs. The English philosopher-historian R. G. Collingwood (1922:445), himself one of the more extreme products of this trend, could note:

> The chief feature of European philosophy in the last generation has been that movement of reaction from nineteenth-century positivism which has tended to degrade science into a false form of knowledge and to find the true form in history.

Commenting specifically on the contest between history and science, M. R. Cohen remarked:

> The fact that literary historians are generally more interested in the concrete picture of the events they portray, while scientific physicists are generally more interested in the laws which physical phenomena illustrate, has given rise in recent times to the view that history is nearer to reality, which is always individual, and that rational or scientific physics is a more or less useful fiction [1925:121].

Emboldened by the "spirit of the times," historians such as Croce could scarcely conceal their contempt for people who were unable to grasp the essence of history on their own but required the feeble crutches of science to do so:

> Do you wish to understand the true history of a Ligurian or Sicilian neolithic man? First of all, try if it be possible to make yourself mentally into a Ligurian or Sicilian neolithic man; and if it be not possible, or you do not care to do this, content yourself with describing and classifying and arranging in a series the skulls, the utensils, and the inscriptions belonging to those neolithic peoples. Do you wish to understand the history of a blade of grass? First and foremost, try to make yourself into a blade of grass, and if you do not succeed, content yourself with analysing the parts and even with disposing them in a kind of imaginative history [1923:233].

MODERATENESS OF BOAS' POSITION

Boas was influenced in a lifelong fashion by the rise of neo-Kantianism, but it must be stressed, contrary to the impression one gains from reading White's scathing manifesto, that he escaped from its worst consequences. It means something in this context that

Boas continued to insist that the laws governing cultural phenomena would eventually be discovered. Indeed, on the very heels of his paper defending the particularist viewpoint in geography, there came another paper, concerned with defining the aims of ethnology. We are not privileged to dismiss the statements which he makes therein, affirming that the most important aim of ethnology is the discovery of scientific laws.

> The frequent occurrence of similar phenomena in cultural areas that have no historical contact suggests that important results may be derived from their study, for it shows that the human mind develops everywhere according to the same laws.
>
> The discovery of these is the greatest aim of our science. To attain it many methods of inquiry and the assistance of many other sciences will be needed. Up to this time the number of investigations is small, but the foundations have been laid by the labors of men like Tylor, Bastian, Morgan and Bachofen [BOAS, 1948:637; orig. 1888].

Instead of a frivolous alternation between the nomothetic and idiographic options, we may now follow Boas' gradual retreat from the position which he took in 1887–88 on the relationship between the collection of facts and the formulation of regularities. We may confidently assign full and typical sobriety to Boas' insistence in the midst of his critique of the comparative method that "the histories of the cultures of diverse tribes . . . [are] not the ultimate aim of our science" (1948:278–79; orig. 1896b).

We must credit the fact that in its origins, the historical particularist movement was conceived as the handmaiden of a nomothetic approach to history. Specific cultures were to be studied in their particular historical context. This was to be done not because the search for uniformities in history is futile, but because the only way in which the amount and nature of such uniformity can be appraised is through a program of inductive historical research. In other words, it was not Boas' intention, as he himself repeated on a number of occasions, to abandon the search for lawful regularities in history. Rather than replace the comparative method, it was his hope that historical particularism would supplement it and facilitate the discovery of the sought-after laws, which remained the ultimate objective of anthropological inquiry.

> When we have cleared up the history of a single culture and understand the effects of environment and the psychological conditions that are reflected in it we have made a step forward, as we

> can then investigate in how far the same causes or other causes were at work in the development of other cultures. Thus by comparing histories of growth general laws may be found. This method is much safer than the comparative method, as it is usually practiced, because instead of a hypothesis on the mode of development, actual history forms the basis of our deductions [*ibid.*:279].

The historical method was thus to be harnessed to the service of the comparative method. By so doing, anthropological theory would be purged of its puerile amateurism, and a new and sounder basis for generalization would be established. Both perspectives were necessary, nor were the methodological reforms restricted to the comparative outlook. Simplistic historicism, which assumed a connection between geographically remote cultural phenomena, without evidence of how the influence actually could have been transmitted, was equally to be condemned. If the parallel evolutionists came in for a worse drubbing than the diffusionists, it was, as I have already suggested, simply because the evolutionists held the field.

WILL THE REAL HISTORIAN PLEASE STAND UP?

Boas and one of his most famous students, Alfred Kroeber, became involved in a curious controversy concerning which was the more historicist-minded. As we shall see at greater length in a subsequent chapter, Kroeber was exposed to trends and reared in a milieu which moved him far closer to the idiographic extreme. The resulting contrast between himself and Boas appeared to him so striking that he reached conclusions concerning Boas which seem incredible, unless placed in the context developed in this chapter. As we have already seen, Kroeber believed that it was Boas' training in physics which was the most fateful aspect of his formative years. How did he reconcile this belief with the main features of Boas' program? Simply by never doubting that Boas meant what he said about the relationship between history and science. But from Kroeber's standpoint this preoccupation with science was a symptom, if not a cause, of Boas' failure to pursue a genuinely idiographic approach. Indeed, incredible as it may seem, Kroeber went so far as to accuse his mentor of neglecting real history! According to Kroeber, the association of Boas with a position of historical particularism was nothing but an error which arose from Boas' attempt to refute the grandiose schemes of his predecessors:

> When he came on the scene, he found anthropology taken up with schematic interpretations—Morgan's will serve as a typical example; and he unhesitatingly proceeded to show that these schemes seemed valid only as long as the fact was ignored that they were built up of subjectively selected pieces of evidence torn out of their historical context, that is, their actual context in the world of nature. In his insistence that this context may not be violated, Boas may have seemed, possibly even to himself, to be following historical method. But it was merely historical method applied as a critical safeguard; the problems with which he concerned himself were not historical except in minor cases, but concerned with process as such [1935:542].

As an example of Boas' interest in process as opposed to history, Kroeber mentions his former teacher's researches into primitive art. What questions does Boas put to the phenomena of art? Supposedly, like a physicist with analogous problems, he considered a gamut of processes: conventionalization, influence of technique, symbolism, secondary interpretation, virtuosity, and "cursive slovening." Nowhere, complains Kroeber, does Boas deal with an art style except as it may serve as a point of departure for some problem concerned with the processes of conventionalization, symbolism, etc. He shows no concern for the styles themselves, for "their essential quality." "The cause is a lack of interest in factual description for its own sake, in other words, in phenomena" (*ibid.*:543). Kroeber goes on to make the flat accusation that Boas was not an historian. Although he observes all the methodological safeguards associated with an historical orientation—the need for context, stress on uniqueness in all phenomena, caution with respect to "generalizations savoring of the universal" —he still does not "*do*" history. "In brief, one may define the Boas position as basically that of the physical scientist" (*ibid.*:554). A similar judgment was rendered by another of Boas' famous pupils, Paul Radin (1933:17).

The only products of Boas' work which were significantly historical in Kroeber's opinion were his monograph on the Eskimo and a presidential address to the New York Academy of Science entitled, "The History of the American Race" (BOAS 1948:324–30; orig. 1911). The Eskimo monograph was historical in spirit, even though it was almost exclusively synchronic, because of its manifest coherence and lucidity! Kroeber's hankering after the essence of history was baffling. Boas found the whole outburst unintelligible. "If Dr. Kroeber calls my first piece of ethnological work, 'The Central Eskimo,' historical, I fail to understand him." Why, wonders Boas, has Kroeber failed to mention the years devoted to trying to unravel the historical development of social organization, secret societies, the spread of art forms and of folktales on the northwest coast of America?

> Is it that painstaking work of this kind does not seem to Dr. Kroeber worth while, but that it requires the flight of an unbridled imagination to have his approval? I cannot understand in any other way his praise of a public lecture which I gave as President of the New York Academy of Sciences on "The History of the American Race," guarding my statement, however, at the very beginning by saying that I should give my fancy freer rein than I ordinarily permit myself [*ibid.*: 307].

Boas used this occasion to refer back across forty-nine years of his career to the paper on "The Study of Geography," thereby confirming the crucial importance of his rejection of the physicalist model. Kroeber, who had been influenced by Windelband and Rickert, simply did not understand Boas' brand of neo-Kantianism:

> In 1887 I tried to define my position in regard to these subjects, giving expression to my consciousness of the diversity of their fundamental viewpoints. I aligned myself clearly with those who are motivated by the affective appeal of a phenomenon that impresses us as a unit, although its elements may be irreducible to a common cause. In other words the problem that attracted me primarily was the intelligent understanding of a complex phenomenon. When from geography my interest was directed to ethnology, the same interest prevailed [*ibid.*: 305].

FIRST PHASE OF BOAS' REJECTION OF CULTURAL LAWS

White has seized upon the similarity between Boas' initial statement of research strategy and the position set forth in the last phases of his career as evidence of an unchanging outlook with respect to the question of regularities in history. He says, regarding the earliest and latest of Boas' statements on laws in history, "it is the same Boas down to the last detail" (WHITE 1963:64). This leads to a view of Boas which suggests a measure of what might almost be called duplicity, or at the very least, an unusual and totally out of character frivolity. For, as we have already seen, and as White points out, at the very moment that Boas adopted the particularist option, he also affirmed the discovery of laws as the most important aim of ethnology. There is every reason to suppose that on this subject Boas meant what he said in 1888, and that between then and his latest writings, a definite development in outlook can be traced. It was in many respects a disastrous kind of development, but it vouches for the integrity and continuity of Boas' belief that particularist studies would lead to the "discovery" of laws.

By accepting Boas' statements that the ultimate objective of his reform of the comparative method was generalization, we shall be able perhaps to state more clearly than White precisely what was wrong with the Boasian research strategy. The great strategic lessons which the Boasian period affords must inevitably elude our comprehension, if we believe that from the outset this movement had no interests other than those which Windelband came to identify as idiographic. Boas, as distinguished from his students, was above all an empiricist. Like Dilthey, and in contrast to the later Neo-Kantians who were to influence Kroeber, Sapir, Radin, and Benedict, a priori insights and conclusions were anathema to him. Nothing would be further from his temperament than to dogmatize an intuited absence of historical regularities. What we find instead is a mounting conviction, based upon the accumulation of ethnographic evidence collected by himself and by other anthropologists, that the search for regularities will end in failure. In his earliest phase as exemplified in "The Limitations of the Comparative Method," universal unilinear sequences are denied but not to the extent of rejecting more limited forms of parallel sequences. The search for the laws governing these uniformities is urged as an important, if not the most important, aim.

SECOND PHASE

By about 1910, Boas had given up the possibility that significant developmental uniformities involving whole congeries of institutions would be found. He continued, however, to stress the probability that the occurrence of similar institutions throughout the world reflected something inherent in the human mind. But it was now his opinion that the expression of this common denominator did not require a uniform cultural matrix. Indeed, he now stressed that convergences under the influence of mental laws could occur in almost any kind of cultural context:

> I do not mean to imply that no general laws of development exist. On the contrary, the analogies that do occur in regions far apart show that the human mind tends to reach the same results, not under similar, but under varying circumstances [1948:341; orig. 1910].

The empirical basis for this shift in emphasis is summarized in Boas' *The Mind of Primitive Man* (1911). In this book, the absence of uniform developmental sequences is for the first time clearly and explicitly related to an absence of a determinative order between the various parts of culture and between culture and the natural environment. He points for example to the various forms of the family and insists that they cannot be correlated with other institutional features.

> Some very primitive tribes, like the Eskimo and the Indian tribes of the Northwest plateaus of North America, count relationships bilaterally . . . other tribes with highly developed culture recognize the maternal line alone, while still others, whose economic and industrial life is of a simpler type, recognize the paternal line [BOAS 1938c:182-83; orig. 1911].

Inventions, social order, intellectual and social life all may develop independently: "There are people, like the Australians, whose material culture is quite poor, but who have a highly complex social organization" (*ibid.*:197). Similarly, the influence of environment is quite unpredictable. Proof of the spontaneous creative influence of the mind is to be found in the great diversity of culture among such pairs of adjacent peoples as the Eskimo and Chuckchee, the Hottentot and Bushman, and the Negrito and Malay (*ibid.*:191). The exploitation of food resources is itself subject to the whim of culture. "Even among the Eskimo, who have so marvelously well succeeded in adapting themselves to their geographical environment, customs like the taboo on the promiscuous use of caribou and seal prevent the fullest use of the opportunities offered by the country" (*ibid.*:191–92). This appeal to sundry ethnographic examples of alleged lack of correlation between the different parts of culture, and hence of the lack of parallel evolution, was accompanied by one of Boas' rare confrontations with economic determinism. Naturally, he saw little merit in such a position:

> There is no reason to call all other phases of culture a superstructure on an economic basis, for economic conditions always act on a preexisting culture and are themselves dependent upon other aspects of culture. It is no more justifiable to say that social structure is determined by economic forms than to claim the reverse, for a preexisting social structure will influence economic conditions and *vice versa,* and no people has ever been observed that has no social structure and that is not subject to economic conditions. The claim that economic stresses preceded every other

> manifestation of cultural life and exerted their influences on a group without any cultural traits cannot be maintained. Cultural life is always economically conditioned and economics are always culturally conditioned [*ibid.*:193].

We cannot stop here to comment on Boas' conclusions except to say that they are unwarranted in fact and theory, but in subsequent chapters we shall examine the relevant ethnographic data. For the moment, let us proceed at once to the final phase of the development of Boas' thought on the question of evolutionary laws.

THIRD PHASE

It was toward the end of his career that Boas reached a position that was fully compatible with Windelband's sharp separation of nomothetic and idiographic studies. This development dates from the appearance in Boas' theoretical writings of a new and strident theme in which it is stated that the search for lawful evolutionary regularities is a chimera; that the aims of anthropology should not include the discovery of laws; and that no amount of additional research could possibly alter the futility of the nomothetic option in the phenomena of culture. In this connection, Boas' dismissal of the possible relevance of the comparison between cultural development in the old and new worlds is especially diagnostic. At the very moment when improved techniques had brought archaeology to the verge of its greatest discoveries, Boas declared: "Although in this case parallelism seems to exist on the two continents, it would be futile to try to follow out the order in detail" (BOAS 1948:287; orig. 1920a). There is a double irony in this unfortunate opinion. Not only were future excavations to prove him wrong, but they were to do so with stratigraphic techniques which he himself helped to introduce (see Chap. 23). It was at some point during the decade of the 1920's that Boas finally abandoned the heritage of the nineteenth-century search for developmental uniformities. By 1930 he had taken the radical step of suggesting that anthropology had become entirely too wrapped up in the attempt to reconstruct particular historical sequences. Since it was now apparent that the structure of the human mind accounted for whatever regularities were manifest in cultural phenomena, anthropology could no longer remain aloof from the study of the relationship between the individual psyche and the forms of culture:

> It should be clearly understood that historical analysis does not help us in the solution of these questions. . . . An error of modern anthropology, as I see it, lies in the overemphasis on historical reconstruction, the importance of which should not be minimized, as against a penetrating study of the individual under the stress of the culture in which he lives [*ibid.*:269; orig. 1930].

It was in this fashion that Boas sired in his maturity a totally unexpected offspring: the field of personality and culture. A more detailed look at this not unmixed blessing must await a separate chapter. Let it simply be noted here that Boas' declining interest in historical reconstruction was accompanied by an increased concern with psychological factors. It was during the twenties that Boas' most famous female students received their training and were sent out with his encouragement to probe the neglected relationship between the individual and culture. It is not necessary at this point to weigh the respective contributions of Boas and his students to this new substantive and theoretical focus. What is essential for the moment is that Boas was prepared to assume full responsibility for the switch in emphasis. The new direction was emphatically defined again in 1932:

> The problems of the relation of the individual to his culture, to the society in which he lives have received too little attention. The standardized anthropological data that inform us of customary behavior, give no clue to the reaction of the individual to his culture, nor to an understanding of his influence upon it. Still, here lie the sources of a true interpretation of human behavior. It seems a vain effort to search for sociological laws disregarding what should be called social psychology, namely, the reaction of the individual to culture. They can be no more than empty formulas that can be imbued with life only by taking account of individual behavior in cultural settings [*ibid.*:258-59; orig. 1932].

Under these circumstances the continued insistence that anthropology was an historical science assumed a significance it lacked at the outset. Anthropology must be an historical science, not because the history of particular cultures is the only way to formulate the lawful ingredients in cultural phenomena, but rather because there is no viable alternative to the study of individual phenomena. If this is so, it follows that the study of the individual human personality is the highest fulfillment of the particularizing trend. Simultaneously with this turn toward psychology, Boas' resistance to a nomothetic approach to history lapsed into dogma. Not only were historical laws undiscovered, but they would for all time remain undiscoverable. His final pronouncement on the subject is contained in an addendum to his reply to Kroeber's accusation that he was no historian:

> In my opinion a system of social anthropology and "laws" of cultural development as rigid as those of physics are supposed to be are unattainable in the present stage of our knowledge, and more important than this: on account of the uniqueness of cultural phenomena and their complexity nothing will ever be found that deserves the name of a law excepting those psychological, biologically determined characteristics which are common to all cultures and appear in a multitude of forms according to the particular culture in which they manifest themselves [*ibid.*:311; orig. 1936].

STACKING THE CARDS AGAINST THE NOMOTHETIC MODE

It is difficult to understand what Boas intended to convey by means of the phrase, "as rigid as [the laws] of physics *are supposed to be*." On the one hand this phrase would seem to indicate that Boas was aware of the changes which the concept of scientific law had undergone as a result of relativity theory and quantum mechanics. But if this were the case, why should anthropology continue to be burdened by Newtonian concepts that physics had abandoned? If probabilities had replaced mechanistic certainties, why should anthropologists demand that their laws admit no exceptions? Actually, as we have seen, it never was the intention of those who spoke of the laws of history in the nineteenth century to obtain anything other than a description of the most probable sequences. But throughout the Boasian period, a unique double standard seemed to prevail against anthropology's nomothetic aspirations. As one ponders the way in which Boas and his students used one or two negative instances to deny hypotheses confirmed by hundreds of other instances, one inevitably becomes impressed by the amount of effort lavished in proving that chaos was the salient feature of the sociocultural realm.

BOAS' GENERALIZATIONS

Boas' students have attempted to combat the impression that he was committed to this self-defeating objective. Boas himself in 1920 replied to the accusation that was being made abroad concerning the futility of trying to disprove everything while proving nothing:

> It may seem to the distant observer that American students are engaged in a mass of detailed investigations without much bearing upon the solution of the ultimate problems of a philosophic history of human civilization. I think this interpretation of the American attitude would be unjust because the ultimate questions are as near to our hearts as they are to those of other scholars, only we do not hope to be able to solve an intricate historical problem by a formula [1948:283–84; orig. 1920a].

As Boas developed his arguments on behalf of historical and psychological particularism, he not infrequently drew upon a small stock of illustrative generalizations. For example, he repeatedly mentions the alleged tendency of an enlargement of food production to give rise to increased population, greater leisure time, and a more elaborate division of labor. (I say "alleged," because it is doubtful that increased productivity in the formative phases of the urban revolution was translated into a decrease in per capita man-hour input [*cf.* HARRIS 1959a].) In offering this generalization, Boas usually tried to make the point that it would require a great deal of qualification in any concrete case. He made similar use of such additional generalizations as the tendency for activities that begin unconsciously later to become "the subject of reasoning"; and the tendency of metallurgy to follow after the invention of pottery, agriculture, and stone-based industries (BOAS 1948:287–88; orig. 1920a). These generalizations are treated only as examples, that is, Boas never discussed them for their own sake. Yet it is on the basis of such snippets of theory that Lesser (1968) has attempted to prove that Boas "did not deny the possibility of regularities or 'laws' in cultural phenomena."

It should be noted that neither Boas nor his students were the originators of these theories—all of them, it will be recalled, were clearly set forth by Turgot in 1750. Nor did Boas and his students orient their fieldwork in relation to them, or make sustained comparative field or library studies specifically intended to test their validity (*cf.* WAX 1956:65). Boas not infrequently offered his examples of generalizations in a context that revealed that he held them in contempt. He repeatedly characterized such statements as "necessarily vague and, we might almost say, so self-evident that they are of little help to a real understanding" (BOAS 1948:258; orig. 1932).

BOAS AS A DETERMINIST

Boas systematically rejected almost every conceivable form of cultural determinism. Of geographical explanations, he wrote: "It is fruitless to try to explain culture in geographical terms" (1948:266; orig. 1930). Of economic factors: "We do not see how art styles, the form of ritual or the special forms of religious belief *could possibly* be derived from economic forces" (*ibid.*:256, orig. 1932; italics added). Of the relationship between religion and art: "We might think that religion and art are closely associated, but comparative study merely shows that art forms may be used to express religious ideas; a result that is of no particular value" (*ibid.*:266; orig. 1930). Of social organization and industrial activities: "There is no significant law that would cover all phases of their relations. We have simple industries and complex organization, or diverse industries and simple organization" (*ibid*). His judgment of the relationship between kinship forms and demographic-economic factors is of special significance in view of the strong theoretical interests that have always centered on these problems: "there is no evidence that density of population, stability of location, or economic status is necessarily connected with a particular system of relationship and of behavior connected with it" (BOAS 1938a:680). The overwhelmingly negative thrust of Boas' empiricism is mitigated only to the extent that he never intended to deny that all of the aforementioned factors were devoid of determinative influence. The point was rather that *all* these factors were determinative in unpredictable degrees and in a pattern unique to each ethnographic instance. In theory, therefore, the Boasian program strongly identified itself with an eclectic outlook in which "complete descriptions" were to be carried out by "all available techniques," and explanations were to be provided by embracing a wide variety of theoretical assumptions. Unfortunately, this is the philosophical position with which probably the vast majority of practicing Western anthropologists would most like to associate themselves.

ECLECTICISM

Eclecticism is certainly the path of least resistance through the frequently strident polemics of the system-mongerers. Most anthropologists simply want to be left in peace to pursue the study of their "people." If one keeps technological, economic, social, political, and ideational factors "in mind," why should one have to get embroiled in the brouhaha of theoretical disputation?

Because of the strong logical affinity between an eclectic and inductive approach, many Boasians have reacted with bewilderment and impatience to the critical evaluation of Boas' influence. The frequent assertion that Boas "founded no school" went along with the belief that the only thing Boas insisted on was higher standards of proof; as long as it was responsible to the data, any theoretical and substantive interest was conceivably compatible with the attempt to preserve the vanishing fragments of primitive languages and cultures.

Eclecticism, however, abounds with hidden dangers. In practice, it is often little more than a euphemism for confusion, the muddled acceptance of contradictory theories, the bankruptcy of creative thought, and the cloak of mediocrity. It bestows upon its practitioners a false sense of security and an unearned reputation for scientific acumen. Science consists of more than responsibility to the data; the data must be made responsible to theory. Neither one without the other suffices. It is impossible to be faithful to the facts and at the same time indifferent to theory.

The history of the Boasian period suggests that the problem of causality in culture can never be solved through a well-rounded eclectic approach. It seems likely that in practice eclecticism will always end by amplifying one's initial impression of randomness and unpredictability. The very idea of a scientific statement demands that some balance be struck among the relevant variables, that they be assigned different weights and values, and that they be segregated into dependent and independent relationships. To say that everything is equally important in every situation is to propose in effect that all situations should be the same.

One deceptively simple solution is to argue that in certain cases one set of factors, e.g., religious beliefs, are the independent variable, while in other cases, another set of factors, e.g., economic organization, takes its place. But this strategy, closely identified with Max Weber and popular among sociologists as well as Boasian anthropologists, is incompatible with historical determinism. Unless one can specify the conditions under which now religion, now art, or then again subsistence comes to the fore, the principles involved will be valid for only one case at a time, much as if mass and gravitational force were related in one way on the earth but in a different way on the moon. A generalization which applies to only one case is a contradiction in terms.

DELIBERATE AVERSION TO SYSTEMATIZATION

But even if we grant that an eclectic approach is admissable as a provisional substitute for a coherent body of theory, we should still have to confront the fact that, in practice, Boas never approached a problem by giving full consideration to the entire range of environmental, technological, economic, social, aesthetic, and ideological factors. With the exception of his study of the Eskimo, he rarely considered environmental influences. His flat rejection of the relevance of economics to art styles has already been cited. Although by no means adequate for assessing the extent of his neglect of economic factors, we may accept his own fiat against relating economics to specific forms of social organization as a temporary estimate. It is thus very difficult to avoid the conclusion that the proof of historical disorder was of greater significance in Boas' mature *Weltanschauung* than was the formulation of orderly principles. Even Lowie, Boas' greatest and most faithful student, was obliged to admit it as "paradoxical" that Boas never integrated his thousands of pages of description of the Kwakiutl into a single work and that he had a "puritanical" resistance to provisional synthesis. "It is this deliberate aversion to systematization that is the despair of many readers and precipitates misunderstanding" (LOWIE 1937:151–52). In the words of Margaret Mead: "No probe must go too far lest it lead to premature generalization—a development which he feared like the plague and against which he continually warned us" (1959b:29).

Boas' achievement of a view of culture in which lawful processes were so vapid as to be unworthy of formulation is associated with egregious epistemological, methodological, and factual errors. In the long run, of course, it will be the errors of fact and of interpretation of fact that will weigh most heavily in the judgment of future generations. We shall turn to these in a moment. But it would be a repetition of Boas' capital mistake to suppose that these errors were unrelated to fundamental philosophical misapprehensions.

BASIC PHILOSOPHICAL ERRORS

From the very earliest period, the Boasian program suffered the embarrassment of a virtue which was at the same time its chief vice. It was inductive to the point of self-destruction. The proposal to substitute concrete historical data for speculative deductions about history needs no defense. On the other hand, to deprive science of speculation altogether is to deprive it of its very life blood. Yet in essence, this is what the Boasian program sought to accomplish. In view of the fragmentary nature of the ethnographic record and in view of the urgency of obtaining data from fast-disappearing tribal groups, all theory was deemed speculative. The need of the moment was fieldwork. As one of Boas' students has put it, "the only corrective was to allow conclusions to follow from the data without the introduction of preconceived philosophical positions" (M. SMITH 1959:49). This "natural history" approach, to which most of Boas' students would probably subscribe, is further elaborated as follows:

> Boas' emphasis on systematic fieldwork led to the collection of whatever data became available. If one found an informant to be particularly well versed in a subject, one concentrated on that subject, getting everything possible from him and following through with other informants, observations, and the like, even though the immediate usefulness of the material might not be apparent. . . . This exhaustive collection of data which seems at the time to have little or no connection with any specific problem is peculiarly a feature of the natural history approach. . . . There is a fascination in following the details of a subject just for its intrinsic interest. . . . Masses of data may therefore be worked over with no clear knowledge of what is to be gained at the end [*ibid.*:54].

In the history of philosophy there is a perfect parallel to Boas' concept of science in the work of Francis Bacon. Reacting to a surfeit of metaphysical final causes and other scholastic theoretical crutches, Bacon insisted on the primacy of induction. Like Boas, he felt that the greatest need of the day was the collection of a corpus of reliable facts: Heretofore, wrote Bacon, "no search has been made to collect a store of observation sufficient either in number, kind, or in certainty to inform the understanding, or in any way adequate."

> The method usually followed by philosophers should be inverted. Instead of coming down from axioms to particular conclusions, as in syllogistic deducation, the scientist should go instead from particular experiments and observations up to axioms—induction, in other words, should replace deduction [GILSON and LANGAN 1963: 37–38].

Science in this view is distinguished by its systematic collection of facts carefully checked for accuracy. "The essence of his [Boas'] method was . . . to gather facts, and ever more facts . . . and permit them to speak for themselves. . . ."(RADIN 1939, quoted in WHITE 1947b:406). If enough facts are collected, the corpus of scientific information will eventually be ripe for the "discovery" of the laws of nature. It is evident, however, both from the history of science in general and from the experience of the social sciences, that a strict adherence to Baconian induction, even if it were culturologically feasible, would not lead to the discovery of regularities. The trouble is that a random sampling of any field of observation will prove beyond the shadow of doubt that nature is chaotic. One has merely to observe birds flying, smoke rising, clouds drifting, feathers floating, and stones plummeting to realize that Galileo's formulation of the laws of motion could not possibly have resulted from the mere collection of facts. If one set out to note all the facts about a single grain of sand, all of the computers in the world could not store the information which could eventually be collected on that subject. Cultural phenomena, with their dependence upon complex levels of logico-empirical abstraction, could undoubtedly provide facts in correspondingly higher degrees of infinity. "Complete descriptions" of anything are impossible. The normal mode of scientific procedure is, therefore, something quite different from what Bacon supposed. For an authoritative opinion in this matter, one can scarcely improve on Einstein (1936):

> There is no inductive method which could lead to the fundamental concepts of physics. Failure to understand this fact constituted the basic philosophic error of so many investigators of the nineteenth century. . . . We now realize with special clarity, how much in error are those theorists who believe that theory comes inductively from experience . . . [quoted in WHITE 1947b: 406].

Facts are limitless, but the resources of science, even in the best endowed branches, are meager by comparison. There are limited quantities of research manpower, funds, and facilities. Moreover, the devotion of research effort to the collection of one set of facts means the neglect of other sets of facts. Under modern laboratory conditions, where funding takes place in relation to competitive proposals, there is less opportunity to confuse mere induction with science. The great instruments of observation, the optical and radio telescopes, the high-energy particle generators, and the rocket-borne telemetry packages operate on the strictist of schedules with each moment of fact collecting justified by thousands of man-hours of previous thought and experiment. Even in conventional laboratories, precious research time is never abandoned to an aimless rushing about from one experiment to another. As Einstein is also reputed to have said, "You've got to itch to scratch." To be sure, the richer the facility, the greater the leeway for relatively unstructured approaches. Thus in the field of cancer research, hundreds of thousands of substances are being tested for their possible curative effects without disturbing the course of more theoretically oriented research. But in the social sciences, especially in ethnology at the turn of the century, only an infinitesimal portion of the social effluent could be diverted. Every expedition, every minor field trip, every conversation with an informant was the equivalent of hundreds of hours of time with the Brookhaven cyclotron or the 200-inch Palomar telescope. In all fields, not only are some facts collected, but others are not collected. And the commission and omission stand as a unit within the research strategy, regardless of whether the research is oriented by a formal conscious hypothesis.

The Boasian Milieu

10

Regardless of the Baconian urge with which Boas has been invested; that is, despite his image as the patient collector of facts on all aspects of culture, neither Boas nor his students conducted their research completely free of hypotheses. These hypotheses were never overtly formulated. Indeed, they resemble nothing so much as what in recent ethnosemantic theory is called a "cognitive map." They were part of the general mode of looking at the phenomena of culture which middle-class Euro-American academics at the turn of the century had acquired through common or parallel enculturation experiences. Only by reference to this milieu can an anthropologically informed understanding be reached of Boas' "aversion to systematization" and of the negative thrust of the entire Boasian program with respect to the formulation of historical regularities.

Anthropologists of all theoretical schools have been strangely lax in applying their own methods of studying cultural phenomena to the study of themselves. One might suppose that anthropologists would not often stand in need of special reminders concerning the capacity of cultural influences to shape the main substance of an individual's cognitive world. Yet it is remarkable how slight has been the attention paid to the relationship between the Boasian program and the sociocultural milieu in which Boas and his students lived. Although this task obviously cannot be attempted in anything less than a major work, we may here at least try to achieve a better definition of the problem than is currently available.

BOAS NOT A REACTIONARY ANTIEVOLUTIONIST

Largely under the influence of Leslie White, critics of the Boasian program have equated its main tenets with "antievolutionism." For White (1949a:110), as we have seen, Boas was the chief representative of the "reactionary and regressive antievolutionist" tendency in the United States. Boas' attack on the comparative method is seen by White as the turning point in American anthropology from evolutionism to antievolutionism (WHITE 1959a:108). In White's analysis of the sociocultural factors responsible for this reaction, a misleading equivalence is established between the forces opposed to Spencer's theories and those opposed to Marx. In White's interpretation, the antievolutionary reaction in the United States was simply an extension of the struggle that had been waged between Darwinism and the "enemies of evolutionism." Although largely unsuccessful in the biological sciences (with such notable exceptions as the Scopes trial), the antievolutionist counterattack is said to have won the field in the social sciences:

> The forces of institutionalized Christianity, especially within the Roman Catholic Church, were arrayed against evolutionism. The use of evolutionist theory in general and Morgan's theories in particular by Karl Marx and the radical socialist labor movement evoked powerful opposition from the capitalist system. Thus, antievolutionism became a creed for certain sectors of society . . . a philosophy in support of the church, private property, the family, and the capitalist state [*ibid.*:109].

White's analysis is encumbered by an unnecessary and confusing rhetoric. It is very difficult to equate Boas with "reactionary and regressive" currents. Of course, White was careful to distinguish Boas the man from Boas the symbol of an intellectual movement, but there is an inevitable association of one with the other. Anyone at all familiar with Boas' career knows that he was a prodigious champion of causes which in the logic of political liberalism are generally acknowledged as being anything but "reactionary and regressive." Boas' lifelong struggle against the notion of a direct feedback between racial and cultural factors is regressive only to the extent that it represents a return to the radical doctrines of the French Revolution. If there is any one theme capable of eliciting an enthusiastic consensus among contemporary American anthropologists, it is that the racist premises of Spencerism blocked the further development of the social sciences. Moreover, Boas had a distinguished record of public protest against racist bigotry. During the First World War he courageously maintained a pacifist position despite the virulent nationalism that had sickened campus life. During the rise of the Nazi race mania, Boas led the struggle against biological reductionism. In 1931, on the occasion of the award of an honorary doctorate at the University of Kiel, he felt it his responsibility to deliver an address on the subject of race and culture. His papers were circulated by the German underground, and his books were conspicuous in the Nazi bonfires. When Boas suffered a fatal heart attack on December 21, 1943, during a luncheon at the Men's Faculty Club at Columbia University, his last words concerned the need for eternal vigilance against racism.

EVOLUTIONISM VERSUS ANTIEVOLUTIONISM

But there is another and more serious defect in White's explanation of the Boasian position. It arises from White's attempt to discuss the functional significance of the Boasian program in terms of a worthless dichotomy: evolutionism versus antievolutionism. As we have seen, if we accept the meaning of evolution to be the transformation of forms, there never has been serious resistance to such an idea in the social sciences. White himself has defined evolution as "a temporal sequence of forms" (see Chap. 22), and to this meaning of evolution, no Boasian could possibly object. Mere transformism, of course, was not the essence of the evolutionism of the Spencerians nor of the doctrinaire Marxists. There were three additional ingredients in the Spencerian version of evolution, and it was to these that the Boasians objected. One was biological reductionism, the other was the tendency to regard parallel evolution as dominant over either convergent or divergent evolution, and the third was a snobbish definition of progress. There was another ingredient in Spencerian evolutionism with which the Boasians were by and large in complete agreement. This was the conviction, shared by Spencer and Darwin, that biological as well as sociocultural evolution was explicable in terms of purely "natural" processes. White's equating of Boas' antievolutionism with the antievolutionism of supernatural explanations of life and mind has been justly criticized by Lowie:

> Thus White's gloomy picture of most contemporary anthropologists plunged into Cimmerian darkness, unrelieved by a single lambent ray of evolution, is preposterous. He ought to realize that Thurnwald, Radcliffe-Brown, Radin, Lesser, Malinowski are professed evolutionists, and that even I have spoken kindly enough of neo-evolutionism.
>
> The questions which worry White, viz., "why Boas and his disciples have been anti-evolutionists" and what may be "the source and basis of the anti-evolutionist philosophy of the Boas group," automatically disappear. In order to infuse sense into such queries they must be re-formulated: Why have Boas and his students attacked not evolution, but Morgan's and other writers' evolutionary schemes [1948a:227]?

White has failed to address himself constructively to this query. The Boasians have done so at length, and we already know *their* answer: the "schemes" were based on shoddy standards of proof. Like White, I reject this explanation. It fails to explain why the normal interplay between theory and research was so drastically restricted; why in the words of Kluckhohn (1939:333), it got to be that "to suggest that something is 'theoretical' is to suggest that it is slightly indecent." To be sure, White is not the originator of the misleading equation between the essence of the Boasian position and a clumsy use of the phrase "antievolution." In his rejoinder to Lowie, White quite properly stressed that some of the Boasians themselves had led the way to misunderstanding by crude expressions of hostility to "evolution." The most splendid example of this debauchery in the ranks of the higher empiricists is that of Berthold Laufer. I quote in extenso, because it represents the nadir of the negativism and antiscientism which was associated with historical particularism.

> The theory of cultural evolution, to my mind the most inane, sterile, and pernicious theory ever conceived in the history of science (a cheap toy for the amusement of big children), is duly disparaged. . . . Culture cannot be forced into the straitjacket of any theory whatever it may be, nor can it be reduced to chemical or mathematical formulae. Nature has no laws, so culture has none. It is as vast and as free as the ocean, throwing its waves and currents in all directions. . . . All that the practical investigator can hope for, at least for the present, is to study each cultural phenomenon as exactly as possible in its geographical

> distribution, its historical development and its relation or association with other kindred ideas. The more theories will be smashed, the more new facts will be established, the better for the progress of our science [LAUFER 1918:90].

White (1947b:402ff.) has shown that Ruth Benedict, Ruth Bunzel, Edward Sapir, Paul Radin, and Alexander Goldenweiser all must share the onus of setting up the false dichotomy between Boas' program and "evolution." But it is clear from the context in which "antievolutionary" statements occur that there is very little White has ever said about evolution per se to which the majority of Boasians would want to raise any objections.

> White summarizes evolutionary doctrine in his "Energy and the Evolution of Culture," laying down propositions which Boasians may find trite and futile, but which do not arouse the Bryanesque ardor imputed to them when evolution is propounded. Boasians do not deny that man requires food, controls his environment with the aid of tools, improves his control by invention and discovery, and alters social structure as a result of technological evolution [LOWIE 1946:416].

DARWIN NOT ATTACKED BY BOASIANS

Nonetheless, we must not fail to take into account the apparent similarity of the "antievolutionary" lapses with the continuing struggle within biology and philosophy between the Darwinists and the special creationists, vitalists, and other varieties of antimaterialists. As was seen earlier, these forces did indeed stage a strong comeback toward the end of the nineteenth century. The vogue of historical particularism corresponded in time with the influence of Henri Bergson in France and William James in the United States, both of whom were concerned to salvage as much as possible of the badly damaged theist position. In Germany, the influence of Windelband and Rickert was reaching its peak. At the same time, despite his many staunch defenders, such as Ernst Haeckel (the hero of Lowie's youth), A. Weissman, F. A. Lange, and E. Krause, there was strong political pressure against the dissemination of Darwin's views: "the theory became entangled with the theories of the Social Democrats and soon assumed a materialistic aspect which the state considered to be so anti-social as to deprecate its teaching in the schools" (FOTHERGILL 1952:121). Within biology, the attack was carried on by the vitalist Hans Driesch (1908) in Germany and by St. George Mivart (1871) in England. In Germany, the historian E. Radl (1930:388) could triumphantly declare in 1910, "Darwinism . . . is dead."

> This complete domination of contemporary thought by the Darwinian point of view did not last long. After the eighties one realm after another was lost to it, until finally it reigned supreme only in the field of biology [*ibid.*:372].

Radl's sketch of the return to theism and orthodoxy leaves no room for doubting that the Boasian movement was part of a widespread cultural phenomenon:

> Interest in religion revives. Scientific attacks on the literal accuracy of the bible are out of date . . . we speak again of the necessity for religion. . . . There came a reaction, too, against the evolutionary view of history. Some workers still believe that science should formulate the empirical laws that govern past events. But the attempts initiated by Buckle and Taine to write history around these laws has long been abandoned [*ibid.*:373].

Like White, Radl equates cultural antievolutionism with anti-Darwinism. But this was an error common to all those who sought to bolster up their own investment in the religious counterattack with references to the opposition that the theory of natural selection was encountering within biology. Radl of course was ridiculously optimistic about the demise of Darwinism within biology. At the very moment of its alleged death, Darwinism, united with the rediscovered Mendelian principles, was on the verge of its greatest victories. The entire field of experimental and paleontological biology was about to fall under its sway. By the twenties, it was vitalism and entelechism which were dead, while the new Synthetic Theory was in full command. This victory proves the essential continuity of evolutionary theory within the discipline of biology. At the height of the reaction, even under men like Hans Driesch, Thomas Hunt Morgan, and Jacques Loeb, all mentioned by Lowie as influential in his own outlook, there was never any question that the doctrine of descent with modification was about to be abandoned. The great issue of the day was whether natural selection was adequate for an explanation of the phenomena of adaptation. As Lowie says, just as these critics of Darwinism did not reject evolution per se, "neither did anthropologists reject all cultural evolution" (LOWIE 1956b:1006). But even this is a drawing of false battle lines. Boas did not reject evolutionism in any degree whatsoever. What he rejected was (1) biological reductionism, (2) cultural parallelism, and (3) universal standards of progress. At no point did Boas and his students, most of whom were atheists or agnostics, embrace a theistic interpretation of either biological or cultural evolution. As a matter of fact, the Boasian model of endlessly divergent cultural transformations is closer to the Darwinian model of the "tree of life," than is White's highly abstract notion of a universal cultural sequence. (We will have more to say about this in Chap. 22.) But at no point either, did the Boasians make the slightest headway toward formulating the general principles—the equivalent of the theory of natural selection—which would account for micro- and macro-evolutionary transformations.

Now in regard to the attack upon parallelism and racism, it is of paramount importance to express without rhetoric the fact that the Boasians rejected *all* coherent (i.e., noneclectic) explanations of sociocultural differences which made any appeal to any deterministic principle whatsoever, with rather marked indifference to whether they were inspired by materialist, idealist, or theist doctrines. This means that if we seek to understand the sociology of knowledge of the Boasian period, we must concentrate on the functional contribution of the rejection of all formulable determinisms.

THE PROBLEM OF SPENCERISM

But there is a minor dilemma that stands in the way. If cultural forces are presumed to be decisive in the unfolding of the Boasian epoch, how is it that Spencerism, so eminently suited to the ideological needs of competitive industrial and international capitalism, was able to be driven out of anthropology by the Boasians? This is the question White is unable to confront because of his inability to reconcile the alleged "reactionary" and regressive antievolutionism with Boas' "progressive" antiracism.

It should not be concluded that Spencerism had to be abandoned because it embraced a determinist view of history. On the contrary, Spencerism was a perfect expression of all individualistic, spontaneous, competitive, and unpredictable impulses. If it was chaos that was needed, the doctrine of the survival of the fittest was beautifully adapted to the wildest surges in Laufer's ocean. The interaction of the sociocultural and biological models of evolution all during the eighteenth and nineteenth centuries in no way produced a decisive adherence to determinist principles. Spencer was a materialist and a determinist. But others could read in the triumph of biological evolutionism a new vindication of the limitless nature of human destiny. Indeed, this was one of the options taken by an influential sector of learned opinion both in Europe and the United States.

> That very theory of evolution which had at first sight appeared to prove the mechanical method afresh, and to give it a new weapon wherewith to subdue the rebel world of life, helped rather to de-

> preciate its value and to shake its foundations. Regarded in the light of evolution, was the world what the mechanical theory had held it to be, an eternal persistence of unchangeable substances, an eternal repetition of necessary movements subject to unchangeable laws; or was it rather a perennial becoming, an incessant renewal of forms which cannot be foreseen, and which cannot therefore be subject to the rigid necessity of determinism? Is not variability, that is to say, the possibility of the new, presupposed in all evolution? Can the new be confined within the limits of any mathematical formula? How can mechanics, the science of eternal types, mirror the transient life of the real? It is not to the motionless ideas of reason that we must turn if we would sound the depths of being and grasp it in the productive moment of its generation, but rather to the free creations of imagination and energy [ALIOTTA 1914:xxi].

In the same vein, the wildly exciting effect that evolutionism had upon Nietzsche, with his uncontrollable "blond beast," is also deserving of note. It is clear, therefore, that the struggle against Social Darwinism by the Boasians is not to be taken for granted. If other aspects of the Boasian program are rooted in cultural forces, one cannot deny a similar derivation of the element of antiracism.

THE CULTURAL SOURCE OF THE ATTACK ON SPENCERISM

The attack on racist theories coincided in the United States with a period of strong democratic countercurrents. Boas was a member of an immigrant minority, who as an individual was obviously unprepared to concede the superiority of the dominant white Anglo-Saxon Protestant intellectual and business elites. Nonetheless, he was no superman; without supporting currents powerfully impelled by the conditions of his adopted social milieu, racism might very well have survived and triumphed in American, as it did in German and Italian, anthropology. But the antiracist countercurrents in the United States were nourished by the vast influx of Poles, Russians, and Italians, whose Catholicism or Judaism was not easily worked up into a master-race complex. These immigrant groups participated in the political and ideological struggle to break the pattern of unrestricted competition, which marks the beginnings of United States welfare capitalism. They provided the pressure for antitrust, pro-labor, and progressive income tax legislation prior to the outbreak of the First World War—the war "to Make the World Safe for

Democracy." In other words, the functional basis for the Boasian attack upon Spencerism had nothing whatsoever to do with the dark reactionary forces summoned up by White. The inappropriateness of the reactionary and regressive label is underscored as soon as we remind ourselves, although this scarcely seems necessary, that Spencerism may be dead in anthropology, but it is still a very conspicuous element in the ideological armamentarium of the American right, the Birchers, Dixiecrats, and right-wing Republicans. Richard Hofstadter's (1944) theory that Social Darwinism has passed out of existence in American life can be sustained only if we regard a belief in the essentials of the doctrine as synonymous with an awareness of who Herbert Spencer was.

In many ways the Boasian program corresponds rather closely with the fundamental ideological outlook associated with left-of-center political liberalism. The belief in multiracial democracy, relativity of custom, maximum freedom for the individual, the importance of material comfort, but the ultimately greater strength of the rational mind, and hence, the ultimate openness of society and history—all these themes are faithfully mirrored in the work of Boas and his pupils. In fact, there is only one point at which the Boasian program can be said to enter into serious conflict with the ideological manifestations of democratized liberalism: the culture concept. This concept, so vital to the destruction of racism, is potentially, if not inherently, deterministic and antidemocratic in its own right.

THE PARADOX OF CULTURAL DETERMINISM

If the enculturation experience determines for life how the individual is to conduct the entire pattern of his affairs, from sex to art, what then becomes of the vaunted freedom of the individual? To push to the furthest wall at once, if culture determines how we behave, then what difference is there between a democratic and totalitarian regime other than the illusion to which the actors in the democratic milieu have been enculturated that they are "freer" to choose their individual and collective destinies? It is no accident that Leslie White, the most outspoken critic of the Boasian program, has driven the concept of culture almost to this very extreme. It is not widely shared, although there are many anthropologists, including myself, who would agree that the association of freedom with political democracy is much more of an illusion than the average well-enculturated ideologue is willing to grant.

Among the Boasians, with one conspicuous exception, namely Alfred Kroeber, the relationship between culture and freedom has been treated in a diametrically opposite fashion. In essence, the Boasian program has pressed forward to a vision of the absolute maximum amount of individual freedom compatible with the continued serviceability of the culture concept. In other words, arguments against historical determinism have stopped just short of destroying cultural determinism.

There are two main routes to this position: (1) by emphasizing the creative role of the individual in cultural change, and (2) by stressing the variability and nonconformity of individuals with respect to culture patterns. The transport of the cultural-determinist position along these paths had a definite chronology. Boas set 1910 as the date which divided the period in which he stressed historical reconstruction from that in which he turned to "the interaction between individual and society" (BOAS 1948:311; orig. 1936). As I have already indicated, it was this concern which led to the development of culture and personality studies during the twenties.

Earlier there was the famous exchange between Sapir and Kroeber (to which we shall turn again in Chap. 12) when Sapir (1917:443) remarked: "I fail to see how we can deny a determining, and in some cases even extraordinarily determining, cultural influence to a large number of outstanding personalities." The culmination of this emphasis on the individual was embodied in the work of Paul Radin, one of Boas' students who shared with Kroeber the belief that Boas didn't really "do history." Radin's prescription for fulfilling the role of historian, however, was diametrically opposed to Kroeber's. To do history properly, one must study individuals. Radin's *Crashing Thunder: The Autobiography of a Winnebago Indian* (1926) represented the ultimate narrowing down of history to a single individual. (Actually, as *The Nature of Cultural Things* [HARRIS: 1964a] demonstrates, there are micro-focused options that even Radin overlooked.) Later, Radin explained his approach as follows:

> The [historical] task, let me insist, is always the same: a description of a specific period. . . . This can be done only by an intensive and continuous study of a particular tribe, a thorough knowledge of the language and an adequate body of texts and this can be accomplished only if we realize, once and for all, that we are dealing with specific, not generalized, men and women, and with specific, not generalized events. But the recognition of specific men and women should bring with it the realization that there are all types of individuals and that it is not, for instance, a

> Crow Indian who has made such and such a statement, uttered such and such a prayer, but a particular Crow Indian. It is this particularity that is the essence of all history [RADIN 1933:184-85].

The most perfect congruence between the culture concept and that of individual freedom has been achieved by David Bidney. Although not a Boasian, Bidney's position is entirely at the mercy of the factual critique that the Boasians employed to demonstrate the openness of history. "Ultimately," insists Bidney (1963:34), "human culture is the product of man's potentiality for freedom of creativity and freedom of choice." But it was not necessary for the Boasians to have moved as far as Bidney toward the *reductio ad absurdum* of cultural indeterminism. The important thing is that the Boasians remained well within the culturally tolerable limits of the ideology of freedom. Even Kroeber, as we shall see, professed and delighted in the unpredictability of cultural evolution. The crucial issue, however, is the probability of parallel and convergent development, informed by an understanding of the causal processes of cultural evolution.

The facts happen to be very much against the kind of situation that Bidney imagines to be the hallmark of humanity. The Boasian treatment of the facts was heavily weighted in favor of making it possible for ideologues to convince a wider public that the doctrines of political liberalism rest on a firm scientific foundation. I hasten to add, however, that in removing that foundation, post-Boasians have no intention of depriving anyone of his illusion of freedom. Rather it is our intention to help clear the way for an objective measurement of the *degree* of historical freedom that cultures and individuals possess. Any other formulation of the problem constitutes a philosophical disputation unworthy of modern anthropology.

The Ethnographic Basis of Particularism

11

Because of the heavy emphasis that the Boasians placed on achieving higher standards of evidence in ethnography, they have exposed themselves to captious and vindictive criticism, based on a re-evaluation of old, or the presentation of new, ethnographic data. Leslie White, the chief architect of the attack on Boas, has generated a considerable amount of resentment within the anthropological fraternity by his sometimes petty innuendos concerning the competence of Boas as a fieldworker. White claims Boas was excessively puritanical and prudish and that the amount of time he actually spent in the field has been inflated. White has also demanded to know why Boas, who was being honored by his students "as the world's greatest anthropologist," could not have formulated the concept of ambilateral descent, which has subsequently turned out to be the key to the understanding of Kwakiutl social organization. "The facts lay right before his eyes," says White (1963:67). Needless to say, one does not criticize Newton for failing to be Einstein.

Furthermore, it is unjust to impugn Boas' performance as a fieldworker in view of the absence of objective standards for measuring the performance of anthropologists in the field. It is of course a commonplace within the fraternity that certain anthropologists will acquire a reputation for being "good" or "bad" fieldworkers and that this judgment will be maintained independently of the evaluation of the substantive and theoretical product that issues from their field or library research. But this kind of thing rarely rises above the level of gossip. It seems unquestionable that Boas functioned quite well in terms of rapport, acceptance, and opportunities for participation and observation; his data-recording techniques were superb; and if one can judge from George Hunt and Henry Tate, whom Boas trained as assistants, no anthropologist has ever had better informants (*cf.* ROHNER 1966). The defective portions of Boas' ethnography have little to do with Boas' capacities as a fieldworker but are entirely a product of the theoretical prospectus of the Boasian program. It therefore remains an essential task, to which White has made important contributions, that the errors involved be publicized and their deleterious consequences upon cultural theory be traced. We must do this not in order to diminish Boas' stature, but rather in order to carry forward the perfection of the discipline to which he dedicated his life.

THE KWAKIUTL

As formulated by Boas, presented to his students, disseminated within anthropology, and diffused beyond to adjacent disciplines, Boas' Northwest Coast ethnography was the main factual armory for the assault on cultural materialism and historical determinism. For those who were interested in proving that the parallelists had grossly exaggerated the amount of order in cultural phenomena, the Northwest Coast Indian tribes were an inexhaustible source of apparent chaos. The Kwakiutl of Vancouver Island, who were the focus of Boas' field interests over a period of almost forty-five years, inhabited an area of great ecological complexity, distinguished by its rain forests, its migratory fish, and its large maritime mammalian species. The Kwakiutl, like the rest of the Northwest Coast peoples, exploited this environment through numerous hunting, fishing, and gathering techniques, but they practiced no agriculture. This mode of existence exposed them to the fluctuations in the size and location of the fish and animal populations, which could be abundant or scarce in conformity with a complex series of environmental circumstances. At the time of Boas' first visit in 1886, however, the Kwakiutl had already been in contact with Europeans for over ninety years. From 1849 on, they had been engaged in intensive trade with the Hudson's Bay Company, and the groups with whom Boas worked had in fact drastically modified their way of life in order to take up residence adjacent to the trading post at Fort Rupert. Toward the end of the nineteenth century, the Kwakiutl and the rest of the Northwest Coast groups were the object of visits by a steady stream of tourists, and their direct or indirect involvement with the events responsible for the development of the Pacific Northwest was steadily intensified all during the years of Boas' research.

The abuse of Kwakiutl ethnography centers on two major issues. At an early point in his study of their social organization in relationship to that of the surrounding tribes, Boas came to believe that the Kwakiutl were undergoing a matrilineal to patrilineal change in descent, contrary to that which the generalists of the nineteenth century had claimed to be the normal sequence. In addition, Boas became fascinated by the occurrence of destructive give-away feasts, or *potlatches,* which he insisted were beyond explanation involving economic causality. Both of these issues are related, since in sum, they involved a misunderstanding of the basic Kwakiutl residence and descent groups, the *numaym,* and the relationship between that group and the techno-environmental conditions under which the Kwakiutl lived during pre-contact times.

KWAKIUTL DESCENT

Boas (1897) presented his view of Kwakiutl social structure under the title, *The Social Organization and the Secret Societies of the Kwakiutl Indians.* It was based upon his belief that the Kwakiutl had kinship groups, originally identified as gens or clans but later simply termed *numaym,* in which membership and privileges were dependent upon a variety of matrilineal descent.

> Here the woman brings as a dower her father's position and privileges to her husband, who however is not allowed to use them himself, but acquires them for the use of his son. As the woman's father on his part has acquired his privileges in the same manner through his mother, a purely female law of descent is secured, although only through the medium of the husband [1897:334-35].

This description was the reverse of Boas' earlier opinion that "The child does not belong by birth to the gens of his father or mother, but may be made a member of any gens to which his father, mother, grandparents, or great-grandparents belonged" (1891a:609). In conformity with his announced interest in historical reconstruction, Boas speculated concerning the nature of the earlier phases of

Kwakiutl social organization. Initially, he seemed to have been convinced that the Kwakiutl had at one time been matrilineal and that they were in transition to the expected patrilineal stage: "The marriage ceremonies of the Kwakiutl seem to show that originally matriarchate prevailed also among them" (quoted in WHITE 1963:52). Within a few years, however, Boas fell victim to the demon of disorder. In 1895 he reversed his thinking, defied the prevailing evolutionary scheme, and argued that the transition that had taken place was in the opposite direction, and that the "organization must have been at one time a purely paternal one" (1897:334–35); hence, the transition had gone from patriliny to matriliny.

His reasoning follows a most tendentious path, which of course is all the more painful with benefit of hindsight. The evidence consisted mainly of the absence of the kinds of survival that should have been found had the former stage been matrilineal. Thus, there was "No trace left of an inheritance from the wives' brothers," matrilocality was absent, and there were no legends or myths which traced the origins of the groups to matrilineal ancestors. There were, however, some legends that mentioned patrilineal ancestors. As for the latter:

> It is true that these traditions are probably not very old and have been modified with the changing social life of the people; but from what we know of the development of myths we should expect to find in them traces at least of the old maternal institutions; but the fact that they are invariably and always are explained by geneaologies seems to my mind conclusive proof that the paternal organization of the tribe preceded the present one [*ibid.*:335].

With the development of the concept of nonunilinear descent through the work of Goodenough (1956) and Davenport (1959), it has become obvious that Boas was trying to force the Kwakiutl *numaym* into one of two categories, both of which were inappropriate. The salient feature of the *numaym* is precisely the fact that there is no rigid adherence to one or the other unilineal principle, but that individuals may make use of ambiguous and flexible principles in aligning themselves and their offspring with various residential and descent groupings.

Actually, by 1920 Boas had once again changed his emphasis and had recognized that something was wrong. Regarding the system of matrilineal descent through a man's daughter's husband's daughter, he now said, "I believe this does not quite correspond to the actual conditions." His analysis, however, seems to have remained in a state of provisional formulation, since it contained contradictory statements. On the one hand, and in conformity with the ultimate solution reached by other analysts, he noted that "The transmission from individual to individual through marriage is most arbitrary." On the other hand, he also maintained that "the *numayms* are based on descent with a preference for the paternal line" (1948b:362; orig. 1920). Despite his evident inability to offer anything like a coherent picture of the observed system, Boas continued to insist upon the validity of the now more than ever tenuous reconstruction: "I do not see any reason for a change of my opinion in regard to the relative antiquity of the transfer of names and privileges through the male or female line" (*ibid.*: 366). It should be noted that in context there are a number of provisos which indicate the speculative quality of this conclusion. But the extreme interest in Boas' handling of the *numaym* stems from the fashion in which he and his students seized upon this case to destroy the supposed universal tendency for patrilineality to follow matrilineality and at the same time to discredit the entire historical determinist position.

On the basis of this one drastically deficient case, there gradually diffused out of Schermerhorn Hall at Columbia, through lecture, word of mouth, article, and text, the unquestioned dogma that Boas had proved that it was just as likely that patrilineality succeeded matrilineality as the reverse. When the case was cited in the general textbook that Boas had edited, Gladys Reichard (1938:425) referred to it as "more convincing" than the other possible instance among the Trobrianders (also highly dubious, however) because "the details of its cause are more positive." Boas' speculations concerning a patrilineal to matrilineal development among the Kwakiutl actually gave rise to an attempt to show that this sequence was the normal one. Thus, John Swanton (1905) tried to demonstrate that it was precisely the matrilineally organized tribes, such as the Haida of the Northwest, the Zuni and Hopi among the Pueblos, and the Creek and Natchez of the Southeast, who were the culturally most advanced peoples, while the groups that were organized on a patrilineal and a bilateral basis were deemed to be more primitive. Lowie (1920:150–55), Kroeber (1923:355–58), and Goldenweiser (1914:436) all fell for this curiously involuted parallelism. As Murdock (1949:189) has shown: "This inverted evolutionistic scheme of a bilateral-patrilineal-matrilineal succession in the forms of social organization became an established dogma in American anthropology." It is clear, therefore, that neither Boas nor his students approached the facts of Kwakiutl social organization free of rather sweeping hypotheses. The pity of it is that their hypotheses were not clearly phrased and that even had they been correct, they would still not have been suitable substitutes for the determinist systems to whose overthrow they were dedicated. For what after all was the explanation of the alleged patrilineal-to-matrilineal shift among the Kwakiutl? Nothing but the proximity of the more northerly tribes who were matrilineal. That is, the functional interpretation of Kwakiutl social structure was left to the mercy of the postulated diffusionary influence.

A MODERN INTERPRETATION OF THE NUMAYM

It was only long after Boas' death that there began to emerge the lineaments of a functional explanation of the *numaym* which at once eclipses and renders superfluous attempts to derive its nonunilinear character from speculative diffusionary impulses. Thomas Hazard (1960) has suggested how the bilateral claims of descent were probably utilized by individuals to associate themselves with chieftains who were best able to provide safety and sustenance. During the sharp population decline brought about by the stresses of the contact period, the ability of a local group to exploit its hereditary fishing and hunting resources depended upon the ability to recruit adequate personnel through all descent lines. Boas' genealogies actually showed the complete scrambling of descent lines as all sorts of claims were pressed and all sorts of exceptions to the allegedly preferred arrangements took place, but he did not attempt a functional analysis of these phenomena. The real force of Hazard's interpretation is that it links the nonunilinear nature of the *numaym* to the Northwest Coast technology, economy, and habitat and, in so doing, at once provides an insight into the situation on Vancouver Island, which, however tentatively offered, opens vistas of fruitful inquiry.

THE POTLATCH

In order to appreciate the advance that this represents over the Boasian position, we must take up that second and by far more influential focus of Boas' fieldwork, the Kwakiutl potlatch. As has already been suggested, if one wished to demonstrate the lawlessness of culture, the Northwest Coast was one of the best places to do it. At the time of Boas' first visit, and probably for several decades prior to that date, the Kwakiutl were practicing a form of feasting that seems to defy any sort of techno-environmental or techno-economic explanation. Here was a whole people caught up in an exchange system that conferred greatest prestige on the individual who gave away the greatest amount of the most valuable goods. Since previous analyses of economic behavior had stressed the importance of husbanding the products of labor and of rationally apportioning work effort in relation to needs and consumption patterns, the Kwakiutl material was in effect the death-knell of *homo economicus*, conceived either in the capitalist or socialist image. Moreover, it was not merely that goods were given away, but that on occasion, so overwhelming was this passion for self-glorification, that blankets were ripped to shreds, valuable fish oil set on fire, whole villages burned, and "slaves" thrown into the sea to drown. Boas' account of the potlatch has probably been the single most influential ethnographic description ever published. It set in motion a series of concentric effects which have yet to lose their strength, centering first among anthropologists, but steadily advancing into adjacent domains and out to a vast educated public.

The continuing pertinence of the potlatch data derives from the fact that Boas' Kwakiutl material was picked up by his student Ruth Benedict and woven into *Patterns of Culture*, probably the most widely read anthropological book of all time. The purport of this book, to which we shall return in a later chapter, was to draw psychological portraits of three different cultures representing three different portions of the spectrum of cultural patterning. In this endeavor, the Zuni were Apollonian, the Dobuans were paranoid, and the Kwakiutl were Dionysians touched with megalomania.

> The object of all Kwakiutl enterprises was to show oneself superior to one's rivals. This will to superiority they exhibited in the most uninhibited fashion. It found expression in uncensored self-glorification and ridicule of all comers. Judged by the standards of other cultures the speeches of their chiefs . . . are unabashed megalomania [BENEDICT 1959:169; orig. 1934].

Looking at the potlatch as seen through the eyes of its participants, especially of its chiefly contestants, the facts that stood out for Boas and his students were the boasting of greatness, the announced intentions of shaming one's rivals, and the compulsion which a man who had been shamed felt to retaliate against his rival by holding an even more lavish give-away. Under Benedict's skillful literary handling, the facts of potlatch took on the appearance of an ultimate mania, without rhyme or reason except the inflated egos of the chiefs and their reckless desire to hold on to or to augment their hereditary claims to prestige. Everything in Kwakiutl life was affected by this strange custom.

> The whole economic system of the Northwest Coast was bent to the service of this obsession. There were two means by which a chief could achieve the victory he sought. One was by shaming his rival by presenting him with more property than he could return with the required interest. The other was by destroying property. In both cases the offering called for return, though in the first case the giver's wealth was augmented, and in the second he stripped himself of goods. The consequences of the two methods seem to us at the opposite poles. To the Kwakiutl they were merely complementary means of subduing a rival, and the highest glory of life was the act of complete destruction [*ibid.*:172].

During the past fifteen years a drastic reinterpretation of the potlatch has been put forward by a number of Northwest Coast specialists. This new synthesis has been achieved by combining historical and ecological interests and by linking the peculiarities of Kwakiutl ethnography to more general types of phenomena.

THE POTLATCH IN HISTORICAL PERSPECTIVE

Helen Codere's *Fighting with Property* (1950) was the first attempt to see the potlatch in relationship to the Euro-American development of the modern Northwest. It is readily established through Boas' and Hunt's family histories and through the records of the trading post and Indian agents, that aboriginal patterns of potlatch bore only a faint resemblance to those observed toward the end of the century. The Kwakiutl, like all other tribal peoples in the path of the Euro-American expansion, were the victims of excruciating ecological and sociocultural pressures, beginning from the moment of the appearance of the first Europeans in the region. These pressures led dramatically and inevitably to the extinction of their aboriginal patterns and to the virtual extinction of the Kwakiutl as a viable breeding population. Even before the explorer Vancouver contacted them in 1792, they were already trading in muskets obtained from the neighboring Nootka and had begun to experience the first effects of European diseases. During the early part of the nineteenth century, a slow increase in trade was accompanied by a drastic decrease in population, brought about by epidemics of smallpox and respiratory diseases to which, like all Amerindians, they lacked immunity. Between 1836 and 1853 their population fell from 23,000 to about 7,000. In 1849 the establishment of the Hudson Bay trading post at Fort Rupert further intensified both the trade with Europeans and the effect of disease. Then in 1858, 25,000 to 30,000 Euro-American males set out for the British Columbia goldfields, making nearby Victoria their jumping-off place. Kwakiutl women in large numbers began to serve these men as prostitutes, and venereal diseases now accelerated the trend toward depopulation. By the eighties, the great Northwest canning industry was in full production with 6,000 boats on the Fraser River alone, and many Kwakiutl responded to the demand for factory workers. At about the same time, lumbering, which during the decade 1870–80 had already produced 350 million board feet, also sought to attract the Kwakiutl. By the time of Boas' first visit, the whole Kwakiutl population had sunk below 2,000!

With the establishment of the Hudson Bay Company trading post, Codere shows how the potlatch involved a preponderance of European trade goods, especially blankets, and hence, how it reflected the new, prodigiously expansive industrial and commercial economy. Another consequence of the Euro-American presence was the prohibition of warfare, and Codere attempts to draw a connection between the cessation of warfare and the development of the flamboyant patterns of hostile potlatching in the late period. According to Codere, when the Indians could no longer wage war, they fought with property, which had become available on an unprecedented scale.

Inasmuch as Codere's book was written as a doctoral thesis under Ruth Benedict's supervision, one scarcely expects it to contain a sustained criticism of the Boasian position. The historical perspective did, however, prepare the way for more penetrating appraisals.

Codere's theory that competitive potlatch substituted for warfare does not by itself involve anything other than a kind of "force of tradition" explanation for the strange phenomena observed by Boas. This may ultimately prove to be a viable perspective, although there are two reasons for withholding judgment. First, the same theory has been used to explain the migratory development of labor patterns to the Rand mines in South Africa but with a noteworthy absence of success (*cf.* HARRIS 1959b). Second, Codere (1956) herself later went on to show that there was a more "amiable" and "playful" side to Kwakiutl life, especially among ordinary people as distinguished from the chiefs, in which the furious competitiveness associated with the great contests of the late nineteenth-century was nowhere in evidence.

As I have said, Codere's modification of the Benedict-Boas version of the potlatch was not intended to lead the way toward a major break with the traditional view. Indeed, in pointing to the amiable side of the Kwakiutl, Codere represented herself as merely elaborating on the caution that Boas had belatedly advised concerning the one-sidedness of Benedict's portrait:

> The amiable qualities that appear in intimate family life are easily overlooked. These are not by any means absent. In contrast to the jealousy with which prerogatives are guarded, everyone within the family circle belittles his position. Husband and wife address each other as "You whose slave I am," or "You whose dog I am" [BOAS 1938a:685].

REVOLT OF THE NORTHWEST SPECIALISTS

By the middle of the fifties a ground swell of dissatisfaction with Boas' Kwakiutl material had set in among other Northwest Coast specialists. The above quote figured prominently in the rear-guard battle that was waged to protect Boas' image. Verne Ray (1955:140) set off a lively exchange in the *American Anthropologist* by demanding to know why Melville Herskovits' biography of Boas had not mentioned the fact that the master had failed to "speak out in correction of the errors of his students, such as Benedict [with] the result that the ethnographic picture for the Northwest Coast as visualized, taught, and accepted by many anthropologists is that which in fact applies only to the nobility of the southern Kwakiutl." Rushing to defend Boas, Lowie (1956a:162) pointed out that it was Boas himself who had indicated the need for mentioning the Kwakiutl's more homely virtues. In his rejoinder, Ray (1956) stressed the omission by Boas of any direct reference to Benedict and of the small amount of space that Boas had devoted to this crucial point.

> It is hard for me to see how this can be considered an adequate answer to, and correction for, the misinterpretations in a book (Benedict 1934) which has sold 600,000 copies. . . . Ruth Benedict's book had appeared four years earlier. But Boas does not mention her or her "Dionysian" formulation in his article and does not list the book in his bibliographical footnotes. I should add that I do not consider that it was mandatory that Boas correct Benedict, but I wish that he had [RAY 1956:167–68].

Ray, in criticizing Herskovits, had elicited sharp rebuttals from both Lowie and Kroeber, thereby entangling himself all at once with three of the most influential living anthropologists (not to mention the spirits of Boas and Benedict). This alone seems to provide a clue as to why Ray failed to mention the fact that Boas was indeed under a special obligation to correct whatever Lowie, Kroeber, and Herskovits conceded was wrong in *Patterns of Culture:* Boas had signed his name to the book's Introduction (about which, more later).

The reformulation of Kwakiutl ethnography by Codere and others (*cf.* DRUCKER 1939:955) failed to cut through the skein of particularism with which Boas had surrounded his description. The Kwakiutl material remained cut off from the world of theory. Nonetheless, the Fort Rupert potlatch could now be seen as a definite product of the contact situation, thereby defeating at once all attempts to prove by means of Boas' data that its explanation was governed by causative factors too complex for nomothetic formulation. The population decline, introduction of wage labor, sudden abundance of goods, repression of warfare, and the earlier pattern of communal feasting taken together indicate that a highly determinate set of factors were at work upon the Kwakiutl. If one objects that the adaptation achieved was rather unique, there remains the obviously predictable fact that their adjustment was not viable, and therefore scarcely the kind of diachronic trajectory with which one would want to construct the laws of history.

THE MYTH OF THE NORTHWEST EDEN

Actually, there is a good chance that we shall eventually be able to make further sense out of the run-away aspects of the Kwakiutl system by taking into consideration the contrasting comparative material characteristic of other contact phenomena. In this regard, the fact that the Kwakiutl resource base was not menaced by the whites and that an attempt was made to lure the Kwakiutl into wage labor and cash trade under free market conditions in a booming economy, without the usual coercive subterfuges, may provide the missing ingredient.

In the meantime, a promising beginning has been made toward interpreting the pre-contact potlatch in conformity with nomothetic ecological principles. Andrew Vayda (1961c) and Wayne Suttles (1960) are responsible for formulating the issues upon which the description and explanation of the aboriginal patterns now seem to depend. From Boas' descriptions, from the accounts of Indian agents, and from superficial acquaintance with the ecology of the Northwest littoral, a deep-seated conviction had developed that the bountifulness of nature in this area was so great that vast surpluses of food were guaranteed to the human population on the basis of a minimum productive effort. Codere pictured the Kwakiutl as having a "fantastic" surplus economy (1950:63) and bases her entire thesis on its unquestioned veracity. In the reformulations of Suttles and Vayda, however, this view is discredited. The salmon and the other river-spawning and off-shore migratory fish, upon which the main subsistence load depended, did not present themselves for harvest in the abundance and with the regularity claimed for them. On the basis of impressionistic accounts of single runs, when salmon "in a solid black mass in aggregate motion" choked a stream from bank to bank, it is possible to exaggerate the long-range harvest potential of delimited portions of the region. Annual variability, both of a general as well as of more localized scope, has been demonstrated not only for fish but for supplemental land products as well. These considerations have been elaborated by Piddocke (1965) specifically for the Kwakiutl. There is evidence that under aboriginal conditions the Kwakiutl were probably the frequent victims of serious food shortages caused by variations in weather and climate, by shifting patterns of migrations, and by uncontrollable variations in the rate of reproduction of the flora and fauna upon which they depended.

But what then are we to make of the abundance that obviously did exist during the period of maximum potlatch? That the remnant Kwakiutl groups toward the close of the nineteenth century were indeed producing what has been called a "superfluous" surplus—food or the means for obtaining food in quantities far beyond ability to consume over a long-range period—is not to be doubted. But one of the theoretical requirements for such a condition is a stable or declining population. With their rapid decrease in numbers, the Kwakiutl certainly could afford to burn their fish oil, destroy their blankets, or ruin their houses. They were a society celebrating its own funeral. And the funeral rites could be all the more lavish because simultaneous with the drop in population there came a vast improvement in the technological repertory for exploiting their environment—guns, iron for harpoons, hooks, and possibly most important, the modern European carpentry kit with which they were able to perfect the construction of their canoes.

THE POTLATCH AND THE NUMAYM

Thus, as soon as we put the Kwakiutl back into nature and proceed on the assumption that their way of life represents an adaptive response to a given techno-economic equation, a whole new panorama of ethnographic comparisons opens before us. To explain the potlatch, we are no longer dependent on the Digger Indian myth with which Benedict lulled her readers into innocence: "In the beginning God gave each people its cup to drink from." For now we see that the bilateral character of the *numaym* as presented in Hazard's analysis is precisely the kind of arrangement that one would expect if the aboriginal potlatch had functioned not to maintain an incomprehensibly self-destructive nobility in the state of bloated ego-satisfaction, but rather a precariously balanced human population in maximum fitness with respect to a bountiful but unpredictable environment. Following Vayda and Suttles, we begin to see the potlatch as a functional response to the problem of minimizing the effects of seasonal and long-term fluctuations in the productivity of the local groups. This was accomplished by the relatively frequent collection of a *numaym*'s economic surplus under the auspices of its chief and by its redistribution again under the auspices of the chief to temporarily disadvantaged *numaym* who inhabited different portions of the tribal area. Like the explanation offered by Codere and the Boasians, this new ecological approach emphasizes the importance of the prestige which the *numaym* potlatch leaders derive from giving gifts of food and other valuables to members of neighboring groups. But whereas this prestige has nothing but a completely inexplicable and unqualified penchant for self-glorification at its base in Benedict's account, we now see that the entire prestige system was probably in definite and controlled articulation with aboriginal techno-environmental and techno-economic conditions vital to the maintenance of individual and collective life. In other words, we see a system, explicable in scientific terms, where previously there was nothing but the unintelligible ravings of megalomaniacs. Under aboriginal conditions, the Kwakiutl potlatch must have been one of the varieties of redistributive systems by which incipiently stratified social systems maintained their productivity levels and maximized their social cohesion. This concept, introduced first by the economist Karl Polanyi, ushered in a new era in Polynesian ethnography, when Marshall Sahlins (1958) showed how it could account for variations in social stratification among Pacific Island groups. The same concept has helped to identify the causal factors responsible for many of the remarkable parallelisms between the evolutionary trajectories of Old and New World civilizations.

It seems highly probable that within the next generation many of the features of primitive cultures that appeared as intractable enigmas to the Boasians will yield their secrets to comparative cultural ecology. This is not to say that we are on the verge of returning to a scheme of universal parallel evolution, but rather that we have within our grasp the ability to formulate the general principles by which both parallel and divergent sequences occur.

BOAS' ETHNOGRAPHIC STRATEGY

In this context it is relevant to return once again to the cardinal inadequacy of the Boasian program—its unadmitted, but nonetheless present, and unfortunately false or inadequate, hypotheses. Under the Boasian program, ethnography was dedicated to the systematic collection of the wrong facts, that is, to the facts about which it could have been declared at the outset that they were precisely those least likely to contribute to an understanding of sociocultural systems. It is for this reason, and not for vindictiveness, that we are obliged to pay full heed to the analysis that White and others have rendered of the nature of the materials with which Boas filled his 5,000 pages of Kwakiutl publications. By far the overwhelming bulk of this labor was concerned with folk tales, mythology, religion, art, ceremony, and mechanical aspects of technology and technique (so-called material culture). Large amounts of space are devoted to food about which we can no longer accept Victor Barnouw's (1949:252) dry optimism:

> When Franz Boas published page after page of blueberry-pie recipes in Kwakiutl, the old man probably knew what he was after; but when his students did the same kind of thing, they often lacked the driving central purpose which animated Boas [1949, quoted in MEAD 1959b:32].

Codere, who has made greater use of Boas' materials than anyone else, has tried to save the day with the conclusion that "Boas' Kwakiutl materials are ready to work with; an important part of his legacy is that the understanding of the Kwakiutl is already far advanced" (1959:73). If this statement refers at all to nomothetic understanding, it is valid only to the extent that we are able to use the Kwakiutl material in spite of having to labor under the dead weight of an enormous amount of *relative* trivia. Granted that one can never tell from which direction the angel of light will descend, we share the obligation of making ourselves responsible for strategic guesses. Boas consistently guessed wrong. How else shall we explain Codere's own admission that the 5,000 pages of Kwakiutl ethnography are an inadequate basis for a general treatment of the culture? "It is not possible to present a synthesized account of Kwakiutl culture based upon

Boas' works" (*ibid.*:66). For reasons previously stated, I cannot agree with Murdock, when in a choleric outburst over not being able to use the Kwakiutl for his World Ethnographic sample, he denounced the "extravagantly overrated" Boas and insisted that "He was not even a good fieldworker" (MURDOCK 1949:xiv). But Murdock's pique is well justified if "Despite Boas' 'five-foot shelf' of monographs on the Kwakiutl, this tribe falls into the quartile of those whose social structure and related practices are least adequately described among the 250 covered in this study" (*ibid.*). Boas may have been a good fieldworker, but he was good about the wrong things.

EMIC AND ETIC ECONOMICS

The evaluation of Boas' ethnographic product and the reason why it was doomed from the outset not to yield insights into the nomothetic principles which govern human history can best be stated by making use of the distinction between emic and etic research strategies. When Ray first gave public utterance to "the cocktail room discussions" of dissatisfaction with Boas' ethnographic monographs, he cited among other inadequacies the lack of economic data. Lowie, with his usual on-the-spot aptitude for citing chapter and verse, flatly denied this accusation:

> Nor were economic phenomena "neglected" by him. In the earlier monograph on the Eskimo he describes their economic life with associated techniques, gives an account of land utilization, and discusses trading (Boas 1888:419-561). Conceivably he might have gathered much more of relevant information on the Northwest Coast, but if property, inheritance, and potlatches are economic phenomena, they were not *neglected* [LOWIE 1956a:161].

Similarly, although admitting that Boas was largely concerned with "symbolic" aspects of culture (mythology, language, and art in that order) Codere (1959:61) insists that he did not slight other types of description and analysis. She forthwith begins to total up the number of Boas' publications in which "non-symbolic" interests are indulged. But both Boas' supporters and his detractors have by and large missed the essential point here. As we shall see in the case of Lowie's own ethnographic interest in things economic, the decision to study "economics" is not at all what is needed if one is to begin to hope that his data may contribute to the formulation of lawful principles. This is because there are emic economics and etic economics. In the former instance, one studies the potlatch as it appears to the potlatchers; in the latter instance, one studies potlatch as it appears within the frame of cross-culturally valid analytical and quantitative categories, such as calories, man-hour in-put, redistribution, stratification with respect to access to resources, and so forth.

EMICS AND THE BOASIAN PROGRAM

In the strategically most decisive sense, the significance of Boas' turn to ethnography from physics and of his selection of the historical method as opposed to the method of science was that thereafter the definitive test of a good ethnography was whether or not it faithfully mirrored the world of the natives *as the natives saw it*. I am not aware of any sustained exception to this viewpoint anywhere in Boas' ethnographic product. Certainly we shall find no exception throughout all of the thousands of pages of texts collected by himself or his two trained informants, Hunt and Tate. The essence of such texts is precisely their unswerving fidelity to what the native said or thought.

To view Boas' fundamental ethnographic strategy in terms of the emic-etic option permits us to see at once the unbroken development that links his initial period of historical reconstruction with the apparently anomalous concern for culture and personality to which it ultimately gave birth. When White accuses Boas of psychological reductionism, and when Boas himself refers to the importance of psychological principles, there is at bottom the issue that divides emics from etics, not that which divides psychology from culture. It is not as a psychologist that Boas turns to his descriptions of potlatch protocol and raven myth elements; it is rather as an ethnographer with an overwhelming bias in favor of emic interpretations. It is as an emicist that he clings to the remnants of Bastian's elementary ideas, gives to his general book the title *The Mind of Primitive Man*, and repeatedly insists that two culture elements are not the same if they *mean* different things to the people who possess them. Margaret Mead's comments on her apprenticeship under Boas seem to confirm this point:

> To get the depth of understanding he required meant submerging his thinking in that of another. It meant learning to think in another's terms and to view the world through another's eyes. The most intimate knowledge of an informant's thought processes was mandatory and could only be obtained by intensive work over a long period. Important concepts and strange viewpoints had to be checked with other material and with a number of in-

> formants; supplementary information had to be obtained elsewhere. But Boas conceived of his main task as the adoption of an informant's mode of thought while retaining full use of his own critical faculties [1959b:58].

Mead associates Boas' interest in the single informant and his indifference or even hostility to statistical treatments of cultural phenomena (despite his skillful use of statistics in physical anthropology) with this same penchant for the natives' point of view. Further confirmation of the saliency of this option in the outlook of Boas and his students may be found in Frederica de Laguna's (1960:792) insistence that the rejection of mechanical or biological analogies as a means of interpreting the world of culture is the most distinctive feature of American cultural anthropology:

> While cultures themselves and their inherent values have become recognized in one sense as phenomena of the natural order, they are not to be understood through mechanical or biological analogies or through an analysis which the scientist can make from outside by confidently appealing to alleged sociological or psychological laws. Rather, this inner world is to be entered with humility, the passport a readiness to listen while the native himself speaks.
>
> For at last we have come full circle, and the savages who first gave us anthropology itself are those through whose eyes and hearts we are to discover not simply the worlds and minds of primitive men, but, in so doing, what it is to be human.

And Boas himself, in one of his last works, forcefully advocated the necessity for interpreting the native's behavior in terms of the native's categories:

> In natural sciences we are accustomed to demand a classification of phenomena expressed in a concise and unambiguous terminology. The same term should have the same meaning everywhere. We should like to see the same in anthropology. As long as we do not overstep the limits of one culture we are able to classify its features in a clear and definite terminology. We know what we mean by the terms family, state, government, etc. As soon as we overstep the limits of one culture we do not know in how far these may correspond to equivalent concepts. If we choose to apply our classification to alien cultures we may combine forms that do not belong together. The very rigidity of definition may lead to a misunderstanding of the essential problems involved. . . . If it is our serious purpose to understand the thoughts of a people the whole analysis of experience must be based on their concepts, not ours [1943:314].

As Codere (1959:72) remarks, "Boas' Kwakiutl work is the product of a consistent, monumental, and unfinished plan motivated by the desire to understand a people." He saw that "desire as understanding the 'mental life' of a people as reflected in their culture."

I take strong exception when Codere goes on to state that "no new anthropological aim" has come along to replace Boas' aim of understanding the mental life of a culture. There has always been the option of seeking to understand a culture in its emic and etic manifestations in terms of the lawful processes governing the generation of similarities and differences in human history. Such an option can only be fulfilled by systematic separation of emics and etics and by the study of both under the guidance of operationalized concepts and overt hypotheses. The error of trying to study culture "without theoretical bias" is laid to rest when we realize that neither Boas nor his students admitted the validity of the logic-empirical procedures that are essential to the study of history, if such a study is to yield nomothetic results.

Kroeber

12

The first of Boas' students to receive a doctorate at Columbia University was Alfred Lewis Kroeber. By the time Kroeber came under Boas' influence, he had already earned a Master of Arts degree in English and was teaching as a lecturer in that subject. He later explained the difference between himself and Boas in terms of this background:

> My education included some contacts with experimental science which I found highly stimulating, but consisted primarily of generalized activity in the linguistic-literary-historical field, remaining rather undifferentiated until I settled upon anthropology as definitive profession [KROEBER 1935:566].

Heightened sensitivity to aesthetic patterns, concern with nuances of style, and a reliance upon intuitive judgments heavily outweighed Kroeber's aspirations toward social science. He never seriously believed that anthropology could become anything other than one of the humanities. But the vast scope of his scholarly erudition, his Olympian geniality, and omnivorous intellect were universally admired among anthropologists and by important segments of the larger academic community. After his "guru's" death, Kroeber became the undisputed "grand old man" of the profession, an image richly reflected by undiminished scholarly activity to the last moments of his eighty-fifth year. I shall leave to his biographers the task of balancing theoretical critique against the erudition and charm of his scholarship. For the present, what seems most relevant is that Kroeber began his career with certain neo-Kantian assumptions concerning history, which were never thrown off and which preserved him in all fundamentals as an historical particularist throughout his life.

VULNERABILITY TO IDEOLOGICAL CURRENTS

Kroeber was fond of saying that he had not really become interested in theoretical issues until he had reached middle age, and he advised others to follow suit. Like Boas, he urged that theory should result from fieldwork conducted as far as possible without theoretical preconceptions. Turning to his earliest anthropological publications, however, one finds an already well-formed theoretical prospectus modeled after Boas' views. Following publications concerned with the folklore of the Smith Sound Eskimo and of the Cheyenne, Kroeber submitted his doctoral thesis, *Decorative Symbolism of the Arapaho* (1901), in which he attempted to show that both decorative and symbolic art forms could occur simultaneously, thus easily defeating Alfred C. Haddon's (1895) notions of a uniform progression of art styles. But neither his brief field exposure prior to 1901 nor his equally brief acquaintance with the literature of the social sciences up to that point furnished a sound basis for his more general conclusion: ". . . all search for origin in anthropology can lead to nothing but false results" (KROEBER 1901:332). This was a large conclusion to reach at age twenty-five at the end of a dissertation whose twenty-eight pages are mainly devoted to the art forms of one badly mauled American Indian society. But as Julian Steward has remarked, "The thesis . . . on Arapaho art . . . clearly set forth Kroeber's basic and life-long point of view" (1961:1043).

The conditions of Kroeber's first employment as an anthropologist illustrate the effective nature of the linkage between the neo-Kantian perspective and the larger milieu in which the Boasian movement unfolded. Starting in 1901, Kroeber began a lifelong involvement with the Department of Anthropology at Berkeley, which, like Boas at Columbia, he was obliged to build practically from scratch. During the first five years of Kroeber's employment his salary came directly from Mrs. Phoebe Hearst, William Randolph Hearst's mother (STEWARD 1961:1044–45). Under these circumstances, it is difficult to imagine how someone from the left end of the intellectual spectrum could personally have achieved a strong institutional base, much less how he could have advanced a whole new branch of learning against its many competitors. The main difficulty that Boas' students confronted may have been a lack of comparative perspective. The milieu in which they operated had so successfully prevented the growth of university-based radical opinion, that in attacking the foundations of nineteenth-century historical determinism, they were exposed only to fundamentally sympathetic critics. Among themselves, the Boasians created an illusion of dialectic exchange, as when Kroeber imagined himself and Boas at opposite sides of the history-science dichotomy, or when Kroeber and Sapir clashed over the need for a concept of the superorganic. But in reality, only a very small part of the spectrum of social-science tradition had achieved academic representation. It cannot be said too often that the progress of intellectual life requires confrontation between the widest possible variety of theories and hypotheses. The penalty of provincialism is always the same: errors are piled on errors, because everyone is tolerant of similar faults.

THE ATTACK AGAINST MORGAN

Laboring under this handicap, Kroeber attempted to enlarge upon the element of randomness that he had exposed in the study of Arapaho art. At approximately the same time that Boas and John Swanton were attacking Lewis Henry Morgan's notions concerning the priority of matrilineal descent, Kroeber turned his attention to Morgan's treatment of descriptive and classificatory kinship terminologies. Kroeber's attack on Morgan, unlike Lowie's, as we shall see in the next chapter, did not arise out of a careful study of Morgan's contribution. It is even possible that Kroeber's knowledge of Morgan was acquired secondhand, or at least he never seems to have taken Morgan seriously, as Lowie was ultimately obliged to do. Kroeber's approach to Morgan was not characterized by the genial toleration he so readily manifested during his maturity on behalf of less qualified contributions, e.g. "leaving room for David Bidney to have God and prayer in his interpretation of culture" (KROEBER 1952:115). By attacking Morgan in a famous article, "Classificatory Systems of Relationship" (1909), Kroeber misled a generation of anthropologists into contempt for Morgan's most enduring contribution. But it was Kroeber's view of the relationship between kinship terminology and social structure that subsequently proved to be incorrect and impoverished.

Morgan, it will be recalled, believed that classificatory terminologies were associated with the evolutionary emergence of unilinear descent groups, that they reflected the great sway of kinship institutions during most of human history, and that they were replaced by descriptive terminologies during the transition from kinship to state-organized societies. Kroeber's attack followed the strategy that had proved successful in his thesis. It was the same strategy that Boas himself was about to sum up in *The Mind of Primitive Man,* namely, an attempt to demonstrate that the allegedly sequential elements can actually be found existing together in the same society at the same time. Thus, Kroeber argued that the kinship terminologies of all cultures, primitive or civilized, consisted of a mixture of classificatory and descriptive tendencies. There was no general rule by which one or the other form could be correlated with social structure. One has only to consider the classificatory nature of such English terms as "uncle" and "cousin" to realize that Morgan must have been carried away by his schemes to have supposed that such practices were confined to cultures on the clan level of organization. But Kroeber was not content to restrict his attack to just this one point; his interest lay in the "toppling" of Morgan's whole developmental scheme. As he explained much later when he wrote a preface for the publication of his collected essays:

> As an anthropologist in the face of Morgan, I could not well stop there; both because his primary segregation into classificatory and descriptive types did not hold water, and because it was easy to show that internal conceptual logic, such as of reciprocity, analogy, and consistency, was sufficiently frequent and strong to prevent sets of kinship terms being construed as mere reflections or indices of marriage or other social institutions. Therewith the whole of Morgan's speculative schema of origin and development of society seemed to me impaired or toppled. I continue to think so until today [1952:172].

Kroeber eventually regretted his dogmatic refusal to accept the principle that kin terminologies reflect social institutions. When the English anthropologist W. H. R. Rivers challenged Kroeber's stand, Kroeber says about himself that he became "intransigent in rebuttal" and that it was this which had led him to declare: "Terms of relationship reflect psychology, not sociology" (KROEBER 1952:181; orig. 1909). It would have been better to say, he admitted in 1952, "that as part of language, kin term systems reflect unconscious logic and conceptual patterning *as well as* social institutions" (KROEBER 1952: 172).

Kroeber had previously proposed several substantial modifications of the obiter dictum in question (1917b; 1917c; 1934). Nonetheless, he continued to reject any remnant of a causal relationship between social organization and terminology. By 1919, he was willing to admit that "institutions and terminologies unquestionably parallel or reflect each other at least to the degree that a marked discrepancy of plan is rare," but in obedience to his basic philosophy of history, and by means of fancy footwork, he continued to hedge on the question of cause:

> Institutions probably shape terminologies causally, but in the main by influencing or permitting a logical scheme. In a sense, this logical scheme underlies both institution and terminology, so that the correlation between them, although actual, can be conceived of as indirect [1952:189; orig. 1919b].

This position, with its emphasis on a "logical scheme" underlying both terminology and social structure, led Kroeber in the direction of an increasing concern with cultural "patterns" as the units of cultural description. In the post-Boasian period, the search for the underlying scheme or plan has been taken up by the "new ethnography" in the guise of ethnosemantic analysis. The debt of this movement to Kroeber's attack on Morgan will be duly noted in subsequent chapters.

MORGAN VINDICATED

The irony in all this is that Kroeber's original attack on the distinction between classificatory and descriptive systems was based on a false rendering of Morgan's meaning. Morgan was aware of the "lumping" characteristics of such terms as "cousin" and "uncle." For Morgan, descriptive terminologies are those in which terms applied to lineal kinsmen are never applied to collaterals. This distinction *does* serve to separate most primitive kinship terminologies from the systems employed by most literate state societies. It *does* have evolutionary significance, and it *is* basic to an understanding of the differential functions of kinship in stratified as opposed to egalitarian social structures.

As White (1959b) indicates, a long list of prominent anthropologists, including Goldenweiser, Tozzer, Stern, Penniman, Gillin,

Hoebel, Murdock, and Lowie, accepted Kroeber's denial of the evolutionary significance of the classificatory-descriptive dichotomy. Fortunately, few anthropologists, even among the Boasians, agreed with Kroeber's "intransigent" insistence that kin-terminological systems and social structure exhibited no orderly relationship. British social anthropologists not only ignored Kroeber in this respect but even managed to preserve Morgan's original sense of the classificatory-descriptive distinction. Thus, A. R. Radcliffe-Brown preceded White by many years in suggesting that the reason for the confusion of Kroeber and other American anthropologists concerning Morgan's meaning was that Morgan had ceased to be consulted in the original. "What Morgan meant by this term is quite clear from his writings . . . but his definition is often ignored, perhaps because people no longer bother to read him" (RADCLIFFE-BROWN, quoted in WHITE 1959b:385). Morgan's approach to kinship terms and kinship groups has been vindicated by scholars who remain as hostile to Morgan's evolutionary schema as Kroeber was back in 1909 and again in 1952. With the publication of George Peter Murdock's *Social Structure,* Morgan's contribution to kinship analysis was re-established as a permanent foundation of contemporary anthropology.

> The scientific significance of kinship systems was first appreciated by Morgan in what is perhaps the most original and brilliant single achievement in the history of anthropology. That many of Morgan's particular interpretations are no longer acceptable does not diminish the luster of his work [MURDOCK 1949:91].

MISPLACED EUPHORIA

Murdock's study owes to Morgan precisely what Kroeber sought to topple, namely, the proposal to search for causal cross-cultural correlations between kin-terminologies, social groupings, and marriage patterns. It is surprising, therefore, to read in the preface to the very volume just quoted that ". . . Kroeber kept American anthropology alive through an ineffectual generation by his originality, his concern with vital issues, and his analytic insight" (MURDOCK 1949:xv)! On the basis of Kroeber's halting concessions to causality, which I have already cited, Murdock strains to achieve a sense of common purpose, declaring, further along in the same book, that he "finds himself in substantial agreement with practically all Kroeber's theoretical statements, save for a few *obiter dicta.*" Apparently, Kroeber was not willing to pay the price of Murdock's praise. In 1952, without the slightest acknowledgment of Murdock's attempt to develop a scientific approach to social structure on the basis first proposed in Morgan's *Systems* (1870), Kroeber once again denied that such an approach was feasible:

> Morgan and Rivers had singled out *particular* terminological features as caused by specific usages. This difference between them and myself I continue to hold to as fundamental in the understanding of cultural manifestations. The causality that is involved in culture has normally accumulated so long and so intricately that on the whole very little of it can be specifically unraveled with authenticity. Boas was big enough to realize this. But the pioneers like Morgan, the men trained in laboratories like Rivers, the ruck of social scientists hoping somehow to imitate physics, kept and keep trying; and yet they achieve either only bits or constructs that are mainly unreal. It is the pattern rather than precise causation that is the meaningful result by and large achievable in the study of culture—as the history of linguistics should long ago have sufficed to teach us [KROEBER 1952:173].

It is not known if Kroeber specifically intended to include Murdock among the "ruck," but there is no doubt that Murdock was practicing social science on the physicalist model or as close as he could get to it when he wrote *Social Structure* (see Chap. 21).

I dwell on this point because Kroeber inspired his colleagues to feel that their irreconcilable theoretical positions were just on the edge of euphoric harmony. The most remarkable instance occurred between him and Leslie White on the issue of the "superorganic," a case to which we shall shortly return. Doctrinaire Marxists have emerged from discussions with Kroeber convinced that if they could only have gone on for a few more minutes, all the differences between them would have evaporated.

KROEBER'S CREDO

Kroeber must have derived a special delight from these encounters, for there was nothing in his writings that justified the widespread confusion surrounding his views on the great issues in social science. The onus for this confusion certainly does not rest with Kroeber, in view of the forthright credo he delivered in his thirty-ninth year under the title "The Eighteen Professions" (1915). This article seems to have suffered an undeserved oblivion. I shall quote or paraphrase all eighteen "professions," since they amount to the best available summary of Kroeber's version of historical particularism.

[1] The aim of history is to know the relations of social facts to the whole of civilization . . . . Relation is actual connection, not cause.

[2] The material studied by history is not man, but his works, i.e., the results of his deeds.

[3] Civilization, though carried by men and existing through them, is an entity in itself, and of another order from life. . . . History is not concerned with the agencies producing civilization, but with civilization as such. The causes are the business of the psychologist.

[4] A certain mental constitution must be assumed by the historian, but may not be used by him as a resolution of social phenomena.

[5] True instincts lie at the bottom and origin of social phenomena, but cannot be considered or dealt with by history.

[6] The personal or individual has no historical value, save as illustration.

[7] Geography, or physical environment, is material made use of by civilization, not a factor shaping or explaining civilization.

[8] The absolute equality and identity of all human races must be assumed by the historian.

[9] Heredity cannot be allowed as a significant factor in history.

[10] Heredity by acquirement is a monstrosity.

[11] Selection and other factors of organic evolution cannot be admitted as affecting civilization.

[12] The so-called savage is no transition between the animal and the scientifically educated man. . . . All men are totally civilized. . . . There is no higher and no lower in civilization for the historian.

[13] There are no social species or standard cultural types or stages. . . . A stage in civilization is merely a preconception made plausible by arbitrarily selected facts.

[14] There is no ethnic mind, but only civilization.

[15] There are no laws in history similar to the laws of physico-chemical science. All asserted civilizational laws are at most tendencies. . . . History does not deny them and may have to recognize them, but their formulation is not its end.

[16] History deals with conditions *sine qua non*, not with causes. The relations between civilizational phenomena are relations of sequence, not of effect.

[17] The causality of history is teleological . . . . this does not suggest theology to those who are free from theology.

[18] In fine, the determinations and methods of biological, psychological, or natural science do not exist for history.

THE SUPERORGANIC

In all essentials save one, Kroeber's "professions" faithfully mirror Boas' influence. The exception is found in number six, "The personal or individual has no historical value, save as illustration."

Whereas Boas' idiography led him increasingly in the direction of interactive problems of personality and culture, Kroeber took the culture concept in the opposite direction and argued for the complete subordination of the individual to his cultural milieu. It was this de-emphasis of the individual, elaborated at greater length in "The Superorganic" (1917a) two years later, which convinced everybody that Kroeber had departed from the Boasian fold. His "culturological" remarks aroused great uneasiness among the Boasians, possibly because of the resemblance to exhortations of soap-box historical determinists against the "great man" theory of history.

In "The Superorganic," Kroeber made extensive appeal to the "principle of the simultaneity of invention" to show that history was determined by cultural patterns, not by individuals. There were those who saw in the simultaneous rediscovery of Mendel's principles by DeVries, Correns, and Tschermak a "meaningless play of capricious fortuitousness." But to Kroeber, this kind of event revealed

> . . . a great and inspiring inevitability which rises as far above the accidents of personality as the march of the heavens transcends the wavering contacts of random footprints on clods of earth. Wipe out the perception of DeVries, Correns, and Tschermak, and it is yet certain that before another year had rolled around, the principles of Mendelian heredity would have been proclaimed to an according world, and by six rather than three discerning minds [KROEBER 1917a:199].

Kroeber went on to claim that the subordination of the individual to the culture pattern held true in all cultures, that everywhere the individual (to return to Hegel) was the mere agent of culturological forces:

> Ericsson or Galvani eight thousand years ago would have polished or bored the first stone; and in turn the hand and mind whose operation set in inception the neolithic age of human culture, would, if held in its infancy in unchanging catalepsy from that time until today, now be devising wireless telephones and nitrogen extractors [*ibid.*:201].

THE CONTROVERSY WITH SAPIR

A reply to this heresy was issued at once by Edwin Sapir, who in addition to setting the pattern of anthropological linguistics, maintained a lifelong interest in the field of personality and culture. Sapir argued that it would require a belief in "social determinism amounting to religion" to accept Kroeber's viewpoint. Although he admitted that the "average historian" tended to exaggerate the determining influence of specific personalities, this was no reason to eliminate the individual from all consideration as a cultural factor. Sapir then threw out a challenge which goes a long way toward explaining the main thread of Kroeber's career. Kroeber was finding his superorganic forces by a kind of trick:

> Shrewdly enough Dr. Kroeber chooses his examples from the realm of inventions and scientific theories. Here it is relatively easy to justify a sweeping social determinism in view of a certain general inevitability in the course of the acquirement of knowledge. This inevitability, however, does not altogether reside, as Dr. Kroeber seems to imply, in a social "force" but, to a very large extent, in the fixity, conceptually speaking, of the objective world. This fixity forms the sharpest of predetermined grooves for the unfolding of man's knowledge. Had he occupied himself more with the religious, philosophic, aesthetic, and crudely volitional activities and tendencies of man, I believe that Dr. Kroeber's case for the non-cultural significance of the individual would have been a far more difficult one to make. . . . One has only to think seriously of what such personalities as Aristotle, Jesus, Mahomet, Shakespeare, Goethe, Beethoven mean in the history of culture to hesitate to commit oneself to a completely non-individualistic interpretation of history [SAPIR 1917:442-43].

PATTERNS

Kroeber spent the rest of his career doing something very similar to what Sapir had said could not be done: showing how patterns of art, religion, philosophy, as well as of technology and science, waxed and waned, acquired their characteristic content and kept rolling majestically along, quite independently of particular individuals. Among American Indians as well as the ancient Greeks, it is the cultural pattern which summons forth geniuses in appropriate numbers, whenever the time is ripe, be they Edisons or Christs.

As a matter of fact, it was Kroeber's special delight to pick out aspects of culture which seemed most vulnerable to the effect of individual fancy and to demonstrate the existence of patterns unknown to the culture carriers. His study of dress fashions, going back to an inspiration first felt in 1909, was an impressive accomplishment along these lines. By 1919 he had measured enough changes of evening gown styles to identify regular pulsations in the width and length of skirt and area of decolletage. There is a note of triumph in his conclusions:

> We are all in the habit of talking glibly of how this year's fashion upsets that of last year. Details, trimmings, pleats, and ruffles, perhaps colors and materials—all the conspicuous externalities of dress—do undoubtedly alter fairly rapidly; and it is in the very nature of fashion to bring these to the fore. They are driven into our attention, and soon leave a blurred but overwhelming impression of incalculably chaotic fluctuations, of reversals that are at once bewildering and meaningless, of a sort of lightning-like prestidigitation to which we bow in dumb recognition of its uncontrollability. But underneath this glittering maze, the major proportions of dress change rather with a slow majesty, in periods often exceeding the duration of human life . . . [KROEBER 1952:336; orig. 1919a].

In 1940, collaborating with Jane Richardson, he published a statistical study which covered three hundred years of fashion changes. The existence of unsuspected periodicities was confirmed, short-run "modes" of style distinguished from the long-run patterns, and the role of the *haute couture* designer explicitly assimilated to that of the genius in biology or physics:

> It is evident that the basic features of style as distinct from more rapidly fluctuating mode, being taken for granted at any given moment, are largely unconscious in the sense that they are felt as axiomatic and derivations are made from them, but they are not tampered with, except again unconsciously.
>
> This in turn seems to imply that the role of particular individuals in molding basic dress style is slight. The influence of creative or important individuals is perhaps largely exerted on the accessories of transient mode [*ibid.*:370; orig. 1940].

Kroeber maintained this diachronic and superorganic orientation right through the period of anthropology's greatest retreat into psychological reductionism and synchronic functionalism. During the twenties and thirties, the unconscious patterns which set the limits for the "in" look in social science and which governed the intellectual behavior of the profession's Christian Diors and Balenciagas cast Kroeber in the role of a potential if not actual wild-eyed radical. It definitely strained "bourgeois" anthropology to the limits of *its* patterns to insist history could be studied without becoming involved in individual biographies. Even his "guru" became alarmed and felt obliged to call for a purge of the mystical patterns that Kroeber claimed were the decisive forces of history: "It has been claimed," wrote Boas, "that human culture is something superorganic, that it follows laws that are not willed by any individual participating in the culture, but that are inherent in the culture itself. . . ." This was too much for Boas' no-nonsense empiricism: "It seems hardly necessary to consider culture a mystic entity that exists outside the society of its individual carriers, and that moves by its own force" (BOAS 1928:245).

CONFIGURATIONS

Kroeber's fascination with the superorganic culminated in the publication of the singularly monumental *Configurations of Culture Growth* (1944). His wife, Theodora, has said that this book was the product of seven years of labor, during which "every summer, every holiday and free hour" (T. KROEBER 1963:xviii) were devoted to it. It was intended as a magnum opus. The task he assigned himself was no less than that of discovering "the common features in the growth" of philology, sculpture, painting, drama, literature, and music in Egypt, Mesopotamia, India, Japan, Greece, Rome, Europe, and China. Although he "cheerfully renounces search for causes" (1944:7), he does ask the question, have civilizations been alike or unlike in producing their "highest manifestations"?

Despite the prodigious research effort expended upon this task, *Configurations* was a failure. Kroeber was able to discover no similarities whatsoever in the abstract growth curves of different civilizations. He did find everywhere the mysterious "patterns" exemplified by sudden simultaneous bursts of creative energy in one or several of the aesthetic domains, but the climaxes were sometimes multiple, sometimes singular, sometimes confined to one or two domains, elsewhere "across the board." At a time when people like Sorokin, Spengler, Toynbee, and other universal historians were propounding all sorts of grand neo-Hegelian national destinies, Kroeber could find nothing but unpredictable culture growths: "In reviewing the ground covered, I wish to say at the outset that I see no evidence of any true law in the phenomena dealt with; nothing cyclical, regularly repetitive, or necessary" (KROEBER 1944:761).

METHODOLOGICAL ABUSES

Added to the painful disappointment of this labor, whose fruit is nothing other than the elaboration of the concept of the superorganic, is the diminishing resistance which Kroeber displays toward reliance upon idiosyncratic and ethnocentric intuitions. Few anthropologists would wish to accompany Kroeber in his self-assigned task, essential to the methodology of *Configurations*, of evaluating the worth of the aesthetic productions of different civilizations and different phases of the same civilization: how far they tend to be "successful" in their several activities simultaneously (*ibid.*:6). We are evidently in the presence of a substantial retreat from the higher standards of evidence demanded by Boas, when the assertion is made that there was no growth of philosophy in Egypt, Mesopotamia, Rome, and Japan; or when we are told that painting did not undergo any significant development in Mesopotamia (*ibid.*:778). Anthropologists, having spent a good part of their lives with peasants and tribesmen, tend to be a rather crusty and skeptical crew. It is disappointing that their "grand old man" could have authored judgments which relied so heavily upon the effete standards of salon gossip:

> In occidental sculpture, Italy holds preeminence—Michelangelo is considered as marking the culmination. But can we be certain that he was inherently by his native gifts, a greater sculptor than Ghiberti, Donatello, Bernini or Canova? . . . We rate Bernini much lower. But can we be at all sure that in his imagination, sense of form, technical skill, he was inferior to Michelangelo? His themes, his invoking of emotions, and perhaps his taste were on a lower level; but they were the emotions and taste of his age. The same holds for Canova. For sculptural ability we cannot with certainty rate him one notch below the highest; it is the tepid neoclassicism of his period which we rate below Renaissance intensity [*ibid.*:14].

Can one seriously propose that "Good sculpture was produced in Dynasties I, IV, V, XII, XVIII, XXVI" (*ibid.*:241), or that "Japanese sculpture was a great art from 600 to 1300," or that "England, which had real music until 1700, has had none since"! According to Steward (1961:1055), "Kroeber always remained a relativist. . . ." Indeed, Kroeber himself reacted with pique to the suggestion by Dorothy Gregg and Elgin Williams (1948) that overt value positions should replace the covert values embodied in the "Dismal Science of Functionalism" (see p. 534). Asserting that this point of view would "quickly undermine and destroy science," Kroeber formulated three professions which were not included in his 1915 article:

[1] The method of science is to begin with questions, not with answers, least of all with value judgments.

[2] Science is dispassionate inquiry and therefore cannot take over outright any ideologies "already formulated in everyday life," since these are themselves inevitably traditional and normally tinged with emotional prejudice.

> [3] Sweeping all-or-none, black-or-white judgments are characteristic of totalitarian attitudes and have no place in science, whose very nature is inferential and judicial.
>
> [KROEBER 1949:319].

If one admits that this affirmation of relativism is an appropriate rejoinder to Gregg and Williams, it certainly merits application to much of the substance and method of *Configurations*.

Although *Configurations* failed to identify any cross-cultural regularities, Kroeber evidently drew satisfaction from demonstrating the cluster effect of patterns upon the appearance of geniuses. This position continued to attract the criticism of Boas and his students. Thus, Ruth Benedict in *Patterns of Culture* (1934:231) accused Kroeber of expressing himself in "mystical phraseology" by calling in "the superorganic to account for cultural process." In 1944 the philosopher David Bidney joined the attack by accusing Kroeber of participating in the "culturalistic fallacy" as shown in the

> tendency to hypostasize culture and to conceive it as a transcendental, superorganic, or superpsychic force which alone determines human historical destiny . . . with . . . the assumption that culture is a force that may make and develop itself [BIDNEY 1944:42, quoted in KROEBER 1948c:407].

Strongest support for Kroeber's superorganic came from an unlikely quarter. In Leslie White's "The Expansion of the Scope of Science" Kroeber is portrayed as one of the few anthropologists who "have undertaken to formulate the philosophy of a science of culture" (WHITE 1949a:90; orig. 1947). It has of course been clear at least since Hegel that a scientific approach to sociocultural phenomena must proceed on the assumption that individual choices are the products of and not the originators of social forces. Hence, the first step toward a science of culture is necessarily the one which Kroeber had taken in the "Superorganic." But Kroeber took just that one step and then no more. It is a curious commentary on White's isolation as an historical determinist that he should have felt obliged to enlist Kroeber among the standard-bearers of his "science of culture." Kroeber, while expressing a high regard for White, never missed an opportunity to dissociate himself from that larger enterprise. He and White merely shared the belief that culture is a distinct level of phenomena which, although reducible to lower levels in theory, cannot in practice be so reduced without diminishing our chances of understanding it. But beyond this reaffirmation of the value of the superorganic concept on exclusively heuristic grounds, Kroeber made certain epistemological concessions to his critics which produced harmony at the expense of enlightenment: "I take this opportunity of formally and publicly recanting," wrote Kroeber, "any extravagances and overstatements of which I may have been guilty through overardor of conviction, in my 'Superorganic.' "

> As of 1948 it seems to me both unnecessary and productive of new difficulties, if, in order to account for the phenomena of culture, one assumes any entity, substance, kind of being, or set of separate, autonomous and wholly self-sufficient forces [1948c:407-8].

> For my part I am ready to concede that culture exists only in persons in the sense that it resides, has its locus, only in them [*ibid.*:408].

As part of this same recantation, Kroeber modified the stand he had taken concerning the relationship between culture and individual behavior. Acknowledging a debt to Bidney, he proposed that Aristotle's distinction between "efficient" and "formal" cause is relevant. Individuals are the efficient causes; culture is the formal cause. But Kroeber further assures us that a formal cause is nothing like the kind of cause with which science is concerned. And indeed it is not. For the only meaning to be derived from Kroeber's proposal that culture is a "formal" cause, in the context of his explicit hostility to historical determinism, is that culture is culture. His new position follows: "So far as the latter (mechanical-scientific causes) are concerned, the prospect seems to me that they will continue to reside in the psychic or psychosomatic level" (*ibid.*:412). But this is precisely the position set forth in Profession Number 3, in 1915, and corresponds exactly to Boas' final conclusion concerning the possibility of formulating cultural laws. The futility of the entire exchange between Bidney, White, and Kroeber is its most salient feature. As far as the epistemological problem of the nature of culture is concerned, Kroeber's retreat to an Aristotelian *deus ex machina* merely intensified the lack of clarity which had characterized his earlier enthusiasm for the superorganic. His "recantation" helped not one bit to set the matter straight and indeed was nothing more than an unnecessary and irrelevant reassurance that he did not believe in ghosts.

THE REALITY OF CULTURAL THINGS

A kindly historian, Philip Bagby, was the first to place Kroeber's recantation in proper perspective. Starting from the position that if culture was anything worth talking about, it was an abstraction built up from the observation of behavior, Bagby disposed at once of the question of the "reality" of cultural things:

> The regularities which the anthropologist studies are just as real as the subjects of the other sciences or indeed as the objects of ordinary discourse. If we had defined culture in terms of some such hypothetical construct as values we should be on shaky ground, but we have defined it in terms of *behavior* and no one doubts the reality of behavior. . . . Of course, it is true that culture has no substance; it is composed of forms and nothing more. But in the view of almost all modern philosophers, idealists as well as positivists, this is equally true of everything else. There was no need for Kroeber to make his famous recantation . . . to object to the reification of culture is to object to talking about it at all [BAGBY 1953:541].

Bagby here pointed the way to the attempt to solve the question of "reductionism" by showing precisely how, starting with the smallest idiosyncratic bits of behavior, it is possible to construct a data language of progressively higher-order abstractions (*cf.* HARRIS 1964a). None of the people who were engaged with Kroeber in arguing the "reality" of cultural things had made themselves face the issue of how one observes such entities in the first place. When this question, the question of operational procedures, is squarely faced, the problem turns out to be not how to reduce cultural entities to psychological phenomena, but rather how to move from the facts of individual behavior to constructs such as "patrisib," "matrilateral cross-cousin marriage," and "Oriental despotism."

STYLES AND SUPER-STYLES

After *Configurations*, Kroeber's substantive contributions became more frankly intuitive and aesthetic. As his wife, Theodora, explains in the introduction to his posthumous *An Anthropologist Looks at History:*

> When *Configurations* was at last behind him, Kroeber came out literally on the sunny side of it, somehow free at last as he had not felt before, to add his sensibility to form, styles, values, and aesthetic truths to his other approaches to the always fascinating phenomena of culture. This sensibility should have been given fuller expression in a book on the arts [T. KROEBER 1963:xviii].

Kroeber's inclination during the last two decades of his life was to deal with the question of growths of civilizations without bothering with the encyclopedic inventories which had given *Configurations* its saving claim as an inductive product. Instead, the free play of intuition characteristic of the more lurid judgments in *Configurations* was now explicitly defended. Each civilization is to be characterized by a multiplicity of patterns whose common denominators added up to its particular style or "super-style." Kroeber himself suggested the comparison between these "super-styles" and the kind of pattern portraits which Ruth Benedict had achieved. The comparisons reveal the fundamental connectedness of Benedict and Kroeber within the historical-particularistic tradition. Although Benedict's patterns are described in a psychological idiom, this is a superficial difference. As far as Kroeber was concerned, the only important distinction between his approach and Benedict's was that his portraits were to be dynamic, covering the early as well as mature phases of style growths (1963:72–74). Thus, the approach Kroeber now favored was that of pluralistic and diachronic formulations, exemplified in Toynbee, Spengler, and Danilevsky (*ibid.*:77–83). His styles are like organic growths, unfolding through time in an irreversible but inexplicable process.

Although Kroeber reaffirmed his belief that "successful insight into the nature and history of human civilizations or cultures will be made via an empirical route, by means of something akin to natural history" (*ibid.*:83), his method for identifying "super-styles" scarcely conformed to empiricist models. "The mental processes called for in dealing with styles are somewhat different from those ordinarily used by the historian or scientist" (*ibid.*:71). What is needed is the kind of faculty we call on when we identify individuals or identify organisms as members of this or that species. It is a "total, immediate and final judgment," and it "is neither inductive nor deductive." Artists and biologists seem to best represent the necessary qualities.

> The creative artist undoubtedly is highly sensitive in his ability to recognize both particular and patterned or stylistic identity in the field of his creativity. However, this faculty is one which is ordinarily not called for to any notable degree in the prosecution of scientific research, especially of the laboratory type. It does enter into many aspects of humanistic scholarship. In science it is perhaps most called for in the basic natural history aspects of biology—the accumulation of a broad organized body of underlying knowledge on which the remainder of biologic science largely rests, and which is often designated as systematic or taxonomic biology [*ibid.*:71].

Kroeber in thus comparing artist to biologist neglected to take into account the relationship between species identification and the formulation of the principles of natural selection and other lawful biological processes. It is the fact that species differences have proven useful in the formulation of these principles that establishes their scientific worth. There is thus a fundamental difference between the paintings hanging on the walls of an art museum and the taxonomies developed within the science of life. One makes possible the systematic exploration of hypotheses concerning the recurrent processes of nature, and the other does not. Kroeber's proposal to classify civilizations on the basis of intuited styles shows little promise of making such a contribution. Indeed, Kroeber himself repeatedly rejected the possibility that anything like a theory of natural selection would ever be achieved by social science.

ANTISCIENCE

The point here is not that room is lacking in anthropology for the kind of artistic empathizing which Kroeber regarded as the central part of his professional legacy. To be against empathy is after all something like being opposed to motherhood or baseball. The objections arise not from one's wish to cut off the approach, but rather in reaction to Kroeber's aggressive opposition to research strategies which could conceivably have led to the formulation of lawful diachronic and synchronic processes. This opposition, because it began as a full-fledged dogma, because it was frequently repeated, and because it often disguised itself in a reflective rhetoric that gave the impression of an open mind, is an onus which all of the historical particularists must shoulder.

Kroeber rejected the possibility of a scientific approach to history in his 1901 thesis on Arapaho art; he repeated the objection in the 1915 "Professions," the 1917 "Superorganic," the 1919 and 1940 dress design papers, and the 1944 *Configurations*. He declared in 1920: "There are in short no causal explanations" (1920b:380). He insisted that parallel evolution was a rarity and he even doubted if "the tendency of agriculture to be followed by town life," constitutes an acceptable example (1923:238). In 1943 he doubted that the patterns of Old and New World agriculture provided a valid basis for cross-cultural comparison (1952:89–91). In 1938 he declared, "the findings of history can never be substantiated like proofs of natural science" (*ibid.*:79). He consistently belittled the nomothetic approach and followed Boas to the conclusion that all generalizations would necessarily be vapid: "Allegations of regular recurrences in culture refer to shadowy, large resemblances which are only dubiously substantiable because they are not precisely definable" (*ibid.*:132). He thought the concepts of the clan and feudalism among others were quite useless

> because actual cultural content of such general concepts has been acquired . . . during . . . historical development, which is always complex and *always tending toward the unique as historians have long ago learned to take for granted* [*ibid.*:134; italics added].

Kroeber was entitled to his empathy, but he was not justified in flicking away two centuries of social science by asserting in 1957 of civilizations: "we know as good as nothing of what produced their wholes" (1957:79).

KROEBER AND STEWARD

There is an increasingly ironic quality in Kroeber's denial of the possibility of a scientific understanding of historical processes. During the forties and fifties a generation of his own students were already pioneering in the renaissance of the comparative method and the quest for historical causal sequences. In Kroeber's *festschrift*, presented to him on his sixtieth birthday, Julian Steward proposed "that every cultural phenomenon is the product of some definite cause or causes." Kroeber seems to have ignored Steward's ecological explanation of hunting and gathering bands, a decisive event in the history of anthropological theory (see p. 666).

At the momentous 1947 Viking Fund conference on Peruvian archaeology, held in New York, Kroeber presided as William Duncan Strong, Pedro Armillas, Gordon Willey, and Julian Steward delivered papers which demonstrated the central influence of techno-environmental factors in the evolution of new world civilizations, and thereby flung wide the door to precisely the kind of scientific explanations that Kroeber had scorned. Steward, in particular, acquired from this conference the boldness to propose that "agricultural proficiency, population density, settlement patterns, sociological complexity, and craft technologies were functionally related" and that there were probably "certain regularities in the development of these features in the different areas of native American high cultures" (STEWARD 1948:103). Kroeber's response to these suggestions which have come to dominate contemporary archaeological research and which show promise of achieving a similar degree of importance in ethnology (see Chap. 23) was uncomprehending as well as patronizing:

> The archaeologist, of course, cannot commence with considerations as remote from evidence as these. He has to begin with objects which are material and which . . . show style. . . . Not

> having worked at first hand in the Peruvian field, [Steward's] desire to convert the stylistic period-concepts into economic-political ones is natural—especially in view of his previous correlations of ecological with socio-political factors. On the other hand, those like Bennet who have been active in Peruvian prehistory for twenty years, and with whom it has been the main specific field of study, are likely to go somewhat more slowly. . . . This is not in the way of a slur, because Steward has had half a dozen years of editing the great South American *Handbook*. But his knowledge is synthetic and tends therefore to be strong precisely on perspective. It is fortunate that we should have here participants like him, pushing eagerly and perhaps straining interpretation to the utmost [KROEBER 1948b:115].

Steward's ideas were interesting baubles. They appear to have been incapable of deflecting Kroeber's determination to regard each civilization as a fundamentally unique stylistic growth. In Kroeber's own approach the cards remained stacked against nomothetic explanations of the Peruvian sequence by avoiding questions concerning the nature of productive and distributive systems in relation to social stratification, political organization, warfare, demography, and settlement patterns. None of these had received sustained treatment in *Configurations.*

Kroeber's rather frigid reception of Steward's ideas reposes at a sharp angle against Steward's own steady respect for his former teacher. Oddly enough, Steward does not appear to be overly uncomfortable with Kroeber's rejection of cultural ecology as a method for the solution of the great questions which Kroeber's own approach so conspicuously failed to achieve. It is of course unlikely that an obituary article would contain strong criticism of a beloved colleague and mentor, but there is one circumstance yet to be discussed which requires us to believe that Steward did not feel as intellectually removed from Kroeber as the surface content of their positions might at first suggest:

> In spite of my views, which differ in some ways from Kroeber's, I am deeply convinced that Kroeber's five hundred odd publications are, and will be for many decades, an almost inexhaustible mine not only of information but of problems, concepts, and hypotheses which have not yet made sufficient impact upon the world of scholarship. I have tried to indicate that Kroeber frequently touched, with deep insights, many problems that searchers for causes might well heed. Some of his syntheses and interpretations could readily be classed as "hard science" [STEWARD 1961:1059].

KROEBER AS ECOLOGIST

Kroeber's early interest in regional surveys of aboriginal cultures, as exemplified in his *Handbook of the Indians of California* (1925), gave priority of treatment to religion and ideology. Later, he approached the construction of culture areas by means of increasingly elaborate statistical manipulations of disjointed trait-element lists consisting of as many as six thousand items (see Chap. 14). But when it came to the formulation of his definitive 1939 statement, *Cultural and Natural Areas of Native North America,* he departed from these earlier methods and followed instead the example set by Clark Wissler (1926) and Otis T. Mason (1894b:148). Kroeber now set up his basic regional categories to reflect modes of subsistence and population density. These in turn he saw as closely related in most cases to the potentialities of the natural habitat. His position with respect to the culture-environment equations was typically eclectic along the lines being proposed by C. Daryll Forde (1934) (see p. 664) and based on the assumption

> . . . that on the one hand culture can be understood primarily only in terms of cultural factors, but that on the other hand no culture is wholly intelligible without reference to the noncultural or so-called environmental factors with which it is in relation and which condition it [KROEBER 1939:205].

There are, however, very few regularities, if any, to be derived from this relationship.

> . . . the interactions of culture and environment become exceedingly complex when followed out. And this complexity makes generalization unprofitable, on the whole. In each situation or area different natural factors are likely to be impinging on culture with different intensity [*ibid.*].

Thus although Kroeber systematically explored North American environment-culture interrelationships, mapping limits of natural floral and faunal provinces against the distribution of cultigens, and evaluating the best estimates of precontact human population, he was far from achieving a consistent ecological approach. For example, in attempting to explain the low population density of the Eastern Woodlands, he quickly retreated to the position that the underlying factor was the absence of the "idea of the state" (1939:149). The theoretical viewpoint harked back to Friedrich Ratzel; Kroeber did not see in the techno-environmental equation much beyond that of a vaguely restrictive or permissive parameter. The creative aspects of the cultural traditions which come to be identified with particular natural provinces are never predictable in any but a negative sense from the environmental givens. He certainly never went so far as to suggest, as Steward had already begun to do, that a similar techno-environmental core would tend to be causally and functionally related to similar social structures. Nonetheless, given Steward's own tendency to withdraw from—or at least to vacillate around—the definition of culture core from which ideology is sometimes excluded and sometimes included (see p. 661), Kroeber's *Cultural and Natural Areas* must be reckoned as an accomplishment that anticipates many of Steward's own interests, especially as expressed in the initial treatment of culture areas in the *Handbook of the South American Indians.* As we shall see later on (Chap. 23), Steward shifted his approach to culture areas in the middle of editing and writing the *Handbook*'s six volumes. Nonetheless, there was enough cultural ecology in Kroeber's treatment of North American culture areas to establish a close affinity between it and both the initial and subsequent treatments in the *Handbook.* Steward's debt to Kroeber is thus more than that of sentiment.

But there is a final irony in the relationship between these two men. *Cultural and Natural Areas* was actually the prelude to Kroeber's fascination with civilizational growths conceived as far as possible without regard to their techno-environmental-economic bases or cores.

CLIMAX AREA AND THE ROAD TO CONFIGURATIONS

Kroeber certainly gave no indication that he regarded the ecological aspects of *Cultural and Natural Areas* as a central theoretical contribution. Instead, he chose to regard the refinements of culture areas by means of the concepts of "cultural intensity" and "climax" as the most important basis for his future work. According to Kroeber, each of the six major North American areas, with the exception of the Eskimo, contained a climax subarea which exhibited the "highest intensity" of the area's patterns. In addition each of the areas relative to each other was depicted as possessing a particular level of intensity on a scale of one to seven. Kroeber admitted that his identification of the climax areas and of their relative intensities was for the time being "no more than a personal estimate" (1939:223).

It is of course symptomatic of Kroeber's inflexible theoretical position that he did not attempt to define intensity and climax in terms of the eminently measurable factors of population density, total population involved in a common production and distribution network, size and duration of armies and concentrated corvée labor, or other factors related to general evolutionary processes. No one has ever taken up his suggestion to measure intensity and climax by counting fragmented trait lists. This procedure would be a waste of time since as long as each trait is weighted evenly and as long as there is no agreement on how to count them, a canoe paddle might count as much as a twenty-million-cubic-foot pyramid.

Comparison of culture areas from the point of view of levels of intensity can be achieved with greater objectivity and theoretical significance by employing Steward's concept of "levels of socio-cultural integration" (see p. 377). Once again, there is the shadowy anticipation of the approach Steward was to develop; but Kroeber was in reality traveling along a rapidly diverging track. He was off on the road to configurations, to the subtleties of unique stylistic growths:

> Parallels with historic civilizations suggest themselves. Wherever one of these attained a clearly recognizable culmination, this seems to have corresponded essentially with a period of successful organization of culture content—organization in part into a conscious system of ideas, but especially into an integrated nexus of styles, standards and values [KROEBER 1939:225].

The relationship between Kroeber's treatment of culture areas and *Configurations* has been correctly understood by Milton Singer:

> It is noteworthy that he developed this concept of "climax" when he was finishing his book *Cultural and Natural Areas of Native North America,* just before he turned to a serious study of civilizations. His theory of civilizations is thus continuous with his theory of preliterate cultures and his work on archaeology. The findings of the *Configurations of Culture Growth* in any case give support to the general conclusions of the *Culture Areas* study on the relations of growth culminations to degree and intensity of organization of culture content: namely, that the growth peak of a civilization tends to coincide with a period of successful organization of culture content—that is, the organization of ideas, styles, and standards. Kroeber sees cultural creativity and assimilation running ahead of organization before the culmination, and running behind it after, as the organization tends more and more to repetition and rigidity [1963:vi].

THE DETERMINIST ILLUSION

Singer's theoretical position, it is interesting to note, is idealist and antideterminist, providing not the slightest opening for reconciliation with that of Steward. Yet Singer has no difficulty in wholeheartedly embracing Kroeber's contributions, even the superorganic. Singer's version of Kroeber's theoretical position is much more accurate than that of Steward. Singer points out three features of Kroeber's theory of culture which have contributed to "an impression of determinism."

> (1) Because culture patterns abstract from the events of history and from the concrete acts of particular individuals the impression arises that individuals and their choices and actions do not count. (2) This impression is reinforced by the fact that, in the long view of history which Kroeber takes, particular individuals are rarely visible or known. (3) Finally, the descriptions of patterns are apt to be read as *laws* of general application [*ibid.*:vii].

These impressions, continues Singer, are misleading. What seems like deterministic laws are merely the patterned way people have of acting, thinking, and doing things. Kroeber's "repression" of individuals is merely a methodological procedure for holding psychological and other noncultural factors constant in order to permit the study of the "quality and sequences" of cultural forms. Kroeber was not concerned to investigate the relationship of these forms to individual personality just as he was not interested in their relationship to social structure, social organization, "and many other factors" (among which presumably Singer was referring to environment, technology, demography, production, and distribution). These other things "were problems to be investigated by others." "Kroeber's theory of culture does not necessarily imply any strict determinism or causality, cultural or otherwise" (*ibid.*).

The attempt by Steward, Murdock, White, and others to identify Kroeber with neo-evolutionism and scientific varieties of determinism is unfounded and wholly misses the point of Kroeber's anthropological style, which in every respect remained well within the Boasian program, inheriting all of its initial limitations of theory and method, adding to them only in ways appropriate to a frank denial of scientific pretense.

Lowie

13

At least as erudite as Kroeber (without the charisma), probably to this day unsurpassed in his knowledge of primitive ethnography, Robert Lowie was by far the most sophisticated advocate of, and later the most effective defender of, the historical-particularist position. In Lowie, the Boasian program came closest to achieving that most essential of all scientific standards, the capacity to sustain a continuous and self-correcting expansion of knowledge. Unlike Kroeber, Lowie's understanding of cultural theory matured along empirically viable and theoretically productive lines. It is Lowie who provides the safest bridge across the abyss of particularist no-nothingism back to the master builders of the nineteenth century. However, despite the clarity and honesty of the personal vision to which his work was devoted, there were barriers to the perfection of his understanding of cultural processes over which he could not rise and which maintained him perpetually within the Boasian mold.

Unlike many of his contemporaries, Lowie's dedication to Boas was rooted in an attempt to appraise the precise epistemological implications of the Boasian program with respect to the main currents of unfolding Western philosophies. He possessed a capacity unique among his contemporaries, to represent that program as the embodiment of the finest flowering of empiricism, by which anthropology could win and hold a proud position among the natural sciences. Intuited visions of art and myth triumphantly veiling the inner mysteries of human life had little appeal for him. Unlike Kroeber, he did not for long propose the futility of science applied to history. Indeed, in most respects, Lowie's conception of scientific method as exemplified in his own programmatic pronouncements is unimpeachable. Whereas Kroeber's errors are clearly the result of imperfect method, of a premature hardening against a nomothetic approach, Lowie's most serious lapses are of a totally different nature. In the long run, one has the impression that he was led astray, not by a faulty model of social science, but by his failure to apply the model he espoused. Lowie is betrayed by facts—by false facts collected to an astonishing degree as part of the Boasian program. But there is no denying that Lowie was also the victim of the antimaterialist current that swirled around him and whose strength he drastically underestimated. In the final analysis these currents impaired the fiber of his skepticism, lowered his resistance to hearsay, and prevented him from challenging the prevailing views of primitive economic life. Exasperatingly rigorous in everything else, he willingly permitted himself to be guided by a pack of veritable old wives' tales whenever he was obliged to consider the claims of cultural materialism.

Initially, there was, by Lowie's own admission, a powerful influence exerted over his own work by the "Southwest German" school of philosophy—Dilthey, Windelband, and Rickert. Thus, Lowie speaks of himself as having been led by the "idiographic conception of history" to "deprecate Schurtz's and Webster's 'belief in a law of social evolution' as 'unhistorical' " (LOWIE 1956b:1008). This influence however, became progressively more diluted. Before mid-career it was distinctly less important in shaping Lowie's outlook than was the influence of Ernst Mach, to whom we return in a moment. Lowie was too firmly committed to the exposure and combat of premature generalizations to permit himself to dogmatize the idiographic proposals that Kroeber incorporated into the "Eighteen Professions." Indeed, Lowie eventually came to regard the dogma that scientific causes could not be found in history as a "pusillanimous" subterfuge:

> The field of culture, then, is not a region of complete lawlessness. Like causes produce like effects here as elsewhere, though the complex conditions with which we are grappling require unusual

> caution in definitely correlating phenomena. It is true that American ethnologists have shown that in several instances like phenomena can be traced to diverse causes; that, in short, unlike antecedents converge to the same point. However, at the risk of being anathematized as a person of utterly unhistorical mentality, I must register my belief that this point has been overdone and that the continued insistence on it by Americanists is itself an illustration of cultural inertia. . . . Nevertheless, in contradistinction to some of my colleagues and to the position I myself once shared, I now believe that it is pusillanimous to shirk the real problem involved, and that in so far as any explanation admits the problem, any explanation is preferable to the flaunting of fine phrases about the unique character of cultural phenomena [1929:88-90].

INFLUENCE OF ERNST MACH

The pedigree that Lowie sought to establish for Boasian anthropology was not the neo-Kantianism of Dilthey, Rickert, and Windelband, but that of the hardest of hardheaded pragmatists, Ernst Mach. The relationship between Mach and Lowie was a prolonged one based upon personal acquaintance and an informal correspondence. Apparently, Lowie's interest in Mach developed out of the discussions of the philosophy of science among the members of a group called the "Pearson Circle." This was a club established by Lowie and other Columbia University graduate students whose members studied the implication of Karl Pearson's portrayal of science as an ethic and a "calling," for their own disciplinary careers. By 1911 Lowie's enthusiasm for Mach had advanced to a point of consummate devotion: In that year, it was he who proposed Mach to honorary membership in the New York Academy of Science.

> In presenting to your notice the name of Ernst Mach, I propose not merely the greatest historian of physics, not only an original experimenter and thinker in the field of psychology and a keen logician of scientific method, but the founder and leader of a new and genuine scientific liberalism [1947:65*n*].

It will not be possible here to digress into a study of Mach's major contributions to philosophy. In main outline however, it can be said that Mach was committed to the rooting out of all vestiges of metaphysics from every branch of science. These vestiges he saw as lingering on especially in the mechanistic categories of space, time, matter, and of causality attributed to mechanical "forces." Radically empiricist in all of his thinking, Mach also showed strong positivist affinities. Like Comte, he stressed the irrelevance of explanation via metaphysical constructs. The business of science is to describe the functional relations between phenomena, not to explain them.

Suffice it to say that one has not the slightest difficulty in accepting Mach's views as a basis for scientific methodology. According to Lowie, Mach was to be admired for his "tough mindedness," and who could object to such a posture? "He abhorred systems, he eliminated the supernatural, he looked askance upon the use of hypotheses, demanding description rather than explanation" (1916a:335). It should not be concluded from the disparagement of hypothesis, that Lowie, following Mach, intended to deprive the scientific method of the interplay between hypothesis and experiment; rather, the emphasis is upon eliminating the nonempirical metaphysical and hypothetical residues from the descriptive end-product:

> Ernst Mach's denial of hypothesis is a denial of the existential character of the conditions or things, supposed in the proposition which are purely imaginative or drawn from analogy, or beyond empirical proof. This is simply a reiteration in slightly varied form, of Mach's . . . thesis that *description* and not explanation is the business of science [WEINBERG 1937:44].

Lowie certainly did not shy away from making hypotheses concerning sociocultural processes; on the contrary, his writings are rich in formulations concerning the origin and functioning of sodalities, kinship groups, and kinship rules. What he objected to was any weakening of the empiricist standards on behalf of preserving poorly studied or imaginary entities as part of the description of a particular domain. This objection is rendered explicit in the enthusiastic exegesis that he performed on Goldenweiser's study of totemism. The latter had cleared away an accretion of fanciful hypotheses associated with such luminaries as Frazer, Freud, and Durkheim by showing that the entity, "totemism," consisted of a number of elements assumed to be in stable association but which in reality were sometimes absent or combined in markedly different ways.

> What was at first supposed to be a necessary connection is reduced to a mere conjunction of elements. Thought is no longer arrested by a contemplation of the mystic underlying units and their relations with the observed elements; to determine the nature and interrelations of those elements themselves becomes the highest, nay the only possible, goal of investigation [LOWIE 1911a, in DU BOIS 1960:306].

There is no doubt that Lowie pictured Boas as the man whose mission it had become to impose Mach's program upon anthropology. Lowie's perspective on Boas was thus always somewhat in the nature of a double image in which Boas and Mach blurred into a single heroic figure:

> In the domain of physical science, a critical reformation of this type has been, within recent decades, effected by Professor Ernst Mach. In ethnology, the school which has set itself a corresponding aim, which endeavors to supplant the traditional belief in mystic ethnological complexes with a deeper, though, it may be, still only proximate, analysis into provisional elements, is the school headed by Professor Franz Boas [*ibid.*].

From this perspective, the negative, picayune, and dilettantish aspects of the Boasian movement take on a bright new clean look. We can accept Lowie's reminiscences about turn-of-the-century anthropology with wholehearted approval. When he writes that the Boasian movement was not the concoction of isolationists, nor the creation of people who abhorred generalization, and whose intellectual aspirations rose no higher than the question of whether the Plains Indians put up tepees on four or five poles, there is certainly no reason to doubt his memory:

> The point is that by 1900 the intellectual climate had changed. . . . What had figured as the quintessence of scientific insight suddenly shrank into a farrago of dubious hypotheses. . . . Critical votaries . . . had simply arrived at higher standards of proof [LOWIE 1956b:1006].

The only question is whether Lowie and his fellow Boasians were willing or able to apply these higher standards of proof when the issues before them related to the validity of cultural materialism and historical determinism.

CRITIQUE OF MORGAN

In 1920, Lowie published the singularly most important and most exasperating book in the historical-particularist tradition. Commencing with its corrective title, *Primitive Society* (with the emphasis upon Primitive), this work served the function of introducing a wide audience to the major flaws in Lewis Henry Morgan's *Ancient Society* (with the emphasis upon Ancient). After the publication of Lowie's book, no one who proposed to make use of anthropological findings could cite Morgan without running the risk of being caught in withering error. Yet, as we look back upon this achievement, across half a century of new evidence and new perspectives, we may detect in Lowie's arguments just about as much chaff as he was able to find in *his* predecessor. To spell out all that is right and all that is wrong in *Primitive Society* would require a book in itself. It is a pity, but symptomatic of contemporary anthropology's bootless, headlong plunge away from its past, that no one has seen fit or found the time to write that book. Yet no understanding of contemporary anthropological theory is admissable which does not begin by righting the balance between Lowie and Morgan. Only the briefest of summaries can be attempted here.

First, on the positive side, we may dispense with the notion that *Primitive Society* was an "antievolutionary" treatise. As we have seen, Lowie rightly objected to Leslie White's characterization of the Boasians as being guilty of a "reactionary philosophy of antievolution." This is a complete misrepresentation of the problem, not only for the Boasians but also for all the other major schools of contemporary anthropology. To confuse Lowie's position with the kind of antievolutionism that the proponents of degeneration theory, such as De Maistre, had offered before Spencer and Darwin swept the field is a grave injustice.

LOWIE'S EVOLUTIONISM

Primitive Society is nothing if it is not a major contribution to the theory of cultural evolution. It is such a contribution because time and again in its pages Morgan's view of the sequence of the emergence of specific institutions on both a worldwide and more localized basis are examined, criticized, and reformulated with the positing of a new sequence. Thus Lowie correctly rejects the notion, shared by Morgan, Lubbock, McLennan, and many other nineteenth-century theorists that the earliest form of marriage was group promiscuity. He does so, not because of antievolutionism but because there is insufficient evidence to establish such a condition. He further rejects Morgan's notion of a succeeding stage of group marriage involving a set of brothers and a set of sisters. He rejects this not because he rejects evolution, but because Morgan's interpretation of Hawaiian kinship terminology as a survival of the time when all fathers and mothers were also brothers and sisters had become utterly untenable in relationship to standard ethnographic knowledge of Polynesia. In the light of such knowledge nothing could be more absurd than to propose that the Hawaiians (who are nowadays seen as having had an incipient form of Oriental despotism) were on the lowest levels of "Savagery." Since almost all contemporary primitives present some form of nuclear family, Lowie comes to the conclusion that the family is a primeval human grouping. This conclusion may run counter to Marxist evolutionary dogma, but it does not constitute, in Lowie's handling of it, a refutation of evolutionary theory in general. On the contrary, he is mainly concerned to show that Morgan was wrong in attempting to demonstrate that sibs (gens in Morgan's terminology) evolved before the monogamous family. Lowie insists that the sequence should be reversed.

Thus, in the chapter entitled "History of the Sib," Lowie pursues the question of the origin of the sib in a manner that is thoroughly compatible with Morgan's own evolutionary approach. To be sure, he substitutes the word history for evolution, but this is a bit of word magic. Since John Swanton had pointed out that virtually all of the "ruder Indian cultures" lacked the sib, a fact unknown to Morgan, there remained little by way of evidence to support its evolutionary priority. Few anthropologists of the neo-evolutionary persuasion would argue the point.

But Lowie's treatment of the origin of the sib is much more than a mere reversal of Morgan's evolutionary scheme. It also happens to be one of the strongest cases ever made for parallel and convergent evolutionary processes. In this respect Lowie's explanation of the origin of the sib far out-Morganned Morgan. To Morgan, as we have seen, the idea of unilinear descent seemed so ingenious that he postulated a single origin for its invention and a subsequent worldwide dispersal on the basis of migration and "blood descent." By comparing the distribution of sibs and the associated elements in the way that Goldenweiser had done for totemism, Lowie came to the conclusion that the sib had been independently invented four and possibly five times in North America alone. This is "evolutionism" with a vengeance! Rejecting Morgan's explanation of the spread of the sib in terms of the psychophysical advantages connected with exogamy, Lowie suggested his own causal mechanisms. The factors he emphasizes—transmission of property rights, mode of residence after marriage, and cooperative association in economic activities—are by neo-evolutionist theories closer to the truth than Morgan's notions of the deleterious effects of inbreeding (LOWIE 1920:157–60).

Lowie also partially rejects Morgan's sequence for the origin of bifurcate merging (Iroquoian or Dakota) kinship terminologies. Whereas Morgan saw this system as a direct product of the invention of the gens, Lowie viewed it as a product of both the gens and the systematic application of the levirate and sororate. Because these marriage forms have a wider distribution than unilinear kinship groupings, Lowie insisted that they were evolutionarily prior to the sib (*ibid.*: 163).

Lowie then proceeded to clear up in a definitive fashion the hoary problem of which came first, matrilineal or patrilineal sibs. His rejection of a universal matrilineal phase prior to the appearance of patrilineal descent corresponds to one of the basic cornerstones of modern ethnology. But Lowie once again does not leave the situation in complete disarray. Instead he carefully examines E. Hahn's (1905) suggestion that plow agriculture, which he admits as being later, is frequently associated with patrilineal descent, while hoe gardening, being women's work, and more primordial, is associated with matrilineal descent. Lowie concludes, however, that there are too many exceptions to make the sequence stick on a universal basis, and this once again is a viewpoint that corresponds to the best modern opinion on the subject.

Lowie's evolutionary contribution is again conspicuously in evidence in his treatment of sodalities and the origin of the territorial as opposed to the kinship principle of achieving political organization. "The soundness of Morgan's and Maine's position," writes Lowie, "in drawing a sharp distinction between kinship (tribal) and territorial (political) organization is beyond cavil" (1920:391). Lowie, however, was unwilling to posit the priority of kinship relations over territorial relations, except perhaps in the most distant past. For the most part, he seeks to emphasize that both kin and non-kin forms of groupings, including those with a territorial ingredient, are present "even in very humble cultural levels" (*ibid.*:395). However, he does try to prove that the state form of organization arises on the basis of the prior evolution of clubs, age grades, and other sodalities which had been neglected by Morgan, but emphasized by H. Schurtz (1902). "It is indeed one of Schurtz's most signal services to have explained the early origin of political society in Morgan's sense without recourse to any deliberate legal enactment" (LOWIE 1920:394–95). Lowie follows this up not only with an evolutionary sequence but one which stands on a foundation of rather classic lack of evidence:

> Even at a very early time and in a very lowly environment there was no necessity for disrupting the ties of kinship in order to found a political state. For concomitantly with the family and the sib there have existed for untold centuries such associations as the men's clubs, age classes and secret organizations, all of them

> independent of kinship . . . and all of them capable of readily acquiring political character if not invested with it from their inception [*ibid.*:395-96].

For confirmation of the intemperate nature of this speculative foray into the evolutionary origins of political institutions, no less an authority than Lowie himself bears witness. In his *The Origin of the State* (1927), Lowie spurns Schurtz's contribution and turns instead to processes associated with military conquest. "Obviously, then," he admitted, "associations do not play the preponderant role in political development which I was at one time inclined to ascribe to them" (LOWIE 1927:111). Summing up the situation later in his article on social organization in the *Encyclopedia of the Social Sciences,* he added: "Although local contiguity creates union among pre-literate peoples, the tie of kinship unquestionably eclipses it" (1933a:142). In this instance, by his honest commitment to hardheaded empiricism, Lowie corrected himself right back to Morgan's and Maine's insistence that kinship systems of solidarity preceded the state on a worldwide basis. It is, of course, the only acceptable view of the matter.

LOWIE'S DEBT TO MORGAN

At the risk of digressing somewhat, let me here emphasize that between Kroeber and Lowie nothing is more revealing of their differences than their respective treatments of Morgan. There is scarcely a single paper on social organization written by Lowie that does not implicitly or explicitly begin where Morgan had left off. It is clear that he had read Morgan and that he had returned to "Systems" and *Ancient Society* throughout his maturity. Lowie, for example, did not share Kroeber's confusion concerning Morgan's distinction between classificatory and descriptive kinship systems:

> Morgan's earliest expressions on the subject indicate that it was the merging of lineal and collateral relatives—the use of a single term, e.g., for mother and mother's sister, for father and father's brother—that impressed this pioneer investigator, and this is the feature that actually characterizes the classificatory systems of all the regions of the globe [LOWIE 1915:347].

Indeed, in this same article, Lowie not only accepts Morgan's distinction, but follows Morgan, Tylor, and Rivers in relating the occurrence of classificatory systems to the development of exogamous, unilinear descent groups. While Kroeber sought to undermine Morgan's classification of kinship terminologies and thereby topple the whole "speculative scheme," Lowie accepted and made use of the basic premises of Morgan's comparative method. Lowie chose the occasion of the celebration of Kroeber's sixtieth birthday to praise Morgan's "magnificent and valid" pioneering efforts and to vindicate Morgan's major postulate that "kinship terminologies in some measure correspond to social facts." He even went so far on that occasion as to uphold the use which Morgan and most of the pre-Boasians had made of terminological "survivals" as a method of reconstructing earlier phases of social organization:

> Trained to view "survival" arguments with suspicion, I have become convinced that the avowed skepticism on this point harbors as much cant as the evolutionary zeal of our predecessors. Indubitably cultural changes proceed with uneven velocity, hence certain elements lag while others spurt ahead; further, linguistic phenomena are markedly conservative. These accepted facts warrant the assumption that a terminological feature in harmony with a certain custom may survive that custom. The only question is whether the social factor is the only possible determinant, whether the really vital factor is not rather one of its correlates, whether the same result may not be effected by a different cause. But when due allowance is made for this, Morgan's principle of survivals remains a valuable procedure [LOWIE 1936:180].

In this connection it is relevant to point out that Lowie went much further than any of the other Boasians in maintaining the legitimacy of the search for regularities, of which kinship and social organizational correlations are the most conspicuous. Denying that there were "absolute laws" he nonetheless insisted that the phenomena of social science point toward certain regularities, and that it is our duty to ascertain these as rigorously as possible. Consistent with this view and in extreme opposition to Kroeber, Lowie held Tylor in highest esteem, not for the tempering of evolutionary sequence with diffusion, but rather for Tylor's suggestions concerning method. Indeed, Lowie completely anticipates Murdock's evaluation of the great "On a Method of Investigating the Development of Institutions Applied to Laws of Marriage and Descent." He might have been a "super-Lang or a super-Frazer," wrote Lowie in 1917, "but the paper on Method raises him at once into an entirely different kind of being" (1917a:266).

All of these considerations make it manifestly unfair to represent Lowie as a typical member of the Boasian school as far as historical determinism and idiographic historicism are concerned. True, there are some unkind words for Morgan, as in his contribution to Kroeber's birthday volume and repeated in *The History of Ethnological*

Theory: There's no better example of Darwin's saying, "It's dogged does it." But in the main, Lowie, at least on his own behalf, was perfectly justified in berating Leslie White for claiming that Morgan had been ignored. "What precisely does White expect?" he inquires. "An academic muezzin at every center of learning who shall lead anthropologists in daily Rochester-ward obeisances and genuflections?" (Lowie 1960:412). Similarly one may find in *Culture and Ethnology*, in *Primitive Society*, and elsewhere statements which seem to be saying that historical explanations are the only admissable explanations in the social sciences, as for example when Lowie notes that "the explanation of a cultural phenomenon will consist in referring it back to the particular circumstances that preceded it" (1917b:82). Or as when he rashly asserts: "One fact, however, encountered at every stage and in every phase of society, by itself lays the axe to any theory of historical laws—the extensive occurrence of diffusion" (see p. 174).

THE SHREDS AND PATCHES INCIDENT

The famous rodomontade of "shreds and patches" appears in the last paragraph of *Primitive Society*:

> To that planless hodgepodge, that thing of shreds and patches called civilization, its historian can no longer yield superstitious reverence. He will realize better than others the obstacles to infusing design into the amorphous product; but in thought at least he will not grovel before it in fatalistic acquiescence but dream of a rational scheme to supplant the chaotic jumble [LOWIE 1920:441].

This statement was widely interpreted as a declaration of an antifunctionalist point of view (p. 520). But no one argued more persuasively than Lowie for the functional interrelationships between kinship terminologies and social organization. There is no doubt that the main import of Lowie's substantive work concels out the extreme implications of his shreds-and-patches remark, and there are plenty of theoretical proposals which counterbalance his more extreme pronunciamentos in favor of diffusionist and particularist interpretations:

> Ethnology is simply science grappling with the phenomena segregated from the remainder of the universe as "cultural." It is a wholly objective discipline, whether it deals with subjective attitudes or not, for its function is the determination of reality in verifiable terms. It coordinates its data spatially, in so far forth duplicating the procedure of geography. It coordinates its data chronologically to that extent sharing the logic of geology, paleon-

> tology, historical astronomy, and political history; the particular techniques employed must vary with the problem, as in other branches of learning. Finally, it coordinates in terms of causality as the concept has been epistemologically purified; and by the demonstration of functional relationships it may attain the degree of generalization consistent with its own section of the universe [LOWIE 1960:410].

ATTACK AGAINST CULTURAL MATERIALISM

These and many other positive scientific and evolutionary contributions emanate from *Primitive Society*. A complete review is not needed for the point at issue. To accuse Lowie of antievolutionism or antiscientism is absurd. On the other hand, Lowie does prove himself to be an implacable opponent of cultural materialism. Again and again Lowie drives home the point that schemes cannot substitute for history; that catchwords and catch phrases must be driven out of respectable discourse; that entities like the sib or exogamy must be resolved into their components, and each of these carefully compared in their real-life context before judgments concerning their similarity or difference can be rendered. And yet in vast domains of social life, wherever social structural and ideological features articulate with the organization of labor, with the production and distribution of goods, and with the other material conditions of human existence, Lowie abandons the hardheaded ethnographic empiricism for which he is otherwise so greatly admired. The most consistent theme in *Primitive Society* is not antievolutionism, but anti-cultural materialism.

What Lowie attacked was a scarecrow of economic determinism, an effigy which no economic determinist would recognize. These attacks occur at points too numerous to permit a case by case examination, but a similar pattern of error characterizes each one. First, a proposition advanced by Morgan or some other evolutionist establishing a relationship between economic factors and social organization is presented. Second, a handful of exceptions to the rule are brought forth. Third, the puerility of economic determinism is proclaimed. His treatment of the economic interpretation of slavery may be taken as an example of this routine.

THE CASE OF SLAVERY

Lowie vehemently attacked the notion (rooted in the Enlightenment) that slavery must have originated at an advanced level of productivity associated with substantial food surpluses:

> Slavery did not commence as Morgan fancied, in communities conversant with the smelting of iron, the domestication of cattle, or the use of irrigation and stone architecture. It occurs in the far ruder stage represented by the Neolithic Polynesians and the non-agricultural Nootka, as does the segmentation of society into castes and gradations of rank [1920:356].

At once Lowie's distaste for metaphysical entities evaporates. Where previously he has poked at, pushed, and pulled apart into a half dozen pieces such concepts as "totemism," the "sib," and "exogamy," now suddenly we have SLAVERY, singular and unfractionable. It is true that many pre-state societies have emic actor-types (role positions), the native terms for which ultimately get glossed into English as "slaves." But the practices behind this word bear no structural resemblance to the slavery that existed among the Oriental hydraulic civilizations or among the Greeks and Romans or among New World capitalist plantation agriculturalists. In the case of the Samoan "slaves" (his example from Polynesia), Lowie himself notes that they were war captives, that "their lot was not one of material degradation," and that "the poorer men of the tribe often married slave women." Contrary to Lowie's view, there is little to indicate that the "slaves" in Samoa constituted a social stratum which played a distinctive or important economic function in Samoan society. On the other hand, that the Samoans had a highly stratified social order is not to be doubted. However, again contrary to Lowie's picture of the situation, the techno-economic-environmental basis upon which that system had been reared was perfectly compatible with a general correlation between productivity and degree of social stratification in Polynesia. In Sahlins' (1958) synthesis of Polynesian social structure, it is demonstrated that Samoa belongs in the same category as Hawaii, Tahiti, and Tonga, the most economically advanced of the Polynesian systems. For Lowie to identify the Samoans as Neolithic on the basis of the absence of metallurgy is as objectionable as for Morgan to have put the Hawaiians in Savagery on the basis of their lack of the bow and arrow.

Equally inappropriate is the use made of the occurrence of so-called slaves among the quixotic "nonagricultural Nootka." Enough has already been said of the failure of Boas and other students of Northwest Coast cultures to identify the extensive changes which had resulted from European contact, depopulation, and intensive trade relations. The Nootka and other Northwest groups took war prisoners, set them to work at menial tasks, and exercised continuing life and death power over them. We shall not here be able to follow the labyrinthine arguments surrounding the interpretation of the economic functions of these low-ranking strata. The essential point, however, is that the existence of slavelike statuses among the postcontact Northwest Coast peoples is again perfectly compatible with an economic interpretation of the development of slavery. The only way that Lowie can make it out to be otherwise is by engaging in a bit of typological legerdemain which is even more metaphysical than his slavery concept. Although these societies did not practice agriculture, they did produce large annual "harvest" surpluses based upon the exploitation of unusually favorable riverine and maritime resources. In addition, they maintained extensive trading relations with European companies which greatly increased their ability to produce nonfood types of surpluses. No more inappropriate ethnographic examples can be found for disproving the general relationship between techno-environmental conditions and features of social organization. After trotting forth these two examples (which even if they were not ethnographically something quite different from what Lowie intends them to be would still not have the power to destroy a generalization based on hundreds of contrary cases), Lowie prepares to administer the *coup de grâce* upon the economic interpretation of history:

> Still another point merits attention. How far do the facts cited harmonize with that economic interpretation of history which we have had occasion to scrutinize once before? It must be confessed, very indifferently. When a Tsimshian chief murders a slave to retrieve the prestige his daughter has lost by a wound or when a Kwakiutl in a paroxysm of vainglory confounds a social rival by destroying a canoe and breaking a copper plate valued at a thousand blankets, the motive is manifestly as far removed from the economic as it can well be [1920:356].

Since the Tsimshian slave is killed for the psychological uplift it brings his owner, Lowie concludes that the institution of slavery does not have economic significance. But if Tsimshian slavery is not an economically significant institution, should it be treated as slavery? Over and above such contradictions, it should be pointed out that the psychological motivations which animate the production or destruction of property and people have nothing to do with the question of whether such phenomena are amenable to economic interpretations. If it were otherwise, the annual destruction of several million American automobiles would emerge as the world's most inscrutable custom. When an American junks his four-year-old car (a vehicle which a taxicab driver in Brazil would give four years of his wages to own), his desire to keep up with the Joneses scarcely eliminates the fact that the underlying determinants of his behavior reside in the structure of the American economy.

THE CASE OF COMMUNAL HUNTING TERRITORIES

To evolutionists like Morgan, Maine, Marx, and even as far back as Turgot, it had seemed a well-established principle that groups which depended upon the hunting of animals for their food supply would not possess strongly individualized proprietary rights over hunting territories and that the land-owning group would tend to correspond to the maximum effective social group. This would seem to be an eminently reasonable deduction in view of the fact that there is no conceivable way to get wild animals to stick to one part of a territory—except by domestication, of course! By 1920, an overwhelming number of ethnographic instances confirming the correctness of this view had accumulated. Lowie accepted the prevalence of family or clan joint ownership of land which had so strongly impressed Sir Henry Maine, but he refused to see joint tenure as being more notably a characteristic of the most primitive hunting and gathering groups. As for the widely accepted relationship between true communal tenure and the hunting and gathering mode of existence, the evidence, Lowie claimed, was all to the contrary:

> It is often assumed that when peoples support themselves by the chase there is of necessity communal ownership of the hunting grounds. This proposition, however, has not only been seriously shaken but invalidated by testimony from a number of distinct regions [1920:211].

Lowie then relentlessly follows out the above-mentioned pattern for discrediting economic-determinist interpetations. Three nonconforming cases, the Vedda, the Algonkians, and the aborigines of Queensland are brought forth. In each case he concludes that less than communal tenure is characteristic of the aboriginal patterns. Among the Algonkians and the Vedda, there is even evidence for private ownership of land in association with the rudest level of cultural development. Lowie ends his argument with the memorable challenge:

> The burden of the proof surely rests with those who believe in a universal stage of communal ownership antecedent to individual tenure of land. Let them advance evidence to show that land was once communally owned in the Torres Straits; that the Algon-

> kians at some definite period failed to recognize the individual hunter's domain; that separate ownership was unknown to the Vedda of some specified period [*ibid.*:231].

One might take up this challenge by inquiring why the burden of proof rests with those who have dozens of cases of band-level societies in which there is an unequivocal correlation between the hunting mode of existence and communal tenure. Given the fact that the three cases advanced by Lowie appear to be aberrant, would it not be more in keeping with the Machian temper to seek the reasons for this departure from the norm than to throw doubt upon the entire generalization? If smoke rises, are the laws of motion less valid? But the matter is much more serious. One would suppose that for Lowie to have issued such an audacious challenge, he must have been arguing from a position of great empirical strength. One can almost see "Fortress Lowie," a wall of impregnable facts. Alas, it now appears that the strength of his position lay exclusively in the improbability that any of his colleagues or students would think it worth their while to call his bluff. All three cases are spurious. Not one of them stands up to careful scrutiny.

CHALLENGE ACCEPTED: THE ALGONKIANS

For the Algonkians we have the ethnographic and ethnohistorical restudy carried out among the Montagnais Naskapi by Eleanor Leacock. This study was specifically dedicated to the examination of the conclusions reached by Lowie's chief source, Frank G. Speck (1915). Leacock denies the existence of individually owned beaver trapping territories (a conclusion toward which Speck's later writings also tended), confirms the existence of joint family tracts, but strongly opposes the contention that such patterns were aboriginal. The introduction of family tracts closely followed the movements of the geographical and chronological centers of the fur trade. She attributes the breakdown in communal tenure to the shift from dependence upon caribou hunting to beaver trapping and beaver-skin trading. Her explanation of the social change consequent upon the shift from hunting to trapping is as follows:

> Owing to the uncertainty of the hunt, several families were necessarily dependent upon each other, thus providing a kind of subsistence insurance or greater security than individual families could achieve. With production for trade, however, the individu-

> al's most important ties, economically speaking, were transferred from *within* the band to *without*, and his objective relation to other band members changed from the cooperative to the competitive. With storable, transportable, and individually acquired supplies—principally flour and lard—as staple foods, the individual family becomes self-sufficient, and larger group living is not only superfluous in the struggle for existence but a positive hindrance to the personal acquisition of furs [LEACOCK 1954:7].

A second and independent study of the Canadian Indian tenure system has been carried out by Rolf Knight in the East James Bay area of Labrador. Knight's conclusions are even more devastating than Leacock's for he doubts that family territories even with the fur trade could have been a viable adaptation for more than a small part of the population for any prolonged period. Knight insists that until the early 1940's hunting and fishing continued to supply the bulk of the food consumed by the Indians but that ". . . any hunting-trapping group that was forced to remain on a particular 'hunting territory' sized tract would probably starve to death, at one time or another, within a generation" (KNIGHT 1965:33).

CHALLENGE ACCEPTED: THE VEDDA

The Vedda, known to Lowie through C. G. Seligman's 1911 monograph, inhabit a small portion of the eastern side of the island of Ceylon. Since the Vedda have been surrounded on all sides by highly stratified kingdoms for at least two thousand years, they immediately strike us as being an unlikely fount of information concerning paleolithic social organization. Seligman tells us that the Makayangana, the oldest Buddhist shrine on Ceylon, is immediately adjacent to Vedda country. We learn further that there are two kinds of Vedda: village-dwelling farmers and those who are "wild" and live from hunting. Yet Knox, an early traveler, writing in 1681, establishes the fact that even the "wild" Vedda have been in constant contact with the Sinhalese, who constitute the majority of the island's population. According to this early authority, the hunting groups regularly sold smoked venison to their sedentary neighbors, from whom in return they received iron arrowheads. In times of crises, the kings of Ceylon employed both "wild" and "tame" Vedda as archers in their armies and they "fought in the service of the king against the Dutch" (quoted in SELIGMAN 1911:7). Seligman further remarks that by 1911 there were very few Vedda living in the forests and that their territory had been encroached upon by the Sinhalese "who are inveterate poachers" (*ibid.*:35). Against this unpromising background Seligman introduces undeniably convincing evidence that the Vedda with whom he had come in contact not only had band territories but that they had in addition family and individual ownership of smaller tracts. As Lowie says, "Dr. Seligman was able to map the territories of distinct Henebedda [i.e., Henebedda band] families." And among the Sitala Wanniya band, as Lowie once again quotes from Seligman, "A man would not hunt even on his brother's land without permission" (SELIGMAN 1911:111). Indeed, for the Sitala Wanniya, Seligman not only provides a map of individual territories but cites five specific transfers of land ownership that had occurred in the memory of his informants. But who are the Henebedda and the Sitala Wanniya? Are they the "wild" Vedda or the "tame" ones? Are they hunters and gatherers or village farmers?

> *The Henebedda*
>
> These people make chenas [i.e., practice slash-and-burn agriculture] on which they live temporarily in bark-covered huts . . . several of them possess guns . . . and some of them rear cattle for the Sinhalese villagers [SELIGMAN 1911:36].
>
> *The Sitala Wanniya*
>
> After visiting so many decaying or degenerate communities a refreshing state of affairs was found at Sitala Wanniya. Here there were at least four families who were living the life their forefathers had lived. . . .They still found game, honey and yams in quantities sufficient not only to support life, but to leave a surplus to barter with the Moormen on their annual visit, or to take into the nearest Sinhalese village to exchange for iron, cloth, pots, and occasional rice and coconuts [*ibid.*:44].

It is clear that Lowie had no right to include the Henebedda in a discussion of tenure among hunters and gatherers. As for the Sitala Wanniya, although there is some ambiguity concerning their status as farmers, there is none concerning their close relations with nearby village communities. Every one of the specific private transfers cited by Seligman involved honey spots, a condition which would at once render intelligible the individualized tenure. No one had ever suggested that a group which can earn its livelihood by trading or selling honey would derive an adaptive advantage from maintaining communal hunting grounds. The false pretense under which this group also appears in Lowie's argument is made even more painful if one inspects the chart which Seligman presents to sum up the extent to which the Vedda bands had surrendered a purely hunting and gathering mode of life. Of the nine nonvillage bands listed, the Sitala Wanniya is the only one said to have no agriculture. However, in the adjacent "remarks," we learn that "The older men of this community had never made chena." This carries with it the unavoidable conclusion that at the time of Seligman's visit, the young men at least *were* making gardens (*ibid.*:58)!

CHALLENGE ACCEPTED: QUEENSLAND

For the Queensland-Torres Straits family hunting territories, Lowie relied on the report of Walter E. Roth, the Australian government's "Chief Protector of Aboriginals" in Queensland. Exactly *twenty-seven lines* of this report are devoted to the matter at hand. The Cape Bedford, Bloomfield River, and Cairns hinterland groups are said to have the usual band-owned territories. In addition and "independently" of this larger area, there are smaller tracts of named portions of the country controlled by families rather than by the band as a whole. The economic significance of these tracts, however, is discussed neither by Lowie nor Roth. We are not told what portion of a family's product comes from the communal territory and what portion from the family's own tract. Whatever may be the answer to that question, however, it is clear that trespass on the family property by fellow band members does not result in very serious consequences. Indeed, among the Bloomfield River groups, trespass produces "a slanging match, with both parties indulging in epithets" (ROTH 1905:8). But Roth assures us that such intraband trespass is seldom committed because "when one family experiences a superabundance of food of any description, its friends and neighbors are generally invited to come and partake of it" (*ibid.*). Roth offers no specific instances of such trespass, and we are left unenlightened concerning the real-life (etic) significance of the jural ideals that he identifies. It is certain that if we wish to speak of these family lands as being "owned," it must be in a sense that is totally different from tenure, which is associated with politically enforced laws of trespass. What is critical for us to know beyond this point is whether family groups within the band generally refuse or generally grant requests by their fellow band members to utilize each other's family territories (in the event that such territories do indeed contain significant strategic resources). Roth's account thus fails to provide a safe basis for any kind of ethnographic conclusion. Least of all does it provide the basis for destroying a generalization which is supported by hundreds of independent observers and dozens of monographs.

Lowie's notion of the quintessence of scientific insight thus shrinks into its own "farrago of dubious hypotheses."

LOWIE'S IDEOLOGICAL BIAS

We have seen that in proposing limited parallelisms and in supporting the possibility of identifying repetitive causal sequences, Lowie contended that the more conservative Boasian outlook was itself an "illustration of cultural inertia." In response to Leslie White's attacks against the supposed antievolutionism of the Boasians, Lowie thus could and repeatedly did demolish the point of view that he and his colleagues were the victims of reactionary antievolutionistic currents allegedly endemic to the intellectual milieu in which they operated. But there is another charge to be brought against the Boasians, the charge of entrenched dogmatic antimaterialism. As Buettner-Janusch (1957:322) has put it, we must recognize that "a powerful ideology against materialism and naturalism" had found spokesmen in the new anthropology. Lowie was quick to take up this challenge in his characteristically peppery idiom by recounting the story of how he helped to vindicate Morgan concerning the existence of clans among the Crow:

> In 1906 I found no such tribal subdivisions among the Lemni Shoshone; my predecessors and successors had the same experience among the Ute and Paiute. On the Plains, investigators discovered no clans among the Arapaho, Kiowa, and Comanche, whence sprang the dogma that Morgan had mistakenly credited the institution to the Crow, Hidatsa, and Mandan. In 1907, as a callow novice, I could not help *stumbling* upon the Crow clan system and so reported. Was I the unwitting tool of reactionary ideologies in 1906 and the unwitting spokesman of enlightenment in 1907? Obviously the idea is preposterous: it was field work, and nothing but field work that corrected Morgan regarding Shoshoneans and vindicated him regarding the Crow (also the Hidatsa and Mandan [1957:884; italics added].

But Lowie missed the point. To "stumble" upon an ethnographic fact is one thing; to deliberately set out to look for it is another. Leacock and Knight did not stumble upon the reinterpretation of Algonkian land tenure. They were able to correct Speck because there existed an established body of scientific theory which Speck's descriptions seemed to falsify, thereby demanding that every aspect of his evidence be gone over with the greatest possible skepticism. In order for Lowie to establish his method as free from the ideological biases of his milieu, he must show that his skepticism is not evenly dispersed, but that it is concentrated precisely upon those critical empirical tests upon whose outcome whole universes of theory were being dashed to smithereens. This Lowie failed to do, not in relation to evolutionism, not in relation to Morgan's and Tylor's theories, for both of whom he had the greatest of respect, but rather in relation to cultural materialism and the theoretical prospectus which like it or not had at the beginning of the century been furthest advanced by Marx and Engels.

Over a span of more than thirty years, Lowie published numerous articles and books in which the same tenuous ethnographic material was brought forth repeatedly to show how a bowdlerized version of economic determinism could be destroyed by the advent of fieldwork and "higher standards of proof." The most important theme running through this span is that the relationship between human populations and their natural habitats is mediated by ideologies and cultural traditions which lead to such wasteful, quixotic, irrational, and useless sorts of relationships as permanently to baffle the creation of generalized "economic" theories of culture history.

The presence of these numerous, powerful, inscrutible, and capricious features of cultures did not disturb Lowie's empiricist posture. He seemed willing to abandon the attempt to achieve a nomothetic understanding of an indefinitely large number of apparently inscrutable patterns because, following Mach, he believed that "there are phenomena which we are obliged to accept as realities without the possibility of further analysis" (LOWIE 1929:96). But it is one thing to accept ignorance in preference to metaphysical forces and essences, and another to revel in it and propound it as a faith. If this sounds uncharitable, how else explain Lowie's dogmatic insistence that an economic explanation could not be found for certain otherwise never-to-be-explained phenomena? As, for example, "among the Toda the cause of female infanticide is obscure, but we know positively that it bears no relation to economic life" (LOWIE 1920:48).

ETHNOGRAPHIC BASIS OF LOWIE'S CRITIQUE OF ECONOMIC DETERMINISM

Let us look a little more closely at the ethnographic basis for Lowie's rejection of economic explanations. Three great domains of allegedly inscrutable and capricious phenomena provided Lowie with the bulk of his arguments. First, he was convinced that in the elaboration of primitive hierarchical systems, the drive for "prestige" was strong enough to efface the adaptive and utilitarian aspects of ranking and stratification. Second, primitive warfare, he believed, for the most part was also a kind of prestige-motivated sport. Third, he pointed over and over again to the way in which religious or other ideological factors prevented many cultures from managing their productive resources in conformity with objective utilitarian standards. Space does not permit the exposure of Lowie's ethnographic blunders in the detail which is merited. For his mistaken notions concerning the unrelatedness of specific techno-environmental conditions and specific hierarchical structures, he was greatly indebted to Boas' Northwest Coast ethnography, some of whose errors have already been discussed. With our heightened understanding of redistributive economic forms, not only the Northwest Coast but many other hierarchical systems, especially in Oceania, which appeared inscrutable to Lowie, now appear eminently intelligible (*cf.* SAHLINS 1958; OLIVER 1955). As we have seen above (p. 356), Lowie claimed in *Primitive Society* that the motive for the potlatch was far removed from economics. Insofar as this opinion confuses individual psychological motivation with the supra-individual nature of cultural adaptations it is irrelevant; insofar as it blocks research into the material conditions responsible for the aboriginal potlatch patterns and their peculiar intensification under acculturative pressures, it is obscurantist and has been condemned to oblivion.

AN EMIC VIEW OF WARFARE

For the interpretation of warfare, Lowie was not the victim of other people's ethnographic biases. He had himself to blame, largely as a result of the peculiar methods of research which he was obliged to maintain in his study of the Crow. In *Primitive Society*, Lowie also claimed that

> the Plains Indian fought not for territorial aggrandizement nor for the victor's spoils, but above all because fighting was a game worth while because of the social recognition it brought when played according to the rules. True, the stealing of horses was one of the principal factors in warfare. But why did a Crow risk his neck to cut loose a picketed horse in the midst of the hostile camp when he could easily have driven off a whole herd from the outskirts? And what was the point in granting distinction not to the warrior who had killed or wounded the foeman but to him who, however lightly, touched his body [1920:356]?

Aside from the confusion between an individual's motivation in carrying out culturally prescribed patterns of action and the nomothetic conditions responsible for the presence of those patterns, we must here consider another and more cutting defect. Lowie was the world's greatest authority on Crow warfare, religion, and social organization. But he appears not to have ever attempted a serious study of Crow economy. Turning to his monograph on the Crow, we search in vain for a chapter in which there is a discussion of the possible links between the vainglory of counting coup and the material conditions of a hunting, marauding, stealing, horse-adapted way of life. Indeed, in the book's six-page double-columned index, the entry "economics" does not appear! In the chapter on warfare, there is scarcely a paragraph dealing with the relationship of the Crow's constant preoccupation with bravery, horsemanship, and martial skills and the means by which the Crow earned their livelihood, protected themselves from the encroachment of the whites and other Plains Indians, and made the best of what with the advent of the horse, rifle, and plow was probably one of the world's most rapidly evolving ecosystems.

It was of course very convenient for Lowie who had to learn about Crow warfare and Crow economics exclusively through the memories of aged informants to adopt the principle that his actors' view of things was the most important ethnographic product. Indeed, it is not for me to detract from the vitality and interest of the monograph in question. But when such material is harnessed to the task of baffling our understanding, we shirk our responsibility if we do not attempt to expose its limitations.

Thus, like all the Boasians, Lowie suffered from a failure to separate emic from etic data. He believed that in the final analysis, the most important kind of data for identifying cross-cultural similarities are the psychological matrix in which etic events unfold:

> The field worker's business is always and everywhere to understand the true inwardness of the beliefs and practices of the people he studies. He is not content to record that infants are suffocated, aged parents abandoned, or enemies eaten. Unless he can also recover the accompanying sentiments, he has failed in his task [LOWIE 1963:534].

This is a defensible option as long as it is not permitted to deteriorate into a rationalization for the omission of the etic context. Yet this is what seems to have happened in Lowie's treatment of the economics of Plains warfare. How else explain the absence of any hard data concerning the role warfare played in spacing out the Plains' population, maintenance of territory, provision of subsistence, distribution of food and nonfood energy rations, regulation of population growth, articulation with the natural biota, and dozens of other crucial "economic questions." And yet we find him asserting with great conviction:

> It is possible to turn the tables on economic determinism and to show how largely economic life is affected by considerations that although irrelevant from our point of view, are of the utmost importance to the people concerned [LOWIE 1938:320].

This is surely an attitude about which we may from our own experience with warfare be profoundly skeptical. There is no more self-evident truth than that the politicians who have been the most eager fomentors of our own wars are usually least capable of explaining why they have done so.

In recent years, dramatic contradictions of Lowie's conclusions concerning the "motivations" of primitive warfare have been achieved by ethnographers who had adopted a consistent etic approach. Andrew P. Vayda for example has suggested that there are commonalities in the ecosystems underlying the warfare patterns of the Maori, Iban, Mundurucu, Tiv, and other swidden agriculturalists (VAYDA 1956, 1960, 1961a, 1961b, 1961c). Roy Rappaport (1966) has shown how an apparently chaotic series of patterns involving warfare, sweet potatoes, pigs, human populations, and magical plants among the Maring of New Guinea fit together to form an ecologically adaptive syndrome. This brilliant tour de force is distinguished by its quantitative richness and its awareness of the demographic, nutritional, caloric, edaphic, medical, and climatological parameters, all of which must be considered before judgments concerning the anti-economic functions of particular institutions can safely be rendered.

MISMANAGEMENT OF RESOURCES

This brings us to the third of Lowie's pet areas of chaos: the alleged mismanagement of resources as a result of historical quirks and ideological idiosyncracies. One thread of this argument is especially long and influential. It is the notion that capricious food taboos and similar ideological quirks frequently prevent the utilization or effective exploitation of potentially significant food sources, especially of certain animal foods. Thus, in *Culture and Ethnology* Lowie attaches considerable significance to the fact that "The Chinaman will not milk his cattle; while the Zulu's diet consists largely of milk" (1966:82; orig. 1917).

> Most startling of all perhaps is the different attitude assumed in different countries towards cattle. To us nothing seems more obvious than that cattle should be kept both for meat and dairy products. This, however, is by no means a universal practice. The Zulu and other Bantu tribes of South Africa use milk extensively but hardly ever slaughter their animals except on festive occasions. On the other hand, we have the even more astonishing fact that Eastern Asiatics, such as the Chinese, Japanese, Koreans, and Indo-Chinese, have an inveterate aversion to the use of milk [*ibid.*:57].

In 1938, in his article on subsistence in the textbook edited by Boas, Lowie elaborated on this theme in the context of a direct attack on economic determinism. Wrote Lowie, "it should be once more emphasized that even where practical considerations play a dominant role, capricious irrationality checks the full and rationalistic exploitation of domestic beasts" (1938:306). As examples, Lowie mentions our failure to milk mares, the Egyptian taboos against pork, the "Negro stockbreeders" lack of cheese, the way the Bantu "spurn" beef, and the Chinese failure to "have conceived the idea of milking their cows" (*ibid.*:306–7). Among Lowie's manuscripts there was found a paper, assumed by Cora DuBois to have been written in 1939 or 1940, which has been published under the title, "Economic Factors and Culture." Once again the same refrain:

> One main objection to the economic interpretations of culture that have hitherto been offered is that they fail to come to grips with those problems that obtrude themselves spontaneously on any unprejudiced observer of the data. The theorists of this school ignore even so obvious a fact as the irrational ingredients of economic activity, a fact so convincingly established by the late Eduard Hahn and so overwhelmingly corroborated by later inquiry. To take a single example, East Africans are enthusiastic stock-breeders; but is their animal husbandry to be gauged by our standards? Far from it. A Shilluk keeps hundreds of cattle, yet slaughters them so rarely that he is obliged to maintain his hunting techniques for an adequate supply of meat. His small cows yield but little milk, his oxen normally serve no purpose at all. But these Negroes, who have failed to perfect their dairying industry and who eschew a beef diet, expend enormous effort on massaging the humps of their beasts and twisting their horns into grotesque shapes [LOWIE 1960:242].

Again in 1942 he drew attention to the mismanagement of pigs.

> Throughout Melanesia the pig greatly affects social prestige without noticeably adding to mass subsistence. Such examples deter us from over-emphasizing rationalistic considerations in reconstructing an undocumented past [LOWIE 1942:541].

CHINESE AVERSION TO MILK

Each of these examples represents an abuse of the comparative method, wrenching out of functional context, comparison of noncomparables, obedience to metaphysical entities, and a serious departure from empirical standards of proof. Consider the Chinese "aversion" to milk as opposed to our own lactic complex. To regard this contrast as capricious is to ignore the basic differences in the food production systems of the two societies. China, with its great dependence upon intensive irrigated rice production, traditionally maintained only as many bovines and buffalos as were needed for draft and draft-breeding requirements. Animal protein and fat were supplied by pigs, more efficient scavengers than cattle. Morton Fried (personal communication) offers a simple explanation for why the Chinese in the village he studied in 1949 would not milk their cows: there weren't any worth milking. The breeds which develop from centuries of adaptive response to the prime requirements of rice agriculture are not going to be Holsteins and Jerseys. Furthermore, to convert a portion of irrigated farmland to dairy pasture under pre-industrial conditions would lower rather than raise the carrying capacity of the ecosystem. Under these circumstances, failure to develop a dairy industry is scarcely an example of a flagrant mismanagement of resources. The density of the Chinese population should have in itself warned Lowie of any such simplistic conclusion. Indeed, it could well be argued that the national "aversion" to cow's milk among the Chinese points to a "rational" adjustment between food tastes and China's basic mode of food production.

THE MYTH OF THE SILLY BANTU

Lowie's case against the Eastern and Southern Bantu fares even worse. The myth of the silly African dairymen had become enshrined by Melville Herskovits as the principle diagnostic of the East African culture area and as such was disseminated among hundreds of Africanists, administrators, and connoisseurs of African exotica. Here the question has been amply explored by Harold Schneider (1957). Among the Pakot, as among the other groups mentioned by Lowie, there is a great love of cattle and much care is lavished upon them. And why not? The animals represent a walking bank account, the living embodiment of surplus production, the best defense against famine, and the next best thing to a woman, if one intends to lead the local *dolce vita*. As for taboos against slaughter, once again the emics of the matter led Lowie to disaster. In East Africa, cattle *are* killed and they *are* eaten in relation to ceremonial occasions. As Lowie says, "they do not slaughter except on festive occasions." But how often do these occasions occur? The answer according to Schneider is that they occur often enough to lead to a constant culling of the herds at a level suited to the carrying capacity of the native ranges. In this connection, care must be taken to evaluate the widespread belief in overstocking and overgrazing among modern Bantu populations. It must be remembered that population increase and the conversion of aboriginal ranges to European-dominated cash-crop agriculture has drastically altered the entire ecosystem.

SACRED COWS, PIGS, AND HORSES

The rebuttal of Lowie's cattle mismanagement argument should also include an analysis of the role of cattle in India. The case is too complex for a brief treatment. Suffice it to say that the relationship between Indian cattle and human populations is demonstrably symbiotic. Cattle and people derive their calorie ration from separate spheres of the ecosystem; cattle are India's prime scavengers; their dung is essential for fuel and fertilizer; their traction contribution is indispensable under the prevailing techno-environmental conditions of agriculture. Dairying is carried out to maximum limits compatible with traction and good planting requirements, while Hindu taboos against slaughter and consumption of beef do not prevent culling of herds nor consumption of beef by low castes and Moslems. There is no evidence that these taboos under present-day techno-environmental conditions adversely affect the welfare of the rural populations. Indeed, insofar as there is a severe shortage of cattle in India, such beliefs may be regarded as an adaption by which the exploitation of cattle, especially during famine, is kept within safe limits (*cf.* HARRIS 1966a).

Similar kinds of analysis have been proposed for the role of Melanesian and New Guinea pigs, another of Lowie's examples (VAYDA, LEEDS, and SMITH 1961). Emic, short-run, and impressionistic data have produced many cases of sensational mismanagement of pig-raising. Few ethnographers have hitherto concerned themselves to assess the nutritional importance of relatively small amounts of animal fat and protein in diets which consist of root crops (*cf.* RAPPAPORT 1966). Similarly, judgments concerning the economic nature of pigs and other animal raising practices have seldom properly weighed long against short-run needs, especially as these may relate to Liebig's law of the minimum; i.e. that adaptations are made not to average, but to extreme, conditions.

Lowie's mention of the failure to milk mares pertains to another set of misunderstood cases in which belong the reluctance to eat insects, dogs, and snails. When alternative sources of nutritional values are available, cultural ecological theory predicts that in the long run, the most efficient will be utilized. It does *not* predict that all of the techno-environmental possibilities will be realized to an equal degree. Why should Western European agriculturalists milk mares? To make any substantial difference in the average calorie, protein, and calcium rations, mares would have to replace cows. Under the techno-environmental conditions which gave rise to the European mixed farming tradition, *that* would indeed have been grist for Lowie's chaos mill.

In these and the remaining cases that Lowie brings forth (e.g., the Moslem resistance to pork), the burden of proof is quite different from what Lowie said it was. We have every good logico-empirical reason to suppose that most human populations reach an adaptive equilibrium within their ecosystem. If a particular culturally induced practice appears to contravene that generalization, it is unequivocally the burden of those who present such cases to make certain that they have carefully examined the allegedly capricious traits in a reasonably real-life functional context. Failure to do this is in essence what the Boasians had charged was the chief defect of their evolutionist predecessors. In post-Boasian ethnography, standards of a reasonably complete real-life functional context, however, were completely overridden by a preference for emic data, even when, as seldom happened, full-scale studies of techno-environmental systems were attempted.

CONCLUSION

I do not wish to create the impression that Lowie's view of economic determinism exhibits no signs of development throughout his career. On the contrary, there are clear indications of a later tendency to give more and more weight to economic factors. In his last major book-length publication, *Social Organization*, Lowie declares in the preface,

> I have pointed out the potency of economic forces, not in abstract, which is hardly necessary nowadays, but by suggesting that certain specific changes in economic life have led to specific modifications in the social life, even affecting sentimental attitudes [1948a:v].

Of course, such daring admissions are carefully hedged by assurances that, come what may, he will never admit any affinity to the devilish proposals made by Marx and Engels. Instead, one should turn to less influential but saner figures, such as Henri Sée:

> As the eminent French scholar Henri Sée has remarked, it is difficult "to unravel the tangle of causes and effects" in history; but "in the infinite sea of historical events economic determinism has helped to furnish us with a guiding thread which keeps us from being lost" [*ibid.*:24].

One must also take note of Lowie's rather pathetic citation of Henry Maine as a guarantor of orthodoxy for economic interpretations: "Any of the material alterations in aboriginal life may, as Maine recognized decades ago, produce far-reaching changes in ideology" (LOWIE 1942:541). We must conclude, however, that Lowie never rose above the restraints of his Boasian heritage to a clear understanding of the cultural-materialist option. He never fully recovered from the historically intelligible but logico-empirically indefensible prejudice that the burden of proof rested upon those who offered "economic" explanations. Immediately after insisting upon the importance of the influence of Potosí silver mining upon Andean culture patterns, of woolen industries upon the urbanization of England, of the introduction of the horse upon the Bannock, and of reindeer among the Chuckchee he lapses back into the glorification of what, for all we know, are some more old wives' tales. Thus, the South American aborigines gain their livelihood in basically similar ways—yet their matrimonial arrangements are far from uniform. Chuckchee old men are respected, Lapp old men are pitiable, yet both Lapps and Chuckchee depend upon reindeers. "The difference must lie in the prior norms of Lapps and Chuckchee," declares Lowie, "and those norms thus codetermine the observed treatment of old people" (1948a:36). The "guiding thread" seems to cut Lowie's hands; he remains all too eager to chase the first "will-o'-the-wisp." And why? Surely not because it can safely be said that the matrilineal as opposed to the patrilineal tropical forest groups in Brazil really have *no* important techno-environmental differences; nor because the Lapps and Chuckchee are identical in their basic material complexes. And for what? To show that culture really is after all inscrutable? No doubt that is so in the ultimate balancing of human intelligence against the infinity of unknowns in nature. But to be faithful to Mach and the empiricist vision is to postpone such admissions to an indefinite future. What Mach had not foreseen, nor Lowie grasped, is that metaphysical residues maintain themselves in both positive and negative guise. A man is known not only by what he declares true and false, but also by what he fails to declare either true or false. Lowie committed few errors of a positive sort; the errors he exposed are legion; but there were many falsehoods he tolerated for no better reason than that they were fashionable.

Diffusionism

14

As the idiographic trend engulfed European and American scholarship, it brought into prominence within anthropology explanatory schemes founded on the nonprinciple of "diffusion." The use to which this concept was put in the Boasian critique of nineteenth-century evolutionism and the falseness of the dichotomies between independent invention and diffusion and parallel and convergent evolution has already been discussed (see Chap. 6). It remains for us to take brief note of the way in which diffusion was actually employed as an explanatory principle characteristic of the idiographic period.

In the United States diffusionist thinking culminated in the elaboration of the concept of culture areas, relatively small geographical units based on the contiguous distribution of cultural elements. In Europe, the same trend gave rise to the notion of *Kulturkreise,* or Culture-Circles, large complexes of traits which had lost their former geographical unity and were now dispersed throughout the world.

ORIGIN OF THE CULTURE-AREA CONCEPT

The culture-area concept had its origin in the practical exigencies of American ethnographic research, as a heuristic device for mapping and classifying the tribal groups of North and South America. The development of ethnographic collections at the American Museum of Natural History and the Chicago Field Museum in particular, coinciding with the trend against evolutionary typologies, fostered the development of geographical categories as display units implicit in the names of sections or halls. In reviewing the history of the concept, Kroeber (1931:250) gave passing credit to Otis T. Mason, referring to a 1907 article in the *Handbook of the American Indian North of Mexico,* in which Mason listed twelve "ethnic environments." Kroeber was apparently unaware that Mason had actually employed the term "culture area" in an 1895 article in the *Annual Report of the Smithsonian Institution,* entitled "Influence of Environment upon Human Industries or Arts." In this article, Mason (1895a:646) identified eighteen "American Indian environments or culture areas: Arctic, Athabascan, Algonkian, Iroquoian, Muskhogean, Plains of the Great West, North Pacific Coast, Columbia Drainage, Interior Basin, California-Oregon, Pueblo, Middle American, Andean, Andean Atlantic Slope, Eastern Brazilian, Central Brazilian, Argentine-Patagonian, Fuegian. In 1899, Mason produced a modified list which went as follows: Arctic, Canadian, Louisiana or Gulf, Plains, Southeast Alaska, Columbian, Interior Basin, California, Pueblo, Middle American, Antillean, Cordilleran, Upper Amazon, Eastern Brazil, Matto Grosso, Argentine-Patagonian, Feugian. Mason's areas were subsequently refined by G. Holmes (1914) and made the basis for a landmark treatment of American Indian ethnology by Clark Wissler (1917) and by Kroeber himself in his *Cultural and Natural Areas* (1939). Despite Mason's clear priority, there is no need to dispute Kroeber's (1931:250) observation that the culture-area concept was "a community product of nearly the whole school of American anthropologists." This follows from the extreme simplicity of the concept. Nothing is more obvious than the prospective utility of an ethnographic map which groups tribal entities in relationship to some geographically delineated aspect of the environment. It is quite another matter, however, to suppose that this geographical grouping in and of itself contributes to an understanding of cultural differences and similarities.

WEAKNESS OF THE CULTURE-AREA CONCEPT

As an explanatory device, the culture area was impaled at the outset on the horns of a dilemma: if too much emphasis is given to the natural geographical substratum, the mapper falls victim to a naïve form of geographical determinism; if simple contiguity is emphasized, the "cause" of each assemblage appears to be wholly capricious and the question of boundaries becomes insuperable. The first "horn" hurts because similar natural environments in different parts of the world are obviously inhabited by peoples with widely different cultures. For example, the tropical rain forests of the New World were inhabited at different times or in different regions by temple-building agriculturalists; village horticulturalists; and semi-nomadic hunters, fishers, and collectors. The prime factor which disturbs the explanatory usefulness of a straightforward arrangement of cultures by natural environmental areas is that it is the techno-environmental interaction which is decisive, not merely the environment. This aspect of the dilemma is well illustrated in Wissler's (1917) attempt to base his culture areas on "food areas," as follows:

Food Areas	*Culture Areas*
Caribou	Eskimo, Mackenzie (and north part of Eastern Woodland)
Bison	Plains
Salmon	North Pacific Coast, Plateau
Wild Seed	California
Eastern Maize	Southeast, Eastern Woodland (except north nonagricultural portion)
Intensive Agriculture	Southwest, Nahua-Mexico, Chibcha, Inca-Peru
Manioc	Amazon, Antilles
Guanaco	Guanaco

Note that three of these "food" areas—Eastern Maize, Intensive Agriculture, and Manioc—refer to domesticated species, while all the rest refer to natural resources. There arises from this partial inclusion of the technological aspect of the techno-environmental equation the further anomaly that the area singled out as "Intensive Agriculture" is divided into three discontinuous sub areas, each of which is several thousand miles away from the others. The existence of two or three widely separated areas of native high civilization in the Americas thus raises at once the question of to what extent mere propinquity may be advanced as an explanation of resemblance.

CENTERS, CLIMAXES, AND THE LAW OF DIFFUSION

Despite these evident anomalies, the American schools continued throughout the twenties and thirties to lavish a great deal of effort on the attempt to make the culture-area concept shoulder the burden for explaining cultural differences and similarities. Wissler sought to overcome some of the difficulties by attributing the characteristic features of each area to a "culture center" from which the assemblage of traits had diffused outward. From the beginning, the concept of this "center" exhibited the full-scale effects of the basic dilemma: how to combine the environmental conditions with the apparently capricious freedom of culture. Hence, Wissler's vague references to "ethnic factors and historic accident":

> The origin of a culture center seems due to ethnic factors more than to geographical ones. The location of these centers is largely a matter of historic accident, but once located and the adjustments made, the stability of the environment doubtless tends to hold each particular type of culture to its initial locality, even in the face of many changes in blood and language [1926:372].

Elaborating further on the notion of "culture center," Wissler (*ibid.*: 183) set forth a "law of diffusion," to wit, "that anthropological traits tend to diffuse in all directions from their centers of origin." This law constitutes the basis of the "age-area principle," which is a method for inferring the relative age of culture traits from their geographical distribution: the most widely distributed traits around a center would be the oldest, if the direction of diffusion were always from the center outwards. Needless to say, the "law of diffusion" is a highly unreliable guide to actual historical events and can be applied only with the greatest caution. Were we to regard it unskeptically, we should soon find ourselves arguing that Coca-Cola must have been bottled long before the invention of the *coup de poing.*

Much to Kroeber's credit, an attempt was initiated during the twenties to define culture areas in terms of comprehensive lists of items. These lists were used to establish coefficients of similarity. The logical extreme of this approach was reached with the University of California element list surveys which compared Indian groups west of the Rockies on the basis of some 3,000 to 6,000 items (KROEBER and DRIVER 1932). Extension of this method to other areas has been blocked, however, by the difficulties encountered in defining unit elements. Thus, even 6,000 traits might be inadequate for measuring overall similarity if the traits utilized were not systematically identified on the same level of detail. (Polygyny might count for one trait, while the bow and arrow might count for four or five.) After the rather inconclusive experience with massive trait lists, Kroeber turned increasingly to impressionistic interpretations of the "culture center," or as he called it, the "culture climax," with ultimate consequences which have been previously discussed.

STEWARD'S CRITIQUE

Although culture-area classifications may be regarded as essential at the initial fact-gathering and fact-ordering levels of ethnography, the concept has been as much of a deterrent to the growth of nomothetic theory as it has been an asset. Steward (1955:82) has discussed the consequences of a reliance upon culture-area typologies with respect to three problems: (1) center and boundary change with passage of time; (2) culture within the area may change so that it resembles cultures in different areas at different times; (3) portions of the area may be regarded as containing radically different cultures despite sharing of many features. All of these problems are well illustrated in the case of Kroeber's Greater Southwest Area. First, archaeological studies of the Southwest do not confirm the notion of a single stable center, nor a small number of climaxes. Second, there are known to be at least two principal developmental sequences: one, the Hohokam sequence, running from the hunting and gathering Cochise through the agricultural but pre-historic Hohokam; the other, the Anasazi sequence, connecting pre-ceramic Basket Maker peoples with the modern Pueblos. Third, the area, despite widespread similarities in culture "content," was inhabited in historic times by peoples whose social organization was as widely contrastive as that of the sedentary Pueblos, the pastoral Navaho, and the marauding Apaches.

STERILITY OF THE CONCEPT OF DIFFUSION

These objections to the culture-area concept expose the fundamental sterility of the attempt to explain cultural differences and similarities by appealing to the nonprinciple of diffusion. Although it is true, as Driver (1966) has shown, that geographical-historical propinquity is often a better *predictor* of traits than psychofunctional causality, under no circumstances can geographical-historical propinquity constitute a valid explanation of cultural differences and similarities. First of all, diffusion is admittedly incapable of accounting for the origin of a given trait, except by "passing the buck" back through an infinite regression: A ⟵ B ⟵ C ⟵ . . . ? As soon as we admit, as the archaeology of the New World now compels, that independent invention has occurred on a massive scale, diffusion is by definition not only superfluous, but the very incarnation of antiscience. But even if we obstinately cling to the assumption that independent invention is a rarity, nothing is more obvious than the fact that there is no simple relationship between distance and cultural type. Indeed, all diffusionists would agree that there is differential receptivity to cultural influences independent of distance. If this is so, then we must inevitably find ourselves involved in the consideration of all the factors of environment, technology, economy, social organization, and ideology which concern those who seek to explain sociocultural differences and similarities in terms of nomothetic principles. Such principles deal with the general classes of conditions under which classes of institutions become more probable. True enough, the specific form in which these institutions are manifested is usually related to whether they are introduced as a result of invention or diffusion. Diffused innovations tend to show greater cross-cultural resemblances in finer detail than independently invented innovations. The focus of nomothetic explanations is not, however, on the fine detail, but on the general structural and functional category of which a particular institution or trait is an example. A diffused innovation, no less than an independently invented one, must withstand the selective pressures of the social system if it is to become a part of the cultural repertory. In this larger sense, the adoption of diffused and independently invented innovations must be viewed as part of a single process. The sterility of the purely historical approach resides ultimately in the fact that nomothetic principles are adequate only to the extent that they can explain specific instances of independent invention *and* of diffusion. Diffusion, however, cannot, by definition, explain independent invention.

If it could be proved, however, that independent invention was indeed an insignificant and rare event and that all of the important inventions in world history had been discovered once and only once, then the need for nomothetic explanations could be challenged in a way that was inadmissible to the Boasians. Given the premium rewards on disproving the nomothetic position, it is not altogether remarkable that precisely this interpretation was fostered and not once but twice—almost simultaneously—in Germany and England.

EXTREME DIFFUSIONISM

The German diffusionists, dominated by members of the Catholic clergy, were responsible for one last grandiose attempt to reconcile anthropological prehistory and cultural evolution with the Book of Genesis. The English school, smaller and less influential, concerned itself with proving that almost all the sociocultural traits of interest to anthropologists had been invented once and only once in Egypt, from whence they had spread to the rest of the world. Both of these movements were palpably bankrupt by mid-century; they require our attention today only as evidence of the international extent of the tide that was running against nomothetic principles. Toward one of the schools—the British "diffusionists"—the Boasians were openly contemptuous. Toward the adherents of the other—the Vienna-based *Kulturkreis*, or "Culture-Circle," approach—the Boasians were critical but not unsympathetic. It can be shown, however, that the English and Germans matched each other very neatly in the extent to which they sought to return the science of history to the study of accidents and miracles.

Both schools have been conventionally categorized as stressing diffusion and therefore as necessarily opposing evolution. The wholly fabricated nature of this dichotomy has already been discussed in relation to the views of the nineteenth-century evolutionists. It was the English idiographers who fostered the error that Morgan and Tylor were unaware of the importance of contact and migration in the spread of cultural innovation (*cf.* LOWIE 1938:172). And it was both the German and British idiographers, who by virtue of their repeated attacks on "evolutionism," had only themselves to blame for their identification as "antievolutionists." This muddled situation has survived Lowie's attempts to draw attention to the Germans' distinction between "evolution" and "evolutionism." But even Lowie failed to do justice to the extent to which the *Kulturkreis* school was dependent upon evolutionary theories and methods, while the evolutionary component in the British schemes has gone virtually unnoticed. This muddle will only be resolved when we freely and emphatically proclaim both the British and the German idiographers as evolutionists. Their distinctive contribution, never quite adequately defined by Lowie, was their denial of lawful regularities in history.

BRITISH DIFFUSIONISM

The most prominent British "diffusionists" were W. H. R. Rivers, Grafton Elliot Smith and W. J. Perry. Rivers, the founder of the trend, converted to diffusionism during the writing of his *The History of Melanesian Society*. Thwarted in his attempt to organize the ethnography of Oceania on the basis of nomothetic principles, Rivers sought the explanation of contrasts among Melanesian and Polynesian cultures in terms of original complexes which had allegedly been spread by successive waves of migrants. For these postulated diffusionary effects to account for the known distribution of Oceanic traits, Rivers had to assume that nonconforming cases had either been brought about by the accidental disappearance of characteristic features of the original complex, or by the advent of small boatloads of migrants whose physical presence could no longer be detected. Insofar as Rivers mainly confined his historical reconstructions to Oceania, he resembled the Boasians more than the remainder of the British school. It was Rivers (1911), however, who first raised the hue and cry against "evolutionism," claiming that anthropology "was wholly under the domination of a crude evolutionary standpoint." Rivers falsely attributed to the evolutionists the view that "after the original dispersal of mankind . . . large portions of the earth had been cut off from intercourse with others, so that the process of evolution had taken place in them independently" (RIVERS, quoted in PERRY 1923:468).

Under G. Elliot Smith and Rivers' pupil, W. J. Perry, the strategy of explaining cultural differences and similarities by appealing to convenient combinations of migrations, additions, losses, and mixings of trait complexes was applied on a worldwide scale. Smith developed the *idée fixe* that practically the entire inventory of world culture had evolved in Egypt. He and Perry believed that this development had begun about 6,000 years ago. Prior to that time, the earth was inhabited by "Natural Man," who not only lacked domesticated animals, agriculture, houses, clothing, but religion, social organization, hereditary chiefs, and formal laws or ceremonies of marriage or burial (SMITH 1928:22). In approximately 4000 B.C. the inhabitants of the Nile Valley "appreciated the fortunate chance provided them" by a "natural crop" of barley and adopted a settled mode of life (*ibid.*:32). Henceforth, in rapid succession they invented pottery, basketry, matting, houses, and flax; learned to domesticate animals; built towns; and began to bury their dead in cemeteries and to develop notions of deity. As the Egyptians progressed in civilization, they set about journeying by land and sea over great distances in search of precious metals and other raw materials. And in so doing, they rapidly spread, through diffusion and colonization, varieties of the original archaic civilization, which had been founded on the banks of the Nile. While many of the new centers of archaic civilization survived and prospered, others, like the New World Maya, declined or died out. Many cultures of contemporary primitive groups thus represent a decline from archaic civilized status rather than an advance from the condition of "natural man"; other primitive cultures represent the mixture of "natural man" and degenerated cultures; while still others represent mixtures of different varieties of degenerated cultures. Despite this emphasis upon degeneration, it is clear that Smith's stages of Egyptian culture history are merely localized versions of conventional eighteenth- and nineteenth-century evolutionary sequences. Even the familiar leisure time and surplus theories of civilization and social stratification are present in Smith's explanation of the Egyptian events:

> It was the agricultural mode of life that furnished the favorable conditions of settled existence, conditions which brought with them the need for such things as represent the material foundation of civilization [*ibid.*].

Smith's account of the evolution of archaic civilization in Egypt and its subsequent spread to other parts of the world greatly resembled the Biblical version of world history, which we have previously treated as folk precedent for the scientific doctrines of cultural evolution. Culture evolves in the scheme of Perry and Smith, no less than it does in Genesis. The problem in both cases is that the explanation of the course it takes cannot be rendered in terms of nomothetic principles. Since the essentials of the Egyptian sequence are alleged to have occurred only once, there can be no correlation analyses, much less assignment of causal priorities. Indeed, the entire weight of the British and German diffusionist schools was bent toward the denial of the possibility that the main sequence of events at the originating center or centers could have been repeated anywhere else.

HISTORY NEVER REPEATS ITSELF

Since Smith and Perry were convinced that the evolution of Egyptian culture was eminently intelligible once the adoption of agriculture was granted, we may very well regard it as puzzling that similar sequences could not have occurred elsewhere. To the charge that the events attributed exclusively to the Nile Valley were simple enough to have been re-enacted many times over in similar river valleys, Smith and Perry replied with the dogma that man was by nature "uninventive":

> Those field-workers who have acquired an intimate acquaintance with relatively uncultured people have repeatedly called attention to the lack of that inventiveness which the theorists are so fond of taking for granted, or rather to their failure to appreciate the need for inventing devices that we regard as obvious and essential in character [*ibid.*:20].

It was nothing but a "fashionable fallacy" which had led anthropologists since the time of William Robertson (described as a "Cartesian scholar") to assume that the ingredients of civilization were obvious and inevitable things for man to have invented. "If there were any truth in this opinion, why did men wait all those hundreds of thousands, perhaps millions, of years before any of them took such a so-called obvious and inevitable step?" (*Ibid.*:25.) Not only did Smith believe that the circumstances which led to the development of civilization were "arbitrary" (*ibid.*:20), but he also asserted that "the distinctive fact in human behavior is the impossibility of predicting the nature of the response to any set of circumstances . . ." (*ibid.*:19). All this adds up to the classic *reductio ad absurdum* of the extreme historicist position: "history does not repeat itself." This position, as we have previously admitted, is unassailable. No one who deliberately seeks to enlarge the apparent chaos of events shall be denied the fruit of his ambition.

From the perspective of the English diffusionists, it would almost appear as if the evolution of culture beyond the hunting and gathering level was a miracle. Although Smith and Perry refrained from any such conclusion, the German diffusionists, under Father Wilhelm Schmidt, did assert that anthropology would get nowhere as long as it attempted to deprive history of its miraculous foundations.

ORIGIN OF THE GERMAN CULTURE-HISTORICAL METHOD

The *Kulturkreis* school traced itself to the inspiration of Friedrich Ratzel, the founder of anthropogeography. Ratzel had criticized his contemporaries, especially Adolf Bastian, for relying too heavily on explanations in terms of psychic unity and independent invention. He had insisted that possible migration or other contact phenomena be ruled out in each particular case before cross-cultural similarities could be attributed to independent invention. "We must beware of thinking even simple inventions necessary," warned Ratzel (1896:79). "It seems far more correct to credit the intellect of 'natural' races with great sterility in all that does not touch the most immediate objects of life." Ratzel was not only impressed by the frequency of migration and other diffusionary processes, but he was at a loss to explain their general principles. Intergroup contacts appeared to him to be "very capricious," and he insisted that "human will takes a hand in the game which, not without caprice, indolently declines some things and all the more readily accepts others" (*ibid.*). For all of his encouragement to the extreme diffusionists, Ratzel may properly be described only as an eclectic. Certainly the difference between Ratzel and Tylor was not so great as to prevent the latter from recommending the English translation of Ratzel's *The History of Mankind* (1896) as "a solid foundation in anthropological study."

On the basis of a study of the similarities in the cross section of the bow shaft, the material and fastening of the bow string, and the feathering of the arrow, Ratzel had concluded that the bow and arrow of Indonesia and West Africa were related. Ratzel's pupil, Leo Frobenius, went further and drew attention to similarities between masks, houses, drums, clothing, and shields in Melanesia, Indonesia, and West Africa. According to Wilhelm Schmidt (1939:26), Frobenius

> thus proved that similarities existed not only between single elements of culture, but also between whole culture complexes and even whole culture circles, so that we have here to reckon not only with migrations of mere individual culture elements but even of entire culture circles.

It was this suggestion of whole large complexes of culture elements, involving all of the categories of the universal pattern, which in 1904 stimulated Fritz Graebner and his fellow assistant, B. Ankermann, at the Berlin Ethnological Museum to write respectively about the culture circles and culture strata in Oceania and the culture circles and culture strata in Africa. In 1906, Graebner went on to apply the culture-circle and culture-strata idea on a worldwide basis. At about the same time, Father Wilhelm Schmidt declared himself a follower of Graebner, founded the journal *Anthropos*, and began to elaborate his own version of the *Kulturkreise*.

CRITERIA OF FORM AND QUANTITY

The high point of Graebner's career came with the publication of his *Die Methode der Ethnologie* (1911), noteworthy for its attempt to elaborate criteria for identifying affinities and chronologies.

The two basic rules were simple enough and were accepted by both Graebner and Schmidt. The first, called by Graebner the "Criterion of Form" and by Schmidt the "Criterion of Quality," states that similarities between two culture elements which do not automatically arise out of the nature, material, or purpose of the traits or objects should be interpreted as resulting from diffusion, regardless of the distance which separates the two instances. The second, called by both the "Criterion of Quantity," states that the probability of historical relationship between two items increases as the number of additional items showing similarities increases; i.e., "several similarities prove more than a single one" (SCHMIDT 1939:150). It is interesting to note that the Criterion of Form, whose discovery Schmidt (1939:143) attributes to Ratzel (*cf.* PENNIMAN 1965:178), had actually been formulated by William Robertson (see p. 34), the very same eighteenth-century "evolutionist" whom G. Elliot Smith proposed as the fountainhead of all "Cartesian" nonsense. This fact serves to strengthen one's suspicion that the two "Criteria" cannot form part of a bona fide "method" and that they are "criteria" only in a purely scholastic sense. How does one distinguish culture elements which arise out of the nature, material, or purpose of a trait or object from elements that are arbitrary? Is patrilineality an arbitrary or inherent aspect of patrilocality? In order to separate the arbitrary from the inherent aspects of culture elements, one must be able to specify the nomothetic conditions under which traits occur—precisely the task which the *Kulturkreis* movement sought to avoid. It should be noted in this regard that there are some very interesting resemblances between the Criterion of Form and the Boasian doctrine known as the "principle of limited possibilities" (see p. 624). By supposing that similarities occurred simply because there was no other way to do certain things (e.g., canoe paddle blades must have broad surfaces), Boas, Lowie, and Goldenweiser vainly sought to eliminate large classes of cross-cultural similarities as evidence for either diffusion or independent invention.

SCHMIDT'S SCHEME

By applying their spurious culture-historical method to the known distribution of contemporary culture traits, Graebner and Schmidt claimed to be able to reconstruct a limited number of original culture circles. All of world history was thus to be understood as the diffusion of these *Kreise* out of the regions in which they were supposed to have evolved. Bearing in mind that there were many points of disagreement among the members of the school, we may take Father Schmidt's list of *Kreise* as the most influential example. Schmidt distinguished four major phases or "grades" of culture circles: Primitive, Primary, Secondary, and Tertiary. Within each of these grades there were several *Kreise*. Thus in the Primitive or hunting and gathering grade we find: (1) the central or exogamous *Kreis*, corresponding to the Pygmy peoples of Africa and Asia, distinguished by their exogamous hordes and their monogamous families; (2) the Arctic *Kreis* (Samoyeds, Eskimo, Algonkians, etc.), exogamous with sexual equality; and (3) the Antarctic *Kreis* (Southeastern Australians, Bushmen, Tasmanians, etc.), exogamous with sex totems. In the next or Primary grade there are also three culture circles: (1) patriarchical cattle-raising nomads; (2) exogamous patrilineal totemic higher hunters; (3) exogamous matrilineal, village-dwelling horticulturalists. The remaining grades and their *Kreise* are as follows:

III. Secondary grade.

Free patrilineal systems (Polynesia, the Sudan, India, western Asia, southern Europe, etc.).	Free matrilineal systems (southern China, Indo-China, Melanesia, northeastern South America, etc.).

IV. Tertiary grade.

Earliest higher civilization of Asia, Europe, and America.

[SCHMIDT 1939:104]

The most striking feature of this scheme is its evolutionism. The succession of "grades" is nothing less than the familiar sequence of "stages" leading from hunting and gathering types of sociocultural systems through horticultural and pastoral types and on to complex stratified civilizations. The evolutionary significance of the *Kreise* is further strengthened by the fact that Schmidt attempted to associate the sequence of grades with the main European archaeological divisions of prehistory:

> With the numerous parallels in points of detail between prehistoric cultures and ethnological spheres of culture, we may establish a twofold parallelism in the classification of these two series of results: (1) the ethnological division into primitive and primary cultures is in fairly complete agreement with the prehistorical division into the earlier and later paleolithic period; (2) the ethnological division into primitive and primary cultures on the one hand and secondary and tertiary cultures on the other, corresponds with the prehistoric division into the paleolithic and the neolithic periods [*ibid.*:104–5].

Schmidt's evolutionism was by no means confined merely to the generalities of the hunting, gathering civilization sequence. His notion of a matrilineal-horticultural *Kreis* was heavily in debt to the evolutionary logic of Bachofen, Morgan, and Eduard Hahn. According to Schmidt, during the hunting and gathering stage, women specialized in the collection of wild plants. This led women to invent horticulture and thus to become the owners of the products of the soil and of the land itself. On the basis of their economic ascendancy, women insisted on matrilocal residence and matrilineal descent. The supreme deity was given feminine attributes, girls' puberty rites were stressed, and the couvade instituted: full gynecocracy reigned. Schmidt (1935:253) called this the "classical phase of mother-right." Since this phase is no longer found in existence, Schmidt had to explain what had happened to it. Gradually, he claimed, the brothers of the ruling women began to take over "duties and tasks which could be better performed by men than by women" (*ibid.*:254). This trend eventually resulted in the usurpation of female rights, with males administering the family property and passing their authority on to their sisters' sons—what Schmidt called a "masculinized mother-right." Thus, despite the absence of examples of the "classic phase," there is no reason, Schmidt argued, for "the astounding conclusion that matriarchy nowhere exists, merely mother-right" (*ibid.*:255).

It is true that Schmidt made no attempt to arrange the three *Kreise* of the Primary Stage in an evolutionary order; i.e., he did not propose that the matrilineal *Kreis* had evolved before the two patrilineal *Kreise*. All three *Kreise* of the Primary Stage apparently existed side by side, having evolved out of the Primitive hunting-gathering stage along separate lines. Nonetheless, the evolutionary sequence which Schmidt outlined for the matrilineal-horticultural *Kreis* covered an extensive series of transformations. Property rights, for example, were supposed to have gone from equality in the Primitive stage, to female-dominated in classic mother-right, to male-dominated under masculine mother-right. The highly speculative nature of these reconstructions did not fail to impress Lowie with their close resemblance to Morgan's privileged insights into sociocultural systems which no one had ever seen. Said Lowie (1933b:290) of Schmidt: "His discussion of the matrilineal *Kulturkreis* . . . is wholly evolutionistic, schematic, unhistorical, and full of *a priori* psychologizing." Actually, the only difference between Morgan's and Schmidt's evolutionistic schemes is that Schmidt's main sequence was supposed to have happened only once, whereas aspects of Morgan's sequence were supposed to have happened over and over again. Yet, as Lowie was quick to grasp, as soon as Schmidt began to argue that there was an "organic" (i.e., causal) relationship between farming and mother-right, the claim that the sequence had happened only once became ludicrous. Since agriculture was supposed to have been invented only once, its appearance all over the world had to be a result of diffusion. What happened, Lowie wanted to know, if it diffused *before* mother-right had evolved?

> Let women invent horticulture in tribe A. What prevents its spread to B, C, D, *before* any matriarchal institutions have time to develop in A? Evidently nothing whatsoever. Now, *ex hypothesi*, feminine ascendancy results from feminine tillage. Hence, in each recipient tribe adoption of the latter sets up a parallel sequence of maternal descent, girls' puberty rites, female deities, ... There would still be a single origin for farming, but the social correlates would arise independently over and over again in parallel series [LOWIE 1933b:291].

Schmidt answered this charge with memorable élan. Noting that Lowie had taunted him with being an evolutionist, he expressed his regrets at not being able to afford his critics any such consolation. His sequence of mother-right is not to be confused with evolutionism, because it is "one of the most firmly established results of modern historical ethnology" (SCHMIDT 1935:250). Evolutionism is aprioristic, and its sequences are unnatural and illogical. The culture-historical method, however, deals with "logical" and "natural" sequences. The male response to female dominance was "to such a degree a natural, almost an inevitable one, that it is not aprioristic evolutionism, but quite logical deduction from the very nature of things and men, to arrange them in a certain series of phases of development" (*ibid.*). This was, of course, precisely the defense given by the nineteenth-century evolutionists on behalf of their own reconstruction of evolutionary sequences.

USE OF THE COMPARATIVE METHOD

Even Lowie failed to grasp the full extent of Schmidt's commitment to evolutionary schema. Lowie apparently regarded the sequence of the matrilineal *Kreis* as some sort of anomaly. He seemed to believe that "in general tendency Father Wilhelm Schmidt's position is unquestionably anti-evolutionary" (LOWIE

1933b:290). But exactly the contrary is true, for both Schmidt and Graebner were fundamentally and inextricably dependent upon the central feature of nineteenth-century evolutionism: the comparative method. It was not the vaunted criteria of form and quantity, but the comparative method, upon which the German "historical" school rested. For their task was precisely the same as that of the evolutionists: they sought to derive from an inspection of contemporary peoples a knowledge of origins and of the successive modifications which cultures had experienced. The *Kreise* were not only "Circles" but they were "Strata"—a part of a universal chronological scheme, which rested entirely on the assumption that contemporary cultures could be arranged according to degree of primitiveness. Schmidt made no attempt to conceal his dependence on the comparative method. Indeed, he called it the "crown" of ethnology and attributed its discovery to Père Lafitau, an association which no doubt enhanced its appeal to the faithful. Criticizing the tendency among ethnologists and sociologists in Britain and America who limit themselves to a purely synchronic interest, Schmidt (1933:9–10) wrote:

> I think that such a scholar would deprive ethnology of its crown by his disbelief in the axiom established already by Père Lafitau in his famous work *Moeurs des sauvages américains comparées aux moeurs des premiers temps* (Paris, 1724), that primitive peoples are stages of the past of humanity and living witnesses of them. And if ethnology should despair of establishing objectively and trustworthily the succession of these stages, it seems to me that it would abdicate its prerogative to be our guide into those first ages of humanity from which sprang the deepest roots of all its institutions, of religion and of ethics, of the family and the state.

It is clear that the culture-historical method was as remote from the methodological reforms of the historical particularists as were Lubbock and McLennan. Yet Lowie (1938:193), for all of his trenchant criticism, went out of his way to declare that in the "final balancing of the books," the German diffusionists are left "with very considerable assets." Lowie was undoubtedly prepared to go to greater lengths to find words of praise for Graebner and Schmidt than he was willing to do for Morgan. He asserted that the diffusionists were "by no means so intransigent" as might appear from some of their writings, and that "a reconciliation with the views of many contemporary and supposedly hostile colleagues is not at all barred" (*ibid.*:191).

SCHMIDT'S AMERICAN DEFENDERS

The *Kulturkreis* school received even higher grades from Clyde Kluckhohn, who was for a time one of Schmidt's students. Kluckhohn lauded Schmidt for his attempt to grasp the archaeological and ethnological facts of the whole world at a time when, under the influence of Boas, American anthropologists were content to "collect and to cull" on a piecemeal basis.

> The followers of the *Kulturkreislehre* have at least resolutely devoted themselves to the true task of scholars: they have endeavored to ferret out and establish unperceived relationships between facts, and we will be unwise to condemn them too austerely if the relations they think to have discovered are not always approved in detail by their fellow scholars [KLUCKHOHN 1936:196].

The most intriguing aspect of the relationship between the American historical school and its German counterpart was the genial acceptance of Schmidt's split allegiance to anthropology and religion. Let me make it perfectly clear that anthropology cannot be represented as opposing this or that article of faith. It is not the business of science to go about intruding into and damaging the private beliefs of religiously orthodox individuals. On the other hand, it cannot be denied that there are certain doctrines of political and religious inspiration which seek to intrude and to damage the integrity of the scientific process. When it becomes certain that religious or political dogmas have set themselves the task of dominating the research strategy of a particular discipline, those who believe in science can scarcely afford to be indifferent. Both Lowie and Kluckhohn were of the opinion that Schmidt's theories were in no way compromised or even seriously influenced by his priestly role. This broad-minded tolerance of Schmidt's ulterior purpose is itself a revealing commentary on the drift of the times. Evidently, neither Kluckhohn nor Lowie believed strongly enough in the possibility of a science of man to feel threatened by Schmidt's attempt to return the discussion of cultural evolution to its pre-Enlightenment premises. Kluckhohn (1936:173) himself painted Schmidt's intellectual heritage in the following terms: rationalistic, deductive logic, "trained theologian," "steeped in the dialectical subtleties of Thomas Aquinas and Albert Magnus," as a priest "almost compelled to reject *Evolutionismus* . . . as based upon the assumption that human beings are subject to the rigid determinism which seems to prevail in nature generally." He also admitted that "some of Schmidt's . . . observations upon anthropological matters . . . seem to have a direct ulterior relation to certain tenets of the Roman Catholic Church . . ." and that "one also rather often gets a sense of their lack of detachment in viewing certain questions" (*ibid.*:173–74). Kluckhohn did not shrink from admitting that "the writers of the *Kulturkreislehre* reject the physico-mathematical notion of causality as meaningless in culture-historical phenomena . . ." (*ibid.*:172). Despite this rather unpromising set of preconceptions, Kluckhohn insisted that there was no reason to accord the *Kulturkreis* school any less respectful a hearing than that which was given to the other schools of anthropology.

> Kant was surely right in maintaining that cognition is impossible without the application of interpretative principles—and those underlying the metaphysics of the Roman Catholic Church are as intellectually respectable as any others in the present state of our knowledge about man and the universe. We must, I think, rigorously avoid the temptation to dismiss the *Kulturkreislehre* as founded upon a "bias" [*ibid.*:173].

Although Kluckhohn was perfectly correct to point out that observation must be carried out in the context of theoretical bias, his defense of Schmidt's bias is inadmissible. The particular bias which declares that physico-mathematical causality is "meaningless in culture-historical phenomena" cannot be tolerated by those who profess themselves interested in a science of human history. To declare in advance that the physico-mathematical model cannot be applied and then to refrain from attempting to apply it is to proceed in a fashion exactly contrary to that which every bona fide scientific strategy requires as an initial condition of research. It is no circumstance other than this intolerable bias which accounts for Schmidt's insistence on the uniqueness of the evolutionary experience of each *Kreis*. The idiographic ingredient in these ideas could not but appeal to Lowie, even though he himself accepted the possibility of "limited parallelism." Evidently this served as enough of a common bond to hold Lowie's sympathy despite the additional consequences which flowed from Schmidt's theological commitment.

SCHMIDT'S SUPERNATURALISM

Not only was Schmidt, like Boas, opposed to a nomothetic explanation of history, but he was also opposed even to a naturalistic explanation. In his reconstruction of cultural evolution, Schmidt was dominated by the necessity of reconciling the findings of anthropology with scriptural precedent. The areas of fact in which specific theological dogmas exerted their most damaging influence concerned, as one might imagine, the origin of religious beliefs themselves. Here Schmidt, like Archbishop Whately, De Bonald, and De Maistre, was an unyielding "degenerationist." His immense, twelve-volume *Der Ursprung der Gottesidee* (*Origin of the Idea of God*) was wholly given over to the proof that those cultures most nearly approximating the condition of the primitive hunting and gathering *Kreis* possessed a purer and more ethical understanding of the nature of God. As culture evolved, perfection in science and technology was accompanied by a degeneration in the religious sphere. The most perfect phase of religion existed at the very outset of prehistory, for religion was given to man by God in a revelation, the memory of which became more and more distorted and confused as time wore on; moreover, by "revelation," Schmidt insisted that he meant a literal, personal appearance such as is described in Genesis. He explicitly denied that this revelation could have been "a merely subjective process" or a "purely impersonal, common experience":

> No; it must have been a tremendous, mighty personality that presented itself to them: capable of captivating their intellect with luminous truths, of binding their will by high and noble moral commands, and of winning their hearts through ravishing beauty and goodness. Moreover, this personality cannot have been a merely internal image of the mind and imagination; for such an image could by no means have possessed the power of awakening those effects which we note in that oldest religion. Rather, it must have been really and truly a personality that presented itself to them from without, and that precisely by the power of its reality convinced and overwhelmed them [SCHMIDT 1939:183].

Schmidt went even further in antiscientism and made it plain that he considered it a matter essential to his conscience to support the teachings of his faith in this matter:

> It is Catholic teaching, binding in conscience and founded on Scripture and the fathers, together with various declarations of the Church, that the very first human beings were not in a merely natural state but were possessed of the supernatural gift of divine sonship and destined to the supernatural end of the immediate vision of God. Men thus endowed entered upon a relationship with God that is properly characterized as supernatural religion [*ibid.*].

When Leslie White (see p. 291) attacked Boas, along with the writers of the *Kulturkreis* school, as reactionary antievolutionists, Lowie rejoined by claiming that not only Boas but Father Schmidt were evolutionists in White's sense of the term. I concur that neither Boas nor Schmidt was an antievolutionist, but it cannot be said of Schmidt that he was uninfluenced by what are usually referred to as reactionary doctrines harking back to the early part of the nineteenth century. The misunderstanding alluded to in the following excerpt from Lowie's (1960:423; orig. 1946) rejoinder is not confined to White:

> Leslie White misunderstands the status of the problem. It is false that any reputable anthropologist nowadays professes an anti-evolutionist philosophy in the sense alleged. The "anti-evolutionism" of the Boasians and of the Kulturkreislehre has nothing to do with, say, the degeneration theory of de Maistre.

The lack of connection between Boas and De Maistre is certainly well founded; but nothing could be more inappropriate than to deny Schmidt's affinities with De Maistre's degenerationism.

Culture and Personality: Pre-Freudian 15

During the interval between the two world wars, the individualizing trend in historical particularism met with and interacted with the doctrines of Sigmund Freud. On the face of it, psychoanalysis and Boasian anthropology seemed to have very little in common. Freud was essentially a nineteenth-century leftover. His theory was a grand scale, evolutionist, materialist, and determinist scheme of precisely the sort most condemned in Boas' attack on the comparative method. Yet there was one overriding favorable predisposition in the Boasian approach. Boas had for long maintained the proposition that cultural anthropology had to be the study of man's "mental life," and no one could deny that Freud had shown more ways of penetrating into man's mind than anyone else before him. Anthropology's drive toward mentalism and the study of the individual eventually was to prove stronger than the taint of Freud's grandiose physicalism, but not before both schools underwent drastic changes: the Freudians gave up their evolutionism and their instinctive universal complexes for cultural relativism; while the Boasians for their part gave up their emphasis upon history and diffusion. The result was the American version of synchronic functionalism: culture and personality.

EPISTEMOLOGICAL BACKGROUND

Care should be taken to extricate this movement, with its specifically Freudian and Boasian inspiration, from the much older and more pervasive occurrence of psychologically oriented ethnology. Psychocultural analyses, carried out in the idiom of mentalistic and ideational data languages and concepts, antedate the modern culture and personality movement by thousands of years. A brief digression into some relevant epistemological issues should make this clear.

Cultural entities are logico-empirical constructs built up out of the observation of the verbal or nonverbal behavior of individual human actors. The scientific vocabulary for the description of these entities is still in a very primitive state. Operationally valid definitions have yet to be achieved for even the most commonly employed terms. Attempts to develop data languages for cultural descriptions have invariably followed the intuitive path of combining etic responses with their emotional and cognitive concomitants.

It is very widely accepted that the statement of psychologically meaningful "goals" and "purposes" is a minimum requirement of ethnographic description. This is obviously true of all the members of the culture and personality movement per se. We have already seen how important the mentalistic or "emic" point of view was in the development of Boas' mature orientation to the theoretical prospects of cultural anthropology. There were many convergences from other backgrounds toward a similar elaboration of mentalistic premises. Ralph Linton, one of the key figures in the neo-Freudian culture and personality movement, defined all cultural traits in a mentalistic idiom. A trait, in Linton's (1936) influential formulation, consisted not only of a particular form and substance with its sociocultural function, but of the meaning of such an entity to the people who manifested or used it. Clyde Kluckhohn, another central figure in the history of personality and culture studies, shared a similar epistemological position (see p. 597). In British social anthropology, Malinowski, an important contributor to the refinement of Freudian and other psychological concepts in anthropology, was also explicit concerning the epistemological and methodological necessity of emic categories.

But most of the anthropologists, such as Boas himself, his student Robert Lowie, and the influential English theoretician S. F. Nadel, who stress the importance of an emic perspective have not been associated with culture and personality research. For this reason, the historical significance of the emic/etic option is discussed in a separate chapter in connection with the so-called New Ethnography. But it must be made clear at the outset that whoever operates with a strong implicit or explicit bias in favor of emics is committed to an epistemological tradition shared by the culture and personality school.

THE PERVASIVENESS OF EMIC AND PSYCHOLOGICAL CATEGORIES

The most obvious diagnostic of this commonality is the occurrence within the average ethnographic monograph of numerous terms and concepts which are derived from vernacular or scientific lexicons devoted to expressing the mental and emotional condition of individual human actors. Actually, from the earliest recorded descriptions of cultural phenomena to the advent of modern anthropology, most ethnographic descriptions have consisted of a melange of data-language concepts drawn partially from a psychological and partially from a sociocultural idiom. Tacitus, writing in the first century A.D., described the marriage arrangements, rules of chastity, weaponry, mode of punishment, military organization, divinatory practices, and many other sociocultural features of the Germanic tribes. He also availed himself of a psychological idiom and attributed to the Germans an ability to endure hard work, a slight capacity for withstanding hunger and cold, and "a taste for peace"; furthermore, he said they were "pleasantly courteous," "neither canny nor cunning," and "devoid of self-control when they drink."

As a modern example of the same practice, one of the monographs of Raymond Firth, whose main theoretical affiliation is with British social anthropology, and certainly not with the culture and personality movement, may serve as an example. Opening *We, the Tikopia* at random, we encounter the following typical description of household patterns:

> A married couple are expected by custom to share such things as areca nut and tobacco, and refusal or evasion is apt to cause a quarrel. Conduct in such matters depends of course upon the temperament of individuals. Food, too, should be shared, though some latitude is given to the claims of differential appetite. The effect of this rule is seen most clearly outside the household. Whenever a visitor calls at another house he is usually offered food, and at meal time such an invitation is never omitted. A close kinsman may eat, but another man, if married, will com-

> monly decline with a "*Makona*," "satisfied." This he will say whether he has eaten or not, since he fears the tongue of slander, which will murmur behind his back, "Ah! There he sits and eats, but what of his wife and children, hungry at home?" An unmarried person may eat without fear, since he has not such responsibilities. Property which is not specifically linked with one sex is shared by husband and wife, or used indifferently by them both. A gift of a string of beads which I made to the Ariki Kafika—beads are highly valued and worn by men as well as women—was calmly appropriated by his wife, who took charge of them at once with the word "Mine," eliciting merely a joking remark from the Ariki [FIRTH 1963:124].

The psychologically derived categories in this paragraph range over a broad spectrum of phenomena. There is not only refusal of sharing but there is *evasion*. The married visitor *fears* being exposed to *slander*. Property is used *indifferently*, beads are *highly valued* and are *calmly* appropriated to the accompaniment of a *joking remark*.

The most "structural" of the British structural-functionalists is Meyer Fortes; theoretically, one can go no further in a direction away from psychological "reductionism." Yet in *The Dynamics of Clanship among the Tallensi*, passages such as the one which follows turn up on almost every page:

> A man who married the former wife of another, even if the marriage was severed for just and accepted reasons, incurs the hostility of the first husband's entire lineage both towards himself personally and towards his clansmen as a group. Reprisals will be taken when an opportunity occurs. When the parties are clansmen, feelings about such acts become very bitter, and the more so the closer the tie. Marriages of this kind take place from time to time, producing conflicts and reprisals but not disruption of clanship ties [FORTES 1945:42].

Note here how the *feelings* of the actors, as expressed in the terms *hostility*, *bitter*, and *conflicts*, are essential for maintaining the ethnographic thread. If one makes an effort to find still more emphatically mentalistic statements, it is not difficult to locate the following sort of descriptions even in *The Dynamics of Clanship*, which is Fortes' most abstract and "structural" book:

> Tallensi say this is just fun (*koohog*); but we see again that this apparently spontaneous jesting acts as a means of reconciling and counter-acting the tensions of a double-edged social relationship. Where two corporate groups are structurally divided from each

> other to the point of having potentially competitive interests likely to lead to conflict at one level of the social organization, but are at the same time bound to each other by strong ties of obligatory co-operation and goodwill in another aspect of their social relations, the undercurrent of hostility and mutual wariness is deflected by jest. You jest with people who must be friendly to you in terms of one set of loyalties and may be hostile to you in terms of another, and with whom you are on an equal footing as far as mutual rights and duties go [*ibid.*:95].

In this vein it is of considerable interest to note that Leslie White, one of the anthropologists who have been most critical of the culture and personality approach, employs in his own ethnography a typical psychologistic lexicon of cognitive and emotional terms:

> In society as in mechanics, the closer moving particles are to each other, the greater is the friction between them. And the distance between individuals in a pueblo is very small. A pueblo is no place for an individualist; an aggressive "go-getter" is especially obnoxious. He makes life unbearable for his neighbors. Close contact within a pueblo tends to wear off the sharp corners and edges of a personality and make it smooth and inconspicuous, like a water-worn pebble. Children are taught that kindness and respect are the greatest virtues. Every effort is made to lubricate social life, to reduce friction to a minimum so that the pueblo will function smoothly like a well-built machine. Quarrelling is intolerable, physical violence rare, murder unheard of.
>
> Although pueblo social life discourages, if indeed it does not penalize, aggressive individualism, and although intimate social intercourse tends to rub down the sharp corners and edges of the individual ego, differences between individuals do, nevertheless, remain and find significant expression in the life of the community. Some men are regarded with more than ordinary respect, others with less; some are influential, others are not [WHITE 1942:190].

These examples should suffice to establish the fact that psychologizing is a deeply rooted habit among cultural anthropologists. It is interesting to note that Mead's (1953:642) paradigm of a cultural as opposed to a psychological statement contains a covert mentalist concept: "In culture X, married men must avoid their mothers . . ." as opposed to "In culture X, the mother-in-law avoidance is enforced through a sense of shame." Although the second statement is obviously more dependent on a psychological frame, the word "must" in the first statement contains a universe of psychological assumptions in its own right. But this merely confirms Mead's point that there is no sharp line in practice between personality and culture and traditional ethnography.

ROOTS OF BENEDICT'S PATTERNS OF CULTURE

One of the characteristics of the modern culture and personality school is simply the intensification and expansion of ethnographic coverage involving psychological terms and concepts. During the 1920's a kind of descriptive threshold was crossed, and the usual mixed data language gave way among the founders of the culture and personality movement to a conscious selection in favor of psychologistic emphases. This transition is associated above all with the work of Ruth Benedict who, under the influence of Edward Sapir and in interaction with Margaret Mead, proposed that the description of entire cultures might be integrated around one or two major psychologistic traits. "Cultures from this point of view are individual psychology thrown large upon the screen, given gigantic proportions and a long time span" (BENEDICT 1932:24).

It is of considerable interest in terms of the continuity between Boasian historical particularism and Benedict's initial "configurationalist" approach in *Patterns of Culture* (1934), that the specific psychological idiom that was utilized owed little if anything to Freudian concepts. Benedict herself traced her major intellectual heritage to "the German school headed by Wilhelm Dilthey" (*ibid.*: 2), and this constitutes an additional reason for associating the Boasians with neo-Kantianism. Mead's objection that Benedict's allusion to Dilthey was a *pro forma* afterthought included to satisfy Boas' demands for scholarly acknowledgment, scarcely modifies the situation. Benedict read Dilthey and recognized her indebtedness. The relevance of Dilthey, as Benedict saw him, was that he approached history through the grouping together of philosophical *Weltanschauungen* expressing distinctive and incommensurable psychological categories which "cannot be resolved the one unto the other" (*ibid.*:3). We do not require Mead's acknowledgment to assert that she too was influenced by the same school, with or without having read Dilthey. As for the source of the particular configurationalist idiom employed in *Patterns of Culture,* it was, as Benedict tells us, Nietzsche's study of Greek drama, *The Birth of Tragedy.* It was here that Benedict picked up the idea of the contrast between Dionysian and Apollonian "psychological types," the "incommensurables" around which *Patterns of Culture* is built (BENEDICT 1928:572).

EARLIER PRECEDENTS

Setting aside for the moment the special history of the Dionysian and Apollonian categories, it is clear that a much more ancient tradition of pithy psychological portraits underlies not only Benedict's scheme, but Dilthey's and Nietzsche's as well. For in addition to the more or less mixed sociocultural and psychological ethnographies produced by the ancients, condensed psychological portraiture slipping imperceptibly into stereotype has always been a vice of learned as well as vulgar observers of cultural phenomena. In her description of anthropology in the sixteenth and seventeenth centuries, Margaret Hodgen (1964:178) attributes the technique of presenting capsular epitomes, stereotypes, and typologies to the brevity characteristic of the medieval scholastic encyclopedias. I would prefer to stress a more vernacular origin in the common tendency of tribes and nations to stereotype each other as a consequence of various forms of intergroup relations. At any rate, early European prototypes of ethnographers such as Sebastian Münster, Henry Agrippa, Johann Boemus, and Gerardus Mercator all indulged in the practice of condensing ethnographic descriptions into pithy psychological formulae. For example, in Muenster's breviary, the Scotch are faithful and vengeful; the Suevi bellicose; the Jews prudent but envious; the Persians steadfast but disloyal; the Egyptians stable and crafty; the Greeks wise but deceitful; and the Spaniards drunken, violent, and sophistic. Writing in 1527, Agrippa declared:

> The Scythians were always infamous for Savageness and Cruelty. The Italians were always eminent for their Magnanimity. The Gaules were reproached for Stupidity. The Sicilians were always Subtile. The Asiaticks Luxurious, the Spaniards Jealous, and great Boasters. . . . Who that sees a man marching in more state than a Dung-hill-Cock, in gate like a Fencer, a confident Look, a deep Tone, grave Speech, severe in his Carriage, and tatter'd in Habit, that will not straight judge him to be a German? Do we not know the French by their moderate Gate, effeminate Carriage, smiling Countenance, pleasing Voice, courteous Speech, modest Behaviour, and careless Habit? The Italians we behold more slow in Gate, their Carriage grave, their Countenances varying, of few words, captious in Discourse, in their Behaviour

> magnificent, and decent in their Habit. In singing also the Italians bleat, the Spaniards Whine, the Germans Howl, and the French Quaver [quoted in HODGEN 1964:180].

Boemus in the 1611 edition of his *Omnium Gentium Mores* associated Suevia with whores, Franconia with thieves and beggars, Bavaria with pilferers and slaves, Helvetia with butchers and bawds, Saxonie with drunkards, Frisia with perjurers, and the Rheinland with gluttons. For Mercator:

> The *Francons* are simple, blockish, & furious; the *Barvarians* sumptuous, gluttons, and brazen-faced; the *Sweeds* light, bablers and boasters; the *Thuringeans* distrustfull, slovens, and quarrelsome; the *Saxons* dissemblers, double-hearted, and opinionative; the *Belgians* good horsemen, tender, docible, and delicate; the *Italians* proud, revengeful and ingenious; the *Spaniard* disdainful, cautious and greedie; the *Gaules* proper, intemperate, rash-headed; the *Cimbrians* high-minded, seditious, and terrible; the *Saramates* gluttons, proud, and theeves; the *Bohemians* cruell, lovers of novelties, filtchers; the *Illyricks* variable, malicious, and ryotous; the *Pannonians* rude, superstitious; the *Grecians* miserable [quoted in HODGEN 1964:181].

ET TU SPENCER

Some idea of the pervasiveness of this kind of psychological portraiture may be gained from the fact that Herbert Spencer, an influence which was highly distasteful to Boas and his pupils, included the rubric *Emotional Characters* as a fundamental heading in his great *Descriptive Sociology*. Spencer's capsule portraits are preposterous amusements:

> *Samoans*. Not so lively as Tahitians. Good humored, social in disposition, very desirous of pleasing, and fond of amusement and traveling. Indolent, fickle, and deceitful.
>
> *Dyaks*. Not very impulsive. Seldom, except on festive occasions going the length of boisterous mirth. Generally mild, polite, and respectful to superiors. Sociable, amiable, sympathetic and capable of strong mutual attachments.
>
> *Andaman Islanders*. Vivacious and affectionate; impulsive and frightfully passionate; revengeful, crafty, and merciless. Suspicious of strangers to an inconceivable degree. Manifest no ferocity when once subdued.
>
> [1873–1933, III]

> *Iroquois*. Show little desire for social intercourse between the sexes, and have been said to be incapable of sexual love. The fa-

ther rarely caresses his children. Fond of jest, repartee and ridicule; also of the excitement of the chase.

[*ibid.*, VI]

Ancient Peruvians. Not impulsive. Patient obedient, industrious, Friendly to one another and kind to animals. Good humored and gentle.

[*ibid.*, II]

OUT OF THE DIFFUSIONIST CUL DE SAC

The taxonomic assumptions of *Patterns of Culture* are of course considerably more sophisticated than anything Spencer or medieval and ancient predecessors had been able to achieve. Benedict based her portraits of the Apollonian Zuni and Dionysian Kwakiutl on a sustained and highly detailed comparison of institutions and ideologies ranging across the entire fabric of sociocultural life, from family to warfare.

In contrast to vulgar stereotypes, which frequently manifest blatant inconsistencies and contradictions (Indians are crafty but dumb, Jews are clannish but cosmopolitan), Benedict's configurations emphasize a culture's strain toward consistency. Indeed, the integration and functional coherence of cultural life when viewed from the configurationist perspective constitutes the main theoretical pretension of Benedict's work.

Benedict's training under Boas had begun in 1921, shortly after the publication of Lowie's *Primitive Society* with its famous "shreds and patches" conclusion. The model of cultures built up out of diffusionary hodgepodges was thrust upon her before she had an opportunity to prepare her own outlook. The influence of Lowie, with whom she took a course at the Museum of Natural History, is prominent in her first publication, "The Vision in Plains Culture" (1922). Margaret Mead (1959a:14) reports her as having said, "I wrote that for Dr. Lowie." This article presents a point of view bearing little resemblance to that of *Patterns of Culture*. It even contains a strident echo of Lowie's "shreds and patches" declaration, which was picked up by Radcliffe-Brown and incorporated into the bogey of the antifunctionalist American school:

> It is, so far as we can see, an ultimate fact of human nature that man builds up his culture out of disparate elements, combining and *re*combining them, and until we have abandoned the superstition that the result is an organism functionally interrelated, we shall be unable to see our cultural life objectively, or to control its manifestations [BENEDICT 1923:84–85].

But Benedict, who was a poetess (publishing under the name Anne Singleton) as much as she was an anthropologist, could not long abide the negativism and emotionally impoverished medium of diffusionist discourse. In Margaret Mead's words, she worked "steadily to find some integrating principle that would explain both the disparate origins of the elements of which a culture was built and the wholeness which she felt was there in each culture" (MEAD 1959a:204). Psychologistic patterns and configurations were the result of this search.

THE END OF EXPLANATION

Mead's use of the term "explanation" in conjunction with the integrative effect of "individual psychology thrown large upon the screen" is misleading. The historical function of *Patterns of Culture* within the Boasian school was its ingenious evocation of a Dilthian feeling of understanding, achieved entirely in the absence of explanation in any scientific sense. However useful the configurationist approach may have seemed to Benedict as a way out of the diffusionist cul de sac, its contribution to the explanation of cultural differences and similarities was miniscule. This result was built into the basic premises upon which she proceeded to employ Nietzsche's categories, for she was careful to insist, in proper neo-Kantian style, that the Apollonian-Dionysian polarity may not be usefully applied to any but a small number of the world's cultures. Moreover, Benedict stressed the improbability that most of the cultures which do not fit into the Apollonian-Dionysian scheme can be fitted into any other comparable well-integrated configuration. "All cultures," she wrote in *Patterns of Culture*, "have not shaped their thousand items of behavior to a balanced and rhythmic pattern; lack of integration seems to be as characteristic of certain cultures as extreme integration is of others" (*ibid.*:196).

Benedict was possibly the student whom Boas in his later years most admired in his paternal fashion. By 1929, she was addressing him as "Dear Papa Franz" and complaining that "It seems very lonely without you," when he was away (MEAD 1959a:400). Upon Boas' retirement in 1937, Benedict became the acting Chairman of the Department of Anthropology at Columbia. The fact that she was Boas' protégée probably helped to obscure the ethnographic defects in *Patterns of Culture*, and Boas' "Introduction" was undoubtedly an important asset in its acceptance by the anthropological community. But there is nothing about her configurationalist ideas which ran counter to Boas' tutelage. On the contrary, Boas undoubtedly felt that his dream of achieving a more intimate knowledge of the workings of the minds of primitive peoples had been advanced by her efforts. At the same time, the care which she took to disassociate the configurations from any global scheme, the strictly limited sample with which she worked, and the absence of causal explanations were fully in accord with historical-particularist beliefs.

The central theme of *Patterns of Culture* is simply that each culture "selects" or "chooses" from the infinite variety of behavioral possibilities a limited segment which sometimes conforms to a configuration and sometimes does not. In its least flattering light, one might sum it up as the observation that some cultures are different and others are similar. One searches in vain through *Patterns of Culture* for any explanation. There is not even the saving grace of the earlier diffusionistic "explanations" by which Apollonian patterns might be traced back to an originating tribe (the Greeks?). All that we get by way of accounting for cultural differences and similarities is the myth of the Digger Indians: "God gave to every people a cup, a cup of clay, and from this cup they drank their life. . . . They all dipped in the water but their cups were different" (BENEDICT 1934:33).

ART, CULTURE, AND FREEDOM

In one sense, of course, it is manifestly unfair to judge Benedict's contribution in the light of the canons and traditions of the social sciences. Like Sapir, with whom she exchanged poems and carried on a voluminous and romantic correspondence, Benedict seems intuitively to have chaffed at the very notion of cultural determinism. The patterns of culture and language had to be given their due (how else could one contemplate a separate discipline of anthropology or linguistics?), but wherever possible the quixotic conditions by which patterns arise, are adopted, or are cast out deserve equal emphasis.

It is in this light that Benedict's discussion of individual deviancy, the subject of the final chapter in *Patterns of Culture*, is most profitably interpreted. Deviants occur in every culture; hence nowhere are men merely puppets dancing on the strings of their cultural destinies:

> Anthropology is often believed to be a counsel of despair which makes untenable a beneficent human illusion. But no anthropologist with a background of experience in other cultures has ever

> believed that individuals were automatons, mechanically carving out the decrees of their civilization. No culture yet observed has been able to eradicate the differences in the temperaments of the persons who compose it. It is always a give-and-take [*ibid.*:220].

It is clear that Benedict's image of cultural anthropology was that of a discipline whose main function it was artfully to describe the varieties of man's cultural traditions and not to explain them. Like Kroeber, she was not at all averse to the prospect of severing anthropology's ties to the social sciences: "To my mind the very nature of the problems posed and discussed in the humanities is closer, chapter by chapter, to those in anthropology than are the investigations carried on in most of the social sciences" (BENEDICT 1948:585). The affinity with the humanistic studies expressed by Benedict is even stronger than that put forth by Kroeber. Her "patterns," as Kroeber himself recognized, were very similar to the configurations of style to which Kroeber devoted his later years. The main difference resides in the diachronic pulsations which Kroeber attempted to discover. But, in the controversy between Sapir and Kroeber, Benedict as we have seen, and as might be guessed from the great sympathy with which she and Sapir regarded each other's poetry, was very much on Sapir's side. "Man is a creature with such freedom of action and imagination that he can, for instance, by not accepting a trait, prevent the occurrence of diffusion, or he can at any stage of technological development create his gods in the most diverse forms" (*ibid.*:589). In *Patterns of Culture* (1934:10) we also find the astonishing remark: "A very little acquaintance with other conventions, and a knowledge of how various these may be, would do much to promote a rational social order."

ETHNOGRAPHIC DIFFICULTIES

The slight theoretical contribution of *Patterns of Culture* fails to justify Benedict's emphasis upon an idiom appropriate to individual psychology. But the larger functional significance of this work cannot be appreciated without reference to the dubious factual foundation on which Benedict reared her psychologistic portraits. Not only was the success of her book unrelated to its theoretical payoff, but it was from the outset the object of intense criticism by anthropologists who possessed relevant ethnographic area specialties. I have already indicated some of the main lines of this critique in reference to Benedict's portrayal of the Kwakiutl. The reaction among

Southwest specialists to her treatment of the Pueblo Indians was more severe, perhaps because so many anthropologists have made this area the focus of their field research. An excellent summary of this critical literature has recently been put together by Victor Barnouw (1963), whose own commitment to the personality and culture movement and whose training under Benedict provide a moderating note.

It is now generally agreed that Benedict's sketch of the Apollonian way of life achieved its beautiful symmetry only as a result of the omission or selective de-emphasis of nonconforming data. For example, one of the first commentators, Li An-Che (1937), noted that Benedict's picture of the allegedly noncompetitive and retiring Zuñi failed to acknowledge historically known incidents of factional internecine strife. ". . . not only do ordinary forms of struggle for individual supremacy exist, but violent forms occur once in a while" (LI AN-CHE 1937:69). One of the deepest splits in the Zuñi pueblo occurred along the lines of rival missionization, and Li An-Che wrote that "a strife of immense magnitude took place between the Catholic and Protestant elements" (*ibid.*). Ruth Bunzel (1952:xv) reported that the Zuñi were frequently split into rival factions over the issue of cooperation or noncooperation with anthropologists. According to Elsie Clews Parsons, Benedict and other Zuñi observers had not had an opportunity to witness the ceremonial of the Zuñi medicine societies which featured walking over red hot coals and sword swallowing. This contributed to the tendency to "underestimate the orgiastic potentiality of Zuñi character" (PARSONS 1939:879).

If Zuñi puberty practices and child training patterns were anything like those of the neighboring Hopi (Benedict did argue that all of the Pueblos were Apollonians), the gentle peace-loving stereotype must be discarded. Benedict knew that initiates were whipped, but she denied that blood was drawn or even that welts were raised. Other eye witnesses report Hopi floggings as "very severe" and as taking place while "pandemonium reigns" (H. R. ROTH, quoted by BARNOUW 1963:46). In the autobiography of a Hopi chief, there appears an account of one very un-Apollonian initiation:

> I stood them fairly well, without crying, and thought my suffering was past; but then the Ho Katcina struck me four more times and cut me to pieces. I struggled, yelled, and urinated. . . . Blood was running down over my body. . . . When they let me go, I wrapped the blanket around my painful body and sat down. I tried to stop sobbing, but continued to cry in my heart. . . . I was led home and put to bed on a sheepskin. The

> next morning when I awoke, the pelt had stuck fast to my body, so that when I tried to get up it came with me [SIMMONS 1942:83, quoted in BARNOUW 1963:46].

Equally distressing is Benedict's failure to provide a balanced picture of Pueblo behavior under the influence of alcohol. Although strong disapproval of drinking exists, actual behavior frequently runs in a definitely Dionysian direction. "Drunkenness is repulsive to them" wrote Benedict (1934:82). But this scarcely tells the whole story:

> After we read this, it comes as a surprise to learn, in Smith and Roberts' recent report on Zuñi law, that by far the most common "crimes" at Zuñi are drunkenness and drunken driving. "In 1949 there were 57 arrests for drunkenness on the first night of the Shalako festival and 150 bottles of liquor were confiscated." The anthropologist E. A. Hoebel informs us that "Field work among the Central Pueblos in 1945 to 1947 revealed the Pueblo governments almost helpless in the face of uncontrollable drunkenness and violence." And Edmund Wilson, describing a visit to Zuñi in 1947, tells how his car was searched for liquor by the police when he entered the Pueblo at the time of the Shalako festival. He adds: "This I was later told, failed almost completely in its purpose, since the Zuñis, by way of their grapevine, would send the word back to Gallup for their bootleggers to come in around the hills" [BARNOUW 1963:44].

DECLINING STANDARDS

There are anthropologists who regard criticism of Benedict's *Patterns of Culture* as a kind of sacrilege. This was admittedly a pioneer work in the field of culture and personality which achieved the unusual distinction of stimulating both professional and lay interest. Because of its great popularity, it has served as the most important single source of recruitment for anthropology as a profession. Moreover, as Barnouw has tried to show, Benedict was aware of some of the inconsistencies in both the Kwakiutl and Pueblo configurations. She herself drew attention to the "amiable side" of Kwakiutl life within the family and noted that "not all situations in Kwakiutl existence require equally the motives that are most characteristic of their lives" (BENEDICT 1934:122, quoted in BARNOUW 1957:533). She further protected herself, according to Barnouw, by stating that "Integration . . . may take place in the face of fundamental conflicts." But Barnouw also tries to show that there was no substantial difference of opinion between Boas and Benedict on the question of configurations and in particular concerning the Kwakiutl configuration. It is this continuity between Boas, Benedict, Mead, and the other configurationists and psychologically oriented anthropologists which raises the central issue to which we must address ourselves. This issue is one of method, of scientific standards, and of the functional significance of the historical-particularist reform. Benedict's "extravagant assertions," such as, suicide being "too violent an act . . . for the Pueblos to contemplate . . . they have no idea what it could be" (BENEDICT 1934:117), cannot be dismissed as a mere peccadillo. It is difficult to shrug off the "easy refutation" which Hoebel (1949:452) achieved in citing three documented Pueblo suicides, in view of the captious negativism with which the Boasians had attacked the use of the comparative method. This is not a matter of spite, but of principle; it is simply impossible to reconcile the Boasian self-image of methodological rigor with the highly impressionistic and scientifically unreliable procedures which characterize the early phases of the culture and personality movement.

EARLY MEAD

Configurationalism, the identification of salient cultural characteristics and their presentation in a familiar psychological idiom, was the forerunner of the rapprochement between historical particularism and psychoanalysis. We see this quite clearly in the case of Margaret Mead, who as a student of both Benedict and Boas made extensive use of the configurationalist frame during her formative period. Indeed, without minimizing Benedict's contribution, Mead claims to have been an active participant in all the important events leading up to the publication of *Patterns of Culture* and attributes to herself the first published statement of the configurationalist idea:

> Historically, the first written application of her conceptualization was in my chapter on "Dominant Cultural Attitudes," in *Social Organization of Manu'a,* written in the winter of 1927-1928, before she wrote her own first formulation in "Psychological Types in the Cultures of the Southwest." None of her theoretical phrasings were included in my chapter, but every detail of the phrasing was thrashed out between us. The clarity of her concept, which owed so much to the lack of a sensory screen between the field worker and the pattern and to her search for meaning within fragments, was also subjected to the test of living field work as I

> marshaled a procession of identified Samoan children to challenge or confirm a formulation [MEAD 1959a:207].

Coming of Age in Samoa (1928), the first major product of Mead's prodigious outpouring of field-based books and monographs, bore the subtitle *A Psychological Study of Primitive Youth for Western Civilization.* Although this book was far richer in psychologistic phrasings than the usual ethnographic report, it cannot be said to reflect an interest in the summing up of a whole culture in terms of a few dominant categories. Mead's mission, chosen for her by Boas, was to emphasize the existence of biopsychological plasticity in human affairs sufficient to permit the cultural conditioning of adolescent behavioral patterns along lines which contrast with the stereotype of adolescence in middle-class Euro-American culture. The use of the phrase "for Western Civilization" in the subtitle and the inclusion of two chapters concerned with the comparison of the Samoan adolescent girl with her counterpart in the United States indicate the importance which Boas and Mead attached to the simple demonstration of the power of cultural conditioning in this area of life. The fact that Samoan sex patterns turned out to be strikingly less inhibited than their Western analogues could not have been unanticipated. That adolescence was not necessarily a stormy and awkward biological epoch was additional support for Boas' emphasis upon the influence of culture as opposed to biology. And it also corresponded well with the contemporary interest in Freudian psychology and the role of sex in pathological personalities. The Samoan's relative freedom from sexually inspired frustrations was eagerly incorporated into the scientific foundation of the "sexual revolution" which the American middle class was the process of experiencing. There was also a strong feminist moral in *Coming of Age in Samoa,* highlighted by the description of a carefree premarital sex life for adolescent girls. But the most important moral proposed by Mead was very similar to that which Benedict was to urge in *Patterns of Culture* six years later: Knowledge of the spectrum of possibilities of enculturation should be made to contribute to our own process of sociocultural change. Like Benedict, Mead found an antidote for cultural determinism in the prospect that once a knowledge of alternative patterns become widespread, significant changes in the Euro-American way of life would necessarily ensue:

> . . . it is unthinkable that a final recognition of the great number of ways in which man, during the course of history and at the present time, is solving the problems of life, should not bring

> with it in turn the downfall of our belief in a single standard [*ibid.*:162].

The artful presentation of cultural differences to a wide professional and lay public by Mead and Benedict must be reckoned among the important events in the history of American intellectual thought. The significance of their contributions as far as cultural theory is concerned cannot be regarded as of a similar magnitude. Mead herself makes this clear in the preface to one of the re-issues of her book, although she would certainly not agree with the construal just rendered: "It was a simple—a very simple—point to which our materials were organized in the 1920's, merely the documentation over and over of the fact that human nature is not rigid and unyielding" (1939:x).

METHODOLOGICAL PROBLEMS

Coming of Age in Samoa did not attempt the configurationalist synthesis of the sort on which Benedict was working. But there are many points of similarity between Mead's and Benedict's early writings, especially from a methodological perspective, and these resemblances increased as time wore on. Mead as much as Benedict succumbed to the temptation to exaggerate the decisiveness with which both individual and cultural personality types can be identified and contrasted. Although the proposal to find out what is going on "inside of peoples' heads"—to find out how they think and feel—is perfectly respectable, it must be admitted that other forms of cultural investigation are decidedly less risky. No one would wish to assert that even a matter so simple as counting the members of a household is without its methodological pitfalls, but the problems associated with developing verifiable statements about how a man feels toward his mother or his wife are more numerous and much more exposed to the observer's moods and fancies.

Mead (1962a:134) has recently argued that the adherence to a physicalist model of science in anthropology is premature, and she has underscored the "need for waiting until appropriate theories and methods have been developed to fit our exceedingly complex materials into an evolving framework." Yet it cannot be said that her own launching into the domain of culture and personality was anything less than precipitous. In the absence of operationally acceptable research techniques, it might very well be argued that the entire configurationalist approach was premature and that the attempt to sketch the typical Samoan girl's feelings and emotions during the transition from puberty to marriage was entirely too ambitious an undertaking.

In this regard it should be stressed that ethnography can easily become overcautious and obsessed with a passion for verifiable minutiae. That is also a grave threat to scientific standards, and I would certainly not wish to be associated with a point of view which demeans the role of impressionistic, nonstatistical data in cultural anthropology. But the most important consideration regarding the appropriateness of research methods, which are relatively "soft" in terms of verifiability, is the nature of the articulation between the data and the corpus of orienting theory. If the data-collecting process is designed to maximize the opportunities for continuous correction in relationship to a set of cross-culturally relevant hypotheses, one may tolerate a considerable amount of guesswork and nonquantitative generalization out of the conviction that some data is better than no data and that the errors will call attention to themselves during the process of cross-cultural comparison. Yet it is precisely the development of systematic cross-cultural comparisons which Mead believes is premature for culture and personality studies and which she believes involve a "violation of the actual complexity of the materials" (*ibid.*).

Let us consider what this means in terms of one of the sweeping ethnographic generalities which leave many of her colleagues in a state of wide-eyed wonder. Samoan girls, according to Mead, move through puberty and adolescence without major psychological conflicts, and this is especially true in the area of sexual development. The result is that "The girls' minds were perplexed by no conflicts, troubled by no philosophical queries, beset by no remote ambitions" (MEAD 1949c: 107). For a generalization which is at once so sweeping and so thoroughly dependent upon "getting inside of heads," Mead's style conveys an unnerving degree of conviction. To be sure, Mead does take up several cases of girls "in conflict." But these are treated as deviants and as requiring no modification in her major point. It is not possible to bring this picture of a serene, even apathetic, passage to maturity into line with a corpus of interrelated and testable hypotheses of cross-cultural and causal significance. There is some evidence from other Oceanic societies which suggests that Mead's Samoan findings were exaggerated. As Barnouw points out, studies in Truk and Ifaluk by Gladwin, Sarason, and Spiro indicate that premarital sexual freedom and an apparently placid and leisurely life is no guarantee that deep inner frustrations and anxieties are not also present.

MEAD'S DEFENSE OF HER METHOD

It would be a grave injustice to one of anthropology's most creative and brilliant personalities to suggest that Mead has not paid sufficient attention to the special methodological issues associated with a psychocultural approach. On the contrary, Mead has always been keenly aware of the need for explicit descriptions of field techniques and methodological assumptions (the same cannot be said for her sense of philosophical and epistemological issues); and in certain research specialties to which we shall refer in a moment, she is without peer. *Coming of Age in Samoa* contains an appendix on method in which Mead anticipated the main outlines of the criticism which she and Benedict were about to provoke. Arguing against the relevance of statistics for the type of study that requires complex situational and emotional statements of context, she compared her role to that of an insightful medical diagnostician:

> As the physician and the psychiatrist have found it necessary to describe each case separately and to use their cases as illuminations of a thesis rather than as irrefutable proof such as it is possible to adduce in the physical sciences, so the student of the more intangible and psychological aspects of human behaviour is forced to illuminate rather than demonstrate a thesis [1949c:169].

This attitude carries through Mead's entire voluminous output and has been the focus of repeated attacks and counterattacks concerning the methodology of psychocultural ethnography. It is once again interesting to note the specific disavowal by one of Boas' most famous students of the physicalist model which Kroeber had insisted was central to Boas' influence. Writing retrospectively, some thirty-six years later, Mead was still unprepared to yield up the intuitive prerogatives of a clinical diagnostician. She declared her continuing lack of sympathy for the attempt to build from the outset, a science of man which "would conform to the ideal science, physics" and her sympathy for "those who have insisted on the complexity and uniqueness of significant events in the life of a bird or the life of a human being" (MEAD 1962a:135).

FLAWS IN THE DEFENSE

This image of the psychologically oriented anthropologist as physician or psychoanalyst is dispelled at once when we consider the differences between applied and "pure" sciences. Although we may deplore the large measure of intuition and guesswork in our doctor's practice, we gratefully pay our bills in the knowledge that there is no alternative. This has never been the case as far as Mead's explorations of the cultural psyche are concerned. I shall make no attempt here to evaluate the possible contribution which Mead may have rendered to the improvement of psychiatric therapy. The tone of breathless urgency in some of her writings seems to promise catastrophic penalties for our failure to come to grips with the most subtle and variable nuances of the human mind in its myriad cultural settings. But this leap into the intuited essences of personality was not a requirement imposed by the profession in which she had elected to achieve eminence. That it was urgent to do an ethnographic study of the Samoans (or other Polynesians) before all traces of the aboriginal patterns were obliterated, none will deny. But from the point of view of experiment design, there is no special reason why Boas' theories about the power of culture could not have been tested in any number of different settings all of which would have permitted the use of statistical controls.

It must be remembered that the kind of psychologizing upon which Mead based her portrait of Samoan adolescence has its analogue in everyday attempts by notably mature and intelligent people to sum up their mutual acquaintances along any of the thousands of available avenues of vernacular characterization. Our common experience in asserting that John is clever, Mary dull, Henry gullible, Fred jealous, and Linda a flirt is that someone who has seen these same people under different circumstances forthwith challenges our opinion and sets forth an entirely different interpretation. Life would be decidedly less complicated were there a larger measure of agreement concerning what it takes to be a beautiful, intelligent, warm, dependable, magnanimous, and charming person. Yet it is just this kind of judgment in which Mead was obliged to indulge in her efforts to obtain a psychological portrait of Samoan youth. Here is an enterprise which plainly requires the courage of one's convictions, a blessing with which Mead has been liberally endowed. Thus in *Coming of Age*, Mead wrote that Lita was "clever and executive"; Sona "overbearing in manner, arbitrary and tyrannous, impudently deferential"; Manita was "haughty and aggressive"; Ana was "mild, quiescent"; Lola was "quarrelsome, insubordinate, impertinent"; Sami was "mild and gentle with a soft undercurrent of resentment"; Nito was "high spirited"; Siva was "passionate and easily aroused"; Pusa was "strong minded"; Fuativa was "cautious and calculating"; Mala was "treacherous"; and poor Tino was "a dull and good child" (*ibid.*:112–20, 168). It should be pointed out that whatever difficulties we might suffer in accepting these vignettes as verifiable statements were they delivered in their usual cultural context, we must now reckon with the additional problem that Mead was twenty-three years old when she left for Samoa and that she had to form her impressions of personality differences through the muffling effect of an imperfectly learned second language, and finally that the ordinary gestural, facial, and behavioral cues associated with personality traits in Western culture could not be assumed to correspond to analogous traits in Polynesia.

INTERPRETATION OF MANUS CHILDHOOD

Mead's next major book, *Growing Up in New Guinea* (1930a), was essentially a repeat performance in a new locale of her Samoan study. It was concerned with the kind of enculturation processes by which the Manus brought their children to adulthood. According to her introductory remarks, she "made this study of Manus education to prove no thesis, to support no preconceived theories," but in the appendix and in retrospective articles she describes how she had originally intended to test the belief propounded by Lévy-Bruhl that the animistic ingredients in primitive mentality were similar to childish thoughtways and that they would therefore be more pronounced among primitive children than among their parents. This hypothesis is interesting for its continuation of the main Boasian thrust against biological determinism. The Manus child turned out to be less animistic than his parents and even less animistic than American children. Left largely to their own devices, Manus children remained stunted and they manifested a conspicuously "dull unimaginative, play life," a fact from which Mead drew the not altogether shattering conclusion that the movement in American education to give more freedom to children would produce no desirable results unless they were given "something upon which to exercise their imagination" (*ibid.*:152).

DIFFICULT PORTRAITURE

In her third major psychocultural study, *Sex and Temperament in Three Primitive Societies,* Mead turned to the question of the degree of malleability of the sexes with respect to culturally assigned, sex-linked behavior (1935a). In this book the parallelism in method between Mead and Benedict is clearly visible and has been pointed out by Mead herself (1962a:126). Perhaps the major difference was that Mead's materials were largely drawn from her own field research. Like

Benedict, Mead compared three different cultures to test the range of variation of cultural patterns. Instead of a psychologistic portraiture of the entire culture, however, Mead restricted herself largely to the problem of typing the varieties of sexually assigned behavioral roles. Nonetheless, there are some unnerving examples of the more general kind of portraiture. Undoubtedly these provoked less criticism (*cf.* THURNWALD 1936; BERNARD 1945; MEAD 1937a) than was directed toward Benedict's treatment of the Pueblos only because of the paucity of relevant area specialists. For instance:

> As the Arapesh made growing food and children the greatest adventure of their lives, and the Mundugumor found greatest satisfaction in fighting and competitive acquisition of women, the Tchambuli may be said to live principally for art [MEAD 1950:170].

In pursuing the main thread, Mead appears to have had the extraordinary good fortune to have selected the Arapesh, Mundugumor, and Tchambuli as the cultures in which to do fieldwork. For as she noted in the *Preface* to the 1950 edition, "many readers felt that her analysis was too pretty" and that "I must have found what I was looking for."

> Here, admittedly looking for light on the subject of sex differences, I found three tribes all conveniently within a hundred mile area. In one, both men and women act as we expect women to act—in a mild parental responsive way; in the second, both act as we expect men to act—in a fierce initiating fashion; and in the third, the men act according to our stereotype for women—are catty, wear curls and go shopping, while the women are energetic, managerial, unadorned partners [*ibid.*].

Mead goes on to insist that although it seemed "too good to be true," she had reported what was actually there and not what she had wanted to find. It is obvious, however, that such oath-takings are irrelevant. The issue is not one of good faith but rather of demonstration, verifiability, and intersubjectivity.

CRITIQUE OF CONFIGURATIONAL HOMOGENEITY

This problem is not restricted to Mead's work but is, of course, a matter of grave concern in all ethnographic research. It does seem, however, to be true that psychocultural studies are especially vulnerable to criticisms which challenge their evidential foundations. This difficulty increases in direct proportion to the size and sociocultural complexity of the population from which the typical impressionistic vignettes are derived. Mead's rejection of statistical validation techniques cannot be justified when one moves from the world of the Arapesh, total population several hundred, to Bali, population several tens of thousands, to Russia, Japan, and the United States, population several tens of millions. Insight, empathy, intuition, everyday experience, training as observer—no matter how highly developed these skills are—provide an inadequate basis for making statements which purport to describe some typical aspect of the personality of millions of human beings. As a matter of fact, evidence has accumulated that even in relatively small populations the amount of emotional and cognitive variability is far beyond that with which nonquantitative psychocultural analysts are prepared to cope.

An early indication of this was implicit in Mead's own data. The very fact that personality of the sexes differed so markedly in some societies —as in Mead's own account of the Tchambuli and as in Bateson's (1936) description of the Iatmul—leads one to expect that other status differences may also be associated with quite different psychic patterns. In stratified societies class and caste differences obviously intrude, and there is every reason to expect that many of the myriad occupational specialties characteristic of the larger state-organized societies are associated with important personality differences.

Actually, the main thrust of the methodological critique to which Mead, Benedict, and the other pioneers of this field have been subjected comes from within the field itself. Among anthropologists, a second generation of culture and personality studies have been approached with a more modest and sober if considerably less exciting regard for methodological complexities. One of the most conspicuous results of the increased use of standardized psychological tests and statistical analysis has been the proof that the variability even in small populations is too great to be ignored. For example, Anthony Wallace (1952) in a highly operationalized approach to the analysis of Iroquois personality, used Rorschach tests to establish statistically meaningful expressions of modal personality. Working with 21 scoring variables and setting arbitrary limits upon deviation from each mode, he counted the number of individuals whose scores on all 21 variables fell within the modal range. By this approach, only 37 percent of the Tuscarora could be said to manifest the "modal" personality of their group (but it should be emphasized that no one can say how much deviation from the mode constitutes an acceptable definition of "shared" traits. B. Kaplan (1954) compared Rorschach responses in four cultures—Zuñi, Navaho, Spanish American, and Mormon—with respect to fourteen variables. Between-group differences turned out to be much smaller than expected with only five of these variables exhibiting statistically valid cross-cultural differences. Moreover, the range of variability within each of the cultures appeared to be comparable to that which Wallace found for the Tuscarora. As Kaplan notes:

> That great variability exists does not argue against the influence of culture on personality; it means merely that cultural influences do not necessarily create uniformity in a group. All individuals interact with their cultures. However human beings are not passive recipients of their culture. They accept, reject, or rebel against the cultural forces to which they are oriented. In many cultures, including our own, there exists a pattern of outward conformity and inner rebellion and deviation. It is probably correct to say that individuals seem a good deal more similar than they really are [1954:32].

In the same vein, but with different methods, C. W. M. Hart has drawn personality portraits of five Tiwi brothers, each of whom showed many striking differences in such patterns as aggressiveness, cheerfulness, sexuality, and other personality dimensions. Hart ironically draws attention to Boas' insistence that there is no uniform mentality to be associated with primitive cultures:

> . . . if the personality and culture literature is leading young anthropologists into the field expecting to find "stereotyped personalities" in the simpler cultures, they are doomed to disappointment [1954:259].

Wallace, speaking of what he calls the "New Culture and Personality," believes that a fundamental shift away from the search for configurational homogeneity on a tribal or national scale has already occurred.

> The magnitude of individual psychological differences within cultural boundaries is recognized as being so large that the analytical problem would appear to be the elucidation of the processes of the organization of diversity rather than the mechanisms of inducing a supposed uniformity [WALLACE 1962:6–7].

MEAD'S USE OF PHOTOGRAPHY

Mead's response to criticism of her methodology has been extremely complex. By 1936 she herself had become convinced that the method she had been using to describe the "ethos" of the Samoans and the New Guineans was unsatisfactory from several points of view:

> This method had many serious limitations: it transgressed the canons of precise and operational scientific exposition proper to science; it was far too dependent upon idiosyncratic factors of style and literary skill; it was difficult to duplicate; and it was difficult to evaluate [BATESON and MEAD 1942:xi].

One of the ways in which Mead has attempted to overcome this difficulty is strictly methodological. She has sought to improve the demonstrative power of her observations by employing cameras and tape recorders to capture characteriologically significant behavioral events in their situational context and to publish or display these records along with word descriptions. The latter are in turn based on a phenomenally skilled facility for note-taking.

Mead's turning to photography, both still and cine, was a direct response to the criticism to which her first three configurational books were subjected. In preparation for her fieldwork in Bali in 1936 jointly with Gregory Bateson, Mead took along an unprecedented array of photographic equipment and film. All together, during the fieldwork period some 25,000 Leica stills and over 22,000 feet of 16 mm. film were exposed. These pioneering experiments in the use of mechanical aids to give ethnography an unimpeachable documentary foundation may very well constitute Mead's most enduring contribution to the development of anthropology as a discipline. The ability to record continuous sequences of specimens of naturally unfolding human behavior—the actual raw material of history and sociocultural evolution—at once raises the scientific prospects of ethnography far beyond its prototechnic horizons. It must be emphasized that these prospects have now become much more obvious than they were only a few years ago. When it first occurred to Mead that part of the answer to her critics lay in the hardware of the communications industry, she had little by way of precedent to guide her. Now, within the next decade, we may anticipate a leap to entirely new levels of machine-assisted ethnography as the technical advances associated with miniaturization are declassified and made available to nonmilitary personnel. (We may of course also anticipate a concomitant intensification of the moral and ethical dilemmas of the ethnographer whose "snooping" has always been likened to gossiping at best and spying at worst.) But Mead was undoubtedly years ahead of her colleagues in this matter, and she quite properly berated her critics with the observation that "the proponents of quantification and 'scientific' accuracy have made very little use of the new tools that make greater accuracy available for all of us" (1962a:135).

Despite its long-run promise, it cannot be said that Mead's and Bateson's utilization of photography solved the immediate methodological problem of documenting the intuited personality differences associated with the large, multivillage, stratified, and specialized Balinese population. Several selective processes, some of them unconscious, intervene between the actual unfolding of Balinese behavior during Bateson's and Mead's sojourn and the printing of the stills and movies, which are intended as proof if not of the representativity at least of the reality of these events. In view of the fact that Bateson and Mead were both the ethnographers and the photographers, it scarcely seems possible that sustained divergences between written observations and the photographic record would come to light. The camera had to be aimed and the shutter made to operate in conformity with the interests, hypotheses, and dramatic and aesthetic inclinations of the moment. The result is that the photographs have superb illustrative value. As far as their demonstrative value is concerned, however, they are not conspicuously less subjective than a straight verbal report. The use of photographs in other words has not solved Mead's difficulties with the problem of intersubjectivity. In this connection the fact that we are asked to accept the visual representation of body motion as clues to the emotional events within the brain places an additional burden upon the verbal interpretations that Mead and Bateson attached to each photograph. Both the problems of representativity and of verifiability have thus remained essentially immune to Mead's photographic innovations.

INFORMANT REPRESENTATIVITY AND NATIONAL CHARACTER

One of Mead's answers to her critics has taken her along quite a different path, of great interest in relationship to the development of a similar strategy by certain proponents of the "New Ethnography," of the "linguistic model," and of French anthropology under Claude Lévi-Strauss.

While recognizing the need for better validation procedures, Mead and her followers and collaborators plunged ahead into a number of ambitious psychocultural projects, none of which are notably more convincing than her analysis of Samoan adolescence, and to which the photographic innovations of her Balinese experiment have not been applied. Studies of the national character of the United States, Russia, and England by Geoffrey Gorer (1948, 1949, 1955); of Japan by Ruth Benedict (1946); and of the United States by Mead herself (1942,

1949a) have all been attacked for their unorthodox methodology. The use of a small number of informants as the basis for generalization about the intimate psychic constellations of great masses of people is the most troublesome aspect of these studies. Mead has responded to such criticism by insisting that a single informant, provided that his social and cultural position is carefully specified, can be a satisfactory source of information about widely distributed patterns:

> Any member of a group, provided that his position within that group is properly specified, is a perfect sample of the group-wide pattern on which he is acting as an informant. So a twenty-one-year-old boy born of Chinese-American parents in a small upstate New York town who has just graduated *summa cum laude* from Harvard and a tenth-generation Boston-born deaf mute of United Kingdom stock are equally perfect examples of American national character, *provided that their individual position and individual characteristics are taken fully into account* [MEAD 1953:648].

Although presented with Mead's characteristic energy and sense of conviction, this statement leaves the major challenge to her position essentially untouched. Mead makes the assumption here that the atypicality of the Chinese American or the deaf mute can be surmounted by *fully* specifying their atypicality; but to do this, we must have already achieved some knowledge of the typical patterns. Although it is doubtless a safe bet that Harvard boys and deaf mutes have noteworthy psychological specialties, what additional varieties of actor types in the United States require special identification? Are tugboat captains and insurance office workers notably different in their sexual standards? Mead in effect runs out from under the methodological requirement for sampling only to have it drop back on her with increased force. For if we are to take *fully* into account individual position and characteristics, then we must either content ourselves with 200 million different national characters or avail ourselves of sampling techniques in order to identify our informants in relationship to the rest of the American population.

THE LINGUISTIC ANALOGY

Like many anthropologists, and among them more than a few who are hostile to her approach, Mead believes that cultural patterns are somehow peculiarly immune to the need for statistically structured samples. In this regard there is a fascinating convergence between Mead's invocation of the linguistic model as a methodological precedent and the similar use of the same model by the practitioners of the "New Ethnography." Unlike the sociologist or the social psychologist, she argues, the anthropologist is not primarily interested in the distribution or incidence of a pattern such as "resistance to paternal authority" but merely in the existence of this pattern as it is manifested in regard to parents, grandparents, siblings, and other sets of relationships. If one wants to know the grammatical structure of a language, "it is sufficient to use very few informants." The same is true of the rest of culture.

> In dealing with culture, the anthropologist makes the same assumptions about the rest of a culture that the linguist makes about the language—that he is dealing with a system which can be delineated by analysis of a small number of very highly specified samples [*ibid.*:655].

Mead attributes to linguistics the belief that the statement "*to be* is an auxiliary verb in English" will not be improved by the collection of more and more samples of English speech. So too, she argues, will our statements about patterns not be improved by additional sampling. The distinction which Mead is making here is also precisely that which Lévi-Strauss has attempted to set up under the rubrics "mechanical" and "statistical" models (see Chap. 18). All of these attempts to circumvent the labor of counting and measuring human responses echo the idealism and intuitionism of Vico, Kant, Hegel, and Dilthey. The strongest case for Mead's point is certainly that furnished by language and other communication systems. But there are important reasons why culture as a whole cannot profitably be looked upon as a communication system. Even in linguistics it is not so apparent that the testing for behavioral variations will not improve the statement of grammatical rules. Were linguists not to test for some additional instances of the use of the sound train "to be," they would be as much victims of philosophical idealism as their colleagues in cultural anthropology. To learn that "to be" occurs not only as an auxiliary verb, but also as three or more intransitive verbs with meanings such as "to exist," "to remain," and "to happen" is the kind of improvement which one might expect from collecting more samples of English speech.

As we shall see, the invocation of linguistics as the patron of intuited regularities is sometimes more appropriate than in the case of personality studies. Some domains of culture are more highly patterned than others. Textbook English obviously lies at one end of a very broad continuum of interpersonal regularities. In between there are such matters as when to plant corn, where to live after marriage, how to greet a chief. At the other extreme, there are such concerns as how one feels and what one thinks in reaction to a mother's nagging, a sexual advance, the death of one's father. It is to the study of this most perplexing of all areas of human behavior that Mead's professional life has been dedicated. And it is precisely in this area that firm statistical control and carefully operationalized and instrumented research methodologies are most urgently required.

Culture and Personality: Freudian

16

The research investment in culture and personality exemplifies the attraction of mentalistic and individualistic themes in American social science. The extraordinary influence of Freudian and other depth psychologies is possibly linked with the heightening of social, political, and economic tension associated with two world wars and the apparently deteriorating prospects of achieving human happiness through sociocultural evolution. It seems to me not without significance for the development of theories of culture that widespread attention to psychocultural analysis among anthropologists historically accompanied the inward-turning of the depth psychologists toward the family's and the individual's responsibility for frustrations and anxieties, and a consequent turning away from the techno-environmental, techno-economic, and social and political conditions that control the destiny of both family and individual.

FUNCTIONALIST PARADIGMS

In addition to constituting an enlargement of the descriptive interests of ethnography, the culture and personality movement has made a number of tentative theoretical contributions toward the explanation of cultural differences and similarities. For the most part these contributions have been phrased in terms of loosely formulated, functionalist paradigms. That is, certain kinds of personality configurations are presented as somehow appropriate to, or consistent with, certain kinds of institutions or other aspects of the group's typical or modal personality. In this sense Benedict's configurations are obviously a form of functional analysis which is fully analogous to the attempt by Radcliffe-Brown and Malinowski to show the interdependence and functional "fit" of less conspicuously psychologistic elements. There is the further resemblance in that most psychological functionalism involves a timeless or synchronic cross-section in which no commitment is made concerning the relative permanence of the observed institutional and psychological concatenation. Milton Singer's (1961:28) observation concerning the timelessness of patterns in the configurational approach actually also applies to the culture and personality movement as a whole:

> The overwhelming impression given by works of this period is that configurations are timeless entities without known antecedents or consequences, but that, once established in a particular territory, they automatically become all-powerful shapers of events and personalities.

A general critique of synchronic functionalism will be found in the chapter, British Social Anthropology. It will then be shown that the strategy is not a viable alternative to historical determinism. Here we may note the philosopher Ernest Nagel's (1953) proof that any logico-empirically meaningful functional statement must be translatable into a cause and effect paradigm. The reverse is also true: any cause and effect statement may also be restated as a functional one. Functional analysis implies that some sort of covariance of a long- or short-range time period can be identified in a set of variables.

HOMEOSTATIC MODEL

Paul Collins (1965) has recently formulated the logical principles which sustain short-range functional analysis and has advanced the analogy of homeostatic control through negative feedback as the basis for functional concatenation between system-maintaining variables. In Collins' view, elements of the system are seen as changing through a range of limited values maintained by sociocultural servomechanisms. The analysis of Melanesian and New Guinea pig populations has been carried out with this paradigm in mind (VAYDA, LEEDS, and SMITH 1961C; RAPPAPORT 1966). Homeostasis is assured by periodic slaughter, under ritual coordination, of herds which place excessive demand on labor input and garden lands. Another variety of short-range covariance involves a safety-valve effect. This admits the existence of "waste" or "noise" in the system and assigns to certain cultural elements the function of ridding the system of potentially disruptive ingredients. In psychocultural analyses, some combination of these two short-time functional paradigms seems to be implied whenever analytic propositions advance beyond the level of mere equivocation. It is this kind of covariance, for example, that is implied when one speaks of the "projective" functions of magico-religious elements. Religious ceremonial is frequently thought of as fulfilling the psychological function of allaying anxiety and also as a coordinating mechanism for heightening cooperation. Translated into the normal cause and effect, covariant statement, this means that the rituals in question drain off individual anxieties when system-destroying levels are approached. It also means that as ceremonials take place, levels of cooperation which had fallen in the direction of system-destroying values are restored to tolerable limits.

EVOLUTIONARY MODEL

Homeostatic functional paradigms should be kept distinct from statements of the conditions under which the system develops new functional or dysfunctional concatenations: in other words, the conditions under which cultural evolution takes place. When the system evolves, changes in the value of the elements in one sector accumulate and in so doing cause changes in other sectors. The cause and effect sequence may produce positive feedback with the consequence that the analytical separation of the dependent and independent variables is made extremely difficult. But the factors responsible for cultural evolution are both functionally and causally related. Nothing could be more futile than to oppose functionalism to historical determinism. An understanding of cultural evolution requires the study of both system-maintaining and system-changing phenomena, and in both cases we are concerned with probabilistic versions of causality. When a functional statement cannot be made to yield a prediction of the changes of state of dependent and independent variables, it is not properly speaking a functional statement, but rather a functional equivocation.

This brings us back to the matter at hand, for any attempt to assess the contribution made by culture and personality studies to cultural theory must grapple with the highly equivocal nature of the relational propositions that dominate the field. These propositions are frequently worded in such a way as to defy all efforts to categorize them as either of the two viable varieties of functionalism. Yet, it is the evident intent of the responsible parties that psychocultural analysis be regarded as more than mere descriptions barren of testable hypotheses.

FREUD'S EVOLUTIONISM

The basic psychological frame of reference for the modern culture and personality school derives directly or indirectly from Sigmund Freud. Paradoxically, there is no equivocation in Freud's psychocultural pronouncements as regarding the category of functionalism to which they are meant to conform. When Freud turned his attention from the analysis of the individual psyche to psychocultural phenomena, it was to identify the causal processes in cultural evolution. This was the avowed objective of *Totem and Taboo* (1913), his first sustained foray into the domain of culture. In every respect, *Totem and Taboo* may be taken as representative of what the Boasians considered to be the worst form of evolutionary speculation. In the grandiosity of its compass, the flimsiness of its evidence, and the generality of its conclusions, it was scarcely approached by anything Morgan had conceived. A direct clash between Freud and the Boasians was thus inevitable.

According to Freud, man began his cultural career under a form of social organization in which a single patriarch held exclusive sexual privileges over his sisters and daughters. At some unspecified moment, his sexually deprived sons plotted their father's murder, killed him, and ate him. But the brothers were overcome with guilt; they henceforth repressed their desire to have sexual relations with their mothers, sisters, or daughters. At the same time, in expiation of their murderous deed and cannibalistic orgy, they created the myth of the totem, the animal symbol of their father, henceforth taboo as food except on ritual occasions. In this fashion, the primal patricide, helped along by hereditary memory traces in the "racial unconscious," gave rise to the Oedipus complex, nuclear family incest taboo, group exogamy, totemism, and many other features of primitive civilization.

Within this anachronistic framework Freud sought to handle the problem of the diversity of cultures. Savage personality was equated with infantile personality; each modern individual in a sense recapitulates the evolution of culture by passing through the various stages of progress toward maturity, and some cultures like some individuals have their development arrested at various points short of "civilization" (maturity). Nothing in these doctrines prepared orthodox Freudians to cope with the great variety of culturally determined personality structures which the data being collected by Malinowski, Mead, Benedict, and other psychologically oriented fieldworkers seemed to demonstrate.

THE ANTHROPOLOGICAL CRITIQUE OF FREUD

The reaction of the Boasians to *Totem and Taboo* is well represented by Kroeber's 1920 review of the book's English translation. Although Freud is called a "gallant and stimulating adventurer into ethnology," his theories are scoffed at wherever they purport to explain social origins and evolutionary phases. The entire historical dimension is associated with the era of discredited speculative anthropology. The Boasians, understandably enough, were not about to substitute the phantasies of neurotic patients for a study of actual historical events. Boas himself was considerably less charitable than Kroeber:

> While, therefore, we may welcome the application of every advance in the method of psychological investigation, we cannot accept as an advance in ethnological method the crude transfer of a novel, one-sided method of psychological investigation of the individual to social phenomena the origin of which can be shown to be historically determined and to be subject to influences that are not at all comparable to those that control the psychology of the individual [BOAS 1948:289; orig. 1920a].

The anthropological critique of Freudian theories centers on Malinowski's (1923; 1927a) "disproof" of the universality of the Oedipus complex. Having had his attention drawn to the strategic value of the matrilineal, avunculocal Trobrianders by C. G. Seligman, Malinowski threatened the entire Freudian edifice with his description of how in a Trobriand family it was mother's brother and not father who was the figure of authority. This meant that repressive discipline did not originate in the man who sexually monopolized ego's mother, thereby depriving the father-son relationship of the ambivalent love-hatred which Freud had observed in his European patients.

To a significant extent, the first three of Margaret Mead's field studies must also be seen as part of the anthropological critique of Freud. Not that Freud was the specific target of her fieldwork, but rather that her main concern was to disprove the widespread belief of which Freud was one of the most prominent advocates, that human nature contained biopsychological components, such as libido and its complexes, which express themselves in definite behavioral stages independently of the specific sociocultural environment. Freud, in other words, in the nature-nurture controversy, leaned heavily toward the side of the physiologists, biologists, instinct psychologists, and Spencerian anthropologists. Boas and his students were concerned to prove that culture has the power to make every human being different from what "nature" has decreed, while Freud and his disciples were convinced that cultural differences were superficial and that in the most significant psychological sense, all human beings were led along similar developmental routes by their common hereditary endowment.

From the morphology of the id, ego, and superego, to the interpretation of dreams, to the origin of civilization, Freud's scheme depended upon the existence of a well-defined universal human instinctual endowment and a definite universal ontogenetic progress through maturational stages (oral, anal, genital). Freud originally gave the name libido to the instinctual source of human behavior. Later, with the publication of *Civilization and Its Discontents* (1930), he spoke of "eros" and opposed this life force to a death instinct (from which he derived such phenomena as masochism, suicide, and war). Everything in Mead's approach weighed against such compulsory psychic freight. It was her mission, set for her by Boas, to defeat the notion of a narrowly fixed racial or panhuman hereditary human nature. And it was for this reason that she tirelessly stressed the absence of maturational regularities: adolescence is not always a time of stress; children are not necessarily more imaginative than adults; women are not necessarily more passive than men (MEAD 1939:x-xi).

THE FREUDIAN PURITY OF RÓHEIM

During the period under discussion there was one field-experienced anthropologist of major stature who argued on behalf of the whole Freudian doctrine: Hungarian-born Géza Róheim. By Róheim's own reckoning, Bruno Bettelheim was the only other authority with possibly comparable credentials (including clinical practice).

Róheim is one of the most flamboyant figures in the history of the culture and personality movement. Although his method of reaching psychoanalytical conclusions is intolerably linked with clinical authority, his didactic "einschnappen" are not appreciably more amazing than those associated with the Mead-Bateson-Gorer axis. On the other hand, Róheim had the virtue of clarity and frankness, always stipulating that the fundamental causal sequence rises from infant experience to adult practice. Everything else is superficial. It is the Oedipus complex which lies at the root of all psychologically significant sociocultural happenings, and from Róheim's perspective anyone who denies this is suffering from a repressed Oedipus complex of his own and should at once rush off to be analyzed. Contrary to popular impression, in the argument between Róheim and Malinowski over the effect of the Trobriand matrilineal organization on the Oedipal situation, it is Róheim who holds the trump card. By Malinowski's own admission, the Trobriand child is brought up largely under the influence of the usual nuclear pairs. Mother's brother enters the picture only when the child is seven or eight years old, an age by which the Oedipal constellation is firmly entrenched.

Róheim's long-running battle with the members of particularist and synchronic anthropological schools on both sides of the Atlantic engendered much acrimonious debate. His rejection of the Boasian emphasis on the alleged uniqueness of each culture, due to its separate historical growth, has many points in common with the neo-evolutionist critique of historical particularism. Yet Róheim's style was so thoroughly calculated to insult the majority of his anthropological peers that he gained few converts, and even those who were influenced by him preferred not to acknowledge his existence. Especially painful was Róheim's accusation that when it came down to it, the Boasian relativists were simply repressed nationalists. The reason why they rejected Freud's evolutionary theory and went about trying to prove that cultural factors could prevent the formation of Oedipal feelings was that they themselves were suffering from unresolved Oedipal urges. His audacious accusations aptly convey both the strength and weakness of his doctrines:

> But the point we are now making is that this impression of complete diversity of various human groups is largely created by the Oedipus complex, that is to say, the Oedipus complex of the anthropologist or psychiatrist or psychologist. He does not know what to do with his own Oedipus complex—he therefore *scotomizes* clear evidence for the Oedipus complex, even when his training ought to enable him to see it [RÓHEIM 1950:362].

Although this seems like a hit below the belt, there are more vicious blows to come. Róheim must have thoroughly enjoyed the sputtering in professional circles which greeted his preposterous notion that Freud was rejected because the Boasians were crypto-racists:

> This repression of the Oedipus complex is paralleled by another *preconscious* tendency, that of *nationalism*. The idea that all nations are completely different from each other and that the goal of anthropology is simply to find how different they are is a thinly veiled manifestation of nationalism, the democratic counterpart of the Nazi racial doctrine or the communist class doctrine. Now of course, I am quite aware of the fact that all those who advocate the study of differences are well-meaning people and that consciously they are in favor of the brotherhood of mankind. The slogan of "cultural relativity" is supposed to mean just this. But I am a psychoanalyst. I know that all human attitudes result from a compromise formation of two opposite trends and I know the meaning of reaction formation: "You are completely different, but I forgive you" is what it amounts to. Anthropology is in danger of being led down a blind alley by being subjected to one of the most ancient tendencies of mankind, that of in-group versus out-group [*ibid.*].

The audacious ironies in which Róheim delighted are not wholly devoid of rational substance. One of the basic requirements of a theory of cultural continuity and change is a description of what used to be called human nature. All cultural items are partially the product of a set of biophysical constants which are shared by most if not all Homo sapiens. Correct though it may be that the explanation of differences and similarities cannot be achieved merely by invoking these constants, it is no less improbable that explanations can be achieved without them. These constants interact with the variables of specific cultural and natural environments, and they form a necessary part of the equation by which we seek to explain specific classes of phenomena of less than universal occurrence. At a minimum, the species-given requirement of metabolism, the conditions and phases of human sexuality, the universals of somatic and psychic health and disease—all must be plugged into the equation by which differences as well as similarities are to be understood. In this respect, despite the obsessive quality of Róheim's search for Oedipal taboos, Oedipal ceremonies, and Oedipal organization, we must maintain an open mind regarding the possibility that much of the recurrent symbolism of dreams and myths reflects an underlying commonality of Oedipal strivings.

In his later years, Róheim's case for the primacy of the Oedipal situation gained immeasurably from his abandonment of Freud's idea of a phylogenetic memory of the primal patricide. Róheim pointed instead to certain species-given characteristics of Homo sapiens which might very well account for a universal sexual complex. There is first the universal affection from mother to child ("sheltered, i.e., libidinal, mother-child situation"); there is second a precocious sexuality which sets in before physical or mental maturity is reached; and third, it is the combination of precocious sexuality and maturing mental processes which fills the human child with libidinal images. Róheim concludes that psychoanalysis is not culture-bound and that its methods are of universal validity: "There can be many types of personality but only one Unconscious" (1950:491).

Róheim recognized that his defense of a single "unconscious" was a restatement of the doctrine of psychic unity, which he attributes to Adolf Bastian, in an acknowledgment almost unique among twentieth-century anthropologists. But Róheim points out that in addition to universal germ thoughts, Bastian was also aware of the specific development which these received in specific cultures. Róheim was similarly unprepared to dismiss individual cultural elaboration as unimportant, but he denied that they could be understood apart from their universal ingredients. This led him to a kind of psychocultural analysis which was clearly antecedent to that of the entire neo-Freudian culture and personality movement. Although he insisted on centering all of his description on the Oedipus complex, he regularly accounted for specific cultural phenomena in terms of the modification of childhood experiences by culturally established customs. Among the Arunta for example, he claimed that the mother slept with her male child under her as if she were copulating with him from the male position. This produces a certain amount of confusion in the child, which gets institutional expression in the famous rite of sub-incision—the slitting of the underside of the penis back to the urethra—an anatomical alteration which Róheim declares is an attempt to possess both a vagina and a penis. The same projective phenomena are invoked to explain the circular patterns which the adult males incise on their sacred phallic stones (tchuringas). Let it not be said therefore that Róheim was insensitive to cultural specialities or that he attempted to reduce them all to a uniform Oedipal situation. On the other hand, the tenuous nature of his interpretation surely requires no further comment.

IRRESISTIBLE LURE OF FREUDIANISM

Despite the isolated situation in which Róheim found himself (not without considerable satisfaction, one suspects), the resistance to Freud was not as great as he seemed to think it was. Freud's doctrines held a great appeal for the intellectual denizens of the interval between the two world wars. Even in the dispute concerning the universality of the Oedipus complex, Freudian doctrine was actually accorded a relatively favorable reception. On closer inspection, Malinowski's point turns out to be rather supportive of Freud's outlook. He himself felt that he was vindicating, not destroying, the essentials of Freud's contributions.

> By my analysis, I have established that Freud's theories not only roughly correspond to human psychology, but that they follow closely the modification in human nature brought about by various constitutions of Society. In other words, I have established a deep correlation between the type of society and the nuclear complex found there. While this is a notable confirmation of the main tenet of Freudian psychology, it might compel us to modify certain of its details, or rather to make some of the formulae more elastic [MALINOWSKI 1923:331].

As Kroeber pointed out, in a reconsideration of *Totem and Taboo* (1952:309; orig. 1939), the orthodox psychoanalytic movement revealed "itself as partaking of a religion—a system of mysticism" from which each deviation was a heresy, and as such, grossly exaggerated the anthropologist's resistance to Freudian psychological principles.

During the 1920's, anthropologists and psychoanalysts were natural allies in the intellectual revolt against the constraints of sexual and other forms of provincialism. Anthropologists enjoyed a reputation for Bohemianism which they earned as proponents of the relativity of morals, as taboo-breaking feminists, or as practitioners of exotic custom picked up in jungle villages and Pacific atolls. Freud's exposure of the pathological results of Euro-American sexual taboos and family organization struck a responsive chord in the Boasian program. Moral relativism was an important side effect of the critique of nineteenth-century evolutionism. Among some of the Boasians, as for example, Melville Herskovits, the disproof of the superiority of Euro-American culture in the realm of religion, social organization, and family life loomed so large that the very word "primitive" came to be regarded as inadmissibly invidious and pejorative.

One of the most important themes running through *Patterns of Culture* is concerned with the alternative ways in which different cultures accommodate deviants, with an explicit psychoanalytically derived critique of our own failings in this respect. The net attractiveness of psychoanalysis is well illustrated by the fact that about the time Kroeber wrote his rather scathing critique of *Totem and Taboo* he himself was undergoing analysis. For two years, Kroeber even maintained an office in San Francisco in which he set himself up as a lay analyst

(STEWARD 1961:1050). Moreover, the drift into ever more individualized versions of historical particularism as practiced and advocated by Sapir, Radin, and Boas also set a premium on achieving a theoretical framework for the description of the cognitive and emotional inner life of one's informants. In brief, the attraction of Freud's psychological, as distinct from his evolutionary and psychocultural, theories was so great that anthropologists were not prepared to read themselves out of the Freudian circle simply because of a few crimes against history. What was needed was a de-mythologized, de-evolutionized, de-Europeanized Freud.

Sapir, responding to W. H. R. Rivers' early criticism, was among the first to realize that this transfiguration would actually take place and that Freud's influence would survive the flames of the anthropological crucible. During the First World War, Rivers had observed that battle-induced hysteria and anxiety neuroses among British soldiers apparently occurred independent of sexual frustrations. Rivers' book, *Instinct and the Unconscious* (1920a), challenged Freud's libido theory. In his review, Sapir looked beyond the specific defects to a remarkably prophetic vision of the neo-Freudian movement:

> Nearly everything that is specific in Freudian theory, such as the "Oedipus-complex" as a normative image or the definite interpretation of certain symbols or the distinctively sexual nature of certain infantile reactions, may well prove to be either ill-founded or seen in a distorted perspective, but there can be little doubt of the immense service that Dr. Freud has rendered psychology in his revelation of typical psychic mechanism. Such relational ideas as the emotionally integrated complex, the tendency to suppression under the stress of a conflict, the symptomatic expression of a suppressed impulse, the transfer of emotion and the canalizing or pooling of impulses, the tendency to regression, are so many powerful clues to an understanding of how the "soul" of man sets to work. Psychology will not willingly let go of these and still other Freudian concepts, but will build upon them, gradually coming to see them in their wider significance [SAPIR 1949:529; orig. 1921].

RECONCILIATION OF ANTHROPOLOGY AND FREUDIANISM

Only after Freud's scheme had been purged of its historical determinism was it embraced by the culture and personality movement (which is not to minimize the importance of the other modifications demanded by the known facts of ethnography). Before this transformation took place, one can vaguely discern Freud's influence being transmitted through Sapir to Benedict and Mead and adumbrating the popular treatment of deviant behavior, early childhood patterns, and comparative sexology. After this transformation the debt to Freud was readily acknowledged. But in the meantime something had been lost: the definiteness of Freud's position as far as causality is concerned. Henceforth, the accent was on synchronic functionalism. It should be noted that this transformation conformed to the Boasian treatment of all other evolutionary schema. The discredited evolutionary section of the Freudian synthesis was eliminated with no attempt made to reformulate the diachronic regularities on the basis of revised ethnographic information. Although many anthropologists now gave their energies and talents to the task of helping the psychoanalysts and psychologists reform Freud's psychological theories, they dumped Freud's evolutionary views into the same dustbin into which Morgan and Spencer had been thrown. But for all its errors, Freud's evolutionary hypothesis was presented in terms of a recognizable cause and effect variety of diachronic functionalism. On the other hand, the neo-Freudian movement in anthropology, for all of its better grounding in ethnographic data, operates with a highly equivocal version of synchronic functionalism. From this circumstance there arose a brand of psychocultural analysis whose relational propositions elude commonly understood standards of scientific verification.

One would need a separate volume to unravel the extent to which anthropological criticism of Freud played a role in bringing about the new approaches to psychoanalysis. Here it can only be mentioned that such neo-Freudians as Karen Horney, Erich Fromm, Abram Kardiner, and Erik Erikson were very much involved in a give and take with anthropologists who insisted upon opening the Freudian system to the effects of cultural variables. The resulting neo-Freudianism was built very much in the image of Sapir's prophecy. It stressed the importance of early childhood experience, especially such matters as toilet training, nursing experience, weaning, sibling rivalry, patterns of sexual discipline, and body contact, which contribute to the human enculturation process. Freud's emphasis upon the oral, anal, and genital phases of sexuality was incorporated into a broader spectrum of conditioning variables, all of which could be presumed to be related to the adult personality in different cultural settings. At the same time an eclectic view was adopted toward the application of Freud's basic psychodynamic principles such as repression, the formation of guilt and anxiety, the relationship between frustration and aggression, sublimation, resistance, and symbolization. They were all to be utilized as needed to draw a connection between childhood experiences and adult personality.

MEAD'S TURN TOWARD FREUD

Mead has set a date—1934—the occasion of the meeting of an interdisciplinary group at Hanover, as the turning point in her own utilization of Freudian principles.

> From the Hanover Seminar I learned how to handle the problem of character formation in what I now believe should be described as a Neo-Freudian way. My understanding of this problem developed out of long discussions at the Seminar and during the following winter with John Dollard, whose approach was also influenced by the work of Karen Horney and Erich Fromm (Dollard 935). These discussions focused on the relationship between character formation and the way in which the developing individual learns to cope with his impulse structure on the one hand, and with the institutions of his society on the other [MEAD 1962a:127-28].

As remarked previously, however, Freud's influence was pervasive. Mead had already adopted certain Freudian premises long before the Hanover Seminar as revealed in her treatment of ambivalence toward the dead in a contribution to the *Psychoanalytic Review* (1930b). Affirming the essential correctness of Freud's use of the ambivalence concept, she simply adds the usual relativist footnote that it is within the power of cultural conditioning to find modes of belief and expression which obviate the need for suppressing either one's sorrow or joy at the death of a kinsman. Nonetheless, her Balinese field trip, already commented on for its methodological innovations, was the first occasion for which Freudian principles provided the major research frame. Even Róheim later referred to the Balinese study as an instance of exemplary Freudian technique. *Balinese Character* is indeed saturated with psychoanalytic terms, concepts, and nuances. Everything from the way men handle their fighting rooster to how infants cross open spaces and women carry their babies is alive with Freudian innuendoes. But few of these hints are brought into a cause and effect focus.

Mead has never formulated a model of how the parts of culture in which she has been interested articulate to produce either homeostasis or predictable transformations. Each of her sustained attempts at psychocultural analysis has involved proposals for connecting one set of institutions with another or with typical character traits. In each case, however, the items that have been singled out and their functional consequences have been different. In Bali, for example, it is proposed that behavior during conventionalized trance performance is related to the frustrated attempts of Balinese children to produce climaxes of affection and anger in their parents (GORER and MEAD 1942:168). None of Mead's other studies take up a similar theme, and although her analysis sounds plausible, we do not know whether a similar relationship can be expected anywhere else in the world. We do have the suggestion that Balinese trance is a "return to repressed patterns of behavior," but the problem of connecting these two features in terms of homeostatic covariance or diachronic transformation is scarcely touched upon. As we shall see in a moment from the case of the swaddling hypotheses, Mead has flatly dissociated herself from all attempts to establish direct causal connections between any given infantile experience and developed cultural forms (*cf.* MEAD 1954:398).

KARDINER'S SYNTHESIS

The neo-Freudian approach which came closest to achieving a theory of psychocultural analysis was that of Abram Kardiner. In 1936 Kardiner, a practicing analyst, organized a seminar at the New York Psychoanalytic Institute in which Sapir, Benedict, and Bunzel were participants. In 1937, the seminar moved to Columbia University, and it was joined by Ralph Linton, Cora DuBois, and Carl Withers, all of whom submitted ethnographic data for Kardiner's psychocultural analysis. Kardiner operated with only the barest remnants of Freud's original scheme. He had dropped the Oedipus complex, with its primal patricide and phylogenetic memory; the three-stage development of sexuality; and the exclusive emphasis upon the sexual aspect of human drives. With this "superstructure" eliminated, what remained was "a method for identifying the reaction of men to the realities of life" (KARDINER 1939:407). Kardiner grasped the fact that the source of personality differences must be sought in a much broader spectrum of conditioning factors than Freud had envisioned. In a sense, Freud's analytic scheme had concentrated only on those aspects of childhood experience which permitted him to identify the processes of gratification, frustration, and discipline relevant to the typical personality of Euro-American man. In different cultures, varieties of frustration, gratification, and discipline, unknown to Freud, would produce personalities having little in common with those familiar to psychoanalysts from their clinical practice. All this had been apparent to the psychologically oriented anthropologists with whom Kardiner had come in contact. But Kardiner now went beyond their documentation of the plasticity of institutions and personalities and attempted to create a theory involving testable hypotheses concerning the relationship between institutional matrix and personality.

Postulating the existence of a "basic personality structure" typical of the members of a given society, he divided the institutional aspects of culture into two categories—primary and secondary. Primary institutions were those responsible for forming the basic personality structure. On analogy with Freudian doctrine, these institutions were the ones most directly concerned with disciplining, gratifying, and inhibiting the infant and young child. However, Kardiner did not produce a fixed list of primary institutions. He believed that the relevant disciplines were administered in different institutional forms from one culture to the next. In general, the indicated research focus is upon family organization, in-group formation, feeding, weaning, care or neglect of children, sexual training, and subsistence patterns. "A primary institution is one which is older, more stable, and less likely to be interfered with by vicissitudes of climate or economy" (*ibid.*:471).

Secondary institutions are those which "satisfy the needs and tensions created by the primary or fixed ones" (*ibid.*:476). Among the secondary institutions Kardiner gave greatest prominence to "taboo systems, religion, rituals, folktales and techniques of thinking" (*ibid.* 471). Between the primary and secondary institutions Kardiner interposed the basic personality structure. Fashioned by the childhood disciplines, the basic personality in turn expressed itself in the group's ideologies, in emotional and cognitive orientation to life and death.

According to Kardiner, it was Freud's *The Future of an Illusion* (1928) which contained the most powerful suggestion for adapting psychoanalytic theory to psychocultural analysis. During his consideration of the illusions which constitute the core of religious phenomena, Freud detected a correspondence between the methods men use to approach, communicate with, and control their deities and the experience which they have had with their parents. The Judeo-Christian God was thus simply the projected image of Western man's stern, patriarchical father. As Kardiner put it, Freud was on the brink of a new technique.

> For the first time, Freud describes here the origin of what may be called a *projective system,* that is to say, a system for structuring the outer world and one's relation to it in accordance with a pattern laid down in an earlier experience during ontogenesis. This is a powerful idea and one with many uses [KARDINER and PREBLE 1961:236].

It should be kept in mind, however, that Roheim had already made similar suggestions in his study of Australian totemism (1925) and that in all essentials Malinowski's critique of the Oedipus theory had envisioned precisely the role which Kardiner was now about to assign to cultural variables. According to Malinowski:

> In that full version of my psycho-analytic results I shall be able to show that in the social life, as well as in the folk-lore, of these natives their specific repressions manifest themselves unmistakably. Whenever the passions, kept normally within traditional bounds by rigid taboos, customs and legal penalties, break through in crime, perversion, aberration, or in one of those dramatic occurrences which shake from time to time the hum-drum life of a savage community—then these passions reveal the matriarchal hatred of the maternal uncle or the incestuous wishes toward the sister. The folk-lore of these Melanesians also mirrors the Matrilineal Complex. The examination of myth, fairy tales and legend, as well as of magic, will show . . . the repressed hatred against the maternal uncle, ordinarily masked by conventional reverence . . . [MALINOWSKI 1923:331].

Kardiner's contribution was to remove Freud's theories further from their culture-bound Viennese-European matrix and enlarge the scope of the basic experiences which have projective consequences. Using the Freudian mechanisms of repression, substitution, and symbolization, he proposed to trace the infantile reactions into the individual's psyche, and out again onto a widened projective screen which included legends, myths, and ceremonial as well as religious doctrine.

SIGNIFICANCE OF KARDINER'S CONTRIBUTION

The great promise of neo-Freudian schemes like Kardiner's is that they embody one of the few suggestions which have ever been made to bring the subtleties of specific magico-religious practices and beliefs within the compass of determinist explanations. We should pause to note that this task has baffled the ingenuity of some of the greatest figures in the social sciences. To achieve a causal explanation of the apparently fortuitous minutiae of magico-religious beliefs and practices was precisely the kind of accomplishment which the historical particularists had regarded as forever unattainable except through the infinite regress of diffusion. Although still only in its most incipient phases, neo-Freudian analysis must be recognized as having the potential of achieving a great advance toward the perfection of the historical-determinist program. It promises to go far beyond the areas blocked out by traditional Marxian theory, and it certainly renders obsolete attempts by Durkheim, Kroeber, Radcliffe-Brown, and White to fight off "psychological reductionism."

In actual practice, of course, no culturologists or superorganicists have been capable of a completely "superorganic" or "culturological" approach. But the psychological principles upon which they depended entered through the back door, so to speak, and were poorly elaborated. Marx and Engels, for example, accorded magico-religious phenomena a homeostatic psychofunctional role in the social system, as suggested in the phrase, "religion is the opiate of the masses." But they had little insight into how the distinctive characteristics of puberty rites, totem designs, myths of winged serpents, etc., might be related to the material conditions of social life. As for Morgan, he despaired of any scientific explanation. Like Freud's predecessors among psychologists, Morgan was prepared to cope only with "sane" ideas. Dreams and religion are irrational, and hence the rational intellect can scarcely aspire to an understanding of them:

> Religion deals so largely with the imaginative and emotional nature, and consequently with such uncertain elements of knowledge, that all primitive religions are grotesque and to some extent unintelligible [MORGAN 1877:5].

To be sure, many of Morgan's contemporaries including Spencer, Tylor, Lang, and Bastian were prepared to offer explanations of recurrent religious phenomena on the basis of "elementary ideas" and common exposure to recurrent natural phenomena (dreams, death, mirror reflections). None of them, however, made noteworthy progress toward the explanation of variable magico-religious content. The same may be said of Frazer, Durkheim, and the British structural-functionalists, all of whom made suggestions as to how to explain the generalities of magico-religious systems, but remained baffled by the problems of the concrete instance.

Kardiner, with the aid of his anthropological collaborators, now attempted to tackle such questions as why female ghosts are unimportant among the Tanala, why the Marquesans believed that certain women could enlist the spirits of dead men called "fanaua" to injure other women but not men, and why the Alorese make slipshod spirit effigies which they use in a perfunctory fashion and then throw away. The answers to such questions lay in the peculiar patterns of childhood disciplines embodied in the primary institutions. For example, the Alorese failure to elaborate religious art was said to be associated with their low expectation of beneficent rewards from supernatural sources: this apathetic attitude toward the supernatural was in turn traced to the relationship between Alorese children and their mothers. The overall treatment of children in Alor was characterized as one of neglect and inconsistency, the basic pattern for which was set by the way Alorese mothers left their children behind in the village while they spent long hours at work in their subsistence gardens.

KARDINER'S MODEL BOTH HOMEOSTATIC AND EVOLUTIONARY

The logical nature of the propositions advanced by Kardiner and his collaborators represent an advance over the equivocation of the Gorer-Mead-Bateson school. Kardiner's scheme provided for both homeostatic and evolutionary cause and effect relations. On the one hand, as we have seen, primary institutions are said to be older and more stable than the secondary ones. This means that in an evolutionary context, the occurrence of certain primary institutions makes the occurrence of certain secondary institutions more probable. The functional reason for this is revealed by an implicit concept of homeostasis in which the mechanism of projection is needed to maintain the typical individual personality in a condition of relative mental well-being. Kardiner specifically rejected the belief of "the extreme relativists who hold that in social patterning anything goes." A penalty must be paid for "bad social patterning" which sooner or later places the entire culture "in jeopardy" (KARDINER and PREBLE 1961:245). Some institutions promote cooperation; others stimulate rage and anxiety. "The success or failure of a society depends on a balance in favor of the former" (*ibid.*). Earlier Kardiner wrote that "secondary institutions must satisfy the needs and tensions created by the primary or fixed ones" (1939:476). If this is the case, then it should be possible within a given culture to show how needs and tensions fluctuate within tolerable limits set by the feedbacks and safety valves of the secondary institutions.

METHODOLOGICAL PROBLEMS

Kardiner and his collaborators attempted to improve the intersubjectivity of their psychocultural analysis. They were painfully aware of the gaps in the ethnographic accounts rendered by anthropologists whose fieldwork had not been planned to feed information into the psychodynamic scheme. To overcome this difficulty, Kardiner obtained the cooperation of Cora DuBois, who set out in 1937 for Alor in the Dutch East Indies in order to gather a corpus of appropriate material. DuBois returned in 1939 with a set of Rorschach test protocols, children's drawings, and most importantly, eight extensive life histories, emphasizing childhood experiences, emotional effect, and dream life. Kardiner then used the interview materials to construct a picture of the Alorese basic personality. At the same time, the drawings and Rorschachs were given to a specialist who performed independent analyses. The conclusions of DuBois, Kardiner, and Emil Oberholzer turned out to be strikingly similar with respect to the main features of Alorese personality. Each analyst independently stressed the shallowness of Alorese emotional life, a prevailing insecurity, suspiciousness, indifference, and apathy. Although this procedure obviously represented a methodological advance as far as the description of Alorese personality was concerned (provided that DuBois' informants were representative), the whole elaborate procedure did little to advance the credibility of the psychodynamic analysis which was to have been Kardiner's crowning contribution.

Kardiner concluded that the main factor in the etiology of the observed basic personality structure was the maternal neglect experienced by the Alorese infant. (Although maternal neglect corresponded to his previous definition of a primary institution, the fact that the Alorese did not formally recognize such a pattern seemed to Kardiner to remove it from institutional status.) But as in all of the other neo-Freudian psychocultural analyses, the linking up of childhood patterns with adult character and cultural forms can be achieved in several alternate ways. Apathy, as DuBois herself pointed out, might be produced by disease. In other instances, similar syndromes have been associated with the suspension of warfare and other contact effects. Furthermore, many cultures practice the kind of division of labor which lies at the basis of Alorese maternal neglect; yet turning the child over to relatives while the mother works in her garden is certainly not uniformly productive of the psychological constellation emphasized for the Alorese. In the Alorese case, therefore, we are left, once again, with an ingenious but highly speculative psychoanalytic tour de force.

The demonstration of the validity of the two varieties of functionalist relation with which Kardiner was involved requires certain kinds of data which he and his group were unable or unwilling to take into consideration. For the homeostatic and safety-valve effects of his secondary institutions, short-run fluctuations in group tensions would have had to be related to fluctuations in the intensity or frequency of the projective constellations. For the long-run evolutionary causal relation between primary and secondary institutions, parallel cases subject to statistical control would have had to be amassed so that correlation between one and the other could be demonstrated. Although Kardiner's seminar concerned itself with several different cultures, the comparative study of parallel cases was not achieved. As in Mead's approach, each of the cases involved a different set of primary and secondary institutions.

MAJOR DEFECT OF KARDINER'S SCHEME

Kardiner's clinically based acceptance of the need for clear cut etiological statements places him in the mainstream of the culture and personality movement. But we can scarcely credit his group with a uniquely satisfactory contribution to the theory of culture and personality. When Mead (1959c:1514) noted that "the major theoretical lines for the study of personality and culture . . . had already been worked out . . ." before Kardiner's seminar began to meet, she was on firm historical footing. The rage into which Kardiner flew at this remark is not justified by the list of accomplishments that he credited to his group and to none other:

> In any case, I request that Mead expose me, not by decree or innuendo, but by documentation. This will require finding a technique (meaning a procedure, based on demonstrable principles, not an ideology, or intention of finding a procedure) that was in existence before 1938 and that could perform the following: derive the personality formation specific to each culture without the aid of the libido theory; demonstrate the relation of this personality to the adaptational problems of the community as a whole; demonstrate the relation of the products of fantasy to this personality; demonstrate the relation of child-rearing practices to the development of affectivity; demonstrate the relation of this latter development to the devices the society has for maintaining . . . social balance . . . [KARDINER 1959:1728].

Had Kardiner actually succeeded in accomplishing all that he here claims as *fait accompli,* one would be obliged to agree with him. But the fact is, his actual achievement was considerably less impressive.

In evaluating Kardiner's contribution we must acknowledge the large defect that his scheme shared with all other psychocultural systems of causality. Kardiner himself, much to his credit, was perfectly aware of this problem and made no attempt to minimize it. The rub is that his scheme could not explain the existence of the primary institutions. These were simply the givens from which basic personality might be predicted but whose origin was inaccessible to psychodynamic techniques:

> . . . psychology can cast no light whatsoever without the aid of history on how these primary institutions took their final forms. So far as we know, no satisfactory explanations have ever been made of primary institutions [KARDINER 1939:471].

This admission betrays the influence of historical particularism passed on to Kardiner through his anthropological collaborators. There is an immense irony in the way the prevailing hostility to diachronic theory obscured from Kardiner's view the possibility of linking his formulations with those of cultural materialism and historical determinism. The domain of cultural phenomena for which he was prepared to offer causal explanations was precisely the most intractable from the point of view of long-range diachronic theory. Contrary to his impressions, garnered from the anthropologists who had turned to culture and personality as a substitute for diachronic interests, excellent hypotheses were available for explaining the origins of the main features of relatively stable techno-environmental, techno-economic, and social systems implicit in his concept of "primary institutions." Indeed, the grand strategy of psychocultural analysis called for giving priority to the examination of the effects upon personality of those categories of the techno-environmental and techno-economic order for which reasonable diachronic hypotheses were already available. Unfortunately, Kardiner could not surmount the barriers which the negativism of the period had erected between him and such an optimal program. Nor does all the blame fall upon the members of the culture and personality school. The uniting of psychodynamic theory and historical determinism has also been made difficult by an overreaction among neo-evolutionists to anything smacking of psychocultural analysis. It will probably take a long time before the interests of the two viewpoints will assume their proper mutually supportive roles.

ERIK ERIKSON'S NEO-FREUDIAN SYSTEM

Kardiner's adaptation of psychoanalytic theory to the task of psychocultural analysis appears to be merely the best formulated of several convergent neo-Freudian approaches which were being tried during the thirties and forties. Somewhat closer to the Freudian model was the work of the psychoanalyst Erik Erikson.

Elaborating on Freud's three-stage ontogeny, Erikson developed a theory of infantile sexuality in which various "organ modes" were seen as modifying the child's progress through the oral, anal, and genital "stages." These modes are "incorporative" (two phases), "retentive," "eliminative," and "intrusive." In this fashion Erikson sought to utilize a much broader spectrum of childhood experience than was allowed for in Freud's three-stage scheme. Thus, "retention," which Freud associated with anal fixation, may in Erikson's scheme arise with respect to oral, anal, and genital functions. In general, Erikson's psychodynamic was less formal than Kardiner's, although there was much in common between the two:

> . . . thus a primitive culture seems to do three things: it gives specific meanings to early bodily and interpersonal experience so as to create the right combination of organ modes and the proper emphasis on social modalities; it carefully and systematically channelizes throughout the intricate pattern of its daily life the energies thus provoked and deflected; and it gives consistent supernatural meaning to the infantile anxieties which it has exploited by such provocation [ERIKSON 1950:160].

When applied to the Sioux and Yurok, this psychocultural approach produced many ingenious connections between stages of growth, type of "organ modes," and adult personality and cultural institutions. The Yurok, for example, are stingy, suspicious, and compulsively dedicated to the amassment of wealth. Prayers and daydreams, accompanied by tearful entreaties, center on getting rich. Erikson related these traits to the retentive mode of the oral stage. The Yurok seem to have no special phobic or pleasurable focus on feces, but they do suffer an abrupt weaning at about the time of the "biting" phase of orality. Erikson's Sioux and Yurok interpretations have certainly failed to convince psychoanalysts of somewhat variant persuasions. Kardiner says that he makes a "feeble case for the Sioux and none at all for the Yurok" (KARDINER and PREBLE 1961:243). Here we may simply draw attention to the vague functionalist framework and its typical inability to deal with the origin of the observed variations in training patterns.

THE CASE OF THE JAPANESE SPHINCTER

Among similar amorphous neo-Freudian synchronic approaches we must now take note of two famous attempts to relate infant training institutions to adult personality and cultural institutions. Both of these involve a group centering on Mead, Benedict, and

Geoffrey Gorer, and both grew out of hot- and cold-war pressures to heighten the combatants' knowledge of themselves and each other.

The first was concerned with the relationship between toilet training and the allegedly compulsive personality of the Japanese as embodied in both national character and cultural institutions. During the height of the Second World War Geoffrey Gorer invoked a toilet-training hypothesis to account for the ". . . contrast between the all-pervasive gentleness of Japanese life in Japan, which has charmed nearly every visitor, and the overwhelming brutality and sadism of the Japanese at war" (GORER 1943, quoted in BARNOUW 1963:121). According to Gorer this brutality was associated with "severe early cleanliness training" which created a repressed rage in Japanese infants because they are obliged to control their sphincters before the appropriate muscular and intellectual development has been acquired. Weston La Barre (1945) had independently been led to the same conclusion. He called the Japanese "the most compulsive people in the world ethnographic museum" (quoted in BARNOUW 1963:122) and like Gorer, emphasized the severity of toilet training. In Ruth Benedict's *The Chrysanthemum and the Sword* (1946:259) there is a similar affirmation of the strictness of Japanese toilet training, but its effects are not interpreted in psychoanalytic terms. Instead, the pattern is seen merely as one of the facets of the Japanese concern for neatness and orderliness.

All of these theories about Japanese national character and toilet training were made without benefit of field research. After the war, when such research was undertaken, it quickly became apparent that a serious error had been committed with respect to the nature of Japanese toilet behavior. Studies by Edward and Margaret Norbeck (1956), B. Lanham (1956), and Douglas Haring (1956) all indicated that Japanese children were not subject to any egregiously severe threats or punishments. Moreover, the rapidity with which the Japanese adapted to their defeat, accepted American influence, changed many basic patterns of behavior, and took the lead in the peace movement in the Orient scarcely seems to confirm the wartime portraits which emphasized their frustration and their brutality.

THE CASE OF THE SWADDLED RUSSIANS

Another notable attempt to achieve a psychocultural analysis of a modern nation state in neo-Freudian terms was embodied in Gorer and Rickman's (1949) study of Russian national character. Gorer has indicated that he owed a debt to Margaret Mead for the suggestion that Russian national character could best be understood in relationship to the long and severely restricting form of infant swaddling allegedly practiced by the Great Russians (*ibid.*:211). This case is very informative because it brings into sharp focus just what kind of functional statements can be expected in the absence of a cause and effect framework. According to Gorer, swaddling was associated with a kind of manic-depressive personality corresponding to the alternating constraint and freedom experienced by the Russian infant, his pent-up rage while swaddled, his sudden freedom when the swaddling bandages are removed. The rage is directed toward a diffuse object since the infant is handled in a very impersonal way and hence never gets a good "fix" on its tormenters. This rage gives rise to guilt, but once again, the emotion is not fixed on any specific set of persons. Gorer attempted to show that such phenomena as the Bolshevik revolution, the Stalin purge trials, the confessions of guilt at these trials, and many other events of recent Soviet history were "related" to the generalized rage and guilt feelings associated with swaddling. He even went so far as to suggest that the Russian interest in the expressiveness of eyes (think of how the song "Dark Eyes" evokes a characteristic Russian feeling) stemmed from the fact that the restriction of the other parts of its body forced the Russian child to depend upon vision for his main contact with the world.

Unfortunately, Gorer had no firm evidence concerning the extensiveness of swaddling. Indeed, the intellectuals who confessed their guilt at Stalin's purge trials were probably not swaddled. The oppressive and fear-haunted ambience of the Stalin period can be found in association with dictatorships from Ghana to Guatemala, and the alleged compatibility between Russian national character and the despotism of the Stalin period is contradicted by the very fact of the Russian Revolution. To attribute the uprising against Tsarist despotism to rage induced by swaddling bandages is to miss the whole point of recent European history. Stalin's tyranny was founded on the corpses of his enemies. Only by filling the Siberian camps with millions of nonconformists and by relentlessly rooting out all vestiges of political opposition did Stalin manage to impose his will on his countrymen. The notion that the mass of Russians were somehow being psychologically fulfilled by the terror of the Stalinist period is absolutely without basis in fact.

Follow-up studies on the character of Russian exiles—groups comparable to those interviewed by Gorer—have drawn conclusions quite opposite to those indicated by the swaddling hypotheses. A high degree of incongruence has been found between the central personality modes of the peasants and workers and the political behavior of the governing clique (INKELES *et al.* 1961). Moreover, Gorer's analysis leaves one absolutely at a loss to explain the whole process of de-Stalinization and the rapidity with which the monolithic structure of the Stalinist apparatus, so essential to his point, suddenly gave way to a more flexible if not yet "open" system.

As an application of Freudian insights into political processes, Gorer's essay is unacceptable. For example, nothing could have been less prophetic concerning the directions of Soviet foreign policy than his comments on the future of the empire which Stalin had put together in Eastern Europe:

> Whatever their conscious intentions may be, it would appear that the Soviet elites find it psychologically impossible to permit their satellites relative independence, because it is a state they cannot envisage. The moment the balance is tipped to the slightest measurable degree from complete equality, they seem to fear that they will become completely subordinate [GORER and RICKMAN 1949:179].

GORER'S DISCLAIMER OF CAUSALITY

While assiduously pursuing the relationship between swaddling and Russian national character, even to the extent of including a twenty-five-page historical appendix entitled "A Note on the Development of the Swaddling Hypotheses," Gorer sought to protect himself from the consequences of his analysis by insisting that he was not attributing any causal efficacy to swaddling.

> It is the argument of this study that the situation outlined in the preceding paragraphs is *one* of the major determinants in the development of the character of adult Great Russians.
>
> It is *not* the argument of this study that the Russian manner of swaddling their children produces the Russian character, and it is not intended to imply that the Russian character would be changed or modified if some other technique of infant training were adopted [*ibid.*:128–29].

A careful reading of this disclaimer does not improve its intelligibility. Swaddling is said to be one of the *major* determinants of Great Russian character in one sentence, while in the next, it is said not to be *any kind* of determinant. Gorer goes on to stress what might be called the heuristic value of the swaddling hypothesis and likens it to a "thread which led through the labyrinth of the apparent contradictions of

Russian adult behavior." But one is hard pressed to understand the epistemological nature of this "thread." What kind of hypothesis is it which does not involve a correlation of some degree of quantity or quality?

MEAD'S DEFENSE OF GORER

In Gorer's defense, Mead has enlarged at length on Gorer's disclaimer, denying that anyone had suggested that Russian national character was attributable to the swaddling practice. Rather than saying that "swaddling makes Russians," Gorer was actually affirming something else:

> From an analysis of the way Russians swaddle infants, it is possible to build a model of Russian character formation which enables us to relate what we know about human behavior and what we know about Russian culture in such a way that Russian behavior becomes more understandable [MEAD 1954:401-2].

According to Mead, this kind of analysis must be clearly separated from the kind of psychodynamic relationships which Kardiner had sought to establish between childhood disciplines and adult character. Kardiner's brand of psychoanalytic extrapolation, she insisted, was rejected by the majority of anthropologists. Gorer was not saying that "swaddling per se by members of any culture will have definite predictable effects of the same sort on all infants, regardless of their culture" (*ibid.*:398). No claim was being made that "swaddling was essential in the Russian pattern" (*ibid.*:403). Given the facts of Russian culture and Russian character, it can be shown that swaddling is one of the techniques by which "Russians become Russians." She admits that there are many other techniques by which the same results might be obtained in different cultures. The Russians themselves might give up swaddling and still maintain the same personality.

All of this would appear to add up to a unique form of scientific statement. The relationship between swaddling and the Russian character is crucial for an understanding of that character, yet there is no reason to suppose that they are causally related in the sense that one makes the other more probable. The vagueness of a statement in which a "major" variable is held to be neither dependent nor independent, neither cause nor effect, neither sufficient nor necessary, is brought out in an additional comment by Mead in which there is a lapse back into a more familiar idiom:

> It is the combination of an unusually confining version of a widespread practice, the age of the child which is thus confined, and an adult insistence on the need to protect the child from itself—the duration and type of swaddling—which are *assumed* to have distinctive *effects* in the formation of Russian character [*ibid.*:402, italics added].

With this statement, the entire argument is returned to its initial form, and the lack of evidence for the "assumed" "effects" once more summons forth its full measure of amazement.

ANTHROPOLOGISTS ARE NOT THERAPISTS

The meeting of anthropology and psychoanalysis has produced a rich harvest of ingenious functional hypotheses in which psychological mechanisms can be seen as intermediating the connection between disparate parts of culture. Psychoanalysis, however, had little to offer cultural anthropology by way of scientific methodology. In this respect the meeting of the two disciplines tended to reinforce the inherent tendencies toward uncontrolled, speculative, and histrionic generalizations which each in its own sphere had cultivated as part of its professional license. The anthropologist carrying out a psychocultural analysis resembled the psychoanalyst whose attempt to identify the basic personality structure of his patient remains largely interpretive and immune to normal verification procedures. In a sense, what the great figures in the formative phases of the culture and personality movement were asking us to do was to trust them as we would trust an analyst, not for the demonstrated truth of any particular item, but for the accumulating evidence of coherence in a believable pattern. Although such faith is essential to psychoanalytic therapy in which it scarcely matters whether childhood events of particular kinds did or did not take place as long as both analyst and patient are convinced that they did, the separation of myth from concrete event is the highest goal of all disciplines which concern themselves with human history.

Culture and Personality: New Directions

17

Shortly after the end of the Second World War, the culture and personality movement was penetrated by an entirely new kind of psychological influence emanating from the development within experimental psychology of neobahaviorist learning theories under the leadership of Clark Hull and, to a lesser extent, B. F. Skinner. The most significant feature of learning theory in the present context is that it embodies a vast eipistemological and methodological reform, the outcome of a deliberate attempt by operationally minded psychologists to raise the standards of intersubjectivity and verifiability. It is through the intermediation of culture and personality studies that this wave of scientism in psychology is now being passed into the entire field of cultural anthropology. Thus in a remarkable turnabout, the adoption of the basic scientific premise of neobehaviorism by social psychologists and cultural anthropologists has meant that culture and personality studies once representative of the most broadly humanistic methods of anthropology have emerged in the last decade as paragons of methodological purity. It is in this area that some of the most sophisticated anthropological research is now being carried out. By the 1960's the methodological and epistemological reforms in the culture and personality movement spreading throughout the entire field of cultural anthropology were threatening to bring about a final rupture of the humanist and scientific traditions.

JOHN WHITING

The main impetus for the revolution in the methodology of the culture and personality movement derives from the work of John Whiting and his coworkers. In this group several lines of development converge, foremost among which are the neo-Freudian, as transmitted through Kardiner; learning theory, through the influence of Hull; and the statistical version of the comparative method, as outlined by Tylor and further perfected through the development of the Human Relations Area Files under George Murdock. In essence, Whiting has carried the work of Kardiner's seminar into its cross-cultural phase and produced the first statistically valid proofs of the feasibility of explaining the details of ideological patterns through a modified version of Kardiner's causal chain. In Whiting and Child's (1953) version this chain runs:

> Maintenance Systems ⟶ Child Training Practices ⟶ Personality Variables ⟶ Projective Systems.

Whiting and Child's "maintenance systems" refers to the entire economic, political, and social organization. This is scarcely an improvement over the huge bundle tied up in Kardiner's "primary institutions." It is noteworthy, however, that specific child-rearing practices have been separated from the rest of the primary institutions. The way is thus prepared for the systematic exploration of the conditions which govern the occurrence of various kinds of child-training procedures, a problem which Kardiner had regarded as insoluble. Using George Murdock's world ethnographic sample or other specially assembled samples, Whiting has systematically explored the basic premise of the neo-Freudian anthropologists, namely that personality serves as a mediator between the maintenance and projective systems. In an overview, Whiting (1961) has brought together an impressive compilation of the most successful hypotheses which have been subject to cross-cultural validation.

One of the most impressive achievements of the Whiting group is their demonstration of the theoretical productivity of the personality concept. Although some of their correlations are suggested by fairly obvious functional chains, which probably could be short-circuited directly from child training to adult practice, others require complicated causal sequences within the personality matrix before the logic of the relationship becomes clear. An example of the former is the correlation between harsh parental treatment of children and the belief that the spirit world is harsh and aggressive. (One might predict such a correlation on the basis of some very simple associational or behavioral generalization: subject to harsh treatment, the child and adult look upon the world in general, including its spirits, as a harsh place in which to live.)

On the other hand, there is the correlation between the length of time during which an infant sleeps with his mother and the occurrence of male initiation rites (WHITING, KLUCKHOHN, and ANTHONY, 1958). This relationship flows easily, if at all, only from the corpus of theory specifically associated with neo-Freudian psychology. In terms of psychological principles, the apparently esoteric connection is demanded by several different hypotheses. One is that the sleeping arrangement intensifies the Oedipal rivalry between father and son and that the puberty rites are a means of asserting social control over the son's hostility. Another is that the sleeping arrangement produces a strong identification between son and mother which must be broken if maleness is to be achieved. A more culturological hypothesis would predict puberty rites as a necessary antidote to the mother's overprotection.

It must be counted a triumph of psychological theory that the negative relationship between couvade and male initiation rites appears to be governed by a similar set of factors. Societies with exclusive mother-child sleeping patterns and patrilocal residence have the initiation rites, while those with similar sleeping arrangements but matrilocal residence tend to have the couvade. This in turn appears to be related to inhibition versus expression of cross-sex identification.

Along similar lines, a correlation has been established between prolonged postpartum sexual taboos and male initiation rites, the explanation being that under such conditions the male child is subject to incestuous seductive temptations which must be controlled at puberty. Other studies inspired by these mixed varieties of psychodynamic and learning-theory hypotheses have related the indulgence of infants to absence of fearful ghosts during funerals; early weaning to the belief that a sick person is responsible for his own illness; severe oral training to the belief that diseases can be cured by eating and drinking; and severe sexual discipline to the belief in sorcery.

Victor Barnouw (1963:356) has noted that "the complexity of the Whiting and Child demonstration sometimes takes on the dimensions of a Rube Goldberg machine," but it is precisely this complexity which carries the approach beyond ordinary culturological perspectives.

DEFENSE OF THE STATISTICAL APPROACH

The accomplishments of this group are somewhat less impressive when one takes into consideration the fact that many of their hypotheses appear to be *post hoc*. That is, the statistical approach permits a certain amount of blind searching for correlations. When these are found, an elaborate causal chain is then set up to serve as the explanation; it is not unusual for several such "Rube Goldberg" explanations to be proposed at the same time without being able to discern which is the correct one. It should also be kept in mind that many hypotheses set up in conformity with the psychological principles under discussion turn out not to be confirmed by the statistical runs. Since it is usually only the successful runs which get written up, the approach has what one might call a "good press." Despite these and other drawbacks, the cross-cultural survey procedure must be reckoned as a major advance in the methodology of the culture and personality movement. Although the data which lies at the basis of the correlations suffers from the usual ethnographic defects, there are strong methodological reasons to believe that such errors can be overcome in a sufficiently large sample.

Donald Campbell (1961:346), a social psychologist who believes that the Whiting movement represents "one of the major events in the social sciences of the past twenty years," defends the use of such admittedly crude instruments as the Human Relations Area Files. Errors in the files, which result from inadequate ethnographies or other unsystematic sources, cannot be used to explain away the correlations. Such errors reduce rather than raise the level of association.

It is a fascinating lesson in the ephemerality of scientific styles to follow Campbell through his closely reasoned defense of Whiting's approach. The main line of resistance to Whiting's methods is precisely the same as that which the Boasians set up against Spencer, Frazer, Tylor, Morgan, *et al.* It is alleged that Whiting's type of survey deals only with fragments. Pieces of culture are wrenched out of context; noncomparables are compared. Unique situations are crammed into a set of inappropriate pigeonholes. The unity of the individual case is shattered, and accuracy is sacrificed for specious generalities. But these objections can no longer be invoked in the name of superior scientism. Despite its limitations, the statistical method is recognized as the only viable substitute for laboratory control. Errors are inevitable in any research procedure; laws are merely approximation; a few exceptions neither prove nor disprove a rule; all generalizations depend on the clause *ceteris paribus*—"other things being equal":

> The healthy infancy of the successful sciences seems to have been predicated upon the stimulating nourishment of crude but effective *ceteris paribus* laws. For example, the force fields of atomic nuclei extend in infinite distance in all directions. However, they decay so rapidly as a function of distance that they can be disregarded in the statement of many crude laws, such as those embodied in Archimedes' mechanics. Were this not so, were Archimedes to have had to limit himself to statements about each particular instance, then physics never could have developed. The critics of the generalizing social scientists are right in cautioning against claiming effective *ceteris paribus* laws when one hasn't got them, but pointing to the obvious idiosyncracy of every person, tribe, or swinging cathedral chandelier provides no *a priori* basis for rejecting the enterprise [*ibid.*:347].

It thus seems quite clear that full methodological initiative has been restored to the nomothetic tradition. The age of the computer will not be held back by the handful of exceptions with which the Boasians brought the machinery of social science to a grinding halt. For Lowie, one negative case out of a hundred meant the triumph of chaos; for the cross-cultural hypotheses in the Whiting manner, a dozen negative cases out of a hundred means the triumph of order.

> The abstractive-generalizing social scientist knows that in dealing with natural groups *ceteris* are not in fact *paribus*, and he therefore expects exceptions which represent the operation of many other laws which he as yet knows nothing of. Such exceptions are repeatedly found in the law-confirming scatter diagrams of biology and psychology. If the over-all significant relationship still persists when the specific errors are corrected and the new cases plotted, the exceptions are not invalidating [*ibid.*].

SOME QUALIFICATIONS

When all of the significant advances in recent culture and personality studies have been accorded the respect due to the hard work and ingenuity which has gone into them, we must take an additional step away from the canvas and ask ourselves just what it all adds up to in terms of a theory of culture. It will then be seen that the picture we have been studying is drastically incomplete. All of the neo-Freudian formulations assume the existence of particular varieties of technology, economics, and social organization. This limitation has not been especially painful in the context of mid-twentieth-century social science since the drift has been toward a permanent anesthesia on the question of cultural causality. The era of "middle-range" theory has grown accustomed to a truncated account of its origin, its significance, and its destiny. Many of the contributors to the culture and personality movement are fully aware of the failure of their specialty to answer the fundamental questions which were set before us in the eighteenth century. Others are more or less like the Emperor without his clothes —victims of a lack of controversy. No cultural determinist can doubt for a moment that Kardiner's primary institutions or Whiting and Child's "maintenance systems" are associated with specific modal personalities. Indeed, this guarantee is built in, since from a behaviorist and operationalist view of personality, the way people make their living, the number of wives they live with, the kinds of political controls they experience—all must have some sort of distinctive effect on the expectation that they will emit determined frequencies of specific responses which are not merely tautological consequences of the initial description. If personality is a measure of probability of verbal or nonverbal response, then every major cultural difference, and not only those associated with the Freudian disciplines, obviously must correlate with personality differences.

But such correlations, even when they are based on the most ingenious Rube Goldberg-Freudianisms and are predictable by *ad hoc* hypotheses, avoid the main arena of theoretical confrontation. Given a particular set of "maintenance," or "primary," institutions and their predictable psychocultural concomitants, what do we then know about the transformation probabilities of maintenance systems and their characterological projections? To speak in the analogy of cybernetics, given the feedback between basic institutions and basic personality, to what extent may this segment of the larger sociocultural network be regarded as an independent and self-sustaining circuit? Since evolution is as much a characteristic of the realm of sociocultural phenomena as it is of the biological realm, we cannot simply posit a steady state and shrug off the question of how and when the feedback loop is broken. This question looms all the more menacing to the euphoria of psychocultural enthusiasts when it is firmly understood that the feedback between basic culture and basic personality does not involve an eradication of nonconforming individuals and psychological complexes. It is a fundamental assumption of the culture and personality movement, and one which is firmly grounded in fact, that every culture has its deviants. These may be more or less numerous, depending one might suppose (the question has not really been studied) on particular constellations of basic conditioning parameters. But regardless of the relative frequency of deviance, everything we have learned about the "simpler" societies, and everything we have always known about our own, indicates that the spectrum of available types is very great. And furthermore, from the same sources of knowledge, it is perfectly obvious that each individual contains within himself resources, potentialities, inhibitions, and anxieties in multitudes and varieties far beyond the manifest content of actual, momentary existence.

There thus arises the fundamental question, the one which is most blatantly ignored throughout the history of the culture and personality movement: to what extent does the existence of a particular momentary feedback between basic institutions and basic personality limit the rate and direction of cultural evolution? For there remains, as a limiting case, the specter of an answer which declares, "every basic cultural change finds its own proper individual agents." That is, when the culturological forces, systematically ignored by the culture and personality school, impinge upon the basic institutions, then those individuals who have harbored in the remote recesses of their personalities the appropriate loves and hates come to the fore, or the deviants, banished to the margins of the system—the "noise" for which there had previously been no use—shunt off into a new circuit, where their behavior is apt to be treated by the functionally minded anthropologist as the very music of the spheres.

Surely, it is wrong to suppose that every modal personality type is equally vulnerable to every wind of change. On the other hand, those who imply that a particular momentary configuration stands for all time as a limitation of the possibilities of basic institutional evolution are sadly in error. The contrary evidence is piled all around us in monumental quantities. The convergence of widely different cultures toward similar evolutionary novelties is the prime source of such evidence. Whatever kinds of people were needed to invent and maintain bifurcate merging kinship terminologies, unilineal descent groups, age grades, slash and burn agriculture, band organization, social stratification, classes, castes, and feudalism, "Yankee ingenuity," capitalism and colonialism, and one party rule, they were obviously available over vast stretches of space and time.

And it is not only from such generalized evolutionary events that we are led to minimize the lag effect of basic personality. Another approach to the same subject is to demand that time perspective be supplied to all psychocultural analyses. We then bear witness to the extraordinary mutability of national character in relation to the evolution of sociopolitical systems. We see the spectacle of enemies become friends and friends become enemies. We see the Mozart-loving Germans transfigured into the beasts of Buchenwald, the authoritarian Japanese become the democrats of Asia, meek Balinese boys joining death squads, American troops turning over Vietcong for torture, the staid Britishers dressed in mini-skirts, the racially democratic Portuguese in league with South African apartheid, promiscuous South Sea Islanders turned Protestant prudes, and Apollonian Pueblo Indians who have become the drunken wards of their former enemies. All this was said a long time ago and with much greater authority:

> Nothing is generally more false and ridiculous than the portraits drawn to represent the characters of different nations. Some paint their own nation after the particular society they frequent, and consequently represent the people as gloomy or gay, dull or witty. . . . Others copy what a thousand writers have said before them; they have never examined the changes necessarily produced in the character of a people, by those which happen in the administration, and the alteration of manners. It has been said, that the French are gay; and this will be repeated to eternity. They do not perceive, that the misfortunes of the times having obliged the princes to lay considerable taxes on the country people; the French nation cannot be gay, because the peasants, who alone compose two thirds of the nation, are in want, and want can never be gay: that even, in regard to the cities, the necessity, it is said, the police of Paris is under of defraying a part of the expence of the masquerades performed on holidays at St. Anthony's gate, is not a proof of the gaiety of the artists and the citizen; spies may contribute to the safety of Paris; but being carried too far, they diffuse a general diffidence through the minds of the people, that is absolutely incompatible with joy, on account of the ill use that may be made of them [HELVETIUS 1810:357; orig. 1748].

PERSONALITY AND HISTORY

The facts of sociocultural convergence and parallelism would work for, rather than against, the attribution of important causal efficacy to basic personality, only if it were maintained that the origin of such regularities resides in the personality configurations themselves. Thus we would have the hypothesis that a particular kind of personality is the necessary and sufficient condition for the occurrence of unilineal descent groups, swidden farming, colonialism, communism, etc. Few of the culture and personality specialists would wish to formulate so vulnerable a proposition. For at the end of this chimeric rainbow there floats a cloud of pure idealism. One can very well understand how appropriate personality types must predominate or come to the fore when basic institutional transformations occur, but it is impossible to understand how personality changes would alone suffice for such transformations. Human personalities, like ideas, are potentially infinite in variety. If one wishes to start the causal chain from personality type and work back toward basic institutions, there shall never be an explanation of why specific cultures manifest regular differences and similarities.

FREUD AND MATERIALISM

The culture and personality movement could scarcely accept the greatness of Freud and at the same time unambiguously proclaim that personality configurations provide the key to the understanding of history. The reason why Freud ranks with Darwin and Marx is that he was the greatest single influence in bringing the phenomena of the human mind within the compass of historical determinism. It was his genius which led the way toward our comprehension of the fact that even the most intimate details of our dreams and wishes—even the dreams and wishes of madmen—are rooted in the intelligible material wants and processes of human childhood. These childhood conditions he derived in turn from the distinctive material components of the human, species-given, biophysical endowment. The entire idiom of the Freudian synthesis with its instinctual drives, its ontogenetic recapitulations, its energy flows and its energy blockages, and its epiphenomenal symptoms and subterfuges is a physicalist and materialist tour de force. But Freud's system could only generate the universals of culture and a few crude stages of a unilinear evolution. Specific cultural differences and similarities were beyond his grasp and interests.

It is also true as we have seen that the neo-Freudians purged Freud of his historical determinism. Despite these modifications, it is impossible to remain a Freudian in any significant sense and adopt an unambiguously idealist position. For if there is one aspect of Freud which cannot be dispensed with, it is the fact that the human personality is not free to shape itself into any form or substance to which an individual may take a fancy. The minimal definition of Freudian theory drives us back ineluctably to the determining conditions of childhood.

The neo-Freudian may yet seek to avoid the materialist option: he may attribute the origin of childhood disciplines to the whim and fancy of some adult generation. To save for himself a determinist image, he may even stop arbitrarily short of an infinite regress somewhere along the route pioneered by the *Kulturwissenschaften.* He would then emerge as an historical particularist suffering from the typical inability to cope with the regularities of cultural evolution.

To sum up: out of the whim and fancy of early or late weaning, postpartum taboos, crawling, creeping or frogging, one cannot construct a theory of history. Let no one minimize the possible historical importance of swaddling or toilet training; but to the extent that these are significant dimensions of the historical process, to that extent they must be linked with other regular features of sociocultural systems. If they are not so linked, if they do not turn out to be articulated with the techno-economic and techno-environmental conditions of sociocultural life, then we shall be left with the *reductio ad absurdum* that personality generates personality according to its idiosyncratic dispositions. Were human cultural systems infinitely divergent, such a view would be tolerable. But infinite divergence is the equivalent of unintelligible chaos, a condition which all previous experience of mankind denies as an apt description of man, culture, or any other segment of the universe.

CRUCIAL DETERMINANTS OF PERSONALITY

In granting the importance of the traditional Freudian or Freudian-inspired enculturation techniques—the anal, the oral, and genital disciplines—as intervening variables in cultural evolution and the maintenance of steady state circuits, we must avoid any implication that these are the most significant psychological factors either for evolutionary or homeostatic analysis. And this reservation might even have to be maintained if it proved to be psychoanalytically correct that the Freudian conditioning factors are crucially relevant to an understanding of *individual* health and disease. For it might very well be that for an understanding of cultural evolution, quite a different set of conditioning factors may have to be taken into consideration. For example, the role which television cartoons, nursery school routines, and children's toys play in the formation of the American basic personality structure might be more important for the homeostasis of the United States sociopolitical system and more diagnostic of historical processes than age of weaning and toilet training. The very fact that the feedbacks being explored by Whiting and his followers require such complicated circuitry may indicate that the more significant functional relations between personality and primary institutions are being neglected. The correlation between Max Weber's Protestant ethic and capitalism or David McClelland's (1961) "need for achievement" and industrial development, with proper readjustment of the causal arrows, need not invoke psychoanalytic mechanisms. There are obviously many other capitalist, industrial, and mass-society personality characteristics which are more easily explained in terms of learning theory than in terms of depth psychology. American children are taught by a system of rewards and punishments, embracing a sociocultural apparatus much larger than the nuclear family, to be aggressively competitive, to seek solace in consumption of commodities, to ignore death, and to fear old age. It is quite possible that the primary and high school experiences of the sort described by Jules Henry (1963) are more determinative of culturally significant personality than all of the Freudian factors put together. The same might be true of the kind of personality factors singled out by David Riesman (1950), Vance Packard, or other non-Freudian observers of the correlation between American anxieties and values and the basic economic and social institutions of mass society under corporate welfare capitalism. General Motors, the Pentagon, and Madison Avenue may have more effect on the vital circuitry of the historically and culturally significant American personality than the nuclear family with all its formal and informal child-training procedures. The significance of Oscar Lewis's (1966a) concept of "the culture of poverty" may also reside in a similar observation: poverty breeds a particular variety of personality configuration regardless of the culture in which it occurs. (Not to be confused with the point of view that poverty is merely a state of mind.) As Aberle (1961b:395) has noted:

> Much of the work on achievement and affiliation, as well as on other features of American child rearing by class and by time period can probably be ultimately related to the nature of the market system in the modern world.

An extension of the same ego-psychology emphasis to cross-cultural situations points to the possibility of major personality correlations to be found among villagers as opposed to band migrants; among swidden horticulturalists as compared with fixed field peasants; among redistributive systems of distribution as opposed to reciprocal systems; among hunters as opposed to gatherers; and among egalitarian societies as opposed to stratified societies.

BACKING INTO CULTURAL MATERIALISM

These fundamental sources of personality differences have not been completely neglected. Ralph Linton's (1937) contrast between the dry and wet rice-producing Tanala provided the basic clues for Kardiner's analysis of Tanala personality structure. Similarly, the Alorese subsistence requirements were seen to be the controlling factor in Alorese infant care. In both of these cases, however, the effect on infant experience was deemed decisive rather than any lifelong series of pressures and expectations as might be the case in market-induced configurations.

A similar observation is called for in connection with the studies carried out by Barry, Bacon, and Child (1959), in which it is shown by the Whiting cross-cultural survey method that where stable harvest surpluses are produced, there is a balance in the socialization process in favor of passive compliance as opposed to individualized assertiveness. The latter is in turn correlated with hunting modes of subsistence. The conclusion that "child training tends to be a suitable adaptation to subsistence economy" (*ibid.*:62) is a welcome confirmation of a somewhat peripheral but nonetheless important aspect of techno-economic determinism. It should not escape our notice however that there is a peculiar slant to the message before us. The study remains fixated on the issue of child training. But it is the adult personality—the product of the socialization process—with which psychocultural theory must come to grips. True enough, the authors of the study claim that their research avoids triviality because it indicates something about adult character:

> Pressures toward obedience and responsibility should tend to make children into the obedient and responsible adults who can best ensure the continuing welfare of a society with a high-accumulation economy, whose food supply must be protected and developed gradually throughout the year. Pressure toward self-reliance and achievement should shape children into the venturesome, independent adults who can take initiative in wresting food daily from nature, and thus ensure survival in societies with a low-accumulation economy [*ibid.*].

But it is a matter of considerable interest to inquire why the research strategy did not involve an attempt to correlate adult personality directly with subsistence practices and then to seek additional sources of the same characteristics in the childhood enculturation disciplines. This question takes us to the heart of the historical role of culture and personality studies in cultural anthropology. The practitioners of this specialty seem to be slowly backing into a position which they might profitably have occupied face-forward from the outset.

WHITING DISCOVERS CULTURAL MATERIALISM

Another example from Whiting's approach will help to make this clear. As a result of several independent studies, a massive set of correlations had been established, linking the following traits: exclusive mother-infant sleeping arrangements, prolonged postpartum sexual taboo, prolonged infant nursing, polygyny, patrilocality, and severe male puberty rites. In searching for a suitable general hypothesis, Whiting literally backed into the possibility that there might be a techno-environmental feedback which is strong enough to generate the entire complex. First, a possible link with climate was explored. This led to the discovery of a correlation between the complex in question and tropical climate. A final link was added when tropical climate was correlated in turn with Kwashiorkor, a disease associated with protein deficiency during infancy. The entire chain could now be read as follows: Protein deficient tropical diets place a premium on prolonged lactation for maintaining infant's protein intake during critical period. Interruption of lactation by demands of a second infant is prevented by prolonged sex taboo while mother nurses. The sex taboo places a premium on the second wife. The husband in the polygynous household sleeps separate from his wife. Hence, exclusive mother-infant sleeping arrangement is the by-product. Polygyny, in turn, also makes patrilocality more probable as the most convenient way to set up a composite household. Patrilocality, in turn, is correlated with patrilineality. With a strong patrilineal, patrilocal emphasis, boys who have spent a prolonged period with a nursing mother are subject to intense pressures to assure proper male role identity (*cf.* WHITING 1964).

I believe we are justified in a spirit of constructive criticism to point out that the strategy of Whiting's research is inferior to its tactics. Why start one's inquiries into personality correlates with exclusive mother-infant sleeping arrangements which turn out to be a mere appendage to the central causal chain? Why not *start* with Kwashiorkor, malaria, tuberculosis, trypanosomiasis, and other pathogenic conditions which we may confidently expect to be associated with both personality and institutional specialties? As A. F. C. Wallace (1961:291) has noted in a brilliant article concerned with tracing arctic hysteria (*pibloktoq*) to hypocalcemia, "The importance of the organic factors in psychopathology has been largely ignored by anthropological theory, which has emphasized psychological factors almost exclusively." But it is not simply anthropological psychopathology which has suffered from a failure to explore organic linkages, it is the entire field of culture and personality. Moreover, it is not merely a neglect of nutritional or epidemiological factors which needs to be pointed out, but a thoroughgoing neglect of the entire parameter of conditioning factors which relate personality to the human ecosystem, to the conditions of production, to the sources of metabolism, to the disease vectors, to climate, to population density, to human and infrahuman competitors and parasites—in short, to the techno-environmental and techno-economic conditions under which people acquire their adult patterns of behavior.

CLINICAL VERSUS ANTHROPOLOGICAL PRIORITIES

The study of personality and culture should be the handmaiden of diachronic functionalism, that is, of the study of cultural evolution and cultural causality. Instead it has all along labored on behalf of questions related to the etiology of individual psychological complexes. The "should be" carries more than a moralistic innuendo. The lack of interest in direct causal connections, sustained throughout life and not just during infancy, between major modes of subsistence and personality type is a consequence of the poverty of cultural theory throughout the Boasian period. The members of the culture and personality movement have themselves grown up in a milieu which has been hostile to diachronic theory. They have thus either been led to believe that the achievement of such theories has been proven impossible, or they have never recognized an obligation to consider the relevance of their work to such matters. But that obligation does exist insofar as a distinction is to be drawn between culture and personality studies which serve the interests of psychology and those which serve the interests of cultural anthropology. To serve the interests of psychology, we operate with the hypotheses which are suggested by the purged synchronic version of neo-Freudian psychoanalysis. We then achieve an understanding of how clinically significant complexes arise in the typical individual. To serve the interests of cultural anthropology, we must begin with the hypotheses suggested by a theory of cultural evolution, and we must follow out the consequences of these hypotheses upon the formation of feedback circuits between basic personality and the parameters designated as vital for an understanding of the behavior not of individuals but of sociocultural systems. The imperative in the "must" will be evident as soon as we seriously contemplate the very large possibility that the principles governing the formation of clinically significant syndromes may be quite devoid of significance in the determination of the main features of sociocultural evolution. We are left therefore with the unavoidable conclusion that here as elsewhere in the recent history of cultural anthropology, a research strategy has been pursued which is almost exactly the one least suited to the solution of the major questions before us.

French Structuralism

18

Émile Durkheim led French social science to its emancipation from biological reductionism. Like Boas in the United States, Durkheim founded a school of anthropology to which at mid-century the great majority of French professional anthropologists still owe their origin. But because of the rigidities and conservatism inherent in the structure of French higher education, it was not until the 1920's that academic curricula resembling the English and American reformulations of anthropology began to appear. To this day, "anthropology" means physical anthropology to the educated Frenchman. Yet Durkheim's "sociological" school from the outset concerned itself as much with the data of primitive ethnography as with Euro-American sociology. Moreover, as Durkheim's interests matured, he became increasingly involved with the study of ethnographic data.

The rejection of Spencerism in France was not related to a vigorous expansion of fieldwork. Indeed, the onset of intensive field studies by French anthropologists began in the 1930's with pupils sent out by Marcel Mauss, himself a pupil of Durkheim (*cf.* BENDER 1965; MERCIER 1966: 104 ff.). Nonetheless, there was much in common between the trajectories of the French and American schools. Both moved steadily away from an evolutionary perspective; both tended to encourage emic approaches on the model of linguistic analysis; and both produced a steady erosion of the strategy which would have sought the lawful principles of sociocultural phenomena in the material conditions of human life. For Durkheim, social facts were entities *sui generis,* but from the beginning they resembled mind more than matter. We shall follow Durkheim's progressive commitment to a Hegelian form of idealism, a trend which by mid-century, in the work of Claude Lévi-Strauss, had returned almost to the rationalism of Descartes.

Durkheim's influence abroad was perhaps even more important than it was at home. Between 1893 and 1897 he published in rapid succession *Division of Labor in Society, The Rules of the Sociological Method,* and *Suicide.* These works eventually provided the basic orientation for the British school of structural-functionalism, the central movement in modern British social anthropology. The accomplishments of this school under the leadership of A. R. Radcliffe-Brown is the subject of the next chapter.

THE SIGNIFICANCE OF DURKHEIM'S POSITIVIST HERITAGE

Durkheim presents a wide variety of facets from which interpretive efforts (*cf.* GEHLKE, 1915) reflect at all sorts of unpredictable angles. He has been classified as everything from a materialist to a mystic. In addition to the fact that his outlook underwent considerable transformation, he seems to have made less than a total effort to avoid ambiguity.

Sociologist Talcott Parsons (1949:307) has properly emphasized Durkheim's debt to Auguste Comte: "Durkheim is the spiritual heir of Comte and all the principal elements of his earlier thought are to be found foreshadowed in Comte's writings." But Parsons' understanding of Comte is quite different from that presented in Chapter 3. For Parsons, Comte's positivism is the opposite of Hegelian idealism. Thus Durkheim is represented as a positivist who gradually converts to a position which mediates between Hegel and Max Weber. Parsons places himself quite accurately at the end of this sequence. We have seen, however, that for Comte as much as for Hegel "ideas govern or overthrow the world." Parsons' family tree, in other words, is much more inbred than he would like us to believe, and French social science is a much more provincial affair than is usually admitted. It has never, not to this day, followed a strategy other than that of cultural idealism.

Actually, Durkheim and Comte struck remarkably similar balances between material and ideational factors at similar stages in their careers. In both cases, they gave increasing emphasis to moral and religious considerations as they grew older.

The suggestion by sociologist Alvin Gouldner (1962:10) that it was Saint-Simon rather than Comte to whom Durkheim owed the greater debt should also be seen in the same context. In the crucial matter of the relationship between ideology and sociocultural change, Comte and Saint-Simon were like two peas in a pod. Durkheim (1962:127) himself provides the decisive quote:

> In point of fact the idea from which he [Saint-Simon] takes his departure and which dominates his entire doctrine, is that a social system is only the application of a system of ideas. Systems of religion, of general politics, morality, of public instruction, says he, are nothing else than applications of a system of ideas, or if one prefers, it is the system of thought considered under different aspects.

Gouldner's case rests on the extent to which Durkheim's first book, *Division of Labor*, may be viewed as a polemic directed against Comte. Because of its divisive effect upon a community's moral consensus, Comte had pictured specialization as a subversive threat to orderly progress. Durkheim, on the other hand, set out to show that the division of labor leads to a different effect, namely an increase in a new and higher form of social cohesion, which he labeled "organic solidarity." According to Durkheim, this new binding ingredient grows up alongside of, and eventually overshadows, the more archaic "mechanical solidarity" based upon cohesion of individuals through the likeness of their "*consciences*" (DURKHEIM 1933:226). But Comte's apprehensions concerning the possible breakdown in social cohesion are fully shared by Durkheim. Indeed, Saint-Simon, Comte, and Durkheim are all aware of the potentially cohesive as well as divisive effects of the increase in the division of labor.

Where Comte spoke of order and progress, Durkheim emphasized "social solidarity." This idiom is the main relevant positivist contribution, serving to maintain a focus upon social evolution which denies the necessity of disorderly structural change.

In this fashion French positivism acted as a buffer between a science of society and the political and industrial revolutionary agitation characteristic of the whole century of French history which preceded the writing of *Division of Labor*.

SOCIAL SOLIDARITY VERSUS CLASS STRUGGLE

The use of the concept of social solidarity by Saint-Simon, Comte, and Durkheim provides an unbroken line of politically conservative theories leading directly to the main varieties of "functionalism" among contemporary British, French, and American social anthropologists. While radical social science followed Marx into a consideration of what it would take to make the social organism fly apart, the conservatives, such as Spencer, Durkheim, Radcliffe-Brown, and Malinowski, busied themselves with calculations of the reasons for its holding together. Let us admit the legitimacy of both interests. In the ultimate stages of theoretical formulation, no doubt both approaches are useful. Marx's effect upon the development of anthropology is felt, in this regard, as in most others, indirectly, by reaction, in the painfully elaborate and only partially successful exploration of self-regulating, sociocultural equilibrium models. Without placing Durkheim's concern with social solidarity in the context of the Marxist predictions concerning the impending violent explosion of the capitalist system, the origins of much of recent cultural theory must remain forever obscure.

Fortunately we have the testimony of Marcel Mauss (1962) and the text of Durkheim's (1962; orig. 1896) study of Saint-Simon and socialism by which the central historical importance of the political issue is established beyond doubt. Mauss tells us that Durkheim's desire to build a new science of society, after the debacle brought about by Comte's popish denouement, arose from schoolboy interest in the "relationship between individualism and socialism." According to Mauss, although this interest was temporarily set to one side, it remained with him throughout his life and coincided with a number of critical biographical events which are relevant to the form in which Durkheim's theories were presented to the world.

> He clashed with touchy moralists and classic or Christian economists for their objections to collectivism which they struck at through his *Division of Labor*. Due to conflicts of this kind, he was excluded from professorships in Paris. Some of the most brilliant among his own students were converted to socialism, especially Marxist, and even Guesdist. In one "Social Study" circle some examined *Capital* as they elsewhere considered Spinoza. Durkheim sensed this opposition to liberalism and bourgeois individualism. In a conference organized by this circle and the Workers' Party at Bordeaux, Juarès in 1893 extolled Durkheim's

> work. However, if it was Lucien Herr who in 1886–88 converted Juarès to socialism, it was Durkheim who in 1889–96 had turned him away from political formalism and the shallow philosophy of the radicals [MAUSS 1962:34].

DURKHEIM, SPENCER, MARX

Between Spencer's military and industrial types of societies (see p. 209) there is a transition which appears to resemble the transition between Durkheim's own mechanical and organic types. This resemblance is only superficial, argued Durkheim. Spencer was in fundamental error concerning the importance of social as opposed to individual factors in the industrial phase. According to Spencer, the sphere of contractual relationships is destined to expand to the point where the entire social organization will consist of nothing but a network of voluntary individual arrangements of convenience. Individuals would depend upon the group to a diminishing degree, inversely related to the number of private conventions.

> Social solidarity would then be nothing else than the spontaneous accord of individual interests, an accord of which contracts are the natural expression. The typical social relation would be the economic, stripped of all regulation and resulting from the entirely free initiative of the parties. In short, society would be solely the stage where individuals exchanged the products of their labor, without any action properly social coming to regulate this exchange [DURKHEIM 1933:202].

Note that there is a curious similarity between Spencer's ultimate industrial phase and the nebulous stateless and classless utopia which Marx had promised would follow the proletarian victory. Both Marx and Spencer continued to expect the triumph of the individual over society as in the dream of Rousseau. For both Spencer and Marx, the withering away of the state was a withering away not only of the political apparatus but of the entire supra-individual, sociocultural nexus of restraint.

Durkheim objected to this predicted diminution of the social factor in the strongest possible terms, and herein lies, as we shall see, the unique twist imparted by Durkheim to cultural theory.

THE STATE SHALL NOT WITHER

According to Durkheim, the growth of the division of labor, and hence of organic solidarity, is accompanied by no weakening of the power of the social organism over the individual; there is rather an intensification of the mutual dependence of individual and social group. Much of the *Division of Labor* is concerned with showing that the evolution of mechanical to organic solidarity is accompanied by a "normal" or "healthy" expansion of the legal and administrative apparatus of sociality and of an appropriate set of moral and ethical rules.

> . . . economists have believed that . . . human societies could and would resolve themselves into purely economic associations. . . . But such a conception is, in all ways, inadequate for the facts. The division of labor does not present individuals to one another, but social functions. And society is interested in the play of the latter; in so far as they regularly concur, it will be healthy or ill. Its existence thus depends upon them, and the more they are divided the greater its dependence. That is why it cannot leave them in a state of indetermination. . . . Thus are formed those rules whose number grows as labor is divided, and whose absence makes organic solidarity either impossible or imperfect [DURKHEIM 1933:407].

THE NEED FOR A SCIENCE OF THE SOCIAL

Out of this refutation of the individualizing effects of the division of labor there arises in Durkheim's outlook the necessity for a discipline which will concern itself with "social," as distinct from individual, "functions." In his next and perhaps his most influential major endeavor, *The Rules of the Sociological Method* (1938; orig. 1895), Durkheim proceeded to set forth the epistemological and methodological principles of such a discipline. In doing so, he reaffirmed the superorganic position which was already explicit in the Marxist tradition, but which for that very reason was elsewhere unacceptable. Durkheim went far beyond Spencer in this regard. Spencer's superorganic was trammeled by bitter opposition to the enlargement of government and was ultimately, despite his denial of free will and his use of an organismic model, perfectly reducible to individual motives and individual strengths and weaknesses in the "struggle for survival."

Durkheim's superorganic is in every way anticipatory of Kroeber's famous exposition of the autonomy of the cultural level, and also of Leslie White's "culturology." It suffered however from an unfortunate idealist and mentalist bias which eventually overwhelmed all of its virtues and produced a distinct heritage within French anthropology of concern with the mystical properties of group minds.

REJECTION OF RACISM

Among Durkheim's basic requirements for a science of social functions was the assumption that sociocultural phenomena could not be understood as the expression of either psychobiological instincts, or individual conscious willful choices. No social phenomenon, he argued, can be placed in indisputable dependence on race since the "most diverse forms of organization are found in societies of the same race, while striking similarities are observed between societies of different races" (1938:108). Unlike Boas, Durkheim rejected the appeal to racial factors largely on methodological grounds. Racial determinism is an evasion of sociological problems whose solution require sociological method:

> In short, when the artistic character of Athenian civilization is related with such facility to inherited aesthetic faculties, we show as little insight as did scholars in the Middle Ages when they explained fire by phlogiston and the effects of opium by its dormitive property [*ibid.*:109].

REJECTION OF INDIVIDUAL PSYCHOLOGICAL FACTORS

To defend the autonomy of the social realm, Durkheim inverted the accepted relationship between consciousness and sociocultural conditions in a manner which is superficially reminiscent of Marx standing Hegel on his head. One of his cardinal methodological rules is that "the determining cause of a social fact should be sought among the social facts preceding it and not among the states of the individual consciousness" (*ibid.*:110). The seeming congruence with Marx is sustained by Durkheim's description of the relationship between the population of human actors, their raw biopsychological capacities, and the materialization of the social forces which act through them and upon them:

> Collective representations, emotions, and tendencies are caused *not* by certain states of the consciousnesses of individuals but by the conditions in which the social group in its totality is placed. Such actions can, of course, materialize only if the individual natures are merely the indeterminate material that the social factor molds and transforms. Their contribution consists

> exclusively in very general attitudes, in vague and consequently plastic predispositions which by themselves, if other agents did not intervene, could not take on the definite and complex forms which characterize social phenomena [*ibid.*:106].

Yet there is actually little resemblance between Durkheim's notions of sociocultural causality and Marx's materialism. We see that Durkheim juxtaposed individual consciousness with the *totality* of social conditions. According to Marx, however, it is not the "totality" of social conditions which deserves emphasis, but rather the techno-environmental and techno-economic aspects of those conditions. It is true that Durkheim, like Marx, believed that individual states of consciousness were molded by social conditions of which the individual remained unaware. But what is the nature of these social conditions?

THE NATURE OF SOCIAL FACTS

What most impressed Durkheim was that there appeared to be a "coercive effect" which social things exerted over individual behavior. Indeed, the principal test of a social "thing" was that it could be shown to have "coercive" power. Therefore, in a manner that Durkheim admitted could not be fully understood by science, such things must have an "existence of their own."

The phenomenological status which Durkheim attributed to social things is operationally unacceptable. Although social science cannot function without vigorously defending the reality of traits, institutions, patterns, and sociocultural forces, we confront an even greater danger if the reality in question is operationally divorced from the observation of the behavior of specific individuals. The solution to this problem is to base the hierarchy of social things upon a series of constructs or logico-empirical abstractions. As the levels of abstractions depart further from the substratum of the historical content of the behavior-stream, they nonetheless preserve concrete, "material" reality defined by the logico-empirical process (*cf.* pp. 333-34, 394).

One must agree completely with Durkheim when he stressed the point that the individual manifestations of a sociocultural entity (such as a particular instance of a phonemic utterance or a given act of avoidance of one's mother-in-law) are not to be regarded as social (cultural) things. From an operational point of view, the idiosyncratic or historical instance is merely the observational raw material out of which the categories of sociocultural discourse are constructed by the community of observers. But for Durkheim, the separation of the specific individual performance from the social thing derives from a drastically different epistemological posture. Individual behavior for Durkheim is rather a "reincarnation" or reflection of social entities (1938:7) enjoying an existence which is independent not only of the concrete expression in a given individual but also of the observer's logico-empirical procedures. Thus when Durkheim states that "sociological phenomena cannot be defined by their universality" and that "a movement repeated by all individuals is not thereby a social fact," he intends a dichotomy for which it is impossible to conceive any operational justification.

The metaphysical enormity of Durkheim's "social things" shows up in his willingness to concede the existence of widely distributed habits acquired by learning which do not reflect or "incarnate" social phenomena. This becomes possible in Durkheim's logic because the generality and coercive restraints of such habits owe their existence to forces "internal" to ourselves, whereas, the generality and coercive restraint of genuine social facts arise from the exterior and collective "consciousness":

> The pressure exerted by one or several bodies on other bodies, or even on human wills, cannot be confused with that which the consciousness of a group exercises on the consciousnesses of its members. . . . It is true that habits, either physical or social, have in certain respects this same feature. They dominate us and impose beliefs and practices upon us. But they rule us from within, for they are in every case an integral part of ourself. On the contrary, social beliefs and practices act on us from without: thus the influence exerted by them differs fundamentally from the effect of habit [DURKHEIM 1938:lv].

THE ORIGIN OF THE IDEA OF GROUP MIND

We see therefore that the independent reality which Durkheim postulates for social things gains its *sui generis* status from the alleged existence of a group mind. Durkheim's group mind is in every respect the heir of a mixture of Hegelian and Comteian idealism.

As we have seen, attempts to confine the Hegelian influence to the later phases of Durkheim's career are based on the false dichotomy between French positivism and German idealism. Yet much of Durkheim's formative period was spent studying philosophy in Germany (*cf.* PARSONS, 1949:307). It is true that Durkheim's idealism is purely secular with no trace at all of gods and world spirits, but these features are easily dispatched without altering the fundamentals of the cultural-idealist strategy.

One should perhaps also take into account Durkheim's own protestations against being identified as an idealist. In the preface to the first edition of the *Rules*, Durkheim assures us that his "reasoning is not at all revolutionary" and that if he is a determinist, he is less dangerous than those who see "in social phenomena only the results of unrestrained manipulation, which can in an instant, by a simple dialectical artifice, be completely upset" (DURKHEIM 1938:xxxviii–xxxix). He expresses the fear that his attempt to study social phenomena objectively will be "judged crude and will possibly be termed 'materialistic.' " Yet he assures the reader that "we would more justly claim the contrary designation." In the final analysis, however, neither the idealist nor materialist appellation is the correct one: the "only designation we can accept is that of 'rationalist' " (*ibid.*).

French intellectuals have always sought surcease from the idealist/materialist dilemma by similar displays of learned ambiguity. It will be recalled that for Comte, positivism was to occupy a neutral ground between the materialism associated with the Revolution and the idealism associated with the counterrevolution. In Durkheim and his successors, this same exaltation of learned ambiguity continued to amuse the "ins" and bemuse the "outs."

But it was as futile for Durkheim as it had been for Comte to pretend that he had found some sort of neutral ground. His postulated superorganic social entity is explicitly modeled after the concept of the individual's subjectively experienced "mind." Social facts are "collective representations," that is, ideas experienced by the group mind and expressed or "reincarnated" in the minds and behavior of the individual members of the social group. "Collective consciousness" is a deliberate play on the ambiguity of the distinction between conscience as a subjectively experienced moral force and the experience of conscious awareness, both of which are incorporated into the concept of the group mind. Every pore of Durkheim's theory is filled with mentalist and idealist images and predilections. If he transcends the individual psychological level, it is in terms of a series of psychological assumptions which stamp social things with an indelible idealist commitment:

> . . . nothing collective can be produced if individual consciousnesses are not assumed; but this necessary condition is by itself insufficient. These consciousnesses must be combined in a certain way; social life results from this combination and is, consequently,

> explained by it. Individual minds, forming groups by mingling and fusing, give birth to a being, psychological if you will, but constituting a psychic individuality of a new sort [*ibid.*:103].

Despite this imagery, Durkheim's critics continued to accuse him of materialism. He was prompted, therefore, to begin his preface to the second edition of the *Rules* with a most emphatic denial of materialist leanings:

> Whereas we had declared repeatedly that the individual consciousness was for us not material, but only a more or less systematized aggregate of phenomena, we were charged with realism and with ontologism. Whereas we had expressly stated and reiterated that social life is constituted wholly of collective "representations," we were accused of eliminating the mental element from sociology [*ibid.*:xli].
> . . . social phenomena, although immaterial, are nevertheless real things [*ibid.*:lvii].

It is thus clear that there is no kernel of truth in Parson's argument that "Idealistic strains appear in Durkheim's thought . . . only at the latest stage of its development" (PARSONS 1949:307). The further development of Durkheim's career brought an intensified commitment to the idealist position already evident in the earliest monographs.

WHAT CAUSES THE DIVISION OF LABOR?

It is Durkheim's answer to this question that is important if one is to understand the rise of the French and English functionalist schools, and the powerful attraction that Durkheim's approach continues to manifest among cultural anthropologists.

From Adam Smith onward, the explanation of the increase in the division of labor had been based upon the common sense notion that greater specialization provided a cheaper and more efficient means for producing the economic goods upon which men depended for their sustenance and pleasure. Although the soundness of this essentially economic explanation would seem to be unassailable, the main purport of Durkheim's first monograph is to deny its validity and to substitute in its place an explanation that emphasizes above all else the functional-causal importance of social solidarity.

To defeat the established view, Durkheim proceeds first to challenge the notion that the division of labor is associated with a general increase in "happiness." Given the condition of Europe's masses toward the end of the nineteenth century, it is not difficult to win the point that a simple utilitarian pleasure-pain principle does not suffice. In this connection, we see that it is no accident that Durkheim's second substantive study (1892) was concerned with suicide—a direct outcome of his somber rejection of utilitarian doctrine.

The specific polemic is once again directed toward Spencer. The latter alleges, in effect, "that happiness increases with the productive power of work" (1933:265). It thus seems to Spencer impossible for us not to utilize each new method for dividing up the work task and increasing output. But we know things do not happen in this way, argues Durkheim. The difficulty is that primitive man, living under arrangements of mechanical solidarity, cannot be assumed to have any desire for material abundance. This remarkable assertion is crucial for all that follows. We have already encountered it in the Boasian attempt to destroy the economic explanation of cultural evolution. It leads in Durkheim's case to the view that productivity is epiphenomenal, that the desire for material abundance is a consequence and not a cause of the division of labor:

> The division of labor appears to us otherwise than it does to economists. For them, it essentially consists in greater production. For us, this greater productivity is only a necessary consequence, a repercussion of the phenomenon. If we specialize, it is not to produce more, but it is to enable us to live in new conditions of existence that have been made for us [*ibid.*:275].

That much of the academic power and intellectual prestige of Durkheim's school rests upon its rejection of economic determinism becomes apparent as soon as we turn to the absurd explanation which Durkheim substituted for that which had satisfied his predecessors. Appealing first to Darwin, Durkheim notes that competition in the biological world is most fierce among the members of the same or similar species: "Darwin justly observed that the struggle between two organisms is as active as they are analogous. Having the same needs and pursuing the same objects, they are in rivalry everywhere" (*ibid.*: 266). In human population this rivalry tends to increase in direct proportion to the rise in what Durkheim calls "social condensation"—an effect related in not too clear a fashion to increases in population size and density. But as the "condensation" progresses, the mechanical cohesiveness which is associated with a small undifferentiated social mass gives way to the organic principle, and the tendency of the social organism to break apart or consume itself in fatal internecine struggle is countered by the rise of organic solidarity. Each break in the equilibrium of the social mass is resolved by a more developed division of labor. The division of labor thus emerges as a social arrangement not for increasing productivity, but for reducing competition. Its principal effect is to increase the amount of heterogeneity among the parts of the social organism, thereby multiplying and intensifying their mutual dependence. In other words, the *function* of the division of labor is to preserve social solidarity.

THERE WILL BE NO REVOLUTION

It seems self-evident that the historical function of Durkheim's explanation lies in the paramount emphasis which Marx had also given to internecine rivalry. Both Marx and Durkheim assign an important role to struggle, but with this difference: social rivalry for Marx is not about to be solved by the division of labor. There is to be an intensification rather than a diminution of social conflict. Social cohesion in Marx's theories would grow only among the proletariat, the social stratum which is destined to be bound ever closer together by increasing "mechanical solidarity." Between the proletariat and the bourgeoisie, that is, between the most differentiated segments of the social organism, instead of organic solidarity, there is to be war.

The crudity of both Marx's and Durkheim's formulations need not detain us. It is clear that one is the obverse of the other and that both suffer from a lack of sensitivity to quantity, refinement of concept, overabundance of conviction, and a lack of data. Between the under- and overestimation of the composability of class struggle, there is little choice. That it was Durkheim's view and not Marx's which provided the basis for British and French functionalism is lamentable, but for quite a different reason. Durkheim's rejection of an irreconcilable class struggle went along with the rejection of economic explanations—a package whose reason for being resided principally in the fact that these two things happened to be put together by Marx. Durkheim's unique contribution was thus the founding of a science of culture which could explain sociocultural phenomena without getting involved in techno-economic causation. Henceforth it would suffice merely to investigate the manner by which a given trait or institution contributed to the maintenance of solidarity among the members of the social organism.

SLOUGHING OFF MALTHUS, SPENCER, AND DARWIN

Durkheim's commitment to an idealist strategy in the *Division of Labor* is obscured by ambiguities associated with the process of "social condensation." Since "social condensation" is produced by an increase in population density, a more general treatment of the conditions responsible for the division of labor would obviously require an explanation of demographic changes. That is, if we accept Durkheim's argument that the division of labor does not derive its functional importance from production, we cannot admit the importance of "social condensation" without re-admitting the factors responsible for production at an even more fundamental level. To this question of what causes the "social condensation" that produces the crises of solidarity whose function it is the division of labor's to solve, Durkheim pays practically no attention. Eventually, as his position matured, the process of "social condensation" was forgotten. His explanations tended more and more to assume the great variety of techno-economic and techno-environmental systems as givens. With economic factors held constant, the analysis of ideology and social structure was carried to a new pitch, while the concept of the collective consciousness assumed an increasingly more autonomous role. Thus, in *The Rules of the Sociological Method,* the growth in the volume and dynamic density of societies is mentioned only peripherally to a discussion which moves toward dismissing concern with ultimate causality in the physicalist sense (DURKHEIM 1938:115ff.). In *Suicide,* as Parsons (1949:327) points out, the question of density and Darwinian competition drops out entirely, never to be heard from again. Instead, in *Suicide,* we have a series of explanations which relate different suicide rates to various intensities of the mechanical and organic components of the collective consciousness. For example, where the collective consciousness is associated with mechanical solidarity, altruistic suicides predominate. On the other hand, where organic solidarity is more important, anomic suicide resulting from an absence of well-defined "collective representations" (i.e., rules of behavior) comes to the fore.

With the further maturation of Durkheim's position, the social milieu, which is after all nothing but a system of ideas in the group mind, achieves a more and more blatant autonomy with respect to the material conditions of individual and collective life. Durkheim's thinking continues along this line until we come, in his last major work, *The Elementary Forms of the Religious Life,* to an affirmation of the power of collective representations, which returns us in unmistakable terms to an idealism patterned after the worst of Hegel's "geists."

THE ORIGIN OF FUNCTIONALIST EXPLANATIONS

The Elementary Forms of the Religious Life, Durkheim's last major work, is an attempt to discover the "origins" of religion. By "origin," Durkheim did not mean simply "first beginning" but rather "the ever-present causes upon which the most essential forms of religious thought and practice depend" (1915:8). The fundamental conclusions reached are that all of the basic concepts associated with religion, such as god, soul, spirit, and totem, originate in the recurrent experience by which human beings feel the force and majesty of the social group. Men collectively invent the basic categories of religion in order to explain the unseen but felt force of the collective consciousness. Several other fundamental ideas, such as logical classes, physical force, space, and time, are also said to owe their origin to a similar sort of apotheosis or concretization of the group mind. Aside from mentioning the slight possibility that these suggestions merit serious consideration from the point of view of social psychology, we shall not attempt to evaluate their empirical status. Of more enduring interest is the kind of explanation they embody. We must note first of all that there is a lack of concern with the explanation of specific variations in religious systems. Once the totem or magical rite has been shown to be functionally compatible or illustrative of certain universal "elementary" collective "structures," the explanatory quest terminates.

In subsequent elaborations of the functional method, among both the French and British social anthropologists, essentially the same strategy was to be followed with respect to such "elementary" principles as the "unity of the sibling" group and other so-called universal structural-functional "laws." In the case of Lévi-Strauss the similarity is even more profound since the French followers of Durkheim do not hesitate to propose universal "elementary" principles cast in an overtly psychological idiom. In addition, the French structuralists have, to a greater extent than their English counterparts, permitted themselves the luxury of ambiguous metaphorical evolutionary sequences in which primitive and derived forms are playfully bandied about in a spirit of *double entendre,* best exemplified, outside of Durkheim, by eighteenth-century discussions of the origin of society in the "social contract."

TRIUMPH OF MIND OVER MATTER

In this final phase of Durkheim's career, considerations of the material conditions such as are implicit in the *Division of Labor* are finally and unequivocally overwhelmed. We confront at last the autonomous power of the "collective representations" to mold themselves into myriads of specific forms. Such forms are intelligible, if at all, only in so far as they continue to represent universal principles of collective psychology. But they are neither predictable nor retrodictable. It is not merely that society has the power to construct ideologies in the processes of "constructing itself" (1915: 423) but that being a higher manifestation of "idea" in its own right, society can construct itself in any image to which it happens to take a fancy.

Paradoxically, Durkheim continues, in the midst of all this, to fend off possible accusations of materialism. The latter, it seems, were brought on by the mere fact that he attributes so little autonomy to the individual. It would almost seem as if Durkheim feared that his colleagues had not heard that there were differences between Hegel and Marx:

> Therefore it is necessary to avoid seeing in this theory of religion a simple restatement of historical materialism: that would be misunderstanding our thought to an extreme degree. In showing that religion is something essentially social, we do not mean to say that it confines itself to translating into another language the material forms of society and its immediate vital necessities. It is true that we take it as evident that social life depends upon its material foundation and bears its mark just as the mental life of an individual depends upon his nervous system and in fact his whole organism. But collective consciousness is something more than a mere epiphenomenon of its morphological basis. . . . In order that the former may appear, a synthesis *sui generis* of particular consciousnesses is required. Now this synthesis has the effect of disengaging a whole world of sentiments, ideas and images which, once born, obey laws all their own. They attract each other, repel each other, unite, divide themselves, and multiply though these combinations are not commended and necessitated by the condition of the underlying reality. The life thus brought into being even enjoys so great an independence that it

> sometimes indulges in manifestations with no purpose or utility of any sort, for the mere pleasure of affirming itself. We have shown that this is often precisely the case with ritual activity and mythological thought [*ibid.*:423–24].

Another way of expressing this triumph of mind over matter is to assert the causal priority of ideology. This Durkheim proceeds to do with the proclamation (validated by nothing more than the tautology deriving from his definition of the collective consciousness) that most great social institutions are the causal products of religious ideas:

> In summing up, then, it may be said that nearly all the great social institutions have been born in religion. Now in order that these principal aspects of the collective life may have commenced by being only varied aspects of the religious life, it is obviously necessary that the religious life be the eminent form and, as it were, concentrated expression of the whole collective life. If religion had given birth to all that is essential in society, it is because the idea of society is the soul of religion [*ibid.*:418–19].

In a footnote to this passage Durkheim himself draws attention to the fact that he has not yet systematically examined how economic activity is governed by religious ideas. He is convinced, however, that there is no dearth of connection: Magic enters into economic processes; economic value is a sort of power or efficacy; richness confers mana. Thus, we see that Durkheim's conception of economics was, like Lowie's, contaminated with the emic sense of rules and ideals. When his pupil Mauss and when Mauss' pupil Lévi-Strauss turned their attention to phenomena which have a manifest relation with the material conditions of habitat and technology, they did so, as we shall see in a moment, in a fashion which preserved the anti-economic and antimaterialist commitment with undiminished ardor, resulting in additional flights of fancy and displays of learned obscurantism.

THE CONSCIOUSNESS OF CONSCIOUSNESS

It remains to be noted concerning the fate of Durkheim's science of society that in the final chapter of *The Elementary Forms* the influence of an Hegelian version of idealism is everywhere conspicuous. Skeptics should review the evidence as presented by Talcott Parsons, who, unlike the writer, detects in this influence a gratifying convergence toward his own formulation of social science. But, in view of the Hegelian heritage which has been identified in Lévi-

Strauss, it is of singular importance that the continuity of such an outlook in and through Durkheim be clearly established. This is additionally imperative, since the British social anthropologists have for the most part failed to understand how much their own position is also based upon an attenuated but nonetheless active and theoretically decisive variety of idealism.

We must recall in this connection that for Hegel, history consists of the world mind working its way into awareness of itself. In Durkheim, the world mind is replaced by the collective consciousness, but the imprint of animistic survivals is unmistakable:

> . . . the collective consciousness is the highest form of the psychic life, since it is the consciousness of the consciousnesses. Being placed outide of and above individual and local contingencies, it sees things only in their permanent and essential aspects, which it crystallizes into communicable ideas. At the same time that it sees from above, it sees farther; at every moment of time, it embraces all known reality; that is why it alone can furnish the mind with the moulds which are applicable to the totality of things and which make it possible to think of them. It does not create these moulds artificially; it finds them within itself; it does nothing but become conscious of them [*ibid.*:444].

The influence of an Hegelian outlook is also evident in Durkheim's approach to the problem of cross-cultural typologies. Durkheim made almost no progress in this matter because he could not rid himself of the romantic notion that each country had a soul which maintained it as a separate social "species" throughout the vicissitudes of historical experience. Especially important in this regard is that the identification of social "species" must eschew dependence upon taxonomic contrasts derived from material differences:

> Since its origin, France has passed through very different forms of civilization; it began by being agricultural, passed to craft industry and to small commerce, then to manufacturing, and finally to large-scale industry. Now, it is impossible to admit that the same collective individuality can change its species three or four times. A species must define itself by more constant characteristics. The economic state, technological state, etc. present phenomena too unstable and complex to furnish the basis of a classification. It is even very probable that the same industrial, scientific, and artistic civilization can be found in societies whose hereditary constitution is very different. Japan may in the future borrow our arts, our industry, even our political organization; it will not cease to belong to a different social species from France and Germany [DURKHEIM 1938:88*n*].

Everything about this passage is backwards or standing on its head. France, a "collective individuality," is declared unique prior to the statement of the logico-empirical procedures by which entities in the domain of sociocultural phenomena are to be identified and classified. Its techno-economic base keeps changing, argues Durkheim, yet France remains; therefore the essence of France must reside elsewhere. That is, Durkheim starts with an operationally undefined and undefinable entity and systematically casts out all the operationally definable concepts which contradict the basic idealist posture. And on what does this idea of France rest if not on the emic conviction of Frenchmen that they are different from everyone else and that France is eternal. Thus we end up with a France that is like Japan in everything but "spirit," with a national "geist" that remains the same no matter how much change occurs. French anthropology continues to pay a high price for this muddled way of thinking.

MARCEL MAUSS

Mauss was the most prominent of the small, close-knit group of scholars who collaborated with Durkheim at the turn of the century, especially in the publication of the journal *L'Année Sociologique* from 1898 to 1912. The group included Henri Hubert, Henri Beuchat, Maxime David, and Robert Hertz. After Durkheim's death in 1917, and as a result of the heavy toll taken by World War I on his younger colleagues, Mauss donned the mantle of leadership. He resumed publication of *L'Année Sociologique* in 1924, and with Lucien Lévy-Bruhl and Paul Rivet, founded the Institute of Ethnology of the University of Paris in 1926. As Seth Leacock (1954: 59) has noted, "Throughout his life, Mauss considered himself a follower of Durkheim and never knowingly violated any of Durkheim's teachings." Of special interest in this connection is the emphasis given by Mauss to explanations of large domains of sociocultural phenomena through the identification of archetypical "collective representations."

ELEMENTARY FORMS

Mauss attributed the worldwide manifestations of sacrificial phenomena to the collective idea of a sacred domain or realm. The sacrificial victim is the medium through which communication with this realm is achieved (MAUSS and HUBERT 1899). Later the explanation of magic was sought in the idea of *mana*, a collective belief in an impersonal force accounting for the efficacy of magical as opposed to religious behavior (MAUSS and HUBERT 1904). In his most influential work, *L'Essai Sur le Don* (*The Gift*), to which we shall return in a moment, Mauss used the idea of "reciprocity" to explain such apparently diverse phenomena as the potlatch and kula.

Lévi-Strauss has pointed out the similarity between Mauss' *modus operandi* and Durkheim's method of reducing complex phenomena to underlying elements: social bonds to organic and mechanical solidarity; suicide to the egoistic, altruistic, and anomic varieties; and god and force to the apotheosis of the social group. To the unsympathetic critic, this procedure is, at best, an attempt to classify together a melange of ideas and practices on the basis of what may be their most trivial resemblances; but for Lévi-Strauss such ideas reach behind superficial differences and similarities to the "hidden, fundamental elements which are the true components of the phenomena" (LÉVI-STRAUSS 1945a:524). "This analytical work, trying to reduce the concrete complexity of the data . . . into more simple and elementary structures is still the fundamental task of sociology" (*ibid.*:525).

FULGURATING INTUITION

Lévi-Strauss' lavish praise of Mauss is instructive for the light it sheds on the professional ideal type after which the French school had modeled itself. Mauss is depicted as having "a bold imagination," "a genius-like feeling of the social stuff," and "unlimited knowledge."

> In his work, and still more in his teaching, unthought-of comparisons flourish. While he is often obscure by the constant use of antitheses, short-cuts and apparent paradoxes which, later on, prove to be the result of a deeper insight, he gratifies his listener, suddenly, with fulgurating intuitions, providing the substance for months of fruitful thinking. In such cases, one feels that one has reached the bottom of the social phenomenon, and has, as he says somewhere, "hit the bed-rock" [*ibid.*:527].

Fulgurating intuitions are, of course, the hallmark of Lévi-Strauss' own dazzling discoveries of hidden elementary structures. But the "bed rock" in both cases is scarcely the kind of stuff which bruises heads or which can be used to build pyramids.

MAUSS' GIFT TO LÉVI-STRAUSS

Lévi-Strauss' magnum opus, (*Les Structures Elémentaires de la Parenté* (*The Elementary Structures of Kinship*), reveals the influence of Mauss and Durkheim in its title, recalling at once Durkheim's search for the "elementary forms" of religion. But Lévi-Strauss himself has pointed out the greater strength of the inspiration transmitted to him by Mauss:

> Few people have been able to read *l'Essai Sur le Don* (The Gift) without experiencing the gamut of emotions described by Malebranche upon his first reading of Descartes: the beating of the heart, the boiling up within the head, the mind overcome by the certainty as yet undefinable but overpowering, of assisting in a decisive event in the evolution of science [LÉVI-STRAUSS 1950: xxxii].

What is this great event? Lévi-Strauss praises *The Gift* because Mauss treats the manifestations of gift-giving as a "total social fact" wherein "all kinds of institutions find simultaneous expression: religious, legal, moral, and economic."

> Everything in a society—even the most special things—everything is above all a function, and is functioning. Nothing can be understood except in relation to everything else, to the complete collectivity and not simply to particular parts. There is no social phenomenon which is not an integral part of the social whole [*ibid.*:139].

Yet according to Lévi-Strauss, this apparently useless truism ushers in a new and superior form of functional analysis. Perhaps the reason for this accolade lies in the connection which Lévi-Strauss draws between "total social fact" and Mauss' developing rapprochement with psychology. Prior to the publication of *The Gift*, Mauss (1924) had expressed an interest in bringing psychological and sociological studies into closer proximity than Durkheim had deemed advisable. Although it is difficult to isolate the portions of *The Gift* that are explicitly dependent upon this new outlook, there are many passages which could be construed as being concerned with the conscious and unconscious meanings of gift-giving from the individual actor's point of view. With his insistence upon a sharp separation between the collective and individual mind, Durkheim had failed to give proper emphasis to the possibility of understanding social phenomena from the inside, so to speak, of the minds of the individual participants. This corresponds, writes Lévi-Strauss, to a general fault of science whereby the subjective properties are left to one side while we seek explanations in purely objective terms:

> When Mauss speaks of total social facts, he implies that on the contrary this facile and convenient dichotomy is inadmissible for sociology. . . . In order to understand a social fact it is necessary to comprehend it *totally*, that is, from without, as a thing of which however, the subjective understanding, both conscious and unconscious, which we have of it is an integral part; as if, being inescapably human, we were to live the fact as the native does, instead of merely observing it as the ethnographer [LÉVI-STRAUSS 1950:xxviii].

In a more modern idiom, which I have had several previous occasions to employ and which is the subject of a separate chapter, Durkheim was not "emic" enough for Lévi-Strauss.

UNCONSCIOUS TELEOLOGY OF THE MIND

Mauss was showing the way toward "elementary structure" not grasped by Durkheim because the master too rigidly excluded the psychological meanings of social facts. It scarcely seems possible to credit Mauss with the dubious achievement of turning French social anthropology back into its subjective rut. That there was a convergence of both Mauss and Durkheim toward essentially psychological categorizations is revealed in their collaborative efforts in the study of religion, which long preceded the writing of *The Elementary Forms of the Religious Life*. Credit Mauss with an intensification of a trend rather than with a sharp break.

Elsewhere, Lévi-Strauss is more explicit concerning the particular kind of emic intensification for which Mauss is to be praised; it is the kind, of course, which Lévi-Strauss employs as the basis of his own analytical posture. It is not merely that Mauss is aware more than Durkheim of the relationship between sociological and psychological phenomena. It is rather that Mauss states that although sociology is a kind of psychology specifically distinct from individual psychology, "it is nonetheless true that one may pass from the facts of individual consciousness to collective representations through a continuous series of intermediaries" (MAUSS 1924, quoted in LÉVI-

STRAUSS 1945a:529). What this boils down to, as we shall have ample occasion to witness, is that Mauss is to be admired for his realization that there might be deep, hidden inner "structures" in the human mind, which are causally prior to collective representations as objective social facts. According to Lévi-Strauss, Durkheim took what appears to be at first glance a strangely intransigent stand against such a possibility. But when he first formulated the concept of the collective consciousness, it was only natural that Durkheim was unable to grasp how social facts might escape the control of individual minds and at the same time be, to any significant extent, projections of individual consciousness. The reason for this is that the fields of depth psychology and structural linguistics had not yet achieved their impact:

> Modern sociologists and psychologists solve such problems by calling upon the activity of the unconscious mind; but at the time when Durkheim was writing the main results of modern psychology and linguistics were lacking. This explained why Durkheim struggled between what he conceived—and this was already a considerable progress upon the thinking of the late 19th century as illustrated, for instance, by Spencer—as an irreducible antinomy: the blindness of history, and the finalism of conscience. Between the two, there is of course the unconscious teleology of the mind [*ibid.*:518].

The special achievement of *The Gift* is related to this reorientation of functionalism toward "unconscious mental teleology." What really set Lévi-Strauss' heart beating and head boiling in *The Gift* was that Mauss had achieved the threshold of a specific discovery concerning the "unconscious teleology of the mind" which was to provide the basis for *The Elementary Structures of Kinship* and for the entire pattern of French "structural" anthropology.

TO GIVE, TO RECEIVE, AND TO REPAY

As I have already indicated, Mauss had endeavored to reduce the worldwide varieties of gift-giving practices, including potlatch, the Kula, Melanesian and Indian feasting and festivals, to their "elementary form." In conformity with the standard practice of Durkheim's school, Mauss is able to discern in these apparently disparate phenomena an underlying principle which is supposed to render them, at one fell stroke, intelligible. All of these phenomena are examples of an "archaic" form of exchange in which there is a "circulation of objects side by side with the circulation of persons and rights" (MAUSS 1954:45). This circulation is maintained neither by barter, purchase, nor economic utility, but rather by the threefold obligation deeply ingrained in the human mind to give, to receive, and to repay (*ibid.*:37ff.).

> All these institutions reveal the same kind of social and psychological pattern. Food, women, children, possessions, charms, land, labour, services, religious offices, rank—everything is stuff to be given away and repaid. In perpetual interchange of what we may call spiritual matter, comprising men and things, these elements pass and repass between clans and individuals, ranks, sexes and generations [*ibid.*:11–12].

In short these are all expressions of the principle of reciprocity upon which the solidary relations between individuals and groups so greatly depend.

We should note in passing that *The Gift* is thus an outstanding example of the use of familiar ethnographic cases of apparently irrational management of resources and labor under ideological or mentalistic pressure. Despite Mauss' talk about viewing social facts in their total functional context, and despite his lip service to the "economic" function, the essay is made possible only by critical lacunae which promote the highest tolerance for wrenching economic behavior out of a structural and dynamic context. Dependence upon the standard anti-economic analysis of Kula and potlatch is especially diagnostic. Mauss' interpretation of the Kula never rises above the fateful decision made by Malinowski not to place the Kula in the context of "ordinary trade" in which admittedly its principal "sociological" significance resided. But this is a theme which requires more extended treatment and to which we shall turn in Chapter 19.

In the meantime, Mauss' misuse of the potlatch should be obvious from our previous discussion of the re-evaluation of this material. Mauss' remark that "It is only our Western societies that quite recently turned man into an economic animal" (*ibid.*:74) is typical of the "emicization" of techno-environmental and techno-economic phenomena.

EMICS AND ECONOMICS

To jump ahead of the story, it is interesting to note how Lévi-Strauss, who again pays lip service to economic functions, follows Mauss into a complete misunderstanding of the difference between the motives which impel an individual to behave in a particular way during the processes of production, distribution, and consumption, and the functional-causal systemic reasons for such behavior. In *The Elementary Structures of Kinship,* Lévi-Strauss elaborates Mauss' suggestion that gift-giving at Christmastime is a modern proof of the strength of the reciprocal principle. With amusing references to his own experiences as a culture-shocked Frenchman in New York, Lévi-Strauss likens the frenzy, competitiveness, and anxiety of the American holiday season to the fiercest of Kwakiutl potlatches.

The comparison of course is perfectly apt on the psychological level, but one does not have to be a Marxist to sense that there is another dimension to our Christmas madness. Why is an intelligence, so subtle in other respects, unable to penetrate to the not-so-deep functions of Christmas purchases in an economy whose productive capacity has raced ahead of the power to buy and consume? It may be "irrational" for Americans to crowd each other over the tinsel and ribbon at Macy's gift-wrapping counter, but the 25 percent of United States retail sales, for which Christmas shopping now accounts, have more serious consequences than tired feet.

This criticism must be distinguished from rejection of the humanistically valuable insight which can be derived from comparing the respective sentiments of Kwakiutl and Americans when they exchange gifts. Thus, one does not object to a comparison between potlatch and Christmas shopping or potlatch and the exchange of wines in cheap French restaurants, if it is made clear that these comparisons are merely intended to bring about a greater degree of insight into the "native point of view." In replying to J. F. Revel's criticism of his method, Lévi-Strauss has indeed invoked just such a defense:

> When, to Revel's great displeasure, I interpret the exchange of wine in the restaurants of southern France in terms of social prestations my primary aim is not to explain contemporary customs by means of archaic institutions but to help the reader, a member of a contemporary society, to rediscover, in his own experience and on the basis of either vestigial or embryonic practices, institutions that would otherwise remain unintelligible to him. The question, then, is not whether the exchange of wine is a survival of the *potlatch,* but whether, by means of this comparison, we succeed better in grasping the feelings, intentions, and attitudes of the native involved in a cycle of prestations [1963a:338].

But Lévi-Strauss' theories concerning the expressions of the principle of reciprocity have been presented by himself and others as relevant to explanations of sociocultural differences and similarities. That task cannot be solved by means of psychedelic "trips" in which we achieve the experience of thinking and feeling like a "native." Although psychic communion may indeed constitute the best result of the French structural school, a much more ambitious program has been announced.

THE PROPHET'S PROPHET

For Lévi-Strauss, the grand achievement of the *Essai Sur le Don* was that it pointed the way toward the understanding of social life in terms of cycles of reciprocity involving the exchange of valuables. It is difficult to know how much of what Lévi-Strauss was able to build upon the foundation provided by Mauss actually was foreshadowed by Mauss' thought. *The Gift* is an extraordinarily disorganized book, as Lévi-Strauss himself admits. According to Lévi-Strauss, Mauss' role was rather that of a prophet: "He stopped at the border of vast possibilities like Moses conducting his people to the very edge of a promised land upon whose splendor he would never gaze" (*ibid.*:xxxvii). But at the decisive point in his journey, Mauss is said to have been distracted by the New Zealand Maori's explanation of reciprocity in terms of *hau*. This concept credits a gift with a kind of transferable spirit which must be returned through the medium of a counter gift in order to avoid harm to the receiver. Mauss was trying to use *hau* to explain reciprocity as he had used *mana* and *sacre* to explain magic and sacrifice. But, says Lévi-Strauss, *hau* is nothing but a native theory, reflecting the underlying structural truth without exposing it. "Reciprocity" is the concept which will conduct us to the underlying mental structure. And this is the task to which Lévi-Strauss devotes himself in his major work.

The Elementary Structures of Kinship is unquestionably the supreme accomplishment of French anthropology. Neither Durkheim nor Mauss was in a position to make use of the ethnographic literature that had accumulated by the time Lévi-Strauss embarked upon the completion of the journey to the promised land. No one before him in the French social sciences could match the combination of literate erudition, in the grand manner, plus extensive firsthand knowledge of primitive tribal groups (based on his fieldwork in Brazil during the late 1930's).

The effectiveness of cultural anthropology, measured in terms of an intellectual influence out of all proportions to the size of its professional membership, undoubtedly relates to the juxtaposition of ivory tower and grass hut. This has been a formidable combination everywhere; but in France, the art of sociological speculation had flourished well into the 1930's. As one of the first French anthropologists who knew what it was like to gather data by living among primitives, Lévi-Strauss spoke with an authority few in France could challenge. On the other hand, in turning to confront the field-hardened professionalism of the English functionalists and the American Boasians, it was his Gallic erudition that frequently placed him at an advantage.

THE GIFT OF WOMEN

The contribution of *The Elementary Structures of Kinship* is the application of Mauss' suggestions concerning the circulation of a particular kind of valuable to the explanation of incest prohibitions, preferential marriages, and the principal varieties of kinship groupings. The valuable in question, merely lumped by Mauss, along with arm bands, feathers, and yams, is the most precious gift which one group can give another, namely, women. The fundamental phenomenon underlying all matrimonial systems is seen as resulting from the prohibition of incest and is always the same: "that is, starting from the moment that I prohibited the use of a woman to myself, who thus becomes available for another man, there is somewhere, a man who renounces a woman who then becomes disposable for me" (LÉVI-STRAUSS 1949:65). The function of incest prohibition is thus to compel the reciprocal exchange of women. From this point onward, the study of kinship resolves itself essentially into the analyses and classification of the various systems of women-exchange, which are more or less implicit in the gamut of institutional arrangements that regulate descent, marriage, and intergroup relations. Given Lévi-Strauss' intellectual pedigree, it is not surprising that at several critical junctures, equivocation and ambiguity overwhelm the often brilliant and always ingenious explication. At the very outset, for example, there is the question of the function of reciprocity. On the one hand, following Durkheim's master strategy and Mauss' specific suggestion, we encounter the theme that reciprocity is the ancient and continuing condition for social solidarity in groups larger than the nuclear family. But what are the reasons for having socially solidary units larger than the nuclear family? Evidently, if the gift of women brings people closer together, fathers and sons would benefit from such an exchange.

RENUNCIATION OF SURVIVAL-VALUE THEORY

Although Lévi-Strauss cites E. B. Tylor's famous aphorism concerning the choice between marrying out and dying out (*ibid.*: 53), the factor of intergroup competition and differential survival is consistently ignored or underplayed.

It is difficult to share Homans and Schneider's (1955:17) enthusiasm with respect to this unfortunate choice: "He does not use, and in this we think him wise, a survival-value theory." It is precisely because of this strategic error that Lévi-Strauss ends up with a theory incapable of explaining specific cultural differences and similarities. Instead of considerations of survival, we are treated to a number of vague suggestions concerning advantages of a secondary or tertiary order: social solidarity, the advantage to the group of being able to control the distribution of women (LÉVI-STRAUSS 1949:55–56), and the sexual advantage to the individual of a larger circle of women from which to choose (*ibid.*:52). By not concerning himself with differential survival effects, Lévi-Strauss is able to ignore the relationships between social structure and productivity, demography, and warfare in bringing about cultural adaptations.

APPEAL TO THE STRUCTURE OF THE MIND

In keeping with his praise of Mauss' "total social facts," our author posits, side by side with the sociocultural advantages of reciprocity, a fundamental universal psychological need for gift-giving and gift-receiving. He argues that historical or geographical studies would not contribute to the explanation of the basic forms of reciprocity as embodied in the nuclear constellation of incest categories and their expression in a simple moiety organization: In order to comprehend these phenomena, "one must appeal to certain fundamental structures of the human mind" (*ibid.*:108). The main "structures" in question are based on a dialectic between "self and others." It is this opposition which is resolved by the idea of reciprocity. To establish the universality of the opposition and its mode of resolution, Lévi-Strauss devotes an entire chapter to psychological studies of children. He concludes that the aptitude for reciprocity is a basic part of the human child's quest for psychological security.

It would be pointless to evaluate the psychological evidence and the use to which it is put. Let it suffice to say that there is no better example of the futility of psychological reductionism. This search for elementary mental "structure" is nothing but a return to the practice of explaining sociocultural phenomena by means of conveniently posited instincts. For a universal instinctual dread of sleeping with one's mother, Lévi-Strauss substitutes a universal mental duality of self and other. The methodological error is identical. If exogamic phenomena are the result of an instinct, why are they so diverse? And if reciprocity is so fundamental to the human psyche, why do we have the ancient and contemporary condition of the opulant and powerful haves (possessing, among other valuables, more than their share of women) and the miserable have nots? In what way is the concept of reciprocity an improvement over the Rousseauan conviction that man in his savage state is a noble creature?

CARTESIANISM

It should be obvious that in order to analyze the variants of marriage and descent as exchange systems, the positing of a subconscious panhuman mental "structure" governing reciprocity is entirely superfluous. The importance attributed to the mental substructure of reciprocity is intelligible only in relation to the history of the French school. Looking back to Mauss and Durkheim, it reveals the devotion to a method which depends upon finding collective archetypes or mental common denominators. Looking ahead, it provides a mid-career manifestation of what looms more and more important in Lévi-Strauss' later development. For, as we shall see, there is a progressively more intense commitment to the discovery of the mental substratum of which social life is the material embodiment. In this regard, one of the most interesting specialties of the French tradition is the lingering influence of a kind of Cartesian rationalism. Cartesian mental structures differ from those which Freud, Jung, and other depth psychologists were convinced lay at the bottom of social behavior. The relevant components are the structures of thought rather than the structures of feeling. If emotions are taken into consideration, they are reduced to mathematized plus and minus qualities. Lévi-Strauss' picture of the human psychological landscape is thus noteworthy for its disregard of the biopsychological, emotional, and affective drives and instincts. Hunger, sex, fear, love, are present, but they seem to be peripheral. More important for the

French structuralist program is the basic propensity of the human mind to build logical categories by means of binary contrasts. For Lévi-Strauss such oppositions or dualities lie at the bottom of large portions if not the totality of sociocultural phenomena.

At this point, a fascinating confluence of sources occurs. On the one hand, binary oppositions suggest the dialectical processes as formulated by Hegel and passed on by Marx. The work of Lévi-Strauss is indeed everywhere pervaded with a dialectic mode of presentation: first the superficial facts, then the hidden negation, and finally the dazzling insight into a new and more fundamental reality. Lévi-Strauss has pointedly sought to achieve some sort of identification with Marx and has consistently promoted his own work as being compatible with the Marxist tradition. This claim, which I shall refute, will be examined at another juncture. Let us take notice, first, of the other methodological world with which the concept of binary opposition joins. By his own admission, the greatest influence upon his method has been the development of linguistics and the convergence of linguistics and cybernetics toward a general science of communication. It is in the work of the Prague linguistic circle, founded by N. Trubetzkoy and passed on to Lévi-Strauss by R. Jakobson, while they were both teaching at the New School, that the main inspiration for Lévi-Strauss' notions of binary contrast analysis has its roots.

THE LINGUISTIC MODEL

The appeal of a linguistic model for general sociocultural analysis is by no means restricted to Lévi-Strauss. The remarkable convergence of French structuralism and the rise of the ethnosemantic approach in the United States is important enough to warrant treatment in a separate chapter. For the moment we shall confine our attention to the profound effect upon Lévi-Strauss of the success achieved by the Prague school in using the principle of distinctive feature contrast. A familiarity with general principles will suffice for an understanding of the school's impact on Lévi-Strauss' thought. The great accomplishment of Trubetzkoy, Jakobson, and their followers was to demonstrate the systemic nature of the set of phonological contrasts employed by each language in building its repertory of significant sounds. The structure of such a system cannot be described by a simple linear catalogue of the significant sounds; the structure consists rather of the matrix or network of oppositions in which binary groupings of sound differences take their position in a multidimensional space. By viewing phonological repertories in this perspective, the apparently infinite variety of sound specialties characteristic of the world's languages is reduced to a small number of systems of contrast in which general categories of contrast substitute for specific phones (e.g., consonants versus vowels and voiced versus unvoiced features). This discovery of the deeper structure underlying surface appearances provides the model scientific achievement toward the emulation of which Lévi-Strauss had already turned his energies during the preparation of his study of kinship. But the advent of structural linguistics constitutes for Lévi-Strauss a scientific revolution comparable to that which flowed from Copernicus or from the development of nuclear physics.

Three basic shifts in emphasis are involved. The study of conscious phenomena is to give way to the study of their "unconscious infrastructure." Second, terms or items are not to be treated as independent entities; the basis of analysis must become the *relationship* between terms or items. Third, general laws in the form of necessary or cross-culturally valid invariant relationships are to be exposed, over against the assumption of random and arbitrary concatenations. A fourth shift, exposited by the linguist Trubetskoy in Lévi-Strauss' paraphrase, is the demonstration of concrete systems in terms of specific cases, as opposed to mere abstract theorizing concerning the systemic nature of phonological phenomena (LÉVI-STRAUSS 1963a:33). This last part of the revolution would appear to be either redundant or trivial with respect to the others, at least as far as applications to extralinguistic analysis is concerned.

It would appear that the relevance of the linguistic structural model to the study of kinship had been worked out by Lévi-Strauss sometime during the preparation of *The Elementary Structures of Kinship*. Not until the last chapter is there a sustained discussion of the similarities between the search for the mental structures which underly kinship systems and the progress made by linguistics in the same direction (611ff.). The book constitutes a bridge between a period in which the characteristic source of structure is found in social solidarity to one in which structure is dominated by the distinctive feature contrasts of the linguistic model. At least this hypothesis helps in understanding some of the ambiguities of the presentation.

MOTHER'S BROTHER/SISTER'S SON

The clearest exposition of the relevance of structural linguistics to the study of kinship appears in an article published in *Word* (1945b). Here Lévi-Strauss attacks the famous problem of the mother's brother/sister's son relationship in order to demonstrate the characteristics of structural as opposed to other brands of sociocultural analysis. The regnant interpretation (discussed at length in the following chapter) was that of Radcliffe-Brown: in patrilineal societies, mother is an indulgent figure with whom her brother is identified; father is an authoritarian figure, with whom his sister is identified. The trouble with this analysis, Lévi-Strauss observes, is that it "arbitrarily isolates particular elements of a global structure which must be treated as a whole" (LÉVI-STRAUSS 1963a:41; orig. 1945b). This larger system (on the analogy with a language's complete system of phonological contrasts) should include not only mother's brother/sister's son and father/son but also brother/sister and husband/wife. The reason for this modification, as expounded at length in *The Elementary Structures of Kinship*, is that the relationships in question constitute the fundamental "unit of kinship" which results from the incest prohibition and the exchange of women:

> The primitive and irreducible character of the basic unit of kinship, as we have definited it, is actually a direct result of the universal presence of an incest taboo. This is really saying that in human society a man must obtain a woman from another man who gives him a daughter or a sister. Thus we do not need to explain how the maternal uncle emerged in the kinship structure. He does not emerge—he is present initially. Indeed, the presence of the maternal uncle is a necessary precondition for the structure to exist. The error of traditional anthropology, like that of traditional linguistics, was to consider the terms, and not the relations between the terms [1949:46].

THE LAW OF NEGATIVE AND POSITIVE KINSHIP RELATIONS

In order to understand the avunculate one must penetrate to the systemic relationships which "organically link" brother/sister, husband/wife, father/son, and mother's brother/sister's son. This penetration is facilitated by grouping together free and familiar relations under one rubric (+) and relations of hostility, antagonism, or reserve under its opposite (—). According to Lévi-Strauss there is a "law" which limits the possible combinations of negative and positive relations as follows:

> . . . the relation between maternal uncle and nephew is to the relation between brother and sister as the relation between father and son is to that between husband and wife. Thus if we know one pair of relations, it is always possible to infer the other [*ibid.*:42].

As Sahlins (1966:134) points out, this does not amount, as one might expect from a literal acceptance of the "law," to a decisive limitation on possibilities, given one relationshp out of four. Instead, we must know two of the relationships in order to predict the other two. For example, if father/son is positive, husband/wife may be either positive or negative, and at the same time, brother/sister may be either negative or positive. Only if we know the sign for both father/son and husband/wife or both uncle/nephew and brother/sister can we complete the paradigm. The possibilities as given in Lévi-Strauss' examples are as follows:

	Trobriand	*Siuai*	*Cherkess*	*Tonga*
uncle/nephew	–	–	+	+
bro/si	–	+	+	–
fa/so	+	+	–	–
hu/wi	+	–	–	+

It would be pointless at this juncture to bring up the issue of whether the relationships in question can in fact be reduced to simple positive and negative contrasts. In real life as a minimum acquaintance with the phenomena of ambivalence would suggest, all the people involved in the formula tend to have, as we say, "mixed feelings" about each other. But let this be a secondary consideration for the moment (in Chapter 20, the inability of the linguistic model to cope with structural ambiguity will receive due emphasis). Yet even if one accepts the schematization into binary contrasts, we are left with a dilemma which is characteristic of the structural approach as embodied not only in the article under consideration but throughout the rest of Lévi-Strauss' work, including his treatment of kinship systems in *The Elementary Structures of Kinship*. Exposed mental structures can only explain similarities; they cannot explain similarities and differences: ". . . to say that one society presents *some* combination of main contrasting characteristics and another society *some* other combination is not very satisfying" (SAHLINS 1966:134). What we want to know is why the Trobriands have the minus, minus, plus, plus rather than some other pattern; why they are matrilineal and avunculocal; why they have exogamous sibs and do not have sections; and so forth. Now Lévi-Strauss is not unaware of this difficulty; indeed, he attempts to meet it head on, but with results that are not worthy of his intellect. If the mother's brother is part of the kinship "atom," he asks, why do we not find the avunculate at all times and places? His answer is that other factors intervene, factors whose relationship to the theory in question cannot be defined:

> Let us point out, first, that the kinship system does not have the same importance in all cultures. For some cultures it provides the active principle regulating all or most of the social relationships. In other groups, as in our own society, this function is either absent altogether or greatly reduced. In still others, . . . it is only partially fulfilled. The kinship system is a language, and a society may prefer other modes of expression and action. From the viewpoint of the anthropologist this means that in dealing with a specific culture we must always ask a preliminary question: Is the system systematic? Such a question, which seems absurd at first, is absurd only in relation to language; for language is the semantic system par excellence; it cannot but signify, and exists only through signification. On the contrary, this question must be rigorously examined as we move from the study of language to the consideration of other systems which also claim to have semantic functions, but whose fulfillment remains partial, fragmentary, or subjective, like, for example, social organization, art, and so forth [1963a:47–48].

The immense latitude of interpretation which this set of qualifications confers upon those seeking to confirm the validity of the "law" of negative and positive relations should be obvious. Here we have the perfect methodological analogue to Merton's "self-fulfilling prophecy": only the corroborative cases are acceptable as evidence. Given this privilege, what structural subtleties cannot be made to obey a convenient hypothesis?

THE EMPEROR'S NEW LAMP

Because of the fact that the entities with which Lévi-Strauss is concerned in the final analysis are mental structures—what to Durkheim were collective representations, and what are best simply called "ideas"—there spreads over the entire corpus of his work a paralysis of reality whose ultimate consequences we shall have occasion to describe at length. In conformity with his interpretation of the linguistic model, the surface of events is always misleading; the structural reality lies beneath and is never accessible to direct measurement. As Sahlins puts it, "what is apparent is false and what is hidden from perception and contradicts it is true" (SAHLINS 1966: 134). Now, this is a perfectly respectable and, indeed, a vital assumption, provided that there are concrete, material expressions, direct or indirect, by which the underlying structure issues forth into some sort of material embodiment. To employ an analogy: if a genie stays in the lamp and never comes out to do anything which his master tells him to do, does the genie exist? Yes, argues our Aladdin. Since the essence of what's in the bottle is nothing but a "mental structure," what right has one to expect that rubbing the lamp will produce a concrete result?

> For a theory like ours, which makes certain logical structures the fundamental basis for understanding matrimonial customs, it is not a matter of indifference that this structure is often visible, in systems where it has not concretely materialized [LÉVI-STRAUSS 1949:184].

STATISTICAL AND MECHANICAL MODELS

The distinction between "mechanical" and "statistical" models is related to an immense debate centering on the reality of certain phenomena which are of central significance in *The Elementary Structures of Kinship*. According to Hugo Nutini (1965:716), "Lévi-Strauss' most distinctive and important contribution to the theory of social structure was his dichotomizing of models into mechanical and statistical." Nutini has to admit, however, that Lévi-Strauss' exposition is "not altogether clear." The definition of the two kinds of models as set forth by Lévi-Strauss is as follows:

> A model the elements of which are on the same scale as the phenomena will be called a "mechanical model"; when the elements of the model are on a different scale, we shall be dealing with a "statistical model" [1963a:283].

As Nutini demonstrates by an analysis of examples provided by Lévi-Strauss, the distinction involved is actually quite simple: statistical models must reflect the frequencies of events, mechanical models are free to ignore such frequencies. Models of marriage systems provide the best illustration. Let us follow Nutini's hypothetical example: in two societies, X and Y, the frequency of polygynous marriages is 10 percent. Yet in X, the ideal cultural standard is monogamy, while in Y, the ideal cultural standard is polygyny. What to do?

> First, we must construct a mechanical model of polygyny for society X and a mechanical model of monogamy for society Y. Second, we subordinate a statistical model of monogamy to the mechanical model of polygyny in society X and statistical model of polygyny to the mechanical model of monogamy in society Y [NUTINI 1965: 722–23].

It may disturb the reader that Nutini would take a frequency of 10 percent and urge that a scientific model can be constructed which takes no account of 90 percent of the cases. But having gone so far, can there be an objection to a mechanical model which is fulfilled in 5 percent, 1 percent . . . or fewer instances? Well then, what about a mechanical model which is never fulfilled in actual practice? As we shall see in a moment, a decade of fierce polemic has centered on just such a case, namely Lévi-Strauss' model of patrilateral and matrilateral cross-cousin marriage. But let us first complete Nutini's train of thought. Why is he convinced that a statistical model should always be "subordinate" to a mechanical one?

> In societies of type X the mechanical model would account for only a fraction of the total number of marriages, and the statistical model for the great majority. Yet I would still maintain that the statistical model should be subordinated to the mechanical model, for, given the proper cultural conditions, the overlapping of ideal and actual behavior would tend to the ideal limit. What I am saying here is . . . the all-important fact that mechanical models are always heuristically superior to statistical models. . . . [*ibid.*:723].

Nutini does not name the corpus of evidence which leads to the conclusion that "actual behavior tends to the ideal limit." The overwhelming evidence to the contrary will be discussed in Chapter 20. Here, let it suffice to say that mechanical and statistical models of *both* actual and ideal culture are possible. Insofar as quantification and science have displayed a conspicuously beneficial partnership in all of the sister sciences, it is a mystification to urge the superiority of nonstatistically based models for anthropology. This is not to say that science and quantification are synonymous, but rather that if we proceed in ethnography to formulate models which lack statistical authority, we do so out of humility, hoping some day to possess the research facilities for correcting our lack of data.

Let us return now to *The Elementary Structures of Kinship* and follow out the consequences of Lévi-Strauss' privileged disregard of the materialization of the structural possibilities of kinship systems.

RESTRICTED AND GENERALIZED EXCHANGE

The aspect of Lévi-Strauss' book which has stimulated the greatest amount of exegesis is concerned with his discovery that marriage systems could be classified into two major types: those which produce "restricted" exchanges of women, and those which produce "generalized" exchanges of women. By a restricted exchange system, he meant one in which the obligation of reciprocity was fulfilled by a direct exchange of females between groups. A moiety situation in which the men of groups A and B exchange sisters for wives is the simplest case. In a generalized exchange system, on the other hand, the reciprocity takes place in a delayed fashion: A gives women to B, B gives women to C, and C gives women to A. Lévi-Strauss must be credited with making the important discovery that these two kinds of exchange are logically associated with different forms of cousin marriage. Restricted exchange would result automatically from regular cross-cousin marriage, provided that there is marriage with both the mother's brother's daughter and father's sister's daughter. This is the symmetrical form of cross-cousin marriage. Generalized exchange, on the other hand, is logically associated with asymmetrical cross-cousin marriage, specifically of the mother's brother's daughter variety. This is called matrilateral cross-cousin marriage. That is, where ego marries mother's brother's daughter and does not marry father's sister's daughter, there logically results a form of circulating connubium in which the cycle A-B-C-A takes place. Lévi-Strauss must be credited with the further important discovery that the patrilateral variety of asymmetrical cross-cousin marriage is not the mirror image of the matrilateral variety. Instead, there logically results a shunting effect such that the cycle A-B-C is reversed to C-B-A in alternate generations.

Although there is a marked reluctance on the part of Lévi-Strauss to place his discussion in an evolutionary context (*cf.* 1949:277), restricted exchange systems have the nuance of being more archaic, and general exchange systems seem modern. This would certainly follow from the emphasis placed upon associating generalized exchange with the achievement of a higher degree of social solidarity than that achieved by restricted exchange:

> In effect, generalized exchange allows, the group remaining the same in extension and composition, the realization, in the heart of this mechanically stable group, of a greater organic solidarity [*ibid.*:548].

From considerations such as these Lévi-Strauss proposes that the peculiar shunting effect of the patrilateral asymmetrical form must be associated with an inferior degree of solidarity:

> Instead of constituting a global system, as do both bilateral and matrilateral cross-cousin marriage each in its own sphere, mar-

> riage with father's sister's daughter is not capable of attaining any other form than a multitude of little closed systems, juxtaposed to one another, without ever realizing a global structure [*ibid.*:553].

Noting that the patrilateral variety has a much more restricted distribution than the matrilateral variety, he offers the following Durkheimian solution:

> If then, in the last analysis, marriage with the daughter of the father's sister is less frequent than that with the daughter of the mother's brother the reason is that the latter not only permits but favors a better integration of the group, while the former never succeeds in creating anything more than a precarious edifice, made of merely juxtaposed materials, obeying no plan of ensemble; and its texture is exposed to the same fragility as that of each of the little local structures of which it is composed [*ibid.*:558].

The first sustained evaluation of *The Elementary Structures of Kinship* was written by Josselin de Jong (1952). Confining his critical comments to matters of detail in the Australian systems, Josselin de Jong chided his colleagues for their lack of response "to one of the most important contributions to anthropological theory of the present century" (*ibid.*:59). But in 1955, a decidedly negative reaction was brought forth by George Homans and David Schneider. Their criticism centered on the explanation of the matrilateral/patrilateral cross-cousin problem, as outlined above; and it touched off an acrimonious debate which is of central importance in the recent history of anthropology.

THE HOMANS AND SCHNEIDER CRITIQUE

Homans and Schneider rejected the postulated relationship between frequency of occurrence of matrilateral and patrilateral cross-cousin marriage and degree of social solidarity resulting from exchange cycles. Although respectful of Lévi-Strauss' erudition and ethnographic competence, they express their suspicion that the invocation of social solidarity as a final cause is mere "rhetoric." To explain the disparity between the incidence of the two asymmetrical forms of cross-cousin rules, a theory involving "efficient causes" is required. That is, the theory must specify how the human actors' short-run personal interests are better served by adopting one form rather than the other. Such a theory, they propose, is already present in Radcliffe-Brown's solution of the avunculate problem. In brief, as

Radcliffe-Brown saw it, the presence of patrilineal descent groups tends to produce a situation where restraint and authority center about father and the male and female members of his descent group. At the same time, informality and indulgence characterize relations with mother and all of the male and female members of mother's patrilineage. Mother's brother is thus a sort of "male mother," while father's sister is a "female father." Homans and Schneider take off from this point by posing the question of what significance this "patrilineal complex" might have for the differential treatment of the mother's brother's daughter as compared with father's sister's daughter. Since indulgent freedom characterizes relations with mother's brother, is it not likely that his daughter will be preferred in marriage? The theory involved could be summed up by the rule: "Where a man finds love in one generation, he will find it in the next" (HOMANS and SCHNEIDER 1955:38). The other cross cousin, associated with the stern and distant father's sister, is less likely to appeal to the sentimental efficient causes of marriage.

Homans and Schneider then take the additional step of postulating that where the descent rule is matrilineal rather than patrilineal, an opposite sort of jural and sentimental complex would exist. Mother's brother now becomes the stern authoritarian figure, while father, father's sister, and father's sister's daughter bask in the warmth of indulgent sentiments. This suggests the hypothesis that matrilateral and patrilateral asymmetrical cross-cousin marriages are respectively correlated with patrilineal and matrilineal descent. This is a prospect that was not considered by Lévi-Strauss, who states that the structure of exchange does not depend upon descent (1949:599). But if the correlation can be demonstrated, it at once explains why the frequency of matrilateral cross-cousin marriage should be so much greater than its opposite: the reason is simply that matrilineal descent occurs much less frequently than patrilineal descent.

With mounting confidence, Homans and Schneider proceeded to formulate a statistical test of their hypothesis. Assisted by the Human Relations Area Files they gathered together all the available cases of preferential asymmetrical cross-cousin marriage and demonstrated a strong statistical correlation in support of their hypothesis. Of twenty-six societies in which mother's brother's daughter is the preferred marriage, twenty-two have patrilineal descent, while of the seven societies which preferred father's sister's daughter, five have matrilineal descent. Homans and Schneider conclude that Lévi-Strauss' theory is not necessarily wrong (solidarity may still have its effect somehow), but that it is now unnecessary. Their own theory "predicts what societies will adopt what form, and Lévi-Strauss's theory will not" (*ibid.*:59).

REPLY TO HOMANS AND SCHNEIDER

In 1958, Lévi-Strauss responded to this critique by means of a page-long footnote to the republication of his article, "Social Structure" (1963a:322; orig. 1958). Homans and Schneider's statistical correlation "proves nothing," he asserts. There was, first of all, the question of statistics. Since both patrilineal descent and matrilateral marriage occur so much more frequently than their opposites, a purely random distribution would result in the kind of correlation which was advanced in favor of Homans and Schneider's hypothesis.

> Societies with patrilineal descent are much more numerous than societies with matrilineal descent. Furthermore, matrilateral marriage is more frequent than patrilateral marriage. Thus, if the distribution occurred at random, we might expect that the incidence of societies characterized by an association between patrilineal descent and matrilateral marriage would be higher, and thus the correlation claimed by my critics would be meaningless [*ibid.*].

We shall note only briefly, as André Köbben (1966:148) points out, that this suggestion is "contrary to simple statistical theory." (Homans and Schneider employed the method of correlation in order to rule out the possibility of "random" effects.) The necessity for this embarrassing comment has scarcely been lessened by J. Pouwer's (1965:155) rejoinder to the effect that Lévi-Strauss did not flatly declare that the correlation was worthless due to random effects (precisely what Homans and Schneider's correlations were intended to eliminate) but that they "*could*" be due to random effects. Translation: the great man may have been in error, but you can't prove it.

Lévi-Strauss did, however, have a telling point to make with regard to the statistical issue. In 1957, Murdock had tested the Homans and Schneider correlations on an enlarged sample, and Lévi-Strauss could now cite Murdock's (1957:687) conclusions: In a sample of 564 societies, patrilateral preference occurred so infrequently that the correlation in question, while still evident, could not be relied upon.

Continuing his rebuttal of Homans and Schneider, however, Lévi-

Strauss went on to express himself as willing to concede, at least for the sake of argument, that matrilateral and patrilateral marriage rules are statistically connected with matrilineal and patrilineal descent. In case this should be so, he is prepared to offer an explanation in conformity with his theory. Since matrilineal systems are (by general agreement) inherently more unstable than patrilineal ones, the long exchange cycle of the matrilateral rule could not be maintained by matrilineal societies, "while the extremely short cycles of patrilateral marriage would be less affected by the conflicts always found in matrilineal societies." He then made the following fateful remark: "If such were the case, matrilateral marriage would be more frequent; but it would not have to be *prescribed*" (LÉVI-STRAUSS 1963a:322).

PRESCRIPTION VERSUS PREFERENCE

It is at this point that Rodney Needham, a British devotee of structural anthropology, enters the scene. The italicized "prescribed" in Lévi-Strauss' footnote appeared to link with certain additional hints in *The Elementary Structures of Kinship* adding up to a crucial distinction between *prescribed* and *preferred* marriage rules. "Prescription" means absolute, exclusive demand for a certain type of alliance to take place, while "preference" is merely suggestion and exhortation. Needham then races ahead to the conclusion that Homans and Schneider have busied themselves with the collection of a lot of data that is irrelevant for Lévi-Strauss' main thesis. For in their cross-cultural test, Homans and Schneider have paid no attention to the difference between mere preference and absolute prescription.

Homans and Schneider were forthwith attacked by Needham (1962), in what must be the most surly if not the most sadistic assault in the annals of scholarly publications. His words dripping with contempt, Needham pushes his opponents into the figurative abyss that their failure to separate preference from prescription seemed to have earned for them. After examining each of the thirty-three societies in the Homans and Schneider sample, Needham throws out twenty-four of them as practicing something other than prescriptive cross-cousin marriage. Of the nine admissible cases, all have the matrilateral form, and one of these is a combination of matrilaterality with matrilineality.

> Now Homans and Schneider claim to explain *both* types of "unilateral cross-cousin marriage." The argument is about prescriptions, and their theory applies in part (specifically, not only by the fact of contending with Lévi-Strauss) to prescriptions. But

> when we examine their test cases we see that they have no prescriptive patrilateral cases at all. Their own evidence thus relates to only *one* form of prescriptive marriage, and cannot therefore yield any support whatever for their claim to explain the differential incidence of both types [*ibid.*: 57].

As for the 8:1 ratio of patrilineal to matrilineal societies with the matrilateral prescription, there is nothing here but a complete vindication of Lévi-Strauss' proposal that there was no *necessary* relation between descent rule and type of prescription:

> He is not concerned with, and says nothing about, statistical frequencies. If it were the case that all societies practicing generalized exchange were patrilineal and patrilocal except one, and that the one were matrilineal and matrilocal, then his proposition would be validated. Even if no such society existed, the proposition would still hold in a formal sense: matrilineal and matrilocal societies exist and form viable systems, and there is no obvious structural reason to deny or doubt that such a society might also practice prescriptive matrilateral cross-cousin marriage [*ibid.*].

I must confess to a total lack of sympathy for Homans and Schneider over the drubbing they received because of their failure to distinguish preference from prescription. They in effect "asked for it" by deliberately confining themselves to mechanical models. That is, by virtue of their own emic and idealist predilections, they chose to criticize Lévi-Strauss on his own home territory. Their test cases are assembled with respect to the ideological norms of rules of marriage. They nowhere inquire into the operation by which the amount of solidarity in a social group can be measured. (Actually, they reject this strategy at the outset—HOMANS and SCHNEIDER 1955:13). More importantly, they do not object to the absence of a discussion of the measurable material manifestations of the rules in question, in terms of actual numbers of historically real marriages involving specific men and women and specific kinship groups at definite times and places. They are content instead to grapple with the phantoms of idealized rules and idealized marriages, from which beautifully logical idealized exchange cycles result. Innocents abroad! They are prepared to deal with phantoms, but not with *elementary* ones. They do not realize that among professional idealists, as distinct from the eclectic American amateurs who have rubbed shoulders with logical positivism and behaviorism too long to know how to really get off the ground, a rule which is manifest in a hundred cases is no better than that which is manifest in none.

THE SEARCH FOR THE UNICORN

The rout of Homans and Schneider appeared complete, but Needham would settle for nothing but unconditional surrender. Statistical correlations are, after all, not very informative, he argued. What we are after is a knowledge of structure. We need "a total structural analysis of all the recorded facts of one society" (NEEDHAM 1962:73). The real question before us continues to be the value of Lévi-Strauss' application of the principle of reciprocity to the understanding of marriage systems. We must take one specific case of matrilateral prescription and see how our understanding of it is enriched by Lévi-Strauss' theory of generalized exchange.

This sounds like a reasonable idea as long as one ignores the fact that Needham was only able to find nine cases of matrilateral prescription in the entire world—nine cases to substantiate empirically the material existence of the long-cycle, generalized exchange system which is supposed to be the more organically solidary of the only two viable elementary exchange systems that have ever existed. If all the remaining thousands of known cases represent "complex" systems, do we not have the obligation to insist upon interpretive principles which are first and foremost responsive to the conditions of the universe in which we happen to be living? In this regard, it cannot be overemphasized that there is not the slightest clue in Lévi-Strauss' tome as to why one finds so few "generalized" exchange systems; nor are there, aside from a few evolutionary innuendos, suggestions of what might be the conditions which lead to the appearance of the restricted rather than the generalized form. But let us follow Needham in his application of the exchange cycle theory to a specific case, for there are more surprises ahead.

ENTER THE PURUM

The society selected for intensive study are the Purum of Manipur, as described by T. C. Das (1945). Needham presents a lucid summary of the rules of the marriage and exchange system which hinges on a firm matrilateral cross-cousin prescription. Various alliance cycles are described, some of them binding wife-giving and wife-receiving lineages in chains involving as many as seven different patrilineages (e.g., A-B-C-D-E-F-G-A). Moreover, Needham goes on to show that many symbolic aspects of Purum ritual life, including such everyday matters as the arrangement of sleeping quarters and household architecture, can be rendered intelligible if they are interpreted as expressing the fundamental "structural" distinction between wife-giving and wife-receiving groups. The symbolic confirmation of the importance of Lévi-Strauss' principle even embraces the ritual difference between left and right, female and male, sun and sky, death and life, and below and above (NEEDHAM 1962:96). Crowing with satisfaction, Needham taunts his victims in the following words:

> All this we are able to see thanks ultimately to the astonishingly fertile notion of "exchange" as an analytical concept, fashioned for us by Mauss and developed in the field of marriage by Lévi-Strauss. It is true that this is only a mediating concept, and that it alone could not bring the analysis quite to the point of radical understanding that I think we have reached here; but it is an essential notion, and it has done for us what a truly scholarly insight should do—it has made things plain. Would Homans and Schneider be prepared to claim as much now for their own theory? Is all this really to be explained, as they say, by "the Oedipus Complex" [*ibid.*:99]?

Now the *raison d'être* of the Purum case is that it is supposed to vindicate Lévi-Strauss by showing: (1) the distinctive results of generalized versus restricted exchange; (2) the analytical advantage of viewing kinship in terms of exchange cycles; (3) the importance of the difference between prescription and preference. Even the skeptical reader, having witnessed the merciless destruction of Needham's enemies, finds it hard to imagine that the Purum could in any way fail to accomplish their assigned task. After all, it is Needham who suggests that a case is necessary to the exposition, and even then, there are several from which to choose. But no reasonably alert graduate student could avoid the tidal wave of disbelief which Needham's presentation of Purum ethnography sets in motion.

PURUM DO NOT ABIDE BY THEIR MATRILATERAL PRESCRIPTION

Needham describes circular connubiums of bride-givers and bride-receivers extending through seven lineages. He lists twenty such cycles and admits that there are many more. Yet of actual historical marriages, Das provides information on only 141. Clearly some of the cycles in entirety or some of the links in some of the cycles reflect ideal, rather than actual, culture. We begin to wonder, therefore, what relationship there might possibly be between the ideal wife-givers and wife-receivers and the actual wife-givers and wife-receivers.

This question has been pursued by Charles Ackerman (1964). The 141 recorded marriages took place between 39 pairs of lineages; but 12 (30 percent) of the members of these pairs were both wife-takers and wife-receivers, *violating the fundamental condition of general exchange.*

In addition, marriage took place between 15 pairs of lineages out of the 39 in the absence of any normative status as either wife-giver or wife-receiver. Yet of the 48 pairs of lineages between whom wives should have been exchanged, only 23 actually were demonstrably linked on the basis of recorded marriages.

Turning to the question of whether the pattern of alliances produced by the actual marriages could have resulted from chance, Ackerman matches actual against potential forms of alliance and concludes that "the probability that the distribution arises from chance and not from any 'avoidance' of direct exchange, is greater than three in ten" (*ibid.*:60). Ackerman further demonstrates that if the observed pattern were to be maintained through a large number of marriages, all of the possible alliances would be realized. That is, the observed alliances could just as well be described as a function of the number of marriages contracted by a particular lineage as of the prescriptive rule.

But the rule itself turns out to be something different from what Needham says it is. The rigorous distinction between prescribed and preferred begins to slip away when the evidence is given careful scrutiny. Das does not specify the procedures which he employed to reach his formulation of the marriage rule. That is, there are no formal eliciting or polling procedures (and Needham never explains what he would do with minority opinions—see Chap. 20). The Purum seem to insist on marriage with either mother's brother's daughter or some other woman of mother's brother's sib, but 48 per cent of the recorded marriages actually contracted are with women outside of this "prescribed" category (*ibid.*:56).

Thus, all the uses for which the Purum case is intended are defeated. Both generalized and restricted exchange occur; reciprocity is fragmentary and unproven; prescription remains a degree of preference rather than a sharply different structural matter. As Ackerman puts it:

> No tendency to avoid the direct exchange of women exists in the distribution of actual marriages. On the contrary, in a series of tests the null hypothesis has been corroborated: the distribution of actual alliances is a function of the marginal distribution among the lineages of the total population of marrying acts. Where direct-exchange cells are not used, the situation is one of few marrying acts and low *a priori* expectation of use; such cells are not "avoided," they are merely not used—yet. Purum marriage choices are not ordered by a matrilateral connubium [*ibid.*: 64].

Lévi-Strauss' basic distinction between restricted and generalized exchange is thus returned to the logical exercise from which it sprang.

There is one escape from this situation for Lévi-Strauss' followers and they were quick to take it; show the bottle instead of the genie. As for Lévi-Strauss, he had another option, to which we refer in a moment. Thus, rising to Needham's defense, David Maybury-Lewis (1965:221) insists:

> When we refer to unilateral cross-cousin marriage as an asymmetric system, we are referring to an asymmetry in the rule, not in its social consequences. The consequences are perhaps likely to be asymmetric but they need not necessarily be so. Similarly it is possible for a society to have a symmetric marriage rule and for the application of the rule to result in asymmetry.

Referring specifically to Ackerman's "erroneous analysis of the Purum material,"

> It can now be seen why there must be a distinction maintained between prescriptive and preferential marriage systems. A prescriptive marriage rule entails . . . the division of Ego's conceptual universe in a determined fashion, irrespective of the percentage of people who marry their actual MBD or into their MB's descent group. These percentages may be of considerable interest in the handling of certain problems. They do not affect the prescription as here defined or its minimum social entailments [*ibid.*:225].

THE OLD ROPE TRICK

There is nothing to be shocked about in the proposal that the existence of the prescribed system depends upon whether or not an appropriate "conceptual" distinction is made by the culture carriers. Setting aside for the moment the nagging operational questions which are to be taken up in the chapter on emics and etics, let us grant the possibility of a neat dichotomization between a preferential and prescriptive conceptual state. But now what becomes of the social solidarity argument? If it doesn't matter whether or not there are material manifestations (i.e., historically specific arrangements of people and their behavior), then there can be no basis for supposing that the matrilateral system occurs more frequently than the patrilateral one because one is associated with more solidary consequences than the other. Unless, of course, the solidary effects are to be viewed as consisting of the same stuff as the rules! Let it be recorded then that in this fashion, the structuralists climb up ropes and disappear off the tops of them.

One of the most impressive exhibitions of this trick is to be found in J. Pouwer's defense of Lévi-Strauss against criticisms proposed by A. J. F. Köbben. The latter supports Homans and Schneider's statistics, noting that their opponents "simply cannot disregard their results" without placing themselves "outside of the sphere of science" (KÖBBEN 1966:147). To which Pouwer (1966:155) replies that Lévi-Strauss cannot be attacked for the failure of his theories to be corroborated by empirical data. Marriage rules cannot be explained by actual marriages. There is no necessary connection between the logic underlying cultural representations and empirical reality! When he wrote his masterpiece, Lévi-Strauss was well aware that "discontinuity and discrepancy can occur between the structuring activities of the human mind and the empirical reality in which those activities manifest themselves": ". . . empirical data yield at most an indication of the direction in which we should seek an explanation for the occurrence of a phenomenon" (POUWER 1966:155). From this remark in its actual context one can only conclude that Pouwer is either beyond the sphere of science or that he would wish science to be defined as the study of nonempirical phenomena.

A VOICE FROM ON HIGH

The Homans and Schneider and Needham clash gave rise to a controversy in which dozens of anthropologists became embroiled and about which scores of learned papers were published in professional journals. In an early draft of this chapter, I had despaired of doing justice to the rival claims of so numerous a swarm of exegetical combatants. At the last minute, however, a new development occurred, which simplifies the problem. This development consists of the publication of a second edition of Lévi-Strauss' *The Elementary Structures of Kinship* with a preface containing the master's comments upon Needham's attempt to protect him from the Homans and Schneider critique. To the astonishment of his entire professional audience, and certainly not least of all of Needham, Lévi-Strauss has denied the validity of Needham's main point. He has expressed himself as follows:

> Led by Needham, several authors today affirm that my book is only concerned with prescriptive systems, or more precisely (since it suffices to glance through it to be convinced of the contrary) that such would have been the case had I not confused the two forms [i.e. prescriptive and preferential marriage rules]. But, since, according to those who defend this distinction, prescriptive systems are very rare, a curious consequence results, if they are correct: I would have written a very big book . . . which was concerned with facts so rare, which applied to such a limited domain, that one no longer comprehends what importance it might have for a general theory of kinship [in press].

Lévi-Strauss goes on to say that if this had been the case he finds it hard to understand why Needham would have busied himself with the task of bringing out an English translation or why his publishers should pay for his work with a "splendid check." The fact, he asserts, is that the distinction between prescriptive and preferential systems does not constitute an important issue as far as he or the groups which practice asymmetrical cross-cousin marriage are concerned:

> If I have indifferently employed the notions of preference and obligation, even sometimes associating them, as I have been reproached for doing, in the same sentence, it's because to my eyes they do not connote different social realities, but correspond rather to slightly different ways by which people think about the same reality [*ibid*].

It cannot but strike the unsympathetic observer that if Rodney Needham and his followers were unable to understand what was going on inside of Lévi-Strauss' head, they show little promise of getting to understand what goes on inside the heads of the Purum. Even more alarming is the possibility that Lévi-Strauss may not even understand what's going on inside his own head. For, in discussing the problems he confronted in bringing out a second edition of *The Elementary Structures of Kinship,* he confesses that once he has finished a book it becomes a strange body to him, no longer capable of engaging his interest, and that "it is with difficulty sometimes, that I come to understand it." All this would be funny were it not for the huge investment in research time and journal space that has been squandered on this issue.[1]

LÉVI-STRAUSS AND MARX

One final aberration requires our attention. Despite all the evidence of actual behavior to the contrary, Lévi-Strauss has repeatedly asserted his fidelity to Marx's teachings. For example, in his reply to M. Rodinson's criticism of his mentalistic use of the concept of "structure," he says Rodinson, "did not think it profitable to inquire about my endeavors to reintegrate the anthropological knowledge acquired during the last fifty years into the Marxian tradition" (LÉVI-STRAUSS 1963b:343).

Just what do Lévi-Strauss and Marx have in common? A number of similarities come to mind, but all of them are superficial. We may note, first of all, that there is a shared suspicion of the devices by which social systems consciously offer up explanations of themselves. Lévi-Strauss is concerned always with the discovery of the "true" social structure as opposed to surface reflexes or epiphenomena. But this attitude merely identifies the basic intellectual posture of every serious modern social scientist and philosopher. If it were peculiar to Marx, then we should have to conclude that Freud, Durkheim, and a hundred other unlikely figures were also working within the Marxist tradition. Secondly, there is the evident infatuation of Lévi-Strauss

[1] As the page proofs of this chapter were being corrected, I was able to inspect the galleys of Rodney Needham's "Introduction" to the forthcoming English translation of the second edition of *Les Structures Élémentaires de la Parenté*. This translation, upon which Needham and two collaborators worked for over six years, includes the startling new "Introduction" described above. But Lévi-Strauss opened this window to his mind only after the hapless Needham had reported that the translation and editing were finished. Indeed, according to Needham, Lévi-Strauss steadfastly refused to examine the translation before it went to press. Needham was thus obliged to add a post-script to his own "Editor's Note," in which he admits that his idol has charged him with a "fundamental misunderstanding of the very title and subject matter of the book"! Needham "can only explain that if the views in question had been published earlier, at a more decisive date, he could never have consented to edit the work (even, as he understood, at the author's wish) or to take any part in its translation." Only those who have not directly experienced Needham's *Structure and Sentiment* will feel sorry for him, but we may all lament the disservice which these antics render to the science of culture.

with a dialectic mode of thought. This may be defined as an aversion to simple dualities, as in his study of Bororo moieties:

> . . . the study of so-called dual organizations discloses so many anomalies and contradictions in relation to extant theory that we should be well advised to reject the theory and to treat the apparent manifestations of dualism as superficial distortions of structures whose real nature is quite different and vastly more complex [1963a:161].

If fascination with the number three makes a Marxist, then perhaps we should include Pythagoras. Or shall we argue that the affectation of a dialectic style is alone sufficient? Shall we make of Hegel the thesis, Marx the antithesis, and Lévi-Strauss the synthesis? Robert Murphy (1963:17) shows quite succinctly that when you stand Marx on his head, you get "Zen Marxism." I should prefer, however, to call it French Hegelianism. Although the phrase lacks the *brille* which Murphy has managed to put into his, it keeps Marx out of it. For Lévi-Strauss no more represents the synthesis of materialism and idealism than Comte did. Every substantative report, every choice of hypothesis, every sustained analysis, from his Nambikwara research to his studies of myth, draws its principal sustenance from the mainstreams of French and German idealism. To protest that Marx was interested in ideology, that Marx also realized that the ideological expressions of social structure were dialectically rather than mechanically related, and that Marx, as well as Lévi-Strauss, assigned creative and determinative roles to human ideas is to pay tribute to Marx, not to Lévi-Strauss. But to count the dialectic and the cautions concerning a rigid exclusion of ideology as his chief contributions is to fail utterly to comprehend Marx's role in the development of the social sciences. Unlike Marx, Lévi-Strauss confronted a great opportunity to which he did not respond. He found Comte, Durkheim, and Mauss standing on their heads, and he joined them.

British Social Anthropology

19

The challenge to nineteenth-century evolutionism in England arose from two unequally endowed groups of scholars. On the one hand W. H. R. Rivers, E. J. Perry, and E. G. Smith paralleled many members of the Boasian school in their idiographic, diffusionist emphasis. At approximately the same time the foundations were being laid for another approach, which spurned both the evolutionists and the diffusionists. Moreover, this second group of scholars, unlike the first, equaled and in many cases surpassed the Boasians in their emphasis upon and actual exposure to fieldwork. Intensive field studies among a small number of aboriginal societies, and intensive analysis of the data from such studies, were organized by this British school around the theme of synchronic functional relations. It was by means of the synchronic functionalist framework that the British "social anthropologists" hoped to preserve the heritage of nineteenth-century scientism while ridding themselves of the accumulated liabilities of the search for diachronic, evolutionary regularities. By the late 1930's this group had gained virtually unchallenged control of the anthropological establishment throughout the British Empire.

DURKHEIM AND STRUCTURAL-FUNCTIONALISM

The fundamental theoretical premises of British social anthropology are based upon Emile Durkheim's apotheosis of social solidarity. Durkheim's influence is especially basic for an understanding of the rise of the so-called structural-functionalists. Alfred Reginald Radcliffe-Brown, the principal theoretician of this movement, was quite explicit about Durkheim's role. On the one hand he hailed Durkheim's definition of "function" as "the first systematic formulation of the concept applying to the strictly scientific study of society" (RADCLIFFE-BROWN 1952b:178). On the other, he explicitly rejected definitions of function which did not relate to "social structure," a concept which can be shown to derive its main inspiration from Durkheim's emphasis upon social solidarity. The combination of "function" with "social structure" gave rise to the awkward but descriptive label, "structural-functional." Radcliffe-Brown placed great emphasis upon distinguishing structural functions from functions that Bronislaw Malinowski and others associated with the biopsychological needs of individuals. For Radcliffe-Brown the only acceptable definition of function was the "contribution" an institution makes to the maintenance of social structure. "This theory of society in terms of structure and process, interconnected by function, has nothing in common with the theory of culture as derived from individual biological needs" (RADCLIFFE-BROWN 1949b:322).

This theory does, however, have everything in common with Durkheim's approach to sociocultural phenomena via the conditions of social cohesiveness or social solidarity. The structural-functionalist's basic assumption is that social systems maintain themselves for significant intervals of time in a steady state during which a high degree of cohesion and solidarity characterizes the relationships among its members. The only difference between Radcliffe-Brown and Durkheim in this regard is that Radcliffe-Brown substituted the terms "unity," "harmony," or "consistency" for Durkheim's "solidarity."

> Such a view implies that a social system (the total social structure of a society together with the totality of social usages in which that structure appears and on which it depends for its continued existence) has a certain kind of unity, which we may speak of as a functional unity. We may define it as a condition in which all parts of the social system work together with a sufficient degree of

> harmony or internal consistency, i.e. without producing persistent conflicts which can neither be resolved nor regulated [RADCLIFFE-BROWN 1952b:181].

COLONIALISM AND THE HYPOTHESIS OF FUNCTIONAL UNITY

It is an error to portray the structural-functionalists as pollyannas, innocent of the occurrence of internal conflict and dissension. Durkheim made ample provision for such phenomena in his assumptions concerning the existence of pathological afflictions to which social systems are prone. Although Radcliffe-Brown disapproved of this effort to identify the structural analogues of disease (*ibid.*:182), neither he nor his students were unaware of the existence of sharp and unresolved conflict. But they were not prepared to accept such conflict as a normal, or fundamental, aspect of the human condition. Assumptions concerning functional unity are, according to Radcliffe-Brown, merely hypotheses which "it seems worthwhile to test by systematic examination of the facts" (*ibid.*:181).

One might very well argue that the concept of functional unity is a necessary heuristic assumption, equivalent to the belief that the system under observation is a phenomenon which lasts long enough to warrant abstraction from the stream of history. As Radcliffe-Brown put it, "In such an analysis we are dealing with a system as it exists at a certain time, abstracting as far as possible from any change that it may be undergoing" (1950:3). In theory, there was nothing to prevent Radcliffe-Brown and his students from exposing and emphasizing the lack of solidarity and cohesion in the larger societies which they were studying. But the argument for heuristic advantage must be placed in the actual research context in which the theory of structural-functionalist ethnography was put to the test. Between 1930 and 1955 the overwhelming bulk of the contributions of the structural-functionalist school was based upon fieldwork in African tribal societies located in European, especially British, territories. Under such circumstances it is impossible not to draw a connection between the proposal to study social systems *as if* they were solidary and *as if* they were timeless, with sponsorship, employment, and indirect association of the members of this school by and with a now defunct colonial system (*cf.* FORDE 1953).

As late as 1950, Radcliffe-Brown's "Introduction" to *African Systems of Kinship and Marriage* included an opening quote from Gobineau advising Europeans who wish their civilizations to spread of the importance of knowing and comprehending those who were to be benefited. This is followed by the author's wish that "this book will be read not only by anthropologists, but by some of those who are responsible for formulating or carrying out policies of colonial government in the African continent." As we shall see, there is something to be said for Gregg and Williams' portrayal of functionalism as a new kind of "Dismal Science" whose function it was to provide a scientific rationalization of the status quo, especially in reference to the British policy of indirect rule. Since this relationship is not peculiar to the structural-functionalist position, but is shared by Malinowski as well, we shall have to return to it later on.

MEANING OF SOCIAL STRUCTURE

As I have already suggested, at the root of the association between structural-functionalism and the Durkheimian heritage there lies an insistence upon viewing functional relations exclusively in the context of social structure.

Just what is this "social structure" which lies at the heart of the structural-functionalist movement? In the context of the research product achieved by Radcliffe-Brown and his students, a pragmatic definition might be offered: the study of groups, especially those organized along territorial, kinship, and political lines and the interrelationships among these constitute the core of social-structural phenomena. In a slightly different sense, all differentiated social positions or statuses derived from a consideration of membership in social groupings constitute parts of social structure (RADCLIFFE-BROWN 1952b:193).

It is of the greatest importance to specify how this notion of social structure is related to the other parts of a sociocultural system. According to Radcliffe-Brown, there are three heuristically separable "adaptational" aspects of the total social system. Social structure, "the arrangements by which an orderly social life is maintained," is one of these three aspects. The other two are the "ecological," or the way the system is adapted to the physical environment; and the cultural, or the mechanisms by which an individual acquires "habits and mental characteristics that fit him for participation in social life" (*ibid.*:9). Substituting the concept "ideology" for the category to which Radcliffe-Brown arbitrarily assigned the term "culture," we are left with the familiar Marxist three-part division of sociocultural systems into techno-economic, social-structural, and ideological phenomena. What is of greatest moment in this arrangement is the separability of social structure from considerations of the techno-environmental and techno-economic complex.

THE PRIORITY OF SOCIAL STRUCTURE

What is the relationship between ecological-economic "adaption" and social-structural "adaption"? Is it the function of the economic and ecological adaptations to sustain the social structure, or is it rather the function of the social structure to maintain the economic and ecological adaptations? According to structural-functionalism, it is the social structure which always deserves priority of analysis. In Radcliffe-Brown's theory and practice of structural-functionalism, it is only legitimate to ask how the economic system results from, or contributes to, the maintenance of a given social structure, never, how a particular social structure results from, and serves to maintain, a given set of techno-economic adaptations:

> The economic machinery of a society appears in quite a new light if it is studied in relation to the social structure. The exchange of goods and services is dependent upon, is the result of, and at the same time is a means of maintaining a certain structure, a network of relations between persons and collections of persons. For the economists and politicians of Canada the potlatch of the Indians of the north-west of America was simply wasteful foolishness and it was therefore forbidden. For the anthropologist it was the machinery for maintaining a social structure of lineages, clans and moieties, with which was combined an arrangement of rank defined by privileges [*ibid.*:197-98].

Although Radcliffe-Brown's threefold division of social systems is not consistently adhered to, either in his own writings or in those of his students, the tactical and theoretical priority of social-structural factors is seldom compromised.

Meyer Fortes, for example, confused a good many American cultural anthropologists by using the term "culture" in a more global sense than that proposed by Radcliffe-Brown. In speaking of "optional frames of reference," Fortes (1953b:21) mentions "ideological," "normative," and "biological viewpoints," omitting the techno-economic altogether. But according to Fortes all the phenomena observable within these frames are to be regarded as facets of social structure: "In this sense social structure is not an aspect of culture, but the entire culture of a given people handled in a special frame of theory" (*ibid.*). It is interesting to note how Lowie reacted to this proposal. He could "admit that it is profitable to view the culture of a people with social structure as a starting point," but he felt that there would be an "appallingly large" residue of other cultural items which would remain unstudied if one approached the "entire culture" from Fortes' point of view (LOWIE 1953:531-32). This seems to suppose that an appalling residue of unstudied facets of culture was not left over by the Boasians. The question cannot be put in the form of why not study the whole of culture rather than a part—a complete ethnography is impossible to achieve. The decisive question is rather, why one part more than some other part?

THE ANTIFUNCTIONALIST BOGEY

Before attempting to learn how Radcliffe-Brown and his students handled this question, let us take time out to bury the misconception that the historical particularists and the structural-functionalists represent, respectively, anti- and profunctionalist positions. This popular notion arose as a result of a breakdown in communication over the meaning of the term "function."

During the late 1920's and early 1930's when the Boasians first began to take cognizance of the structural-functionalist program, there seems to have been little comprehension of the highly specific meaning which Radcliffe-Brown was giving to the concept of function. At a joint session of the American Anthropological Association, the American Folk-Lore Society, and Section H of the American Association for the Advancement of Science at Pittsburgh in 1934, Radcliffe-Brown was invited to comment on a paper by Alexander Lesser in which function was treated as follows:

> In its logical essentials, what is a functional relation? Is it any different in kind from functional relations in other fields of science? I think not. A genuinely functional relation is one which is established between two or more terms or variables such that it can be asserted that under certain defined conditions (which form one term of the relation) certain determined expressions of those conditions (which is the other term of the relation) are observed. The functional relation or relations asserted of any delimited aspect of culture must be such as to explain the nature and character of the delimited aspect under defined conditions [LESSER 1935:392].

Radcliffe-Brown understandably enough felt that there was so little in common between his "function" and the one which Lesser had that he declined to "offer any real criticism of his paper" (RADCLIFFE-BROWN 1935:394). But instead of taking advantage of the opportunity to advise Lesser on the Durkheimian meaning of function, Radcliffe-Brown added to the confusion by declaring that the "functional hypothesis" was in conflict with the view held by some ethnologists. He called this view "the 'shreds and patches' theory of culture," from Lowie's phrase, "when he speaks of that planless hodge-podge, that thing of shreds and patches called civilization" (RADCLIFFE-BROWN 1952a:186).

The indignation which this produced in the ranks of the Boasians was certainly justified. Lowie's phrase, as we have seen, although it appears on the last page of *Primitive Society,* bears little resemblance to the main substance of that work, which at every point emphasized the importance of examining cultural traits in relationship to their larger cultural context. Unfortunately, in rebuttal, Lowie shifted the focus of criticism of both Radcliffe-Brown and Malinowski toward proof that "In his functionalist approach, Boas . . . antedates others by decades" (LOWIE 1938:142).

It was unwise for Radcliffe-Brown to have mixed up the shreds and patches heresy with the structural-functionalist program; any kind of functionalism was an antidote to extreme diffusionism, and Lesser, Boas, and Lowie scarcely needed to be warned about the dangers of diffusionist schemes. In addition, all the Boasians operated with an implicit model of total sociocultural systems. On the other hand, the Americans were certainly guilty of failing to grasp the significance of Radcliffe-Brown's Durkheimian heritage.

As a result of this kind of off-center parrying, plus Malinowski's crusade against Graebnerian "museum moles," too many scholars have befuddled themselves with the question of who was and who was not a functionalist. It was left for Kingsley Davis to declare that functional analysis as a special method of social research was nothing but a myth. Much as Lesser had insisted twenty-six years before him, Davis (1959) declared that sociological analysis is inseparable from an attempt to show the relationship between the parts of social systems. Therefore, sociological analysis and functional analysis should be treated as synonyms. Although Davis is essentially correct, his understanding of the problem suffers from a lack of historical perspective. If functionalism is a matter of showing the contribution that one part of culture makes to another part, teleologically, or by mathematical correlation, then Turgot, Malthus, Marx, Boas, Lowie, and yes, even Graebner and Grafton Elliot Smith, were functionalists of sorts. There is no name of consequence in the history of the social sciences who is not in some measure concerned with the relationships among the parts of culture.

The contrast between different kinds of sociocultural theories is not built around the question of whether sociocultural systems have parts which are integrated with or effected by other parts, but rather which parts, and how often and with what kind of effect and for how long? In this sense we may distinguish the functionalism of Radcliffe-Brown from the functionalism of Boas from the functionalism of Marx, etc. To cut through the verbiage, the *ad hominem* sniping, the prestige-building value of obscurantism which baffles our understanding of the development of the social sciences, we must revert to the fundament of all such inquiry: how does a particular theoretician propose to explain observable cultural differences and similarities? If he is to provide any explanation at all, he must sooner or later commit himself to the assumption that he is dealing with systems—i.e., sets of causally related variables. What we want to know, what we must know, is why he emphasizes certain sets of variables rather than others.

STRUCTURAL-FUNCTIONAL LAWS

This brings us back to the question of why the structural-functionalists insist that social structure provides the central set of variables for orienting social anthropology. Ostensibly, the answer lies in the claim that by concentrating on social structure anthropology could be cured of the explanatory impotence which had followed upon the demise of evolutionary schemes. This pretension to superior understanding or explanation is an explicit feature of the program set forth by Radcliffe-Brown, and it was explicitly opposed to the Boasian conclusion that the search for sociocultural laws was futile. Radcliffe-Brown's displeasure with the dogma of no sociocultural laws was expressed as early as 1923:

> Now while ethnology with its strictly historical method can only tell us that certain things have happened, or have probably or possibly happened, social anthropology with its inductive generalizations can tell us how and why things happen, i.e., according to what laws [1958:29].

This attempt to return anthropology to social science deserves our admiration and reflects with credit upon the guiding influence of Durkheim. Later, responding to his American critics, who insisted that there were "no discoverable significant laws such as the functionalist is seeking," Radcliffe-Brown delivered a telling blow, very reminiscent of Spencer's attack on his nineteenth-century opponents of a social science.

> I have found it impossible to know what they mean, or on what sort of evidence (rational or empirical) they would base their contention. Generalisations about any sort of subject matter are of two kinds: the generalisations of common opinion, and generalisations that have been verified or demonstrated by a systematic examination of evidence afforded by precise observations systematically made. Generalisations of the latter kind are called scientific laws. Those who hold that there are no laws of human society cannot hold that there are no generalisations about human society because they themselves hold such generalisations and even make new ones of their own. They must therefore hold that in the field of social phenomena, in contradistinction to physical and biological phenomena, any attempt at the systematic testing of existing generalisations or towards the discovery and verification of new ones, is, for some unexplained reason, futile, or, as Dr. Radin puts it, "crying for the moon". Argument against such a contention is unprofitable or indeed impossible [1952a:187].

The structural-functionalist school thus came forward to be judged on the basis of the adequacy of its explanations of sociocultural differences and similarities according to the common standards of science. For Radcliffe-Brown at least, structural-functionalism was not to be valued merely for its stimulus to improved standards of fieldwork or for its organizing contribution to ethnographers in search of a theme to hang their data on. The tests of adequacy were to be the ability to generate lawful statements in terms of which explanations of sociocultural phenomena could be achieved that were superior in accuracy, generality, and economy to rival theories. It is by these standards that the structural-functionalists will be judged here.

Other British social anthropologists have exercized greater caution in their declarations concerning the ultimate objectives of social anthropology. For some, the concentration upon social structure was probably little more than a matter of personal taste, to which they are of course inalienably entitled (but not in the name of science). Many of the British social anthropologists often allude to the need for specialization, and it is, after all, impossible for a small group of scholars to study everything. Raymond Firth, for example, rejected what he called "an old-fashioned and spurious-unified science of man. . . . What a 'cultural' upbringing does seem to mean in some cases is too great diversification of interest and lack of opportunity to get a really specialized training" (FIRTH 1951:484). Piddington (1957:49) puts this notion into more picturesque, if no more accurate, terms:

> The British trend toward specialization has had a stimulating effect on ethnographic research. Social anthropologists no longer clutter up their minds with information about skulls and potsherds but look instead to cognate social sciences (such as economics, jurisprudence and psychology) for a stimulus in extending and deepening their research.

In this vein, the structural-functionalists have repeatedly expressed their antipathy to the concept of culture as employed by Malinowski and the Boasians, arguing that it is too vast and shapeless a notion to be of much use for the individual researcher. As Fortes (1953b:20) put it, "A serious limitation to this point of view is that it is bound to treat everything in social life as of equal weight, all aspects as of equal significance." "Malinowski, in common with all who think in terms of a global concept of culture, had no answer to it" (*ibid.*:21). Although Fortes does not specifically claim that the structural-functionalists do have the answer to this problem, his exposition of the accomplishments of social anthropology is set in the context of superior explanatory power: Says Fortes, "Anyone who has tried to understand African religious beliefs and practices in the field knows, for example, that one cannot get very far without a very thorough knowledge of the kinship and political organization" (*ibid.*:22). One can only conclude that social structure is to be regarded as "the foundation of the whole of social life of any *continuing* society" (*ibid.*:23) because by so doing one achieves superior "understandings" or explanations of sociocultural phenomena.

In view of all that has been said in previous chapters, it is perhaps repetitious to declare my deepest sympathy for Radcliffe-Brown's attempt to return anthropology to social science. His role in keeping alive and nourishing the study of sociocultural regularities has earned for him a distinguished place in the history of cultural theory. As an opponent of the relativism, quixoticism, and psychological reductionism which had brought the end of nomothetic theory in the United States, Radcliffe-Brown was a lonely voice in a wilderness interlude. But there remains the nagging question of why the path back to science was to be paved with social structure. It is not, I trust, ungrateful to point out that there is no theoretical justification for this strategy. Certainly none can be found in the works of Radcliffe-Brown and his students. Appeals to the richness of the ethnographic reporting achieved under the structural-functionalist banner are not relevant to this discussion. It might be possible to justify the theoretical infatuation with social structure by appeal to the pragmatic results obtained from such studies in terms of lawful generalizations. One might possibly say, "Well, but you see, it works," without specifying the underlying reason for why it is so conspicuously productive of powerful nomothetic statements. But the tragedy of Radcliffe-Brown's contribution to theory is that the "laws" which he produced were distinguished by their weakness, their low capacity for prediction and retrodiction, and their vapidity.

HISTORY, ORIGINS, EVOLUTION

This failure to formulate significant sociocultural laws is not the simple consequence of the structural-functionalist pursuit of Durkheim's grail. The deliberate subordination of techno-economic parameters would of course constitute a serious flaw in any program concerned with discovering the causes of sociocultural differences and similarities. But in Radcliffe-Brown's case, even if the Durkheimian mystique of social solidarity is set aside, there remains an additional, and perhaps even more injurious, ingredient, which cannot be laid at the door of French anthropology. Radcliffe-Brown set himself the task of discovering sociocultural laws under the rigid and unprecedented handicap of restricting anthropology to the data collected from a single time level, namely the mid-twentieth century.

Uncharitable and not too well-informed critics have turned this feature around to mean that the structural-functionalists were "opposed to the study of history." This is a vulgar distortion. It is impossible to suppose that reasonable men would deny the importance of history for achieving a full explanation of sociocultural phenomena. Indeed, Radcliffe-Brown repeatedly urges the importance of historical inquiry. If the structural-functionalists seldom concerned themselves with historical perspectives, it was because they remained convinced that little useful historical information could be obtained with respect to primitive societies. It was not history, but "pseudo history" to which they objected:

> In the primitive societies that are studied by social anthropology there are no historical records. We have no knowledge of the development of social institutions among the Australian aborigines

> for example. Anthropologists, thinking of their study as a kind of historical study, fall back on conjecture and imagination, and invent "pseudo-historical" or "pseudo-causal" explanations. We have had, for example, innumerable and sometimes conflicting pseudo-historical accounts of the origin and development of the totemic institutions of the Australian aborigines. . . . The view taken here is that such speculations are not merely useless but are worse than useless. This does not in any way imply the rejection of historical explanation but quite the contrary [RADCLIFFE-BROWN 1952b:3].

Like Boas, Radcliffe-Brown was scornful of the evolutionary schemes which his nineteenth-century predecessors had elaborated. Again, like Boas, this did not mean that he was an antievolutionist in the sense of being opposed to the Darwinian version of evolution (1947:80). Radcliffe-Brown even declared himself to be a *social* evolutionist, defined as one who is interested in studying the process of diversification by which "new and different forms of societies are produced" (*ibid.*:80-81). His expressed objections to evolutionism provide a curious counterpoint to the complaints of the Boasians. According to Radcliffe-Brown, the trouble with the evolutionists was that they got lost in the search for origins when what they should have been doing was looking for laws.

> All that I am concerned with here is to point out that the anthropologists of this school considered culture and the history of culture from one standpoint only, namely, as a process of development, and were interested only or chiefly in the problem of development, and that they regarded the development of culture from the historical standpoint as a succession of stages rather than from the inductive standpoint as the action of specific laws . . . [1958:11].
>
> The effect of the historical bias of the early anthropology, and of the false idea of evolution to which it led such writers as Morgan, was to set anthropologists seeking not for laws, but for origins [*ibid.*:19].

This rejection of nineteenth-century evolutionism because classic evolutionary theory did not lead to laws is, of course, contradicted by the Boasians who allegedly gave up evolutionism because it was predicated upon the assumption that the search for evolutionary laws had perverted the search for historical origins. Since it is clear that Radcliffe-Brown was doctrinally opposed to the possibility of formulating laws of parallel and convergent evolution, and that the lawfulness to which he alludes is merely that of synchronic regularity, the contradiction here is more apparent than real. What is essential in the passage just quoted is that the search for origins could not be carried out by means of evolutionary formula. Here Boas and Radcliffe-Brown concur. Immediately thereafter, however, a fundamental difference in strategy separates the two schools. For the Boasians, the remedy for false evolutionary reconstructions are specific historical inquiries; for Radcliffe-Brown, the remedy is more drastic: avoid all historical inquiry for which historical documents are not available. Up until the 1950's, this restriction resulted in a *de facto* separation of synchronic structural-functional studies from diachronic inquiry.

We need not concern ourselves at any great length with the question of to what extent the alarm over pseudo history with the resulting synchronic emphasis was another convenient rationalization for avoiding fundamental issues. I shall present evidence in a moment which proves that the structural-functionalists did not take advantage of reputable or otherwise useful historical sources even when these were available in great abundance. Had they used these sources, vital sectors of sociocultural inquiry would possess a set of assumptions different from those which prevail at the moment.

STRUCTURAL-FUNCTIONALISM AND THE ORGANISMIC ANALOGY

The theoretical case for Radcliffe-Brown's synchronic laws depends on the validity of the biological organismic model upon which he explicitly based his exposition of the principles of structural-functional analysis. The aspect of the model to which attention is directed is the set of relations among an organism's parts which constitute its morphology or physiology. This analogy, which goes back at least to Hobbes, and which received its highest elaboration by Spencer, is not necessarily ill-advised. There is much with which we may agree in Radcliffe-Brown's defense of it:

> In using the terms morphology and physiology, I may seem to be returning to the analogy between society and organism which was so popular with medieval philosophers, was taken over and often misused by nineteenth century sociologists, and is completely rejected by many modern writers. But analogies, properly used, are important aids to scientific thinking and there is a real and significant analogy between organic structure and social structure [1952b:195].

To accept the appropriateness of this analogy is not to concede the possibility of a synchronic science, from which statements similar to those describing life-sustaining functions of the pancreas, or the kidneys, or some other physiological relationship concerning the parts of delimited categories of organisms, can be expected. The situation is scarcely so simple, however, and in practice there results a significant abuse of the analogy in question. At the core of the matter there lies an unanswered problem in epistemology, one which I have sought to attack with draconian measures in *The Nature of Cultural Things*. Individual biological organisms, at least as far as all higher forms are concerned, enjoy an epistemological status which is radically different from that of sociocultural organisms. It is part of a species-given biopsychological gestalt, a product of man's adaptive phylogeny, that boundaries of individual organisms are delimited by unequivocal intersubjective criteria. We see whole bio-organisms, regularly, effortlessly, and infallibly. We do not see whole sociocultural organisms. These, and all their parts, including social structure, must be constructed through a process of logico-empirical abstraction out of the material furnished by the observation of the behavior of specific human beings. The structural-functional analysis of the functions of parts of sociocultural organisms is thus obliged to proceed without reasonably certain knowledge that the whole organism has been laid out, so to speak, on the dissecting table.

It is as if in attempting to discover the functions of the spinal columns of amphibia, we ran the risk of examining a series of headless frogs. By virtue of the same species-given gestalt, the various sectors of an organism, if not its organs, present themselves to the community of observers in a fixed and orderly spacial arrangement. But when I look at an African society, I see whole sets of vital organs, great throbbing nerves and sinews, which the structural-functionalists either do not consider part of the organism at all, or which they relegate to the position of toenails. That this is no idle danger as far as our sociocultural specimens are concerned is evident in the announced program of the structural-functionalists and abundantly demonstrated in their handling of specific cases to which we shall now turn.

MOTHER'S BROTHER AGAIN

The classic attempt by Radcliffe-Brown to offer a synchronic explanation of a structural feature is that of the relationship between the mother's brother and sister's son among the Bathonga of Moçambique. This relationship, an asymmetrical joking relationship, was characterized by the extraordinary liberties which sister's son took with his maternal uncle's property and wives. In his uncle's absence, sister's son would enter his hut, steal his favorite spear, carry on a lewd conversation with his wife, demand to be fed, and in many ways comport himself in an utterly disrespectful fashion, all without fear of retaliation or remonstrance. These liberties extended even to the solemn occasion of uncle's funeral when sister's son was expected to snatch the sacrificial chicken from amid the grave offerings and run off with it to his own house. In marked contrast to this behavior was the great respect which the same man would be obliged to display in all of his dealings with his father's brother. Junod (1913:253) had treated this situation in the typically evolutionary style of the times:

> Now having enquired with special care into this most curious feature of the Thonga system, I come to the conclusion that the only possible explanation is that, in former and very remote times, our tribe had passed through the matriarchal phase.

Radcliffe-Brown took up this challenge by proposing to offer, if not to prove, an alternate hypothesis which would require no reference to history. His explanation, which was alluded to in the previous chapter, went about like this: among the patrilineal Thonga, there is a tendency to extend to all of the members of ego's mother's patrilineage the kind of behavior and attitudes which characterize ego's relation with his mother, and to all of the members of ego's father's patrilineage, the kind of behavior and attitudes which characterize ego's relations with his father. Since mother is a warm and indulgent figure, so will be her brothers and sisters; since father is a stern patriarch, so will be his brothers and sisters. But this equivalence is disrupted by the principle of sexual differentiation. Generally speaking, argues Radcliffe-Brown, the greatest degree of familiarity is possible only between people of the same sex. If mother and mother's sisters are indulgent, then mother's brother, the term for whom (*malume*) actually means "male mother," will be even more so. Conversely, if father demands respect, father's sister should be even more aloof, since she is called by a kinship term (*nanani*) which means "female father." And that is indeed the case. Although not spelled out in the original article, it would be correct, I believe, to add that the structural-functional significance of the Thonga joking relationship is the contribution which it made to the maintenance of the patrilineages.

A CULTURAL-MATERIALIST ALTERNATIVE

One of the problems which such an explanation confronts is that the structural-functionalists have not cornered the market on the stuff out of which "just so stories" can be made. Granting Radcliffe-Brown's ingenuity in drawing attention to a set of variables which are analytically ignored by Junod, how do we know that there are not other functional relationships which are equally relevant or more so? Let me offer an alternative: Ego takes advantage of mother's brother because he has an economic claim on that man's wife and children, a claim which by virtue of the corporate nature of the lineage involves everyone in it to some extent. The claim arises because mother's brother has married his bride directly, or indirectly, with the brideprice furnished by ego's patrilineage to mother's patrilineage. When ego steals mother's brother's spear, propositions his wife, and runs off with his grave goods, this all functions to remind the members of mother's patrilineage that sister's husband's patrilineage gave them the cattle to which they owe so much of their welfare.

In this connection, it should also be mentioned that the most important "respect relationship" which exists among the Bathonga is that between a man and his wife's brother's wife, i.e., between ego's father and ego's maternal uncle's wife, a relationship the Thonga explain in terms of the temptation a man feels to sleep with a woman who has been bought with his cattle. It is not ego alone therefore who enjoys the joke on mother's brother; all the members of his patrilineage, who must maintain proper decorum with their in-law and his wife, rejoice at the nephew's antics. For father to do those things would endanger the intricate web of marriages, which have been built up around the exchange of women for cattle, but everyone knows that sister's son is merely joking.

Which of these is the correct explanation? I prefer mine, because it does not involve the assumption that the mother-son relationship is the basic one from which the other kinship positions derive their value. It also seems to me preferable insofar as it links the lineage system to the economic domain through the emphasis on cattle. For the Bathonga lineages are not, in my view of the Bathonga "organism," the be-all and end-all of the Bathonga life. The lineages arise from and reflect the adaptation of the Bathonga population to a mixed pastoral-horticultural way of life in which cattle are a vital resource and in which the techno-economic patterns of cattle breeding and gardening are more important sociocultural "organs" than the lineages. That is, the function of the mother's brother-sister's son relationship is to maintain the population's techno-economic adaptation. Of course, this institution may also contribute to the maintenance of lineage solidarity, but if that solidarity did not contribute to the maintenance of the techno-environmental adaptation, or to a better one, it probably would not long endure.

TIME AND THE ORGANISMIC ANALOGY

It is not essential to my point that a choice be made between the above explanations of the mother's brother-sister's son phenomenon. Although I believe that definite criteria can be elaborated for preferring one to the other, these criteria demand that a diachronic perspective be adopted. In effect, in order to assign priorities of functional order within a sociocultural organism, that is, in order to be able to describe its structure, we must simultaneously study its history and the history of similar organisms. From such a study there emerges a conception of how the parts of sociocultural systems relate to each other in general and specific terms, for we observe the phenomena of parallel and convergent development and note how the changes in one part are regularly succeeded by changes in another. Parallel and convergent evolution made manifest through comparative and diachronic anthropology is the anthropologist's equivalent of the physiologist's laboratory. To ignore the results of the natural experiments which constitute the stuff of history is to abandon all hope of understanding how sociocultural systems are put together in the present.

SOCIOLOGICAL LAWS, STRUCTURAL PRINCIPLES, AND PSYCHOLOGICAL REDUCTIONISM

What, then, are the sociological laws which emerge from synchronic structural-functionalism? In what sense can they be said to fulfill Radcliffe-Brown's intentions of achieving a science of society?

Radcliffe-Brown's thought and technique followed a smooth and continuous development stemming directly from the analysis of the mother's brother-sister's son. He gradually came to see the joking relationship as an aspect of a larger complex of phenomena which included kinship terminologies, the treatment of lineage members as a unit, cross-sex differentials, and the differential treatment of adjacent and alternate generations. These notions were gradually formulated as structural principles and presented as satisfying the quest for sociological laws.

Eggan (1955b:503) refers to two of these principles, "the lineage principle and the principle of the unity and solidarity of the sibling group," as "the most important concepts guiding the analysis of social structure today. . . ." Under the direct stimulation of Radcliffe-Brown, during the latter's stay at the University of Chicago, Tax (1955b:19ff.) proposed twelve such principles, or rules, which are listed here in order to convey an idea of the nature of the "structural" laws associated with this movement: the rule of uniform descent, uniform reciprocals, uniform siblings, uniform mates, uniform ascent, equivalence, terminological correlation, reciprocal behavior, equivalence of siblings, sex differentiation, generation principle, and the sex principle.

As discussed in the next chapter, Coult (1966b) has re-established the relevance of Tax's structural principles to the ethnosemantic analysis of kinship terminologies. But for Radcliffe-Brown and his American students, these principles were regarded as useful for the analysis of both kinship terminologies and social structure. The connection with ethnosemantics is instructive because it highlights the heavy psychological component in the generalizations produced by the structural-functionalists.

Bottomore (1962:44) correctly associates functionalism with the interpretation of institutions in terms of the values and purposes of individuals. He seems to regard Radcliffe-Brown as an exception, or at least as an instance of a functionalist who also managed somehow to remain on the sociological level. Of course, Radcliffe-Brown shared Durkheim's doctrinal opposition to psychological reductionism, but neither he nor Durkheim, nor the French school, including Lévi-Strauss, has found a way to avoid dependence upon phychological universals as one of their main explanatory devices.

The theoretical penalty of this form of reductionism is always the same: since all men are equipped with the same psychobiological tendencies, all sociocultural systems should be the same. As White (1949a:139) correctly insists, constants cannot explain variables. If alternate generations everywhere tend to have friendly relations, while adjacent generations are more agonistically inclined, then why don't all societies have the Australian four-section system in which alternate generations are formally distinguished? Or why, if the unity of siblings is universal, do some systems distinguish collaterals from lineals while others do not? The answer is that these universals, important and valid as they may be, cross-cut each other and are embedded in still other cross-cutting skeins of additional universal tendencies (e.g., a principle of least effort, or a principle of Aristotelian logical consistency, or a Freudian Oedipus principle or a behaviorist reinforcement principle).

SOME PECULIAR LAWS

There were also, to be sure, structural-functional principles which were less conspicuously psychological. Thus, in 1935 Radcliffe-Brown named three sociological, but otherwise no less peculiar, laws, as follows:

> . . . if we could define any universal condition to which a social system would have to conform, we would thereby have a sociological law. . . . One such law or necessary condition of continued existence is that of a certain degree of functional consistency amongst the constituent parts of the social systems. . . . To this law we may add a second . . . rights and duties need to be defined in such a way that conflict of rights can be resolved without destroying the structure. Another sociological law is the necessity not merely for stability, definiteness, and consistency in the social structure, but also for continuity [1952b:44-45].

But the best that can be expected from the application of all such universals, be they psychological or sociological, in the explanation of particular concrete varieties of sociocultural arrangements is a weak form of "interpretation." Indeed, the general instructions for achieving such interpretations were given in 1929 as follows:

> The functional method aims at discovering general laws and thereby at explaining any particular element of culture by reference to the discovered laws. Thus, if it is a valid generalization to say that the chief function of ritual or ceremonial is to express and thereby maintain in existence sentiments that are necessary for social cohesion, we can "explain" any given ritual or ceremonial by showing what are the sentiments expressed in it and how these sentiments are related to the cohesion of the society [RADCLIFFE-BROWN 1958:40].

In other words, given the variety of systems, we can show how one or another principle is reflected in it. But we cannot explain the particular variety of system in terms of the conditions which yield a generation terminology here, a lineage organization there, now a moiety system, sometimes an eight-section system, and then again, no sections at all.

It must be said that Radcliffe-Brown from the outset was probably quite well aware of the limitations which the synchronic approach imposed upon the predictive and retrodictive powers of the laws he intended to discover. It was, however, easy to become confused, as when in his haste to oppose the Boasian position, he proposed "to tell how and why things happen" (see above, p. 521). This stirring invitation to science was indeed followed by a series of studies culminating with a now classic examination of Australian kinship in which the main synchronic structural-functional principles were blocked out. But Radcliffe-Brown could not resist the temptation to assimilate psychosocial interpretation to the standards of genuine scientific explanations, and hence made the mistake of referring to "a universal sociological law though it is not yet possible to formulate its scope, namely that in certain specific conditions a society has need to provide itself with a segmentary (clan) organization" (RADCLIFFE-BROWN 1931:109, quoted in LOWIE 1937:224-25). Lowie's (1937:225) scornful retort was perhaps not completely justified:

> Whoever heard of a universal law with an as yet undefinable scope, of a law that works in certain specific but unspecified conditions? Is it a law that some societies have clans, and others have not? Newton did not tell us that bodies either rise or fall.

CONFESSION OF EXPLANATORY IMPOTENCE

Radcliffe-Brown by this time had actually achieved a more realistic appraisal of his "laws" quite on his own. His 1935 paper on patrilineal and matrilineal succession, after in effect showing how all societies must somehow or other handle the question of lineality in conformity with the laws of consistency, control of conflict, and continuity, leaves the reader with slight expectation of ever getting to know anything about the classic problems of descent: namely, why are some descent systems matrilineal, others patrilineal, double, bilateral, etc?

> It might well be expected that such a paper as this would deal with the question of what general factors determine the selection by some people of the matrilineal and by others of the patrilineal principle in determining status or succession. My opinion is that

> our knowledge and understanding are not sufficient to permit us to deal with this problem in any satisfactory manner [RADCLIFFE-BROWN 1952b:48].

This admission of explanatory impotence was repeated in 1941 for the entire field of kinship terminology, one of the lifelong foci of his search for lawful principles: "If you ask the question, 'how is it that the Omaha (or any tribe we have considered) have the system they do?', then it is obvious that the method of structural analysis does not afford an answer" (1952b:85). With this admission we are brought back to a point remarkably close to that of the Boasians. For, not only is structural-functional analysis incapable of answering the kinds of questions which have occupied the minds of social scientists since the eighteenth century and the dreams and myths of primitive and folk philosophers since the dawn of time, but let it be known, henceforth and forever more, that no one, no other school, shall ever find the answers to these riddles. For the structural-functional method "is the only method by which we hope ultimately to arrive at valid generalizations about the nature of human society" (*ibid.*:86). Anything that a synchronic study cannot do, cannot be done; and, as we have seen, causal explanations have no place in a synchronic study. The missing ingredient is, of course, history, but to establish any probability for historical explanations, "we should need to have a knowledge of the preceding conditions and events which we certainly do not possess and to which I do not think we shall ever attain" (*ibid.*:50). It is the "cannot be done" which must strike a generation already accustomed to the search for the origin of life in the conditions of the primal atmosphere five billion years before our time as oddly unprophetic. To adopt a sociological perspective, which Radcliffe-Brown, were he alive today, might appreciate, does science shackle itself to such narrow prospects, if not out of obedience to a social function?

THE NEW DISMAL SCIENCE

For an explanation of this function, Dorothy Gregg and Elgin Williams (1948) proposed an analogy between the entire synchronic functionalist movement and the classical laissez-faire doctrines of economics. Although frequently incorrect in fact and ethically entirely too wild and presumptuous (KROEBER 1949:318 called it an "Authoritarian Panacea"), this analogy, nonetheless, requires serious consideration. It is an undeniable consequence of both the Malinowskian and Radcliffe-Brownian versions of functionalism that every sort of institution, from witchcraft to war, receives its due as a functional contribution to the welfare and maintenance of the social system. As the outraged left-leaning economists saw it, ". . . predisposed to think that all's well, social scientists will devote their time to metaphysical eulogy, inventing high sounding purposes for the most absurd and pernicious customs while their actual social consequences go unregarded" (GREGG and WILLIAMS 1948:598).

I believe that an objective appraisal of the contribution of the structural-functionalists requires one to acknowledge the streak of intellectual know-nothingism which flourished in their work despite the ostensible emphasis upon scientism and orderliness. This negative, narrowed-down view of the world, brought on by the deliberate use of blinders to blot out the significance of history, is not as pronounced as in the case of the Boasians, nor is it as politically reactionary as Gregg and Williams claim it to be. Like the Boasians, most of the British social anthropologists would probably pass muster as left-wing liberals or socialists. Their emphasis upon the orderliness of contemporary systems was not, as Gregg and Williams would have it, part of an attempt to prove that all was well in the world in order to sustain the belief that "Capitalism is human nature, and the social organization of modern times, with its depressions, imperialism and war," is a necessary part of the human condition. The functionalists may have been naïve, but they were not insensitive. I venture to guess that the question was not so much whether the world contained evils, but rather whether there was any likelihood that less evil substitutes were about to be found.

The point here, however, is not to criticize the functionalists for their political and ethical beliefs, about which we are at any rate very badly informed. The know-nothingism to which I refer is a scientific rather than an ethical problem. It is an affliction which leads the functionalists to ignore, or even deliberately obscure, the amount of order that human history exhibits. Its most serious intellectual consequence is that it fails to come to grips with the fact that the evolutionary careers of both bioforms and sociocultural systems consist of an array of eminently functional structures, all doomed to extinction. Dinosaurs were no less a marvel of consistency, coordination, and continuity than the mammals which replaced them; similarly there is ample justification for the sympathetic wonder with which an anthropologist describes the subtle perfections of a beautifully organized patrilineal, patrilocal Omaha system. What history teaches us, however, is that the great issues of any period are not bound up with the question of which element in the structure or which structure as a whole is functional. Rather, it is a matter of which of a number of alternative structures is the *most* functional under the specific conditions which evolution has provided for them. Without recourse to diachronic data, the whole question of degrees of functional adaptiveness is shut out, and yet surely there is no subject of more vital concern to social science than the prospects for survival of our own way of life and of the ways of life of our contemporaries, both primitive and civilized. Failure to come to grips with this domain of problems is not an ethical fault, or at least need not, as Gregg and Williams demand, be phrased as such. It may very well be that many of those functional adaptations, which "liberals" and "leftists" find most odious, are going to survive for a long time to come. This does not relieve social science of the burden of studying the diachronic and synchronic conditions responsible for the origin, perpetuation, and dissemination of cultural differences and similarities any more than the likelihood of a more pleasant prospect would constitute by itself sufficient reason for ignoring the blights of the past.

THE DISMAL CASE OF POLITICAL ORGANIZATION

The treatment accorded the subject of political organization was perhaps the most serious victim of the synchronic approach. In 1940 Meyer Fortes and E. E. Evans-Pritchard edited a volume of contributions by their fellow social anthropologists in which the structure of African political systems was defined in a lasting manner for a large professional audience. Yet, it is difficult to imagine a less propitious combination of place and subject for synchronic analysis. The fact that direct European political control, especially of the interior, goes back only about one hundred years does not mean that in the days of Stanley and Livingstone a pristine ethnographic situation existed in Africa. For as surely as the slave-run plantation system of the New World sounded the death knell of American aboriginal societies, it also marked the beginning of vast upheavals of human populations in Africa. For something like three hundred and fifty years the "Dark Continent" was utilized as a breeding ground for cheap and docile labor. It is estimated that forty million Africans were caught up in the slave trade in one way or another, although possibly only as few as fourteen million were still alive when they got to their destinations overseas. Advancing before this scourge were shock waves of wars, migrations, political upheavals, and vast demographic changes. In such a context, restriction to an ethnographic present of the 1930's, in the name of empiricism, has little to commend it.

UNDOING THE DAMAGE

Distortions introduced by means of the synchronic focus in *African Political Systems* threatened to reduce our understanding of state formation to a shambles. Apparently oblivious of, or uninterested in, the fact that for every other continent a close correspondence between state systems and high population density had been established beyond a doubt, Fortes and Evans-Pritchard reached the conclusion that "it would be incorrect to suppose that governmental institutions are found in those societies with greatest densities. The opposite seems to be equally likely judging by our material" (FORTES and EVANS-PRITCHARD 1940:7-8). This conclusion was based on the evidence provided by six case studies, the Zulu, Ngwato, Bemba, Nuer, Tallensi, and Logoli. R. F. Stevenson (1965) has taken each of these cases, applied a diachronic perspective, utilizing sources available in any major library, and reversed or seriously modified every negative instance.

Stevenson shows how Zulu territory and population were influenced by the compression of the Bantu frontier under the shock of British and Boer penetration. M. Gluckman's 3.5 persons per square mile estimate accepted by Fortes and Evans-Pritchard is replaced with a figure of 20 per square mile for the Shaka period (pre-1850), with the possibility of densities as high as 46 per square mile. The historical data requires a similar upward revision for nineteenth-century Ngwato population. For the Bemba, Stevenson shows that the paradox of low population density and state apparatus is "an illusion" created by the collapsing of history into the ethnographic present and the consequent neglect of the effect of the advent of British indirect rule upon the aboriginal local political monopoly over slave and ivory trade. The Nuer paradox of acephalous polity combined with "high density" also turns out to be illusory. With the upward revision of the nineteenth-century Zulu and Ngwato densities, the figure of 7 per square mile for the Nuer fits into the theoretically expected sequence. The Logoli, who have a population of 391 per square mile, but allegedly no state system, probably had a nineteenth-century density closer to 70 per square mile. They were surrounded on all sides by state-organized societies and, in addition to possessing a number of statelike features, were partially under the control of their neighbors. The most startling case is that of the Tallensi, who have come to serve as the classic instance of an "acephalous society" due to Fortes' (1945:1949) elaborate descriptions of their kinship ideology. Elliot Skinner had previously pointed the way for Stevenson:

> Fortes' insistence on the acephalous nature of Tallensi society stems from his failure to consider that these people had been defeated and dispersed by the British at the turn of the century and had probably lost a great deal of their organization. The society he describes can be compared to a modern community arbitrarily divorced from its nation state [SKINNER 1964:7].

Far from being acephalous, as Stevenson shows, the Tallensi inhabited an area which had been controlled before the advent of the British by the Mamprusi kingdom.

It must be emphasized that Stevenson's brilliant defense of the population density–state formation hypothesis in Africa does not rest with the reformulation of the Fortes and Evans-Pritchard materials. Historical and demographic evidence from all over the continent is also reviewed, including the most puzzling case of all, the Ibo. In total, the evidence is overwhelming that African political systems, like those found almost everywhere else, show a definite relationship to density phenomena. Stevenson's use of readily available and abundant historical sources to correct the conclusions of the structural-functionalists jeopardizes the credibility of the "pseudo-history" excuse for synchronic specialization. At any rate, Radcliffe-Brown's (1950:2) assertion that "We cannot have a history of African institutions" can no longer be taken as anything more than a rationalization for avoiding a confrontation with the past.

WAS JUNOD RIGHT?

Among the more sensational rebuttals of Radcliffe-Brown's position is Murdock's (1959a) culture history approach to African institutions, in which there is a fateful return to the article which started it all, "The Mother's Brother in South Africa." Reviewing the evidence for Junod's "pseudo history" of matrilineal descent, Murdock strikes at the roots of the structural-functionalist movement. According to Murdock, the speculative shoe belongs on the other foot. Radcliffe-Brown's argument with Junod represented an "opposition between sound historical scholarship and untrammeled sociological speculation" (*ibid.*:378). There is every reason to believe that the Bathonga had passed through an earlier matrilineal phase. This does not, of course, signify that Radcliffe-Brown's synchronic interpretation was incorrect but that his conclusions require further interpretation in relationship to the probable trajectory of Thonga history.

FRED EGGAN AND THE RESUMPTION OF DIACHRONIC RESEARCH

It must be made clear that the end of the synchronic obsession has been brought about less by this kind of attack than by a gradual drift among the younger generation of British social anthropologists toward combining diachronic and synchronic interests. This reconciliation may actually have been stimulated by Radcliffe-Brown himself, upon his return to Oxford in 1937 as a result of his American experience.

Certainly, the most profound effect of his sojourn at Chicago was the development of a point of view, most impressively represented in the work of Fred Eggan, by which structural-functionalist principles were combined with the Americanist's concern with historical documents. By the time of Radcliffe-Brown's departure, Eggan (1937) had already achieved a brilliant synthesis of the structural-functional and the historical-particularist approaches. Using what he later called the "method of controlled comparison," Eggan (1954) attempted to explain puzzling variations in Crow terminology among the Choctaw, Creek, Chickasaw, and Cherokee, a group of southeastern United States tribes which had been exposed to a similar set of acculturative pressures. Eggan demonstrated that length of time and degree of exposure matched the amount of departure in the terminological systems from a matrilineal Crow type to something more closely resembling a patrilineal Omaha type.

It is difficult to discover any definite historical link between Eggan and Radcliffe-Brown's students and colleagues in England. Among the contributors to *African Systems of Kinship and Marriage* (FORDE and RADCLIFFE-BROWN 1950), only Audrey Richards shows an inclination toward the kind of comparison which Eggan had proposed. Eggan's name does not appear in the volume's index, although he was a contributor to the Radcliffe-Brown *Festschrift* (FORTES 1949).

THE COLLAPSE OF SYNCHRONISM

In 1954, Eggan was still predicting that the social anthropologists would eventually become more interested in diachronic studies: "Ultimately the British anthropologists will discover that time perspective is also important and will encourage archaeology and historical research" (1954:755). According to Raymond Firth (1951), however, this interest had already reached important dimensions before the

1950's. Rejecting Murdock's (1951) characterization of social anthropology as not interested in history, Firth cites a number of cases in which his colleagues had made an attempt to concern themselves with social change (e.g., MAIR 1938; WILSON and HUNTER 1939; EVANS-PRITCHARD 1949). Firth (1951:486) correctly emphasizes the importance of culture-contact studies, a theme coincident with the formalization of acculturation research by American scholars (REDFIELD, LINTON, and HERSKOVITS 1936), as one of the sources of diachronic comparisons. For example, Monica Hunter (Wilson) had written extensively of Pondoland acculturation as early as 1936. During the Second World War, the interest in contact phenomena intensified, and both Malinowski (1945) and Wilson and Hunter (1945) came out with elaborate theoretical statements concerned with the trajectory of colonial relations, especially in Africa. Firth (1954) cites Read (1942), Schapera (1947), Hogbin (1939), Richards (1954), Freedman (1950), Gluckman (1955a), and Berndt (1952), among others, as having produced social anthropological studies involving the analysis of social change. It must be made clear that important ethnological contributions employing a wide variety of historical research methods have become an accepted feature of the most recent period of British social anthropology (*cf.* STENNING 1959; M. G. SMITH 1960; J. A. BARNES 1954). According to C. Daryll Forde (1965:19):

> There is no need to labour the point that outsiders may have provided documents concerning the forebears of an unlettered people which can be of great value to a social anthropologist. The recovery of such documentation and its study, when this is done with detailed knowledge and understanding of the contemporary ethnography, has enabled social anthropologists to analyse developments of structure and process over considerable time spans. The importance of the search for, and the use of, documentation both indigenous (where it exists) and foreign, is accepted as obvious by the anthropologist as by any other student of some phase or aspect of the life of a people. We need to recognise however, that the extent to which such documentation can be found is very variable, and that for many peoples in Africa it may be nonexistent before the turn of the century.

It must also be emphasized, however, that this return to diachronic interests has not as yet contributed to a revival of diachronic theory. Indeed, as Leach (1961a:1) has commented, "Most of my colleagues are giving up the attempt to make comparative generalizations; instead they have begun to write impeccably detailed historical ethnographies of particular peoples."

EDMUND LEACH

Leach himself is responsible for one of the most effective critiques of the structural-functional model. In his *Political Systems of Highland Burma* (1954), he was obliged to analyze a region-wide process involving slow but drastic changes of democratic dispersed hill peoples (*gumlao* type) to democratic-in-theory intermediate types (*gumsa*), to stratified lowland irrigation rice kingdoms (*Shan*). This dynamic could lead to change in the reverse direction as well, involving the progressive alteration of peoples of *Shan* background to the *gumlao* condition. Leach refused to see this situation in terms of a static model: "We can no longer be satisfied with attempting to set up a typology of fixed systems. We must recognise that few if any of the societies which a modern field worker can study show any marked tendency towards stability" (LEACH 1954:285). Leach's treatment of evolving political modalities in Burma leaned heavily on an ecological analysis, since the extreme types, *Shan* and *gumlao*, were obviously dependent upon contrasting forms of cultivation and occupied different habitats. The promise of greater attention to such matters has not been fulfilled. Instead, as we shall see in a moment, Leach's fancy has been captured by Lévi-Strauss.

RAYMOND FIRTH

Among those who have long been dissatisfied with the synchronic limitations of structural-functionalist theory, the name of Raymond Firth is outstanding. Through his concept of social organization, Firth hoped to achieve a closer approximation to actual behavior-stream events, especially to the variations which are largely ignored in the static formulations of social structure. From a study of these variations, Firth hoped to be able to discover the processes by which fundamental structural changes occurred (FIRTH 1954; 1961:40ff.). According to Firth, neglect of such variations was responsible for the fact that "structural analysis alone cannot interpret social change" (*ibid.*: 35). In 1951 Firth saw British social anthropology, after a quarter of a century of structural-functional typologies, moving "slowly and unevenly toward a more systematic study of variation, including variation over time" (1951:488). But in 1954 he admitted, "We are hardly yet on the threshold of any general theory of a dynamic kind which will enable us to handle comprehensively the range of materials within our normal anthropological sphere" (quoted in FIRTH 1964:7). In 1962

Firth went so far as to base most of his discussion of "dynamic theory" upon a reconsideration of the contributions of Marx (*ibid.*:7-29). Although scarcely prepared to embrace a Marxist-derived variety of historical determinism, Firth has recently made it clear that he believes no approach to a theory of change can be attempted which does not seriously reconsider Marx's proposals concerning the importance of the material conditions of production. In Firth, we seem almost to have come full circle, to a social anthropology whose main concern is the understanding of sociocultural change. Firth's explanation of this phenomenon is as follows:

> The present day interest in dynamic theory for social anthropology is partly a response to increasing perception of deficiencies in earlier theoretical approaches. But it is partly a response to changed conditions in our field of observation itself, and it has been influenced by modern intellectual movements of a more general kind [*ibid.*:28].

One assumes that, above all, the change in question reflects a Britain no longer interested in preserving the world's largest colonial empire.

MYSTICISM, CYNICISM, AND MINI SKIRTS

With the collapse of the structural-functionalist program, British social anthropology has entered a phase of confused and conflicting trends. It is clear, however, that the return to diachronic data has not as yet contributed to a revival of diachronic theory. Nor should we expect, from all that has been said about historical particularism, that mere attention to change over time will produce theoretically interesting results. Indeed, British social anthropology may be on the verge of something quite different from a return to the formulation of diachronic-synchronic regularities. For some famous Britishers, the waning of influence of Radcliffe-Brown and the intensification of historical research has resulted in complete disillusion with the entire scientist pretension. Evans-Pritchard is the most outspoken heretic in this regard. For him, the end of Radcliffe-Brown's reign has meant a return to the dichotomy between history and science as proposed by the Southwest German school of philosophy (see p. 344) and, closer to home, by the philosopher Karl Popper (1957). The resemblance to Kroeber is striking:

> Social anthropology has more in common with history than with natural science . . . it studies societies as moral or symbolic sys-

> tems and not as natural systems . . . is less interested in process than in design . . . seeks patterns and not laws, demonstrates consistency and not necessary relations . . . interprets rather than explains . . . [EVANS-PRITCHARD 1951:60–61].

> Up to the present nothing even remotely resembling what are called laws in the natural sciences has been adduced—only rather naive deterministic, teleological, and pragmatic assertions. The generalizations which have so far been attempted have, moreover, been so vague and general as to be, even if true, of little use, and they have rather easily tended to become mere tautologies and platitudes on the level of common sense deduction [*ibid.*:57].

> I do not believe that there can ever be a science of society which resembles the natural sciences . . . [*ibid.*:117].

> Social anthropology is best regarded as an art and not as a social science [*ibid.*:85].

Fortes, who has been the most faithful of Radcliffe-Brown's pupils, warns that Evans-Pritchard "contrived to throw out the baby of functionalist theory with the bath-water of evolutionary speculation" (1953a:32). To save the baby, Fortes recommends that we return to a view of man which places him squarely in the midst of nature and which invokes a remembrance of his origin in the processes of organic evolution. Although these reminders of the material basis of sociocultural systems are better than nothing, Fortes' defense of the scientist posture does not really break new ground:

> I hold with Frazer and Haddon, Malinowski and Radcliffe-Brown that there are regularities independent of period and place in social organization and culture, and that the main aim of social anthropology is to investigate the general tendencies, or laws, manifested in them [*ibid.*:35].

There is no room to doubt that what is meant here are the uniformities which occur in social life *despite the lack* of regularity in history, rather than the uniformities which result *because of* historical regularity: "It is perhaps superfluous to add that this view does not imply a belief in mechanical determinism in human life or a denigration of man's intellectual and spiritual qualities" (*ibid.*).

Leach has been no less outspoken than Evans-Pritchard concerning his "dislike" of the comparative method as proposed by Radcliffe-Brown (LEACH 1961a:2). Instead of circling back to the historical-particularist position, which is implicit in the reaction of Firth and Evans-Pritchard, and even in Fortes when he invokes "evolution,"

Leach has extended himself along the lines which have made of Lévi-Strauss a French national treasure. As an "intellectual" (one who knows how to say less than what he means but more than you can understand), Leach believes that the "butterfly-collecting followers" (*ibid.*:1) of Radcliffe-Brown have got to start rethinking the really basic issues. However, what Leach considers the basic issue can only leave the rest of us trembling over our failure to appreciate what is really important in life. We have not properly conceptualized the difference between incorporation (as into a lineage) versus alliance (as through marriage). Previous models of this duality have been overly ethnocentric. A correct formulation requires a mathematical approach, preferably a topological one, because topology is nonmetric, thus conforming to the criteria of Lévi-Strauss' "mechanical models" (see p. 498). It turns out, however, that the topological presentation can easily be omitted. The central concern settles down to the rather simple idea that relations of incorporation are emically phrased as those of common substance (blood, milk, bone, etc.), whereas alliance relationships are viewed in terms of metaphysical forces. In keeping with this distinction, there are different kinds of witches: those found in one's own lineage have an ability to control their powers to do evil and theirs is a deliberate witchcraft. But affinal or alliance-type witches are like fate: they do their evil as a result of "uncontrolled mystic influence." Other conclusions relating the varieties of witchcraft to intensities of political power are also advanced, but we are warned that there can be such a thing as too much "popshy" (to use Leach's term) for one night (*ibid.*:27). In the same volume of essays, Leach attempts an interpretation of the myth of Cronos and the representation of time in worldwide ritual calendars. One is amazed at the imaginative fashion in which Durkheim's conception of time as a projection of the collective consciousness is vindicated. For more daring myth fanciers, there is "Lévi-Strauss in the Garden of Eden" (LEACH 1961c), a Biblical exegesis the nature of whose correspondence to empirically verifiable facts is exceeded in ambiguity only by what Lévi-Strauss has achieved in his flirtations with Hegel's dialectic.

There are, of course, more serious sides to Leach. His contribution to the typology of the varieties of cross-cousin marriage will endure as a solid achievement. But what is most distressing to view is the veritable debauchery of method which has succeeded Radcliffe-Brown's puritanical reign. This weakening of the empirical fibers (can it be the same influence which has made London the exporter of all manner of musical and sartorial novelty?) stands out in morbid contrast to the utilization of the linguistic model by American cultural anthropologists in their study of emic categories.

The path along which Leach has followed Lévi-Strauss leads in a remarkably parallel fashion to the swamp of linguistic analysis, where a search for systems of contrastive meanings is now being carried out by some of the best brains in the United States. Leach undoubtedly deplores the cramped vision of the world which serves its scholars a steady diet of componential, transformational, and algorithmic analyses of how to distinguish rashes from boils in Subanum, types of firewood in Chiapas, and varieties of rice in Hanunóo. But there is a limit to the amount of "popshy" which anthropology can absorb, even when it comes wrapped up in pages torn from topological texts. With the discovery that synchronic structural-functional models were of little use for the analysis of the Kachin, with the realization that after fifty years of polemic concerning the meaning of descent and marriage, no one yet could define them to his liking, Leach indeed had a lot of "rethinking" to carry out. Instead of rethinking his way to an unoperational, intuitive, synchronic form of the dialectic, he might well have pondered why he so devoutly believes, "Now whether or not evolutionary doctrine is true, it is certainly quite irrelevant for the understanding of present-day human societies . . ." (LEACH 1957:125).

THE UNCLEAN AND UNHYPHENATED

The publicly announced bankruptcy of the structural-functional school provides us with a fresh perspective on one of the most animated controversies in the history of anthropological theory, that between Radcliffe-Brown and Malinowski. From Radcliffe-Brown's "Protest" (1949b) over Gregg and Williams' "The Dismal Science of Functionalism," one gathers that the worst of the injuries sustained appears not to have been the accusation of reactionary politics but the lumping of the two functionalists in the same category. The indignation of Radcliffe-Brown was monumental, as he took the opportunity not only to chastise Gregg and Williams, but to deride Malinowski:

> Malinowski has explained that he is the inventor of functionalism, to which he gave its name. His definition of it is clear; it is the theory or doctrine that every feature of culture of any people past or present is to be explained by reference to seven biological needs of individual human beings. I cannot speak for the other writers to whom the label functionalist is applied by the authors, though I very much doubt if Redfield or Linton accepts this doc-

> trine. As for myself I reject it entirely, regarding it as useless and worse. As a consistent opponent of Malinowski's functionalism I may be called an anti-functionalist [RADCLIFFE-BROWN 1949b: 320-21].

> I have no wish to follow further the irresponsible extravagances of the authors. They certainly do not deserve to be taken seriously. I only ask to be permitted to register a personal protest against a procedure, for which they can find no possible justification or excuse, by which, having applied to me the label "functionalist," they attribute to me, first, acceptance of the Malinowskian theory of culture, which I reject, and second, the quite impossible view that all customs and institutions of any society are right and good, and I suppose they might add that all socially accepted beliefs are true [*ibid.*:322].

> It is true that I make use of the concept of function, and I did so in my lectures at Cambridge and the London School of Economics before the time when Malinowski began to study anthropology. All physiologists make use of the same concept, but they are not called functionalists [*ibid.*].

To the outsider, and in retrospect, this fuss about being identified as a Malinowskian functionalist seems rather like a tempest in a teapot. Both brands of functionalism arose in opposition to the diachronic schools of the evolutionary and diffusionist traditions. Both devoted their major efforts to intensive field experience, and both employed an organismic analogy as their main analytical crutch. As one of Malinowski's students has said,

> Both denied the value of speculative reconstruction of history; both emphasized the need to study existing social institutions; both conceived of cultures as wholes; both developed a concept of function in terms of the social effect of any custom or institution [KABERRY 1957:75].

The Radcliffe-Brownians, it is true, tended to be more comparative and were guided, initially at least, by the hope of achieving synchronic laws. We have seen, however, that these laws turned out to be statements concerning universal psychosocial tendencies by which cultural differences and similarities could be "interpreted" but by which they could not be predicted or retrodicted. In compensation, Malinowski's ethnographic contributions were unexcelled. His Trobriand Island monographs (MALINOWSKI 1922; 1929b; 1935) still constitute the greatest ethnographic description ever achieved. Although Malinowski's concept of function developed along a trajectory, which removed it further and further from Radcliffe-Brown's formulation, there initially was a very strong resemblance between them.

EARLY MALINOWSKI

Malinowski's earliest publication was about the family in Australia and bore the subtitle, "A Sociological Study." It contained a defense of Edward Westermarck's position on the universality of the nuclear family. Although the theme of social solidarity is not conspicuous, the conclusions pay lip service to Durkheimian functions:

> Social institutions should in the first place be defined by their social functions; if the functions—religious, magical, legal, economic, etc.—of the totemic class, the exogamous class, and other divisions be known and compared with the functions of the individual family, each of these institutions will appear as occupying a definite place in the social organization, and playing a determinate part in the life of the community. And such a knowledge would afford a firm basis for further speculations.
>
> In the foregoing investigations we have omitted this side of the problem partly in order to avoid increasing the bulk of the monograph, but above all, that we might develop more clearly the features of the institution described [1913a:303].

In a footnote to this passage, Malinowski promised to go beyond the family to study the clans and sections in terms of their "social functions." It was in fact Radcliffe-Brown (1931) and not Malinowski who was to achieve the promised analysis. As J. A. Barnes (1963:xvi) has noted, Radcliffe-Brown's review of this book already contained the seeds of their future disagreements:

> Radcliffe-Brown reviewed Malinowski's book in 1914 and after commenting that "it is by far the best example in English of scientific method in dealing with the descriptions of the customs and institutions of a savage people" went on to argue that Malinowski's statement of the theoretical framework for the study of kinship (Chapter VI) was "the least successful in the book. The Australian notions relating to kinship cannot be studied without reference to what the author calls 'group relationships'; in other words, the relationship systems, classes, and clans. As Mr. Malinowski has confined himself, quite justifiably, to a study of the individual family relationships, this part of his work remains imperfect." Here we have the criticism, often repeated, that Malinowski could not see a descent system existing save as an "extension" of relationships within the elementary family.

SEX, FAMILY, AND THE INDIVIDUAL

Malinowski's interest in the family provided a major focus for his work up until the ill-fated switch to problems of Colonial acculturation. It led him quite logically to a confrontation with the theories of Freud, which he put to the test, guided by books sent to him by C. G. Seligman (MALINOWSKI 1927a:ix), during his Trobriand fieldwork. The matrilineal inclinations of this group provided the world with the first field examination of Freud's theories concerning the universality of the Oedipus complex, as well as of many other Freudian notions such as racial conscience and infant sexuality. Barnouw (1963:59ff.) points out that Malinowski's conclusions were not unequivocal. But the net impression of *Sex and Repression in Savage Society* is that of a substantial blow from which Freud's original doctrines were never able fully to recover. It was certain at least that relations between father and son in a matrilineal and avunculocal descent system were radically different from what Freud had been able to observe in his Viennese patriarchy.

The influence of Malinowski's work on sex and the family earned for him a reputation outside of anthropology which was in no way matched by Radcliffe-Brown's arid discussions of the lineage principle. He had a predilection for juicy titles (*The Sexual Life of Savages*), and his flamboyant treatment of the Trobriands as a Rousseauan sexual paradise is properly emphasized in Leach's (1965a:36) attempt to explain Malinowski's public success. But I do not accept Leach's sour conclusion, obviously intended to include Radcliffe-Brown, that "there are many lesser, more pedantic men who in some ways can be considered much better anthropologists." Malinowski's concern with sex, family life, and individual psychology is no evidence of his lack of awareness of the Durkheimian kind of functional relations with which the structural-functionalists had become obsessed. Malinowski's functionalism was a bigger, potentially more powerful, and emically more interesting armamentarium than anything Radcliffe-Brownians could muster. It both included and surpassed the principles with which the structural-functionalists operated.

TEMPEST IN A TEAPOT

Malinowski's explanation of the universality of nuclear family incest prohibitions is not at variance with a structural-functional approach. Indeed, his appeal to individual biopsychological givens is a necessary part of any structural-functional "explanation." Malinowski's interpretation of all incest prohibitions is that they originate within the family and function to preserve the family and thus the rest of social organization (see p. 198 for earlier precedents):

> In any type of civilization in which custom, morals, and law would allow incest, the family could not continue to exist. At maturity we would witness the breaking up of the family, hence complete social chaos and an impossibility of continuing cultural tradition. Incest would mean the upsetting of age distinctions, the mixing up of generations, the disorganization of sentiments and a violent exchange of roles at a time when the family is the most important educational medium. No society could exist under such conditions. The alternative type of culture under which incest is excluded, is the only one consistent with the existence of social organization and culture [MALINOWSKI 1927a:251].

There can be no basis other than scholastic snobbism for setting this interpretation in opposition to a more "sociological" approach which would start with extrafamilial group incest prohibition and extend these to the nuclear family. Many of Radcliffe-Brown's structural principles assume the existence of the nuclear family (as in the case of the "male mother"); in both approaches it is not the survival of the individual which is at stake but that of the "social organization and culture."

MALINOWSKI'S SCHEME

With the gradual formalization of Malinowski's theory of culture during the 1930's, a propagandistic exaggeration of the incompatibilities between the two approaches took shape. Malinowski came up with a list of seven basic individual biopsychological needs for the satisfaction of which the social organism or culture was a "vast instrumental reality." The latter was made effective by a series of direct and indirect, primary and secondary collective needs and collective instrumentalities in the form of institutions and symbolic projections, presentations, and defenses. The scheme, as laid out in 1939, is illustrated in the table on pp. 550–51.

It is obvious that in a scheme so vast as Malinowski's, *everything* has its place. Thus, the set of "instrumental needs" is very close to the Durkheimian notion of social structure. But Malinowski chose the same occasion to insist that everything rested on the individual needs and that therefore an unbridgeable gap had opened between on the one

Basic Needs	*Direct Responses*	*Instrumental Needs*
NUTRITION	Commissariat	Renewal of cultural apparatus
REPRODUCTION	Marriage and family	
BODILY COMFORTS	Domicile and dress	Charter of behavior and other sanctions
SAFETY	Protection and defense	
RELAXATION	System of play and repose	Renewal of personnel
MOVEMENT	Activities and system of communication	Organization of force and competition
GROWTH	Training and apprenticeship	

hand "pure functionalism" and, on the other, "hyphenated functionalism" (a splendid riposte upon Radcliffe-Brown's structural-functionalism—*cf.* BRADSHAW-MORREN 1966):

> Professor Radcliffe-Brown is, as far as I can see, still developing and deepening the views of the French sociological school. He thus has to neglect the individual and disregard biology.
> Functionalism differs from other sociological theories more definitely, perhaps, in its conception and definition of the individual than in any other respect. The functionalist includes in his analysis not merely the emotional as well as intellectual side of mental processes, but also insists that man in his full biological reality has to be drawn into our analysis of culture. The bodily needs and environmental influences, and the cultural relation to them, have thus to be studied side by side [MALINOWSKI 1939:939].

Admittedly, Malinowski's listing of needs is rather *ad hoc*—physiologists and psychologists would certainly want to make substantial emendations—and the logic connecting the various instrumentalities to their biopsychological base is never more than arbitrary. Nonetheless, the "hyphenates" cannot convert the virtue of Malinowski's vivid concern with the full amplitude of individual and social functions into a

Responses to Instrumental Needs	Symbolic and Integrative Needs	Responses to Symbolic and Integrative Needs
Economics	———	Knowledge
Social control	———	Magic, religion
Education	———	
Political organization		Art, sports, games

[MALINOWSKI 1939:942]

vice. It would be a less questionable matter were the hyphenates able in any consistent fashion to stay away from a larger framework of their own. But one can easily find statements among Radcliffe-Brown's definitions of function which are so broad as obviously to require an accommodation with Malinowski's ideas, as for example: "Function may be defined as the *total* set of relations that a single social activity or usage or belief has to the *total* social system" (RADCLIFFE-BROWN 1948:85, italics added).

MALINOWSKI AND EVOLUTIONISM

As we have seen, Radcliffe-Brown accepted a "sociological" type of evolutionism, of which he considered Spencer to be an early representative. In Malinowski's case, there is an even more positive relationship to evolutionary doctrines. Edward Westermarck, "to whose personal teaching and to whose work" he acknowledged owing "more than to any other scientific influence" (FIRTH 1957:5), was, of course, an armchair evolutionist of the classical mold. It was to Westermarck that Malinowski owed his conception of the diachronic and synchronic universality of the family, an orientation which pervades every aspect and period of his scholarly work. The second most influential figure in Malinowski's background was James Frazer, whose evolutionary view of magic as a pragmatic instrumentality, the forerunner of science, is a constant theme in Malinowski's treatment of both magic and religion.

The recent attempt by philosopher Karl Popper's student I. C. Jarvie (1964) to set Frazer, the evolutionist, off against Malinowski, the antievolutionary functionalist, has been properly rebuffed by Leach (1965a). Jarvie displays a poverty of historicism, which is a dismal science all its own, in failing to apprehend the strength of Malinowski's evolutionary interests. As Malinowski put it, "The functional view obviously does not dispose of a sound and limited evolutionary conception of culture, though it discourages any hope of giving an exact reconstruction of human development" (1927b:41). Malinowski's conviction that "savage" cultures in general were inferior to civilized cultures provides an essential clue to his long-term devotion to "practical anthropology." Although I shall discuss this aspect of Malinowski's career in a separate section, it should suffice to silence Jarvie that as Malinowski matured, he displayed increasing permissiveness toward evolutionary reconstructions which were anything but "exact." During the Second World War, which Malinowski spent in the United States, he wrote an effulgent paean on "freedom." Aside from its frankly political commitment, the book is remarkable for its wedding of functional theory to a universalistic variety of evolutionism (MALINOWSKI 1944a). Sweeping generalizations about primitive stages and developmental sequences are tossed about with no noticeable indications of restraint:

> We cannot imagine the earliest beginnings of culture without at least two social groupings, the family and the horde [*ibid.*:227].
>
> Inequality in wealth, in the distribution of valuables, of privileges and enjoyments, starts in human evolution with the first advent of war [*ibid.*:194].
>
> Only gradually there emerges a centralized authority within the tribe, such as the council of elders . . . [*ibid.*:234].
>
> The earliest ways of using wealth as power are related to magic and religion [*ibid.*:247].
>
> We can apply in all evolutionary arguments the principle of the survival of the fittest cultural constitution. . . . Were we to imagine a primitive community where the making of fire, the shaping of stones, the techniques of food collecting (etc.) . . . had

> become the monopoly of one or a few lineages, such a culture would have become wiped out within a few generations [*ibid.*:238].

The central animus of Malinowski's attacks on evolution concern the use of "survivals" to reconstruct past evolutionary phases. Here, antievolutionism and antidiffusionism were merged in a loud chorus of protest against explanations of cultural facts without due attention to their fullblooded, living context. Just as Radcliffe-Brown argued that the mother's brother/sister's son relationship was not necessarily a survival of a matrilineal phase, so too did Malinowski repeatedly substitute functional interpretations for diffusionist or evolutionist reconstructions. If you want to know the origin of a fork, he would argue, then pay heed to the service it renders in conveying food to the mouth. This attitude, however, reflects a concern with a question of method rather than fact and was perfectly compatible with evolutionary ideas. Indeed, both men seem rather to have enjoyed the image of themselves as having remained aloof from the fashionable disdain which the Boasians were supposed to have conferred upon evolutionary theories. (But as we have seen, the Boasians were, in their own intimate circle, fully convinced that they too were not really antievolutionists.) Obviously both Malinowski and Radcliffe-Brown made the most of this opportunity of distinguishing themselves from the Americans. Said Malinowski: "Evolutionism is at present rather unfashionable. Nonetheless, its main assumptions are not only valid, but they are also indispensable to the field worker as well as to the student of theory" (1944b:16). Said Radcliffe-Brown:

> Back at the beginning of the century I accepted the theory of *social* evolution as a useful working hypothesis. In 1931, when I spoke of social evolution in my lectures in Chicago, one of the students pointed out to me that "Boas and Lowie have proved that there is no such thing as social evolution." I found that this was a generally accepted view in the United States. But to my mind the arguments of Boas, Lowie, and other anti-(cultural)-evolutionists have no bearing at all on the theory of social evolution [1947:80].

But the fact remains that, despite their acceptance of more or less well-defined evolutionary stages, neither Malinowski nor Radcliffe-Brown can be credited with contributing to the development of evolutionary theory, except in the negative and critical sense in which the Boasians can also be said to have made such a contribution.

PEOPLE WHO LIVE IN GLASS HOUSES

This brings us to the question of whether as an evolutionist, openly admiring Spencer's organismic scheme, in which the superorganic is related to "the physical and biological environment and the physical, emotional, and mental characteristics of social individuals" (SPENCER 1896:8), Radcliffe-Brown's disdain for Malinowski's more earthy functions can be taken seriously. It would scarcely seem consistent with Radcliffe-Brown's professed interest in adaptation (1952b) to insist upon the irrelevance of the parameters with which Malinowski was concerned. Indeed, Meyer Fortes, clinging to the functionalist baby which Evans-Pritchard has almost washed out of existence, berates the latter for not viewing man in evolutionary perspective and adds:

> When we speak of kinship, chiefship, magic, witchcraft, and so on, we are using abstractions. But it is not true to say that their meaning is purely symbolic. For we arrive at them by observing the general features of human relationships and activities in exploiting the environment, in speech and in work, in bringing up children and waging wars, in coming to intellectual and emotional grips with the inexorable facts of birth and death. Concepts become meaningless in social anthropology if they cannot be related to such real activities in their full context of human social life, the artifacts in which knowledge and skill, beliefs and aspirations are given enduring form and without which mankind could not survive [FORTES 1953a:34].

The cheapest of all the invidious comparisons between Radcliffe-Brown and Malinowski is that Malinowski's list of needs, insofar as they are universals, cannot explain observed cultural differences and similarities. (PIDDINGTON 1957:39 attempts to refute this argument.) But this is precisely the main defect and major characteristic of Radcliffe-Brown's "laws." For those of us outside the teacup, the major difference on this score is that Malinowski more or less starts out with his major principles as given, accessible to anyone who wished to erect a heuristic scheme of necessary biocultural conditions in the manner of Wissler's universal pattern. Radcliffe-Brown's principles, on the other hand, are much narrower and result from an attempt to interpret specific sociocultural contrasts. But in both instances, all that happens is that an institution gets "explained" by a functional requirement which could just as well serve to "explain" any other institution you might care to name. It is especially distressing to recall how Max Gluckman poked fun at this aspect of Malinowski's theories without seeming to be aware that he and the rest of the structural-functionalists were equally vulnerable:

> There is a myth among anthropologists that one of Malinowski's students ended a long thesis: "Our survey of the facts has forced us to conclude that the function of leadership in primitive societies is to initiate and organize activities." Is this much more of: "There's ne'er a villain, dwelling in all Denmark but he's an arrant knave" than Malinowski's . . .. "We could state that the function of the tribe as a political unit is the organization of force for policing, defence, and aggression . . . the function of age-groups is the coordinating of physiological and anatomical characteristics as they develop in the process of growth, and their transformation into cultural categories. In occupational groups we see that the carrying out of skills, techniques, and such activities as education, law, and power, constitute the integral function of the group." [GLUCKMAN 1949:24]

Granted that this is an appropriate point at which to make fun of Malinowski's functionalism, is it any less appropriate with respect to the hyphenated variety? Consider, for example, Radcliffe-Brown's attempt to turn Malinowski's explanation of magic inside-out by stressing social rather than individual needs. For Malinowski, the most dangerous and uncertain occasions were filled with magic, a pragmatic attempt to cope with the reality of human means and ends. For Radcliffe-Brown, magic and ritual in general arise out of requirements imposed by the social system. The individual's perception of what is dangerous is guided at every point by the community (RADCLIFFE-BROWN 1952b:149). Thus if an Andaman Islander is afraid to eat dugong during his wife's pregnancy, it is because the social structure has put the fear into him in order to mark the importance of his social responsibilities toward his wife and offspring:

> The primary basis of ritual . . . is the attribution of ritual value to objects and occasions which are either themselves objects of important common interest linking together the persons of a community or are symbolically representative of such objects [*ibid.*:151].

The latitude this formula provides is surely no less than that which Gluckman attributes to Malinowski. If the members of a community repeatedly spend a good deal of time and effort on sacrificing pigs, making canoe magic, or cutting off foreskins, one can be sure that in some fashion or other these rituals relate to important common interests linking them together. Or at least it would be a dull anthropologist who could not come up with a couple of guesses along these lines. Incidentally, it is symptomatic of the whole internecine fracas that both interpretations of magic are transparently complementary rather than exclusive. In the words of George Homans:

> A study of the theories of Malinowski and Radcliffe-Brown illustrates a common feature of scientific controversies: two distinguished persons talking past one another rather than trying to find a common ground for discussion, presenting their theories as alternatives when in fact they are complements [HOMANS 1941: 172].

MALINOWSKI'S APPROACH TO CULTURAL CHANGE

Between 1929 and 1943 Malinowski published about thirteen articles on culture change. The ideas they embody, together with sundry unpublished materials, were put together by Phyllis Kaberry and brought out after Malinowski's death as *The Dynamics of Culture Change* (1945). Although the point of view adopted may have seemed quite daring at the time of publication, in retrospect it bears a heavy burden of conservatism, if not of unreality. The essence of Malinowski's theory is that Europeans and Africans are involved in a give-and-take which must balance out through the development of "common measures" or compromises in "tasks of common interest" (1945:72). In order to assess the likelihood of such peaceful and mutually beneficial adjustments, a scientific contribution which the anthropologist is duty bound to make to colonial administrators, the full cultural context of the African and European institutions and alternatives must be examined. The anthropologist should accept the task of performing this analysis, making a special effort to withhold no facts concerning the failure of the Europeans to give as much as they have taken from the African, without, however, succumbing "to an outburst of pro-native ranting" (*ibid.*:58). Moderation, compromise, and civil service decorum are the ethical bases for the aspiring "practical anthropologist":

> The ethnographer who has studied culture contact and has assessed its active forces, its potentialities and dangers, has the right and duty to formulate his conclusions in a manner in which they can be seriously considered by those who frame policies and those who carry them out. He also has the duty to speak as the Natives' advocate. But he can go no further. Decisions and the practical handling of affairs are outside his competence. His pri-

> mary duty is to present facts; to develop concepts theoretically valid and practically useful; to destroy fictions and empty phrases, and thus to reveal the forces and factors which are relevant and active. Through comparative study he can discover and define the common factor of European intentions and of African response. He can lay bare the sources of maladjustment. These, at times, he will find are due to real intrinsic conflict of interests; at times they arise from faulty assessment of African realities; or again, from almost adventitious misunderstandings. . . . Knowledge gives foresight, and foresight is indispensable to the statesman and to the local administrator, to the educationalist, welfare worker, and missionary alike. This discovery of long-run tendencies; the capacity of foreseeing and forecasting the future in the light of full knowledge of all the factors involved; competent advice on specific questions—these are the tasks of the contact-ethnographer as a practical expert [*ibid.*:161-62].

INCOMPETENT ADVICE

Much has happened in Africa since Malinowski's tour in 1934. We have the benefit of hindsight. But it would scarcely seem accidental that amid all the events which have taken place, the one thing that has not happened is compromise. Instead, everywhere in Africa there occurred a polarization of African nationalist versus white settler and colonial interests, leading to decisive victories for the Africans in west, central, and east Africa and continuing struggle or sharp setbacks in the Portuguese and southern sectors. The judgment of history lies heavy on those anthropologists who believed themselves free of ethical involvement because they were advocates of the "Native" cause before the tribunals of the European racists while at the same time preaching moderation to the exploited and underprivileged.

Were it constructive in this context to plunge into a discussion of ethics, I should raise the question, never entertained by Malinowski, of why the Africans who had been invaded, conquered, enslaved, and exploited owed the Europeans anything else in return. The basic premise of Malinowski's position involved him in the assumption that the Europeans had a right to be governing the Africans and that every future adjustment rightfully demanded that the European interests be given their legal and customary due. Despite the admonitions to the Europeans that they had better be nice to the natives or the natives would go on misbehaving, there is a sanctimonious note in Malinowski's theory which helps to explain why anthropology is still a dirty word among many African nationalists:

> I suggest that first and foremost it would be well to unify, coordinate, and harmonize various policies. For we have already noted the considerable discrepancy between the enthusiasm of good-will and educational zeal, and the existence of the color bar; between the requirements of the settler and the activities of the agricultural department, which may develop economic ambitions beyond the legitimate scope of their realization. Whenever Europeans plan the settlement of large portions of any colony, segregation and color bar become inevitable. This ought to be remembered by the enthusiastic minority of good-will, who may involuntarily raise high hopes through such doctrines as the Brotherhood of Man, the Gospel of Labor, and the possibilities of assimilation through education, dress, manners, and morals. If, from the outset, it were possible to make quite clear in preaching the gospel of civilization that no full identity can ever be reached; that what are being given to the Africans are new conditions of existence, better adapted to their needs but always in harmony with European requirements, the smaller would be the chances of a strong reaction and the formation of new, potentially dangerous nationalisms [*ibid.*:160].

A LARGE GRAIN OF DISMAL TRUTH

Perhaps Kroeber's (p. 331) reaction to Gregg and Williams' link-up of functionalism with a conservative political position was just a little too self-righteous. It was, after all, Malinowski himself who said in a context different but not altogether remote from colonialism: "Functional anthropology is thus an essentially conservative science" (1930a:168). Ironically enough, Malinowski's basic errors, with respect to a theory of change, reflect his lingering Frazerian evolutionist biases. I would say that he never quite achieved the ability to distinguish between the native as a primitive, and the "Native," as an actor-type in a definite Euro-American colonial order. We suffer from the lack of this distinction even in the Trobriand monographs. Failure to make it in Africa can lead to disastrous mistakes. We have, at any rate, a clear-cut statement from the very beginning of Malinowski's involvement in practical anthropology which it is very difficult to shrug off:

> The practical value of such a theory (functionalism) is that it teaches us the relative importance of various customs, how they dovetail into each other, how they have to be handled by missionaries, colonial authorities, and those who economically have to exploit savage trade and savage labor [MALINOWSKI 1927b:40-41].

INABILITY TO EXPLAIN CHANGE

But it is not the ethic of one form or another of political collaboration which constitutes the main subject matter of this book. Here we must inquire instead into the adequacy of the theory of cultural change which Malinowski had sought to erect on the unlikely basis of his previous synchronic functionalist principles. It must be admitted that at one point Malinowski appears to be on the verge of proposing an interesting and truly dynamic theory of culture change. Invoking his own ethnic background, he contrasts the experience of Polish Americans and Africans in the following terms:

> Successful culture change in Africa demands enormous expenditure. For it is one of the soundest and most important principles of social science that people are prepared to pass only from worse to better. Only such change is encompassed without much friction and with relative rapidity. This of course is the reason why the national minorities in the United States changed culturally with comparatively amazing ease, with little resistance, and with a rapidity incredible to a European brought up as one of a minority. . . . The main reason for this, though there are also others, is that in the United States they are offered all along the line substantial economic, political, and social advantages, which was by no means the case under Russian or Prussian rule [MALINOWSKI 1945:56].

This being the case, it then would seem a prime requisite of any theory of cultural change applicable to Africa to assess the probability that substantial economic, political, and social advantages were about "to be offered" to the Africans. Or if one is more ambitious, to inquire, what in general are the conditions under which such offers are likely to be made? Or, even more to the point, under what conditions have colonial peoples or other minority groups sat around for tens or even hundreds of years waiting for advantages which never came?

MAX GLUCKMAN'S CRITIQUE

It is in large measure because Malinowski could not shake loose from the functionalist emphasis upon equilibrium that his theory never gets off the ground. His system of cultural instrumentalities can only explain how tensions and conflicts are reduced or eliminated, never why or how they originate or why or how they intensify. Thus, instead of producing a theory of change, all he succeeded in doing was to enlarge upon a theory of no-change. Events in Africa have since rendered his analysis superfluous, since the situation for which it was intended no longer exists.

I find myself in complete agreement, therefore, with Max Gluckman's appraisal of Malinowski's attempt at a theory of change.

> This is a bad book. . . . His "theory" does not bear examination from any point of view. It is analytically sterile, and it ends in the worst kind of practical anthropology: welfare work without morality, based on naive oversimplification . . . [1949:21].

Moreover, Gluckman's perception of the source of so much of what is wrong with this in part at least corresponds to my own: "He cannot admit 'conflict' into his frame of integrated institutions; that is, conflict as an inherent attribute of social organization" (*ibid.*: 8). But the ironical rub in this fierce criticism is that Gluckman's ability to handle conflict is not that different from Malinowski's. Although Gluckman and other social anthropologists have written extensively of the matter of conflict, and unresolved tension, they have done so only within the framework of their Durkheimian heritage, in terms of how, despite such conflict, social solidarity is maintained. Gluckman, for example, has expended his main theoretical thrust in attempting to show how conflicts are a normal (even "healthy") part of social life not at all incompatible with the maintenance of social order. This is because "conflicts in one set of relationships, over a wider range of society or through a longer period of time, lead to the re-establishment of social cohesion" (GLUCKMAN 1963:2). Feuds, hostility to chiefs, estrangements within the family, witchcraft, and even South African apartheid are all grist for his mill. This is not to say that Gluckman is unaware of structure-breaking conflict, but rather that he is unprepared to deal with it through a theory of sociocultural change. We are much in debt to Gluckman for his honesty on this point. Still referring to *The Dynamics of Cultural Change*, he comments:

> It is also a humbling book. For if, on the positive side, Malinowski's thesis remains descriptive, no social anthropologist has yet put forward an alternative. The Marxists have a theoretical framework. Among ourselves the Wilsons have tried to formulate one. But we have still to establish a right to maintain that we are more than good recorders of contemporary events [*ibid.*:21].

With this much admitted, the remarks of one of the very few frankly Marxist British anthropologists deserve special emphasis:

> Malinowski's basic sociological heritage like that of Radcliffe-Brown, derived from Durkheim in whose writing conflict was primarily treated as a form of social pathology, and where attention was focussed on the normative and integrative elements in social life. The problem of order was considered to be logically prior to the problem of change. . . . Neither showed much interest in structural change [WORSELEY 1961:28].

I hasten to express my agreement with Firth (1964), an agreement which incidentally is shared by Worsley to judge from his treatment of cargo cults (1957), that an adequate theory of sociocultural change cannot confine itself to considerations of overt and irreconcilable conflict. Even in orthodox Marxism, class struggle is after all relevant only to the evolution of class-structured society. An anthropological theory of sociocultural change obviously must include more subtle and covert selective mechanisms, and these must be admitted as having their effect at the state as well as the pre-state level. But there is surely a monument to the power of culture that will long endure in Malinowski's attempt to analyze colonialism as if the Europeans and Africans were about to become part of one big happy Kula ring.

GLUCKMAN DID NOT GET TO THE HEART OF THE MATTER

It does not seem to me to get at the heart of the matter to stress Malinowski's difficulties with deepening and irreconcilable conflict situations at the state level. Even if the functionalists of either variety had somehow made over their schemes to accept conflict as an important engine of change, there would yet remain a profound impotence with respect to the explanation of cultural differences and similarities in terms of lawful diachronic-synchronic principles. As I have already indicated, the main defect of both kinds of functionalism is the attempt to interpret differences and similarities in terms of constants. In the case of Radcliffe-Brown, the issue of whether one part of the system is causally more significant than the others was given an illusory solution by relating everything to social structure. It is Radcliffe-Brown's failure to inquire systematically into the causal relationship between techno-environmental adaptation, productive and distributive arrangements, and social structure, which should most disturb my own generation of anthropologists. In Malinowski's case, however, given the vastly expanded notion of function with which he operated, the failure to give special weight to techno-economic functions is not a case of omission, but a result of deep commitments to anti-economic determinist dogma. In the chapter which follows, I describe Malinowski's strong attachment to the emic option in the context of the development of the linguistic model, and the "New Ethnography." Some advance reference to this matter is required at this juncture.

ATTACK AGAINST CULTURAL MATERIALISM

Only by considering Malinowski's treatment of techno-economic factors in connection with the emic/etic distinction can we appreciate the extent to which his theories participated in and contributed to the downgrading or obstruction of techno-environmental and techno-economic research options. Superficially it would seem that no subject was of greater import to Malinowski than that of primitive economics. Nutrition and reproduction topped his list of needs, and in all of his work there appears to be an intense concern for all manner of mundane detail. His first Trobriand monograph, *The Argonauts*, was largely devoted to a description of the Kula ring and contained a Preface by Frazer in which Malinowski was congratulated for his emphasis upon economics:

> Little reflection is needed to convince us of the fundamental importance of economic forces at all stages of man's career from the humblest to the highest. After all, the human species is part of the animal creation, and as such, like the rest of the animals, it reposes on a material foundation; on which a higher life, intellectual, moral, social, may be built, but without which no such superstructure is possible. That material foundation, consisting in the necessity of food and of a certain degree of warmth and shelter from the elements, forms the economic or industrial basis and prime condition of human life. If anthropologists have hitherto unduly neglected it, we may suppose that it was rather because they were attracted to the higher side of man's nature than because they deliberately ignored and under-valued the importance and indeed necessity of the lower . . . Be that as it may, Dr. Malinowski has done well to emphasise the great significance of primitive economics by singling out the notable exchange system of the Trobriand Islanders for special consideration [FRAZER 1922:viii].

As Frazer goes on he becomes even more enthusiastic, for Dr. Malinowski has not confined himself merely to the surface phenomena but at every point has searched out the full complexity of human nature and found the "motives and feelings," the "emotional as well as rational basis" of Trobriand life.

But there is a great muddle in all this. If there is any single theme pervading *The Argonauts,* it is precisely that the motives and feelings which arise from noneconomic needs dominate the whole Kula enterprise. The fact of the matter is that Malinowski deliberately refrained from carrying out a genuine economic study of the productive and distributive system of the Trobriand Islands because his ethnographic orientation was overwhelmingly opposed to any such option. Malinowski himself is my authority for this statement, for he was perfectly aware of what he was doing and of how his monographs would have looked had he really been concerned to examine the "material foundation" of Trobriand culture.

The Kula, that splendid example of commerce inscrutable in its risk of life on long sea voyages all for the sake of a few spondylus and *Conus millepunctatus* shells, is to the functionalists what potlatch is to the Boasians. But economic analysis is properly a matter of a system of production and distribution: of energy, of time and labor in-put, of the transformation, transportation, mechanical and chemical interplay between a human population and their habitat and of the distribution of the products of this interaction in terms of energy, especially food energy, and the mechanical and biological apparata upon which all these processes depend. Malinowski treats us instead to a vastly elaborate account of the ritual aspects of the preparations for open-sea expeditions in which the subjective motivations of the actors in terms of prestige and magical aspirations dominate every aspect of the ethnography. We learn only incidentally, never in detail, that the whimsical voyagers circulate not only arm bands and necklaces but coconuts, sago, fish, vegetables, baskets, mats, sword clubs, green stone (formerly essential for tools), mussel shells (for knives), and creepers (essential for lashings). Malinowski's explanation is as follows:

> Both the canoe-building and the ordinary trade have been spoken of as secondary or subsidiary to the Kula proper. This requires a comment. I do not, by thus subordinating the two things in importance to the Kula, mean to express a philosophical reflection or a personal opinion as to the relative value of these pursuits from the point of view of some social teleology. Indeed, it is clear that if we look at the acts from the outside, as comparative sociologists, and gauge their real utility, trade and canoe-building will appear to us as the really important achievements, whereas

> we shall regard the Kula only as an indirect stimulus, impelling the natives to sail and to trade. Here, however, I am not dealing in sociological, but in pure ethnographical description, and any sociological analysis I have given is only what has been absolutely indispensable to clear away misconceptions and to define terms [1961:100; orig. 1922].

In this passage, "ethnographic" and "sociological" correspond to emic and etic, respectively. The result of Malinowski's option is to submerge the entire issue of the significance of the techno-economic subsystem in an irrelevant and obscurantist context. For we next find that the opposite strategy of giving priority to the techno-economic factors is attacked on the very grounds which an etic approach to sociocultural systems is designed to overcome. We are thrown back upon the ethnosemantic categories and subjective psychological appraisals and reactions of the actors, who constitute those elements in the whole array least capable of comprehending the sociocultural system to which they have been conditioned. We are henceforth denied a picture of the whole system as it moves through time, related to an island habitat, rich in ecological specialties, fluctuating in population, variable in annual production, precarious for human existence during droughts, typhoons, and war, and progressively subject to European blackbirding, pearl diving, and copra trading.

A TATTERED SCARECROW

In his South Sea Island paradise, experienced through the eyes, minds, and ears of the "native," Malinowski attempted to confront Marx in much the same way as he had confronted Freud. But the paradox is evident: emics are essential for psychoanalytical comment; they in no way prepare one to come to grips with the issues raised by Marx. Thus we see Malinowski's Trobriand material falling into place among the long line of anthropological attacks against the scarecrow called "economic man." The economic determinists, so the refrain goes, treat man as motivated by purely rationalistic calculations of self-interest. But ethnology shows that even the savage has his ideals, his values, his occasions of self-sacrifice, and his postponement of gratification. Therefore, the priority given by some to the economic factors in history is patently false.

All of *The Argonauts* is in fact harnessed to this non sequitur. Throughout the book there are numerous outbursts concerning "economic man," any one of which would serve to make the point. But it is in the concluding chapter, during the discussion of "The Meaning of the Kula" that the climax is reached:

> At one or two places in the previous chapters, a somewhat detailed digression was made in order to criticise the view about the economic nature of primitive man, as it survives in our mental habits as well as in some text books—the conception of a rational being who wants nothing but to satisfy his simplest needs and does it according to the economic principle of least effort. This economic man always knows exactly where his material interests lie, and makes for them in a straight line. At the bottom of the *so-called materialistic conception of history* lies a somewhat analogous idea of a human being, who, in everything he devised and pursues, has nothing but his material advantage of a purely utilitarian type at heart. Now I hope that whatever the meaning of the Kula might be for Ethnology, for the general science of culture, the meaning of the Kula will consist in being instrumental to dispell such crude, rationalistic conceptions of primitive mankind, and to induce both the speculator and the observer to deepen the analysis of economic facts [1922:316, italics added].

SO-CALLED MATERIALISTIC CONCEPTION OF HISTORY

No informed critic of the historical-materialist position could confuse the utilitarian doctrines of classical economic theory with the research strategy associated with Marx. For what is more conspicuous in Marx's analysis of capitalism than that millions of people spend their lives making choices and upholding values which are not only "irrational," but positively contradictory to their own "enlightened self-interest"? The promise of the research strategy which lies buried under the political debris churned up by the clash of capitalism and communism is that these irrational ingredients are nonetheless "functional" features of the particular sociocultural systems in which they are found.

Whether this means that they are rational in terms of the actors' short- or long-run "goals" (whatever these are) is a philosophical issue into which we need not venture. What is vital to a science of culture is that an attempt be made to relate such apparently inscrutable phenomena to the basic techno-economic arrangements by which the total sociocultural system interacts with its natural and cultural habitat. Historical materialism as proposed by Marx did not consist of attempts to explain particular sociocultural systems by reference to individual economic motivations. Nothing could be more contrary to Marx's position. He rather sought to explain the peculiar conditioned forms of a group's collective and individual economic behavior in terms of an adaptive evolutionary sequence. In a modern anthropological formulation, it is the techno-environmental and techno-economic conditions in which the human population finds itself which demand priority of analysis because there exists overwhelming evidence that these are the parts of the total sociocultural system which in the long run and in most cases swing social structure and ideology into functional conformity.

To take another example from Malinowski: The Trobrianders, like many other Melanesian groups, apparently produce a temporary surplus of yams which they display at harvest time on special racks. Malinowski reached the conclusion that the prestige derived from the display of this surplus is an adequate account of why it occurs. Many other anthropologists have emphasized how in Melanesian villages yams devoured in gluttonous feasts or left to rot in conspicuous displays demonstrate that prestige motives will lead people to produce more than they "need." As in the case of the potlatch and the anti-economic food taboos associated with the mismanagement of animal foods (see Chap. 11), the bias against etic interpretations has been overwhelming. In Malinowski's ethnography, failure to consider the possibility of a relationship between "overproduction" of yams and certain basic features of the techno-environmental equation, brings to mind his weakness for sensational titles and his penchant for titillating oddments. It was perhaps important for Malinowski's presentation of the Trobrianders as freely fornicating noble savages (*cf.* LEACH 1965a:35) that they live in a world of tropical abundance in which the other basic necessities were also rather easily taken care of. We learn only in passing and in a separate context that the Trobrianders not infrequently confront years of disastrous drought-induced famines (MALINOWSKI 1935:160–61; *cf.* HARRIS 1959a:192). But this is enough to raise certain lively alternatives to the prestige interpretations of the rotting yams. Might not these seemingly superfluous foodstuffs actually represent the innocuous side effect of an adaptive relationship between Trobriand labor in-put and the conditions of the Trobriand habitat? The extra effort annually expended to produce a superabundant crop of yams, some of which will rot in times of abundant rainfall, might be just enough to ward off starvation in years of scanty rainfall.

At any rate, no value system which induces heavy labor in-puts by pinning "medals" on its Stakhanovite producers can be regarded as totally anti-economic. It would have been a real coup for the camp of the antideterminists and culture-by-whimsy school if Malinowski had discovered the Trobriand practicing a custom whereby, among the commoners, the man who produced the least number of yams had the biggest house and the most wives.

Emics, Etics, and the New Ethnography 20

At mid-century there arose within cultural anthropology a movement dedicated to the improvement of standards of ethnographic descriptions and analysis, having as its source and inspiration the techniques of linguistics. This movement, for which the name "The New Ethnography" has been proposed (STURTEVANT 1964), originated at Yale and has spread rapidly throughout the United States. Known variously as "ethnolinguistics," "ethnoscience," or "ethnosemantics," its manifest appeal lies in its promise to achieve the precise and highly operationalized paradigmatic renderings of cultural phenomena which have come to be associated with the linguist's descriptions of phonology and grammar. Its covert appeal, however, is that it carries forward the tradition of cultural idealism in anthropology while supplying that tradition with impressive new scientific credentials. These credentials are fully merited within certain domains and under certain restrictions which I will shortly attempt to specify. In larger perspective, however, the movement suffers from the accumulated liabilities of the past two hundred years of cultural-idealist thought.

As we have seen, a convergent, if operationally unsound, mo based on the linguistic model, has arisen in France under th ship of Lévi-Strauss. The primary aim of the present chapt show that the convergence toward the strategy embodied in t ethnography derives from an epistemological outlook widely held among contemporary social scientists of many different theoretical persuasions. Despite its unique attachment to explicitly linguistic paradigms, there are certain epistemological assumptions, of questionable value, which link the new ethnography with schools as diverse as the Boasians, Culture and Personality, French Structuralism, and both varieties of British functionalists. In order to demonstrate this convergence and in order to locate the new ethnography in relationship to the "old ethnography," we are obliged to undertake a discussion of the difference between emic and etic research options.

Recourse to the emic/etic dichotomy, reference to which has been made at several points throughout the preceding chapters, is imperative if we seek to identify the prospects of cultural materialism within the context of modern social science. The concepts of emics and etics provide an epistemological and operational basis for distinguishing between cultural idealism and cultural materialism in an age dedicated to eclectic middle-ground theories. In order to evaluate the historical significance of these eclectic preferences, certain epistemological issues must be confronted, at the deepest level of research design, rather than at the level of sociocultural hypotheses and theories. We have already pointed to the need for this confrontation in discussing the way in which techno-economic and techno-environmental data have been "emicized" on behalf of the disproof of economic-determinist theories. A similar "emicization" of social-structural phenomena is also common. In order for there to be a fair test of the cultural-materialist strategy, the predominantly emic corpus of extant ethnography must be supplemented by etic descriptions.

PIKE'S DEFINITIONS

The terms themselves were coined by the missionary linguist Kenneth Pike (1954:8) on analogy with the "emic" in phon*emic* and the "etic" in phon*etic*. In conformity with this analogy, Pike stressed "the structural results" obtained by phonemic analysis as opposed to the "nonstructural" results characteristic of phonetics. From a linguistic point of view, etic analyses cannot achieve structural results, since a purely etic *system* of sound differences is inconceivable. With all deference to the linguistic origin of the dichotomy, a nonlinguist must object to Pike's extrapolation of the correlation between etics and nonstructural results to nonverbal behavior. What does "structure" mean in this context? To avoid tautology, it must be taken as suggesting something like the "order in an orderly arrangement." Structure is the order in a system. The pairing of structural results with emics and nonstructural results with etics accords with the history of linguistics. But there is no reason to suppose that this equation must hold for nonlinguistic phenomena. There are structures in an atom, a molecule, a cell, and an organism, the description of none of which depends upon emic operations. Why should we not also assume that there are sociocultural systems whose structure can be exposed independently of procedures modeled after phonemic analysis? Pike's failure to make provision for this alternative was rooted deeply in religious convictions which cannot be ignored if one wishes to understand *his* meaning (PIKE 1962). It is of course possible to utilize etic categories which will not contribute to an understanding of sociocultural systems. But many phonological analyses, because of poor technique, also end up with partial or spurious structures.

In further defining the consequences of the two approaches, Pike elaborates a theme which he considers to be secondary, but which assumes primary importance as soon as we disregard the gratuitous equivalence between emics and structure. Outlining the operations for the identification of nonverbal emic units (behavioremes), he makes it clear that emic structure must correspond to the actor's "purpose" during the observed performance. That is, an emic description must be related to a set of logico-empirical procedures by which the actor's meaning and purpose is made known: "In spite of the problems which are involved, it is absolutely essential if one is to study behavior *as it actually functions*, that one assume that the analyst can detect the presence and to some degree the nature and meaning of purpose" [PIKE 1954:80] The behavioreme itself is partially defined as "an emic segment or component of purposive human activity" (*ibid.*:57). Moreover, the same definitional ingredient is paramount in an extensive quote from Edward Sapir (1927) who is regarded by Pike as having anticipated the distinction at issue:

> It is impossible to say what an individual is doing unless we have tacitly accepted the essentially arbitrary modes of interpretation that social tradition is constantly suggesting to us from the very moment of our birth. Let anyone who doubts this try the

> experiment of making a painstaking report (i.e. an etic one) of the actions of a group of natives engaged in some activity, say religious, to which he has not the cultural key (i.e. a knowledge of the emic system). If he is a skillful writer, he may succeed in giving a picturesque account of what he sees and hears, or thinks he sees and hears, but the chances of his being able to give a relation of what happens, in terms that would be intelligible and acceptable to the natives themselves, are practically nil. He will be guilty of all manner of distortion; his emphasis will be constantly askew. He will find interesting what the natives take for granted as a casual kind of behavior worthy of no particular comment, and he will utterly fail to observe the crucial turning points in the course of action that give formal significance to the whole in the minds of those who do possess the key to its understanding [quoted in PIKE 1954:9-10].

It is the "formal significance" in the "minds" of the actors which needs to be stressed. The "created" significances of etic descriptions are not dependent upon the subjective "meanings" and "purposes" of the actors. Emic distinctions, on the other hand, require one to enter the world of purpose, meaning, and attitudes. Emic study "helps one to appreciate not only the culture or language as an ordered whole, but it helps one to understand the individual actors in such a life-drama—their attitudes, motives, interests, responses, conflicts, and personality development" (*ibid.*:11).

DEFINITION OF EMIC

In keeping with the broader uses to which the emic/etic distinction has been put and in the tradition which ties Pike to Sapir, I propose the following definition:

Emic statements refer to logico-empirical systems whose phenomenal distinctions or "things" are built up out of contrasts and discriminations significant, meaningful, real, accurate, or in some other fashion regarded as appropriate by the actors themselves. An emic statement can be falsified if it can be shown that it contradicts the cognitive calculus by which relevant actors judge that entities are similar or different, real, meaningful, significant, or in some other sense "appropriate" or "acceptable."

EMICS AND PREDICTABILITY

At least two prominent advocates of the emic approach have insisted upon establishing unusual and, to my view, unacceptable criteria for verifying the truth content of emic statements. According to Charles Frake (1964a:112):

> . . . an ethnography should be a theory of cultural behavior in a particular society, the adequacy of which is to be evaluated by the ability of a stranger to the culture (who may be the ethnographer) to use the ethnography's statements as instructions for appropriately anticipating the scenes of the society. I say "appropriately anticipate" rather than "predict" because a failure of an ethnographic statement to predict correctly does not necessarily imply descriptive inadequacy as long as the members of the described society are as surprised by the failure as is the ethnographer. The test of descriptive adequacy must always refer to informants' interpretations of events, not simply to the occurrence of events.

A similar position is adopted by Harold Conklin (1964:26) who also specifies "appropriate anticipation" rather than prediction. Since no attention has been devoted to the question of how to proceed with this operation, it cannot be taken at once both literally and seriously.

THE NATIVE'S POINT OF VIEW

The unsatisfactory formulation of emic predictability (to which of course not all ethnosemanticists would subscribe) need not deter us from setting rather clear-cut limits to the logico-empirical domains embraced by emic studies. It is convenient to begin by demarcating two broad, overlapping subfields: The first is concerned with semantic and communication phenomena; the second, with inner psychological states and feelings. All phonological, grammatical, and semantic analyses carried out by linguists and ethnographers constitute emically oriented studies. Regardless of how one chooses to define phonemes, the range of sounds involved must produce systematic sound contrasts which are significant to the native speaker. Similarly, in stating the rules by which grammatical utterances are generated in a specific language, the "test of adequacy" is the native speaker's intuitive knowledge of the grammaticality of the sample utterances generated according to such rules.

It is a fundamental premise of linguistic analysis that the phonemic system or the grammatical rules need not correspond to the analysis which the native speaker is usually capable of performing. Indeed, the native speaker may emphatically reject the linguist's analysis. That analysis does not therefore cease to be the product of logico-empirical operations in which emic distinctions provide the basis for subsequent logical manipulation as well as for the ultimate tests of logico-empirical adequacy.

"Componential analysis," an analytic procedure first employed by Ward Goodenough (1956), fits in here as an activity devoted to the formulation of the rules by which semantic domains are logico-empirically ordered. As in the case of phonemic and syntactic rules, the componential formula need not (one can say, probably never will) correspond to the rules which the native is capable of expressing. Goodenough's componential definition of an American's grandmother's second husband goes something like this: a kinsman at less than two degrees collateral distance; at two units of genealogical distance; in lineal relationship; in a senior generation; of male sex; in the presence of a marital tie; senior party involved, senior party being the first person in the particular relationship to become known to the junior party (1965a:279). Goodenough appears unconcerned by the possibility that some natives might not share his convictions concerning the adequacy of the definition. (Actually, few Americans can confirm or deny Goodenough's analysis from personal experience.)

> One test of the adequacy of this account, I have said, is that it not do violence to my own feel, as informant, for the structure of what is described. This is the subjective test of adequacy. An equally important test is that it provide an alien with the knowledge he needs to use my kinship terminology in a way I will accept as corresponding with the way I use it. This is the objective test of adequacy. An account is deficient to the extent that it fails the test [*ibid.*:261].

OTHER COMMUNICATIONS SYSTEMS

Another kind of ethnography which should be explicitly associated with the emic point of view is that which Ray Birdwhistell (1952) has called "kinesics," the study of the communication functions of body motions. At least some of the body motions of interest to Birdwhistell link up with the earlier field of gesture study and clearly constitute emic entities insofar as they involve the statement of the rules of a public communication *system*. The study of other body motions, such as the particular walking gait or sitting slump of a psychiatric patient, cuts across the second large category of emically oriented research shortly to be discussed and is not so easily classified.

It seems obvious that whenever we deal with phenomena that are part of a communication system, and that when our research program calls for "cracking" the code which the native communicators employ, then that program incorporates the strategy of emic studies. In this enterprise it is of no epistemological importance that the native users of the system know how to formulate the rules of the code. Humans share with other organisms the ability to communicate information without being able to say just how the communication task gets done. This is a most interesting psychological fact, but it does not alter the emic nature of the phenomena under consideration.

INNER PSYCHOLOGICAL STATES

The second great domain of emic studies is concerned with the analysis of the behavior stream in terms of the intentions, purposes, motives, goals, attitudes, thoughts, and feelings of the culture carriers. Benjamin Colby (1966:3) has explicitly linked these phenomena with formal semantics by making them the object of "ethnographic semantics." "The ultimate goal is the understanding of the evaluations, emotions, and beliefs that lie behind word usage." Although not touched upon by Colby—he specifically rejects the suggestion that Morris Opler and Ruth Benedict are relevant (*ibid.*: 28)—this is a universe regularly studied by psychologists as well as by social scientists.

Two traditions within psychology diverge with respect to the treatment of these phenomena. The division corresponds roughly to the emic/etic distinction in the social sciences. On the one hand there is the approach which emphasizes the validity of introspective descriptions and verbal reports of inner psychological states. On the other, there is the approach, represented by the major neobehaviorist learning theory schools, which systematically avoids dependence upon states or dispositions which cannot be defined by means of operations performed on the external parts and conditions of the behaving organism.

In ethnography, an emic approach to purposes, goals, motivations, attitudes, etc., is premised on the assumption that between the actor and the observer, it is the actor who is better able to know his own inner state. Furthermore, it is assumed that access to information concerning the actor's inner state is essential for an understanding of his behavior and for a proper description of the behavior-stream events in which he participates. In most cases, this assumption is quite overt, and the postulation of the existence of inner states is carried out on such a lavish scale that there is no danger of mistaking the emic nature of the research. This is certainly true whenever the ethnographer takes the familiar Boasian position that if only he had been brought up as a member of X tribe then his descriptions of purposes, goals, motives, etc., would be so much richer by virtue of being able to think and feel like a member of that tribe.

CONFOUNDING THE EMIC/ETIC DISTINCTION

There are certain options which in their most subtle form defeat the emic/etic distinction. Thus it is a commonplace of psychoanalytical research and practice that the actor is regarded as a poor observer of his own inner state. The analyst's task is to penetrate behind the façades, symbols, and other defenses to the unconscious feelings and thoughts of which the actor is unaware. This much is etic: the analyst's statements are not falsified even if it is shown that the contrasts which he draws are not significant, meaningful, real, or appropriate from the point of view of the actor. On the other hand, there also seems to be an assumption that if the actor accepts the analyst's description as corresponding to his own "true" inner state, then verification has occurred. To that extent, psychoanalytic descriptions are emic. But it should be noted that this apparent defeat of the emic/etic distinction suffers a penalty in the form of a low standard of verifiability and a dubious empirical status. This penalty is always suffered by those who indiscriminately shift back and forth from emic to etic strategies.

DEFINITION OF ETICS

Let us now turn to a provisional definition of etics. Etic statements depend upon phenomenal distinctions judged appropriate by the community of scientific observers. Etic statements cannot be falsified if they do not conform to the actor's notion of what is significant, real, meaningful, or appropriate. Etic statements are verified when independent observers using similar operations agree that a given event has occurred. An ethnography carried out according to etic principles is thus a corpus of predictions about the behavior of classes of people. Predictive failures in that corpus require the reformulation of the probabilities or the description as a whole.

The definitions set forth here will be best clarified by viewing them in the context of some of the major misconceptions which have attached themselves to the emic/etic distinction.

EMICS NOT NECESSARILY LESS EMPIRICAL THAN ETICS

In theory, an emic ethnography need be neither more nor less empirical, scientific, or intersubjective than an etic ethnography. Historically, of course, emic imponderables have been more prevalent than etic ones, if for no other reason than that almost all traditional ethnography is heavily biased in favor of an emic approach. There is no reason, however, why emic statements cannot be operationalized to the point of achieving high standards of intersubjectivity, verifiability, and predictability. Presumably, it is the upgrading of such standards which animates the current concern with rigorous paradigmatic treatments of emic phenomena.

INFORMANTS MAY SUPPLY EMIC OR ETIC INFORMATION

The relationship between an etic perspective and the traditional dependency upon native informants for ethnographic information deserves special comment. An ethnography of etic statements is not incompatible with operations involving recourse to the information to which an informant has access by means of verbal exchanges with him. The critical issue here is whether the information in question is etic or emic information. It is emic if the informant's native distinctions, significances, and meanings provide the semantic ground for communication between him and the ethnographer. An example of the use of an informant to maximize the emic content of ethnography is Duane Metzger and Gerald Williams' (1963a; 1963b) "eliciting heuristic." This method involves a prolonged educational exposure during which the ethnographer teaches the informant how to teach the ethnographer to think in appropriate emic terms. An equivalent amount of effort can be (and often is) devoted to teaching the informant to think in the *ethnographer's* terms, as for example, when native assistants learn to measure fields, weigh harvests, take censuses, and describe past and present events in conformity with the categories of significance which the ethnographer has brought to the task. When an informant is used etically, he joins the community of observers. He becomes the ethnographer's assistant, part of a team which can produce more information in less time than one man working alone. If the behavior-stream events which he reports are scenes in which he himself is involved, then it is expected that his report of his own behavior will be as close as possible to that which would have been obtained had the scene been recorded on film and tape.

EMICS CANNOT BE TRANSMUTED INTO ETICS

One of the categories of etic, "nonstructural" classifications foreseen by Pike allows for a mixture of emic and etic operations:

> The units of behavior, though classified without reference as such to the individual systems from which they were abstracted, may nevertheless be classified in reference to the fact that they were in fact abstracted from purposive human behavior, so that elements of meaning or purpose constitute one of the sets of criteria for such etic classification [1954:9].

This type of etic description is an anomaly for which there can be no epistemological justification. By admitting units which are simultaneously emic and etic, we reduce the distinction to the "anemic" status assigned to it by Gerald Berreman (1966).

It is this misconception which led Sturtevant (1964) to make the historically misleading claim that Kroeber's 1909 treatment of the semantic dimensions of kinship was "the basic paper on the etics of kinship." But as we have seen, (p. 321ff.), the whole point of Kroeber's famous article was to replace Morgan's sociological treatment of kinship with a linguistic treatment. The eight "principles or categories of relationship" proposed by Kroeber are categories alleged to underly "the hundreds or thousands of slightly varying relationships that are or can be expressed by the various languages of man" (KROEBER 1952:176). If a semantic distinction is found in more than one culture this does not mean that such distinctions cease to be semantic in nature. Concepts such as filiation, agnation, territoriality, ownership, affinity, religion, unilineal descent group, etc., are applied in a wide variety of cross-cultural contexts. The test of whether these are etic or emic concepts resides in their logico-empirical relationship to cognitive processes. If the verifiability of an ethnographic statement involves a confrontation with cognitive adequacy or appropriateness, then we are dealing with emic categories, no matter how many cultures contribute to that confrontation. Identification of similar emic categories merely establishes such categories as cross-culturally valid logico-empirical abstractions; it does not transform them into etically derived phenomena. As we have seen, the data language of cultural and social anthropologists derives from a melange of emic and etic operations which it will undoubtedly take several generations to unscramble.

KINSHIP AS A MIXED DOMAIN

The domain of kinship has not escaped this confusion between emic and etic phenomena. Floyd Lounsbury's (1965:191) assertion that "kin types" are a composite of the semantic discriminations made in many societies (*cf.* HAMMEL 1965:67–68) is historically inaccurate. Genealogical reckoning was not invented by anthropology. The apparent success of a mating, reproduction, and genealogy frame for eliciting categorizations which are amenable to contrastive analysis has an etic basis: mating, reproduction, and genealogical relationships have a rather precise biological meaning. The ethnographic mating, reproduction, and genealogy frame, however, is a lethal mixture of emic and etic categories. For a biologist, all fertile matings are equally relevant for tracing genealogical connections; for the ethnosemantics of kinship, only those matings and genealogical connections which occur in and through "marriage" are relevant. In order to elicit questions about kinship, the ethnographer must first discover an intercultural gloss for the particular kind of mating which in English goes by the name of "marriage." Incidentally, in the search for the native equivalent, it must be remembered that the informant, if he has not already fallen victim to a standardized equivalence, is also straining to find the proper gloss for the ethnographer's concept. Murdock (1949:1) defines the family in such a way as to commit us to a consideration of whether there is a "socially approved sexual relationship between mated pair." Having children and feeding and housing them is an etic phenomenon, but doing it in a socially approved manner puts the whole matter in an eminently emic frame.

Lounsbury's "kin types" are thus etic and emic composites, and Goodenough's (1964b:10–11) claim that the analogue of phonetic notation has already been developed for kinship studies is true only for the biological frame. It does not apply to the emic aspects of kinship. How else do we explain the seemingly endless quest for the meaning of marriage and descent? A recent exchange between David Schneider (1964; 1965b) and John Beattie (1964b; 1965) rests on the conviction that there must be a cross-culturally valid emic definition of kinship distinct from a biological genealogy; but they are unable to agree on what it might be. Beattie solves the problem in a highly instructive fashion:

> What kinship as an anthropological concern is all about are those social relationships, whatever their social and cultural content, which the people who have them think about and talk about in the idiom of kinship [1965:123].

Aside from the biological reproduction frame, the content of kintypes is emic and must always remain emic until the observers decide what bits of behavior (analogous to phones) will constitute the minimum etic definition of marriage and descent. It is an error of capital importance to suppose that the scrambling of the etic and emic components in the study of kinship will convert one into the other. Indeed, as far as American cultural anthropology is concerned, there is a strong presumption of cause and effect between this misconception and the fact that no consistent etic treatment of marriage and kinship has been attempted.

CAN EMICS BE STUDIED ETICALLY?

An etic approach, by definition, avoids the premises of the emic approach. From an etic point of view, the universe of meaning, purposes, goals, motivations, etc., is thus unapproachable. But to insist upon the separateness of emic and etic phenomena and research strategies is not to affirm a greater or lesser "reality" or a higher or lower scientific status for either of them.

BOTH EMIC AND ETIC DATA CAN BE STUDIED CROSS-CULTURALLY

It should be obvious that emic phenomena can be studied cross-culturally. The question of whether patrilineal descent rules or Omaha kinship terminology recurs in different societies has nothing to do with the emic/etic distinction per se. Rather what is involved is the setting of intersubjective standards of similarity and difference. Both emic and etic phenomena may be defined with an abundance of detail sufficient to confound an attempt to find replicative instances anywhere in the behavior stream. The previous chapters demonstrate, however, that a conscious and overt commitment to the study of inner meaning and psychic complexities has usually been associated with a considerable amount of indifference toward the quest for the scientific explanation of sociocultural differences and similarities. In the case of the new ethnography, the prevailing research strategy frequently seems to be unconcerned with whether new insights into diachronic and synchronic regularities will result from the higher standards of emic descriptions that are being developed at heavy costs in research and publication resources. Harold Conklin (1964:26), for example, has listed (1) appropriateness of anticipation, (2) replicability or testability, and (3) economy as the criteria by which ethnographic statements must be evaluated. A number of other ethnosemanticists have concerned themselves at length with the question of whether their models represent as closely as possible the way in which the natives actually think (A. F. C. WALLACE 1965; BURLING 1964; HYMES 1964a; ROMNEY and D'ANDRADE 1964). But few if any of the ethnosemanticists have considered the question of how to distinguish important from unimportant ethnographic descriptions. With all due regard to the need for the widest latitude of interests in a common scientific endeavor, it cannot be said that an important ethnographic description is one which is merely accurate, elegant, and economical. Scientific ethnographic models pay their way to the extent that they link up with theories which explain diachronic and synchronic differences and similarities. Admittedly it is not always possible to know in advance when and how such a link-up will be achieved; but in the case of ethnosemantic studies there are a number of historically demonstrated adverse considerations, of which the practitioners seem unaware.

EMICS/ETICS VERSUS IDEAL/ACTUAL

On superficial inspection the contrastive research strategies suggested by the well-worn phrases "ideal versus actual behavior" or "ideal versus actual culture" would seem to be aimed at the same distinction as that which is involved in emics versus etics. But the two sets of strategies do not share much in common; indeed they derive from very different epistemological positions. The ideal/actual distinction is not grounded in the consideration of how one can know that cultural things are what they are said to be by the ethnographer. Instead it merely assumes that there is one set of patterned regularities consisting of what people say or believe about what they do or should do and another set of patterned regularities concerned with what they "actually" do. In the ideal/actual contrast, the problem of specifying the operations by which one gets to know what people "actually do" is not even broached, whereas in the emic/etic frame this problem is fundamental. The entire weight of the latter dichotomy rests upon the epistemological significance of describing cultural things through categories and relations which are necessarily isomorphic with those appropriate or meaningful to the actors, as opposed to categories and relations which arise independently in the ethnographer's data language. Thus, actual behavior can be treated in both an emic and an etic fashion. An informant's description of what is actually happening at a festival, during a work scene, or inside a household need not correspond to what the ethnographer sees or would see in the same situations.

Let us take as an example the ideal behavior by which captains of certain Bahian fishing boats are said to locate the ocean spots over which their boats anchor and the fishing lines are dropped. Identification of the proper spot, as small as a room, seven or eight miles out at sea, is supposed to depend upon the lining up of two or more pairs of landmarks. The memorization and sighting of these landmarks is the special responsibility of the captain, whose reputation can be measured by the size of the catch, ability to attract and hold good crews, and keenness of memory and eyesight. Now it is quite possible to describe this whole complex as actual behavior in terms of the emically significant categories of spots, landmarks, eyesight, and memory. Indeed, one can *actually* see and hear the captain look for the landmarks, maneuver the boat into position, order the sails down and the anchor dropped; and one can actually watch the fishing commence over the "spot." Actual culture here corresponds to a large degree to ideal accounts of it. But both accounts are emic. There is another way to look at the performance in question. The clue to this additional perspective resides in the fact that when the captain locates the spot and the men start to fish, they not infrequently fail to catch a single fish. On such occasions the captain explains that the fish are not home, that they have gone visiting elsewhere, and he orders the boat off to another spot. The etics of the matter do not commit us to a description of this behavior in terms of the captain's emically appreciated skills. One also observes the constant use of a plumb line, and there is a widespread knowledge of the relationship between type of bottom, water depth, and type of fish likely to be found in broad zones as opposed to "spots." An etic account of the fishing complex includes a description of the patterns of behavior by which the captain maneuvers his craft, but the activity involved in his peering at the horizon does not carry the meaning it has in an emic account of actual behavior. Instead of accepting the emic version of actual culture as an adequate description of what it takes to be a successful captain of a fishing boat, the etic categorizations open quite a different ethnographic trail. An analysis of the relationship between age of captain, size of catch, and stability of crew reveals that younger, more active and vigorous men who do not drink, who work hard, and who manifest a "protestant" kind of behavior (an eminently etic category since they are all "Catholics") are the ones who are likely to be successful captains around whom the reputation for keen landmark sighting and good "spot memory" will develop (KOTTAK 1966:210 ff.).

Cultural anthropology will not easily overcome its heritage of ethnographies of actual behavior carried out in a manner which permits slipping back and forth from an emic to an etic frame in an unconscious and unpredictable fashion. The effect of the lack of attention to the emic/etic distinction has been especially deleterious in the ethnography of primitive and peasant economic systems where descriptions of essential economic processes have been obscured and distorted by emic descriptions of actual behavior. Malinowski's description of the Kula (p. 563) is a classic instance, to which we have already referred.

SHOULD ETICS REPLACE EMICS?

One no sooner suggests that an etic research option deserves special emphasis than he is represented as proposing that all studies of semantic domains, goals, and purposes should cease at once. Even if some advantage accrued to such a proposal, it is difficult to imagine a more unlikely development in the context of the research establishment's vested interests in emic matters. But no advantage would accrue to a research strategy concerned exclusively with etic phenomena. The whole point of insisting upon etic studies is that one wishes to explain the emic universe to which as actors in our own culture we are ineluctably bound. Actually, the shoe is on the other foot. If there is danger of intradisciplinary imperialism whereby one strategy deliberately denies the validity of alternative research options, it is the etic approach which has suffered the effects of sweeping programmatic manifestos. Let it be recalled that Sapir declared that it was "impossible" to describe behavior-stream events in an etic data language. The declarations of Frake (1964b) and Sturtevant (1964), which are discussed below, are simply the latest in a long series of strategically extreme proposals directing the attention of cultural anthropologists away from the etic substance of human behavior. Comparably exclusionist proposals have never been made against emic studies.

AMBIGUITY AND THE LINGUISTIC MODEL

The fundamental error of the new ethnography is that it is based upon a patently false analogy between vernacular codes on the levels of phoneme, morpheme, and syntax on the one hand,

and on the other, the higher-order codes which are in some way related to the semantics of everyday speech behavior and the historical unfolding of nonverbal behavior-stream events. In linguistic analysis, it is assumed in theory and followed in practice that the phonemic, morphemic, and syntactic descriptions of a language can be achieved by working with a very small group of informants. This procedure is justified by the empirically established fact of the uniformity of the sound discriminations which constitute the basis for verbal communication. Whatever else a speaker must accomplish, he must be able to convince his fellows that he has something to say that they could understand if they wanted to. The actor who speaks gibberish, who mumbles or garbles his words, who uses deviant pronunciations or otherwise fails to demonstrate that he is in a condition to deliver an intelligible message, is seldom accorded a serious audience (except for ceremonial or ritual performances in which paralinguistic codes bear the burden of the message). The lack of tolerance for such deviations emanates from the most primordial functional conditions underlying the evolution of language, whereby viable ratios of signal to noise have become established. These linguistic features evidently enjoy a selective advantage of the highest magnitude.

The theory and fact of vernacular communication on the level of pragmatics, however, point to another and opposite set of conditions. To be sure, many complex messages derive their functional significance from their high signal to noise ratio; however, there are also powerful psychological and sociocultural functions which are fulfilled by complex messages which are perfectly communicative on the phonemic, morphemic, and syntactic levels, but ambiguous or quite unintelligible in other respects. Such messages are demonstrably characteristic of whole cognitive domains. The semantic ambiguity characteristic of such activities as poetry, art and literary criticism, eschatology, traditional philosophy, and theology in our own cultural experience cannot be dismissed as epiphenomenal or as subcultural variations. There is no reason to suppose that uniformity of understanding in such domains has a functional significance which outweighs the obvious benefits of ambiguity, obfuscation, and individual variation. What our ethnoscientists seem to be unprepared for is the contingency that in human cultural repertoires there may actually be more domains which derive their salient semantic order from ambiguity and variation than there are domains whose orderliness reflects consensus and uniformity.

Brazilian racial categories, of which several hundred have been discovered, constitute an example of an eminently ambiguous and highly idiosyncratic semantic domain (HARRIS and KOTTAK 1963; HARRIS 1967). Precision and clarity in this domain would conflict with the main etic features of Brazilian social structure. A similar functional utility is associated with the emic definition of class in contemporary United States stratification hierarchies (*cf.* VIDICH and BENSMAN 1958). The functional nature of the ambiguity in caste and kindred in Ceylon has been impressively demonstrated by S. J. Tambiak (1965). Stanley Freed (1963) has measured the degree of consensus concerning caste ranking in Uttar Pradesh without considering the possible functional significance of the demonstrated lack of agreement. Yet such an interpretation is clearly warranted by Bernard Cohn's (1955) description of caste mobility through litigation and violence. The structural significance of cognitive ambiguity is also implicit in Leach's analysis of the "gumsa" ideology of Kachin social structure. As Leach (1965b:10) points out, "The ethically correct action for a Christian businessman is often equally ambiguous." Leach's conceptualization of matrilateral prescription involves a rigid dichotomization of wife-giving and wife-taking groups. According to William Wilder (1964:1370): "Granted the uniqueness and permanence of the mayu-dama relationship (the alliance set up by cross-cousin marriage), the whole kinship terminology falls into place as a consistent whole . . . ; *without that assumption the classifications are chaotic.* It can be said with equal emphasis however that without the observed ambiguity in the mayu-dama ideology, Kachin social structure would be reduced to chaos.

The vast and acrimonious debate which has centered on the attempt to distinguish prescriptive from preferential marriage rules (see Chap. 18) derives its monumental futility from the same error. Given the fact that 30 percent of the recorded Purum alliances are contrary to the rule of matrilateral prescription, it seems likely that the mental state of some of the Purum is not compatible with Rodney Needham's splendid certainty regarding how they should behave.

It is interesting to note that Pike's (1954:80) advice on how to handle emic ambiguity has been largely ignored:

> A theory of the structure of behavior must leave room for variants in both form and meaning, but without being able to provide any absolute measure of just how much alike or just how different either form or meaning or the form-meaning composite may be before one can no longer equate two items. In our present theory we state that the indeterminacy lies in the data, within the struc-

> ture, and that any arbitrary attempt to force a decision one way or another in certain instances does violence to the structure rather than clarifying it.

In view of this admonition, the attempt to maximize the order in emic phenomena by regarding ambiguity as either inconsequential or as the result of error is a false strategy.

Before a domain is subjected to formal analysis, we must be told something about the generality of the distinctions and contrasts in terms of specific historic events and people. It is remarkable how little attention has been paid to this issue especially when one considers the importance of statistical data-gathering techniques among the operations of contemporary social psychology. Indeed, much of the new ethnography appears to be social psychology shorn of its statistical base. At least one ethnosemanticist, Goodenough (1965b), appears to have settled down with the data obtained from only one informant. Although Conklin (1955:340) reports that he obtained color naming responses from "a large number of informants," the relationship between individual responses and the four-way classification about which there is said to be "unanimous agreement" (*ibid.*: 341) is not specified, despite the fact that this agreement exists side by side with "hundreds of specific color categories, many of which over-lap and inter-digitate" (*ibid.*).

Charles Frake (1961:125) reports that "informants rarely disagree in their verbal descriptions of what makes one disease different from another." It would seem important for us to know just what this "rarely" means. Did Frake's informants represent all Subanum actor types? Given the fact that medical expertise is seldom uniformly distributed in a population, it would not be unexpected that "rare" disagreement was frequent disagreement at least in certain sex and age categories.

PROBLEM OF THE WELL-INFORMED INFORMANT

Since much of the terminological data which provides the basis for the ethnosemantics of kinship derives from fieldwork that can no longer be repeated, there is little hope of correcting for overagreement in the formal accounts. All too often, the data have been obtained from a few "well-informed informants" (BACK 1960). My own encounter with individual variation and ambiguity in the terminology of the Bathonga of southern Moçambique may serve as an example. Convinced by my reading of Radcliffe-Brown (1950:34) that I was dealing with an Omaha system, I shrugged off the responses of a half dozen informants until I finally found someone who "really knew" the system. The justification for this was that the Bathonga were undergoing intensive acculturation, in an area where a considerable mixture of Zulu, Ronga, and Shangane "tribes" was taking place. It seemed best to work with someone who remembered the old system. But Henri Junrod (1913), who had studied the Bathonga sixty years ago, had already noted four alternate terms for mother's brother's son: *makwabu* (sibling); *nwana* (child) (1912: 220); *malume* (mother's brother); and *kokwana* (grandfather) (*ibid.*:229). What I encountered in some of my "ill-informed informants" was an even greater measure of confusion. Thus, while Junod attributed the substitution of the grandfather term (*kokwana*) for mother's brother (*malume*) as a dialect difference, I kept running across people who insisted that both *malume* and *kokwana* were appropriate! Now these departures from the Omaha system are of the precise order of difference which Lounsbury (1964:354) regards as requiring the establishment of separate subtypes of Crow and Omaha terminology. It may be that these variations can be handled as subcultural or dialect differences taking place inside different heads. On the other hand, it is equally plausible that these variations take place inside the same head. Indeed, this is true for many Bathonga in the modern situation. If that is the case, then an "adequate" ethnography must express the ambiguity of the system, and it must do so statistically.

The way in which the emic formalists have handled this problem in the treatment of American kinship terminology is scarcely reassuring. Goodenough has referred to his "dialect" as a means of escaping the fact that *his* understanding of "correct" kin terminological usage does not correspond to *mine*. Several important foci of functionally important ambiguity in the American cognitive calculus of kinship probably get swept under the rug by this maneuver. One strongly doubts, for example, that Goodenough's (1965a:206) lumping of Pa Pa Pa Sb Ch and Pa Sb Ch Ch Ch along with Pa Sb Ch as "my first cousin" is merely a matter of dialect or subcultural variation. Is it a valid cognitive principle of American kinship that "first cousin" need not be included in the basic corpus of kinship terms because it is not a lexeme? Goodenough proposes that he is representative of significant numbers of Americans in believing that we cannot say "No, he is my half brother" but that we can say "Yes, he is my half brother" (*ibid.*:265) in response to the question, "Is he your brother?" Such convictions mask the fact that many Americans have trouble applying kinship terms to relatives outside of a small span of kin types with whom they have significant etic transactions. In this connection, Schneider (1965a), who uses a more generously functional approach to the question of American kinship, refers to the "fuzzy boundary and fadeout principles" (*ibid.*:291) but does not drive home the consequences of this fuzziness for a strategy which is inherently incapable of accommodating ambiguity.

Goodenough's assumptions need to be tested against sample population responses under standardized conditions. This is especially true of some of the basic themes which are taken as underlying the construction of a componential grid. For example, it is claimed that an American husband cannot disown his wife's child and keep his wife (*ibid.*:287*n*). Yet it is common knowledge in welfare circles that such cases frequently show up in adoption courts; it cannot be left to intuition to decide the rules by which Americans in general cognize extramarital pregnancies in wedlock.

A potentially important step has been taken by A. K. Romney and Roy D'Andrade (1964) in their use of samples of public high school students to obtain lists of kinship terms and other relevant responses. Unfortunately, the implications of their findings are not developed out of deference to the task of finding *the* correct set of rules in conformity with the linguistic model. Thus, in one of Romney and D'Andrade's samples, modifier terms which occurred with a frequency of less than 25 percent with a core term (e.g., *great* uncle) were excluded from consideration. Then, an additional simplification was achieved by excluding responses of subjects whose use of modifiers constituted a pattern found in less than 10 percent of the sample of 105 (*ibid.*:156). By this sloughing off of "idiosyncratic or variant" answers, the conclusion is reached that "cousin" in our terminology takes only one modifier, "second" (*ibid.*:156, Table II).

None of the attempts to define the basic cognitive features of American kinship terminology has thus far made concessions to the possibility that ambiguity is one of the salient characteristics of this domain. Wallace and Atkins (1960), Romney and D'Andrade (1964), and Goodenough (1965a) each operate with a different inventory of basic American kinship terms. Variant treatments by David Schneider (1965a) and Munroe Edmunson (1957) ought also to be considered in estimating the scope of the problem which has yet to be met head on. Conklin has suggested that American anthropologists who do not know their native terminology had better take steps to learn it. They are urged to consult:

> an explanatory note on "The Mathematics of American Cousinship" in a recent issue of the Kroeber Anthropological Society Papers (Roark, 1961). There, the purpose in providing such a de-

> vice is explicitly the resolution of a frequently met ambiguity and lack of common knowledge among American anthropologists as to the steps required in reckoning degrees of cousinship in English [1964:34]!

This advice carries an implicit warning concerning the kinship terminologies of the natives in other cultures: If you don't know your own minds, we'll teach you. In this vein, one is reluctant to share Dell Hymes's (1964a:34) nostalgic reverie over "The nights of beer drinking and brain wracking spent in the Rainbow Cafe at the edge of Warm Springs reservation" with Philip Kahclamet, "the most knowledgeable and fluent speaker of Wishram." There is also the experience reported by Anthony Wallace (1965:237) with a Japanese informant who brought along a friend "to check the accuracy" of her kinship definitions: "The informant never completely accepted our view that her task was to give personal usage; she felt that she was a representative of Japan and should be 'correct.' "

Among the ethnosemanticists, Hymes has cautioned against transferring data-gathering techniques appropriate to phonemics and grammar to higher-order semantic phenomena. Hymes sees an "ethnography of speaking" as providing the antidote for the lack of information about the settings and variations in speech behavior which derive from "the implicitly normative stance long characteristic of linguistic theory in prescribing its object" (HYMES 1964a:41). He goes on to point out that other functions fulfilled by agreement about referential meaning are not always the prime function of speech behavior:

> (e) From the standpoint of a general theory of language and its functioning, it is simply the case that *some* of the functions of languages in communities do call for approximation to independence of context, simple uniformity, and primacy of organization about the function of reference, three assumptions so common to descriptive linguistic theory—*and some do not* [*ibid.*].

It is to be hoped that Hymes's suggestions for placing the study of speech behavior in a more realistic and more ample functional context will be given the attention they merit. In the meantime, the failure of American ethnologists to agree on the analysis of their own native terminology, the evident tendency among ethnosemanticists to accept the cognitive expertise of the well-informed informant, and the failure to accommodate the possibility of functional ambiguity suggest that the ethnosemanticists must take a more critical look at their basic assumptions. The brilliant efforts lavished upon placing second cousin, half brother, and grand niece in a single paradigmatic semantic space may actually result in a serious distortion of emic facts. At the very least, the difficulties and shortcomings of the treatment of American terminology provide a firm basis for skepticism regarding the attempt to push the study of major terminological systems into the numerous refinements which are possible if terms for kin types representing all shades of ambiguity and psychological and social significance are jammed into the same frame.

EMICS AND ACTUAL VERBAL BEHAVIOR

Consideration must be given to the prominence of operations involving artificial eliciting situations in the construction of the formal analyses of the new ethnography. This has meant that much of the basic data employed consists of verbal statements in which people say what they would say under given hypothetical circumstances. As Frake (1961:63) has put it: "Given a set of contrasting disease names, the problem remains of determining the rules which govern the assigning of one name rather than another in a particular diagnostic situation." This is the problem of referential as distinct from abstract meaning (HARRIS 1964a:156). For example, most Brazilians verbally agree on the contrasts out of which rules for distinguishing between a "preto" ("black") and a "branco" ("white") can be constructed. Yet these rules are demonstrably inadequate for predicting when a specific individual will call another "preto" or "branco." In real life a whole new set of factors enter which may involve calculi from domains far removed from "racial" categories. Thus as Hymes implies, there is an air of scholasticism or of arm chair detachment about much of the formal analysis of the new ethnography, even when we restrict ourselves to the question of the rules which govern *verbal* behavior-stream events. It is as if a generation of anthropologists had never observed hesitation, "change of mind," "groping for the right word," argument, lying, puzzlement, and many other ordinary speech phenomena.

EMICS AND NONVERBAL BEHAVIOR

But social and cultural anthropology enjoys a more ample scientific mandate than the study of what people say they will say. There remains the question of what they say they will do, and of the relationship between these sayings and the nonverbal happenings of history.

Now whatever doubts may exist concerning the appropriateness of the linguistic model for verbal behavior, the application of that model to nonverbal behavior is even more powerfully ill-advised. Evidence of both a logical and empirical nature from many different quarters and cultures indicates that emic rules of behavior are a poor guide to historical events and etic regularities in economic, social, and political subsystems. If permitted to develop unchecked, the tendency to write ethnographies in accord with the emic rules of behavior will result in an unintentional parody of the human condition. Applied to our own culture it would conjure up a way of life in which men tip their hats to ladies; youths defer to old people in public conveyances; unwed mothers are a rarity; citizens go to the aid of law enforcement officers; chewing gum is never stuck under tables and never dropped on the sidewalk; television repairmen fix television sets; children respect their aged parents; rich and poor get the same medical treatment; taxes are paid in full; all men are created equal; and our defense budget is used only for maintaining peace. Elsewhere it would turn the Chinese family into a Confucian fantasy (FRIED 1953); invent Hindu farmers who starve in order to avoid harming their sacred cows (HARRIS 1966a); spread the idea that the Portuguese have no racial prejudice (HARRIS 1964b; 1966b); and convince a whole generation of introductory anthropology students that the Zuñi never get drunk (see p. 406). If Jules Henry's recent study of American culture is at all accurate, American anthropologists should be especially skeptical of ethnographies in which the rules of behavior dominate the rules for breaking rules. Commenting upon the pervasiveness of cheating among American school children, Henry (1963: 205–6) writes: "An honest adolescent life could be a crippling preliminary for many phases of contemporary culture." Granted that this may be a specialty of industrial civilization, it nonetheless poses an empirical question which cannot be left unanswered when Panglossian grammars are attempted for other cultures.

In attempting to demonstrate that the grammar of normative status and role behavior among the Trukese is not "an exercise in sterile formalism," Goodenough (1965b:19–20) presents the case of a father who struck his married daughter. This act violated five of the six rules in Goodenough's emic "Duty Scale": Trukese fathers should crouch or crawl if a married daughter is seated; they should avoid initiating action; honor any request; avoid speaking harshly; and never assault the daughter "regardless of provocation" (*ibid.*:11–12). Instead of being dismayed by the discovery that all of these rules were flouted right before his eyes, Goodenough takes comfort from the fact that the woman in question had in turn been breaking another series of rules! "Her petulant behavior had been getting on her kinsmen's nerves for some time . . .," and she had indulged in "an early morning tirade against her husband whom she suspected of having just come from an amorous visit to her lineage sister next door." It was therefore "poetic justice," remarks Goodenough, for the woman's father to hit her: "A good hard jolt was just what she deserved," he says. It seems to me that Goodenough derives the wrong moral from this episode. So blatant a failure of a set of rules to predict behavior requires a rewriting of the rules. Just how often do these good hard jolts get delivered? And do the injured ladies agree with the anthropologist that a good hard jolt is just what they need?

EMICS AND THE SCIENCE OF TRIVIA

Referring to the accomplishments of ethnosemantics listed by Frake (1964b:143), Berreman (1966:351) notes:

> None of these descriptions, whatever the virtues, can in themselves be called very significant . . . they remind of Mills' warning that many sociologists have gotten to the point where they overlook what is important in their search for what is verifiable . . . many have worked so hard on what is trivial that it comes to appear important. . . .

It is no accident that formal analysis has so often been taken to task for its involvement with trivia (KEESING 1966:23; SWEET 1966:24–25). It is probably only with respect to statistically insignificant or scientifically trivial performances that behavior-stream events can be predicted from a small set of emic rules. The insistence by Frake, Conklin, and Goodenough that "appropriateness or acceptability" be substituted for predictability among the canons of good ethnography is nothing so much as a tacit admission of this dilemma. The problem is not that behavior is not governed by cognitive plans, maps, rules, themes, ideologies, etc. Since these phenomena take place inside people's heads in great abundance and on all sorts of conscious (WARD 1965), preconscious, and unconscious levels with all degrees of strength and persistence, and in all manner of logical or illogical, rational or irrational combination, it would be most unlikely that at some levels, in some degree, and in some combination, behavior-stream events were not based on or at least accompanied by some form of cognitive calculus. In all societies, concrete manifestations of behavior, verbal or nonverbal, result from complicated interactions of specific personalities whose repertories of rules, especially when it comes to the rules for interpreting or breaking rules, often seem to have little in common. Unless the new ethnographers are a breed apart, they must surely have noted by this time that their lives have consisted largely of trying to figure out what rules one ought to live by or, what amounts to the same thing, what rules one ought to invoke in a particular situation. There is little indication that the normal condition of social life is one in which conformity to emic norms predominates. The judgment expressed by Hugo Nutini (1965:723) that "mechanical models" (i.e. models constructed out of ideal behavior) "are always superior to statistical models" (i.e. models constructed out of actual behavior) is dangerously detached from empirical foundations (see pp. 498–99). There is no evidence which indicates that under "the proper cultural conditions"—whatever these may be—"the overlapping of ideal and actual behavior would tend to the ideal limit" (*ibid.*). Instead, there is a vast literature in anthropology and related disciplines which indicates that emic norms and etic events never quite match and that not infrequently the main function of the norms is to obscure the etic reality. A case in point is Marshall Sahlins' suggestion about how to resolve the "E.-P. (Evans-Pritchard) paradox" wherein, as among the Nuer, there is an inverted relation between commitment to agnation in principle and commitment to it in deed: "Then too, the agnatic dogma may only be strengthened by a deepening contradiction with kin group membership, as ideology undertakes its Mannheimian function of keeping people from knowing what's going on in the world" (SAHLINS 1965: 105).

I hasten to acknowledge certain recent attempts to link formal analysis with social-structural or comparative generalizations. It would appear on balance, however, that the net contribution to substantive theory is less than what usually results from equivalent labor in-puts. For example, Conklin's conclusion that the Hanunóo's terminological specialization in cousin terms reflects payment of fines in accordance with degree of incest scarcely requires the elaborate descriptive apparatus with which it is juxtaposed (1964:48).

THE CASE OF CROW TERMINOLOGY

Among formal analysts, the most ambitious claim for sociological significance has been set forth by Floyd Lounsbury (1964; 1965). Lounsbury suggests that Crow and Omaha kinship terminologies and their variants, including Trobriand, are best understood as expressions of the extension of nuclear family terminological categories outward to other kin types on the basis of what he calls "status succession." It is the passing on of statuses such as "head of family, other positions in the domestic group, headship of lineage or kin-based corporation, hereditary political office, religious office, etc." (1965: 383) which accounts for the overriding of generational distinctions typical of Crow and Omaha terminologies. This principle is set forth in opposition to that endorsed by Leach (1958), derived from Radcliffe-Brown, subscribed to by Lowie, Murdock, and White, and ultimately traceable to Morgan that Crow and Omaha terminologies reflect first and foremost the alignment of people into unilinear groupings.

In the first place, we should note that Lounsbury's interpretation at no point contradicts the principle of lineage solidarity; instead his "status successions" might all be viewed as measures of the degree of lineage corporateness. But Lounsbury is really not interested in his analysis as a means of discovering the causal ingredients in the evolution of kinship systems. What he actually tries to show is that given the Crow-type terminologies it is possible to write rules for extending nuclear family kin terms which "account for" the system. These rules account for *all* of the terminology, whereas the principle of lineage solidarity accounts for only the bulk of the terms, leaving certain residues which are anomalous (as when certain Crow-types call ego's Fa Mo Br by a general grandfather term rather than Fa) (*ibid.*: 355). The disparity in completeness, however, is not a legitimate test of theoretical adequacy. Lounsbury is privileged to keep adding transformation rules precisely until the point is reached at which all of the features of the particular case have been taken care of. In writing these rules, Lounsbury chose not to employ an extensional principle which explicitly incorporates or depends upon the principle of lineage solidarity. Instead he employs such principles as "skewing rules," "half-sibling rule," and "merging rule." In rejecting the established lineage principle, Lounsbury makes no sustained attempt to evaluate the possibility that the terminological phenomena it does not account for are sociologically or statistically insignificant, or semantically ambiguous or that the principle could be made to account for them with minor addenda. As we have seen, the Bathonga's Omaha terminology involves ambiguities at a number of points. Similar alternate manifestations are regarded by Lounsbury as having separate sociological significance. Furthermore, although admitting the general correlation between strong lineage principle and Crow-Omaha terminologies, Lounsbury chooses to emphasize the fact that there are five deviant cases in which Crow terminologies are associated with patrilineal descent (*ibid.*:354–55). He does not elect to study these cases in the light of the special conditions which, had he done so, would, for at least three of the instances, permit an interpretation perfectly compatible with the lineage principle.

THREE ETHNOGRAPHIC CASES

These three cases deserve our attention because they are indicative of what happens when supersophisticated formal analyses are reared on a foundation of shoddy primary materials. Lounsbury (1964:388) cites Murdock (1949:168) as the source of three of his five cases in which Crow terms occur with patrilineal descent and patrilocal residence. These are the Bachama of Nigeria, the Koranko of Sierra Leone, and the Seniang of the Solomon Islands. First of all, it must be made perfectly plain that Murdock's definition of a Crow terminology is scarcely the equivalent of what Lounsbury is interested in subjecting to formal analysis. For Murdock, the Crow form exists when cross cousins are distinguished from parallel cousins and siblings, while the Fa Si Da is classed with Fa Si *and/or* the Mo Br Da with Br Da (MURDOCK 1949:224). This says nothing about the treatment of the uncle and aunt terms in relationship to each other and to Mo and Fa, and little about these uncle and aunt terms in relation to the sibling and cousin terms. Turning to the Bachama in the original source (MEEK 1931:18–20), we find not only that Fa Si and Mo Si are terminologically equated, but that Mo Bro, Fa, and Fa Bro are also terminologically equated. Worse, the terms for both kinds of grandmothers and grandfathers are the same as those used for cross uncle and for father's elder brother. As for the patrilineality of the Bachama, Meek (*ibid.*:15–17) makes it perfectly clear that a form of double descent is operating; that the sister's son inherits horses, goats, clothes, cash, and cattle, and the mother's brother's widow or her brideprice, his standing crops, and the contents of his granary; and that the system was in transition from an earlier form of still greater emphasis upon "mother right" in which: "The sense of kinship with the mother's family was undoubtedly in former times greater than that with the father's family" (*ibid.*:16).

Turning to the Koranko (N. THOMAS 1916) we find that the Fa Si Da is *not* equated with Fa Si although the rest of Murdock's conditions are met. The system thus barely survives as Crow by virtue of invoking the *and/or* in the definition. It is incredible, however, to discover in the setting of the refined analysis presented by Lounsbury an appeal to this ethnographic case. The Koranko terminology appears as part of a foldout in which the terminological systems for eight Sierra Leone peoples are set forth in tabular fashion. The only statement specifically concerned with Koranko descent and locality is herewith reproduced: "Descent is reckoned in the male line, and there are no clear traces of the existence of matrilocal marriage, though some of the birth customs seem to suggest it" (*ibid.*:107). The ethnographic standard of Thomas's account is unacceptable (except in a large sample), and any attempt to hinge an important theoretical issue on the Koranko is as good as resorting to scapulimnancy.

Finally, there is the Seniang division of Malekula, subtitled "A Vanishing People in the New Hebrides." It is relevant to point out that not only had the Seniang been afflicted by the worst sort of biocultural collapse at the time of A. B. Deacon's (1934) visit, but that the monograph in question was put together from Deacon's field notes by Camilla Wedgwood, who comments:

> . . . it must be stressed here that, far from finding a living society, Deacon found at South-West Bay only relatively few survivors of several districts. He was therefore unable here to study the social, economic, and religious life of a living community, but had to acquire his knowledge of what that life had once been by means of the tedious and not wholly reliable method of questioning the older men [1934:xxxii].

The Seniang satisfy Murdock's criteria for Crow terminology. Fa Si Da is classed with Fa Si and Fa Si So with Fa, but there is no information concerning the terms for the children of these cross cousins. Because of this and other gaps it is difficult to assess the strength of the Crow pattern. There is at least one anomaly: Wedgewood directs special attention to the fact that Fa Fa Fa Fa is called by the term for elder brother and that So So So So is probably called by the term for younger brother. This is not the kind of terminology on the basis of which one would predict strong matrilineal or matrilocal clans, although admittedly, it also is not at all suggestive of the reported rather strong patrilineal and patrilocal principles. Additional reasons for rejecting Malekula as a negative case for the correlation in question arise on all sides. The neighboring Newun with whom the Seniang intermarry and who recognize descent from each other's localized patrisibs classify Fa Si with Fa Si Da but the same root term is also used for Mo. The classification of Mo, Fa Si, and Fa Da under the same term is repeated among many of the other Malekulan groups, including the Lambumbu (DEACON 1934:98); Senbarei (*ibid.*:121); Uripiv (*ibid.*:124); Nesan, Uerik, Bangasa, and Niviar (*ibid.*:125). This is a most un-Crow-like feature and is certainly not provided for by Lounsbury's sub-types. It should be mentioned that definite traces of double descent crop up to the north among the Lambumbu (*ibid.*:101) and Lagalag (*ibid.*:110); although nothing like a reliable description is anywhere available concerning relations with matrilineal kinsmen. Both Deacon and Wedgewood were convinced that Malekula has been invaded by a succession of different cultures, the last of which were strongly patrilineal. To what extent this may have obscured the observation of de facto matrilineal groupings among the Seniang is unclear. Similarly in doubt is Deacon's ability to have salvaged information of such a nature from the cultural wreckage in which he was working, even if it had occurred to him that the Crow cousin terminology required special attention in the light of the heavy patri-bias which he attributed to the entire island. One point is clear, however, this is not a very convincing case of anything.

THE QUEST FOR FORMAL ELEGANCE

The critical test of Lounsbury's thesis concerning the shortcomings of the lineage solidarity principle hinges on the question of whether a set of emic rules can be written which build upon or incorporate the lineage principle and which will be as productive and parsimonious as Lounsbury's. Allan Coult (1968) claims to have done just that. Starting with a set of principles first proposed by Tax (1955a; orig. 1937), and adding the principle of lineage solidarity, Coult says that he "accounts for" all of the features which Lounsbury "accounts for," and that he does it in a more simple and elegant fashion. Coult disposes of the anomalies in the relationship between lineage membership and terminological lumping by applying logical, as opposed to sociological, principles: "the terms applied to relatives outside of either own or M's patriline are determined, given the terms applied within these two lines, and the operation of the principles of uniform succession and uniform reciprocals" (COULT 1968:11).

But the significance of Coult's achievement is not to be judged by these purely formalistic criteria. As Coult himself expresses it, "A good theory should be phrased in such a way that not only can it predict empirical phenomena, but the reasons why it predicts should also be apparent" (*ibid.*:10). That is, as stated earlier, a good ethnographic description must link up with a corpus of explanatory theory. "Lounsbury in fact has no theory, he has merely a set of empirically observed relationships . . ." (*ibid.*:11).

THE NEW OLD ETHNOGRAPHY

Formal analysis presents itself as a new and revitalizing movement, whereas, in fact, it is actually the latest in a series of cultural-idealist proposals for intensifying cultural anthropology's commitment to emic research strategies. The "new approach to ethnography," what Sturtevant (1964:99) is tempted to call "the New Ethnography," has a definite and highly compromised historical position of which its practitioners seem unaware. In one important sense, this is not the new ethnography, but the new old ethnography. It is a better operationalized but narrower version of a research strategy which has already proved itself incapable of solving the major substantive issues of the social sciences.

In evaluating ethnosemantics' claim to newness, we must bear in mind the fact that almost every major theoretical school in anthropology has expended the bulk of its research effort in the pursuit of some form of emic analyses. The main historical lines of influence have been set forth in the previous chapter. Here it must suffice merely to recall the heritage of what Lowie (1956b:1007) has called the Southwest German school of philosophy—Windelband, Dilthey, Rickert—which transmitted eighteenth-century rationalism and idealism through its Hegelian culmination into contemporary anthropology (see Chap. 12). In the twentieth century many prominent spokesmen representing a nominally wide variety of theoretical positions have exhorted anthropologists to give priority to emic analysis. Among the Boasians, Lowie's opinion as previously quoted, was typical. The fieldworker's business is to understand the "true inwardness" of the beliefs and practices of the people he studies. The fieldworker does not simply record that there is infanticide or cannibalism. If he does not also record how his informants feel about these practices, "he has failed in his task" (see p. 365).

Kluckhohn (1949:300) may be taken as representative of another broad spectrum of American anthropologists: "The first responsibility of the anthropologist is to set down events as seen by the people he is studying." Malinowski, in the *Argonauts*, wrote of "the final goal, of which the ethnographer should never lose sight."

> This goal is, briefly, to grasp the native's point of view, his relation to life, to realise his vision of *his* world. To study the institutions, customs, and codes or to study the behavior and mentality without the subjective desire of feeling by what these people live, of

> realising the substance of their happiness—is, in my opinion, to miss the greatest reward which we can hope to obtain from the study of man [MALINOWSKI 1961:25].

Furthermore, although David Schneider (1965c:38) contrasts Radcliffe-Brown's position on social structure with that of Needham, Lévi-Strauss, and Homans, the common heritage which the structuralists and the structural-functionalists derive from Durkheim provides a common emic bias for both groups. The overwhelming commitment among contemporary British anthropologists to the analysis of descent, affinity, filiation, prescriptive and preferential alliance should suffice to establish the emic thrust of their research interests. On the other side, as we have seen, Lévi-Strauss and Needham have carried Durkheim's notion of "collective representations" to the purest pinnacle of mentalism. As Schneider points out, even the question of social *order* is for Needham a question of underlying logical and symbolic congruence. Although Needham writes about "groups pragmatically distinguished," "The word pragmatic can only make sense if it is taken to mean 'conceptually,' and this in turn can mean that some native will talk about it. A figment of a figment of a figment of a native's imagination will do" (*ibid.*:39).

CONVERGENCE TOWARD MENTALISM

It is a fact of salient importance, however, that the emic bias of the new ethnography derives its vigor from an infusion of a mentalism which has more recent origins. The new ethnography represents a confluence of the interests of the older empathetic, humanist, emic approach with a newer, narrower, and less humanistic mentalism arising out of linguistics. Hymes has traced this influence in terms of Sapir, the "Yale School: complementary distribution, and Jakobsonian distinctive features, and Chomskyian generative grammar" (1964a:10). The linguistic model has also been influential among French and British anthropologists who have been led by a remarkable convergence toward an emic strategy in which logic and reason have taken the place of emotional meaning. In Europe, again specifically influenced by Jakobson, it is Lévi-Strauss who has led the way to this new form of idealism (HYMES 1963; 1964a:15; 1964b). Although formal analysis is deeply committed to the image of "hard science," it has its precise parallel in the structuralist position of Lévi-Strauss, whose essence is captured in the inspired phrase, "Zen Marxism" (see p. 512). For Lévi-Strauss as for the ethnosemanticists, a quasi-mathematical, linguistic model should be the model for all cultural analysis: "language can be said to be a condition of culture because the material out of which language is built is of the same type out of which the whole culture is built: logical relations, oppositions, correlations and the like" (LÉVI-STRAUSS 1963a:68–69). Frake's image of ethnography precisely parallels this view:

> . . . descriptive linguistics is but a special case of ethnography since its domain of study, speech messages, is an integral part of a larger domain of socially interpretable acts and artifacts. It is this total domain of "messages" (including speech) that is the concern of the ethnographer. The ethnographer, like the linguist, seeks to describe an infinite set of variable messages as manifestations of a finite shared code, the code being a set of rules for the socially appropriate construction and interpretation of messages [1964b:133].

It will be seen that Lévi-Strauss' "incredible ingenuity" (SAHLINS 1966) in discovering the hidden mental structures of society is the French analogue of Frake's (1964b:133) invocation: "We must get inside our subjects' heads." When one takes into consideration the objections which have been raised concerning the lack of statistical validation of the mental structures which ethnosemantics has sought to discover, the gap between Lévi-Strauss and the new ethnography narrows still further. Lévi-Strauss' (1953:528) justification of the so-called mechanical model parallels the arguments employed by ethnosemantics to justify a lack of concern with sampling and prediction. As I have already indicated, the mentalism of Lévi-Strauss and his American counterparts departs from previous emic approaches in laying stresses upon the logical functions of mind as opposed to the emotional and irrational components: "Lévi-Strauss emphatically rejects recourse to affectivity or emotion. Emotion is vague, where structure is precise, merely sentimental where structure is logical" (SAHLINS 1966:136). An implicit disdain for the emotional events which go on inside people's heads is also a conspicuous hallmark of ethnosemantics. Emics for a previous generation of American anthropologists meant the discovery of the unconscious psychological complexes which were assumed to underly ideal and actual behavior. The linguistic model, however, has no means of accommodating the Freudian conflict between id, ego, and superego. One might as well try to squeeze blood from a stone as obtain from Hammel's "algorithmic" masterpiece on Comanche kinship, the kinds of emotions the Comanche experienced in the presence of their sisters and mothers. It is indeed a new experience for anthropologists to be exposed to an analysis which "does not pretend to offer solutions which have sociological, psychological or historical relevance in any necessary sense . . ." (HAMMEL 1965:104).

BACK TO PLATO

Another novel ingredient in the ethnosemantic approach is the exclusionist insistence that anthropology must be emic if it is to be anything at all. Although idealism and mentalism have always dominated our outlook, this was traditionally combined with an eclecticism by which at least one anthropological foot could touch the ground. In the past, emic commitments have seldom been so blatant, insistent, and parochial. Earlier idealist and mentalist programs were pragmatically capable of and interested in describing and explaining techno-economic, social, and political systems on the basis of concrete historical events. In the new ethnography, however, culture is a timeless system of logical categories. Hegel's historicism, his only redeeming feature, has been dropped in favor of a synchronic idealist dialectic known as "distinctive feature analysis." Although the ethnosemanticists enjoy the illusion that they are deriving nourishment from new springs of wisdom, even as idealists they may actually have taken a giant step backward. Thus, according to Goodenough:

> The great problem for a science of man is how to get from the objective world of materiality, with its infinite variability, to the subjective world of form as it exists in what, for lack of a better term, we must call the minds of our fellow man. . . . Structural linguistics has, I think, made us conscious, at last, of their nature, and has gone on to convert this consciousness into a systematic method [1964a:39].

The notion that the objective world of materiality represents the shadowing forth of the forms which exist in the mind takes us all the way back to Plato's cave. Goodenough fails to consider that although materiality is infinitely complex, this is a condition which has not inhibited the development of generalization in all the other sciences, none of which have had to search out subjective worlds of form. Furthermore, as I have already indicated, if the subjective world of form appears less infinitely variable, it is because the ethnosemanticists have ignored the variability which each of us knows exists. Goodenough's rejection of the material world as too complex reflects an opinion which is widelv shared (more in conversation than in print) that ethnography must be emic, and emic in the new linguistic sense, if it is to be anything at all. Indeed, there is the insistence by some of the ethnosemanticists that the cultural field of inquiry is only definable in emic terms: "Actually, I find it difficult to conceive of any act, object, or event which can be described as a *cultural* artifact, a manifestation of a code, without some reference to the way people talk about it" (FRAKE 1964b:133).

CULTURES ARE MORE THAN CODES

Are all cultural artifacts—acts, objects, or events—as Frake puts it, only conceivable as manifestations of a code? Referring to the earlier discussion of variation and ambiguity, let me rejoin that acts, objects, or events relevant to the human behavior stream seldom express one or a few simple code rules. Some examples will be helpful at this point. Among the Bathonga there is a strong agnatic bias with a rule that brothers and sons rear their families within or immediately adjacent to their father's compound. Many additional rules stress the order in which brothers and sons are to marry, the allocation of lineage brideprice resources, the treatment of co-wives and of junior sons. There are additional rules which refer to how to make witchcraft, how to make accusations of witchcraft, and how to react to such accusations. There are still more rules which indicate how a man is to become successful in life, the importance of plural marriage, the importance of having many children. All of these rules are in turn related to rules of treating the ancestors with proper respect and attention. Now it is a regular etic feature of Bathonga life that the local lineage fissions when population exceeds 100 or 200 people, that the break involves the establishment of new households with a junior son and his mother at the core, and that the break is accompanied by all sorts of hostile expressions, including witchcraft accusations, which violate the rules of lineage solidarity, but which give the young man a chance to achieve a measure of success in life and marriage that he could not otherwise hope to achieve. To regard the fission event as a result of the intersection of all of the codes that might conceivably have influenced the behavior of the agnates, elder and younger brothers, junior and senior wives, as they wrestled each in their own way with the problem of which rule to invoke, or as the rules themselves intersected on some unconscious level in an untraceable skein of guilt and anxiety in each of the actors, is a hopeless task. The fission of the Bathonga homestead is a cultural event and is *not* conceivable in any operational sense as a manifestation of a code. On the contrary, it is simply and clearly and operationally conceivable as an etic phenomenon in which the rate of fission expresses not a mental code, but the density and spacing of the animal and human population under the techno-environmental conditions of southern Moçambique (HARRIS 1959b).

A similar but highly quantified example is found in Roy Rappaport's (1966) study of the relationship between secondary growth, sweet potato production, the pig and human populations, warfare, and major pig-slaughtering festivals among the Maring of New Guinea. Each of these activities has its emic rules, which cross each other at numerous points. Thus pigs are to be fed with inferior grades of sweet potatoes. But as the pig population goes up, the pigs consume more and more of the labor input that goes into the sweet potato crop. There is no rule among the Maring that pigs should multiply to the point of menacing the human calorie ration. Yet without specifying the cyclical etic regularities in the ratio, between pigs, people, and garden lands, the ethnography of Maring warfare and feasting behavior cannot be properly described, i.e., it cannot be linked up with a corpus of diachronic and synchronic theory.

Among the ethnosemanticists, Frake (1962b) has gone so far as to attempt to treat the interaction between a human group and its habitat primarily in emic terms. Noting that there is no explicit rule among the Subanum by which their settlement pattern can be accounted for, Frake proposes to derive the implicit rule from the intersection of a number of "quite explicit principles about the desirable relations among houses and fields" (*ibid.*:56). The analysis is presented largely as a methodological proposal and hence starts off with the major features of the agricultural system as given. But we are assured that these givens, for example, that new swiddens are started every year, can also be derived from a calculus of emically informed individual decisions. Three emic rules are offered by which an emic "accounting" of settlement pattern is to be achieved: minimum number of wild vegetation boundaries; minimum house to swidden distance; and maximum house to house distance (*ibid.*:56–57). These rules, even with the givens of no larger than nuclear family work groups and an annual shift in locus of the main swidden input, are obviously incapable of predicting (as distinguished from "accounting for") the spatial distribution of Subanum households. Even if they all invoke the same rules at the same time in Subanum land, it cannot be that everyone gets the same result in terms of size of household, size of swidden, and productivity of swidden. Somewhere the emic rules must confront the etic reality of how much is produced under the given techno-environmental conditions. Whatever else must be taken into consideration, it is obvious that the diminishing returns for labor input must figure prominently in the etic formula governing house site shifts among swidden farmers. It is symptomatic of the mentalism and formalism of the ethnosemanticists that Frake does not describe the actual pattern of dispersal of household sites. One description of such a pattern showing long-term stability or change in relationship to population size and production factors would be worth a thousand emic rules. Subanum settlement pattern, a characteristic distribution of people across a portion of the earth and through a specific portion of the earth's history, is a cultural artifact. It is not necessary, indeed, it is impossible to derive this pattern solely from the emic principles, explicit or implicit, by which the Subanum think they conduct their lives.

In northeastern Brazil, peasant fathers accept the pan-Brazilian rules emphasizing the importance of the kindred and of *compadrazco*. Family size, both in terms of the number of kinsmen per household and total effective kinship network, varies from fifteen to twenty to several hundred, according to class. Within a given village, the most economically successful peasant has the largest circle of kinsmen. Unlike his upper-class metropolitan counterparts, however, the circle of kinsmen which surrounds him is associated with the siphoning off of his wealth rather than its consolidation. It is a cultural fact that the pressure upon the Brazilian peasant to expand his family size reduces his chances for upward mobility; yet I challenge the ethnosemanticists to find a mental locus for the rule which links large families to the maintenance of poverty. This problem may be viewed on a still broader scale: Is the poverty of the world's peasant masses a cultural artifact? If so, and it is hard to imagine a negative answer, then are we to suppose that this poverty results from a set of emic rules to which the poor obstinately subscribe?

ETHNOSEMANTICS AND ARCHAEOLOGY

Finally, the relationship between ethnosemantics and the diachronic approach to sociocultural phenomena through ethnology, history, archaeology, and the comparative method deserves comment. Ethnosemantics may be able to develop valid and, within limits, useful descriptions of contemporary social systems, but the linguistic model, even more strongly than the model employed by the British structural-functionalists, is inherently incapable of making discoveries about the content of history and the nature of historical processes. If anthropology is to have a diachronic component, that component cannot consist of an inventory of cognitive rules. The reason for this is that for most human history we have no operational basis for getting inside people's heads in the manner proposed by Frake. But even if we did, we would still confront an insuperable difficulty. The archaeologically recoverable portion of most of human history consists of the environmental modifications which different varieties and expressions of energy quanta have brought into being. Binary oppositions, contrastive features, skewing rules, etc., have this in common: they have no measurable energy cost.

Statistical Survey and the Nomothetic Revival

21

The Boasians themselves would occasionally remark upon the emptiness of the anthropoligical landscape. Kroeber's (1920b:380) review of Lowie's *Primitive Society* was one of the earliest expressions of misgiving:

> As long as we continue offering the world only reconstructions of specific detail, and consistently show a negative attitude toward broader conclusions, the world will find very little profit in ethnology.

Noting that Lowie's achievement is a great improvement over Morgan's "brilliant illusions," Kroeber nonetheless "sighs regretfully that the honesty" of Lowie's method "is not stirred into quicker pulse by visions of more ultimate enterprise" (*ibid.*:380–81). Some years later, Sapir, elsewhere opposed to Kroeber's hankering after ultimate determinisms, came out with a similar expression of discomfort:

> But anthropology cannot long continue to ignore such stupendous facts as the independent development of sibs in different parts of the world, the widespread tendency toward the rise of religious or

> ceremonial societies, the rise of occupational castes, the attachment of differentiating symbols to social units, and a host of others. Such classes of phenomena are too persistent to be without deep significance [SAPIR 1927:204].

But historical particularism continued to exercise its sway over anthropological theory well into the middle of the century. If we include not only those who are historical particularists, but the related viewpoints represented within culture and personality, the new ethnography, and structural-functionalism, we must acknowledge the continued dominance of idiographic currents right through to the present moment. Beginning with the mid-1930's, however, currents of thought and practice associated with a recommitment to nomothetic inquiry have steadily gained strength and stature within the anthropological community. We have already entered a new era of creative theory in which once again a science of man based upon the comparative method boldly confronts the great questions of origins and causality. Although this renaissance has already transformed the research strategies and teaching practices at a number of major university and museum departments, the effects seem not yet to have been noticed in sociology, political science, academic history, philosophy, and related disciplines. But to paraphrase Sapir, the social sciences cannot continue to ignore the stupendous innovations of fact and theory which are associated with the end of the Boasian era.

The mid-century collapse of historical particularism was brought about by the critique of two very different revivals of the comparative method. On the one hand, through the efforts of George Peter Murdock, the statistical form of the comparative approach, which had been originated by Tylor, reasserted itself, greatly strengthened by new techniques and enlarged facilities. Although deeply committed to a physicalist model and nomothetic perspective, this school, as we shall see in the present chapter, has remained aloof from, or even antagonistic toward, cultural materialism. The second line of attack against the Boasians, led by Julian Steward and Leslie White, explicitly embraces the strategy of techno-environmental and techno-economic determinism, although it has for the most part either obfuscated or shied away from an acknowledgment of its debt to Marx. We shall leave the discussion of this manifestation of the nomothetic revival to the next chapter.

Murdock has not only rejected Boas' criticism of the comparative method, but he has gone far beyond any other figure in the nomothetic revival in utilizing statistical techniques to provide testable generalizations. Nonetheless, Murdock's position remains heavily compromised by particularist residues. If we were to arrange White, Steward, and Murdock in order of furthest departure from the Boasian strategy, Murdock would fall closest to the Boasian extreme. The distance between him and Steward is made up of the issue of relatively long-run versus relatively short-run evolutionary parallels. Although Murdock has devoted himself to proving that in the short run, the evolution of kinship terminologies, postmarital residence, and descent rules are obliged to follow a highly predictable sequence, he has denied that anything similar exists over an extended period of time. We find him offering therefore a strange counterpoint to both Steward and Boas. Murdock's position in this respect is actually very similar to that of the synchronic functionalists for whom the laws of functional relation were to be expressed independently of long-range diachronic implications. But in other respects, especially in the manner of treatment of data with regard to functional context, Murdock and the British functionalists have little in common.

SPENCER, SUMNER, KELLER

Murdock has long been an outstanding critic of historical particularism, charging, as we have seen, that Boas was "extravagantly overrated by his students" (see p. 315). But the sources of Murdock's nomothetic interests are remote from the experiences of White and Steward. One set of influences represents, in large measure, a specialty confined in its effects, practically to Yale and to two men, William Graham Sumner and his intellectual executor, Albert Keller. These two figures accounted for a unique prolongation into the twentieth century of Spencerism. To understand Murdock's position, we must revert briefly to Sumner and Keller.

The vast, four-volume masterpiece, *The Science of Society* (1927), which Keller completed on the basis of Sumner's notes, carried forward Spencer's grandiose plan for a total picture of world evolution. Although not a typical Spencerian product by virtue of its cautions concerning the biological transmission of cultural patterns, it is heavily committed to analogy with bio-evolution. As explained in the "Note to Index" in the fourth volume, "the text of this treatise is adjustment, as resulting from the factors of variation, selection, and transmission" (1927:1269).

It would be impossible in the space available to describe Sumner and Keller's vast scheme of cultural evolution. It must suffice merely to indicate that no attempt to limit their perspective to one of

Steward's three categories of evolutionism could be justified (see p. 642). Although perfectly well aware of specific adjustments to local environmental and historical conditions, they experienced no difficulty in stepping back from the canvas for the general view. Perhaps a partial list of topics drawn from the tables of contents of the first three volumes may serve to convey some idea of the enormous scope of this extraordinary work: there are first the "maintenance systems" under which fall such items as subsistence, division of labor, specialization and cooperation, the accumulation of capital, and advances in energy utilization; then the effects of domestication of plants and animals and of men as slaves, evolution of property ideas, and property types, evolution of war, associations, government, fraternities, classes, types of justice, antecedents of the state; and religion, animism, "eidolism," ghost-cult, "daimonism," fetishism, totemism, sin, sacrifice, shamanism; also, marriage, endogamy and exogamy, purchase and dowry, status of women, divorce; and finally evolution of marriage forms, family forms, "transition to patriarchate," and hundreds of subtopics.

Volume 4 is wholly given over to cases linked to the other three volumes by an elaborate index system. This index provides a direct link between Murdock's attempt to set up a universal file of ethnographic materials and the great compendia organized by Frazer, Westermarck, Tylor, and, most important, by Spencer's *Descriptive Sociology*. The actual evolutionary sequences in the various branches of sociocultural life tend toward a consensus drawn from Morgan, Tylor, and Spencer. Of paramount interest is the avowedly materialistic determinism upon which the overall argument is hung. Despite a conservative political position based on their Spencerian support of competition as the agent of evolutionary improvement, Sumner and Keller's acceptance of cultural materialism goes far beyond that of any of their non-Marxian predecessors.

> Our contention is briefly this: that if society is to endure, no considerations whatever can take precedence over success in self-maintenance, that is, in the food quest and in the provision of protection of all kinds to life. . . . Unless the earth provides sufficient sustenance, men may fail. They fail in any case if there are too many of them; they will succeed with a minimum of effort if they are few in comparison with resources; the sort of struggle they will be forced to make will vary according with the proportion of numbers to resources.
>
> What they can do in ranges outside of material self-maintenance cannot but vary, and will be seen to vary, with the type of

> struggle they have to maintain in order to supply basic necessities. Ways outside of self-maintenance proper must take their general tone from self-maintenance ways [SUMNER and KELLER 1927, I:42].

MATERIALISM AT YALE

Keller was perfectly aware of the resemblance between this point of view and that of Marx. If we are moved to wonder how he managed to survive at Yale, it must be remembered that Sumner's and Keller's views were categorically opposed to socialism. They were convinced of the victory of capitalism on the grounds of superior maintenance institutions. Class competition would not dissolve into socialism but rather would lead to a superior form of adaptation. Their position confounds at once any attempt to equate evolutionism in a blanket fashion with leftist politics, as in White's denunciation of the Boasians.

If this is "economic determinism," so be it.

> [The] objection to that theory seems to inhere in its application rather than in its own validity. Marx had a therapeutic plan, based upon his doctrine, for changing the maintenance mores, a plan of selection from which most men of perception would dissent. Doctrinaire socialists do not study to adjust to verities, but challenge them in utopian fashion. Their assumption that the mores must be changed wholesale gives many a student of society pause. It is possible, however, to believe in the basic nature of the economic life and then, when it comes to planning action, modestly try to help society adapt to the conditions of life as learned: it is not necessary to have in view the radical alteration of the whole social order, rejecting the experience of the race and testily setting out to change human nature and other somewhat permanent elements, rather than accommodate one's self, even though it is not so easy, speedy, or grandiose, to actual life-conditions. Belief in some of the Marxian positions, together with entire distrust in the plan for their application, does not make one a socialist or a communist, any more than disbelief in the doctrine of absolute state power and control renders one anarchistic, with leanings towards bomb-throwing [KELLER 1931: 249–50].

Murdock, as we shall see in a moment, has reflected Sumner and Keller's emphasis upon economic determinism but only in a highly evasive and cryptic fashion.

DARWIN AND SPENCER

In Keller's (1931) summary of the evolutionary principles embodied in *The Science of Society*, we find an insistence upon the literal appropriateness of Darwin's model, with "adjustment" changed to the more fashionable "adaptation":

> It is clear enough that the idea of taking the issue up, as it is done here—of exploring the nature of social variation, social selection, social transmission and social adaptation—was suggested by the Darwinian system . . . [KELLER 1931:18].

But in *The Science of Society* the debt to Spencer is expressed no less emphatically. Speaking of the results which justify the possibility of such a science, Sumner and Keller accord Spencer the kind of praise of which he was seldom the object in the twentieth century:

> The credit of this demonstration of results belongs, above all, to Herbert Spencer, and can never be taken from him. It has worked out, in brief, to a conception of society as a unified whole—as a great entity, self-maintaining and self-perpetuating, something more and greater than the sum of its parts, whose evolution and life are susceptible of investigation, whose forms pass from phase to phase, from the most primitive up to the most sophisticated, remaining yet constantly interdependent in the most intimate and intricate of relations. The local form of society is seen to be an adaptation to environment, and the phases of institutions are found to be due to mutual adjustments between them. Democracy did not simply happen, nor was it revealed; it is a characteristic form under certain conditions—and so were and are communalism, polygyny, fetishism. Property and marriage are seen to be closely interlocked; likewise property and religion, religion and government, government and economic organization, economic organization and property. Fossil forms of institutions—survivals—exist, as in organic evolution, and afford links with phases of the evolutionary far past. In short, the conception of the nature of society and of the rise and decline of societal institutions has come to be a broader one, and it has entered into and vitally affected all subsequent study and thought along social lines [1927 III:2194].

THE SCIENCE OF SOCIETY

One part of Murdock's historic role appears to center on his transmission of Sumner and Keller's interest in a "science of society," especially in terms of the emphasis that cultural evolution is "orderly adaptive change" (MURDOCK 1949:xii). In his most significant book,

Social Structure, Murdock acknowledges that the Sumner-Keller approach is "perhaps the most influential single intellectual stimulus behind the present volume" (*ibid.*:xiii). This book is dominated by the promise that the study of sociocultural phenomena can be carried out in conformity with the strictest physicalist model of science:

> It seems clear that the elements of social organization, in their permutations and combinations, conform to natural laws of their own with an exactitude scarcely less striking than that which characterizes the permutation and combination of atoms in chemistry or genes in biology [MURDOCK 1949:183].

It is to Sumner and Keller that Murdock owes his confidence on this issue. Yet he insists that *The Science of Society* is "permeated with survivals of nineteenth-century evolutionism which historical anthropologists have long since disproved" (*ibid.*:xiii).

SCALING DOWN THE SCIENCE OF SOCIETY

In response to historical-particularist currents, Murdock's approach to evolution and causality is heavily compromised by his adoption of a short time-scale and by a failure to combine his comparative approach with the nomethetically relevant data of prehistory or, indeed, with any macro-temporal view of the human condition. Murdock joins White, Steward, and Sumner-Keller in urging that evolution is the central concept in sociocultural studies. But the evolutionary model with which he works is so close to the endlessly branching tree of life that there is actually little difference on this score between him and the historical particularists. Indeed, all of Murdock's contributions are suffused with a painful paradox: While arguing persuasively for a nomothetic interpretation of the varieties of sex-regulating and kinship institutions, he has denied that whole sociocultural systems also exhibit diachronic regularities and that long-range parallel and convergent evolution are significant features of culture change.

In *Social Structure,* this paradox is manifest in the studied failure to relate kinship structures and kinship ideologies to the development of political institutions; by the failure to treat the rise of caste and class hierarchies as a category of "social structure." Murdock's great predecessors at Yale treated these subjects in ways which deserved to be improved upon, rather than to be negated or ignored. We shall return anon to the basis of Murdock's rejection of macro-evolutionary sequences.

THE ORIGIN OF THE HUMAN RELATIONS AREA FILES

But first, we must credit Murdock with his historic contribution, the triple linking up of modern ethnography, modern statistics, and the statistical comparative cross-cultural survey method. His great achievement along this line was the creation of the Human Relations Area Files (until 1949, the Cross-Cultural Survey), a catalogue of indexed ethnographic summaries collated under uniform headings. Begun in 1937, the files in 1967 contained the description of the relevant portions of more than 240 cultures. These files are the culmination of an unbroken line of statistically oriented enthusiasts extending back from Murdock to Tylor (1889), whose essay, "On a Method of Investigating the Development of Institutions; Applied to Laws of Marriage and Descent," was the originating impulse (see p. 158).

The earliest sustained follow-up to Tylor's suggestion was embarked upon by the founder of the Dutch School of inductive sociology, S. R. Steinmetz (1930; orig. 1900). Like Spencer and other mass compilers of ethnographic data, Steinmetz set about establishing a catalogue of world tribes and cultures. He hoped eventually to have at his disposal coded information on 1000 to 1500 "peoples and phases" (*ibid.*:209–10*n.*). Although Steinmetz did not come close to completing his proposed catalogue, several of his students used samples and statistical correlations to explore important evolutionary issues. H. J. Nieboer's (1900) *Slavery as an Industrial System* is one of the most important achievements of this school. Drawing upon Steinmetz's tables, Nieboer investigated the distribution of slavery on an area basis and then attempted to discover the causes of this distribution. Assuming that economic factors are most potent in accounting for slavery, he proceeded to a classification of his sample in terms of economic types (which are carefully distinguished from evolutionary stages). Nieboer's tables are based on 65 hunting and fishing societies, 22 pastoral groups, and 219 agricultural groups.

The next great book in this line is *The Material Culture and Social Institutions of the Simpler Peoples* by L. T. Hobhouse, G. C. Wheeler, and M. Ginsberg (1915). Although not students of Steinmetz, the authors of this "Essay in Correlation" built upon Nieboer's techno-economic classification of societies to establish their major rubrics: lower, higher, and dependent hunters; three grades of agriculturalists;

and two grades of pastoralists. Their main interest was to discover to what extent varieties of modes of food production were correlated with the evolution of other aspects of culture. Using an initial sample of about 640 ethnic units, they carried out simple correlation calculations on five major categories, namely political and juridical organization, family, warfare, social stratification, and control over property. They concluded that "upon the whole the variations accord with general probability, for the economic development may be taken as a rough index of the amount of intellect and organizing power available for the shaping of the life of a society" (*ibid.*:254).

Hobhouse, Wheeler, and Ginsberg placed considerable emphasis on the point that "economic development has no necessary connection with improvement in the relations between members of society" (*ibid.*). This issue of "improvement" loomed large in their overall approach to sociocultural studies, and its injection into the argument concerning the extent to which modes of food production influenced the other categories of cultural phenomena obscured the strong positive correlation which most of their tables exhibit.

Among several additional studies directly inspired by Steinmetz, we must mention especially J. H. Ronhaar's (1931) neglected treatment of matrilineal societies, Jan Tijm's (1933) study of the role of women in North American Indian culture, and T. S. Van Der Bij's (1929) study of warfare.

HUMAN RELATIONS AREA FILES

Murdock's development and utilization of the Human Relations Area Files surpasses all precedents in several crucial respects. First, the files have been available on a subscriber basis in Xerox and microfilm form to large numbers of institutions and scholars, all of whom thus have or will have access to the same set of primary materials. Second, the quality, quantity, and depth of information available in the files go far beyond what had hitherto been possible. Over 450,000 pages of source material already had been filed by 1967 (*cf.* MOORE 1961:335). Third, the growth of the files has been accompanied by a steady improvement in the capacity of anthropologists to make use of statistical expertise and thus to coax maximum significance from the techniques of correlation.

Although it can scarcely be maintained that the files have suddenly made the results of ethnographic inquiry more secure, or more scientific, we must admit that they have helped to generate a number of valuable nomothetic essays among which the works of Murdock (1949), Whiting and Child (1953), and Whiting (1964) may be taken as representative.

Murdock's *Social Structure*, aspects of which we shall discuss in a moment, would alone probably justify the enterprise. But the creation of the files must be seen as ushering in a whole new era of the comparative method in which the search for nomothetic regularities has led to the development of a number of additional world samples. Most of these take the Human Relations Area Files as their starting point. Murdock himself (1957) has led the way here with the development of a "World Ethnographic Sample" and an *Ethnographic Atlas* of that sample in which some 600 societies are described with respect to several dozen coded features. This atlas is being issued in serial form in the journal *Ethnology*, which Murdock founded in 1962.

SIGNIFICANCE OF THE FILES

The principle upon which all of this activity has proceeded seems unassailable and to be representative in large measure of the future course of ethnology. Ethnological statements which aspire to nomothetic status must be checked for their degree of correspondence to the ethnographic reality in as large a number of cases as possible. This requirement is imposed on us by virtue of our inability to perform laboratory tests on human history. Dependent as we are on the unfolding of the natural continuum of events, our generalizations must be couched in probabilistic terms derived from the observation of the frequencies with which predicted or retrodicted events occur. Synchronic and diachronic causal relations, so often hitherto expressed in terms of approximate trends or tendencies, can only benefit from more precise statements of operationally defined measures of probability. Once the practice of stating causal relationships in terms of probabilities of association becomes firmly established, many problems which have plagued generations of determinists and antideterminists will dissolve themselves into a more profitable level of discourse. Furthermore, it is obvious that the social sciences are about to glut the conventional library channels of information storage and retrieval with indigestible quantities of raw data. We must welcome all attempts to enlarge the utility of the data on hand and to maximize the effectiveness of the yearly crop.

To appreciate these information devices as technical assets implies, of course, that one is aware of their technical shortcomings. Problems exist on many levels and manifest varying degrees of resistance to improvement. The Files, for example, are dependent upon ethnographic monographs whose scope, quality, and theoretical design are highly variable. Answers to many ethnographic questions simply cannot be extracted from the sample as it is now constituted. There is very little which the Files can do, for instance, by way of compensating for the relative paucity of reliable quantitative information on all aspects of primitive economics and social organization (*cf.* KÖBBEN 1967:10). The need to overcome the unevenness of the monographic resources prevented Murdock from establishing a random sample of cultures, since cultures were included or rejected partially in accordance with the quality of the available literature. It may very well be that this factor biases the sample in unknown ways, as would happen, for example, if the best known and best reported groups were the most peaceful, or the most acculturated. This in turn places limitations on the kinds of statistical measures which can legitimately be applied to the typical correlation analysis end-product.

DIFFUSION AND THE PROBLEM OF UNITS

The Files and all similar ethnographic samples are plagued by difficulties in establishing the boundaries of discrete sociocultural systems. Some cultures in the sample may actually consist of several such systems, whereas others, counted separately, may actually deserve to be lumped together.

In addition, there is the notorious question, first raised by Sir Francis Galton, of how to distinguish correlations which arise from nomothetic influence from those which reflect diffusion (e.g., gasoline and aeroplanes as distinguished from bow ties and aeroplanes). It is interesting to note that it was this issue which discouraged Boas, despite an interest in statistics, from adopting Tylor's method, about which he was initially enthusiastic (LOWIE 1946:227).

Since 1961 Raoul Naroll (1961; 1964) and Naroll and D'Andrade (1963) have proposed a total of five solutions to the problem which baffled Galton. These solutions involve the establishment of arcs of contiguous cultures extending over hundreds and preferably thousands of miles within which various mathematical devices are employed to sift out the probable effects of contact.

Murdock (1957:193) has argued persuasively on behalf of the point of view which minimizes the diffusionary effect, in conformity with the viewpoint generally adopted by Steward and other critics of the extreme diffusionists and historical particularists:

> The mere fact of historical relatedness does not disturb the author, for the evidence now seems clear that societies borrow from one another, much as they invent for themselves, cultural elements for which they have a need and which are at least reasonably consistent with preexisting usages, and that borrowed like invented and traditional elements undergo a continual process of integrative modification leading to the emergence of new independent configurations. Diffusion negates the independence of two cultures only if it has occurred too recently for the integrative process to have run its course.

Additional study of this problem by Harold Driver (1966), J. Jorgensen (1966), and Driver and Sanday (1966) has failed to sustain Murdock's optimism on this point. Analysis both of North American distributions and of world samples shows that at least one problem, namely that of the explanation of mother-in-law/son-in-law avoidance, cannot be solved by ignoring the possibility of diffusionary influences. (This is especially galling, if I may be permitted the pun, because it is the first trait which Tylor sought to explain in the article which provoked Galton's critique.) The trouble is that higher correlations of association can be demonstrated for temporal and spatial propinquity than for any of the variables which are said to have a nomothetic causal relationship to the avoidance patterns (e.g., kinship terminology, residence, descent). Driver's suggestions for improving the reliability and significance of the statistical cross-cultural method go beyond Naroll's solution to Galton's challenge. In order to control for diffusion and at the same time to have a permanent sample adaptable to any number of problems, Driver advocates an initial group of 1,000 societies (1966:147). Jorgensen goes even further and suggests that "exhaustiveness of data should be sought" rather than sampling, implying that perhaps 2,000 cases may have to be consulted in order to overcome Galton's objections. Jorgensen's solution also calls for the collation of data from at least two time periods per culture (1966:168–69), a requirement which it would seem difficult to reconcile with the need for exhaustiveness.

THE PROBLEM OF FUNCTIONAL CONTEXT

One of the most persistent criticisms of Murdock's strategy comes from those who are alarmed by the mechanical nature of the operations by which cross-cultural correlations are established. This is the point on whose behalf Boas sought to abandon the comparative method: items are wrenched out of context by coders unknown to the reader or to the original ethnographer. Items which should be treated separately are lumped together and those which should be lumped together are counted as examples of different traits. The British social anthropologists, as might be expected from their functionalist heritage, have been especially disturbed by this aspect of the comparative survey. A. J. F. Köbben's (1952:142) critique in the *Journal of the Royal Anthropological Institute* may be taken as representative:

> A consequence of Murdock's insufficiently functional approach is that his product often amounts to no more than mere classifying. Where he enters into the minutiae of a problem, as occasionally happens, his argument at once becomes more lively and interesting. More often, however, he simply formulates rules or produces columns of figures. A Dutch sociologist once called a certain book "a work without a heart," and in reading Murdock's *Social Structure* one is constantly reminded of this description. Of course, the author may well protest that what he writes has gained in exactness what it lacks from a functional point of view and that a functional treatment is hardly compatible with mathematical precision. Now every effort to be exact is welcome in our discipline, which certainly does not suffer from an overdose of this tonic, but it must be real and not *quasi*-exactness. Can quasi-exactness be denied if different phenomena are placed in the same category and treated as though strictly comparable when in fact they are not?

The reply to this sort of criticism is best stated in its most general form. Does one object to the isolation, codification, and cross-cultural comparison of traits in general? Or is it that one objects to the *mistakes* which are made in the name of this procedure? In the former instance, carried to its logical conclusion, we reach the impasse of Ruth Benedict's Digger Indians, wherein cultures can be compared only as wholes and as such are really noncomparable. As Murdock has put it in his critique of cultural relativism:

> Benedict held, not only that cultures must be viewed in the context of the situations faced by the societies that bear them—a position with which few modern social scientists would quarrel—but also that they must be viewed as wholes. To her, every culture is a unique configuration and can be understood only in its totality. She strongly implied that the abstraction of elements for comparison with those of other cultures is illegitimate. An element has no meaning except in its context; in isolation it is meaningless. I submit that this is nonsense. Specific functions, of

> course, are discoverable only in context. Scientific laws or propositions, however, can be arrived at, in anthropology, as in any other science, only by abstracting and comparing features observable in many phenomena as they occur in nature [1965:146].

This defense of the comparative method, with which all who aspire to nomothetic expression must concur, does not eliminate the technical difficulties associated with the statistical survey approach. Until such time as the method under consideration approaches more closely to the ideal model, there is one firm conclusion which must be kept in plain view of those who are working with the considerably less than perfect ones: Statistical cross-cultural surveys can, indeed must, be used to supplement other modes of generating and testing hypotheses, but they cannot be used alone or even as the primary sources of nomothetic statements.

THE PROBLEM OF CAUSALITY

That the technique as it now stands cannot be used in isolation is evident in one glaring defect which is characteristic of all of the statistical comparative studies carried out since Tylor's pioneering essay. None of them have been capable of showing causal relations. The reason for this is that the samples consulted have all been synchronic. None of the studies have concerned themselves with time-structured data and as a result they merely show probabilities of association between elements which as far as the statistical methods are concerned may be indifferently regarded as either dependent or independent. As Jorgensen (1966:162) observed: "Statistics cannot validate functional hypotheses or hypotheses about origins when the data are synchronic."

THE CASE OF THE DETERMINANTS OF KINSHIP TERMINOLOGY

One of the most illuminating examples of this limitation on synchronic correlations may be found at the very heart of Murdock's *Social Structure*. In the chapter entitled "Determinants of Kinship Terminology," twenty-seven theorems are put to the test of the statistical comparative method. These theorems are divided into three sets, each of which is characterized by a particular class of "determinant," namely, (1) marriage form, (2) descent rule, and (3) postmarital residence. After validating all twenty-seven theorems by demonstrating various associations between the "determinants" and kinship terminology, Murdock turns to the question of the relative "efficacy" of these "determinants."

He notes first of all that the coefficients of association found in the tables used to confirm the theorems involving marriage form are generally lower than those found in the tables used to confirm descent. He interprets this to mean that marriage forms have less "efficacy" than descent. The same relative standing is suggested by a test in which marriage form is pitted against descent rule by enumerating cases in which they both occur in a fashion which theoretically should tend to produce contradictory results in the relationship terminology. For example, in societies in which there is patrilineal descent, bifurcate merging terminologies are very common. On the other hand, in societies with nonsororal polygyny, bifurcate collateral terminologies are very common. When both patrilineal descent and nonsororal polygyny are present, what happens? The descent-produced tendency toward bifurcate merging terminology takes precedence over the "effect" of the marriage rule; bifurcate merging terms are more common than bifurcate collateral ones. By similar kinds of steps, Murdock (1949:182) concludes that "the efficacy of marriage forms is greater than that of residence rules." Finally separate proof is offered that descent is also "a more effective factor" than residence. This leaves us with residence as the *least* "effective" of the three "determinants."

AND THE LEAST EFFECTIVE SHALL BE THE MOST POWERFUL

It quickly becomes apparent, however, that the so-called determinants are misnomered and that none of the correlations per se prove the existence of causal relations. Were this not the case, the most important assumption in the entire book would be wrong. For it is central to Murdock's explanation of varieties of descent and kinship terminology, as well as of the probable direction of the evolution of "social structure," that residence is the most powerful determinant of all the factors considered. "Powerful" here means that "the rule of residence is normally the first aspect of a social system to undergo modification in the process of change from one relatively stable equilibrium to another . . ." (*ibid.*:183). It means that "it is in respect to residence that changes in economy, technology, property, government, or religion first alter the structural relationships of related individuals to one another, giving an impetus to subsequent modifications in forms of the family, in . . . kin groups, and in kinship terminology" (*ibid.*:202). It means also that "no place is allotted in this hypothesis for the influence of such factors as preferential marriage customs" (*ibid.*:222). That is, one does not ordinarily expect changes in marriage rules or descent rules to initiate changes in residence, but one does expect changes in residence to initiate changes in marriage and descent rules. Some additional indication of the importance of this deterministic order can be gained from Murdock's lavish praise of Lowie for having been the first anthropologist to demonstrate the causal significance of residence (actually Tylor long preceded Lowie on this point): "This is by far the most important contribution of any modern anthropologist to our knowledge of the evolution of social organization" (*ibid.*:202). It should be noted that the argument of about half of *Social Structure* is directly or indirectly contingent upon the validity of this appraisal. Before pursuing the question of the method which Murdock employs to validate the importance of residence, the negative significance of the positive correlations should be stressed.

If residence is the most powerful determinant of kinship terminology, why does an analysis of the coefficients of association show that descent and marriage forms are more "effective" in producing particular varieties of kinship terminologies? The answer is that they do nothing of the kind. They show nothing about one factor "producing" another; all they do is predict the frequency with which two factors will be found in association. They show nothing about the causes of kinship terminologies. They are not determinants; they are merely predictors.

CAUSALITY IS ALIVE AND LIVING EVERYWHERE

It is fashionable in contemporary social science to ignore the difference between a causal relationship and an associational one. This haughty attitude no doubt has its roots in Hume's famous critique of the inductive method. When we say that x causes y we merely declare a regular relationship between the two. Thus, the notion of cause as a metaphysical property is superfluous. But in a causal statement, the association of x with y has a temporal component, namely that y follows x. A nomothetic statement which lacks a causal arrow is a contradiction in terms; its absence can be tolerated only as a token of work in progress. If mere statistical associations are offered in lieu of statements of cause and effect, science is defeated, for it is knowledge and not ignorance which deserves to be counted.

The difference between causal factors and mere predictive ones is not to be taken lightly. It is the difference in knowing whether wounds cause gunshots or gunshots cause wounds. Bullet holes are excellent predictors of gunshots. As all devotees of Hercule Poirot know, there is a high correlation between gunshots and bullet holes, but no murder has yet admitted of the possibility that it was the fatal wound which caused the gun to discharge its contents. Along the same lines, one might note how reliably rain predicts clouds, or how frequently fire engines are found near burning buildings. If any additional examples are needed, they are available to anyone who has a movie projector which can be run in reverse.

I am tempted to elaborate further on the method by which the time relationship between two variables is utilized to separate cause from effect, since once again it is obviously not merely a matter of correlating any two variables which happen regularly to occur in sequence (*cf.* BLALOCK 1961:19ff.). But it is sufficient for our present discussion that we realize why additional logico-empirical operations are necessary before synchronic cross-cultural statistical comparisons can be made to contribute to the advance of knowledge. Perhaps it is even more important that we realize that the mere multiplication of correlation studies, as in Robert Textor's (1967) 20,000 computer-calculated correlations, may actually be the equivalent of running a movie backwards and hence a source of ignorance and confusion as well as of correlations.

THE PRIMARY IMPORTANCE OF MURDOCK'S CAUSAL HYPOTHESES

It would be unfair to attribute to Murdock a lack of interest in separating causal from predictive variables. Indeed, Murdock's theory of the determinants of kinship groups and of kinship terminologies must be acknowledged as the most important nomothetic advance in the study of social organization since Morgan's *Systems of Consanguinity and Affinity of the Human Family* (1870). But the methodological structure of Murdock's achievement has been obscured by the razzle-dazzle of his statistical tables and by his ritualistic avoidance of the consequences of his own major causal premises.

The manifest structure of Murdock's presentation would have us believe that the twenty-seven theorems concerning the "determinants of kinship terminology" are set forth in order to validate a single postulate which is given formal expression in the following terms:

> Postulate 1. The relatives of any two kin-types tend to be called by the same kinship terms, rather than by different terms, in inverse proportion to the number and relative efficacy of (a) the inherent distinctions between them and (b) the social differentials affecting them, and in direct proportion to the number and relative efficacy of the social equalizers affecting them [1949:138].

Although it sounds impressive, this postulate is rather trivial once the jargon is stripped away. In translation, what Murdock is really saying is that kinship terminologies are determined by all the factors that determine them. He himself practically admits as much in the very next paragraph:

> Rephrased in looser language, the postulate states that the extension and differentiation of kinship terminology is the product of the joint interplay of all inherent and cultural factors which significantly affect the degree of similarity or dissimilarity between particular categories of relatives [*ibid.*].

In order to understand the logico-empirical structure of Murdock's magnum opus, we must go back to an earlier portion of the same chapter wherein Murdock undertakes to make explicit all assumptions upon which Postulate 1 is based. There are thirteen such assumptions, most of which are merely definitional and need not concern us here. There is one, however, namely the twelfth, which provides the key to Murdock's theoretical position:

> Our twelfth assumption is that the forms of social structure are not determined by kinship patterns or terminology, or influenced in any major degree by them, but are created by forces external to social organization, especially by economic factors. It is assumed herewith, for example, that the available sources of food and the techniques of procuring it affect the sex division of labor and the relative statuses of the sexes, predisposing peoples to particular rules of residence, which can eventuate in the formation of extended families, clans, and sibs. It is further assumed that the prevailing types and distribution of property favor particular rules of inheritance, that wealth or its lack affects marriage (e.g. encouraging or inhibiting polygyny), and that these and other factors external to social structure can strongly influence rules of residence and marriage and through them the forms of social organization and kinship structure. This assumption is derived from the analysis by Lowie of the origin of sibs, from our own supportive evidence as presented in Chapter 8, and from the

> various theorists from Marx to Keller who have stressed the importance of economic factors in cultural change [*ibid.*:137].

What is the relationship between this assumption and the 27 theorems which it is alleged to underly? None. If anything, as we have seen, the analysis of the theorem leads to contradictory conclusions concerning the "effectiveness" of residence. Indeed Murdock is forced to go through an extraordinary turnabout in order to make the two ends of his argument meet without the one destroying the other.

> Despite our tentative conclusion that rules of descent and the kin groups resulting from them rank highest in relative efficacy among the major groups of kinship determinants, followed by forms of marriage and the consequent family types, the influence of residence rules should not be too heavily discounted [*ibid.*:182].

Note the remarkable understatement embodied in the phrase "the influence of residence rules should not be too heavily discounted." How can we reconcile this hesitancy with the bold language of assumption 12 or the even bolder: "when any social system which has attained a comparatively stable equilibrium begins to undergo change, such change regularly begins with a modification in the rule of residence" (*ibid.*:221)?

In terms of the larger theory with which Murdock approaches his subject, the relatively poor predictive value of residence is easily explained as a result of a lag in the responsiveness of terminology—precisely the same argument as that used by Morgan to justify the use of kinship terminology for the reconstruction of earlier phases of social organization:

> Hence in systems undergoing transition, of which any large and random sample of human societies will necessarily include a considerable number, kinship terms will more often be consistent with the conservative rule of descent than with the progressive rule of residence [*ibid.*:183].

THE LOST STRATEGY OF THE TWELFTH ASSUMPTION

But what is of interest here is that "the adaptive changes" in kinship terminology described in the twenty-seven theorems are explicitly said to take place *after* the initiation of residence changes. And yet this supremely important causal statement remains throughout the book nothing but an "assumption" (*ibid.*:137, 221). What we should like to know at once is why this assumption, upon which rests Murdock's entire subsequent treatment of the "evolution of social organization," is not the focus of intense inquiry.

As Keller freely acknowledged (see p. 609), this assumption commits one to the strategy of cultural materialism. Applied to kinship terminology and residence, it calls for the study of the techno-economic and techno-environmental causes of residence changes. But the strategy which Murdock actually pursues is highly ambiguous. On the one hand he establishes himself as the representative of the hard, statistical approach and on the other hand, he carefully detaches his deterministic assumptions from any deterministic theory of history. Although this would not seem possible in view of assumption 12 and in view of other achievements associated with his study of kinship systems, it is accomplished by what I should like to describe as the "miracle" of the "principle of limited possibilities." And it is to this extraordinary doctrine that we must now turn our attention.

THE PRINCIPLE OF LIMITED POSSIBILITIES

Murdock's first reference to limited possibilities occurs in his article "The Common Denominator of Cultures" (1945), where it is used to explain why the universal pattern exists. The nature of man, the world in which he lives, the physical and chemical properties of materials, the physical and behavioral characteristics of other animals, set conditions for successful responses: "These conditions introduce into cultures the principle of limited possibilities, which is of extreme importance in determining the universal culture patterns" [1945:139]. In this form, the principle of limited possibilities is unobjectionable and merely states that cultural similarity is "not a mere artifact of classificatory ingenuity but rests upon some substantial foundation . . . ," namely, adaptive responses to the conditions of human existence. In this form it is merely a reaffirmation of Sumner and Keller's belief in the lawfulness of the domain of history since it predicts that cultures will not diverge endlessly, but will be confined to a limited number of adaptations to the conditions of human life.

Murdock's next use of the principle, however, introduces a rather new emphasis. In *Social Structure* (1949:115) he calls it "the crucial criterion" for deciding whether a comparative or "sociological" as contrasted with a "purely historical" approach is warranted:

> Where there are no practical limits to the variety of responses which people can make in particular situations, cultural forms can vary endlessly with little comparability between those of unrelated societies, with the result that satisfactory interpretation must depend very heavily upon historical investigation of local and regional influences [*ibid.*].

Murdock here informs us that the principle of limited possibilities applies to some domains of culture but not to others. The list of domains to which it allegedly does not apply is staggering: language, ceremonial, folktales, art, technology, and "other aspects of culture." "In all such cases, the overwhelming majority of cross-cultural similarities must necessarily be attributed to diffusion" (*ibid.*). The only exceptions which Murdock admits are "kinship terms and their determinants." He proceeds to demonstrate this by asserting that a group may either "recognize or ignore sex," affinity, etc., may either be monogamous, polyandrous, or polygynous; recognize either levirate, sororate, or cross-cousin marriage; have either bilateral, matrilineal, or patrilineal rules of descent; practice either patrilocal, matrilocal, avunculocal, neolocal, or bilocal residence; and so on through family forms and types of kin groups (*ibid.*:116).

Two problems which escape Murdock's attention have now reached the crisis stage. First, it is obviously false that when parallels occur in the domains which Murdock singles out as being exempt from his principle, that they must be attributed to diffusion. He is wrong even in the best case, namely, linguistics, in which parallelisms and convergences in phonetics, phonemics, and syntax have been demonstrated by a long line of linguists, from Zipf (1935) to Greenberg (1963). But much more distressing is the promulgation of a point of view which asserts that technology is less subject to limitations than social structure! It was to explain technological parallels that the concept was originated.

ONE OAR IS NOT AS GOOD AS ANOTHER

The anthropologist who first introduced and elaborated the principle of limited possibilities—Alexander Goldenweiser—employed as his favorite examples sword handles, knives and other technological items. Goldenweiser's most cherished case, however, was the technology of nautical propulsion:

> It may be observed here incidentally that the operative conditions or use to which an article is to be put, often provide limiting

> conditions which in a sense predetermine the technical solution, thus leading to comparable results whenever such a solution is reached. Take, for example, an oar. Abstractly speaking, an oar can be long or short, light or heavy, circular in cross section or flat, wide or narrow, of even width throughout its length or otherwise; it can also be made of more than one material. Now in accordance with local conditions or chance, most of these shapes and materials may have been used for oars at one time or another, and a variety are still being used in a pinch. . . . But if you want a *good* oar—and this is what at length you do want—the end result is limited by conditions of use. . . . These limitations are so drastic that every oar is—emphatically—an oar, implying numerous points of similarity between all oars [1942:124–25].

Let us translate Goldenweiser's point about "a *good* oar" into less anthropocentric terminology: a good oar is an *evolutionarily viable* propulsion device adapted to small boats in which energy is transmitted from the human arm to the water. And now we perceive the second crisis in Murdock's version of nomothetic propriety: It is simply false that there are only nine possible ways to classify kinsmen, three ways to get married, three (or four) ways to reckon descent, and five ways to take up postmarital residence. What Murdock means to say is that there are only a limited number of ways under certain conditions (not specified by him) to make "a good oar," or in less anthropocentric terms, only a limited number of *evolutionarily viable* terminological systems, marriage arrangements, descent rules, and residence practices.

Early in the century Lowie (1912:37) had asked the rhetorical question, "How many ways of fastening a skin membrane to a drum are conceivable?" He actually thought there were only "limited possibilities." But with Goldenweiser as a guide, it is clear that what Lowie had in mind was not how many kinds of drums are conceivable, but rather, how many kinds could be expected to survive the selective tests (durability, loudness, cost, etc.) to which drums are exposed under specific biocultural conditions.

It is easy to imagine kinship terminologies which Murdock has not considered. (Actually, since his major types of "kinship organization" are based only on cousin terms, hundreds of variants are known from fact and not fancy.) Why, for example, is it a nonpossibility for a terminological system to recognize not two, but three or four sexes; for new marriages to take place after each pregnancy, the first monogamous, the second polyandrous, the third polygynous; or why not descent which is patrilineal in the morning, matrilineal in the afternoon, bilateral in the evening, and double on Sundays? Shall we not ask, in other words, why elephants do not have two heads, why cabbages do not grow on clouds, and why the moon is not made of Swiss cheese? The limited possibilities of nature are none other than the forms which evolution has produced. The task of science is to explain why they were produced. They cannot be explained by saying the other possibilities are illogical.

EVOLUTION IS FORTUITOUS AND UNPREDICTABLE

During a discussion commemorating the one hundredth anniversary of the publication of *Origin of Species,* Murdock explicitly opposed the doctrine of limited possibilities to a nomothetic view of history. Objecting to White's version of evolutionism, he insisted that the true model of cultural evolution was, as in biology, an endlessly diverging "tree." He proposed:

> 1. That evolution is an actual process of change, not a classificatory characterization of sequences.
> 2. That evolution consists of real events, not of abstractions from events, so that evolutionary development is historical in the strictest and most literal sense.
> 3. That the course of evolution is fundamentally divergent or multilinear. When parallel development occurs in more than one evolutionary line, the sequences and results are similar only in a typological sense, and are never in any respect identical.
> 4. That evolution operates by a purely fortuitous mechanism, and is neither predictable, predetermined, nor purposive [1959b:129].

Murdock next proceeds to identify this model with Steward's concept of multilinear evolution: "Unless I completely misread him," he says of Steward, "he considers all cultural evolution to be basically multilinear and regards cases of parallel development as exceptions demanding special investigation" (*ibid.*:130–31). Murdock then concludes that multilinear evolution is really nothing but what anthropologists have all along been calling "cultural change":

> The group of processes usually designated collectively as those of culture change, and on which we possess an immense literature, corresponds closely in practically every respect to the processes of organic change known to the biologist as evolution. Culture change meets exactly the criteria embedded in our four statements. It refers to actual processes of change, not to abstracted typological sequences. Its events are historical in the most literal sense, and in their totality constitute culture history. Its course or direction

> is fundamentally multilinear. And it operates in a fortuitous, not in a predictable or predetermined manner. Moreover, it is adaptive, producing cultural adjustments to the geographical environment and to the other basic conditions of life [*ibid.*:131].

But if cultural evolution is "fundamentally multilinear," "not predictable" and "fortuitous," how do we account for the fact that, as Murdock himself assures us, only "five major kinship systems" are found in "an analysis of 447 societies drawn from all parts of the world and from all levels of culture" (*ibid.*:135)? Murdock's explanation is as follows:

> The resemblances are typological, not historical or necessarily even functional. They occur because only a certain limited number of combinations of rules of descent, residence patterns, forms of family organization, and methods of classifying kinsmen constitute configurations whose elements are genuinely consistent with each other, so that they represent states of equilibrium toward which other combinations tend to gravitate over time [*ibid.*].

Were it not for the stipulation in the first sentence that the consistency and equilibrium in question are not necessarily functional, but may merely be typological, the second sentence might pass muster as an assertion of evolutionary determinism in the realm of social organization. But the two together constitute a classic case of eating cake and having it.

Ordinarily one might suppose that the principle of limited possibilities was nothing more than an improvisation, like the "ether" or "phlogiston," for dignifying a lack of knowledge about causal processes. But Murdock's cryptic commitment to cultural materialism profoundly complicates the issue. This is not the usual case of theoretical bafflement, but rather a highly original form of retrenchment: the causal theory is abandoned, not because it fails to give results, but because it shows signs of becoming too successful. That only five major kinship systems emerge from a study of a representative sample of 447 societies drawn, according to Murdock, "from all parts of the world and from all levels of culture," suggests the existence of extraordinarily powerful, selective, deterministic, evolutionary forces.

THE EVIDENCE FOR EVOLUTIONARY UNPREDICTABILITY

To conclude in the face of his own lifework that evolution operates in a "fortuitous, not in a predictable or predetermined manner" (1959b:131) surely must imply an overpowering mass of evidence in support of the historical-particularist view. And this is just what Murdock asserts in *Social Structure*: "The forms of social organization, indeed, appear to show a striking lack of correlation with levels or types of technology, economy, property rights, class structure, or political integration" [1949:187]. What kind of evidence is presented to justify this extravagant statement, so clearly refuted by Sumner and Keller; by Hobhouse, Wheeler, and Ginsberg; by Nieboer; by Spencer, Tylor, Morgan, Marx, and Engels; not to mention White, Childe, Steward and Wittfogel?

Since the methodological strength of *Social Structure* lies in the statistical cross-cultural survey technique, one might suppose that "the striking lack of correlation" refers to a set of relevant tables. But there are no such tables in the book. Not only are tables correlating technology, economy, property rights, class structure, and political organization absent from *Social Structure*, but the book lacks altogether anything remotely resembling a systematic treatment of these subjects. "Technology" does not even appear in the index! The "evidence" consists rather of the following taxonomic decision:

> As will appear below, an objective classification of societies in terms of their similarities in social structure results in grouping together under the same specific type and sub-type such dissimilar peoples as the New England Yankees and the forest-dwelling Negritoes of the Andaman Islands, the imperialistic Incas and the Vanimo Papuans of New Guinea, the Mayan Tzeltal of Yucatán and the backward Miwok of California, the civilized Nayars of India and the primitive nomadic Veddas of the interior of Ceylon. Nowhere does even a revised evolutionism find a shred of support [*ibid.*].

DO NEW ENGLANDERS AND ANDAMANESE HAVE THE SAME TYPE OF SOCIAL STRUCTURE?

The only reasonable conclusion which can be drawn from a classification which lumps the social structures of the New England Yankees with that of the Andaman Islanders is that the originator of the classification has made a singularly poor choice of taxonomic criteria. Let us examine the criteria employed by Murdock for bringing together into one category such unlikely bedfellows. There are nine traits which the Yankees and Andamanese share in common: (1) Bilateral descent, (2) Eskimo cousin terms, (3) Neolocal residence, (4) Absence of clans, (5) Incest prohibitions extended to first cousins, (6) Monogamy, (7) Nuclear family, (8) Lineal aunt terms, and (9) Lineal niece terms (*ibid.*:228). Since three of these nine (2, 8, 9) refer to kinship terminology, we might very well argue that there are really only seven traits in common. But there is no need for pressing in this direction. Let us quickly mention some of the items of social structure which are present among the Yankees, absent among the Andamanese, and ignored by Murdock. Such a list might be expected to contain towns and cities, social classes, endogamous minorities, religious congregations, political parties, benevolent associations, universities, manufacturing companies, jails, state legislatures, municipal councils, law courts, and street corner groups. The Andamanese, for their part, have a few items which Murdock has not managed to squeeze into his check list: the levirate (RADCLIFFE-BROWN 1933:73), infant betrothal (*ibid.*), communal ownership of land (*ibid.*:41), gerontocracy (*ibid.*:44), and the corporate hunting and gathering band. Especially interesting is their highly elaborated adoption system (*ibid.*:77). This institution reduces to a shambles Murdock's claim that the forms of family organization among the Yankees and Andamanese are of the same nuclear family type:

> It is said to be of rare occurence to find any child above six or seven years of age residing with its parents, and this because it is considered a compliment and also a mark of friendship for a married man, after paying a visit, to ask his hosts to allow him to adopt one of their children. The request is usually complied with, and thenceforth the child's home is with his (or her) foster-father; though the parents in their turn adopt the children of other friends, they nevertheless pay continual visits to their own child, and occasionally ask permission (!) to take him (or her) away with them for a few days [*ibid.*].

Is this a way to run a Yankee household?

THE CASE OF THE CHINESE CLAN

The lumping together of Yankee and Andaman social structure fulfills Boas' worst apprehensions concerning the comparative method. Murdock is betrayed into this error by his expectation (is it a hope?) that the blessings of the principle of limited possibilities are reserved only for residence, descent, and terminology. His conclusion strongly suggests the need for a revision of the categories upon which it is based. At the very least, one would expect that it not be paraded to and fro as a wholesome product of superior scientism.

One additional example of violence to context must suffice for our rejoinder to Murdock's denial of evolutionary regularities. Among the allegedly false correlations of the discredited "evolutionists" is the belief that the sib and clan tend to disappear at the state level of organization. "That the sib disappears with the development of the state," writes Murdock, "is negated by the Chinese and the Manchus." (1949:187). This case has been taken up by Morton Fried (1957), who has demonstrated the capricious nature of a taxonomic principle which would lump together the egalitarian, land-owning Iroquois or Tungus sib with the highly stratified Chinese descent groups:

> Chinese social organization includes units which are clearly recognizable as unilineal descent groups. These groups, however, have a number of features which distinguish them from apparently analogous groups. In China there is relative emphasis on familial independence, marked differences between the wealth and authority of the family units, and a formal emphasis on written genealogies. There is also a highly developed ancestor cult which stresses the importance of direct descent from influential progenitors [*ibid.*:16].

It is clear that Murdock can justify the inclusion of his state-level instances of sibs under the same rubric as that under which egalitarian sibs are placed only by ignoring the profound functional differences which pertain in the two classes of instances (*cf.* FREEDMAN 1958: 138ff.). But even were he to insist on the residual similarities which characterize "sibs" under all conditions, he would yet remain very far from sustaining his point about lack of *correlation* between state organization and the disappearance of the sib. To begin to make any headway in this enterprise, one would have to show *correlation*—use a sample—and that he has not done. Why do some theories require a hundred statistical runs to be proven partially true, while others require no statistics whatsoever to be proven entirely false?

This issue is further complicated by Murdock's admission that a statistical treatment of the sib-state relationship would confirm the generally accepted nineteenth-century position: "Political evolution from a gentile to a territorial state, for example, has frequently been followed in Africa, Asia, and Europe, by the disintegration of clans and the weakening of unilinear ties" (*ibid.*:203). But why are there no tables on this subject?

TOWARD A BETTER KIND OF SAMPLE

Part of the answer lies in the nature of the sample which is contained in the Human Relations Area Files. Murdock's basic preoccupation has always been to achieve representativity of world regions and of culture areas within these regions. Although this concern is important and should be maintained, it leaves the question of the representativity of the sample with respect to major types of social structure entirely at the mercy of chance. It thus ignores Steward's critique of the traditional culture area classification. As a result one can not approach the Files with questions involving the frequency with which state-level societies are associated with unilinear descent groups, nor can one inquire how frequently chiefdoms lack such groups, or how frequently band-organized societies practice polygyny.

Nonetheless, it should be pointed out that in the construction of the World Ethnographic Sample, Murdock (1957) has made provisions for overcoming this kind of problem by including at least one example of each basic type of economy represented in each of sixty culture areas. It may be taken as a further sign of Murdock's retreat from the exposed position of *Social Structure* that his contribution to the *Festschrift* for Steward (*Process and Pattern in Culture*) contains the admission that "Levels of political integration, as many studies have shown, tend to be correlated with complexity in subsistence economy and technology and with demographic factors" (MURDOCK 1964:405). With the inclusion of column 38 in the World Ethnographic Sample (MURDOCK 1962), it is now possible to choose a sample which will be approximately representative of different levels of sociocultural integration.

THROW IT AGAINST THE WALL AND SEE IF IT STICKS

A closer look at *Social Structure* thus reveals why the statistical cross-cultural survey method should never be the lone or primary instrument of nomothetic research. The correlations achieved by what has been called "the-throw-it-against-the-wall-and-see-if-it-sticks" technique are unlikely to build on their own toward macrotheory. Let us admit that positive correlations established in the face of the hazards of coding and the unreliability of the sources may nonetheless, barring systematic bias, merit our confidence (*cf.* D. CAMPBELL 1961; 1964; 1965). There remains, however, the problem of the noncorrelations which arise from poor ethnography, biased analysis, faulty coding, and improperly phrased hypotheses. It is quite possible by the throw-it-against-the-wall method to write a hundred trivial equations none of which relate to the others, or all of which relate to each other indiscriminately, and at the same time to get a negative result on the theory which subsumes them all. If we wish to achieve an orderly picture of history, we must begin by assuming that there are certain orderly principles which are at work. And we must use these principles to order and classify the data. We cannot simply throw our data against the wall to see if it sticks according to the predicted pattern. Rather, we must process the data, question it, classify it, and code it, in relation to the expectations of our major premises. Then and only then can we accept a failure to stick to the wall as evidence against the major premise. At the same time, it is only from such a procedure that the particular correlation on each trial may be seen as connected and governed by the general principles of sociocultural evolution.

A close look at Murdock's *Social Structure* in other words reveals that there is no substitute for macro-theory founded on detailed diachronic and synchronic causal-functional analysis of specific cases. It is out of such studies, imperfect as they may have been, that a view of the macro-evolutionary tendencies of sociocultural systems was gradually built up during the past two centuries. The general framework of sociopolitical evolution from paleolithic bands to several different varieties of tribes, chiefdoms, and states is firmly established (*cf.* FRIED 1967). The relative fruitfulness of the techno-economic and techno-environmental explanations is also well established. Classifications which ignore the broad levels of sociocultural evolution and which evade the consequences of cultural materialist causality in the name of inductive purity pursue a false image of science. On the other hand, the utility of the statistical cross-cultural survey is beyond dispute and Tylor's belief that "in statistical investigation the future of anthropology lies" still holds true when statistical investigation is used as a method for revealing unsuspected connections among institutions, for identifying exceptions to regularities, as a measure of probability, and as an indicator for research needs. But it holds true only if we accept the larger theoretical frame within which Tylor sought to encourage the use of his method of "adhesions." It remains true only if we also acknowledge that the major "institutions of man are as distinctly stratified as the earth on which he lives" (1889:269).

Cultural Materialism: General Evolution 22

It is a misfortune, some of whose consequences have already been described, that the return to diachronic and synchronic generalization has acquired the name "neoevolutionism." This label confounds our understanding of the developmental continuities within anthropology by its suggestion of a revival of a doctrine which is associated with the struggle to establish the fact of speciation. Historical particularism, culture and personality, and synchronic functionalism are all perfectly compatible with both biological transformism and cultural transformism. Even the *Kulturkreis* school, in which religious doctrine played a definite supporting role, experienced no difficulty in accepting the fact that cultures evolve and that an explanation for such transformations could be achieved independently of hypothesis of sustained animistic interference. It scarcely strains the canons of scientific respectability of emic and idealist schools to associate their research with causal and evolutionary relations. Mead has made this clear in her recent expression of interest in evolutionary problems. She is perfectly correct in her observation that "most of the interests of cultural anthropologists are embraced by this concept" (MEAD 1964:327). And when she traces the causes of change in Manus society to an eclectic mixture of personalities and cultural setting, she evidently intends more than a local lesson in evolutionary causality. Yet Mead's theoretical position remains largely uninfluenced by the specific kind of causal and evolutionary formulations which are distinctive of the post-Boasian period.

No one has ever denied that cultures evolve in the sense that sociocultural systems undergo cumulative changes roughly analogous to those which eventuate in speciation or stellar and galactic transformations. The point at issue has always been the nature of the process of cultural change. And this dispute has two principal facets: how much parallelism and convergence has there been in sociocultural evolution and what has caused both the observed differences and observed similarities in the evolutionary careers of sociocultural systems?

Neither of the two most important figures associated with the nomothetic revival, namely Leslie White and Julian Steward, has adequately described the shared, novel, and strategically decisive ingredient in their approach. Although White has on occasion (e.g., 1949b) discussed the main issues in anthropological theory in terms of "spiritualistic, vitalistic, or idealistic" versus "mechanistic, materialistic" views, he has given much greater emphasis to, and has become almost exclusively identified with, the defense of evolution. An even more conspicuous avoidance of the discussion of the materialist and idealist options has been characteristic of Steward's treatment of evolution and causality. Yet by objective standards it is the application of the cultural-materialist strategy to the understanding of history which distinguishes their point of view from that of their predecessors and contemporaries.

THE INFLUENCE OF SPENCERISM ON LESLIE WHITE

In order to evaluate the debate between Steward and White, it is necessary first of all to recall our previous discussion concerning the miniscule role of cultural materialism in the works of Tylor and Morgan, by whom White alleges himself to be directly inspired (see Chap. 5). Indeed, White has so adamantly insisted on the continuity of his theories with those of Morgan and Tylor that he has refused to accept the label "neoevolutionist" on the grounds that his own role extends only to the resurrection and not to the remodeling of nineteenth-century anthropological evolutionary theory:

> But let it be said, and with emphasis, that the theory set forth here cannot properly be called "neoevolutionism," a term proposed by Lowie, Goldenweiser, Bennett, Nunomura (in Japan), and others. Neoevolutionism is a misleading term: it has been used to imply that the theory of evolution today is somehow different from the theory of eighty years ago. We reject any such notion. The *theory* of evolution set forth in this work does not differ one whit in principle from that expressed in Tylor's *Anthropology* in 1881, although of course the development, expression, and demonstration of the theory may—and does—differ at some points. "Neo-Lamarckism," "neoplatonism," etc. are valid terms, but "neoevolutionism," "neogravitationism," "neoerosionism," etc., are not [WHITE 1959b:ix].

Although White has repeatedly stressed his indebtedness to Tylor, Morgan, and Darwin, there are two fundamental discrepancies in this picture. First, insofar as materialism figures in the outlook of these founding fathers, it is the materialism of Spencerism—the explanation of sociocultural differences in terms of biological selection. White, on the other hand, has devoted a massive effort to the criticism of both psychological and biological reductionism. His refrain, "Culture must be explained in terms of culture" (1949a:141), is opposed not only to Steward's admission of the importance of environmental factors but to the theories of Morgan and Tylor as well. Second, White's "Basic Law of Evolution" has no precedent among the nineteenth-century evolutionists with whom he seeks to align his work. This law reads as follows:

> Other factors remaining constant, culture evolves as the amount of energy harnessed per capita per year is increased, or as the efficiency of the means of putting the energy to work is increased [*ibid.*:368–69; orig. 1943].

White's "law" sounds like a definition more than a statement of covariance. From the actual context, however, it is clear that it is neither a law nor a definition but rather a statement of research strategy.

WHITE'S BASIC STRATEGY

This strategy is the strategy of cultural materialism, phrased in energy terms. It is employed by White as the point of departure for the analysis of major trends with respect to both local and worldwide evolutionary modifications. The linkage with cultural materialism and with Marx (and not with Morgan, Tylor, and Spencer) is made clear during the course of the application of the "law of evolution" to the explanation of the major outlines of world history. For White proposes to regard sociocultural systems as consisting of three parts: techno-economic, social, and ideological; and he states the causal relationships among these divisions in unmistakable terms:

> Culture thus becomes primarily a mechanism for harnessing energy and of putting it to work in the service of man, and, secondarily, of channelling and regulating his behavior not directly concerned with subsistence and offense and defense. Social systems are therefore determined by technological systems, and philosophies and the arts express experience as it is defined by technology and refracted by social systems [*ibid.*:390–91].

UN-AMERICAN ANTHROPOLOGICAL ACTIVITIES

In her contribution to the *Festschrift* for White (*Essays in the Science of Culture*), Betty Meggers (1960:302–3) wrote:

> The law of energy and cultural evolution was first set forth by White in 1943. . . . This law is based on the recognition that all cultures are composed of three general classes of phenomena: technology, social organization, and philosophy. Of these, technology is primary and determines the content and form of the other two components.

This provided the occasion for an illuminating exchange between Meggers and Morris Opler, one of the relatively few figures in anthropology who may be reckoned as well-acquainted with Marxist theory. Opler's point was that it was Marx and the Marxists, especially Nikolai Bukharin (1925), who were the true authors of "White's Law," despite the failure of White and his followers to cite these sources. Opler was intent on making this point because he apparently sought to damage the scientific status of the cultural-materialist position by emphasizing its incorporation into Communist dogma: "Apparently the 'practical tool kit' Dr. Meggers urges upon the field anthropologists is not quite so new as she represents, and its main contents seem to be a somewhat shopworn hammer and sickle" (1961:13). The impropriety of this remark is made all the more noteworthy by Opler's failure to point out the reasons why White's ideas could not conceivably be embraced by Communist doctrine. With his knowledge of Marxist literature, Opler is in no need of being reminded that it takes more than cultural materialism to qualify for Communist approval. One must also accept the dialectic nature of evolutionary process, especially as related to the primacy of conflict in structural change. One must at least be a dialectical materialist, accepting the

Hegelian element in Marx, in order to put the "hammer and sickle" in one's tool kit. White, who has never indicated the slightest interest in dialectics, qualifies therefore for one of the worst epithets in the Communist arsenal of antiheretical verbiage: he is what Engels was the first to call a "mechanical materialist."

It would be pointless to elaborate the aspects of White's views which falsify Opler's innuendo. The question of whether or not cultural materialism is a sound strategy for social science cannot be left to depend on whether those who espouse it would or would not be acceptable to the House Un-American Activities Committee. Scientific facts and theories cannot be tested by loyalty oaths. That the Russian geneticists were ultimately triumphant over their government's attempt to purge them of "bourgeois" Mendelian principles is an encouraging sign for all of the sciences. Although the pressure to purge Western social science of theories of cultural materialism has not been as direct (barring the McCarthy interlude), its palpable effects are ubiquitous: Western social scientists confront a situation strictly analogous to the former plight of the Soviet Mendelian geneticists. It is as if merely by virtue of the fact that Communists have politicized the meaning of cultural materialism that it must therefore be rejected as a valid strategy for nomothetic inquiry. But we cannot permit ourselves to be cut off from the valid contributions of Marx simply because our national ideology is deeply committed to the suppression of Marxist thought in total. Just as our physicists, chemists, physiologists, and mathematicians have established for themselves the right to use the products of scientific discovery regardless of the political milieu in which these have originated, so, too, must cultural anthropology feel free to use the discoveries of social scientists wherever and whenever they help to answer the questions in which we are interested.

THE ANTHROPOLOGIST IS NOT FOR BURNING

Opler expressed amazement that anyone discussing White's variety of techno-economic determinism could have attributed its beginnings to the early 1940's (actually, all that Meggers intended to do was to give the date of White's statement, not the origin of the law).

> It seems incredible that anyone seeking to place in time and in the history of theory a point of view which systematically subordinates the social and ideological to the technological should completely overlook Marx and Engels and their heirs. It is curious

> that our neo-evolutionists constantly acknowledge their debt to Darwin, Tylor, and Morgan and never have a word to say about the relation of their ideas to those of Marx, Engels, Bukharin, Plekhanov, Labriola, Suvorov, Lenin, Stalin, *et al.* Yet it is patent that their formulations are a great deal closer to those of Bukharin and, indeed, to those of any thoroughgoing historical materialist than they can ever be to those of Tylor or Morgan. What they share with Tylor and Morgan is a conviction that cultural evolution has taken place. With Marx, Engels, Bukharin, Plekhanov, Labriola, and the others they share, in addition, convictions concerning the elements and mechanisms through which the process occurs. This close correspondence may be an instance of parallelism. It may be the result of stimulus diffusion. There is the possibility of lineal or collateral descent. It could reflect still other dynamic forces. It might be helpful to know what is involved. At any rate, before it becomes a matter of total assimilation, anthropologists might well take a closer look at recent intellectual history and at some recent trends in American ethnology [*ibid.*:18].

Yet Opler's incredulity is misplaced; what is hard to believe is that Opler does not know from firsthand experience the real reason for the avoidance of Marxist references by anthropologists who have discovered, or rediscovered, Marx's contribution to the strategy of cultural materialism. It is incredible, since Opler himself, with his political innuendo, reveals himself fully prepared to expose and jeopardize his colleagues before the political passions of the times.

WHITE'S CONVERSION

Despite the almost complete lack of reference to Marx and the Marxist literature in White's books and articles, White's involvement with cultural materialism need not be ferreted out by lengthy citations of Bukharin's treatment of energy and technology. In Harry E. Barnes's "Foreword" to White's *Festschrift*, the same volume in which Meggers provoked Opler's attack, there appears a clear-cut statement of the relationship between White's conversion to evolutionism and his exposure to Marxist theories. During his graduate studies, White had acquired a strong Boasian outlook. At the New School in New York, he was taught by Alexander Goldenweiser; and at the University of Chicago, where he obtained his degree in 1927, he was influenced by the Boasians, Fay-Cooper Cole and Edward Sapir. His first anthropological article (1925) was a typically Boasian plea for the importance of the cultural factor in the determination of personality and was in many ways parallel to the program upon which Margaret Mead was about to embark. The beginning of White's shift to an implacably anti-Boasian position took place during the two years that he taught at the University of Buffalo. Since this was Iroquois territory, he was obliged to read Morgan for the first time. And he was shocked as anyone must be who had accepted Morgan as a worthless example of speculative philosophy on the basis of secondhand opinion. It was at this point that he discovered that Morgan was a "remarkable scholar, savant, and personality." The step from Morgan to Marx via Engels was inevitable, and in 1929 White was deeply enough involved in Marxist matters to take time out for a trip to the Soviet Union.

> The final step in Dr. White's conversion to enthusiastic evolutionism was a tour through Russia and Georgia in 1929, during which he first made his acquaintance in any thorough manner with the literature of Marx and Engels, particularly those portions dealing with the nature and development of civilization. In his treatment of the origins of the family, Engels had made especially wide use of the views of Morgan on social evolution and thus tended to impress Dr. White still further with the validity and importance of the evolutionary approach. The writings of Marx and Engels also helped to reveal the reasons that Morgan's theory of the role of property in cultural development was so vigorously attacked by Catholic scholars and by capitalist historians and economists [H. E. BARNES 1960:xxvi].

There is no need to repeat here the arguments against White's equation of antievolutionism with the central theoretical and factual errors of the historical-particularist school. We may take this whole issue as evidence of the extraordinary trauma which social science in the United States had experienced as a result of its isolation from Marxist viewpoints. White returned from the Soviet Union to take up a teaching position at the University of Michigan, where he ultimately succeeded in building one of the country's major centers of anthropology. Although White was uncompromisingly and outspokenly hostile to historical particularism, to psychological reductionism, to doctrines of free will and theological teleology, and to almost every other shibboleth of the Midwestern milieu in which he operated, he managed to avoid placing his critique within the arena of Marxist disputation. Perhaps this was made possible because the level of anthropological theory had slipped back so far toward a prescientific condition that there was enough to do merely by way of recapturing the ground upon which Marx had built without going beyond or even equaling Marx's own contributions. Nonetheless, many themes in White's publications were fully anticipated by Marx and Engels. This should be understood to include Marx and Engels's reworking of Morgan, for when White speaks of himself as an evolutionist following in Morgan's footsteps, it is the Morgan as reinterpreted by Engels in the *Origin of the Family, Private Property, and the State* of whom we must think.

WHITE'S DEFENSE OF MORGAN AND TYLOR

White's crusade on behalf of the defeat of the "antievolutionists" in order to restore *the* theory of evolution to its former prominence has produced irrelevant polemics. Kroeber (1948c), Lowie (1946; 1957), and Steward (1955) joined with him in discussions which have obscured the basic simplicity of White's point. The theory of evolution for White is "the old and simple concept so well expressed by Tylor: . . . the great principle that every scholar must lay firm hold of, if he intends to understand either the world he lives in or the history of the past" (WHITE 1959b:125). Returning to the full context of this "great principle," we find:

> On the whole, it appears that wherever there are found elaborate arts, abstruse knowledge, complex institutions, these are results of gradual development from an earlier, simpler, and ruder state of life. No stage of civilization comes into existence spontaneously, but grows or is developed out of the stage before it. This is the great principle which every scholar must lay firm hold of . . . [TYLOR 1881:20].

The perfect acceptability of this kind of evolutionism to the Boasian stalwarts has already been discussed.

As long as there is no claim to the effect that all cultures must pass through a specific set of stages, no Boasian would ever deny that a series of worldwide evolutionary stages can be identified. Yet White has insisted over and over again in his defense of his nineteenth-century evolutionist heroes that they never proposed that all cultures necessarily passed through the same set of stages, e.g., Savagery, Barbarism, Civilization. To speak of the position of Morgan and Tylor in terms of such an impoverished antinomy is misleading. It was not an all or nothing question for them nor is it one for us. As Sahlins and Service (1960:12) have observed, Tylor "laid out the study of cultural evolution both stage by stage as well as along its many lines." The only issue worth discussing is the frequency of convergence and parallelism; not whether there are exceptions to the regularities of history, but rather how frequently these occur.

In the perspective of Tylor and Morgan, there is no doubt that the parallelism and convergence were often assumed to be far more frequent than the facts have subsequently justified. For example, it was because of Morgan's faith in the uniformity of the historical experiences of widely separated cultures that he was led to argue, on the basis of fragmentary evidence, that the Aztec were in a stage of culture which was not significantly different from that of the Iroquois. It was a similar faith in the uniformity of history which led Morgan to suppose that his fragmentary data on archaic Greece was adequate for identifying the matrilineal stage.

When Tylor spoke of the tendency of the experience of mankind to move through uniform channels, it was not to say that mankind in general as distinct from mankind in particular cultures shared these channels. Such a distinction is a refinement for which White's heroes had no need. Tylor meant that most (not all) cultures unfolded along similar lines (see p. 171). The exceptions, recognized by both Tylor and Morgan, were explicable in terms of race, diffusion, and environmental specialties.

White has used this recognition of diffusion and local perturbations in the evolutionary sequence to distort the theories of the nineteenth-century evolutionists into a shape convenient for the maintenance of "evolutionism" as the center of twentieth-century controversy. He has argued that their evolutionism was not one of particular times and places but rather of the world as a whole. It is clear, however, that their interests encompassed both levels of generalization.

UNILINEAR, UNIVERSAL, AND MULTILINEAR EVOLUTION

In an attempt to formalize the differences between himself and White on the issue of evolutionism, Steward (1955) has proposed a threefold classification of evolutionary approaches: unilinear, universal, and multilinear. The unilinear, says Steward, was characteristic of the "classical" evolutionists who "dealt with particular cultures, placing them in stages of a universal sequence" (1955:14). Morgan and Tylor fit in this category. But every one of the "classical" evolutionists also fit in Steward's second ("universal") category: "a rather arbitrary label" to designate White's "revamping of unilinear evolution" and which "is concerned with culture rather than cultures." Steward's third brand of evolutionism is called "multilinear evolution." This is defined as follows:

> . . . it is interested in particular cultures, but instead of finding local variations and diversity troublesome facts which force the frame of reference from the particular to the general, it deals only with those limited parallels of form, function, and sequence which have empirical validity [*ibid.*:19].

The inadequacy of this classification is shown by the fact that the two anthropologists whom Steward nominates for universal evolutionism, namely White and V. Gordon Childe, are equally good contenders for at least one of the other categories. White, as much as the classical evolutionists, has attempted to locate specific cultures in relationship to universal schemes (i.e., unilinear evolutionism). And in his most sustained substantive treatment of evolution, *The Evolution of Culture* (1959b), White not only attempts to trace the whole course of cultural development, from the transition of anthropoid to human society to the beginnings of the iron age, but he also reconstructs specific cultural sequences in the light of the general trends manifest in the universal sequence. In Australia, for example, the Arunta system of marriage classes is said to have evolved from the Kariera type of relationship to "a higher stage of cultural development and social evolution" when "the maximum effectiveness of the cooperative group formed by marriage could not be achieved by union between first cousins" (1959b:173). More commonly, it is White's practice to interpret the significance of various institutions in particular societies on the assumption that the culture has reached a certain level of evolution. Thus, his treatment of social stratification in Polynesia and the Northwest Coast draws heavily on the universalistic generalization (first advanced by the Edinburgh School in the eighteenth century) that "it is not until kinship has ceased to be the basis of social systems and society has become organized on the basis of property relations and territorial distinctions that true classes of subordination and superordination come into being" (*ibid.*:203).

WHITE AND CHILDE AS MULTILINEAR EVOLUTIONISTS

In every respect, White's *The Evolution of Culture* is the modern equivalent of Morgan's *Ancient Society*, the only difference being the updating of some of the ethnography and the greater consistency of the cultural-materialist thread. White has explicitly rejected Steward's attempt to make the "house of evolutionism" . . . "falsely divided against itself" (1959a:125). Programmatically, at least, he has embraced all of the varieties of evolution set forth by Steward:

> It follows from the foregoing that culture may be regarded as a one or as a many, as an all-inclusive system—the culture of mankind as a whole—or as an indefinite number of subsystems of two different kinds: (1) the cultures of peoples or regions, and (2) subdivisions such as writing, mathematics, currency, metallurgy, social organization, etc. Mathematics, language, writing, architecture, social organization, etc. may each be considered as a one or a many, also; one may work out the evolution of mathematics as a whole, or a number of lines of development may be distinguished. Evolutionist interpretations of culture will therefore be both unilinear and multilinear. One type of interpretation is as valid as the other; each implies the other [WHITE 1959b: 30–31].

As for the universal evolutionism of V. Gordon Childe, there must be taken into consideration not only Childe's adherence to Morgan's universal stages of Savagery, Barbarism, and Civilization in the presentation of the Middle Eastern archaeological sequences, but also Childe's highly particularistic treatment of the emergence of a distinctly European culture area (CHILDE 1946; 1958). In actual practice, Childe is even more inclined toward multilinear evolution than is Steward:

> So on the whole archaeology does not hold out much prospect of correlating social institutions with stages of cultural development as defined in economic terms. But, after all, we have seen that such stages, apart from the three main status, are themselves hard, if not impossible to define. For within the status of barbarianism at least, the observable cultural sequences do not follow parallel lines [CHILDE 1951a:165–66].

As a matter of fact, Childe goes on to compare the diversity of cultural evolution with the Darwinian model of a tree "with branches all up the trunk and each branch bristling with twigs" (*ibid.*:166), and this is none other than the extreme limiting case of multilinear evolution.

EVOLUTIONARY MODES AND EPISTEMOLOGY

It is evident that the three evolutionary modes defined by Steward are not mutually exclusive. It is also evident that the logic of Steward's categories rests on a continuum involving degrees of abstraction away from the description of specific cases.

At one end of this continuum there is the evolutionary transformation which is characterized by or known through one case. For example, one might want to consider the development of a four-caste apartheid system (Africans, Europeans, Coloreds, and Asians) as an evolutionary product peculiar to South Africa. Similarly, the Natchez system of exogamous castes is not reported elsewhere, yet it is obviously resultant of a process of transformation (whose stages are as yet unknown).

On a slightly higher level of generality, we may note the evolutionary products characteristic of several societies within a single culture area. The peculiar Australian speciality involving eight marriage sections is an evolutionary product of the transformation of two- and four-section systems. Parallelisms involving one or two cultures in several different culture areas also occur, as in the case of matrisibs in the Eastern Woodlands, West Africa, and Melanesia.

Finally, there are the universal evolutionary products such as the nuclear family incest taboos or the belief in animism.

All of these categories can be expanded or contracted indefinitely in accordance with the amount of ethnographic detail which is required before we are willing to grant that two instances are the "same" or different. Universal evolutionism merely represents an extreme expansion of the tolerated degree of abstraction. Distinctions otherwise relevant between patrilateral and matrilateral marriage exchange system are canceled out and the remainder scooped up under the rubric "kinship regulation of marriage"; or endogamous hierarchies in India, the United States, and South Africa are treated as "caste system." By ignoring millions of trivial differences, in order to emphasize a few significant similarities, we arrive at such theoretically vital notions as egalitarian societies, state organization, feudalism, capitalism, or oriental despotism. Conversely, with a sufficiently intense historical-particularist mandate, we may prove to our satisfaction that the state of affairs in eleventh century France had no parallel anywhere else in Europe, much less in Japan or West Africa. The mutual failure of both White and Steward to grasp the epistemological issues which underly our judgments concerning evolutionarily significant similarities and differences goes a long way toward explaining the prolongation of their controversy beyond useful limits. This failure is especially acute in relationship to White's refusal to admit that certain transformations studied by Steward qualify as "evolutionary" phenomena.

WHEN IS CHANGE EVOLUTION?

My intent here is not to arbitrate the controversy over what is or is not evolutionary. Nothing could be more fruitless. The point at which the accumulation of changes in an old form results in the identification of a new form—in a "temporal sequence of forms"—is not a matter for research. The predictable end result of the further discussion of this theme is that differences of opinion will be resolved by introducing a few new terms (how about "minor," "major," and "mega" evolution?). The matter for research as distinct from philosophical disputation is: What causes the observed changes, be they small or large, "systems" or "mere aggregates"? Whatever causes small-scale changes must be important for an understanding of large-scale changes; conversely, whatever causes large-scale changes must be important for an understanding of the small-scale ones. Thus we have the mutual relevance of genetics and natural selection in the theory of bio-evolution; and of the physical chemistry of stars and the evolution of galactic forms.

WHITE'S CRITERIA OF EVOLUTION

Phrasing the nomothetic revival in terms of evolutionism has meant that the search for the underlying causal processes responsible for cultural differences and similarities has become mired in scholastic dichotomies. White has attacked Steward for studying nonevolutionary changes on the model of historical particularism, and Steward has attacked White for his grandiose generalizations. In reviewing Steward's *Theory of Culture Change*, White (1957:541) declares:

> Steward falls between the two poles of idiographic and nomothetic interpretation, between the particular and the general. He is not content with mere particulars, but he cannot go the whole hog of generalizations. He wants generalizations but, as he says repeatedly, they must be of limited scope (*Theory*, p. 22 et passim). Try to imagine a law of falling bodies, or of gravitation, of limited scope. Steward resembles one who discovers that this river and that flow down hill but is unwilling to go so far as to assert that "rivers flow down hill."

The particular transformation which White rejects as an example of evolution concerns two American Indian groups, the horticultural Brazilian Mundurucu Indians and the Algonquin hunters and gatherers of Canada. In a convergent fashion these tribes responded to

European contact by shifting to dependence upon the production of trade goods—furs in one case and rubber in the other. One group became "tappers," the other, "trappers." But the involvement with the trading post through debt obligations followed a similar line of development despite the different techno-environmental relationship (MURPHY and STEWARD 1955). For Steward these transformations represent convergent evolutionary sequences. White (1959a:122), however, demands to know, "What justification is there for calling them lines of evolution?"

In other studies by Steward, such as the comparison of the development of civilization in Mesopotamia and Peru, White is willing to grant that we have examples of "true evolutionary processes." But this

> . . . is a fundamentally different kind of process than the simple like cause, like effect occurrences in Steward's tappers and trappers example. Thus some, or at least one, of the "lines of evolution" he describes (Steward, 1956) turns out to be a genuine evolutionary process; others are not evolutionist at all [*ibid.*].

But if evolution is "a temporal sequence of forms" (WHITE 1959b:30), how is it possible to deny that the Munducuru have undergone evolutionary change during their transformation from horticultural tribesmen to debt-bound rubber collectors? Perhaps an answer could be built around White's declaration that "only systems can evolve; a mere aggregation of things without organic unity cannot undergo evolution" (*ibid.*). But he would have great difficulty in convincing the majority of anthropologists that the Munducuru's subsistence patterns are a "mere aggregation." Or perhaps, in order for White to accept a cultural change as evolutionary, it must have produced a transformation on a certain scale, measured perhaps in energy quanta. If so, White has nowhere proposed what quantitative operations would be required.

STEWARD'S CRITIQUE OF WHITE

Steward, on his part, has condemned the universal evolutionist approach of White and Childe for its inability to come to grips with the question of specific cultural differences and similarities as distinct from the vague and unilluminating generalities of universal laws. Steward's comments hark back to the Boasian response to highly generalized evolutionism:

> The postulated cultural sequences are so general that they are neither very arguable nor very useful. No one disputes that hunting and gathering, which is Childe's diagnostic of "savagery," preceded plant and animal domestication which is his criterion of "barbarism," and that the latter was a precondition of large populations, cities, internal social differentiation and specialization, and the development of writing and mathematics, which are characteristics of "civilization." . . . It is certainly a worthy objective to seek universal laws of cultural change. It must be stressed, however, that all universal laws thus far postulated are concerned with the fact that culture changes—that any culture changes—and thus cannot explain particular features of particular cultures [STEWARD 1955:17–18].

In Steward's (1960:146) review of White's *Evolution of Culture* the same point is directed specifically at White's own evolutionary formulations:

> Regarding the causal chain that begins with technology and control of energy and runs through society to religion, there can be little disagreement with the self-evident proposition that "as the amount of energy harnessed by sociocultural systems increases per capita per year, the systems not only increase in size, but become more highly evolved, i.e. . . . more differentiated structurally and more specialized functionally" (pp. 39-40). But this does not at all explain what kinds of social structures arise from the utilization of technologies in particular environments. White concedes (p. 41) that "technological and environmental factors both operate to produce cultural differences quite apart from the source and magnitude of energy harnessed," but he is not interested in these differences and states (p. 51) that "if one . . . wishes to discover how cultural systems are structured and how they function . . . then *one does not need to consider the natural habit at all*," for he is really concerned with "*how and why the culture of mankind as a whole has grown*" [italics Steward's].

WHITE'S DEFENSE

White's response to such criticism is singularly unconvincing. He argues that general laws are not supposed to explain particular events. The kinds of problems which Steward wishes to handle under multilinear evolution really belong in the historical-particularist tradition. It is Steward's training in the "atomistic, idiographic, there-is-no-rhyme-or-reason-to-cultural-phenomena tradition of the Boas school" which is at fault:

> The predicament in which we find Steward, suspended between the particular on the one hand and the general on the other, may also be illustrated by citing his objection to broad generalizations or "universal laws," as he calls them: they "cannot explain particular features of particular cultures" (Theory, p. 18). Of course they cannot! This is precisely the characteristic of a generalization or law; particulars are subsumed under the universal. The law of gravitation cannot tell us whether the falling body is a rock or a feather, much less whether the one is sandstone or the other a heron plume. And this is precisely why the law of gravitation—or any other scientific law—has value: because it is a universal, i.e., tells us nothing about particulars as particulars [WHITE 1957:541].

Does the law of gravitation tell us nothing about particulars? When one predicts a particular eclipse on a particular planet of a particular sun by a particular moon, has this no relation to the general law? White undoubtedly means to say something else, to wit: no general law tells us *everything* about particulars. Hence our lack of information about whether falling bodies are rocks or feathers. But if a generalization tells us *nothing* about particulars, it can scarcely enjoy the status of an empirical proposition.

THE NEED FOR STATEMENTS OF COVARIANCE

A closer look at what White means by cultural "laws" or generalizations will help us overcome the muddle of evolutionism and antievolutionism. Two very different kinds of propositions are offered by White, only one of which might conceivably qualify for the status of lawful generalization. The kind which definitely does not qualify is that which sums up universal cultural evolution with observations like:

> As society evolved under the impetus of increased technological control over nature, the processes of exogamy and endogamy operated to increase the size of the cooperative group of kindred while at the same time maintaining its solidarity and effectiveness. The radius of kinship was extended until the boundaries of the community were reached; eventually the whole tribe became a unified, integrated group of kindred living together on terms of mutual aid.
>
> Custom in general and special codes of etiquette and ethics served to integrate and regulate societies. Classes were defined

> and kept intact by rules of etiquette; the general welfare was fostered by ethical rules. Division of labor and specialization of function marked the course of social evolution [WHITE 1959b:275].

If we take White's separation of the particular from the general at face value, these statements all reduce to the form: in the history of hominid culture on planet earth, cultural form *x* was followed by cultural form *y* at unknown times and places. It is of absolutely no significance in the logico-empirical structure of these statements whether each stage in the alleged sequence occurred often, sometimes, or only once. These are not, in other words, statements of covariance.

In order to achieve nomothetic status these summaries of world history must be rephrased into the form of propositions about covariance, from which probabilistic predictions and retrodictions about specific cultures can be made. Thus: At a certain level of technological control (to be more precisely defined), we expect to find kinship extended to the boundaries of the community with a probability greater than chance. Of course, as soon as we phrase White's generalization in this form, we see at once that the disdain for the particular case cannot be reconciled with the quest for generality. The generality is nothing but the sum or average of the particular case.

Of greater interest in the context of our discussion concerning cultural materialism is the task of converting White's alleged "law" of evolution to genuine nomothetic status. A statement of covariance of a sort implicit in White's techno-economic determinism ("culture evolves as the energy in the system increases") might take the form: When the ratio of technological efficiency in food production (calorie output per calorie input per total man hours of production) exceeds 20:1, the probability that stratified endogamous descent groups will be found is greater than chance (*cf.* HARRIS 1959a). As we shall see in a moment, not only does this reformulation oblige us to become concerned with particular measurements of particular culture systems, but it also obliges us to calculate the effect of specific environments on technologically mediated productive processes.

CULTURAL MATERIALISM AND THE EXPLANATION OF SPECIFIC CASES

There is another kind of interpretation of White's energy "law" which possesses utility as a kind of meta-generalization rather than as a statement of covariance. It is this reformulation which actually deserves our greatest attention, because it amounts to nothing less than a statement of the research strategy through which one proposes to arrive at the formulation of the most productive statements of diachronic and synchronic regularities. This is the strategy which often reluctantly acknowledges its debt to Marx: The most powerful generalizations about history are to be found by studying the relationship between the qualitative and quantitative aspects of culture energy systems as the independent variables and the quantitative and qualitative aspects of the other domains of sociocultural phenomena as the dependent ones. It needs to be emphasized in this context that the meta-generalization embodied in the cultural-materialist research strategy is fully analogous to and at least as well vindicated by specific cases as the vaunted "principle of natural selection" in biology.

The implication in White's proposals concerning nomothetic explanations to which we must take vigorous exception is that cultural materialism as a general strategy leads only to highly abstract evolutionary sequences. It must be affirmed that this strategy need not limit itself to the vapid generalizations with which White has sometimes tried the patience of his colleagues. It leads as well to the understanding of particular cases in all their detail in so far as such an understanding can be achieved with reference to nomothetic, as distinct from strictly historical, relations. We may credit White therefore with the formulation of this strategy (under the pseudonym of evolutionism), but we must also note his failure to apply it to specific cases.

SPECIFIC AND GENERAL EVOLUTION

Recently, an attempt has been made to reconcile Steward's and White's views through the recognition of two different varieties of evolution, "specific" and "general." The authors of this proposal, Marshall Sahlins and Elman Service, have been students and colleagues of both White and Steward, a circumstance which accounts in part for their mission of reconciliation. The failure to keep in mind the dual character of evolution, a concept well expressed by Tylor and upheld by the biologist Julian Huxley, is alleged to be "at the very heart of the confusion and polemical controversy about such terms as 'unilinear,' 'multilinear,' and 'universal evolution' as well as about the differences between 'history' and 'evolution'" (SAHLINS and SERVICE 1960:12). According to Sahlins and Service:

> . . . evolution moves simultaneously in two directions. On the one side, it creates diversity through adaptive modification: new

> forms differentiate from old. On the other side, evolution generates progress: higher forms arise from, and suppress, lower [*ibid.*:12-13].

Specific evolution thus seems to be equated with divergence and adaptation to local natural and cultural habitats; general evolution, with stages of progress.

It cannot be said that this formulation achieves the desired reconciliation of Steward's cultural ecology with White's universal evolutionism. Neither specific nor general evolution is readily applicable to the facts of cultural transformations. By seeming to equate adaptation with divergence, Sahlins and Service appear to overlook a salient characteristic of both cultural and biological evolution: convergence and parallelism. That is, adaptation produces both divergence *and* convergence.

These impressions are reinforced when they further insist that the study of specific evolution requires a "phylogenetic" approach to taxonomy as opposed to the taxonomy of general evolution which requires "stages" or "levels" (*ibid.*). It is a capital error to employ the concept of phylogeny (even as analogy) in relation to cultural forms, since (as Sahlins and Service very well know) there is no resemblance between the mechanisms responsible for cultural continuity and those responsible for biological reproduction. Phylogeny is an expression of the capacity of bioforms to differentiate to the point where gene exchange no longer takes place. Phylogeny implies speciation, and there is no concept less applicable to cultural evolution than that of biological "species." The adaptive significance of culture in the evolution of the biosphere is precisely its exploitation of a nongenetic feedback circuit which permits adaptation without speciation. All sociocultural systems can exchange parts with each other, a situation whose startling effects in biology would be appreciated were pigeons and elephants to mate and reproduce whenever they enjoyed each other's company for any length of time.

That the difference between Steward and White cannot be composed by equating Steward's approach with specific evolution is immediately apparent if we consider Steward's interest in limited parallels. The taxonomy which results from, or is appropriate to, such a study can scarcely be called phylogenetic (even after making due allowances for the inappropriateness of the term for *any* cultural process), since it is avowedly concerned with regularities which occur in widely scattered parts of the world. Yet Steward calls the process "adaptation." Obviously this "adaptation" is concerned not with specific cultures in specific environments but with a class of cultures in a class of environments, mediated by a class of technological inventories. Indeed, it can be argued that in both biological and cultural evolution, the only practical method for identifying "adaptive" traits is to employ the comparative method, which, of course, is nothing but the search for nonphylogenetic regularities under conditions of controlled comparison. The only way to compose the difference between Steward and White is to realize that the problem is quantitative, not qualitative. As we have already seen, if Steward's regularities occur with sufficient frequency and embrace sufficiently broad categories of transformations, White experiences no difficulty in admitting the process as evolutionary.

PROGRESS AGAIN

Sahlins and Service's concept of "general evolution" suffers from an additional grave defect. Insofar as Sahlins and Service follow White's lead and emphasize the importance of energy quanta as a measure of general evolution, their discussion conforms to the cultural-materialist strategy and is unobjectionable, if highly programmatic. It is regrettable, however, that these same criteria are offered as measures not only of successively better adapted sociocultural systems but also as a measure of evolutionary "progress."

In the former case, we merely predict that adapted systems tend to be replaced by other adapted systems, the later ones in the series being thermodynamically larger and more efficient than the earlier ones. There is no doubt that this generalization is broadly true of both biological and cultural evolution. It is quite another matter, however, to affix the term "progress" to the observed trend. This seems like a deliberate re-exposure of all the raw nerves associated with nineteenth-century Euro-American ethnocentrism and with the discredited attempt to read a moral lesson out of the facts of biological evolutionary processes. It is obvious that no matter how certain it is that thermodynamically smaller and less efficient cultures will be replaced by larger and more efficient ones, we are under no obligation to like it or to believe it to be morally good and proper. Calling negative entropy "progress" does not enhance our understanding of the conditions under which culture energy systems evolve to higher levels of productivity and efficiency.

Cultural Materialism: Cultural Ecology 23

The attempt to reconcile Steward with White does not require further elaborations of a typology of evolutionism. The central question is to what extent the strategy employed by Steward corresponds to the cultural-materialist formulation which underlies White's evolutionary and energetistic pronouncements. It can be shown that Steward has led his contemporaries in actually applying cultural-materialist principles to the solution of concrete questions concerning cultural differences and similarities. Unlike White, Steward has sought to identify the material condition of sociocultural life in terms of the articulation between production processes and habitat. His cultural materialism resides in this pragmatic venture to which he himself gives the title "the method of cultural ecology."

It will obviously not be possible to review any significant proportion of the anthropological research which has been undertaken in conformity with ecological versions of cultural materialism. Even to give summary treatment to the work carried out by those who have been directly influenced by Steward—Sidney Mintz (1956), Eric Wolf (1957; 1966), Morton Fried (1952; 1967), Elman Service

(1955; 1962), René Millon (1967), Andrew Vayda (1956; 1961c), Robert Manners (1956), F. Lehman (1963)—could prove an exhausting task.

The list of anthropologists who have benefited indirectly from Steward's treatment of techno-environmental and techno-economic interactions is proportionally larger and includes, at this date, many younger figures who take their cultural ecology for granted, and who acknowledge Steward's contribution only by means of criticism aimed at disproving some of his specific ecological explanations on the basis of new data.

Nothing would be more contrary to the general frame of reference advocated in this book than to explain the recent prominence of ecological studies as a result of Steward's personal influence. The mounting interest in techno-environmental and techno-economic relationships reflects a broad movement aimed at strengthening the scientific credentials of cultural anthropology within the prestigious and well-funded natural sciences. Cultural ecology, precisely because it links emic phenomena with the etic conditions of "nature," strengthens the association between social science and the "harder" disciplines. In a synchronic mode it thus promotes research involving cooperation with the general medical sciences, biology, nutrition, demography, and agronomy, all of which enjoy high levels of economic support. Applied diachronically, the ecological approach establishes a similar set of ties between archaeology and numerous specialties within geology and paleontology. The contemporary premium upon scientism thus makes the expansion of cultural ecological research almost inevitable. Predictably, however, the movement to take up the cultural-materialist option in the guise of cultural ecology has failed to link itself with the historical precedent of Marx's proposals. Indeed, one of the most fascinating aspects of Steward's contribution to the revival of nomothetic inquiry is the slow but unacknowledged rediscovery or reinvention of principles long ago made explicit in Marx's "Preface" to *The Critique of Political Economy* (see p. 229).

MULTILINEAR EVOLUTIONISM NOT A METHODOLOGY

The link between cultural ecology and cultural materialism has been obscured by the spurious issue of evolutionism. This has provided Steward with the impetus to think of cultural ecology as a kind of evolutionism rather than as a kind of determinism. Indeed, he would have us believe that "Cultural evolution may be regarded as a special type of historical reconstruction or as a particular methodology or approach" (1955:27). "Multilinear evolution is essentially a methodology based on the assumption that significant regularities in cultural change occur, and it is concerned with the determination of cultural laws" (*ibid.*). Now, the establishment of the lines of cultural evolution might be an important result of research oriented by the assumption that there are regularities in cultural change. Such regularities would presumably eventuate in certain lines occurring repeatedly in separate regions of the world in which similar conditions obtain. But to call multilinear evolutionism the *method* by which this assumption is brought to the research phase is a malapropism which has the unfortunate consequence of distracting us from the true nature of Steward's methodological contribution. In contrast to that method and its brilliant concrete results, to which we shall turn in a moment, Steward's concept of multilinear evolution is all the more regrettable.

HOW MANY IS MULTI-?

Multilinear evolution, Steward says, "deals only with those limited parallels of form, function, and sequence which have empirical reality" (*ibid.*:19). This is equivalent to the statement that other forms of evolutionism have not been rigorously empirical and have as a result discovered too many parallels. Where have we heard it before? Is this not precisely the message which Boas delivered from Morningside Heights?

> Multilinear evolution, therefore, has no a priori scheme or laws. It recognizes that the cultural traditions of different areas may be wholly or partly distinctive, and it simply poses the question of whether any genuine or meaningful similarities between certain cultures exist and whether these lend themselves to formulation [*ibid.*].

This misnomered "methodology" is scarcely a decisive invention. It is encumbered by a lingering acceptance of the possibility that endless diversity may still turn out to be the best model of cultural evolution.

> A taxonomic scheme designed to facilitate the determination of parallels and regularities in terms of concrete characteristics and developmental processes will have to distinguish innumerable culture types, many of which have not as yet been recognized [*ibid.*:24].

If the "innumerable" tends toward the infinity side, we have historical particularism. Moving in the other direction, we have multilinear evolutionism. But it must be remembered that even in the biological model of the tree of life, "innumerable" convergences and parallelisms have their place. Furthermore, the so-called unilinear evolutionists, despite their emphasis upon parallelism, certainly did not deny "innumerable" divergences. Finally, Steward himself questioned the utility and not the validity of White's universal sequence.

The question of how much parallelism has existed during the course of culture history is a logico-empirical matter which cannot be settled by adhering to one or another brand of evolutionism. The most important considerations here are the operations by which judgments of similarity or difference are rendered. It should be possible to demonstrate the similarities of band organization among the Arunta and Bushmen regardless of the type of evolutionism adhered to by the community of observers. This of course is not to say that the identification of parallel sequences is equally possible under all research options. In the case of historical particularism, differences are deliberately enumerated until they overwhelm similarities, and we should not expect the discovery of many parallels. I must repeat, however, that the issue here is not evolutionism, but rather the triumph of the nomothetic mode over the idiographic. In this respect, both Steward and White stand opposed to the Boasian school, regardless of their differences of opinion concerning the kind of evolutionism one ought to "practice." They both believe that causal explanations of cultural phenomena are within our grasp.

THE SIGNIFICANCE OF PARALLEL AND CONVERGENT CASES

One of the most unfortunate consequences of the subordination of the question of causality to that of "evolution" is that it has deflected our attention away from an understanding of the central importance of parallel cases in the social sciences. To look for and collect parallel sequences is not a methodology; the methodology comes in when one looks for parallel cases in order to establish the causal principles which account for both parallel and divergent evolution. If the evolutionary trajectory consequent upon the introduction of irrigation agriculture were associated with the development of "oriental despotism" in Egypt and nowhere else, it would be difficult to establish any kind of causal relation between the two phenomena. It is the fact that a similar sequence is repeated in several different cases that makes it possible for us to talk about nomothetic causal relationships. The special significance of parallel developmental sequences therefore is that they provide the natural history analogues to laboratory controls in the experimental sciences. In this respect they potentially offer a highly satisfactory form of cross-cultural correlation analysis since actual chronological sequence may be invoked to determine the direction of causality.

Although Steward has not participated in the development of statistically oriented cross-cultural theories, his understanding of the methodological function of parallelisms actually assumes both diachronic and synchronic forms of correlation:

> . . . it is our basic premise that the crucial methodological feature of evolution is the determination of recurrent causal relationships in independent cultural traditions. . . . Whether it requires ten, twenty, or several hundred years for the relationship to become established, development through time must always take place. Therefore parallel developments which require only a few years and involve only a limited number of features are no less evolutionary from a scientific point of view than sequences involving whole cultures and covering millennia [*ibid.*:27].

Removing the emphasis from the sterile question of whether a phenomenon is or is not evolution, we may rephrase Steward's point to read as follows: cross-culturally valid correlations indicate that causality is operative. As we shall see in a moment, one of Steward's most important contributions, namely the ecological analysis of hunting and gathering bands, actually follows the paradigm of synchronic correlation analysis, rather than a diachronic model.

STEWARD AS CULTURAL MATERIALIST

In order to show that cultural ecology is a subcase of cultural materialism, two points must be established: (1) in the cultural-ecological strategy, techno-environmental and techno-economic variables are accorded research priority; (2) this is done in conformity with the hypothesis that social organization and ideology tend to be the dependent variables in any large diachronic sample of sociocultural systems.

It is clear that Steward is the author of many statements which conform to the definition of cultural materialism. One of the most succinct is embedded in the discussion which led him to revise the culture area classification in the *Handbook of the South American Indians.* In explaining why a diffusionist interpretation of South American culture is unsatisfactory, he states that the acceptance or rejection of diffused items "was always contingent upon local potentialities." These "potentialities" are

> . . . a function of the local ecology, that is, the interaction of environment, exploitative devices, and socioeconomic habits. In each case, the exigencies of making a living in a given environment with a specific set of devices and methods for obtaining, transporting, and preparing food and other essential goods set limits to the dispersal or grouping of the people and to the composition of settlements, and it strongly influenced many of their modes of behavior [STEWARD 1949a, V:674].

There will be critics of this interpretation who will fix upon the phrase "strongly influenced many of their modes of behavior" to prove that Steward's position is not that of "cultural materialism." But if provision for "accident," "historical factors," and short-run and relatively rare reversals of causality from superstructure to base remove one from the heritage of cultural-materialist theory, then Marx as well as Steward must be so removed.

Dogmatic and otherwise degraded versions of historical materialism may insist on a one-to-one absolute correlation between material base and the rest of the social system. But our interest does not encompass such aberrations. Any rejection of cultural materialism on the grounds that it represents a less empirical, less skeptical, less operational or, in brief, an inferior scientific method is unworthy of serious consideration. Empiricism, skepticism, operationalism are scarcely the exclusive property of any particular anthropological school or theoretical orientation. These are the minimum conditions of science in general. If they are not met, as is frequently enough the case, it is a disaster regardless of the theoretical orientation in whose name the lapse has occurred.

The essence of cultural materialism is that it directs attention to the interaction between behavior and environment as mediated by the human organism and its cultural apparatus. It does so as an order of priority in conformity with the prediction that group structure and ideology are responsive to these classes of material conditions. Turning to Steward's statement of the research strategy of cultural ecology, we find all of these attributes of cultural materialism clearly delineated. He states that there are three fundamental procedures of cultural ecology:

> First, the interrelationship of exploitative or productive technology and environment must be analyzed. . . . Second, the behavior patterns involved in the exploitation of a particular area by

> means of a particular technology must be analyzed. . . . The third procedure is to ascertain the extent to which the behavior patterns entailed in exploiting the environment affect other aspects of culture [STEWARD 1955:40-41].

This is Steward's research strategy. It is the procedure actually followed in his substantive work to which we turn in a moment.

CORE, BASE, SUPERSTRUCTURE

In connection with his misnomered "method of multilinear evolution," Steward attempts to set up a taxonomy of the empirically identified instances of parallel lines of development. By what congeries of traits shall we identify these sequences? Steward's answer is that they should be classified in accordance with the kinds of "cultural cores" which they manifest. Such cores he defines as "the constellation of features which are most closely related to subsistence activities and economic arrangements" (*ibid.*:37). It is inevitable that this definition of "cultural core" should summon up comparison with Marx's distinction between base and superstructure. One thinks immediately that the core is that part of the sociocultural system which in the long run determines all the other parts. Steward's explication, however, leads to other conclusions:

> *cultural core*—the constellation of features which are most closely related to subsistence activities and economic arrangements. The core includes such social, political, and religious patterns as are empirically determined to be closely connected with these arrangements. Innumerable other features may have great potential variability because they are less strongly tied to the core. These latter, or secondary features, are determined to a greater extent by purely cultural-historical factors—by random innovations or by diffusion—and they give the appearance of outward distinctiveness to cultures with similar cores. Cultural ecology pays primary attention to those features which empirical analysis shows to be most closely involved in the utilization of environment in culturally prescribed ways [*ibid.*].

If we proceed on the assumption that "core" is analogous to "base," we shall find on closer inspection that the logic of the above statement leaves much to be desired.

On this assumption, the core would be essential to the understanding of the causality responsible for a type, yet it would not determine the type's secondary features. These are determined by purely chance cultural-historical factors, that is, by variables which cannot be put into nomothetic generalizations. What about the subsistence activities, economic arrangements, the social, political, and religious patterns, all of which are to be included in the core? Is there any indication that we are to regard some of these factors as causally more significant than the others? None at all. Why then, we may very well wonder, should certain types tend to occur frequently enough to produce the parallel sequences which constitute the subject matter of multilinear evolution? How can we speak of "causality" when it appears to be a matter of indifference whether it is one, several, or all of the respective subsistence, economic, political, or religious variables which can summon into existence the whole pattern of the cultural-ecological type? But this quandary has not exhausted itself.

> Obviously, the diagnostic features of any given era—*the cultural core*—will depend in part upon particular research interest, upon what is considered important; and there is still a healthy if somewhat confusing disagreement regarding these matters. It should be noted, however, that functionally interrelated economic, social, political, religious, and military patterns as well as technological and esthetic features have become the basis for developmental taxonomies. These features do not constitute total cultures. They form *culture cores*, which are defined according to the empirical facts of *cross-cultural type* and level [*ibid.*:93].

Not only must we now admit military and aesthetic features into the culture core, thus rounding out the entire universal pattern, but the reasons for including some and excluding others may depend upon what each anthropologist appears to consider important!

THE CORE OF CONFUSION

It is clear that the interests of coherent and systematic theory cannot be served by the interpretation of Steward's "cultural core" as a statement of causal relations. The concept of cultural core makes sense only in relation to the misguided polemic surrounding the multilinearity of cultural evolution. It cannot be reconciled with Steward's cultural-ecological method. Steward has confused the causal implications of the cultural-ecological strategy with the typological requirements of multilinear sequences. The stress on multilinearity, in turn, is intelligible only as a counterweight to dogmatized versions of Marxism, as a means of dissociating cultural ecology from the political stigma attached to historical materialism. We do not otherwise require to be told over and over again that cultural ecology cannot explain everything, that there are exceptions, that not all cultures conform to the same type, and that there is divergence as well as convergence and parallelism in human history. What anthropologists can deny these challenges to nomothetic understanding?

But that is not the issue. Rather, the issue is what kinds of results have been achieved by following historical particularism, culture and personality, and the other emic and idealist alternatives? Let those who know how to explain what the cultural-materialist strategy has thus far failed to explain step forward with their nomothetic alternatives. We do not demean a theory by its failures to explain everything, but rather by its failure to explain as much as its nearest rivals. In this frame of reference, the alternatives to cultural materialism have failed and have as often obscured as enlightened our understanding of sociocultural evolution.

EARLY INFLUENCES ON STEWARD

When we turn to the substantive applications of Steward's cultural-ecological method, the confusion associated with his concept of cultural core is somewhat attenuated. In each of his major undertakings he has stressed the techno-economic and techno-environmental parameters as the first order of business and has demonstrated the advantages of such a strategy by rendering intelligible cultural phenomena which are otherwise inscrutable. It will obviously not be possible to recount all of Steward's achievements; only those of the highest theoretical significance can be touched upon.

Steward was trained at Berkeley, where he received his Ph.D. in 1931, and his earlier work was dominated by particularist influences emanating from Kroeber and Lowie. One must also reckon with the influence of Carl Sauer, whose interest in human geography helped to strengthen Kroeber's awareness of environmental factors (see pp. 339ff.).

Steward's own interest in environmental factors was first consolidated by fieldwork among the Eastern Mono and Paiute of Owens Valley, California, in 1927 and 1928. Up to the publication of his "The Economic and Social Basis of Primitive Bands," however, Steward's position corresponded essentially to that of a rather large number of anthropologists who regarded the natural environment as a vaguely limiting or enabling factor in culture history. Let us pause for a moment to consider the background.

EARLIER TREATMENTS OF THE RELATIONSHIP BETWEEN CULTURE AND ENVIRONMENT: WISSLER

The salient feature of the anthropological discussions of the influence of environment on culture prior to Steward's essay was that they were carried out within the particularist frame of culture area classifications, and hence did not rise to nomothetic status. Both Kroeber and Clark Wissler for example, basing themselves on the still earlier formulations of Otis Mason (1895a), were convinced that there was a correspondence between cultural and natural areas over the entire New World (see Chap. 14). Wissler in particular indicated that some kind of determinist influence had to be operating from environment to culture. He was especially impressed by the fact that when a map of North American "ecological" areas was placed over a map of the cultural areas, not only did the two line up, but the centers of the respective areas were the same for both the cultural and natural features. He was baffled, however, as to why this should be so.

> We have, then, made progress in our search for the environmental factor, since it appears the rule that, wherever in aboriginal America, a well marked ecological area can be delineated, there one will find a culture area and that the centers of distribution for the constituent traits will fall in the heart of the ecological area. There must then be some determining condition that produces this uniformity, some ecological relation here, and no doubt a mechanism involved, which when laid bare, will give an adequate scientific explanation of the phenomenon. This discussion has at least set us on the trail of this mechanism, for its place of function is the ecological area, and it is most in evidence at the center [WISSLER 1926:216-17].

Wissler was further convinced that in so far as the environment influenced the formation of cultural areas, it was through effects of food production.

> In a large measure the particular economic type followed by the community shapes the entire mode of life. . . . As we have stated repeatedly, the most basic of all economic conditions are those related to food, and the specific food habits of a people are among the most resistant to change [WISSLER 1929:79].

But Wissler was also capable of such statements as: "The influence of the environment thus appears as a passive limiting agency rather than as a causal factor in tribal life" (*ibid.*:339), and his notion of determinism becomes utterly befuddled when he tries to explain the uniformity of subsistence practices within a cultural area. This he attributed not to the adaptive advantages of a particular mode of subsistence but rather to the alleged advantage which accrues to the tribes of a region when they all exploit the same resources:

> The environment really holds together the tribes occupying a region, and develops a community of interest and concentrates leadership within itself. The tendency for a bison-hunting tribe is, first, to confine its wanderings to the bison range; secondly, to observe and to fraternize with other bison-hunting tribes. Under such circumstances, it seems inevitable that the tribes within a region should follow much the same round of life [*ibid.*:338-39].

Wissler was thus unable to formulate the essential ingredients in a nomothetic approach to the culture-environment relationship. Such an approach can be stated only in terms of relationships that are found in different culture areas—indeed, on different continents—as a result of recurrent ecological exigencies. Furthermore, Wissler had no idea how, in general, the techno-environmental conditions could be nomothetically related to social organization and ideology. All in all, Wissler's approach represented only a slight advance over the work of Ratzel, to whom he himself attributed many of his ideas.

CULTURE AND ENVIRONMENT: C. DARYLL FORDE

One additional approach to the culture-environment problem must be mentioned, namely that of C. Daryll Forde. Like Wissler, Ford was convinced that the environment was important, but he was also incapable of and disinclined toward expressing the relationship in nomothetic terms. In effect, his main contribution was to warn geographers that they could not hope to understand cultures as mere reflexes of environment since each culture had the power to take out of the environment or to stress those aspects of it which historical (i.e., cultural) events inclined it to take into consideration:

> Physical conditions enter intimately into every cultural development and pattern, not excluding the most abstract and nonmaterial; they enter not as determinants, however, but as one category of the raw material of cultural elaboration. The study of

> the relations between cultural patterns and physical conditions is of the greatest importance for an understanding of human society, but it cannot be undertaken in terms of simple geographical controls alleged to be identifiable on sight. It must proceed inductively from the minute analysis of each actual society. The culture must in the first place be studied as an entity, and as an historical development; there can be no other effective approach to interrelations of such complexity. The most meticulous knowledge of physical geography, whether of great regions or of small areas, will not serve to elucidate these problems unless the nature of cultural development is grasped. The geographer who is unversed in the culture of the people of the land he studies, or in the lessons which ethnology as a whole has to teach, will, as soon as he begins to consider the mainsprings of human activity, find himself groping uncertainly for geographical factors whose significance he cannot truly assess [FORDE 1934:464–65].

What we have here is merely a restatement of the historical-particularist position with an emphasis upon accumulating techno-environmental data instead of folktales. The failure to reach a nomothetic point of view is yet more evident when Forde goes on to say that even if we could discover determinist principles by which techno-economic patterns could be related to the environment, we should still confront an impasse in trying to relate these patterns to the rest of the culture. One more citation is required at this point in order that the full measure of Steward's achievement may be taken:

> But if geographical determinism fails to account for the existence and distribution of economies, economic determinism is equally inadequate in accounting for the social and political organizations, the religious beliefs and the psychological attitudes, which may be found in cultures based on those economies. . . . The tenure and transmission of land and other property, the development and relations of social classes, the nature of government, the religious and ceremonial life—all these are parts of a social superstructure, the development of which is conditioned not only by the foundations of habitat and economy, but by complex interactions within its own fabric and by external contacts, often largely indifferent to both the physical background and to the basic economy alike [*ibid.*].

The phrase "complex interactions within its own fabric" is a noteworthy example of how an admission of ignorance, properly celebrated, can convey a sense of wisdom.

ECONOMIC AND SOCIAL BASIS OF PRIMITIVE BANDS

Against this background, Steward's "The Economic and Social Basis of Primitive Bands" must be reckoned among the important achievements of modern anthropology. It constitutes the first coherent statement of how the interaction between culture and environment could be studied in causal terms without reverting to a simple geographical determinism or without lapsing into historical particularism. This achievement has a double focus: first, the identification of a cross-culturally valid form of social organization, the "primitive band"; second, its explanation. The band occurs among widely separated hunting and gathering peoples in many different parts of the world. It is a type of social organization distinguished in its most general form by political autonomy and a small population, in that it consists of several nuclear families whose access to land is controlled by ownership privileges vested in the larger group. Incidentally, in defining this unit Steward had to cut through the issue of family and individual land ownership which Boas' student Speck (1928) had succeeded in bringing to a point of almost complete confusion (see pp. 357ff.) by his failure to separate acculturation effects from aboriginal patterns. Having established the existence of the major type by reference to several dozen recorded cases, Steward classified them into three subtypes: patrilineal, composite, and matrilineal. He then proceeded to supply causal explanations for the existence of the major type and its three subtypes. These explanations involve a consideration of the relationship between the productive capacity of low-level technologies applied to various types of habitats. Where Steward triumphed over the earlier expressions of determinism linking habitat and social organization going back as far as Turgot (see p. 28) was in being able to explain how, despite the diversity of environments and technologies associated with band-organized societies, there remained underlying ecological commonalities which gave rise to the general type and other commonalities which gave rise to the subtypes. Where the older tradition of geographical determinism was baffled by the fact that similar organizations occurred among the desert-dwelling Arunta, the Negritoes of the Congo rain forest, and the California Miwok, Steward's analysis focused attention on the structural similarities which resulted from the interaction of habitats and cultures whose specific content masked a fundamentally similar ecologic adjustment.

The nature of this adjustment may be summed up in reference to the low productivity of hunting and gathering techniques in adverse environments with a consequent limitation of population density to less than one person per square mile. Social aggregates are therefore necessarily small (averaging thirty to fifty persons per band) yet they are larger than the nuclear family because of the greater efficiency of the larger group in "subsistence insurance" and "security in warfare and feuds" (STEWARD 1936:332–33). According to Steward, the patrilineal type results from patrilocal residence which in turn is associated with the subsistence and defense advantages stemming from organizing the local group around a core of resident males. Composite forms of the band result from the intrusion of factors which reduce the advantages of patrilocality, as when subsistence depends on migratory animals.

Not only did this formulation surpass crude environmental determinism, which makes no provision for cultural variables, but it also surpassed that form of human geography known as "possibilism," in which the recognition of the cultural factor ends in a morass of indeterminacy. Steward was not merely saying that a particular combination of technology and environment made it possible for man to create a particular type of social organization; the whole weight of his argument was in the direction of insisting that a similar techno-environmental relationship regularly caused a similar effect (i.e., made it highly probable) regardless of whether the people involved were "creatively inclined" or not. Despite subsequent critical evaluations of certain aspects of Steward's data (*cf.* SERVICE 1962; MEGGITT 1962), the strategy of Steward's explanation continues to warrant approval.

SOME SUPERFLUOUS LIMITATIONS

It should not be concluded, however, that Steward had in one stroke severed his ties to particularism. In the actual listing of causal factors responsible for the band and its subtypes, Steward included a number of fortuitous and quixotic ingredients which, if taken as integral to the argument, greatly reduce its novelty. Thus in his summary of the factors responsible for the patrilineal band, Steward noted that band size is sometimes restricted not by ecological relations but rather by "some social factor which nevertheless has brought about occupation of small parcels of territory by correspondingly small groups" (*ibid.*: 343). Similarly in the explanation of the conditions responsible for composite bands he included such intrusive factors as "adoption of children between bands" and legitimacy of parallel cousin marriages; for matrilocal bands he listed: "Desire to secure the assistance of the wife's mother in child rearing"; and "strength of borrowed matrilineal institutions" (*ibid.*). Despite these lapses, there is no doubt that Steward intended to produce a statement of nomothetic causality based upon techno-environmental regularities. In his own words:

> Underlying this paper is the assumption that every cultural phenomenon is the product of some definite cause or causes. This is a necessary presupposition if anthropology is considered a science. The method of this paper has been first to ascertain the causes of primitive bands through analysis of the inner functional or organic connection of the components of a culture and their environmental basis. Next, through comparisons, it endeavored to discover what degree of generalization is possible. It is not assumed, of course, that generalizations may be made concerning all culture traits. On the contrary, it is entirely possible that the very multiplicity of antecedents of many traits or complexes will preclude satisfactory generalization and that the conclusion with respect to some things will be that "history never repeats itself." The extent, however, to which generalizations can be made may be ascertained by further application of the methods followed here [*ibid.*].

What Steward failed to realize is that the idiosyncratic, social, and ideational factors included among the determinants of band organization preclude "satisfactory generalization" and thus should have been removed from the statement of the lawful conditions.

CONSEQUENCES OF NONSTATISTICAL GENERALIZATION

It is regrettable that Steward operates with a nonstatistical concept of causality: "The method will be to analyze functional or necessary relationships. It will not undertake statistics or correlations" (*ibid.*:331). Had he approached the statement of ecological causality in terms of statistical probabilities, then we might have been spared a long series of curiously self-defeating theoretical forays, each of which undermines an important substantive nomothetic achievement by putting back into the ecological formula the indeterminacy which it was designed to overcome.

The significance of Steward's analysis of bands is that it showed how the interaction between technology and environment could explain *most* of the important structural and ideological features of low-energy hunters and gatherers in *most* of the known examples without utilizing historical or other idiographic modes of explanation. If we do not clearly state that the issue is a matter of probabilities, then before long we find ourselves retreating to the cupboard of eclecticism in order to achieve an explanation of *all* of the important structural and ideational features in *all* of the known cases. But such explanation ceases to be nomothetically viable. We already know beforehand that if we could be given an account of all of the events in the history of each of the peoples who have band organization, we should be able to offer an explanation which would be more "complete" than that which can be obtained through the nomothetic option. But such a program is the antithesis of science, and we do not improve our nomothetic formulations by tacking on the additional bit of advice that the exceptions to our rules can be understood by dragging in other factors, *unless these additional considerations are couched in nomothetic terms.*

ECOLOGY OF THE SOUTHWEST

In his analysis of the development of multi-matrisib villages among the Pueblos and multi-patrisib villages among the Yuman tribes of the Colorado River, Steward repeated the performance which made his treatment of the origin of bands a landmark. Rejecting the prevailing theories which derived the Yuman sib organization from the Pueblos, he emphasized instead the effect which the introduction of agriculture had upon the population density of the Colorado groups. This combined with pressure of warfare produced the evolution of the Yuman groups from patrilineal bands to multi-patrisib villages. Similar processes account for the gradual conversion of the semisedentary seed gatherers of Basket Maker times into the multi-matrisib villages of the late Basket Maker and Pueblo times.

It is noteworthy for an assessment of Steward's total impact upon anthropological theory during the last three decades that his utilization of archaeological data for the reconstruction of the Pueblo sequence helped to usher in a new era of archaeological interpretations, one whose influence continues to expand exponentially at the moment of writing. But I shall return to the interrelationship between cultural ecology and archaeology in a moment.

First we must record Steward's reiteration of the importance of the cultural-ecological approach:

> The present analysis of Southwestern society assumes that cultural process, and therefore sound historical reconstruction, can be

> understood only if due attention is paid to the economic and ecological factors that shape society. This requires analysis of the degree and manner in which economic factors have combined with kinship, ceremonialism, inheritance, and other factors to produce observed social patterns [1955:155]

Once again, however, we confront not only the nomothetic factors but the peculiar idiographic ones which negate the entire effort if we accord them their literal significance. In explaining the concentration of formerly localized and independent units in Pueblo III times, for example, Steward asserts that the change was "made possible but not caused by ecological factors" (*ibid.*:166–67).

> Village concentration must, therefore, have been produced by a factor of a nonecological order. Many causes are conceivable but in this instance it does not seem imperative to seek beyond the need for defense; for, whatever the danger, increasinging pains taken to choose impregnable dwelling sites attest an important motive for banding together. This tendency to concentrate in large villages, aided by the development of multistoried architecture and probably stimulated by some threat, began to spread. But at this time the total Pueblo area also began to shrink. The communal dwelling has persisted to the present, but now that the motives for constructing it have vanished, the reverse tendency has set in, houses becoming more widely scattered. The unilateral organization presumed to have been created during the original concentration of the Pueblo population continues in effect to the present day [*ibid.*:167].

A slight amount of reflection should suffice for establishing the point that an increase in warfare in the Pueblo area could easily have resulted from factors consistent with Steward's notion of ecology, namely from population increase. Once again, it should be emphasized that the peculiarly hesitant formulation would be rendered redundant by rephrasing the determinism to accord with statistical notions of causality. What Steward was really saying in this paper on the formation of multisib communities is that given a certain set of environmental and technological conditions, the transition from band to sib is highly predictable in a sufficiently large sample. But this is all we can ask of nomothetic statements in any realm of science.

CULTURAL LAW AND CAUSALITY

We turn now to an historically decisive paper, Steward's "Cultural Causality and Law; A Trial Formulation of Early Civilization." This article elaborated on Steward's contribution to the 1947 Viking

Fund Conference on Peruvian Archaeology at which the first stratigraphically based syntheses of the independent evolution of civilization in the New World had been set forth (see p. 337). Juxtaposing the New World sequences as known from northern Peru and central Mexico with available summaries of events in Mesopotamia, Egypt, and North China, Steward demonstrated a degree of developmental parallelism which dwarfed all of the "stupendous" phenomena referred to by Sapir (see p. 605). In all five regions Steward identified a sequence which involved a roughly parallel development through the following stages: Hunting and Gathering; Incipient Agriculture; Formative; Regional Florescent; Cyclical Conquests. The importance of this synthesis will emerge from the following discussion of the background of Steward's theory. We shall have to consider first the relationship of Steward's formulation to the "hydraulic hypothesis" as proposed by the comparative historian and sinologist Karl Wittfogel. Second, the relationship between Wittfogel, Steward, and Marxist theory must also be considered. And finally we shall have to assess the relationship between archaeological research and the rise of cultural-materialist theories.

WITTFOGEL AND THE HYDRAULIC THEORY

Steward's trial formulation of the developmental sequence in the five centers of ancient civilization was not intended to exhaust all of the possible routes which cultures have followed toward complex state-organizations. Rather, the trajectories he outlined were those assumed to be the characteristic sequences of one particular type, namely, irrigation, or "hydraulic civilizations."

> The formulation here offered excludes all areas except the arid and semiarid centers of ancient civilizations. In the irrigation areas, environment, production, and social patterns had similar functional and developmental interrelationships [STEWARD 1949b: 17].

Steward's ideas at this point converged with the theories of Karl Wittfogel.

As early as 1926 Wittfogel had begun to apply a cultural-ecological approach to the explanation of the peculiarities of Chinese and other "Asiatic" societies. In Wittfogel's early formulation these systems were characterized as "mighty hydraulic bureaucracies" whose despotic control over the densely populated ancient states in China, India, and Egypt arose from the techno-environmental exigencies of large-scale irrigation and other forms of water control in regions of scant rainfall. Although inspired by Max Weber, this analysis owed its central thrust, its clarity, and its success to Marx. The realization that the evolution of Oriental societies had followed a path substantially different from those of Europe was quite common among the scholars of the Enlightenment. Marx accepted this difference and postulated an Oriental mode of production.

As Wittfogel tells us, he employed "Marx's concept," in conformity with what he understood to be Marx's own conclusions (WITTFOGEL 1957:5–6). Wittfogel's analysis of the functional interdependence of the main features of the social organization and techno-economic patterns of irrigation civilization led him to stress the general importance of environmental parameters in the application of historical materialism to the understanding of social systems. His proposal to emphasize the interplay between economics and environment to account for phenomena which had baffled Marx was published in the Marxist journal *Unter dem Banner der Marxismus* (1929), and was clearly conceived as an expansion of the scope and effectiveness of the historical-materialist strategy.

WITTFOGEL ABANDONS CULTURAL MATERIALISM

Wittfogel's views on hydraulic society clashed with several cardinal items of dogma in the Stalinist version of world history. Marx's notion of an Asiatic mode of production indicated a degree of divergence in sociopolitical evolution which the international Communist parties were unwilling to accept. The Asiatic mode of production with its despotic centralized bureaucratic state was the very opposite of European feudal society. If there could be no feudalism in the evolutionary careers of the hydraulic civilizations, how could they develop capitalism? And without capitalism, how could they develop communism? As a result of the communist expurgation of Marx's ideas on the multilinearity of sociocultural evolution, Wittfogel's research and writing gradually took on the coloration of a crusade against communism and totalitarianism in general. Initially this crusade was closely linked with a defense of the cultural-materialist strategy and was inspired by "Marx's insistence on an unbiased pursuit of truth" (1957:6). Gradually, however, Wittfogel came to see the phenomena of Oriental despotism as capable of surviving in, and diffusing to, societies whose techno-economic relationships bore little resemblance to the conditions underlying the pristine state. Oriental society, he has recently declared, "cannot be explained in purely ecological or economic terms; and the spread of Oriental despotism to areas lacking a hydraulic agriculture underlines the limitations of such an explanation" (WITTFOGEL 1964:46).

Disturbed by a vision of the Soviet Union and Communist China as new installments in an age-old pattern, Wittfogel permitted himself to serve as a government witness in the McCarran committee's investigation of the Institute of Pacific Studies. Tragedies resulting from this episode have ill-served the cause of scholarship and have contributed to the suppression of the cultural-materialist strategy in American social science. Wittfogel's crusade to prove the multilinearity of evolution has centered more and more on the alleged moral implications of closed and open models of history:

> Marx and Engels' acceptance of Asiatic society as a separate and stationary conformation shows the doctrinal insincerity of those who, in the name of Marx, peddle the unilinear construct. And the comparative study of societal conformations demonstrates the empirical untenability of their position. Such a study brings to light a complex sociohistorical pattern, which includes stagnation as well as progress. By revealing the opportunities, and the pitfalls, of open historical situations, this concept assigns to man a profound moral responsibility, for which the unilinear scheme, with its ultimate fatalism, has no place [1957:7–8].

THE POLITICS OF HYDRAULICS

Although Wittfogel's model of history is more correct than anything proposed in the name of Stalinist orthodoxy, it is regrettable that the issue of moral responsibility should be employed in support of multilinear evolutionism. One could argue that there is not the slightest evidence that a world view in which human behavior is determined by material processes leads to any greater or lesser amount of "fatalism" than is to be found among peoples who believe in the determinism of an omnipotent God. Under either alternative mature individuals learn to accept responsibility for their actions. But I shall not elaborate on this aspect of the issue, because we have before us not a question of morality but one of scientific fact and theory. If we want to know to what extent human history is determined along parallel and convergent lines, we must turn to our measuring instruments and to our evidence and not to the moral premises of theologians, philosophers, and politicians.

Wittfogel's concern with the need to defeat the Stalinist world view has led him away from the cultural-materialist strategy—the strategy which was responsible for the formulation of his original theory of Oriental despotism. The irony of this situation is that in the meantime the evidence in favor of his theory has accumulated far beyond that which was available in the 1920's. Wittfogel's emigration to the United States corresponded to the period during which the revival of interest in large-scale nomothetic formulations was just getting under way. And by the end of the 1930's, this interest could for the first time in history avail itself of an abundance of archaeological facts adequate to the scientific solution of some of the most formidable riddles of human life.

ANTHROPOLOGICAL CONTRIBUTIONS TO THE STRATEGY OF CULTURAL MATERIALISM

As we shall see, the central hypothesis in Steward's "Cultural Causality and Law" was taken over bodily from Wittfogel. It would appear that knowingly or unknowingly, Steward had thus succeeded in wedding anthropology to the materialist strategy of which Marx had been the pioneer. But "Cultural Causality and Law" also represents the coming together of a number of distinctively anthropological achievements, whose substance and nature must now be set forth.

There was first of all the heritage of research carried out among non-European and precivilized groups with all its advantages in terms of the relative simplicity of the techno-environmental and techno-economic feedbacks. Field techniques applied to living people in their natural habitat gave anthropologists an advantage over the scholars who like Marx and his orthodox followers depended upon documents and historiography as their principal source of information about the structure and dynamics of sociocultural systems. Steward himself was an important contributor to this heritage, having carried out additional field studies in 1934–36 among the Great Basin Shoshone seed gatherers.

Secondly, anthropology was rapidly expanding the scope of its ethnographic studies over areas which provided maximum contrast with the cases most familiar to the European historians and even to scholars such as Wittfogel, whose great knowledge of Chinese history freed him from the typical Eurocentric parochialism of Western historiography.

Steward, for example, enjoyed an especially advantageous ethnological perspective as editor of the six-volume *Handbook of the South American Indians* (1946–50). This monumental collection immersed him in ethnographic material covering an entire continent with an extraordinary variety of environments and sociopolitical types.

In his struggle to organize the contributions of some ninety collaborators from a dozen different countries, Steward had at first accepted the historical-particularist trait-inventory frame of culture areas. In the fifth volume, however, he expressed his dissatisfaction with the definition of the four culture areas which provided the typological basis for one of each of the preceding volumes: *Marginal, Tropical Forest, Circum-Caribbean/Sub-Andean,* and *Andean.* In retrospect, he announced, "it is evident that many tribes were improperly classified" (1949a:670–71), and he called for and carried out a reclassification in accordance with patterns "which integrate the institutions of the sociopolitical unit" (*ibid.*:672).

The resulting reclassification corresponded roughly to the levels of sociocultural development which Elman Service (1962) later came to designate as band, tribe, chiefdom, and state. Steward himself was obliged to continue to speak of the culture types in question in terms of the continental-specific rubrics in the titles of the first four volumes. Within the *Handbook,* Steward (1949a:674) refrained from pressing "the developmental implications" of his classification, preferring instead, in a work so clearly a product of many different collaborators, to offer a more conventional historical reconstruction of diffusionist routes within South America. "Cultural Causality and Law," however, was a direct outgrowth of this revised classification since it answers the question of the origin of the Andean civilization in nomothetic rather than historical terms.

THE LINK WITH ARCHAEOLOGY

The third great anthropological contribution to the cultural-materialist approach was perhaps the most important. It was largely through cultural-ecological reconstructions, first of the Southwest and then in regard to the hydraulic hypothesis, that a link was established between cultural materialism and the discoveries of New World archaeologists. This relationship was beneficial in two directions; that is, it played a key role both in bringing the results of archaeology to bear upon nomothetic issues as well as in bringing the benefits of cultural-materialist strategy to the conduct and interpretation of archaeological research.

To appreciate the scope of this contribution and to understand the strategic significance of "Cultural Causality and Law," we must digress for a moment and consider the condition into which archaeology had lapsed during the Boasian period.

ARCHAEOLOGY DURING THE REIGN OF PARTICULARISM

If the hand of historical particularism rested heavily upon the study of cultural regularities among ethnologists, its weight was even more deadening among the archaeologists. If each ethnologist had his tribe, each archaeologist had his "site." If the ethnologist described his tribe in terms peculiar to and literally borrowed from the lexicon of the people he was studying, the archaeologist concentrated upon the pattern of rim sherd incisions found at his site and possibly at one or two adjacent localities. If culture was a thing of shreds and patches to Lowie, to the majority of his contemporaries working in archaeology it was a thing of sherds and scrapers and little else.

Speaking of the period from 1910 to 1936, the archaeologist Alfred Kidder lamented the particularism into which archaeology had lapsed as a result of what he called "pre-1910 speculations about the vast antiquity of the American Indians" with its consequent loss of "historical perspective" and its "taboo" on questions concerning origins:

> Archaeology accordingly became preponderantly descriptive; effort was directed toward identification of ancient sites with modern tribes; research upon American prehistory, striking forward rather than back, upward rather than downward, was left without foundations . . . many of us merely dodged the issue of origins and comforted ourselves by working in the satisfactorily clear atmosphere of the late periods [KIDDER 1936:146].

THE PROBLEM OF NEW WORLD ORIGINS

What kind of attitude prevailed concerning the universally accepted belief (ushered in with the defeat of the Morgan-Bandelier reconstruction of Aztec "democracy") that highly elaborate state-organized societies existed in the New World as well as the Old? We have already seen that the Boasians tended to adopt an ambivalent position on this question. On the one hand almost all of the Boasians were convinced that the attempts by the diffusionists to explain the native American civilizations exclusively by migrations and contact processes across either the Atlantic or Pacific were without foundation in fact. On the other hand, the Boasians were willing to admit that it was by no means unlikely that transoceanic influences had occurred. The task of separating the diffused from the independently invented items was regarded as an empirical question, the unraveling of which might require many years of research for each item in the list of parallels. There was certainly slight expectation that when the final balance was reckoned, any of the major tenets of the Boasian position would require restatement.

In the reiterated assurance that no one doubted that certain technological events would have to precede others and that civilization could result only from an increasingly more stable food supply and enlarged population, the Boasians thought that they had already exhausted the entire inventory of generalizations which the further study of the origin of New World civilizations could make possible. From their eclectic and particularist viewpoint they were willing to concede that states and empires had to have a basis in "surplus" production and "leisure time" made available by intensive agriculture. But since cultural evolution was conceived of as a hodgepodge of independent inventions and capricious diffusions, it was of no special importance that similar traits such as supreme god-priest rulers, monumental architecture, standing armies, state corvee, urbanization, astronomical and mathematical specialists, writing and calendars, and hundreds of other traits and institutions should appear in a number of different places throughout the world.

Kroeber, it will be recalled, explicitly warned against any expectation that any but the vaguest resemblance of sequence could be expected. The discussion of the theoretical significance of the New World civilizations thus remained in a state of suspended animation (see p. 336).

NEW TECHNIQUES, NEW DATA

The foundation of this murky mixture of diffusion and invention, however, rested upon a precarious situation in the archaeological realm. Here vast uncertainties of chronology and seriation fed the prevailing fashions of particularism. In this connection, it must be recalled that techniques of excavation adequate to an understanding of nongeologically stratified sites were not perfected and certainly were not widely used until the mid-twenties. The new techniques and their consequences have been outlined by the archaeologist Gordon Willey:

> The method was applicable to refuse deposits which had grown by occupational accretion. Marked physical stratification of deposits was not necessary. The technique consisted of removing detritus and artifacts from arbitrary depth levels. In studying artifact change by levels, percentage fluctuations of types were noted from level to level, so that rising or declining percentage frequencies of types were correlated with time. Deriving in large part from the mechanical nature of the operation, "continuous stratigraphy" of this kind had important theoretical repercussions on the nature of culture continuity and change. With the continuous depositional record of a site occupation before his eyes, the archaeologist could not help being impressed with the evidence for culture dynamics [WILLEY 1953:365].

During the twenties and early thirties, the impact of the numerous but far-flung applications of these new techniques on both simple and complex societies was obscured by an inability to establish a coordinated chronology for the entrance of man into the New World and his subsequent dispersal to the southernmost limits of the hemisphere. Although, as J. A. Mason (1966) has pointed out, many archaeologists accepted a Pleistocene date for the migration from Siberia, providing for some 10,000 years of evolution, diffusion, and migration, it was not until 1926, with the discovery of a point embedded between the ribs of an extinct form of bison at Folsom, New Mexico, that really convincing evidence could be brought forth to buttress the logical arguments for the time span in question.

TIME AND THE SIGNIFICANCE OF THE NEW WORLD CIVILIZATIONS

Few archaeologists appreciated the theoretical significance of the possibility of an independent origin for New World civilizations. An exception was Herbert Spinden, who, during the course of his arguments with the doctrinaire diffusionists, remained alert to the theoretical import of the independent inventionist position. If America "was the home of a family of civilizations independent of the family of civilizations in the Old World," observed Spinden, this fact would ". . . have a tremendous bearing on the innate potentialities of mankind, and thus, in turn, on the future course of political and social evolution" (SPINDEN 1927:60–61). In very general terms,

Spinden's view of evolution in the New World appears to have anticipated Steward's treatment of the subject:

> The American record indicates in very complete fashion the natural history of civilizations, from the family hunting band type of association up through the farmer's and fisherman's villages to nationalities, including all the members of a language group and even to empires based on conquest and tribute [*ibid.*:62].

Spinden, however, was far from having achieved a clear understanding of the scope and pattern of the evolution of New World culture. This is shown by his curious change of heart about the antiquity of the Paleo-Indian migration. In his 1936 presidential address to the American Anthropological Association he insisted that the Amerindian migration from the Old to the New World could not have occurred before 2500 B.C. Few anthropologists were willing to compress the entire sequence from the first appearance of Folsom-type hunters, their dispersal over the hemisphere, and the appearance of the first civilizations into such a short time period. Spinden's theory nonetheless reveals how doubtful the whole chronology of the New World continued to be as late as the mid-thirties. Clark Wissler, writing in 1933, summed up the situation in the following words:

> While it is true that the great number of living tribal units and their various cultures suggest a fair lapse of time, no satisfactory way has been found to express this interval in years or even in the relative terms of Old World chronology [WISSLER 1933:216].

The picture was especially unclear precisely in those areas such as the Valley of Mexico and the Central Andean highlands in which the best known of the New World civilizations had flourished at the time of conquest. Thus, the archaeologist Alfred Kidder observed in 1936 that "Kroeber and Vaillant believe that the oldest remains so far discovered in Peru and Mexico are not older than the time of Christ" (1936:146). Indeed, even in 1949, the entire Incipient Agricultural phase in Steward's chart was supported by nothing more than a question mark.

DISCOVERY OF THE ENERGY BASIS OF THE NEW WORLD CIVILIZATIONS

The turning point in the relationship between archaeological data and cultural materialism came in the late thirties and early forties with the excavations in Peru carried out by W. D. Strong,

Steward's classmate at Berkeley, and Gordon Willey, one of Strong's students at Columbia. In the Viru Valley, a complex of domesticated beans, squash, and cotton was identified at the base of a large mound with an estimated date of 2500 B.C. A continuous evolutionary sequence was obtained in the mound and in adjacent sites leading from Incipient Agriculture through several stages of village life up to the lowland irrigation states which were ultimately absorbed by the Inca Empire. Of special interest in this sequence was the phase identified by Steward as the Formative, when maize was introduced and irrigation techniques took over the main subsistence load. The entire sequence is wholly intelligible as a product of endogenous forces; increasing productivity, increasing population density, multiplication of village sites, warfare, intervillage and later intervalley coordination of productive processes, increasing social stratification and bureaucratic control of production and distribution, centralization of power, feedback to greater productivity, and population density. If contacts with the Old World had occurred during the 2500 to 3000 years which were required for the shift from autonomous village to state organization, nothing vital to the dynamic of the process seems to have resulted therefrom.

The only possible exception was maize, which obviously had not been domesticated on the Peruvian coast. At the time of Steward's analysis of the New World irrigation sequence the wild ancestors of the plant had yet to be identified. A few die-hard diffusionists continued to insist that it was not a native American cultigen, despite the fact that it was grown nowhere outside of the New World prior to the European conquest. In recent years not only have the wild ancestors of corn been identified in highland Mexico, but radiocarbon 14 dates have confirmed a period of gradual experimentation with domesticated varieties extending back to 7000 B.C. in the Tehuacán Valley of Central Mexico and in southern Tamaulipas (MANGELSDORF, MACNEISH, and GALINAT 1964; MAC NEISH 1964a; 1964b)! Proof that the Amerindians domesticated corn is tantamount to proof that they were capable of achieving every other technological innovation associated with the New World sequence independently of diffusion from the Old. Given the combination Homo sapiens, a nutritive and hardy grain, semiarid valleys, ample sources of water, terrain adaptable to irrigation, it was highly probable that irrigation civilizations would evolve, not once, but again and again.

Steward's provisional comparison of the main evolutionary sequences in the Old and New World was thus an epochal event because it marked the beginning of the use of the New World archaeological evidence to support a cultural-materialist interpretation of the origin of civilization. Hitherto, few archaeologists had accepted cultural materialism as a valid strategy. There were, of course, a number of exceptions, one of whom, V. Gordon Childe, must now be considered.

V. GORDON CHILDE AND THE STRATEGY OF CULTURAL MATERIALISM

A key figure in English archaeology, Childe was a Marxist who, like Leslie White, staunchly supported the validity of Morgan's stages of Savagery, Barbarism, and Civilization. But when it came to the specific sequences of the Middle East and of Europe, Childe actually seems closer to historical particularism than to historical materialism. As previously discussed (p. 644), Childe's working model of evolution was that of the divergent Darwinian tree of life. Despite his explicit Marxist leanings, Childe was unsuccessful in achieving a reconciliation between the abstract overall transition from savagery to civilization and his superb knowledge of the specific developmental sequences in the Middle East and Europe. He did of course recognize certain parallels in the end product, but he saw these as resulting more from diffusion than from parallel evolution. "The intervening steps in development did not exhibit even abstract parallelism" (1951a:161).

> So the observed developments in rural economy do not run parallel; they cannot therefore be used to define stages common to all the sequences examined. . . . In fine, the development of barbarians' rural economies in the regions surveyed exhibits not parallelism but divergence and convergence [*ibid.*:162].

CHILDE'S POSITION ON THE IRRIGATION QUESTION

Childe was not unfamiliar with the importance of irrigation in Mesopotamia and Egypt both from the perspective of productivity and organizational exigencies and controls:

> Conditions of life in a river valley or other oasis place in the hands of society an exceptional power for coercing its members; the community can refuse a recalcitrant access to water and can close the channels that irrigate his fields. Rain falleth upon the

> just and the unjust alike, but irrigating waters reach the fields by channels that the community has constructed. And what society has provided, society can also withdraw from the unjust and confine to the just alone. The social solidarity needed by irrigators can thus be imposed owing to the very circumstances that demand it. And young men cannot escape the restraint of their elders by founding fresh villages when all beyond the oasis is waterless desert. So when the social will comes to be expressed through a chief or a king, he is invested not merely with moral authority, but with coercive force too; he can apply sanctions against the disobedient [CHILDE 1946:90].

Childe's views on irrigation were transmitted by Pedro Armillas (1948) to the Conference on Peruvian Archaeology sponsored by the Viking Fund. It was at the same conference that Steward read a paper entitled "A Functional-Developmental Classification of American High Cultures" (1948), which provided an outline of the sequence that was incorporated, one year later, in "Cultural Causality and Law." However, Steward at this point made no mention of the hydraulic hypothesis. Armillas, on the other hand, citing Childe, gave extensive attention to the possible role of irrigation in the Formative and Regional Florescent, but he rather tended to postpone and limit its influence to the later Classic and post-Classic periods. That he was far from postulating a hydraulic base for the Formative as Steward was to do after adapting Wittfogel's theories to the Meso-American sequence may be seen from the following passage:

> In considering the role which irrigation works may have played in the social development of Meso-America it is necessary to note that water for irrigation was obtained from many local sources —various rivers and arroyos, springs and also wells—making unnecessary the constitution of large political entities. In fact, irrigation in Meso-America may have favored cantonalism, making each valley self-sufficient in nearly all of its basic economic products [ARMILLAS 1948:107].

We shall turn to the question of irrigation in Meso-America in just a moment.

THE SIGNIFICANCE OF THE SECOND EARTH

Childe's most serious shortcoming was his lack of interest in the civilizational sequences outside of the Middle East and Europe. Having concluded correctly at an early point in his career that there was little resemblance between the specific steps involved in the development of civilization in Europe, on the one hand, and in Mesopotamia and Egypt on the other, he was unprepared to look for parallels in Mexico or Peru.

Childe's views are extremely instructive with respect to our understanding of Steward's relationship to Marxism and historical materialism. Observe the irony: Both Steward and Wittfogel appear embarrassed by the relationship between Marxism and cultural materialism. Childe, on the other hand, openly pleads for the importance of a cultural-materialist strategy. Yet it is Childe who argues that environmental differences are too great in the earliest centers of civilization to expect parallel sequences, while it is Steward and Wittfogel—the cultural ecologists and doctrinaire multilinear evolutionists—who propose that hydraulic types, wherever they occur, tend to evolve through a similar series of stages.

Thus it was in Steward's trial formulation that for the first time archaeological evidence from the New World was harnessed to the task of providing a cultural-materialist interpretation of cultural evolution on a global scale. At last, it could be seen through archaeological data that American Indian populations, starting with paleolithic tool kits and restricted to a life of hunting and gathering, had slowly advanced through various degrees of complexity in a direction fundamentally similar to that taken by racially and culturally separate populations in the Old World. There was no longer any possibility that either area had depended on the other for any of the vital steps in the sequence. The New World in other words had finally emerged as the equivalent of a second earth; and on that second earth, due to the fact that in the psychocultural realm, as in all others, similar causes under similar conditions lead to similar results, hominid cultures tended to evolve along essentially similar paths when they were confronted with similar techno-environmental situations.

THE NEW ARCHAEOLOGY

We have already seen that the analysis of the development of the sibs in the Southwest and California integrated a knowledge of both ethnographic and archaeological facts. We also should note in this connection that Steward himself had been trained in seriational stratigraphy by Kroeber and that he had worked with William Duncan Strong in a project at The Dalles on the Columbia River in 1926 (STRONG, SCHENCK, and STEWARD 1930). Firsthand familiarity with the techniques of modern archaeological research gave Steward both the authority and the motivation for criticizing the failure of his colleagues to articulate their findings with significant nomothetic issues:

> When complexes have been identified and history in the narrow sense reconstructed, what task remains for archaeology? Someday world culture history will be known as far as archaeological materials and human intelligence permit. Every possible element of culture will be placed in time and space. . . . When taxonomy and history are thus complete, shall we cease our labors and hope that the future Darwin of anthropology will interpret the great historical scheme that will have been erected? There has been a marked tendency to avoid these questions on the assumption that they are unimportant at present. It is held that the urgent need of the moment is to record data which are rapidly vanishing. . . . We believe that it is unfortunate that attempts to state broad objectives which are basic to all cultural anthropology . . . should be relegated to a future time of greater leisure and fullness of data.
>
> One wonders whether the frequent limitations of interest to measurements and tabulations of data and refinement of technique is an unwillingness to grapple with the problem of objectives. And it is by no means improbable that in spite of our refined techniques of excavation, ceramic studies, and classification, we are actually overlooking important data, even when doing field work.
>
> Often ten pages are devoted to the minutiae of pottery types . . . while one page or less describes subsistence and the relationship of the culture to the geographical environment. . . . Even less space is usually accorded data concerning social groups and population distribution and concentration which are indicated by such elements as house remains and village locations [STEWARD and SELTZER 1938:5–7].

To a marked degree, Steward's image of what archaeology should have been doing in the 1930's has become true in the fifties and sixties. The dominant orientation in contemporary American anthropological archaeology now conforms to Steward's understanding of cultural ecology. Whether it be shell middens on Long Island, ancient burial grounds in Peru, or pyramids in Mexico, the questions now being asked and the theories being framed to answer them reflect a growing convergence toward the strategy of cultural materialism.

Mere dating and classification have ceased to guarantee respectability in archaeological circles. The demands of the moment are to be met by data on population size, density, minima and maxima in short-

and long-time runs; seasonal and climatic cycles; response of settlement pattern; rate of population increase; food production techniques; total exploited habitat; short- and long-run changes in natural biota; techno-environmental effects; size of food producing and non-food producing groups; incidence of warfare; contribution of disease vectors to mortality; nature of social organization defined in terms of house groups, village or town units; and intercommunity organization (BINFORD 1962; 1967; STEWARD 1967). These interests link archaeology to ethnology in a powerful new symbiosis, providing the two disciplines with a common set of assumptions emphasizing etic events and a joint strategy which has already begun to yield a better understanding of evolutionary processes.

TESTING OF THE HYDRAULIC HYPOTHESIS

One of the most interesting manifestations of the new strategy of archaeological research is the attempt to test the hydraulic hypothesis. Research has centered on the role of irrigation in the evolution of Classic period Meso-American urban civilizations. The case of the Valley of Teotihuacán, a short distance to the north of the Valley of Mexico, is a good example of recent efforts along these lines. It was in this valley that one of the largest man-made structures in the world, the great Pyramid of the Sun, was erected a thousand years before Columbus' voyage. In 1948, when Steward formulated his developmental typology, very little was known about the circumstances which had led to the construction of this great pyramid, or of any of the other monuments which were part of the total Teotihuacán complex. Very little was known, either, about the role of irrigation in the formation of Meso-American civilizations. Although there was no doubt that the Aztecs had carried out extensive hydraulic projects in connection with *chinampa* cultivation (misnomered "floating gardens") and the drainage of Lake Texcoco, the date at which these installations were introduced and their causal significance remained uncertain.

In the case of Teotihuacán, nothing at all was known about the agricultural practices which had provided the energy for building the great monuments. Excavations carried out under the direction of René Millon (1967) of the University of Rochester have now established the fact that Teotihuacán was the site of one of the New World's largest aboriginal cities. Its estimated population of 70,000 to 100,000 people could only have been surpassed, if at all, by Tenochtitlán, capital of the Aztecs. Like Tenochtitlán, Teotihuacán was the center of an empire that covered a large part of Central Mexico. The question of whether it was based on hydraulic modes of production appears now to have been settled. Studies carried out by William Sanders of Pennsylvania State University show that the change from rainfall farming to irrigation was correlated with rapid population growth, nucleation, monument construction, intense social stratification, and expansionist warfare. "The water for the permanent irrigation systems derives from 80 springs, all located within a single very small area (20 hectares). This was the most significant single ecological resource" (SANDERS 1965:201). Sanders and Price (1968) have gone on to interpret the difference between Maya civilizations and the Highland Mexican hydraulic empires. The former were based not on irrigation agriculture but on slash-and-burn (swidden) farming. These were true civilizations, but they lacked the nucleated settlements of urban civilization. The hierarchical divisions within the lowland Maya states appear to have been much less severe than those in Teotihuacán.

MEXICO AND MESOPOTAMIA

It would be unreasonable to suppose that substantial criticisms of the details of Steward's irrigation sequence would not have been forthcoming from archaeologists and historians with specialized knowledge of the areas in question. Nor should the impression be conveyed that Wittfogel's hydraulic hypothesis has everywhere received support from our rapidly expanding knowledge of prehistory. It is not possible to review all the negative and positive bits of information and favorable and unfavorable interpretations which are accumulating around this vital question. I shall mention only the most recent attempt by Robert Adams (1966) to compare the evolution of Meso-American and Mesopotamian urban civilizations.

Although Adams acknowledges the existence of irrigation agriculture in Early Dynastic times in Mesopotamia, he does not believe that its scale was large enough to account for the concentration of political power which is characteristic of the later or Classic phases. He is also skeptical of the organizational role of irrigation in Meso-America although his argument is based more on the Aztec than on the Teotihuacán situation. A major difficulty appears to be the lack of coordinating measures of the irrigation works and size of polity in the two regions through successive periods of growth and expansion. Adams' position is weakened when we consider that there is, in the long run, a step-by-step increase in the size of the Mesopotamian waterworks and the size and power of the ruling bureaucracy. Thus, even if Adams is correct in maintaining that the first consolidation of political power was achieved independently of the organizational requisites of the hydraulic system, the achievement of Wittfogel's Oriental despotic type remains closely associated with maximum hydraulic dependency.

But the most interesting aspect of Adams' critique lies elsewhere. Despite his rejection of the hydraulic theory, his entire perspective on the Mesopotamian data bears the imprint of the nomothetic revival, and everywhere implicitly acknowledges the inspiration of the search for law and causality. Indeed, in the final reckoning, Adams reaches conclusions that vindicate Steward's method to a remarkable extent if we reflect how fragmentary were the data upon which Steward was obliged to base his "trial formulation":

> What seems overwhelmingly most important about these differences is how small they bulk even in aggregate, when considered against the mass of similarities in form and process. In short, the parallels in the Mesopotamian and Mexican "careers to statehood," in the forms that institutions ultimately assumed as well as in the processes leading to them, suggest that both instances are most significantly characterized by a common core of regularly occurring features. We discover anew that social behavior conforms not merely to laws but to a limited number of such laws, which perhaps has always been taken for granted in the case of cultural subsystems (e.g., kinship) and among "primitives" (e.g., hunting bands). Not merely as an abstract article of faith but as a valid starting point for detailed, empirical analysis, it applies equally well to some of the most complex and creative of human societies [ADAMS 1966:174–75].

We may note that Adams, who deals with time scales on the order of millennia, appears to have misunderstood recent anthropological history in suggesting that elements of the nomothetic revival were always "taken for granted." It has been a long hard struggle all the way. In concluding our review of this centuries-old struggle to achieve a science of history, it cannot be overemphasized that the vindication of the strategy of cultural materialism does not depend on the verification of the hydraulic hypothesis or of any other particular techno-environmental, techno-economic theory. Rather, it lies in the capacity of the approach to generate major explanatory hypotheses which can be subjected to the tests of ethnographic and archaeological research, modified if necessary, and made part of a corpus of theory equally capable of explaining the most generalized features of universal history and the most exotic specialties of particular cultures.

Bibliography

Original dates of publication are given only when they are important to the historical discussion in text.

ABERLE, D.

1961a "Matrilineal Descent in Cross-cultural Perspective." D. Schneider and K. Gough, eds., *Matrilineal Kinship*. Berkeley: University of California Press, 655-727.

1961b "Culture and Socialization." F. Hsu, ed., *Psychological Anthropology: Approaches to Culture and Personality*. Homewood, Ill.: Dorsey Press, 381-99.

ACHELIS, T.

1889 *Die Entwicklung der modernen Ethnologie*. Berlin: E. S. Mittler und Sohn.

ACKERKNECHT, E. H.

1954 "On the Comparative Method in Anthropology." R. F. Spencer, ed., *Method and Perspective in Anthropology*. Minneapolis: University of Minnesota Press, 117-25.

ACKERMAN, C.

1964 "Structure and Statistics: The Purum Case." *American Anthropologist*, 66:53-65.

1965 "Structure and Process: The Purum Case. *American Anthropologist*, 67:83-91.

ADAMS, R. MC C.

1966 *The Evolution of Urban Society*. Chicago: Aldine.

ADELUNG, J. C.

1782 *Versuch einer Geschichte der Cultur des menschlichen Geschlechts*. Leipzig: C. G. Hertel.

AGASSI, J.

1960 "Methodological Individualism." *British Journal of Sociology*, 11:244-70.

ALIOTTA, A.

1914 *The Idealistic Reaction against Science*. Agnes McCaskill, trans. London: Macmillan and Co.

ANKERMANN, B.

1905 "Kulturkreise und Kulturschichten in Ozeanien und Afrika." *Zeitschrift für Ethnologie*, 37:54-84.

ARBUTHNOT, J.

1751 (orig. 1733) *An Essay Concerning the Effects of the Air on Human Bodies*. London: J. and R. Tonson, and S. Drap.

ARGYLE, M.

1957 *The Scientific Study of Social Behavior*. London: Methuen.

ARMILLAS, P.

1948 "A Sequence of Cultural Development in Meso-America." W. J. Bennett, ed., *A Reappraisal of Peruvian Archaeology*. Memoirs of the Society for American Archaeology, 4:105-11.

BACHMAN, J.

1850 *The Doctrine of the Unity of the Human Race Examined on the Principles of Science*. Charleston: C. Canning.

BACHOFEN, J. J.

1861 *Das Mutterrecht*. Basel: Benno Schwabe.

1966 (orig. 1880) "Antiquarische Briefe." J. Dormam, W. Strasser, and H. Lommel, eds., *Johann Jacob Bachofen's gesammelte Werke*, VIII. Basel: Schwabe and Co.

BACK, K.

1960 "The Well-informed Informant." R. Adams and J. J. Priss, eds., *Human Organization Research*. Homewood, Ill.: Dorsey Press, 179-88.

BAGBY, P.

1953 "Culture and the Causes of Culture." *American Anthropologist*, 55:535-54.

BAGEHOT, W.

1872 *Physics and Politics, or Thoughts on the Application of the Principle of Natural Selection and Inheritance to Political Society*. New York: Appleton.

BANCROFT, H. H.

1883 *The Early American Chronicles*. San Francisco: A. L. Bancroft.

BANDELIER, A.

1879 *On the Social Organization and Mode of Government of the Ancient Mexicans*. Reports of the Peabody Museum, 12:577-699.

1885 *The Romantic School in American Archaeology*. New York: Trow and Co.

BARKER, R. and L. BARKER

1961 "Behavior Units for the Comparative Study of Culture." B. Kaplan, ed., *Studying Personality Cross-Culturally*. Evanston: Row, Peterson, 456-76.

BARKER, R. G.

1963 "The Stream of Behavior as an Empirical Problem." R. G. Barker, ed., *The Stream of Behavior*. New York: Appleton-Century-Crofts, 1-21.

1965 "Explorations in Ecological Psychology." *American Psychologist*, 20:1-14.

BARNES, H. E.

1948 *Historical Sociology: Its Origins and Development*. New York: Philosophical Library.

1960 "Foreword." G. Dole and R. Carneiro, eds., *Essays in the Science of Culture*. New York: Thomas Y. Crowell, xi-xlvi.

1965 *An Intellectual and Cultural History of the Western World*. New York: Dover.

BARNES, J. A.

1954 *Politics in a Changing Society*. Cape Town: Oxford University Press.

1960 "Anthropology in Britain before and after Darwin." *Mankind*, 5:369-85.

1961 "Physical and Social Kinship." *Philosophy of Science*, 28:296-98.

1963 "Introduction." B. Malinowski, *The Family among the Australian Aborigines*. New York: Schocken, xi-xxx.

BARNOUW, V.

1949 "Ruth Benedict: Apollonian and Dionysian." *University of Toronto Quarterly*, 3:241-53.

1957 "The Amiable Style of Patterns of Culture." *American Anthropologist*, 59:532-36.

1963 *Culture and Personality*. Homewood, Ill.: Dorsey Press.

BARRY, H.

1957 "Relationships between Child Training and the Pictorial Arts." *Journal of Abnormal and Social Psychology*, 54:380-83.

BARRY, H., M. K. BACON, and I. L. CHILD

1957 "A Cross-Cultural Survey of Some Sex Differences in Socialization." *Journal of Abnormal and Social Psychology*, 55:327-32.

1959 "Relation of Child Training to Subsistence Economy." *American Anthropologist*, 61:51-63.

BARTLET, F.C. *et al.* (eds.)

1939 *The Study of Society*. New York: Macmillan.

BARZUN, J.

1937 *Race: A Study in Modern Superstition*. New York: Harcourt, Brace.

BASTIAN, A.

1860 *Der Mensch in der Geschichte*. Leipzig: O. Wigand.

1895 Ethnische Elementargedanken in der Lehre vom Menschen. Berlin: Weidmann'sche Buchhandlung.

BATESON, G.

1949 "Bali: The Value System of a Steady State." M. Fortes, ed., *Social Structure: Essays Presented to A. R. Radcliffe-Brown*. Oxford: Clarendon Press.

1958 (orig. 1936) *Naven*. Stanford: Stanford University Press.

BATESON, G. and M. MEAD

1942 *Balinese Character: A Photographic Analysis*. Special Publications of the New York Academy of Sciences, 2. New York: New York Academy of Sciences.

BAUMHOFF, M.

1963 "Ecological Determinant of Aboriginal California Population." *University of California Publications in American Archaeology and Ethnology*, 49:155-236.

BEALS, R.

1960 "Current Trends in the Development of American Anthropology." A. Wallace, ed., *Selected Papers of the Fifth International Congress of Anthropological and Ethnological Science*, 11-18.

BEATTIE, J. H. M.

1955 "Contemporary Trends in British Social Anthropology." *Sociologus*, 5:1-14.

1964a *Other Cultures: Aims, Methods and Achievements in Social Anthropology*. New York: Free Press.

1964b "Kinship and Social Anthropology." *Man*, 64:101-3.

1965 "Reply to Schneider." *Man*, 108:123.

BECKER, H. and H. BARNES

1961 *Social Thought from Lore to Science*. New York: Dover.

BENDER, D.

1965 "The Development of French Anthropology." *Journal of the History of the Behaviorial Sciences*, 1:139-51.

BENDYSHE, T.

1865 "The History of Anthropology." *Memoirs Read before the Anthropological Society of London*, 1:335-60.

BENEDICT, R.

1922 "The Vision in Plains Culture." *American Anthropologist*, 24:1-25.

1923 *The Concept of the Guardian Spirit in North America.* Memoirs of the American Anthropological Association, 29.

1928 "Psychological Types in the Cultures of the Southwest." *Proceedings of the Twenty-Third International Congress of Americanists,* 572-81.

1932 "Configurations of Culture in North America." *American Anthropologist,* 34:1-27.

1934 *Patterns of Culture.* New York: Houghton Mifflin.

1943 "Obituary of Franz Boas." *Science,* 97:60-62.

1945 *Race: Science and Politics.* New York: Viking Press.

1946 *The Chrysanthemum and the Sword.* Boston: Houghton Mifflin.

1948 "Anthropology and the Humanists." *American Anthropologist,* 30:585-93.

1959 (orig. 1934) *Patterns of Culture.* New York: New American Library, Mentor Books.

BENNETT, W. J.

1943 "Recent Developments in the Functional Interpretations of Archaeological Data." *American Antiquity,* 9:208-19.

BENNETT, W. J. and M. NAGAI

1953 "The Japanese Critique of the Methodology of Benedict's *Chrysanthemum and the Sword.*" *American Anthropologist,* 55:404-11.

BERGER, P.

1963 *Invitation to Sociology: A Humanistic Perspective.* Garden City, N. Y.: Doubleday.

BERGMANN, C.

1848 "Über die Verhältnisse der Wärmeökonomie der Thiere zu ihrer Grösse." *Göttingen Studien,* No. 8.

BERNARD, J.

1945 "Observation and Generalization in Cultural Anthropology." *American Journal of Sociology,* 50:284-91.

BERNDT, R. M.

1952 "A Cargo Movement in the Eastern Central Highlands of New Guinea." *Oceania,* 23:40-65; 137-58; 202-34.

BERREMAN, G.

1966 "Anemic and Emetic Analysis in Social Anthropology." *American Anthropologist,* 68:346-54.

BIDNEY, D.

1944 "Concept of Culture and Some Cultural Fallacies." *American Anthropologist,* 46:30-44.

1946 "The Concept of Cultural Crisis." *American Anthropologist,* 48:534-51.

1963 "The Varieties of Human Freedom." D. Bidney, ed., *The Concept of Freedom in Anthropology.* The Hague: Mouton, 11-34.

BIGO, P.

1953 *Marxisme et Humanisme.* Paris: Presses Universitaires de France.

BINFORD, L. R.

1962 "Archaeology as Anthropology." *American Antiquity*, 28:217-25.

1967 "Comment on K. C. Chang, 'Major Aspects of the Interrelationship of Archaeology and Ethnology.'" *Current Anthropology*, 8:234-35.

BIRDWHISTELL, R.

1952 *Introduction to Kinesics*. Louisville: University of Louisville Press.

BIRNBAUM, N.

1953 "Conflicting Interpretations of the Rise of Capitalism: Marx and Weber." *British Journal of Sociology*, 4:125-41.

BLACK, M.

1949 *Language and Philosophy: Studies in Method*. Ithaca: Cornell University Press.

BLALOCK, H.

1961 *Causal Inferences in Non-Experimental Research*. Chapel Hill: University of North Carolina Press.

BLUMENBACH, J. F.

1865 (orig. 1775) *The Anthropological Treatises of Johann Friedrich Blumenbach*. Thomas Bendyshe, trans. and ed. London: Longman, Green, Longman, Roberts and Green.

BOAS, F.

1884 "A Journey in Cumberland Sound and on the West Shore of Davis Strait in 1883 and 1884." *Journal of the American Geographical Society*, 16:242-72.

1885 "Baffin-Land: Geographische Ergebnisse einer in den Jahren 1883 und 1884 ausgeführten Forschungsreise." Ergänzungsheft No. 80 zu *Petermanns Mitteilungen*, Gotha: Justus Perthes.

1887a "The Study of Geography." *Race, Language and Culture*. New York: Macmillan, 639-47.

1887b "Museums of Ethnology and Their Classification." *Science*, 9:587-89.

1888 *The Central Eskimo*. Report of the Bureau of Ethnology 1884-1885. Washington: Smithsonian Institution, 399-669.

1891a "The Indians of British Columbia." *Sixth Report of the Committee on the North-Western Tribes of Canada*. Report of the British Association for the Advancement of Science 1890, 801-93.

1891b "The Dissemination of Tales among the Natives of North America." *Race, Language and Culture*. New York: Macmillan, 437-45.

1894 "Human Faculty as Determined by Race." *Proceedings of the American Association for the Advancement of Science*, 43:301-27.

1896a "The Growth of Indian Mythologies." *Race, Language and Culture*. New York: Macmillan, 425-36.

1896b "The Limitations of the Comparative Method of Anthropology." *Race, Language and Culture*. New York: Macmillan, 271-304.

1897 *The Social Organization and the Secret Societies of the Kwakiutl*

Indians. Report of the U.S. National Museum, 1895. Washington.
1899a "Some Recent Criticism of Physical Anthropology." *American Anthropologist*, 1:98-106.
1899b "Review of Frobenius' *Die Weltanschauung der Naturvölker*." *American Anthropologist*, 1:755.
1902 "Rudolph Virchow's Anthropological Work." *Science*, 16:441-45.
1904 "The History of Anthropology." *Science*, 20:513-24.
1907 "Anthropology." A lecture delivered at Columbia University in the series on Science, Philosophy and Art. Dec. 18, 1907.
1909 "The Mind of Primitive Man." W. Thomas, ed., *Source Book for Social Origins*, Chicago: University of Chicago Press, 143-55.
1910 "Ethnological Problems in Canada." *Journal of the Royal Anthropological Institute*, 13:529-39.
1911 *The Mind of Primitive Man*. New York: Macmillan.
1912 "Changes in the Bodily Form of Descendants of Immigrants." *Race, Language and Culture*. New York: Macmillan, 60-75.
1916 "The Origin of Totemism." *American Anthropologist*, 18:319-26.
1920a "The Methods of Ethnology." *Race, Language and Culture*. New York: Macmillan, 281-89.
1920b "The Social Organization of the Kwakiutl." *Race, Language and Culture*. New York: Macmillan, 356-69.
1924 "Social Organization of the Tribes of the North Pacific Coast." *Race, Language and Culture*. New York: Macmillan, 375-76.
1928 *Anthropology and Modern Life*. New York: Norton.
1930 "Some Problems of Methodology in the Social Sciences." *Race, Language and Culture*. New York: Macmillan, 260-69.
1932 "The Aims of Anthropological Research." *Race, Language and Culture*. New York: Macmillan, 243-59.
1936 "History and Science in Anthropology: A reply." *Race, Language and Culture*. New York: Macmillan, 305-11.
1938a (ed.) *General Anthropology*. New York: Heath.
1938b "An Anthropologist's Credo." *The Nation*, 147:201-4.
1938c (orig. 1911) *The Mind of Primitive Man*. New York: Macmillan.
1943 "Recent Anthropology." *Science*, 98:311-14; 334-37.
1948 *Race, Language and Culture*. New York: Macmillan. The essays in this volume are individually noted above in the chronological order of their original publication.
1967 *Kwakiutl Ethnography*. Helen Codere, ed. Chicago: University of Chicago Press.

BOBER, M. M.
1927 *Karl Marx's Interpretation of History*. Cambridge: Harvard University Press.

BOCHNER, S.
1965 "Defining Intolerance of Ambiguity." *Psychological Record*, 15:393-400.

BOCK, K. E.

1956 *The Acceptance of Histories: Toward a Perspective for Social Science.* Berkeley: University of California Press.

BOGARDUS, E. S.

1960 *The Development of Social Thought.* New York: Longmans, Green.

BOPP, F.

1816 *Über das Conjugationssystem der Sanskritsprache in Vergleichung mit jenem der griechischen, lateinischen, persischen und germanischen Sprache.* Frankfurt-am-Main: K. J. Windischmann.

BOSSUET, J. B.

1748 *Discours sur l'Histoire Universelle.* Paris: David.

BOTTOMORE, T. B.

1956 *Marx's Social Theory.* London: Watts.

1962 *Sociology: A Guide to Problems and Literature.* London: Allen & Unwin.

1965 "Karl Marx: Sociologist or Marxist." *Science and Society,* 30:11-24.

BOUCHER DE PERTHES, J.

1860 *De l'Homme Antédiluvien et de Ses Oeuvres.* Paris.

BOYD, W. C.

1958 "Has Statistics Retarded the Progress of Physical Anthropology?" *American Journal of Physical Anthropology,* 16:481-84.

BRADSHAW-MORREN, G. E.

1966 "A Catalogue of Hyphenated Anthropologists." *American Anthropologist,* 68:1020-21.

BRAND, J.

1905 (orig. 1855) *Popular Antiquities.* London: Reeves and Turner.

BRANDON, S. G. F.

1951 *Time and Mankind, an Historical and Philosophical Study of Mankind's Attitude to the Phenomena of Change.* London: Hutchinson.

BRINTON, D. G.

1896 "The Aims of Anthropology." *Proceedings of the 44th Meeting of the American Association for the Advancement of Science,* 1-17.

BROCA, M. P.

1863 "Review of the Proceedings of the Anthropological Society of Paris." *Anthropological Review,* 1:274-312.

BROWN, I. C.

1960 "Review of *The Testing of Negro Intelligence* by Audrey M. Shuey." *American Anthropologist,* 62:544.

BROWN, R.

1964 *Explanation in Social Science.* Illinois: Aldine.

BROWNE, P.

1856 *Trichologia Mammalium, or a Treatise on the Organization, Properties, and Uses of Hair and Wool.* Philadelphia: Hart.

BRYSON, G.

1945 *Man and Society: The Scottish Inquiry of the Eighteenth Century.* Princeton: Princeton University Press.

BUCKLAND, W.

1823 *Reliquiae Diluvianae.* London: J. Murray.

BUCKLE, H. T.

1857 *History of Civilization in England.* London: J. W. Parker and Sons.

BUETTNER-JANUSCH, J.

1957 "Boas and Mason: Particularism vs. Generalization." *American Anthropologist,* 59:318-24.

BUFFON, G. L. L. DE

1740-1804 *Histoire Naturelle.* Paris: De l'Imprimerie Royale.

BUKHARIN, N.

1925 (orig. 1921) *Historical Materialism: A System of Sociology.* New York: International Publishers.

BUNZEL, R.

1929 *The Pueblo Potter.* New York: Columbia University Press.

1933 *Zuñi Texts.* Publications of the American Ethnological Society, vol. 15. New York: G. E. Stechert.

1938 "The Economic Organization of Primitive Peoples." F. Boas, ed., *General Anthropology.* New York: Heath, 327-408.

1952 *Chichicastenango, A Guatemalan Village.* Monographs of the American Ethnological Society, vol. 22. New York: J. J. Augustin.

BURCKHARDT, J. C.

1943 *Force and Freedom: Reflections on History.* New York: Pantheon.

BURLING, R.

1964 "Cognition and Componential Analysis: God's Truth or Hocus-Pocus?" *American Anthropologist,* 66:20-28.

BURROW, J. W.

1966 *Evolution and Society: A Study in Victorian Social Theory.* London: Cambridge University Press.

BURY, J. B.

1909 *The Ancient Greek Historians.* New York: Macmillan.

1932 *The Idea of Progress.* New York: Macmillan.

BUTTEKOFER

1893 "Note." *American Anthropologist,* Old Series 6:337.

BUTTERFIELD, H.

1960a *The Origins of Modern Science.* New York: Macmillan.

1960b *Man on His Past. The Study of Historical Scholarship.* Boston: Beacon Press.

CAMPBELL, D.

1961 "The Mutual Methodological Relevance of Anthropology and Psychology." Francis Hsu, ed., *Psychological Anthropology: Ap-*

proaches to Culture and Personality. Homewood, Ill.: Dorsey Press, 333-52.

1964 "Distinguishing Differences of Perception from Failures of Communication in Cross-cultural Studies." F. S. C. Northrop and H. Livingston, eds., *Cross-Cultural Understanding: Epistemology in Anthropology*. New York: Harper and Row, 308-36.

1965 "Pattern Matching as an Essential in Distal Knowing." K. R. Hammond, ed., *The Psychology of Egan Brunswik*. New York: Holt, Rinehart and Winston, 81-106.

CAMPBELL, J.

1851 *Negro Mania: Being an Examination of the Falsely Assumed Equality of the Various Races of Man*. Philadelphia: Campbell and Power

CAMPER, P.

1791 *Sur les Différences que Présente le Visage dans les Races Humaines*. Utrecht: B. Wild and J. Altheer.

CAREY, H. C.

1858 *Principles of Social Science*. Philadelphia: Lippincott.

CARLYLE, T.

1849 "Occasional Discourse on the Nigger Question." *Fraser's Magazine*, London, 40:670-79.

CARNEIRO, ROBERT (ed.)

1967 "Introduction." *The Evolution of Society: Selections from H. Spencer's Principles of Sociology*. Chicago: University of Chicago Press, ix-lvii.

CARROLL, J. B.

1959 "An Operational Model for Language Behavior." *Anthropological Linguistics*, 1:37-54.

CASSIRER, E.

1944 *An Essay on Man*. New Haven: Yale University Press.

CHAGNON, N.

1966 "Yanomanö Social Organization." Unpublished Ph.D. dissertation, University of Michigan.

CHAMBERLAIN, G. L.

1963 "The Man Marx Made." *Science and Society*, 27:302-20.

CHAMBERS, R.

1844 *Vestiges of the Natural History of Creation*. London: J. Churchill.

CHAMBLISS, R.

1954 *Social Thought*. New York: Dryden.

CHARDIN, J.

1927 *Sir John Chardin's Travels in Persia*. London: Argonaut.

CHESNEAUX, J.

1966 "Où En Est la Discussion sur le Mode de Production Asiatique?" *La Pensée*, 129:33-46.

CHILD, I. L., T. STORM, and J. VEROFF

1958 "Achievement Themes in Folk Tales Related to Socialization Practice." J. W. Atkinson, ed., *Motives in Fantasy, Action and Society.* Princeton: Van Nostrand, 479-92.

CHILDE, V. G.

1925 *The Dawn of Western Civilization.* New York: Knopf.

1935 "Changing Methods and Aims in Prehistory." *Proceedings of the Prehistoric Society,* vol. 1. Cambridge. 1-15.

1944 "Archaeological Ages as Technological Stages." *Journal of the Royal Anthropological Institutes,* 74:1-19.

1946 *What Happened in History.* New York: Pelican.

1951a *Social Evolution.* New York: Henry Schuman.

1951b *Man Makes Himself.* New York: New American Library, Mentor.

1953 *What Is History?* New York: Henry Schuman.

1958 *The Dawn of European Civilization.* New York: Knopf.

CHURCHILL, A.

1728 (orig. 1704) *Collection of Voyages.* London: A. and J. Churchill.

CODERE, H.

1950 *Fighting with Property.* Monographs of the American Ethnological Society, vol. 18. New York: J. J. Augustin.

1956 "The Amiable Side of Kwakiutl Life." *American Anthropologist,* 58:334-51.

1957 "Kwakiutl Society: Rank without Class." *American Anthropologist,* 59:473-85.

1959 "The Understanding of the Kwakiutl." W. Goldschmidt, ed., *The Anthropology of Franz Boas.* Memoir 89. American Anthropological Association, 61-75.

COHEN, M. R.

1925 "The Insurgence against Reason." *Journal of Philosophy,* 22:120-23.

COHN, B.

1955 "The Changing Status of a Depressed Caste." McKim Marriott, ed., *Village India: Studies in the Little Community.* Memoir 83. American Anthropological Association, 53-78.

COLBY, B. N.

1966 "Ethnographic Semantics: A Preliminary Survey." *Current Anthropology,* 7:3-32.

COLDEN, C.

1902 (orig. 1727) *The History of the Five Indian Nations of Canada.* New York: Barnes.

COLE, G. D. H.

1964 *The Meaning of Marxism.* Ann Arbor: University of Michigan Press.

COLLINGWOOD, R. G.

1946 *The Idea of History.* Oxford: Oxford University Press.

COLLINGWOOD, R. G., A. E. TAYLOR and F. C. S. SCHILLER

1922 "Are History and Science Different Kinds of Knowledge?" *Mind,* 31:442-66.

COLLINS, P.

1965 "Functional Analyses in the Symposium on Man, Culture, and Animals." A. Leeds and A. Vayda, eds., *Man, Culture and Animals*. Washington: American Association for the Advancement of Science, 271-82.

COLSON, E. and M. GLUCKMAN (eds.)

1951 *Seven Tribes of British Central Africa*. London: Oxford University Press for Rhodes-Livingstone Institute.

COMAS, J.

1961 " 'Scientific Racism Again?" *Current Anthropology*, 2:303-40.

COMBE, G.

1819 *Essays on Phrenology*. London.

COMTE, A.

1830-1842 *Cours de Philosophie Positive*. Paris: Bachelier.

1851-1854 *Système de Politique Positive*. Paris: E. Thunot.

1875-1877 *System of Positive Polity, or A Treatise on Sociology*. London: Longmans, Green.

1896 *The Positive Philosophy*. Trans. and condensed by Harriet Martineau. London: G. Bell.

CONDILLAC, E. B. DE

1746 *Origine des Connaissances Humaines*. Amsterdam.

CONDORCET, MARQUIS DE

1822 (orig. 1795) *Esquisse d'un Tableau Historique des Progrès de l'Esprit Humain*. Paris: Masson.

1955 *Sketch for a Historical Picture of the Progress of the Human Mind*. Jean Barraclough, trans. New York: Noonday Press.

CONKLIN, H. C.

1955 "Hanunóo Color Categories." *Southwestern Journal of Anthropology*, 11:339-44.

1964 "Ethnogenealogical Method." Ward H. Goodenough, ed., *Explorations in Cultural Anthropology*. New York: McGraw-Hill, 25-55.

COOK, M.

1936 "Jean Jacques Rousseau and the Negro." *Journal of Negro History*, 21:294-303.

COON, C. S.

1962 *The Origin of Races*. New York: Knopf.

COULBOURN, R.

1952 "Causes in Culture." *American Anthropologist*, 54:112-16.

COULT, A. D.

1962 "An Analysis of Needham's Critique of the Homans and Schneider Theory." *Southwestern Journal of Anthropology*, 18:317-35.

1966a "On the Justification of Untested Componential Analyses." *American Anthropologist*, 68:1014-15.

1966b "A Simplified Method for the Transformational Analysis of Kinship Terms." *American Anthropologist,* 68:1476-83.

1968 "Lineage Solidarity, Transformational Analysis, and the Meaning of Kinship Terms." *Man,* in press.

COULT, A. and R. W. HABENSTEIN

1965 *Cross-tabulation of Murdock's World Ethnographic Sample.* Columbia: University of Missouri Press.

COUNT, E. (ed.)

1950 *This Is Race.* New York: Henry Schuman.

COWGILL, G.

1964 "Statistics and Sense: More on the Purum Case." *American Anthropologist,* 66:1358-65.

COX, O.

1948 *Caste, Class, and Race, A Study in Social Dynamics.* Garden City, N. Y.: Doubleday.

CRAWLEY, A. E.

1902 *The Mystic Rose: A Study of Primitive Marriage.* London: Macmillan.

CROCE, B.

1923 *History—Its Theory and Practice.* D. Ainslie, trans. New York: Harcourt, Brace.

CULL, R.

1852 "Recent Progress of Ethnology." *Journal of the Ethnological Society of London,* 3:165-77.

CUNNINGHAM, J. D.

1908 "Anthropology in the 18th Century." *Journal of the Royal Anthropological Institute,* 38:10-35.

CURTIN, P.

1964 *The Image of Africa: British Ideas and Action, 1780-1850.* Madison: University of Wisconsin Press.

1967 *Africa Remembered.* Madison: University of Wisconsin Press.

CURTIS, E.

1915 *The North American Indian.* Vol. X, *The Kwakiutl.* Norwood, Mass.: Plimpton Press.

CUVIER, G.

1811 *Recherches sur les Ossements Fossiles.* Paris: G. Dufour and E. d'Ocagne.

DAMPIER, W.

1729 *A Collection of Voyages.* London: J. J. Krapton.

D'ANDRADE, R. G.

1961 "Anthropological Studies of Dreams." Frances Hsu, ed., *Psychological Anthropology: Approaches to Culture and Personality.* Homewood, Ill.: Dorsey Press, 296-332.

DANIEL, G. E.

1943 *The Three Ages: An Essay on Archaeological Method.* Cambridge: Cambridge University Press.

1950 *A Hundred Years of Archaeology*. London: Duckworth.
1964 *The Idea of Prehistory*. London: Watts.

DAPPER, O.
1686 *Description de l'Afrique*. Amsterdam: Wolfgang, Waesberge, Boom and van Someren.

DARGUN, L.
1883 *Mutterrecht und Raubehe und ihre Reste im germanischen Recht und Leben*. Breslau.

DARWIN, C.
1871 *The Descent of Man and Selection in Relation to Sex*. New York: D. Appleton.
1903 *More Letters of Charles Darwin*. Francis Darwin, ed. London: J. Murray. 2 vols.
1958 (orig. 1859) *Origin of Species*. New York: New American Library, Mentor.

DARWIN, C. and A. R. WALLACE
1859 "On the Tendency of Species to Form Varieties; and on the Perpetuation of Varieties and Species by Natural Means of Selection." *Journal of the Linnaean Society*, 3:45-63.

DAS, T. C.
1945 *The Purum: An Old Kuki Tribe of Manipur*. Calcutta: University of Calcutta Press.

DAVENPORT, W.
1959 "Nonunilinear Descent and Descent Groups." *American Anthropologist*, 61:557-73.

DAVIS, K.
1959 "The Myth of Functional Analysis as a Special Method in Sociology and Anthropology." *American Sociological Review*, 24:757-73.

DAWES, B.
1952 *A Hundred Years of Biology*. London: G. Duckworth and Co.

DEACON, A. B.
1934 *Malekula: A Vanishing People in the New Hebrides*. London: George Routledge.

DE BONALD, L.
1826 *Sur les Premiers Objets des Connaissances Morales*. Paris: D'Adrien Le Clere.

DE MAISTRE, J. C.
1959 (orig. 1810) *On God and Society. Essay on the Generative Principle of Political Constitutions*. Chicago: H. Regnery.

DEMEUNIER, J. N.
1776 *L'Esprit des Usages et des Coutumes des Différents Peuples*. London: Chez Pissot.

DENNIS, W.
1940 "Does Culture Appreciably Affect Patterns of Infant Behavior?" *Journal of Social Psychology*, 12:305-17.

DE SOLLA PRICE, D. J.

1962 *Science Since Babylon.* New Haven: Yale University Press.

1963 *Little Science Big Science.* New York: Columbia University Press.

DEVEREUX, G.

1945 "The Logical Foundations of Culture and Personality Studies." *Transactions of The New York Academy of Science.* Series II, 7:110-30.

1956 "Normal and Abnormal: The Key Problem of Psychiatric Anthropology." *Some Uses of Anthropology: Theoretical and Applied.* Washington: Anthropological Society of Washington, 23-48.

DEXTER, R.

1966 "Putnam's Problems Popularizing Anthropology." *American Scientist,* 54:315-32.

D'HOLBACH, P. H. T.

1770 *Système de la Nature.* London: M. Mirabaud.

1774 *Système Social, ou Principes Naturelles de la Morale et de la Politique.* London.

DIAMOND, S. and M. SCHEIN

1966 "The Waste Collectors." Unpublished Master's thesis, Columbia University.

DICKMAN, H. R.

1963 "The Perception of Behavioral Units." Roger G. Barker, ed., *The Stream of Behavior.* New York: Appleton-Century-Crofts, 23-41.

DIDEROT, D.

1772 (orig. 1754) *Pensées sur l'Interprétation de la Nature. Oeuvres Philosophiques de M. Diderot.* Amsterdam: Chez Marc-Michel Ray.

1875-1879 *Oeuvres Complètes.* Paris: Garrier.

1943 *Interpreter of Nature.* J. Stewart and J. Kemp, trans. New York: International Publishers.

DIETERLEN, G.

1957 *Introduction to Marcel Griaule's Méthode de l'Ethnographie.* Paris: Presses Universitaires de France.

DILLON, W. S.

1961 "Giving, Receiving, and Repaying: An Examination of the Ideas of Marcel Mauss in the Context of International Technical Assistance." Unpublished Ph.D. dissertation, Teachers College, Columbia University.

DILTHEY, W.

1883 *Einleitung in die Geisteswissenschaften.* Leipzig: Duncker and Humbolt.

1954 (orig. 1907) *The Essence of Philosophy.* S. Emery and W. Emery, trans. Chapel Hill: University of North Carolina Press.

1959 "The Understanding of Other Persons and Their Life-Expressions." P. Gardiner, ed., *Theories of History.* New York: Free Press, 213-26.

1961 *Meaning in History*. H. P. Richman, ed. London: Allen & Unwin.

DIXON, R.

1963a *Linguistic Science and Logic*. The Hague: Mouton.

1963b "A Trend in Semantics." *Linguistics*, 1:30-57.

1964 "A Trend in Semantics: Rejoinder." *Linguistics*, 3:14-18.

DOBB, M.

1966 "Marx on Pre-Capitalist Economic Formations." *Science and Society*, 30:319-25.

DOBRIZHOFFER, M.

1822 (orig. 1783) *An Account of the Abipones*. London: J. Murray.

DOBZHANSKY, T.

1960 "Individuality, Gene Recombination and Non-Repeatability of Evolution." *Australian Journal of Science*, 23:71-74.

1962 *Mankind Evolving: The Evolution of the Human Species*. New Haven: Yale University Press.

DOBZHANSKY, T. and M. F. ASHLEY MONTAGU

1963 "Two Views of Coon's Origin of Races with Comments and Replies." *Current Anthropology*, 4:360-68.

DREGER, R. M. and K. S. MILLER

1960 "Comparative Psychological Studies of Negroes and Whites in the United States." *Psychology Bulletin*, 57:361-402.

DRIESCH, H.

1908 *The Science and Philosophy of the Organism*. London: A. C. Black.

DRIVER, H. E.

1956 *An Integration of Functional, Evolutionary, and Historical Theory by Means of Correlations*. Indiana University Publications in Anthropology and Linguistics. Memoir 12.

1964 *Indians of North America*. Chicago: University of Chicago Press.

1965 "Survey of Numerical Classification in Anthropology." Dell Hymes, ed., *The Use of Computers in Anthropology*. The Hague: Mouton, 304-44.

1966 "Geographical versus Pyscho-functional Explanations of Kin Avoidances." *Current Anthropology*, 7:131-82.

DRIVER, H. E. and A. KROEBER

1932 "Quantitative Expression of Cultural Relationships." University of California Publications in American Archaeology and Ethnology, 31:211-56.

DRIVER, H. E. and P. SANDAY

1966 "Addendum: Factors and Clusters of Kin Avoidances and Related Variables." *Current Anthropology*, 7:169-82.

DRUCKER, P.

1939 "Rank, Wealth and Kinship in Northwest Coast Society." *American Anthropologist*, 41:55-65.

1955 *Indians of the Northwest Coast.* New York: McGraw-Hill.

DU BOIS, C.

1944 *The People of Alor: A Social-Psychological Study of an East-Indian Island.* Minneapolis: University of Minnesota Press.

1960 (ed.) *Lowie's Selected Papers in Anthropology.* Berkeley: University of California Press.

DUIJKER, J. C. J. and N. H. FRIJDA

1961 *National Character and National Stereotypes: A Trend Report for the International Union of Scientific Philosophy.* New York: Humanities Press.

DUNCAN, D. (ed.)

1908 *Life and Letters of Herbert Spencer.* London: Methuen.

DUNDES, A. (ed.)

1966 *The Complete Bibliography of Robert Lowie.* Berkeley: Robert H. Lowie Museum.

DUNN, R.

1865 "Some Observations on the Psychological Differences Which Exist among the Typical Races of Man." *Transactions of the Ethnological Society of London,* 3:9-25.

1866 "Civilization and Cerebral Development." *Transactions of the Ethnological Society of London,* 4:1-33.

DUNNING, W. A.

1926 *A History of Political Theory from Rousseau to Spencer.* New York: Macmillan.

DUPUIS, C. F.

1835 (orig. 1795) *Origine de Tous les Cultes.* Paris: Rosier.

DURKHEIM, É.

1897 "Review of A. Labriola, Essai sur le Conception Matérialiste de l'Histoire." *Revue Philosophique de la France et de l'Étranger,* 44:645-51.

1915 (orig. 1912) *The Elementary Forms of the Religious Life.* J. W. Swain, trans. London: Allen & Unwin.

1933 (orig. 1893) *Division of Labor in Society.* G. Simpson, trans. New York: Macmillan.

1938 (orig. 1895) *The Rules of the Sociological Method.* S. Solovay and J. Mueller, trans. New York: Free Press.

1951 (orig. 1897) *Suicide.* J. Spaulding and G. Simpson, trans. New York: Free Press.

1960 (orig. 1893) *Montesquieu and Rousseau: Forerunners of Sociology.* Ralph Manheim, trans. Ann Arbor: University of Michigan Press.

1962 (orig. 1896) *Socialism.* C. Sattler, trans. New York: Collier Books.

EDMUNSON, M.

1957 "Kinship Terms and Kinship Concepts." *American Anthropologist,* 59:393-433.

EDWARDS, W. F.

1841 "Des Caractères Physiologiques des Races Humaines, Considérés dans Leur Rapport avec l'Histoire." Mémoires de la Société Ethnologique, 1:1-108. Paris.

EGGAN, D.

1943 "The General Problem of Hopi Adjustment." *American Anthropologist*, 45:357-73.

EGGAN, F.

1937 "Historical Changes in the Choctaw Kinship System." *American Anthropologist*, 39:34-52.

1950 *Social Organization of the Western Pueblos*. Chicago: University of Chicago Press.

1954 "Social Anthropology and the Method of Controlled Comparison." *American Anthropologist*, 56:743-63.

1955a "The Cheyenne and Arapaho Kinship System." F. Eggan, ed., *Social Anthropology of North American Tribes*. Chicago: University of Chicago Press, 35-93.

1955b "Social Anthropology: Methods and Results." F. Eggan, ed., *Social Anthropology of North American Tribes*. Chicago: University of Chicago Press, 485-551.

1966 *The American Indian: Perspectives for the Study of Social Change*. Chicago: Aldine.

EINSTEIN, A.

1936 "Physics and Reality." *Journal of the Franklin Institute*, 221:349-82.

EISENSON, J. (ed.)

1963 *Psychology of Communication*. New York: Appleton-Century-Crofts.

EISELEY, L.

1958 *Darwin's Century: Evolution and the Man Who Discovered It*. Garden City, N. Y.: Doubleday.

ELLEGARD, A.

1958 *Darwin and the General Reader: The Reception of Darwin's Theory of Evolution in the British Periodical Press*, 1859-1872. Gothenburg Studies in English, 8. Goteborg: Elanders Boktrycheri Aktiebolag.

ENGELS, F.

1933 *Revolution and Counter Revolution*. London: Lawrence.

1947 (orig. 1888) *Herr Eugen Dühring's Revolution in Science*. Moscow: Foreign Languages Publishing House.

1954a (orig. 1884) *Origin of the Family, Private Property, and the State*. Ernest Untermann, trans. Moscow: Foreign Languages Publishing House.

1954b (orig. 1876) *Dialectics of Nature*. Moscow: Foreign Languages Publishing House.

1963 (orig. 1890) "Letter to Joseph Bloch." H. Selsam and H. Martel, eds., *Reader in Marxist Philosophy*. New York: International Publishers, 204-6.

ERASMUS, C.

1953 *Las Dimensiones de la Cultura: Historia de la Ethnología en los Estados Unidos entre 1900 y 1950*. Bogotá: Editorial Iqueirna.

1962 "Review of *The Achieving Society* by D. C. McClelland." *American Anthropologist*, 64:622-25.

ERASMUS, C. and W. SMITH

1967 "Cultural Anthropology in the United States since 1900: A Quantitative Analysis." *Southwestern Journal of Anthropology*, 23:111-40.

ERIKSON, E.

1950 *Childhood and Society*. New York: Norton.

ETKIN, W.

1964 "Theory of Socialization and Communication." W. Etkin, ed., *Social Behavior and Organization among Vertebrates*. Chicago: University of Chicago Press, 167-206.

EVANS-PRITCHARD, E. E.

1949 *The Sanusi of Cyrenaica*. London: Oxford University Press.

1951 *Social Anthropology*. New York: Free Press.

EVANS-PRITCHARD, E. E. and M. FORTES

1940 *African Political Systems*. International African Institute. London: Oxford University Press.

EWING, A. C.

1934 *Idealism: A Critical Survey*. London: Methuen.

FABER, M.

1955 "The Study of National Character." *Journal of Social Issues*, 11:52-56.

FAIRCHILD, H. N.

1928 *The Noble Savage: A Study in Romantic Idealism*. New York: Columbia University Press.

FANFANI, A.

1935 *Catholicism, Protestantism and Capitalism*. New York: Sheed and Ward.

FEBVRE, L. and L. BATAILLON

1925 *A Geographical Introduction to History*. New York: Knopf.

FERGUSON, A.

1819 (orig. 1767) *An Essay on the History of Civil Society*. Philadelphia: A. Finley.

FINOT, J.

1906 *Race Prejudice*. Florence Wade-Evena, trans. New York: Dutton.

FIRTH, R.

1929 *Primitive Economics of the New Zealand Maori*. London: George Routledge.

1951 "Contemporary British Social Anthropology." *American Anthropologist*, 53:474-90.
1954 "Social Organization and Social Change." *Journal of the Royal Anthropological Institute*, 84:1-20.
1957 *Man and Culture: An Evaluation of the Work of Bronislaw Malinowski*. London: Routledge & Kegan Paul.
1961 *Elements of Social Organization*, 2d ed. Boston: Beacon Press.
1963 (orig. 1936) *We, the Tikopia*. Boston: Beacon Press.
1964 *Essays on Social Organization and Values*. London: Athlone Press.

FIRTH, R. and B. S. YAMEY
1964 *Capital, Savings and Credit in Peasant Societies*. Chicago: Aldine.

FISON, L. and A. W. HOWITT
1880 *Kamilaroi and Kurnai, Group Marriage and Relationship, and Marriage by Elopement*. Melbourne: George Robertson.

FLINT, R. F.
1894 *History of the Philosophy of History*. New York: Scribner.

FLORENCE, P. S.
1927 *Economics and Human Behavior*. New York: Norton.

FORD, C.
1966 "On the Analysis of Behavior for Cross-cultural Comparisons." *Behavior Science Notes*, 1:79-97.

FORDE, C. D.
1934 *Habitat, Economy and Society*. London: Methuen.
1953 "Applied Anthropology in Government: British Africa." A. L. Kroeber, ed., *Anthropology Today*. Chicago: University of Chicago Press, 841-65.
1965 "Social Anthropology in African Studies." *African Affairs*. Spring, 1965, 15-28.

FORDE, C. D. and A. R. RADCLIFFE-BROWN
1950 *African Systems of Kinship and Marriage*. London: Oxford University Press.

FORTES, M.
1936 "Culture Contact as a Dynamic Process." *Africa*, 9:24-55.
1945 *The Dynamics of Clanship among the Tallensi*. London: Oxford University Press.
1949a "Preface." *Social Structure: Studies Presented to Radcliffe-Brown*. Oxford: Clarendon Press, v-xiv.
1949b *The Web of Kinship among the Tallensi*. London: Oxford University Press.
1953a *Social Anthropology at Cambridge since 1900: An Inaugural Lecture*. Cambridge: Cambridge University Press.
1953b "The Structure of Unilineal Descent Groups." *American Anthropologist*, 55:17-41.
1953c "Analysis and Description in Social Anthropology." *The Advancement of Science*, 10:190-201.

1955 "Radcliffe-Brown's Contribution to the Study of Social Organization." *British Journal of Sociology*, 6:16-30.

1957 "Malinowski and the Study of Kinship." R. Firth, ed., *Man and Culture*. London: Routledge & Kegan Paul, 157-88.

1959a *Oedipus and Job in West African Religion*. Cambridge: Cambridge University Press.

1959b "Descent, Filiation and Affinity: A Rejoinder to Dr. Leach." *Man*, 59:193-97; 206-12.

1962 (ed.) *Marriage in Tribal Societies*. Cambridge Papers in Social Anthropology, No. 3. Cambridge: Cambridge University Press.

FORTES, M. and E. E. EVANS-PRITCHARD (eds.)

1940 *African Political Systems*. London: Oxford University Press.

FORTUNE, R.

1932 *The Sorcerers of Dobu*. New York: Dutton.

FOTHERGILL, P.

1952 *Historical Aspects of Organic Evolution*. London: Hollis and Carter.

FRAKE, C.

1961 "The Diagnosis of Disease among the Subanum of Mindanao." *American Anthropologist*, 63:113-32.

1962a "The Ethnographic Study of Cognitive Systems." T. Gladwin and W. G. Sturtevant, eds., *Anthropology and Human Behavior*. Washington: Anthropological Society of Washington, 72-85.

1962b "Cultural Ecology and Ethnography." *American Anthropologist*, 64:53-59.

1964a "A Structural Description of Subanum 'Religious Behavior.' " W. Goodenough, ed., *Explorations in Cultural Anthropology*. New York: McGraw-Hill, 111-29.

1964b "Notes on Queries in Anthropology." *American Anthropologist*, 66, part 2:132-45.

FRANK, A. G.

1967 "Sociology of Development and Underdevelopment of Sociology." *Catalyst*, Summer:20-73.

FRANK, L. K.

1950 *Society as the Patient: Essays on Culture and Personality*. New Brunswick: Rutgers University Press.

FRAZER, J. G.

1887 *Totemism*. Edinburgh: Adams and Charles.

1911-1915 (orig. 1890) *The Golden Bough*, 3d ed. London: Macmillan.

1922 "Preface." B. Malinowski, *Argonauts of the Western Pacific*. New York: Dutton, vii-xiv.

1958 *The Golden Bough*. New York: Macmillan.

FREED, S.

1963 "An Objective Method for Determining the Collective Caste Hierarchy of an Indian Village." *American Anthropologist,* 65:879-91.

FREEDMAN, M.

1950 "Colonial Law and Chinese Society." *Journal of the Royal Anthropological Institute,* 80:97-126.

1958 *Lineage Organization in Southeastern China.* London: Athlone Press.

FRERE, J.

1800 "Account of Flint Weapons Discovered at Hoxne in Suffolk." *Archaeologia,* 13.

FREUD, S.

1918 *Totem and Taboo.* A. A. Brill, trans. New York: Moffat, Yard.

1928 *The Future of an Illusion.* W. D. Robson-Scott., trans. London: Institute of Psychoanalysis.

1930 *Civilization and Its Discontents.* New York: Jonathan Cape and Harrison Smith.

1938 (orig. 1913) *Totem and Taboo.* London: Penguin Books.

FRIED, M.

1952 "Land Tenure, Geography and Ecology in the Contact of Cultures." *American Journal of Economics and Sociology,* 11:1.

1953 *The Fabric of Chinese Society.* New York: Praeger.

1957 "The Classification of Corporate Unilineal Descent Groups." *Journal of the Royal Anthropological Institute,* 87:1-29.

1967 *The Evolution of Political Society.* New York: Random House

FROBENIUS, L.

1898 *Die Weltanschauung der Naturvölker.* Weimar: E. Felber.

GAGE, W.

1863 *Geographical Studies.* Boston: Gould and Lincoln.

GALL, F. J.

1825 *Sur les Foncions du Cerveau et sur Celles de Chacune de Ses Parties. Paris: J. B. Ballière.*

GARCILASO DE LA VEGA

1609 *Primera parte de los comentarios reales que tratan del origin de los Yncas.* Lisbon: En la officina de Pedro Crasbeeck.

GARDIN, J.

1965 "On a Possible Interpretation of Componential Analysis in Archaeology." *American Anthropologist,* 67, part 2:9-22.

GARDINER, P.

1959 *Theories of History.* New York: Free Press.

GARN, S.

1957 "Race and Evolution." *American Anthropologist,* 59:218-24.

1961 *Human Races.* Springfield: Thomas.

GAY, P.

1964 *The Party of Humanity.* New York: Knopf.

1966 *The Enlightenment: An Interpretation. The Rise of Modern Paganism.* New York: Knopf.

GEHLKE, C. E.
1915 "Emile Durkheim's Contribution to Sociological Theory." Unpublished Ph.D. dissertation, Columbia University.

GELLNER, E.
1957 "Ideal Language and Kinship Structure." *Philosophy of Science*, 24:235-43.
1958 "Time and Theory in Social Anthropology." *Mind*, 67:182-202.

GEOGHECAN, W. and P. KAY
1964 "More Structure and Statistics: A Critique of C. Ackerman's Analysis of the Purum." *American Anthropologist*, 66:1351-55.

GEORGE, K.
1958 "The Civilized West Looks at Primitive Africa: 1400-1800. A Study in Ethnocentrism." *Isis*, 40:62-72.

GERARD, R. W.
1957 "Units and Concepts of Biology." *Science*, 125:429-33.

GERTZ, C.
1963 *Agricultural Involution*. Berkeley: University of California Press.

GIANTURCO, E.
1937 "Joseph de Maistre and Giambattista Vico." Unpublished Ph.D. dissertation, Columbia University.

GIBBON, E.
1804-1805 (orig. 1776) *The History of the Decline and Fall of the Roman Empire*. Philadelphia: William Birch and Abraham Small. 7 vols.

GIBSON, A. and J. H. ROWE
1961 "A Bibliography of the Publications of Alfred Louis Kroeber." *American Anthropologist*, 63:1060-87.

GILLISPIE, C.
1951 *Genesis and Geology*. Cambridge: Harvard University Press.
1960 *The Edge of Objectivity*. Princeton: Princeton University Press.

GILSON, E. and T. LANGAN
1963 *Modern Philosophy: Descartes to Kant*. New York: Random House.

GINSBERG, M.
1932 *Studies in Sociology*. London: Methuen.

GLADWIN, T.
1961 "Oceania." F. Hsu, ed., *Psychological Anthropology: Approaches to Culture and Personality*. Homewood, Ill.: Dorsey Press, 135-71.

GLUCKMAN, M.
1949 *Malinowski's Sociological Theories*. Rhodes Livingstone Papers 16. New York: Oxford University Press.
1955a *Custom and Conflict in Africa*. Oxford: Basil Blackwell.
1955b *Judicial Process among the Barotse of Northern Nigeria*. Manchester: Manchester University Press.
1962 *Essays on the Ritual of Social Relations*. Manchester: Manchester University Press.
1963 *Order and Rebellion in Tribal Africa*. New York: Free Press.

GOBINEAU, J. A. DE

1856 (orig. 1853) *The Moral and Intellectual Diversity of Races.* Philadelphia: J. B. Lippincott.

GOLDENWEISER, A.

1914 "The Social Organization of the Indians of North America." *Journal of American Folk-Lore,* 27:411-36.

1925 "Diffusionism and Historical Ethnology." *American Journal of Sociology,* 31:19-38.

1933 *History, Psychology and Culture.* New York: Knopf.

1937 *Anthropology: An Introduction to Primitive Culture.* New York: Appleton-Century-Crofts.

1940 "Leading Contributions of Anthropology to Social Theory." H. E. Barnes *et al.*, eds., *Contemporary Social Theory.* New York: Appleton-Century, 433-90.

1941 "Recent Trends in American Anthropology." *American Anthropologist,* 43:151-63.

1942 *Anthropology: An Introduction to Primitive Culture.* New York: F. S. Crofts.

GOLDFRANK, E.

1945 "Socialization, Personality, and the Structure of Pueblo Society." *American Anthropologist,* 47:516-39.

GOLDMAN, I.

1950 "Psychiatric Interpretations of Russian History: A Reply to Geoffrey Gorer." *American and Slavic East European Review,* 9:155-61.

GOLDSTEIN, L.

1967 "Theory in Anthropology: Developmental or Causal." L. Cross, ed., *Sociological Theory: Inquiries and Paradigms.* New York: Harper and Row.

GOODENOUGH, W.

1949 "Premarital Freedom on Truk: Theory and Practice." *American Anthropologist,* 51:615-20.

1956 "Componential Analysis and the Study of Meaning." *Language,* 32:195-216.

1964a "Cultural Anthropology and Linguistics." D. Hymes, ed., *Language in Culture and Society.* New York: Harper and Row, 36-39.

1964b "Introduction." W. Goodenough, ed., *Explorations in Cultural Anthropology.* New York: McGraw-Hill, 1-24.

1965a "Yankee Kinship Terminology: A Problem in Componential Analysis." *American Anthropologist* 67, part 2:259-87.

1965b "Rethinking 'Status' and 'Role': Toward a General Model of the Cultural Organization of Social Relationships." *The Relevance of Models for Social Anthropology.* New York: Praeger, 1-22.

1967 "Componential Analysis." *Science,* 156:1203-9.

GOODY, J.

1959 "The Mother's Brother and Sister's Son in West Africa." *Journal of the Royal Anthropological Institute,* 89:61-88.

GORER, G.
1943 "Themes in Japanese Culture." *Transactions of the New York Academy of Sciences.* Series II, vol. 5:106-24.
1948 *The American People.* New York: Norton.
1955 *Exploring English Character.* London: Cresset.
GORER, G. and M. MEAD
1942 *Balinese Character: A Photographic Analysis.* Special Publication of New York Academy of Sciences.
GORER, G. and J. RICKMAN
1949 *The People of Great Russia.* London: Cresset.
GOSSETT, T. F.
1963 *Race: The History of an Idea in America.* Dallas: Southern Methodist University Press.
GOTTSCHALLS, L. (ed.)
1963 *Generalization in the Writing of History.* Chicago: University of Chicago Press.
GOUGH, E. K.
1959 "The Nayars and the Definition of Marriage." *Journal of the Royal Anthropological Institute,* 89:23-34.
GOULDNER, A. W.
1962 "Introduction." É. Durkheim, *Socialism.* New York: Crowell-Collier, 7-31.
GOULDNER, A. W. and R. PETERSON
1962 *Technology and the Moral Order.* Indianapolis: Bobbs-Merrill.
GRAEBNER, F.
1903 "Kulturkreise und Kulturschichten in Ozeanien." *Zeitschrift für Ethnologie,* 37:28-53.
1911 *Die Methode der Ethnologie.* Heidelberg.
GREENBERG, J.
1963 *Universals of Language.* Cambridge: M.I.T. Press.
GREENE, J.
1959 *The Death of Adam.* Ames, Iowa: Iowa State University Press.
1961 *Darwin and the Modern World View.* Baton Rouge: Louisiana State University Press.
GREGG, D. and E. WILLIAMS
1948 "The Dismal Science of Functionalism." *American Anthropologist,* 50:594-611.
GRIMM, J.
1831-1840 *Deutsche Grammatik.* Goteberg.
GRINNELL, G. B.
1897 "Review of Mooney's Ghost-Dance Religion." *American Anthropologist,* 10:230.
GROSSE, E.
1896 *Die Formen der Familie und die Formen der Wirtschaft.* Freiburg: J. C. B. Mohr.

GROSSMAN, M.
1926 *The Philosophy of Helvetius.* New York: Bureau of Publications, Teachers College, Columbia University.

GURVICH, G. and W. E. MOORE (eds.)
1945 *Twentieth Century Sociology.* New York: Philosophical Library.

GUY, B.
1963 "The French Image of China before and after Voltaire." Theodore Besterman, ed., *Studies on Voltaire and the Eighteenth Century,* Genève: Institut et musée Voltaire, 21.

HABER, F. C.
1959 *The Age of the World—Moses to Darwin.* Baltimore: Johns Hopkins Press.

HADDON, A. C.
1895 *Evolution in Art.* London: W. Scott.
1908 *The Study of Man. London:* J. Murray.
1910 *A History of Anthropology.* New York: Putnam.
1927 *The Wanderings of Peoples.* Cambridge: Cambridge University Press.
1934 *History of Anthropology.* London: Watts.

HAHN, E.
1905 *Das Alter der wirtschaftlichen Kultur der Menschheit.* Heidelberg: Winter.

HAIMSON, L. H.
1955 *The Russian Marxists and the Origins of Bolshevism.* Cambridge: Harvard University Press.

HALE, M.
1677 *The Primitive Origination of Mankind.* London.

HALLOWELL, A. I.
1955 *Culture and Experience.* Philadelphia: University of Pennsylvania Press.
1959 "Behavioral Evolution and the Emergence of the Self." B. Meggers, ed., *Evolution and Anthropology: A Centennial Appraisal.* Washington: Anthropological Society of Washington, 36-60.
1960 "The Beginnings of Anthropology in America." Frederica deLaguna, ed., *Selected Papers from the American Anthropologist 1888-1920.* Evanston: Row, Peterson, 1-96.
1965 "The History of Anthropology as an Anthropological Problem." *Journal of the History of the Behavioral Sciences,* 1:24-38.

HAMMEL, E.
1965 "A Transformational Analysis of Comanche Kinship Terminology." *American Anthropologist* 67, part 2:65-105.

HANKE, L.
1959 *The Spanish Struggle for Justice in the Conquest of America.* Philadelphia: University of Pennsylvania Press.

HANKIN, F. H.
1908 "Adolphe Quételet as Statistician." New York: Longmans, Green.

HARDING, T. and E. LEACOCK
1964 "Morgan and Materialism; A Reply to Professor Opler." *Current Anthropology*, 5:109-10.

HARING, D.
1956 "Japanese National Character: Cultural Anthropology, Psychoanalysis, and History." D. Haring, ed., *Personal Character and Cultural Milieu*. Syracuse: Syracuse University Press, 424-37.

HARRIS, M.
1959a "The Economy Has No Surplus?" *American Anthropologist*, 61:185-99.
1959b "Labour Migration among the Moçambique Thonga: Cultural and Political Factors." *Africa*, 21:50-64.
1964a *The Nature of Cultural Things*. New York: Random House.
1964b *Patterns of Race in the Americas*. New York: Walker.
1966a "The Cultural Ecology of India's Sacred Cattle." *Current Anthropology*, 7:51-66.
1966b "Race, Conflict, and Reform in Moçambique." S. Diamond and F. Burke, eds., *The Transformation of East Africa*. New York: Basic Books, 157-84.
1967 "The Cognitive Calculus of Brazilian Racial Categories." Unpublished manuscript.

HARRIS, M. and C. KOTTAK
1963 "The Structural Significance of Brazilian Racial Categories." *Sociologia*, 25:203-8.

HARRIS, M. and G. MORREN
1966 "The Limitations of the Principle of Limited Possibilities." *American Anthropologist*, 68:122-27.

HART, C. W. M.
1938 "Social Evolution and Modern Anthropology." H. A. Innes, ed., *Essays in Political Economy in Honour of E. J. Urwick*. Toronto: University of Toronto Press, 99-116.
1954 "The Sons of Turimpi." *American Anthropologist*, 54:242-61.

HART, J.
1964 *Political Writers of Eighteenth Century England*. New York: Knopf.

HARTLAND, S.
1917 *Matrilineal Kinship and the Question of Its Priority*. Memoir 4. American Anthropological Association.

HAYS, H. R.
1958 *From Ape to Angel*. New York: Knopf.

HAZARD, T.
1960 "On the Nature of the Numaym and its Counterparts Elsewhere on the Northwest Coast." Unpublished paper read at the 127th

Annual Meeting of the American Association for the Advancement of Science.

HECKER, J. F.

1934 *Russian Sociology*. New York: Wiley.

HEEREN, A.

1817 *Ideen über die Politik, den Verkehr, und den Handel der vornehmsten Völker der alten Welt*. Wien: Harter.

HEGEL, G. W. F.

1910 *The Phenomenology of Mind*. J. J. B. Baillie, trans. London: Allen & Unwin.

1956 (orig. 1837) *The Philosophy of History*. J. Sibree, trans. New York: Dover.

HEINE-GELDERN, R.

1960 "Recent Developments in Ethnological Theory in Europe." A. Wallace, ed., *Selected Papers of the Fifth International Congress of Anthropological and Ethnological Sciences*. Philadelphia: University of Pennsylvania Press, 49-53.

HEIZER, R.

1962 "The Background of Thomsen's Three-age System." *Technology and Culture*, 3:259-66.

HELM, J.

1962 "The Ecological Approach in Anthropology." *American Journal of Sociology*, 67:630-39.

1966 (ed.) *Pioneers of American Anthropology*. Seattle: University of Washington Press.

HELVETIUS, C. A.

1810 (orig. 1748) *De L'Esprit or Essays on the Mind and Its Several Faculties*. London: Albion Press.

1818 (orig. 1772) *De l'Homme*. Paris: Mme. Ve Lepetit.

1946 *A Treatise on Man. Introduction to Contemporary Civilization in the West*, I. New York: Columbia University Press, 1004-24.

HENRY, J.

1959 "Culture, Personality, and Evolution." *American Anthropologist*, 61:221-26.

1963 *Culture against Man*. New York: Random House.

HERDER, J. G. VON

1803 (orig. 1784) *Outlines of a Philosophy of the History of Man*. T. Churchill, trans. London: Luke Hansard.

HERSKOVITS, M.

1948 *Man and His Works*. New York: Knopf.

1953 *Franz Boas*. New York: Scribner.

1957 "Some Further Notes on Franz Boas' Arctic Expedition." *American Anthropologist*, 59:112-16.

HERTZ, R.

1960 (orig. 1909) *Death and the Right Hand*. R. Needham and C. Needham, trans. New York: Free Press.

HIELD, W.
1954 "The Study of Change in Social Science." *British Journal of Sociology*, 1-12.
HIMMELFARB, G.
1959 *Darwin and the Darwinian Revolution*. London: Chatto and Windus.
HIPPOCRATES
1881 *On Airs, Waters, and Places*. London: Wyman and Sons.
HOAGLAND, H. and R. W. BURHOE (eds.)
1962 *Evolution and Man's Progress*. New York: Columbia University Press.
HOBBES, T.
1958 (orig. 1642) *Leviathan*. New York: Liberal Arts Press.
HOBHOUSE, L. T., G. C. WHEELER, and M. GINSBERG
1915 *The Material Culture and Social Institutions of the Simpler Peoples: An Essay in Correlation*. London: Chapman-Hall.
HOBSBAWM, E. (ed.)
1965 *Introduction to Pre-Capitalist Economic Formations: Karl Marx*. New York: International Publishers, 9-65.
HOBSON, J. A. and M. GINSBERG
1931 *Hobhouse, His Life and Work*. London: W. H. Allen.
HOCKETT, C. and R. ASCHER
1964 "The Human Revolution." *Current Anthropology*, 5:135-68.
HODGE, F. W. (ed.)
1907 *Handbook of American Indians North of Mexico*. Washington: Bureau of American Ethnology, Bull. 30.
HODGEN, M.
1936 *The Doctrine of Survivals*. London: Allenson.
1964 *Early Anthropology in the Sixteenth and Seventeenth Centuries*. Philadelphia: University of Pennsylvania Press.
HODGES, H. A.
1944 *Wilhelm Dilthey: An Introduction*. London: Kegan Paul, Trench, Trubner.
1952 *The Philosophy of Wilhelm Dilthey*. London: Routledge & Kegan Paul.
HODGKIN, T.
1848 "Progress of Ethnology." *Journal of the Ethnological Society of London*, 1:27-45.
HODSON, T. C.
1925 "Notes on the Marriage of Cousins in India." *Man in India*, 5:163-75.
HOEBEL, E. A.
1949 *Man in the Primitive World*. New York: McGraw-Hill.
1960 "William Robertson: An 18th Century Anthropologist-Historian." *American Anthropologist*, 62:648-55.

HOERNLÉ, A. W.
1933 "New Aims and Methods in Social Anthropology." *South African Journal of Science*, 30:74-92.
HOFSTADTER, R.
1944 *Social Darwinism in American Thought, 1860-1915*. Philadelphia: University of Pennsylvania Press.
HOGBEN, L.
1960 *Man, Race and Darwin*. London: Oxford University Press.
HOGBIN, H. I.
1939 *Experiment in Civilization: The Effects of European Culture on a Native Community of the Solomon Islands*. London: George Routledge.
1963 *Kinship and Marriage in a New Guinea Village*. London: Athlone.
HOGEN, E. E.
1962 *On the Theory of Social Change*. Homewood, Ill.: Dorsey Press.
HOLMES, G.
1914 "Areas of American Culture Characterization Tentatively Outlined as an Aid in the Study of Antiquities." *American Anthropologist*, 16:413-16.
HOLMES, L.
1957 "The Restudy of Manu'an Culture: A Problem in Methodology." Unpublished Ph.D. dissertation, Northwestern University.
HOMANS, G.
1941 "Anxiety and Ritual: The Theories of Malinowski and Radcliffe-Brown." *American Anthropologist*, 43:164-72.
HOMANS, G. and D. M. SCHNEIDER
1955 *Marriage, Authority and Final Causes*. New York: Free Press.
HONIGMANN, J. J.
1954 *Culture and Personality*. New York: Harper and Row.
1961 "North America." F. Hsu, ed., *Psychological Anthropology: Approaches to Culture and Personality*. Homewood, Ill.: Dorsey Press. 93-134.
1963 *Understanding Culture*. New York: Harper and Row.
HOOTON, E. A.
1946 *Up from the Ape*. New York: Macmillan.
HORKHEIMER, M.
1939 "The Relation between Psychology and Sociology in the Work of Wilhelm Dilthey." *Zeitschrift für Sozialforschung*, 8:430-43.
HOROWITZ, I. L.
1954 *Claude Helvetius: Philosopher of Democracy and Enlightenment*. New York: Pane-Whitman.

HOUSE, F. N.

1936 *The Development of Sociology*. New York: McGraw-Hill.

HOWARD, G. E.

1904 *A History of Matrimonial Institutions Chiefly in England and the United States, with an Introductory Analysis of the Literature and the Theories of Primitive Marriage and the Family*. Chicago: University of Chicago Press.

HOWELL, F. C. and F. BOURLIERE

1964 *African Ecology and Human Evolution*. Chicago: Aldine.

HOWETT, W.

1838 *Colonization and Christianity: A Popular History of the Treatment of the Natives by Europeans in All Their Colonies*. London: Longman Orne, Brown, Greene and Longman.

HSU, F.

1961 "Kinship and Ways of Life." F. Hsu, ed., *Psychological Anthropology: Approaches to Culture and Personality*. Homewood, Ill.: Dorsey Press, 400-56.

HULSE, F.

1948 "Convention and Reality in Japanese Culture." *Southwestern Journal of Anthropology*, 4:345-55.

HUME, D.

1822 (orig. 1780) *The Rise and the Progress of the Arts and Sciences. Essays and Treatises on Several Subjects, Containing Essays, Moral, Political, and Literary*. London: J. Jones.

1898 (orig. 1742) *Of National Character. The Philosophical Works of David Hume*, III. London.

1953 *David Hume's Political Essays*. C. W. Hendel, ed. New York: Liberal Arts Press.

HUNT, J.

1863 "Introductory Address on the Study of Anthropology." *Anthropological Review*, 1:1-20.

1866a "Race in Legislation and Political Economy." *Anthropological Review*, 4:113-35.

1866b "On the Application of the Principle of Natural Selection in Anthropology." *Anthropological Review*, 4:320-40.

HUNTER, J.

1865 (orig. 1775) "Inaugural Disputation on the Varieties of Man." T. Bendyshe, ed. and trans., *The Anthropological Treatises of Johann Friedrich Blumenbach*. London: Longman, Green, Longman, Roberts, and Green, 357-94.

HUNTER, M.

1936 *Reaction to Conquest: Effects of Contact with Europeans on the Pondo of South Africa*. London: Oxford University Press for International Institute of African Languages and Cultures.

HUTTON, J.

1788 *Theory of the Earth, or an Investigation of the Laws Observable in the Composition, Dissolution and Restoration of Land upon the Globe.* Edinburgh: Royal Society of Edinburgh Transactions.

1899 (orig. 1795) *Theory of the Earth, with Proofs and Illustrations.* London: Geological Society.

HUXLEY, J. S.

1942 *Evolution: The Modern Synthesis.* London: Allen & Unwin.

HYMES, D.

1963 "Toward a History of Linguistic Anthropology." *Anthropological Linguistics,* 5:59-103.

1964a "Directions in (Ethno-) Linguistic Theory." *American Anthropologist* 66, part 2:6-56.

1964b "A Perspective for Linguistic Anthropology." Sol Tax, ed., *Horizons of Anthropology.* Chicago: Aldine, 92-107.

IDRISI, AL

1836 (orig. 1154) *Geographie D'Édrisi.* P. A. Jaubert, trans. Paris: La Société de Geographie, Recueil de Voyages et de Memoires, 5.

IMANISHI, K.

1963 "Social Behavior in Japanese Monkeys." C. H. Southwick, ed., *Primate Social Behavior.* Princeton: Van Nostrand, 68-81.

INGRAM, J. K.

1894 *A History of Political Economy.* New York: Macmillan.

INKELES, A., E. HAUFMAN and H. BEIER

1961 "Modal Personality and Adjustment to the Soviet Socio-political System." B. Kaplan, ed., *Studying Personality Cross-Culturally.* Evanston: Row, Peterson, 201-24.

INKELES, A. and D. J. LEVINSON

1954 "National Character: The Study of Modal Personality and Sociocultural Systems." G. Lindzey, ed., *Handbook of Social Psychology.* Cambridge: Addison-Wesley, 977-1020.

JABLOW, A.

1963 "The Development of the Image of Africa in British Popular Literature, 1530-1910." Unpublished Ph.D. dissertation, Columbia University. Ann Arbor: University Microfilms.

JACOBS, M.

1964 *Pattern in Cultural Anthropology.* Homewood, Ill.: Dorsey Press.

1966 "A Look Ahead in Oral Literature Research." *Journal of American Folklore,* 79:413-27.

JARVIE, I. C.

1964 *The Revolution in Anthropology.* London: Routledge & Kegan Paul.

JEFFERSON, T.

1801 (orig. 1785) *Notes on the State of Virginia.* Newark, N.J.: Pennington and Gould.

JENNESS, D.
1932 "The Indians of Canada." Canada Department of Mines. *National Museum Bulletin*, 65.

JOACHIM OF FLORIN
1928 (orig. 1254) *L'Évangile Éternel; Première Traduction Française*. Paris: Rieder.

JORGENSEN, J.
1966 "Addendum: Geographical Clusterings and Functional Explanations of In-law Avoidances: An Analysis of Comparative Method." *Current Anthropology*, 7:161-82.

JOSSELIN DE JONG, J. P. B.
1952 *Lévi-Strauss's Theory on Kinship and Marriage*. London: E. J. Brill.
1962 "A New Approach to Kinship Studies." *Bijdragen. Tot de Taal-, Land En Volkenkunde*, 118:42-67.

JUDD, N.
1967 *The Bureau of American Ethnology: A Partial History*. Norman: University of Oklahoma Press.

JUNOD, H.
1913 *The Life of a South African Tribe*. Neuchâtel: Imprimerie Attinger Frères, 2 vols.

KABERRY, P.
1957 "Malinowski's Contribution to Fieldwork Methods and the Writing of Ethnography." R. Firth, ed., *Man and Culture: An Evaluation of the Work of Bronislaw Malinowski*. London: Routledge and Kegan Paul, 71-91.

KAMES, H. H., LORD
1774 *Sketches of the History of Man*, I and II. Edinburgh: W. Creech; London: W. Strahan and T. Cadell.

KANT, I.
1798 *Anthropologie in pragmatischer Einsicht abgefasst von Immanuel Kant*. Königsberg: F. Nicolovius.
1946 (orig. 1784) *What Is Enlightenment? Introduction to Contemporary Civilization in the West*, I. New York: Columbia University Press, 1069-76.
1951 (orig. 1790) *A Critique of Judgment*. J. H. Bernard, trans. New York: Hafner.

KAPLAN, A.
1964 *The Conduct of Inquiry. Methodology for Behavioral Science*. San Francisco: Chandler.

KAPLAN, B.
1954 *A Study of Rorschach Responses in Four Cultures*. Harvard University. Papers of the Peabody Museum of American Archaeology and Ethnology, vol. 42.
1961a (ed.) *Studying Personality Cross-Culturally*. Evanston: Row, Peterson.

1961b "Cross-Cultural Use of Projective Technique." F. Hsu, ed., *Psychological Anthropology: Approaches to Culture and Personality.* Homewood, Ill.: Dorsey Press, 235-54.

KARDINER, A.

1939 (ed.) *The Individual and His Society.* New York: Columbia University Press.

1959 "Psychosocial Studies." *Science,* 130:1728.

KARDINER, A., R. LINTON, J. WEST, *et al.*

1945 *The Psychological Frontiers of Society.* New York: Columbia University Press.

KARDINER, A. and E. PREBLE

1961 *They Studied Man.* Cleveland: World Publishing Co.

KATZ, J. and J. FODOR

1962 "The Structure of Semantic Theory." Unpublished manuscript.

KEANE, A. H.

1896 *Ethnology.* Cambridge: Cambridge University Press.

KEESING, R. M.

1966 "Comment on B. N. Colby (1966)." *Current Anthropology,* 7:23.

KELLER, A. G.

1915 *Societal Evolution.* New York: Macmillan.

1931 *Societal Evolution: A Study of the Evolutionary Basis of the Science of Society,* rev. ed. New York: Macmillan.

KERLINGER, F. N.

1953 "Behavior and Personality in Japan: A Critique of Three Studies of Japanese Personality." *Social Forces,* 250-58.

KIDDER, A. V.

1936 "Speculations on New World Prehistory." R. Lowie, ed., *Essays in Anthropology.* Berkeley: University of California, 143-51.

KILZER, E. and E. J. ROSS

1954 *Western Social Thought.* Milwaukee: Bruce.

KLEIN, H.

1967 *Slavery in the Americas.* Chicago: University of Chicago Press.

KLEMM, G.

1843 *Allgemeine Cultur—Geschichte der Menschheit.* Leipzig: Leubner.

KLINEBERG, O.

1935 *Race Differences.* New York: Harper.

1944 "A Science of National Character." *Journal of Social Psychology,* 19:147-62.

1951 *Race and Psychology.* Paris: UNESCO.

1963 "Negro-White Differences in Intelligence Test Performance: A New Look at an Old Problem." *American Psychologist,* 18:198-203.

KLOOSTERBOER, W.

1960 *Involuntary Labor since the Abolition of Slavery.* Leiden: E. J. Brill.

KLUBACK, W.
1956 *Wilhelm Dilthey's Philosophy of History*. New York: Columbia University Press.

KLUCKHOHN, C.
1936 "Some Reflections on the Method and Theory of the Kulturkreis Lehre." *American Anthropologist*, 38:157-96.
1938 "Participation in Ceremonials in a Navaho Community." *American Anthropologist*, 40:359-69.
1939 "The Place of Theory in Anthropological Studies." *The Philosophy of Science*, 6:328-44.
1940 *The Conceptual Structure in Middle American Studies. The Maya and Their Neighbors*. New York: Appleton-Century, 41-51.
1943 "Bronislaw Malinowski, 1884-1942." *Journal of American Folklore*, 56:208-19.
1944 "The Influence of Psychiatry on Anthropology in America during the Last 100 Years." J. K. Hall, G. Zilboorg, and H. A. Bunker, eds., *One Hundred Years of American Psychiatry*. New York: Columbia University Press, 589-617.
1947 *Some Aspects of Navaho Infancy and Early Childhood. Psychoanalysis and the Social Sciences*, I. New York: International Universities Press, 37-86
1949 *Mirror for Man*. New York: McGraw-Hill.
1954 "Southwestern Studies of Culture and Personality." *American Anthropologist*, 56:685-97.
1958 "The Evolution of Contemporary American Values." *Daedalus*, Spring edition: 78-109.
1961 *Anthropology and the Classics*. Providence: Brown University Press.

KLUCKHOHN, C., H. A. MURRAY and D. M. SCHNEIDER (eds.)
1953 *Personality in Nature, Society and Culture*, 2d ed. New York: Knopf.

KLUCKHOHN, C. and O. PRUFER
1959 "Influences during the Formative Years." *The Anthropology of Franz Boas*. Memoir 89. American Anthropology Association, 4-28.

KNIGHT, R.
1965 "A Re-examination of Hunting, Trapping and Territoriality among the Northeastern Algonkian Indians." A. Leeds and A. Vayda, eds., *The Role of Animals in Human Ecological Adjustments*. Washington: The American Association for the Advancement of Science, 27-42.

KNOX, R.
1850 *Races of Men: A Fragment*. Philadelphia: Lea and Blanchard.

KÖBBEN, A. J. F.
1952 "New Ways of Presenting an Old Idea: The Statistical Method in

Social Anthropology." *Journal of the Royal Anthropological Institute,* 82:129-45.

1966 "Structuralism versus Comparative Functionalism; Some Comments." *Bijdragen. Tot de Taal-, Land En Volkenkunde,* 122:145-50.

1967 "The Logic of Cross-cultural Analysis." *Current Anthropology,* 8:3-34.

KOMAROV, V. L.

1935 "Marx and Engels on Biology." N. S. Bukharin, ed., *Marxism in Modern Thought.* New York: Harcourt, 190-234.

KOTTAK, C.

1966 "The Structure of Equality in a Brazilian Fishing Community." Unpublished Ph.D. dissertation, Columbia University.

KROEBER, A.

1901 "Decorative Symbolism of the Arapaho." *American Anthropologist,* 3:308-36.

1909 "Classificatory Systems of Relationship." *Journal of the Royal Anthropological Institute,* 39:77-84.

1915 "The Eighteen Professions." *American Anthropologist,* 17:283-89.

1917a "The Superorganic." *American Anthropologist,* 19:163-213.

1917b *California Kinship Systems.* University of California Publications in American Archaeology and Ethnology, 12:339-96.

1917c "Zuñi Kin and Clan." American Museum of Natural History. *Anthropological Papers,* 18:39-204.

1919a "On the Principle of Order in Civilization as Exemplified by Changes of Fashion." *American Anthropologist,* 21:253-63.

1919b "Kinship in the Philippines." American Museum of Natural History. *Anthropological Papers,* 19:69-84.

1920a "Totem and Taboo: An Ethnologic Psychoanalysis." *American Anthropologist,* 22:48-55.

1920b "Review of *Primitive Society.*" *American Anthropologist,* 22:377-81.

1923 *Anthropology.* New York: Harcourt, Brace.

1925 (ed.) *Handbook of the Indians of California.* Washington: Bureau of American Ethnology, Bull. 78.

1931 "The Culture-area and Age-area Concepts of Clark Wissler." S. Rice, ed., *Methods in Social Science.* Chicago: University of Chicago Press, 248-65.

1934 *Yurok and Neighboring Kin Term Systems.* University of California Publications in American Archaeology and Ethnology, 35:15-22.

1935 "History and Science in Anthropology." *American Anthropologist,* 37:539-69.

1938 "Basic and Secondary Patterns of Social Structure." *Journal of the Royal Anthropological Institute,* 68:299-310.

1939 *Cultural and Natural Areas of Native North America.* University of California Publications in American Archaeology and Ethnology, vol. 38.

1944 *Configurations of Culture Growth*. Berkeley: University of California Press.

1947 "My Faith." *The American Weekly*, April 6, vol. 33.

1948a *Anthropology*. New York: Harcourt, Brace.

1948b "Summary and Interpretations." W. Bennett, ed., A *Reappraisal of Peruvian Archaeology*. Memoirs of the Society for American Archaeology, 4:113-21.

1948c "White's View of Culture." *American Anthropologist*, 50:405-15.

1949 "An Authoritarian Panacea." *American Anthropologist*, 51:318-20.

1952 *The Nature of Culture*. Chicago: University of Chicago Press.

1954 "Critical Summary and Commentary." R. F. Spencer, ed., *Method and Perspective in Anthropology*. Minneapolis: University of Minnesota Press, 273-99.

1956 "The Place of Boas in Anthropology." *American Anthropologist*, 58:151-59.

1957 *Style and Civilizations*. Ithaca: Cornell University Press.

1963 *An Anthropologist Looks at History*. Berkeley: University of California Press.

KROEBER, A. and H. DRIVER

1932 "Quantitative Expression of Cultural Relationships." University of California Publications in American Archaeology and Ethnology, 29:253-423.

KROEBER, A. and C. KLUCKHOHN

1952 "Culture: A Critical Review of Concepts and Definitions." Harvard University. Papers of the Peabody Museum of American Archaeology and Ethnology, vol. 47.

KROEBER, A. and J. RICHARDSON

1940 "Three Centuries of Women's Dress Fashions: A Quantitative Analysis." *University of California Anthropological Records*, 5:111-54.

KROEBER, T.

1963 "Introduction." A. Kroeber, *An Anthropologist Looks at History*. Berkeley: University of California Press, xvi-xix.

KRONICH, D. A.

1962 A *History of Scientific and Technical Periodicals*. New York: Scarecrow Press.

LA BARRE, W.

1945 "Some Observations on Character Structure in the Orient: The Japanese." *Psychiatry*, 8:326-42.

1954 *The Human Animal*. Chicago: University of Chicago Press.

1958 "The Influence of Freud on Anthropology." *American Imago*, 15:275-328.

LABRIOLA, A.
1904 *Essays on the Materialistic Conceptions of History.* C. H. Kerr, trans. Chicago: C. H. Kerr.

LAFITAU, J. T.
1724 *Moeurs des Sauvages Amériquains, Comparées aux Moeurs des Premiers Temps.* Paris: Saugrain l'aîné.

LAGUNA, F. DE (ed.)
1960 *Selected Papers from the American Anthropologist.* Evanston: Row, Peterson.

LAMARCK, J. B.
1964 (orig. 1802) *Hydrogeology.* A. V. Carozzi, trans. Urbana: University of Illinois Press.

LAMB, D. S.
1906 "The Story of the Anthropological Society of Washington." *American Anthropologist,* 8:564-79.

LAMBERT, W. W., L. TRIANDIS, and M. WOLF
1959 "Some Correlates of Beliefs in the Malevolence and Benevolence of Supernatural Beings: A Cross-cultural Study." *Journal of Abnormal and Social Psychology,* 58:162-69.

LAMENNAIS, F.
1822-1823 *Essai sur l'indifférence en Matière de Religion.* Paris.

LA METTRIE, J. O. DE
1912 (orig. 1748) *Man a Machine.* G. Bussey, ed. Chicago: The Open Court.

LANG, A.
1893 (orig. 1885) *Custom and Myth.* London: Longmans, Green.
1898 *The Making of Religion.* London: Longmans, Green.

LANGE, F. A.
1925 *The History of Materialism.* E. C. Thomas, trans. London: Kegan Paul, Trench, Trubner.

LANHAM, B.
1956 "Aspects of Child Care in Japan: Preliminary Report." D. Haring, ed., *Personal Character and Cultural Milieu.* Syracuse: Syracuse University Press, 565-83.

LANTIS, M. (ed.)
1955 "The U.S.A. as Anthropologists See It." *American Anthropologist,* 57:1113-1295.

LA PEYRÈRE, I. DE
1656 (orig. 1655) *Men before Adam.* London.

LASKI, H. J.
1920 *Political Thought from Locke to Bentham.* New York: Holt.

LATHAM, R. G.
1859 *Descriptive Ethnography.* London: J. Van Voorst.

LAUFER, B.

1918 "Review of R. H. Lowie's *Culture and Ethnology*." *American Anthropologist*, 20:87-91.

LAWRENCE, SIR W.

1823 (orig. 1819) *Lectures on Physiology, Zoology and the Natural History of Man*. London: James Smith.

LEACH, E.

1950 "Review of Murdock's *Social Structure*." *Man*, 50:107-8.

1954 *Political Systems of Highland Burma*. Boston: Beacon Press.

1957 "The Epistemological Background to Malinowski's Empiricism." R. Firth (ed.), *Man and Culture: An Evaluation of the Work of Bronislaw Malinowski*. London: Routledge & Kegan Paul, 119-37.

1958 "Concerning Trobriand Clans and the Kinship Category Tabu." J. Goody, ed., *The Developmental Cycle of Domestic Groups*. Cambridge Papers in Social Anthropology, No. 1. Cambridge: Cambridge University Press, 120-46.

1961a *Rethinking Anthropology*. London: Athlone Press.

1961b *Pul Eliya, A Village in Ceylon*. New York: Cambridge University Press.

1961c "Lévi-Strauss in the Garden of Eden." *Transactions of the New York Academy of Sciences*, 23:386-96.

1964 "Anthropological Aspects of Language: Animal Categories and Verbal Abuse." E. H. Lenneberg, ed., *New Directions in the Study of Language*. Cambridge: M.I.T. Press, 23-63.

1965a "On the 'Founding Fathers.' " *Encounter*, 25:24-36.

1965b *Political Systems of Highland Burma*. Boston: Beacon Press.

1966 "On the 'Founding Fathers.' " *Current Anthropology*, 7:560-67.

LEACOCK, E.

1954 *The Montagnais Hunting Territory and the Fur Trade*. Memoir 78. American Anthropological Association.

1963 "Introduction." L. H. Morgan, *Ancient Society*. New York: Meridian Books, World, i-xx.

LEACOCK, S.

1954 "The Ethnological Theory of Marcel Mauss." *American Anthropologist*, 56:58-73.

LE BON, G.

1914 (orig. 1896) *The Crowd, A Study of the Popular Mind*. London: T. Fisher Unwin.

LE CAT, C. N.

1765 *Traite de la Couleur de la Peau Humaine*. Amsterdam.

LEE, D.

1959 *Freedom and Culture*. Englewood Cliffs: Prentice-Hall.

LEEDS, A. and A. VAYDA (eds.)

1965 *Man, Culture and Animals: The Role of Animals in Human Eco-*

logical Adjustments. Washington: American Association for the Advancement of Science, Pub. No. 78.

LEHMAN, F.

1963 *The Structure of Chin Society*. Illinois Studies in Anthropology, No. 3. Urbana: University of Illinois Press.

LEHMANN, W. C.

1960 *John Millar of Glasgow*. Canterbury: Canterbury University Press.

LENIN, N.

1934 *Selected Works*. New York: International Publishers.

LENNEBERG, E.

1953 "Cognition in Ethnolinguistics." *Language*, 29:463-71.

1960 "Language, Evolution, and Purposive Behavior." S. Diamond, ed., *Culture in History*. New York: Columbia University Press, 869-93.

LE PLAY, F.

1877-1879 (orig. 1855) *Les Ouvriers Européens*. Tours: A. Mame et fils.

LEROY, O.

1925 *Essai d'Introduction Critique à l'Étude de l'Économie Primitive*. Paris: Paul Guenther.

LESSER, A.

1935 "Functionalism in Social Anthropology." *American Anthropologist*, 37:386-93.

1968 "Franz Boas." *Encyclopedia of the Social Sciences*. In press.

LETOURNEAU, C.

1888 *L'Évolution du Mariage et de la Famille*. Paris: A. Delahaye and E. Lecrosnier.

1903 *La Condition de la Femme dans les Diverses Races et Civilisations*. Paris: V. Giard and E. Brière.

LÉVI-STRAUSS, C.

1945a "French Sociology." G. Gurvitch and W. Moore, eds., *Twentieth Century Sociology*. New York: Philosophical Library, 503-37.

1945b "L'Analyse Structurale en Linguistique et en Anthropologie." *Word*, 1:1-21.

1949 *Les Structures Élémentaires de la Parenté*. Paris: Presses Universitaires de France.

1950 "Introduction à l'Oeuvre de Mauss." *Sociologie et Anthropologie*. Paris: Presses Universitaires de France, ix-lii.

1953 "Social Structure." A. Kroeber, ed., *Anthropology Today*. Chicago: University of Chicago Press, 524-53.

1958 *Anthropologie Structurale*. Paris: Plon.

1960a "On Manipulated Sociological Models." *Bijdragen. Tot de Taal-, Land En Volkenkunde*, 116:45-54.

1960b *Ce Que l'Ethnologie Doit à Durkheim*. Annales de l'Université de Paris. Vol. 1.

1961 *Tristes Tropiques*. J. Russel, trans. New York: Criterion Books.
1963a *Structural Anthropology*. C. Jacobson, trans. New York: Basic Books.
1963b *Totemism*. R. Needham, trans. Boston: Beacon Press.
1964 *Mythologiques: Le Cru et le Cuit*. Paris: Plon.

LÉVY-BRUHL, L.
1910 *Les Functions Mentales dans les Sociétés Inférieures*. Paris: F. Alcon.
1966 *The 'Soul' of the Primitive*. L. Clare, trans. New York: Praeger.

LEWIS, I. M.
1965 "Problems in the Comparative Study of Unilineal Descent." *The Relevance of Models for Social Anthropology*. A.S.A. Monographs, No. 1. London: Tavistock, 87-112.

LEWIS, O.
1951 *Life in a Mexican Village*. Urbana: University of Illinois Press.
1961 *The Children of Sanchez*. New York: Random House.
1966a "The Culture of Poverty." *Scientific American*, 215:19-25.
1966b *La Vida*. New York: Random House.

LI AN-CHE
1937 "Zuñi: Some Observations and Queries." *American Anthropologist*, 39:62-77.

LICHTENBERGER, J. P.
1923 *Development of Social Theory*. New York: Century.

LICHTHEIM, G.
1963 "Marx and the 'Asiatic' Mode of Production." St. Anthony's Papers, No. 14, 86-112.

LIENHARDT, G.
1964 *Social Anthropology*. London: Oxford University Press.

LINDESMITH, A. R. and A. L. STRAUSS
1950 "Critique of Culture-Personality Writings." *American Sociological Review*, 15:587-600.

LINGUET, S. N. H.
1767 *Théorie des Loix Civiles ou Principes Fondamentaux de la Société*. Paris.

LINTON, R.
1936 *The Study of Man*. New York: Appleton-Century.
1937 "The Tanala of Madagascar." A. Kardiner, ed., *The Individual and His Society*. New York: Columbia University Press, 251-90.
1945 *The Cultural Background of Personality*. New York: Appleton-Century-Crofts.
1950 "An Anthropologist Views Point IV." *American Perspective*, Spring: 113-21.
1951 "The Concept of National Character." A. H. Stanton and S. E. Perry, eds., *Personality and Political Crisis*. New York: Free Press, 133-50.

1953 "An Anthropological View of Economics." A. Dudley Ward, ed., *Goals of Economic Life*. New York: Harper, 305-44.

LIPPERT, J.

1884 *Die Geschichte der Familie*. Stuttgart: Enke.

1931 (orig. 1886-87) *The Evolution of Culture*. G. P. Murdock, trans. New York: Macmillan.

LIPS, J.

1935 "Fritz Graebner." *American Anthropologist*, 37:320-26.

1937 *The Savage Hits Back*. New Haven: Yale University Press.

LITTLE, K.

1965 *Social Anthropology in Modern Life*. Edinburgh: University of Edinburgh Press.

LIVINGSTONE, F. B.

1959 "A Formal Analysis of Prescriptive Marriage Systems among the Australian Aborigines." *Southwestern Journal of Anthropology*, 15:361-72.

1962 "On the Non-Existence of Human Races." *Current Anthropology*, 3:279-81.

LOCKE, J.

1894 (orig. 1690) *An Essay Concerning Human Understanding*. Oxford: Clarendon Press.

1947 (orig. 1690) *Two Treatises of Government*. New York: Hafner.

LONG, E.

1774 *History of Jamaica*. London.

LORIA, A.

1899 *Economic Foundations of Society*. New York: Scribner's.

LOUNSBURY, F.

1955 *The Varieties of Meaning*. Institute of Languages and Linguistics Monograph No. 8. Washington: Georgetown University Press.

1956 "Semantic Analysis of the Pawnee Kinship Usage." *Language*, 32:158-94.

1964 "A Formal Account of the Crow and Omaha-Type Kinship Terminologies." W. Goodenough, ed., *Explorations in Cultural Anthropology*. New York: McGraw-Hill, 351-93.

1965 "Another View of the Trobriand Kinship Categories." *American Anthropologist*, 67, part 2:142-85.

LOVEJOY, A.

1923 "The Supposed Primitivism of Rousseau's Discourse on Inequality." *Modern Philology*, 21:165-86.

1933 "Monboddo and Rousseau." *Modern Philology*, 30:275-96.

1960 (orig. 1936) *The Great Chain of Being*. New York: Harper Torchbooks.

LOWETH, K.

1949 *Meaning in History*. Chicago: University of Chicago Press.

LOWIE, R.

1911a "A New Conception of Totemism?" *American Anthropologist*, 13:189-207. Reprinted in C. DuBois, ed., *Lowie's Selected Papers in Anthropology*. Berkeley: University of California Press, 283-311.

1911b "A Forgotten Pragmatist: Ludwig Feuerbach." *Journal of Philosophy*, 8:128-29.

1912 "Dr. Radosavljevich's 'Critique' of Professor Boas." *Science*, 35:537-40.

1915 "Exogamy and the Classificatory Systems of Relationship." *Proceedings of the National Academy of Sciences*, 1:346-49.

1916a "Ernst Mach." *The New Republic*, 6:335-37.

1916b "Historical and Sociological Interpretations of Kinship Terminologies." *Anthropological Essays Presented to William Henry Holmes*. Washington, 293-300.

1917a "Edward B. Tylor." *American Anthropologist*, 19:262-68.

1917b *Culture and Ethnology*. New York: D. C. McMurtrie.

1920 *Primitive Society*. New York: Boni and Liveright.

1927 *The Origin of the State*. New York: Harcourt, Brace.

1929 *Are We Civilized?* New York: Harcourt, Brace.

1933a "Land Tenure, Primitive Societies." *Encyclopedia of the Social Sciences*, 9:76-77.

1933b "Queries." *American Anthropologist*, 35:288-96.

1936 "Lewis H. Morgan in Historical Perspective." *Essays in Anthropology Presented to A. L. Kroeber*. Berkeley: University of California Press: 169-81.

1937 *History of Ethnological Theory*. New York: Farrar and Rinehart.

1938 "Subsistence." F. Boas, ed., *General Anthropology*. New York: Heath, 282-326.

1942 "The Transition of Civilizations in Primitive Society." *American Journal of Sociology*, 47:527-43.

1944 "Franz Boas." *Journal of American Folklore*, 57:59-64.

1946 "Professor White and 'Anti-evolutionist' Schools." *Southwestern Journal of Anthropology*, 2:240-41.

1947 "Letters from Ernst Mach to Robert Lowie." *Isis*, 37:65-68.

1948a *Social Organization*. New York: Rinehart.

1948b "Some Facts about Boas." *Southwestern Journal of Anthropology*, 4:69-70.

1953 "Ethnography, Cultural and Social Anthropology." *American Anthropologist*, 55:525-34.

1954 *Toward Understanding Germany*. Chicago: University of Chicago Press.

1955 "Contemporary Trends in American Cultural Anthropology." *Sociologus*, 5:113-21.

1956a "Boas Once More." *American Anthropologist*, 58:159-63.

1956b "Reminiscences of Anthropological Currents in America Half a Century Ago." *American Anthropologist*, 58:995-1015.

1957 "Generalizations, Field Work, and Materialism." *American Anthropologist,* 59:884-85.
1959 *Robert H. Lowie, Ethnologist.* Berkeley: University of California Press.
1960 *Lowie's Selected Papers in Anthropology.* C. DuBois, ed. Berkeley: University of California Press.
1963 "Religion in Human Life." *American Anthropologist,* 65:532-42.
1966 (orig. 1917) *Culture and Ethnology.* S. Diamond, ed. New York: Basic Books.

LUBBOCK, J.
1865 *Pre-Historic Times, as Illustrated by Ancient Remains and the Manners and Customs of Modern Savages.* London: Williams and Norgate.
1870 *The Origin of Civilization and the Primitive Condition of Man; Mental and Social Condition of Savages.* London: Longmans, Green.
1872 *Prehistoric Times as Illustrated by Ancient Remains and the Manners and Customs of Savages.* New York: D. Appleton.

LUCRETIUS
1910 *On the Nature of Things.* C. Bailey, trans. London: Oxford University Press.

LUTZ, B. F.
1927 "The Sumerians and Anthropology." *American Anthropologist,* 29:202-9.

LYELL, C.
1850 (orig. 1830) *Principles of Geology,* 8th ed. London: J. Murray.
1863 *The Geological Evidences of the Antiquity of Man.* Philadelphia: G. W. Childs.

MC CLELLAND, D. C.
1961 *The Achieving Society.* Princeton: Van Nostrand.

MC EWEN, W.
1963 "Forms and Problems of Validation in Social Anthropology." *Current Anthropology,* 4:155-83.

MC GEE, W. J.
1894 "The Citizen." Second Prize Essay. *American Anthropologist,* 7:352-57.
1895a "Some Principles of Nomenclature." *American Anthropologist,* 8:279-86.
1895b "The Beginning of Agriculture." *American Anthropologist,* 8:350-75.
1896a "Review of Giddings' *The Principles of Sociology.*" *American Anthropologist,* 10:19-24.
1896b "The Beginning of Marriage." *American Anthropologist,* 9:371-83.
1901 "Man's Place in Nature." *American Anthropologist,* 3:1-13.

MACHIAVELLI, N.
1948 *The Prince.* W. K. Marriott, trans. New York: Dutton.

MACKINTOSH, SIR J.

1798 *A Discourse on the Study of the Law of Nature and of Nations.* London: T. Cadell, Jr., W. Davies, J. Debrett, and W. Clarke.

MC LENNAN, J. F.

1865 *Primitive Marriage.* Edinburgh: Adam and Charles Black.

1876 *Studies in Ancient History.* London: Macmillan.

MAC NEISH, R.

1964a "Ancient Mesoamerican Civilization." *Science,* 143:531-37.

1964b "The Origins of New World Civilization." *Scientific American,* 211:5, 29-37.

MAC PHERSON, C. B.

1962 *The Political Theory of Possessive Individualism: Hobbes to Locke.* Oxford: Clarendon Press.

MAC RAE, D. G.

1958 "Darwinism and the Social Sciences." S. A. Barnett, ed., *A Century of Darwin.* London: Heinemann, 296-312.

1960 "Race and Sociology in History and Theory." P. Mason, ed., *Man, Race, and Darwin.* London: Oxford University Press, 76-86.

1961 *Ideology and Society.* London: Heinemann.

MAINE, H. S.

1861 *Ancient Law.* London: J. Murray.

1873 (orig. 1861) *Ancient Law: Its Connection with the Early History of Society and Its Relations to Modern Ideas.* New York: Holt.

1883 *Dissertations on Early Law and Custom.* London: J. Murray.

1887 (orig. 1871) *Village Communities in the East and West.* London: J. Murray.

1888 (orig. 1875) *Lectures on the Early History of Institutions.* New York: Holt.

MAIR, L.

1938 *The Place of History in the Study of Culture Change: Methods of Study of Culture Contact.* Africa Memoirs, vol. 15. Oxford: Oxford University Press.

MALINOWSKI, B.

1913a *The Family among the Australian Aborigines: A Sociological Study.* London: University of London Press.

1913b "Review of Durkheim's Les Formes Élémentaires de la Vie Religieuse." *Folklore,* 24:525-31.

1920 "Kula: The Circulating Exchanges of Valuables in the Archipelagos of Eastern New Guinea." *Man,* 20:97-105.

1922 *Argonauts of the Western Pacific.* New York: Dutton.

1923 "Psycho-analysis and Anthropology." *Psyche,* 4:293-322.

1926 *Crime and Custom in Savage Society.* London: Kegan Paul, Trench, Trubner.

1927a *Sex and Repression in Savage Society.* London: Routledge and Kegan Paul.

1927b "The Life of Culture." G. E. Smith, *et al.*, eds., *The Diffusion Controversy*. New York: Norton, 26-46.

1929a *The Sexual Life of Savages in Northwestern Melanesia*. London: George Routledge.

1929b "Social Anthropology." *Encyclopaedia Britannica*, 14th ed., 862:70.

1930a "Parenthood the Basis of Social Structure." V. F. Calverton and S. D. Schmalhauser, eds., *The New Generation*, 113-68.

1930b "Race and Labour." *The Listener*. Suppl. No. 8.

1931 "Culture." *Encyclopedia of the Social Sciences*, 621-46.

1935 *Coral Gardens and Their Magic*. London: Allen & Unwin, 2 vols.

1939 "The Group and the Individual in Functional Analysis." *American Journal of Sociology*, 44:938-64.

1944a *Freedom and Civilization*. New York: Roy Publisher.

1944b *A Scientific Theory of Culture*. Chapel Hill: University of North Carolina Press.

1945 *The Dynamics of Culture Change: An Inquiry into Race Relations in Africa*. P. Kaberry, ed. New Haven: Yale University Press.

1961 (orig. 1922) *Argonauts of the Western Pacific*. New York: Dutton.

1962 *Sex, Culture and Myth*. New York: Harcourt, Brace and World.

1967 *A Diary in the Strict Sense of the Term*. New York: Harcourt, Brace and World.

MALTHUS, T. R.

1803 (orig. 1798) *An Essay on the Principle of Population*. London: J. Johnson.

1817 *An Essay on the Principle of Population*. London: J. Murray.

MANDELBAUM, D. G. (ed.)

1949 *Selected Writings of Edward Sapir in Language, Culture, and Personality*. Berkeley: University of California Press.

MANGELSDORF, P., R. MAC NEISH, and W. C. GALINAT

1964 "Domestication of Corn." *Science*, 143:538-45.

MANNERS, R.

1956 "Tabara: Subculture of a Tobacco and Mixed Crop Municipality." Julian Steward, ed., *The People of Puerto Rico*. Urbana: University of Illinois Press, 93-170.

1964 (ed.) *Process and Pattern in Culture: Essays in Honor of Julian H. Steward*. Chicago: Aldine.

1965 "Reply to Morris Opler." *Current Anthropology*, 6:319-20.

MANUEL, F. E.

1959 *The Eighteenth Century Confronts the Gods*. Cambridge: Harvard University Press.

MARCHANT, J.

1916 *Alfred Russel Wallace; Letters and Reminiscences*. London: Cassell.

MARCUSE, H.

1960 (orig. 1941) *Reason and Revolution: Hegel and the Rise of Social Theory*. Boston: Beacon Press.

MARETT, R. R.

1914 (orig. 1909) *The Threshold of Religion*. London: Methuen.

1927 *The Diffusion of Culture*. Cambridge: Cambridge University Press.

MARKHAM, F. M. A.

1952 *Claude Henri Comte de Saint-Simon: Selected Writings*. Oxford: Blackwell.

MARTINDALE, D. A.

1960 *The Nature and Types of Sociological Theory*. Boston: Houghton Mifflin.

MARTINEAU, H.

1896 *The Positive Philosophy of Auguste Comte*. London: G. Bell.

MARX, K.

1859 *Zur Kritik der Politischen Ökonomie*. Berlin: Franz Dunker.

1888 (orig. 1848) *The Communist Manifesto*. London: W. Reeves.

1904 (orig. 1859) *The Critique of Political Economy*. I. N. Stone, trans. Chicago: International Library Publication Co.

1909 (orig. 1867) *Capital*. E. Unterman, trans. Chicago: C. H. Kerr.

1941 (orig. ms. 1845) "Theses on Feuerbach." F. Engels, ed., *Ludwig Feuerbach and the Outcome of Classical German Philosophy*. New York: International Publishers, 82-84.

1960 (orig. 1853) *The British Rule in India*. Moscow: Foreign Language Publishers.

1963 (orig. 1847) *The Poverty of Philosophy*. New York: International Publishers.

1965 (orig. ms. 1857-58) "Pre-Capitalist Economic Formations." E. Hobsbawm, ed., *Pre-capitalist Economic Formations: Karl Marx*. J. Cohen, trans. New York: International Publishers, 67-120.

MARX, K. and F. ENGELS

1942 *The Selected Correspondence: 1846-1895*. New York: International Publishers.

1956 (orig. 1845) *The Holy Family*. Moscow: Foreign Languages Publishers.

1957 *Marx and Engels on Religion*. Moscow: Foreign Languages Publishers.

1965 (orig. ms. 1846) "The German Ideology." E. Hobsbawm, ed., *Pre-capitalist Economic Formations: Karl Marx*. J. Cohen, trans. New York: International Publishers, 121-39.

MASON, J. A.

1966 "Pre-Folsom Estimates of the Ages of Man in America." *American Anthropologist*, 68:193-96.

MASON, O.

1894a "Migration and the Food Quest: A Study in the Peopling of America." *American Anthropologist*, 7:275.

1894b "Technogeography, or the Relation of the Earth to the Industries of Mankind." *American Anthropologist*, 7:137-61.

1895a "Influence of Environment upon Human Industries or Arts." *Annual Report of the Smithsonian Institution,* 639-65.
1895b "Similarities in Culture." *American Anthropologist,* 8:101-17.
1899 "Aboriginal American Zootechny." *American Anthropologist,* 1:45-81.
1907 "Environment." *Handbook of American Indians North of Mexico,* Part I. Washington: Bureau of American Ethnology, Bull. 30, 427-30.

MAUS, H.
1962 *A Short History of Sociology.* London: Routledge and Kegan Paul.

MAUSS, M.
1913 "L'Ethnographie en France et à l'Étranger." *La Revue de Paris.* September, October: 537-60; 815-937.
1920 "L'Extension du Potlatch en Melanésie." *Anthropologie* 30:396-97.
1924 "Rapports Réels et Pratiques de la Psychologie et de la Sociologie." *Journal de Psychologie Normale et Pathologique,* 31:892-922.
1954 (orig. 1924) *The Gift.* I. Cunnison, trans. New York: Free Press.
1950 *Sociologie et Anthropologie.* Paris: Presses Universitaires de France.
1962 "Introduction." E. Durkheim, *Socialism,* 1st ed. New York: Collier Books, 32-36.

MAUSS, M. and H. BEUCHAT
1906 "Essai sur les Variations Saisonnières des Sociétés Eskimos." *L'Année Sociologique,* neuvième année (1904-1905), 39-132.

MAUSS, M. and H. HUBERT
1899 "Essai sur la Nature et la Fonction du Sacrifice." *L'Année Sociologique, deuxième année* (1897-1898), 29-138.
1904 "Esquisse d'une Théorie de la Magie." *L'Année Sociologique,* septième année (1902-1903), 1-146.

MAYBURY-LEWIS, D.
1965 "Prescriptive Marriage Systems." *Southwestern Journal of Anthropology,* 21:207-30.

MAZLISH, B.
1955 "Burke, Bonald, and de Maistre: A Study in Conservatism." Unpublished Ph.D. dissertation. Columbia University.

MEAD, G. H.
1936 *Movements of Thought in the Nineteenth Century.* Chicago: University of Chicago Press.

MEAD, M.
1928 *Coming of Age in Samoa.* New York: Morrow.
1930a *Growing Up in New Guinea.* New York: Blue Ribbon.
1930b "An Ethnologist's Footnote to Totem and Taboo." *The Psychoanalytic Review,* 17:297-301.
1933 "More Comprehensive Field Methods." *American Anthropologist,* 35:1-15.
1935a *Sex and Temperament in Three Primitive Societies.* New York: Morrow.

1935b "Review of *The Riddle of the Sphinx*, by Géza Róheim." *Character and Personality*, 4:85-90.

1937a "A Reply to a Review of *Sex and Temperament in Three Primitive Societies*." *American Anthropologist*, 39:558-61.

1937b *Cooperation and Competition among Primitive Peoples*. New York: McGraw-Hill.

1939 *From the South Seas*. New York: Morrow.

1941 "Review of *The Individual and His Society*, by Abram Kardiner." *American Journal of Orthopsychiatry*, 11:603-5.

1942 *And Keep Your Powder Dry: An Anthropologist Looks at America*. New York: Morrow.

1949a *Male and Female*. New York: Morrow.

1949b "Character Formation and Diachronic Theory." M. Fortes, ed., *Social Structure: Studies Presented to A. R. Radcliffe-Brown*. Oxford: Clarendon Press, 18-34.

1949c (orig. 1928) *Coming of Age in Samoa*. New York: New American Library, Mentor Books.

1950 *Sex and Temperament in Three Primitive Societies*. New York: New American Library, Mentor Books.

1951a "The Study of National Character." D. Lerner, and H. D. Haswell, eds., *The Policy Sciences*. Stanford: Stanford University Press, 70-85.

1953 "National Character." A. L. Kroeber, ed., *Anthropology Today*. Chicago: University of Chicago Press, 642-67.

1954 "The Swaddling Hypothesis: Its Reception." *American Anthropologist*, 56:395-409.

1955 *Cultural Patterns and Technical Changes*. New York: New American Library, Mentor Books.

1958 "Cultural Determinants of Behavior." A. Roe and G. G. Simpson, eds., *Behavior and Evolution*. New Haven: Yale University Press, 480-503.

1959a *An Anthropologist at Work: Writings of Ruth Benedict*. Boston: Houghton Mifflin.

1959b "Apprenticeship under Boas." W. Goldschmidt, ed., *The Anthropology of Franz Boas*. Memoir 89. American Anthropological Association, 29-45.

1959c "Reply to Kardiner." *Science*, 130:1728, 1732.

1961a "National Character and the Science of Anthropology." S. M. Lipset and L. Lowenthal, eds., *Culture and Social Character: The Work of David Riesman Reviewed*. New York: Free Press, 15-26.

1961b *Cooperation and Competition among Primitive Peoples*. Boston: Beacon Press.

1962a "Retrospects and Prospects." T. Gladwin and W. C. Sturtevant, eds., *Anthropology and Human Behavior*. Washington: Anthropological Society of Washington.

1962b "Review of *National Character and National Stereotypes: A Trend Report Prepared for the International Union of Scientific Philosophy,* by H. C. J. Duiker and N. H. Frijda." *American Anthropologist,* 64:688-90.

1964 *Continuities in Cultural Evolution.* New Haven: Yale University Press.

MEAD, M. and R. BUNZEL (eds.)

1960 *The Golden Age of Anthropology.* New York: George Braziller.

MEAD, M. and E. CALAS

1955 "Child-training Ideals in a Post-revolutionary Context: Soviet Russia." M. Mead and M. Wolfenstein, eds. *Childhood in Contemporary Cultures.* Chicago: University of Chicago Press, 179-203.

MEAD, M. and F. M. C. MAC GREGOR

1951 *Growth and Culture: A Photographic Study of Balinese Childhood.* New York: Putnam.

MEAD, M. and R. METRAUX (eds.)

1953 *The Study of Culture at a Distance.* Chicago: University of Chicago Press.

MEEK, C. K.

1931 *Tribal Studies in Northern Nigeria.* Vol. 1. London: Kegan Paul, Trench, Trubner.

MEGGERS, B.

1946 "Recent Trends in American Ethnology." *American Anthropologist,* 48:176-214.

1960 "The Law of Cultural Evolution as a Practical Research Tool." G. Dole and R. Carneiro, eds., *Essays in the Science of Culture.* New York: Thomas Y. Crowell, 302-16.

1961 "Field Testing of Cultural Law, a Reply to Morris Opler." *Southwestern Journal of Anthropology,* 17:352-54.

MEGGITT, M. J.

1962 *Desert People; A Study of the Walbiri Aborigines of Central Australia.* Sydney: Angus and Robertson.

1965 *The Lineage System of the Mae-Enga of New Guinea.* Edinburgh: Oliver and Boyd.

MEHRING, F.

1935 *Karl Marx, The Story of His Life.* E. Fitzgerald, trans. New York: Covici Friede.

MEINERS, C.

1785 *Grundriss der Geschichte der Menscheit.* Lemgo: im Verlage der Meyerschen Buchhandlung.

MERCIER, P.

1966 *Histoire de l'Anthropologie.* Paris: Presses Universitaires de France.

MERZ, J. T.

1965 (orig. 1904-11) *A History of European Thought in the Nineteenth Century.* New York: Dover.

METZGER, D.
1965 "Review of *The Nature of Cultural Things*," by Marvin Harris. *American Anthropologist*, 67:1293-97.
METZGER, D. and G. WILLIAMS
1963a "Tenejapa Medicine: The Curer." *Southwestern Journal of Anthropology* 19:216-34.
1963b "A Formal Ethnographic Analysis of Tenejapa Ladino Weddings." *American Anthropologist*, 65:1076-1101.
1966 "Some Procedures and Results in the Study of Native Categories, Tzeltal 'Firewood.'" *American Anthropologist*, 68:389-407.
METZGER, W.
1965 "The Historical Background for National Trends in Psychology: German Psychology." *Journal of the History of the Behavioral Sciences*, 1:109-14.
MEYER, A. G.
1954 *Marxism, The Unity of Theory and Practice*. Cambridge: Harvard University Press.
MILL, J. S.
1923 (orig. 1848) *Principles of Political Economy*. London: Longmans Green.
MILLAR, J.
1771 *Observations Concerning the Distinction of Ranks in Society*. London: J. Murray.
MILLON, R.
1967 "Teotihuacán." *Scientific American*, 216:38-48.
MILLS, C. W.
1962 *The Marxists*. New York: Dell.
MINS, H.
1965 "Marxists and Non-Marxists: Theoretical Schemes and Political Creeds." *Science and Society*, 30:25-31.
MINTZ, S.
1956 "Canamelar, the Sub-culture of a Rural Sugar Plantation Proletariat." J. Steward, ed., *The People of Puerto Rico*. Urbana: University of Illinois Press, 314-17.
MIVART, ST. G.
1871 *Genesis of Species*. London: Macmillan.
MONBODDO, J. B., LORD
1774 *Of the Origin and Progress of Language*, vol. 1. Edinburgh: J. Balfour and T. Cadell.
MONTAGU, A. (M. F. ASHLEY MONTAGU)
1945 *Man's Most Dangerous Myth: The Fallacy of Race*. New York: Columbia University Press.
1952 *Darwin, Competition and Cooperation*. New York: Henry Schuman.
1964 *The Concept of Race*. New York: Free Press.

MONTESQUIEU

1949 (orig. 1748) *The Spirit of Laws.* T. Nugent, trans. New York: Hafner.

MOONEY, J.

1896 *The Ghost-Dance Religion and the Sioux Outbreak of 1890.* Fourteenth Annual Report. Washington: Bureau of American Ethnology.

MOORE, F. (ed.)

1961 *Readings in Cross-Cultural Methodology.* New Haven: Human Relations Area Files.

MORET, A. and G. DAVY

1926 *From Tribe to Empire.* V. Gordon Childe, trans. New York: Knopf.

MORGAN, L. H.

1851 *League of the Ho-de-no-sau-nee, or Iroquois.* Rochester: Sage and Broa.

1868 *The American Beaver and His Works.* Philadelphia: J. B. Lippincott.

1870 *Systems of Consanguinity and Affinity of the Human Family.* Washington: Smithsonian Institution.

1876 "Montezuma's Dinner." *North American Review,* 122:265-308.

1877 *Ancient Society.* New York: World Publishing.

1881 *Houses and House Life of the American Aborigines.* Washington: U. S. Geological Survey. Contributions to Ethnology.

1963 (orig. 1877) *Ancient Society.* E. Leacock, ed. New York: Meridian Books. World Publishing.

MORTON, S. G.

1839 *Crania Americana.* Philadelphia: J. Penington.

1844 *Crania Aegyptica; or Observations on Egyptian Ethnography, Derived from Anatomy, History and the Monuments.* Philadelphia: Transactions American Philosophical Society, IX.

MURDOCK, G. P.

1932 "The Science of Culture." *American Anthropologist,* 34:200-15.

1937 *Statistical Correlations in the Science of Society.* New Haven: Yale University Press.

1943 "Bronislaw Malinowski." *American Anthropologist,* 45:444-51.

1945 "The Common Denominator of Cultures." R. Linton, ed., *The Science of Man in the World Crisis.* New York: Columbia University Press, 123-42.

1949 *Social Structure.* New York: Macmillan.

1951 "British Social Anthropology." *American Anthropologist,* 53:465-73.

1957 "World Ethnographic Sample." *American Anthropologist,* 59:664-87.

1959a *Africa—Its Peoples and Their Culture History.* New York: McGraw-Hill.

1959b "Evolution in Social Organization." B. Meggers, ed., *Evolution and Anthropology*. Washington: Anthropological Society of Washington, 126-45.

1963 *Outline of World Cultures*. New Haven: Human Relations Area Files.

1964 "Cultural Correlates of the Regulation of Premarital Sex Behavior." R. Manners, ed., *Process and Pattern in Culture*. Chicago: Aldine, 399-410.

1965 *Culture and Society*. Pittsburgh: University of Pittsburgh Press.

1967 *Ethnographic Atlas*. Pittsburgh: University of Pittsburgh Press.

MURPHREE, I.

1961 "The Evolutionary Anthropologists: The Progress of Mankind." *Proceedings of the American Philosophical Society*, 105:265-300.

MURPHY, R.

1963 "On Zen Marxism: Filiation and Alliance." *Man*, 63:17-19.

MURPHY, R. and J. STEWARD

1955 "Tappers and Trappers: Parallel Processes in Acculturation." *Economic Development and Culture Change*, 4:335-55.

MYRES, J. L.

1908 "Herodotus and Anthropology." *Anthropology and the Classics*. Oxford: Oxford University Press.

1916 "The Influence of Anthropology on the Course of Political Science." *University of California Publications in History*, 4:1-81.

NADEL, S. F.

1951 *The Foundations of Social Anthropology*. New York: Free Press.

1957 *The Theory of Social Structure*. New York: Free Press.

NAGEL, E.

1948 "The Development of Modern Science." J. L. Blau, J. Buchler, and G. T. Mathews, eds., *Chapters in Western Civilization*. New York: Columbia University Press, 241-84.

1953 "Teleological Explanation and Teleological System." H. Feigl and M. Brodbeck, eds., *Readings in the Philosophy of Science*. New York: Appleton-Century, 537-58.

1961 *The Structure of Science*. New York: Harcourt, Brace and World.

NAROLL, R.

1961 "Two Solutions to Galton's Problem." *Philosophy of Science*, 28:15-39.

1964 "A Fifth Solution to Galton's Problem." *American Anthropologist*, 66:863-67.

NAROLL, R. and R. G. D'ANDRADE

1963 "Two Further Solutions to Galton's Problem." *American Anthropologist*, 65:1053-67.

NEEDHAM, R.

1962 *Structure and Sentiment*. Chicago: University of Chicago Press.

1964 "Explanatory Notes on Prescriptive Alliance and the Purum." *American Anthropologist*, 66:1377-85.

1966 "Comments on the Analysis of Purum Society." *American Anthropologist*, 68:171-77.

NIEBOER, H. J.

1900 *Slavery as an Industrial System: Ethnological Researcher.* The Hague: Martinus Nijhoff.

NILSSON, S.

1868 (orig. 1838) *The Primitive Inhabitants of Scandinavia.* J. Lubbock, trans. London: Longmans, Green.

NORBECK, E. and NORBECK, M.

1956 "Child Training in a Japanese Fishing Community." D. Haring, ed., *Personal Character and Cultural Milieu.* Syracuse: Syracuse University Press, 651-73.

NOTT, J. C. and G. R. GLIDDON

1854 *Types of Mankind.* Philadelphia: J. B. Lippincott, Grambo.

1857 *Indigenous Races of the Earth.* Philadelphia: J. B. Lippincott.

NUTINI, H.

1965 "Some Considerations on the Nature of Social Structure and Model Building: A Critique of Claude Lévi-Strauss and Edmund Leach." *American Anthropologist*, 67:707-31.

OGBURN, W. F. and A. GOLDENWEISER (eds.)

1927 *Social Sciences and Their Interrelation.* Boston: Houghton Mifflin.

1950 *Social Change.* New York: Viking Press.

OLIVER, D.

1955 *A Solomon Island Society, Kinship and Leadership among the Siuai of Bougainville.* Cambridge: Harvard University Press.

OPLER, M.

1943 "On the Method of Writing Anthropological Monographs." *American Anthropologist*, 45:329-32.

1947 "Rule and Practice in the Behavior Pattern between Jicarilla Apache Affinal Relatives." *American Anthropologist*, 49:452-62.

1961 "Cultural Evolution, Southern Athapaskans, and Chronology in Theory." *Southwestern Journal of Anthropology*, 17:1-20.

1962 "Integration, Evolution, and Morgan." *Current Anthropology*, 3:478-79.

1964a "Cause, Process, and Dynamics in the Evolution of E. B. Tylor." *Southwestern Journal of Anthropology*, 20:123-45.

1964b "Reply to T. G. Harding and E. Leacock." *Current Anthropology*, 5:110-14.

1965 "The History of Ethnological Thought." *Current Anthropology*, 6:319.

ORLANSKY, H.

1949 "Infant Care and Personality." *Psychological Bulletin*, 46:1-48.

OSBORN, H. F.

1929 *From the Greeks to Darwin.* New York: Scribner's.

PALEY, W.

1963 (orig. 1802) *Natural Theology.* Indianapolis: Bobbs-Merrill.

PANCHANANA, M.

1933 *A History of American Anthropology*. Calcutta: The University of Calcutta Press.

PARSONS, E. C.

1939 *Pueblo Indian Religion*. Chicago: University of Chicago Press.

PARSONS, T.

1949 (orig. 1937) *The Structure of Social Action*. New York: Free Press.

1957 "Malinowski and the Theory of Social Systems." R. Firth, ed., *Man and Culture: An Evaluation of the Work of Bronislaw Malinowski*. London: Routledge and Kegan Paul, 53-70.

PEARCE, R. H.

1953 *The Savages of America. A Study of the Indian and the Idea of Civilization*. Baltimore: Johns Hopkins Press.

PEARSON, K.

1901 *National Life from the Standpoint of Science*. London: A. & C. Black.

1949 (orig. 1892) *The Grammar of Science*. London: J. M. Dent.

PEDERSEN, H.

1931 *Linguistic Science in the Nineteenth Century*. J. W. Spargo, trans. Cambridge: Harvard University Press.

PESCHEL, O.

1876 (orig. 1874) *The Races of Man*. London: H. S. King.

PELTO, P.

1966 "Cognitive Aspects of American Kin Terms." *American Anthropologist*, 68:198-202.

PENNIMAN, T. K.

1965 *A Hundred Years of Anthropology*. London: Gerald Duckworth.

PERRY, W. J.

1923 *The Children of the Sun*. London: Methuen.

PIDDINGTON, R.

1957 "Malinowski's Theory of Needs." R. Firth, ed., *Man and Culture: An Evaluation of the Work of Bronislaw Malinowski*. London: Routledge and Kegan Paul, 33-51.

PIDDOCKE, S.

1965 "The Potlatch System of the South Kwakiutl: A New Perspective." *Southwestern Journal of Anthropology*, 21:244-64.

PIKE, K.

1954 *Language in Relation to a Unified Theory of the Structure of Human Behavior*, vol. 1. Glendale: Summer Institute of Linguistics.

1962 *With Heart and Mind, A Personal Synthesis of Scholarship and Devotion*. Grand Rapids, Michigan: William B. Eerdmans Publication.

PITT-RIVERS, A. L.-F.

1906 *The Evolution of Culture and Other Essays*. J. L. Myres, ed. Oxford: Clarendon Press.

PLEKHANOV, G.

1934 *Essays in the History of Materialism.* R. Fox, trans. London: John Lane.

1940 (orig. 1898) *The Role of the Individual in History.* New York: International Publishers.

POCOCK, D. F.

1961 *Social Anthropology.* London: Sheed and Ward.

POPPER, K. R.

1946 *The Open Society and Its Enemies.* London: George Routledge.

1957 *The Poverty of Historicism.* Boston: Beacon Press.

PORTEUS, S. D.

1937 *Primitive Intelligence and Environment.* New York: Macmillan.

POTT, A. F.

1833-1836 *Etymologische Forschungen auf dem Gebäude der indogermanischen Sprachen.* Lemgo.

POUWER, J.

1966 "Referential and Inferential Reality: A Rejoinder." *Bijdragen. Tot De Taal-, Land En Volkenkunde,* 122:151-57.

POWELL, J. W.

1899 "Sociology or the Science of Institutions." *American Anthropologist,* 1:695-733.

PRENANT, M.

1943 *Biology and Marxism.* C. D. Greaves, trans. London: Lawrence and Wishart.

PRICHARD, J. C.

1826 (orig. 1813) *Researches into the Physical History of Man.* London: J. and A. Arch.

1836-1847 *Researches into the Physical History of Man.* London: Sherwood, Gilbert and Piper.

1855 (orig. 1848) *The Natural History of Man.* London: Hippolyte Baillière.

PROUDHON, P. J.

1849 *De la Création de l'Ordre dans l'Humanité.* Paris: Garnier.

PUTNAM, C.

1961 *Race and Reason, A Yankee View.* Washington: Public Affairs Press.

QUATREFAGES, A. DE

1867 *Rapport sur les Progrès de l'Anthropologie.* Paris: Imprimerie Impériale.

QUÉTELET, A.

1832 *Recherches sur la Loi de la Croissance de l'Homme.* Nouveaux Mémoires de l'Academie Royale des Sciences et Belles Lettres. Brussels: M. Hayez, Imprimeur de I'Académie de Bruxelles, 1-32.

1842 *A Treatise on Man and the Development of His Faculties.* Edinburgh: Wm. and Rbt. Chambers.

1848 *Du Système Sociale et des Lois qui le Régissent.* Paris: Guillaumin.

1871 *Anthropométrie, ou Mesure des Différentes Facultés de l'Homme.* Bruxelles: C. Muquardt.

RADCLIFFE-BROWN, A. R.

1914 "Review of Malinowski's *The Family among the Australian Aborigines.*" *Man,* 14:31-32.

1924 "The Mother's Brother in South Africa." *South African Journal of Science,* 21:542-55.

1931 "The Social Organization of Australian Tribes." *Oceania,* 1:426-56.

1933 (orig. 1922) *The Andaman Islanders.* Cambridge: Cambridge University Press.

1935 "On the Concept of Function in Social Science." *American Anthropologist,* 37: 394-402.

1947 "Evolution, Social or Cultural. *American Anthropologist,* 49:78-83.

1948 *A Natural Science of Society.* New York: Free Press.

1949a *Social Structure, Studies Presented to A. R. Radcliffe-Brown.* Oxford: Clarendon Press.

1949b "Functionalism: A Protest." *American Anthropologist,* 51:320-23.

1949c "White's View of a Science of Culture." *American Anthropologist,* 51:503-12.

1950 "Introduction." A. R. Radcliffe-Brown and C. D. Forde, eds., *African Systems of Kinship and Marriage.* London: Oxford University Press, 1-85.

1952a "Historical Note on British Social Anthropology." *American Anthropologist,* 54:275-77.

1952b *Structure and Function in Primitive Society.* London: Oxford University Press.

1958 *Method in Social Anthropology.* Chicago: University of Chicago Press.

RADIN, P.

1913 "Personal Reminiscence of a Winnebago Indian." *Journal of American Folklore,* 26:293-318.

1926 *Crashing Thunder: The Autobiography of a Winnebago Indian.* New York: D. Appleton.

1929 "History of Ethnological Theories." *American Anthropologist,* 31:9-33.

1933 *The Method and Theory of Ethnology.* New York: McGraw-Hill.

1939 "The Mind of Primitive Man." *The New Republic,* 98:300-3.

1958 "Robert Lowie." *American Anthropologist,* 60:359-61.

RADL, E.

1930 *The History of Biological Theories.* E. J. Hatfield, trans. London: Oxford University Press.

RAMSAY, J.

1784 *Essay on the Treatment and Conversion of African Slaves in the British Sugar Colonies.* London: J. Phillips.

RANDALL, J.
1965 *The Career of Philosophy: From the German Enlightenment to the Age of Darwin.* New York: Columbia University Press.
RANKING, J.
1827 *Historical Researches on the Conquest of Peru, Mexico, Bogotá, Natchez and Talomeco in the Thirteenth Century by the Mongols, Accompanied with Elephants.* London: Longmans, Green.
RAPPAPORT, R.
1966 "Ritual in the Ecology of a New Guinea People: An Anthropological Study of the Tsembaga Maring." Unpublished Ph.D. dissertation. Columbia University. Ann Arbor: University Microfilm.
RASK, R. K.
1818 *Investigation on the Origin of the Old Norse or Icelandic Language.* Copenhagen: Gyldendal.
RATZEL, F.
1896 (orig. 1885-88) *The History of Mankind.* A. J. Butler, trans. London: Macmillan.
1899 (orig. 1882) *Anthropogeographie.* Stuttgart: J. Engelhorn.
RAY, V.
1955 "Review of *Franz Boas: The Science of Man in the Making,* by M. Herskovitz." *American Anthropologist,* 57:138-41.
1956 "Rejoinder." *American Anthropologist,* 58:164-70.
RAYNAL, G. T. F.
1788 *A Philosophical and Political History of the Settlements and Trade of the Europeans in the East and West Indies.* London: Printed for W. Strahan, etc.
READ, M.
1942 "Migrant Labour in Africa and Its Effects on Tribal Life." *International Labour Review,* 45:605-31.
RECLUS, E.
1876-1894 *The Earth and Its Inhabitants.* E. G. Ravenstein, ed. London: J. S. Virtue and Co.
REDFIELD, R.
1947 "The Folk Society." *American Journal of Sociology,* 52:293-308.
1955 "Introduction." F. Eggan, ed., *Social Anthropology of North American Tribes.* Chicago: University of Chicago Press, ix-xiv.
REDFIELD, R., R. LINTON, and M. HERSKOVITS
1936 "Memorandum on the Study of Acculturation." *American Anthropologist,* 38:149-52.
REED, E.
1957 "Anthropology Today." *International Socialist Review,* Spring, 18:54-60.
REICHARD, G.
1938 "Social Life." F. Boas, ed., *General Anthropology.* New York: Heath, 409-86.

RESEK, C.

1960 *Lewis Henry Morgan: American Scholar*. Chicago: University of Chicago Press.

RETZIUS, A.

1864 *Ethnologische Schriften, nach dem Tode des Verfassers gesammelt*. Stockholm.

RICHARDS, A. I.

1932 "Anthropological Problems in Northeastern Rhodesia." *Africa*, 5:121-44.

1939 "The Development of Field Work Methods in Social Anthropology." F. C. Bartlett, *et al.*, eds., *The Study of Society*. New York: Macmillan, 272-316.

1950 "Some Types of Family Structure amongst the Central Bantu." A. R. Radcliffe-Brown and D. Forde, eds., *African Systems of Kinship and Marriage*. London: Oxford University Press, 207-51.

1954 *Economic Development and Tribal Change*. Cambridge: Cambridge University Press.

RICKERT, H.

1896 }
1902 } *Die Grenzen der naturwissenschaftlichen Begriffsbildung*. Tubingen.

1924 *Die Probleme der Geschichtsphilosophie*. Heidelberg.

RIESMAN, D.

1950 *The Lonely Crowd: A Study of Changing American Character*. New Haven: Yale University Press.

RITTER, K.

1863 (orig. 1822-59) *Geographical Studies*. W. Gage, trans. Boston: Gould and Lincoln.

RITTERBUSH, P.

1964 *Overtures to Biology*. New Haven: Yale University Press.

RIVERS, W. H. R.

1901 "On the Functions of the Maternal Uncle in Torres Strait." *Man*, 1:171-72.

1906 *The Todas*. New York: Macmillan.

1911 "The Ethnological Analyses of Culture." Presidential address to Section H of the British Association for the Advancement of Science. *Report of the British Association for the Advancement of Science*, 81:490-99.

1912 "The Disappearance of Useful Arts." *Festskift tillägnad Edvard Westermarck: Helsingford*, 190-230.

1914a *The History of Melanesian Society*. Cambridge: Cambridge University Press.

1914b *Kinship and Social Organization*. London: Constable.

1920a *Instinct and the Unconscious: A Contribution to a Biological Theory of the Psycho-Neuroses*. Cambridge: Cambridge University Press.

1920b "Review of *Primitive Society*," by Robert Lowie. *American Anthropologist*, 22:278-83.
1922 *History and Ethnology*. New York: Macmillan.
1923 *Conflict and Dream*. New York: Harcourt, Brace.

RIVET, P. (ed.)
1957 *Les Origines de l'Homme Américain*. Paris: Gallimard.

ROARK, R.
1961 "The Mathematics of American Cousinship." *The Kroeber Anthropological Society Papers*, 24:17-18.

ROBERTS, J. M.
1951 "Three Navaho Households: A Comparative Study in Small Group Culture." *Papers of the Peabody Museum of American Archaeology and Ethnology*, vol. 40, no. 3. Cambridge: Harvard University Press.

ROBERTSON, J. M.
1929 *A History of Free Thought in the Nineteenth Century*. London: Watts.

ROBERTSON, W.
1812 (orig. 1777) *The History of America*. Philadelphia: J. Broien and T. L. Plowman.

RÓHEIM, G.
1925 *Australian Totemism: A Psychoanalytical Study in Anthropology*. London: Allen & Unwin.
1934 *The Riddle of the Sphinx*. London: Hogarth.
1947 "Psychoanalysis and Anthropology." *Psychoanalysis and the Social Sciences*, 1:9-33.
1950 *Psychoanalysis and Anthropology*. New York: International University Press.

ROHNER, R.
1966 "Franz Boas, Ethnographer on the Northwest Coast." J. Helm, ed., *Pioneers of American Anthropology*. Seattle: University of Washington Press, 151-222.

ROMNEY, A. K. and R. G. D'ANDRADE
1964 "Cognitive Aspects of English Kin Terms." *American Anthropologist*, 66:146-70.

RONHAAR, J. H.
1931 *Women in Primitive Motherright Societies*. The Hague: J. B. Walters Groningen.

ROSE, F. G. G.
1960a "The Australian Aboriginal Family: Some Theoretical Considerations." *Forschen und Wirken: Festschrift zur 150-Jahr-Feier der Humboldt-Universität zu Berlin*. Berlin: VEB Deutscher Verlag der Wissenschaften. 3:415-37.
1960b *Classification of Kin, Age Structure and Marriage amongst the Groote Eylandt Aborigines: A Study in Method and a Theory of*

Australian Kinship. Berlin: Akademie-Verlag. Deutsche Akademie der Wissenschaften zu Berlin 3: Sektion für Völkerkundliche Forschungen.

ROTH, W. E.

1905 *Notes on Government, Morals, and Crime*. Brisbane: Department of Home Secretary.

ROUSSEAU, J. J.

1964 (orig. 1751) *The First and Second Discourses*. R. and J. Masters, trans. New York: St Martin's Press.

1938 (orig. 1762) *The Social Contract*. G. D. H. Cole, trans. New York: Dutton.

ROWE, J. H.

1961 "Stratigraphy and Seriation." *American Antiquity*, 26:324-30.

1965 "The Renaissance Foundations of Anthropology." *American Anthropologist*, 67:1-20.

RUMNEY, J.

1934 *Herbert Spencer's Sociology*. London: Williams and Norgate.

RUSH, B.

1797 "Observations Intended to Favor a Supposition That the Black Color (as it is called) of the Negroes Is Derived from the Leprosy." *Transactions of the American Philosophical Society*, 4:289-97.

SAGARD-THÉODAT, G.

1936 *Le Grand Voyage du Pays des Hurons*. Paris: Chez Denys Moreau.

SAHLINS, M. D.

1958 *Social Stratification in Polynesia*. Seattle: University of Washington Press.

1965 "On the Ideology and Composition of Descent Groups." *Man*, 65:104-7.

1966 "On the Delphic Writings of Claude Lévi-Strauss." *Scientific American*, 214:131-36.

SAHLINS, M. and E. SERVICE

1960 *Evolution and Culture*. Ann Arbor: University of Michigan Press.

SANDERS, W.

1965 *The Cultural Ecology of the Teotihuacán Valley*. Unpublished manuscript.

SANDERS, W. and B. PRICE

1968 *Mesoamerica: The Evolution of a Civilization*. New York: Random House.

SANDOW, A.

1938 "Social Factors in the Origins of Darwinism." *Quarterly Review of Biology*, 13:315-26.

SAPIR, E.

1917 "Do We Need a Superorganic?" *American Anthropologist*, 19:441-47.

1921 *Language*. New York: Harcourt, Brace.

1924 "Culture, Genuine and Spurious." *American Journal of Sociology*, 29:401-29.

1927 "Anthropology and Sociology." W. F. Ogburn and A. Goldenweiser, eds., *The Social Sciences and Their Interrelation*. Boston: Houghton Mifflin, 97-113.

1932 "Cultural Anthropology and Psychiatry." *Journal of Abnormal and Social Psychology*, 27:229-42.

1937 "The Contribution of Psychiatry to an Understanding of Behavior in Society." *American Journal of Sociology*, 42:862-70.

1949 (orig. 1921) "Review of W. H. R. Rivers' *Instinct and the Unconscious: A Contribution to a Biological Theory of Psycho-Neurosis*." D. G. Mandelbaum, ed., *Selected Writings of Edward Sapir*. Berkeley: University of California Press, 528-29.

1951 "Sound Patterns in Language." D. G. Mandelbaum, ed., *Selected Writings of Edward Sapir*. Berkeley: University of California Press, 33-45.

SARGENT, S. S. and M. W. SMITH (eds.)

1949 *Culture and Personality*. New York: Viking Fund.

SCHAPERA, I.

1947 *Migrant Labour and Tribal Life*. London: Oxford University Press.

1953 "Some Comments on Comparative Method in Social Anthropology." *American Anthropologist*, 55:353-62.

SCHAPIRO, J. S.

1934 *Condorcet and the Rise of Liberalism*. New York: Harcourt, Brace.

SCHEFFLER, I.

1963 *The Anatomy of Inquiry*. New York: Knopf.

SCHEIN, M. and S. DIAMOND

1966 "The Waste Collectors." Unpublished Master's thesis. Columbia University.

SCHER, J. (ed.)

1962 *Theories of the Mind*. New York: Free Press.

SCHLEGEL, F. VON

1808 *Über die Sprache und Weisheit der Indier*. Heidelberg.

SCHMIDT, W.

1926-1955 *Der Ursprung der Gottesidee*. 12 vols. Münster i.W.: Ascherdorff.

1933 *High Gods in North America*. Oxford: Clarendon Press.

1934 "Primitive Man." E. Eyre, ed., *European Civilization*. Oxford: Oxford University Press.

1935 "The Position of Women with Regard to Property in Primitive Society." *American Anthropologist*, 37:244-56.

1939 *The Culture Historical Method of Ethnology*. S.A. Sieber, trans. New York: Fortuny's.

SCHNEIDER, D.

1964 "The Nature of Kinship." *Man*, 64:180-81.

1965a "American Kin Terms and Terms for Kinsmen: A Critique of Goodenough's Componential Analysis of Yankee Kinship Terminology." *American Anthropologist* 67, part 2:288-308.

1965b "The Content of Kinship." *Man*, 65:122-23.

1965c "Some Muddles in the Models. The Relevance of Models for Social Anthropology." *A. S. A. Monographs* 1. London: Tavistock, 25-85.

1965d "Kinship and Biology." A. J. Coale *et al.*, *Aspects of Family Structure*. Princeton, N. J.: Princeton University Press.

SCHNEIDER, H. K.

1957 "The Subsistence Role of Cattle among the Pakot and in East Africa." *American Anthropologist*, 59:278-301.

SCHOOLCRAFT, H. R.

1851 *Personal Memoirs of a Residence of Thirty Years with the Indian Tribes*. Philadelphia: J. B. Lippincott.

1851-1857 *Historical and Statistical Information Respecting the History, Condition, and Prospects of the Indian Tribes of the United States*. Philadelphia: J. B. Lippincott, Grambo.

SCHRADER, O.

1890 *Primitive Antiquities of the Aryan Peoples*. F. Jevons, trans. London: C. Griffin.

SCHUMPETER, J. A.

1954 *History of Economic Analysis*. Oxford: Oxford University Press.

SCHURTZ, H.

1902 *Altersklassen und Männerbunde*. Berlin: Reimer.

SCOTT, J. P.

1963 "The Process of Primary Socialization in Canine and Human Infants." *Child Development Monograph*, 28:1-47.

SEGERSTEDT, T. T.

1966 *The Nature of Social Reality*. Stockholm: Svenska bokforlaget Bonniers. Scandinavian University Books.

SELIGMAN, C. G.

1924 "Anthropology and Psychology: A Study of Some Points of Contact." *Journal of the Royal Anthropological Institute*, 54:13-46.

1932 "Anthropological Perspective and Psychological Theory." *Journal of the Royal Anthropological Institute*, 62:193-228.

SELIGMAN, C. G. and B. SELIGMAN

1911 *The Veddas*. Cambridge: Cambridge University Press.

SELIGMAN, E.

1961 (orig. 1902) *The Economic Interpretation of History*. New York: Columbia University Press.

SELLARS, R. (ed.)

1949 *Philosophy for the Future: The Quest of Modern Materialism*. New York: Macmillan.

SELLNOW, I.

1961 *Grundprinzipien einer Periodisierung der Urgeschichte.* Berlin: Akademie-Verlag.

SELSAM, H. and H. MARTEL

1963 *Reader in Marxist Philosophy.* New York: International Publishers.

SEMPLE, E. C.

1911 *Influences of Geographic Environment: On the Basis of Ratzel's System of Anthropogeography.* New York: Holt.

SERVICE, E.

1955 "Indian-European Relations in Colonial Latin America." *American Anthropologist,* 57:411-25.

1962 *Primitive Social Organization.* New York: Random House.

SHAPIRO, H. L.

1964 "Anthropology and the Age of Discovery." R. A. Manners, ed., *Process and Pattern in Culture.* Chicago: Aldine, 337-48.

SHELDEN, W. H.

1919 "Dr. Goldenweiser and Historical Indeterminism." *Journal of Philosophy, Psychology and Scientific Method,* 16:327-30.

SHMELEV, N. P.

1964 "Critique of Bourgeois Theories of Economic Development." *The Journal of Development Studies,* 1:71-92.

SHOTWELL, J. T.

1922 *An Introduction to the History of History.* New York: Columbia University Press.

1939 *The History of History.* New York: Columbia University Press.

SHRYOCK, R. H.

1944 "The Strange Case of the Wells' Theory of Natural Selection." M. F. Ashley Montagu, ed., *Studies and Essays in the History of Science and Learning in Honor of George Sarton.* New York: Henry Schuman, 195-207.

SHUB, B.

1950 "Soviets Expose American Baby." *The New Leader,* June 17, 11-12.

SIEGEL, B. J. (ed.)

1963 *Biennial Review of Anthropology, 1963.* Stanford: Stanford University Press.

SIMMONS, L. W. (ed.)

1942 *Sun Chief, The Autobiography of a Hopi Indian.* New Haven: Yale University Press.

SIMONDE DE SISMONDI, J. C. L.

1827 *Nouveaux Principes d'Économie Politique.* Paris: Delaunay.

SIMPSON, G. G.

1964 *This View of Life. The World of an Evolutionist.* New York: Harcourt, Brace and World.

SINGER, M.

1961 "A Survey of Culture and Personality Theory and Research." B.

Kaplan, ed., *Studying Personality Cross-Culturally*. Evanston: Row, Peterson: 9-90.

1963 "Foreword." A. Kroeber, *An Anthropologist Looks at History*. Berkeley: University of California Press, v-xiv.

SKINNER, E.

1964 *The Mossi of the Upper Volta*. Stanford: Stanford University Press.

SLOTKIN, J. S.

1965 *Readings in Early Anthropology*. Chicago: Aldine.

SMALL, A.

1924 *Origins of Sociology*. Chicago: University of Chicago Press.

SMITH, G. E.

1928 *In the Beginning: The Origin of Civilization*. New York: Morrow.

1933 *The Diffusion of Culture*. London: Watts.

SMITH, M.

1959 "Boas' 'Natural History' Approach to Field Method." W. Goldschmidt, ed., *The Anthropology of Franz Boas*. Memoir 89. American Anthropological Association, 46-60.

SMITH, M. G.

1960 *Government in Zazzau: 1800-1950*. London: Oxford University Press.

SMITH, S. S.

1965 (orig. 1787; reprinted 1810) *An Essay on the Causes of the Variety of Complexion and Figure in the Human Species*. Harvard: The Belknap Press.

SMITH, W. R.

1903 (orig. 1885) *Kinship and Marriage in Early Arabia*. London: Charles and Black.

1956 (orig. 1889) *The Religion of the Semites*. New York: Meridian Books, World Publishing.

SNYDER, L.

1962 *The Idea of Racialism: Its Meaning and History*. Princeton: Van Nostrand.

SONTAG, S.

1963 "Review of *Structural Anthropology*, by Claude Lévi-Strauss." *New York Review of Books*, 1, No. 7, 6-8.

SOROKIN, P.

1928 *Contemporary Sociological Theories*. New York: Harper.

1950 *Social Philosophies of an Age of Crisis*. Boston: Beacon Press.

SPECK, F. G.

1915 "The Family Hunting Band as the Basis of Algonkian Social Organization." *American Anthropologist*, 13:289-305.

1928 "Land Ownership among Hunting Peoples in Primitive America and the World's Marginal Areas." Rome: Proceedings of the 22d International Congress of Americanists, 2:323-32.

1936 "Inland Eskimo Bands of Labrador." R. Lowie, ed., *Essays in Anthropology*. Berkeley: University of California Press, 313-30.

SPELLER, G. (ed.)

1911 *Papers on Inter-Racial Problems*. London: P. S. King and Son.

SPENCER, H.

1852a "A Theory of Population, Deduced from the General Laws of Animal Fertility." *Westminster Review*, 57:468-501.

1852b "The Development Hypothesis." *The Leader*, vol. 3.

1857 "Progress: Its Laws and Causes." *Westminster Review*, 67:445-85.

1859 "What Knowledge Is of Most Worth?" *Westminster Review*, 72:1-41.

1860 "The Social Organism." *Westminster Review*, 17:90-121.

1866 (orig. 1864) *Principles of Biology*. New York: D. Appleton.

1871 (orig. 1855) *Synthetic Philosophy; Principles of Psychology*. New York: D. Appleton.

1873 *The Study of Sociology*. New York: D. Appleton.

1873-1933 *Descriptive Sociology*. New York: D. Appleton.

1883 (orig. 1850) *Social Statics*. New York: D. Appleton.

1896 (orig. 1876) *Principles of Sociology*. New York: D. Appleton.

1912 (orig. 1864) *First Principles*. 6th ed. New York: D. Appleton.

1926 *An Autobiography*. London: Watts.

SPINDEN, H. J.

1927 "The Prosaic vs. the Romantic School in Anthropology." E. Smith, ed., *Culture: The Diffusion Controversy*. New York: Norton, 47-98.

1937 "First Peopling of America as a Chronological Problem." G. G. MacCurdy, ed., *Early Man*. London: J. B. Lippincott, 105-14.

SPINOZA, B.

1934 (orig. 1632) *Ethics*. A. Boyle, trans. New York: Dutton.

SPIRO, M. (ed.)

1965 *Context and Meaning in Cultural Anthropology*. New York: Free Press.

SPOEHR, A.

1947 *Changing Kinship Systems*. Anthropological Series. Chicago Natural History Museum, 33.

STANTON, W.

1960 *The Leopard's Spots*. Chicago: University of Chicago Press.

STARCKE, C. N.

1901 (orig. 1889) *The Primitive Family in Its Origins and Development*. New York: D. Appleton.

STEINMETZ, S. R.

1894 *Ethnologische Studien zur ersten Entwicklung der Strafe*. Leiden: S. C. Van Doesburgh.

1930 *Classification des Types Sociaux et Catalogue des Peuples. Gesam-*

melte kleinere Schriften zur Ethnologie und Soziologie, vol. II. Groningen: P. Noordhoff, 96-210.

STENNING, D.

1959 *Savannah Nomads*. London: Oxford University Press.

STERN, B. J.

1931 *Lewis Henry Morgan*. Chicago: University of Chicago Press.

1948 "Engels on the Family." *Science and Society*, 12:42-64.

STERN, F. (ed.)

1956 *The Varieties of History, Voltaire to the Present*. New York: Meridian Books, World Publishing.

STEVENSON, R. F.

1965 "Population Density and State Formation in Sub-Saharan Africa." Unpublished Ph.D. dissertation. Columbia University.

STEWARD, J.

1929 "Diffusion and Independent Invention: A Critique of Logic." *American Anthropologist*, 31:491-95.

1936 "The Economic and Social Basis of Primitive Bands." R. Lowie, ed., *Essays in Anthropology Presented to A. L. Kroeber*. Berkeley: University of California Press, 331-45.

1937 "Ecological Aspects of Southwestern Society." *Anthropos*, 32:87-104.

1938 *Basin-Plateau Aboriginal Sociopolitical Groups*. Washington: Bureau of American Ethnology, Bull. 120.

1946-1950 *Handbook of the South American Indians*. Washington: Bureau of American Ethnology, Bull. 143. 6 vols.

1948 "A Functional Developmental Classification of American High Cultures." W. Bennett, ed., *A Reappraisal of Peruvian Archaeology*. Memoirs of the Society for American Archaeology, 103-4.

1949a "The Native Populations of South America." J. Steward, ed., *Handbook of the South American Indians*. Washington: Bureau of American Ethnology. Bull. 143. Vol. 5:655-88.

1949b "Cultural Causality and Law; A Trial Formulation of Early Civilization." *American Anthropologist*, 51:1-27.

1955 *Theory of Culture Change*. Urbana: University of Illinois Press.

1956 "Cultural Evolution." *Scientific American*, 194:69-80.

1960 "Review of White's *The Evolution of Culture*." *American Anthropologist*, 62:144-48.

1961 "Alfred Louis Kroeber 1876-1960." *American Anthropologist*, 63:1038-60.

1965 "Some Problems Raised by Roger C. Owen's *The Patrilocal Band*." *American Anthropologist*, 67:732-34.

1967 "Comment on K. C. Chang, *Major Aspects of the Interrelationship of Archaeology and Ethnology*." *Current Anthropology*, 8:239-40.

STEWARD, J. and F. SELTZER

1938 "Function and Configuration in Archaeology." *American Antiquity*, 4:4-10.

STEWARD, J. and D. SHIMKIN

1962 "Some Mechanism of Sociocultural Evolution." H. Hoagland and R. Burhoe, eds., *Evolution and Man's Progress*. New York: Columbia University Press, 67-87.

STOCKING, G.

1960 "Franz Boas and the Founding of the American Anthropological Association." *American Anthropologist*, 62:1-17.

1964 "French Anthropology in 1800." *Isis*, 55:134-50.

1965a "From Physics to Ethnology: Franz Boas' Arctic Expedition as a Problem in the Historiography of the Behavioral Sciences." *Journal of the History of the Behavioral Sciences*," 1:53-66.

1965b "On the Limits of Presentism and Historicism in the Historiography of the Behavioral Sciences." *Journal of the History of the Behavioral Sciences*, 1:211-17.

1965c "Cultural Darwinism and Philosophical Idealism in E. B. Tylor: A Special Plea for Historicism in the History of Anthropology." *Southwestern Journal of Anthropology*, 21:130-48.

STOETZEL, J.

1955 *Without Chrysanthemum and Sword: A Study of the Attitudes of Youth in Postwar Japan*. New York: Columbia University Press.

STOLPE, H.

1891 *Evolution in the Ornamental Art of Savage Peoples*. H. C. Cooley, trans., Rochdale: Transactions of the Rochdale Literary and Scientific Society.

STRONG, W. D.

1936 "Anthropological Theory and Archaeological Fact." R. Lowie, ed., *Essays in Anthropology Presented to A. L. Kroeber*. Berkeley: University of California Press, 359-70.

STRONG, W. D., W. E. SCHENCK, and J. STEWARD

1930 "Archaeology of the Dallas-Deschutes Region." *University of California Publications in American Archaeology and Ethnology*, 29:1-154.

STURTEVANT, W.

1964 "Studies in Ethnoscience." *American Anthropologist*, 66, part 2:99-131.

SUMNER, W. G. and A. KELLER

1927 *The Science of Society*. New Haven: Yale University Press.

SUTTLES, W.

1959 "Cultural Relativism, Cultural Evolution, and Popular Ideology." *Western Humanities Review*, 13:311-19.

1960 "Affinal Ties, Subsistence and Prestige among the Coast Salish." *American Anthropologist*, 62:296-30.

SWANSON, G. E.

1960 *The Birth of the Gods*. Ann Arbor: University of Michigan Press.

SWANTON, J. R.

1904 "The Development of the Clan System and of Secret Societies among the Northwestern Tribes." *American Anthropologist*, 6:477-85.

1905 "The Social Organization of American Tribes." *American Anthropologist*, 7:663-73.

1906a "Review of Frazer's Lectures on the Early History of the Kingship." *American Anthropologist*, 8:157-60.

1906b "Review of Lang's *The Secret Totem*." *American Anthropologist*, 8:160-65.

1908 "Review of Webster's *Primitive Secret Societies*." *American Anthropologist*, 10:457-59.

1917 "Some Anthropological Misconceptions." *American Anthropologist*, 19:459-70.

SWEET, L.

1966 "Comment on 'Ethnographic Semantics' by B. N. Colby." *Current Anthropology*, 7:24-25.

TACITUS

1948 (orig. A.D. 98) *Tacitus on Britain and Germany*. London: Penguin.

TAMBIAK, S. J.

1965 "Kinship Fact and Fiction in Relation to the Kandyan Sinhalese." *Journal of the Royal Anthropological Institute*, 95:131-73.

TAX, S.

1955a "Some Problems of Social Organization." F. Eggan, ed., *Social Anthropology of North American Tribes*. Chicago: University of Chicago Press, 3-32.

1955b "From Lafitau to Radcliffe-Brown: A Short History of the Study of Social Organization." F. Eggan, ed., *Social Anthropology of North American Tribes*. Chicago: University of Chicago Press, 445-81.

1964 (ed.) *Horizons of Anthropology*. Chicago: Aldine.

TAYLOR, S.

1956 *Conceptions and the Theory of Knowledge*. New Haven: Bookman Associates.

TAYLOR, W. C.

1840 *The Natural History of Society. The Barbarian and Civilized State*. London: Orme, Brown. 2 vols.

TEGGART, F.

1916 "Prolegomena to History." *University of California Publications in History*, 4:156-292.

1941 *Theory and Processes of History*. Berkeley: University of California Press.

TEXTOR, R. B.

1966 *A Cross-Cultural Summary*. New Haven: Human Relations Area Files.

THOMAS, F.
1925 *The Environmental Basis of Society: A Study in the History of Sociological Theory*. New York: Century.

THOMAS, N.
1916 *Law and Custom of the Timne and Other Tribes*. London: Harrison.

THOMAS, W. (ed.)
1955 *Yearbook of Anthropology*. New York: Wenner-Gren Foundation.

THOMAS, W. I.
1909 "The Mind of the Savage." W. I. Thomas, ed., *Sourcebook in Social Origins*. Chicago: University of Chicago Press, 155-73.

THOMSEN, C. J.
1848 (orig. 1836) *A Guide to Northern Antiquities*. London.

THORNER, D.
1966 "Marx on India and the Asiatic Mode of Production." *Contribution to Indian Sociology*, 9:3-66.

THURNWALD, R.
1936 "Review of *Sex and Temperament in Three Primitive Societies*," by Margaret Mead. *American Anthropologist*, 38:558-61.

TIJM, J.
1933 *Die Stellung der Frau bei den Indianern der Vereinigten Staaten und Canada's*. Zutphen: W. J. Thieme.

TIMASHEFF, N. S.
1955 *Sociological Theory*. Garden City, N.Y.: Doubleday.

TINKER, C. B.
1922 *Nature's Simple Plan*. Princeton: Princeton University Press.

TODOROV, T.
1965 "L'Héritage Méthodologique du Formalisme." *L'Homme*, 5:64-83.

TOKEI, F.
1964 "Le Mode de Production Asiatique dans l'Oeuvre de K. Marx et F. Engels." *La Pensée*, 114:7-32.

TOLSTOY, P.
1952 "Morgan and Soviet Anthropological Thought." *American Anthropologist*, 54:8-17.

TOPINARD, P.
1885 *Éléments d'Anthropologie Générale*. Paris: Delahaye et *Leecrosnier*.

TOURNAL, M.
1959 (orig. 1833) "General Considerations Concerning the Phenomena of the Bone-Bearing Caves." Translated in *Kroeber Anthropological Society Papers*, 21:6-16.

TOZZER, H. F.
1964 *A History of Ancient Geography*. New York: Biblo and Tannen.

TROTTER, W.
1916 *Instincts of the Herd in Peace and War*. New York: Macmillan.

TRUBETZKOY, N.

1933 *Le Phonologie Actuelle. Psychologie du Langue.* Paris: Librairie F. Alcan.

TRUMBULL, H. C.

1898 (orig. 1887) *Blood Covenant, A Primitive Rite and Its Bearing on Scripture.* Philadelphia: John D. Wattles.

TURGOT, A. R. J.

1844 (orig. 1750) *Plan de Deux Discours sur l'Histoire Universelle. Oeuvres de Turgot.* Paris: Guillaumin.

1895 *Life and Writings.* W. W. Stephens, trans. and ed. London: Longmans, Green.

TYLOR, E. B.

1861 *Anahuac or Mexico and the Mexicans, Ancient and Modern.* London: Longmans, Green, Longman, and Roberts.

1865 *Researches into the Early History of Mankind and the Development of Civilization.* London: J. Murray.

1871 *Primitive Culture: Researches into the Development of Mythology, Philosophy, Religion, Language, Art and Custom.* London: J. Murray.

1878 "Anthropology." *Encyclopaedia Britannica,* 9th ed., 2:107-23.

1889 "On a Method of Investigating the Development of Institutions; Applied to Laws of Marriage and Descent." *Journal of the Royal Anthropological Institute,* 18:245-69.

1899 (orig. 1881) *Anthropology: An Introduction to the Study of Man and Civilization.* New York: D. Appleton.

1905 "Obituary: Adolf Bastian." *Man,* 5:138-43.

1958 (orig. 1871) *Primitive Culture.* New York: Harper Torchbooks.

UNESCO

1961 *The Race Question in Modern Science.* New York: Columbia University Press.

VAN AMRINGE, W. F.

1831 *An Investigation of the Theories of the Natural History of Man.* New York: Baker and Scribner.

VAN DER BIJ, T. S.

1929 *Ontstaan en Eerste Ontwikkeling van de Oorlog.* Groningen: Wolters.

VAN GENNEP, A.

1910 "Une Ethnographe Oublié du XVIIIe Siècle: J. N. Demeunier. *Revue des Idées,* 7:18-28.

VARTANIAN, A. (ed.)

1960 *La Mettrie's L'Homme Machine: A Study in the Origins of an Idea.* Princeton: Princeton University Press.

VAYDA, A.

1956 "Maori Conquests in Relation to the New Zealand Environment." *Journal of the Polynesian Society,* 65:204-11.

1960 "Maori Warfare." *Polynesian Society Maori Monographs*, No. 2. Wellington: Polynesian Society.

1961a "Maori Prisoners and Slaves in the Nineteenth Century." *Ethnohistory*, 8:144-55.

1961b "Expansion and Warfare among Swidden Agriculturists." *American Anthropologist*, 63:346-58.

1961c "A Re-examination of Northwest Coast Economic Systems." *Transactions of the New York Academy of Sciences*. Ser. 2, Vol. 23, No. 7: 618-24.

VAYDA, A., A. LEEDS, and D. SMITH

1961 "The Place of Pigs in Melanesian Subsistence." *Proceedings of the 1961 Annual Spring Meeting of the American Ethnological Society*. Seattle: University of Washington Press, 69-77.

VICO, G.

1948 (orig. 1725) *The New Science*. T. G. Bergin and M. H. Fisch, trans. Ithaca: Cornell University Press.

VIDICH, A. and J. BENSMAN

1958 *Small Town in Mass Society*. Princeton: Princeton University Press.

VIREY, J.

1837 *Natural History of the Negro Race*. Charleston, South Carolina.

VITRUVIUS

1914 *The Ten Books on Architecture*. M. Morgan, trans. Cambridge: Harvard University Press.

VOEGELIN, C.

1965 "Sociolinguistics, Ethnolinguistics and Anthropological Linguistics." *American Anthropologist*, 67:484-85.

VOGET, F. W.

1960 "Man and Culture: An Essay in Changing Anthropological Interpretation." *American Anthropologist*, 62:943-65.

VOLTAIRE

1829 (orig. 1745) *Essai sur les Moeurs et l'Esprit des Nations*. Paris: Chez Werdet et Lequien Fils.

WAFER, L.

1934 (orig. 1699) *A New Voyage and Description of the Isthmus of America*. Oxford: Hakluyt Society.

WAGLEY, C.

1965 (orig. 1958) "On the Concept of Social Race in the Americas." D. Heath and R. Adams, eds., *Contemporary Cultures and Societies of Latin America*. New York: Random House, 531-45.

WAGLEY, C. and M. HARRIS

1958 *Minorities in the New World*. New York: Columbia University Press.

WAISSMAN, F.

1959 "The Decline and Fall of Causality." A. C. Crombie, ed., *Turning*

Points in Physics. Amsterdam: North-Holland Publishing Co., 84-154.

WAITZ, T.

1859 *Anthropologie der Naturvölker*. Leipzig: G. Gerland.

1863 *Introduction to Anthropology*. J. F. Collingwood, trans. London: Longmans, Green, Longman, and Roberts.

WAKE, C. S.

1967 *Primitive Marriage*. R. Needham, ed. Chicago: University of Chicago Press.

WALLACE, A. F. C.

1952 "The Modal Personality of the Tuscarora Indians as Revealed by the Rorschach Test." *Washington: Bureau of American Ethnology, Bull.* 150

1961 "Mental Illness, Biology and Culture." F. Hsu, ed., *Psychological Anthropology: Approaches to Culture and Personality*. Homewood, Ill.: Dorsey Press, 255-94.

1962 "The New Culture-and-Personality." T. Gladwin and W. Sturtevant, eds., *Anthropology and Human Behavior*. Washington: Anthropological Society of Washington, 1-12.

1965 "The Problem of the Psychological Validity of Componential Analysis." *American Anthropologist*, 67, part 2:229-48.

1966 *Religion, An Anthropological View*. New York: Random House.

WALLACE, A. F. C. and J. ATKINS

1960 "The Meaning of Kinship Terms." *American Anthropologist*, 62: 58-80.

WALLACE, A. R.

1905 *My Life*. London: Chapman and Hall.

WALLACE, S. E.

1965 *Skid Row as a Way of Life*. Totowa, N. J.: Bedminster Press.

WALLIS, W.

1930 *Culture and Progress*. New York: McGraw-Hill.

1957 "Anthropology in England Early in the Present Century." *American Anthropologist*, 59:781-90.

WARD, B.

1965 "Varieties of the Conscious Model: The Fishermen of South China." *The Relevance of Models for Social Anthropology*. A.S.A. Monograph 1. London: Tavistock Publications: 113-38.

WARD, L.

1904 "Review of *Where Did Life Begin?* by G. H. Scribner." *American Anthropologist*, 6:151-52.

1905 "Relation of Sociology to Anthropology." *American Anthropologist*, 8:241-56.

WASHBURN, S.

1951 "The New Physical Anthropology." *Transactions of the New York Academy of Sciences*, 13:298-304.

1963 "The Study of Race." *American Anthropologist,* 65:521-31.

WATERMAN, T. T.

1917 "Bandelier's Contribution to the Study of Ancient Mexico." *University of California Publications in Archaeology and Ethnology,* 12:249-83.

WAX, M.

1956 "The Limitations of Boas' Anthropology." *American Anthropologist,* 58:63-74.

WEDGWOOD, C.

1934 "Introduction." A. B. Deacon, *Malekula: A Vanishing People in the New Hebrides.* London: George Routledge, xxxi-xxxviii.

WEINBERG, C. B.

1937 "Mach's Empirio-Pragmatism in Physical Science." Unpublished Ph.D. dissertation. Columbia University.

WEINER, P. and A. NOLAND, (eds.)

1957 *Roots of Scientific Thought.* New York: Basic Books.

WELLS, W. C.

1818 *An Account of a Female of the White Race of Mankind, Part of Whose Skin Resembles That of a Negro: With Some Observations on the Causes of the Differences in Color and Form between the White and Negro Races of Men Appended to Two Essays: One Upon Single Vision with Two Eyes and the Other on Dew.* London: A. Constable.

WESTERMARCK, E.

1894 (orig. 1891) *The History of Human Marriage.* New York: Macmillan.

WHATELY, R.

1855 *On the Origin of Civilization.* London: Young Men's Christian Association.

1861 *Miscellaneous Lectures and Reviews.* London: British Museum.

WHITE, C.

1799 *An Account of the Regular Gradation in Man and in Different Animals and Vegetables from the Former to the Latter. London:* C. Dilly.

WHITE, LESLIE

1925 "Personality and Culture." *The Open Court,* 39:145-49.

1939 "A Problem in Kinship Terminology." *American Anthropologist,* 41:566-73.

1940 *Pioneers in American Anthropology: The Bandelier-Morgan Letters, 1873-1883.* Albuquerque: University of New Mexico Press.

1942 *The Pueblo of Santa Ana, New Mexico.* American Anthropological Association. Memoir 60.

1943 "Energy and the Evolution of Culture." *American Anthropologist,* 45:335-56.

1945 "Diffusion Versus Evolution: An Anti-evolutionist Fallacy." *American Anthropologist,* 47:339-56.

1947a "The Expansion of the Scope of Science." *Journal of the Washington Academy of Sciences*, 37:181-210.
1947b "Evolutionism in Cultural Anthropology: A Rejoinder." *American Anthropologist*, 49:400-11.
1949a *The Science of Culture*. New York: Grove Press.
1949b "Ethnological Theory." R. W. Sellars, ed., *Philosophy for the Future: The Quest of Modern Materialism*. New York: Macmillan, 357-84.
1957 "Review of Steward's *Theory of Culture Change*." *American Anthropologist*, 59:540-42.
1958 "What Is a Classificatory Kinship Term?" *Southwestern Journal of Anthropology*, 14:378-85.
1959a "The Concept of Evolution in Cultural Anthropology." B. Meggers, ed., *Evolution and Anthropology*. Washington: The Anthropological Society of Washington, 106-25.
1959b *The Evolution of Culture*. New York: McGraw-Hill.
1963 *The Ethnology and Ethnography of Franz Boas*. Austin: Bulletin of the Texas Memorial Museum, no. 6.
1966 "The Social Organization of Ethnological Theory." *Rice University Studies*, 52:1-66.

WHITE, LYNN
1962 *Medieval Technology and Social Change*. Oxford: Clarendon Press.

WHITING, J.
1941 *Becoming a Kwoma: Teaching and Learning in a New Guinea Tribe*. New Haven: Yale University Press.
1961 "Socialization Process and Personality." F. Hsu, ed., *Psychological Anthropology: Approaches to Culture and Personality*. Homewood, Ill.: Dorsey Press, 355-80.
1964 "Effects of Climate on Certain Cultural Practices." W. Goodenough, ed., *Exploration in Cultural Anthropology*. New York: McGraw-Hill, 511-44.

WHITING, J. and I. CHILD
1953 *Child Training and Personality: A Cross-Cultural Study*. New Haven: Yale University Press.

WHITING, J., C. KLUCKHOHN, and A. ANTHONY
1958 "The Function of Male Initiation Ceremonies at Puberty." E. Macoby, T. M. Newcomb, and E. L. Hartley, eds., *Readings in Social Psychology*. New York: Holt, 359-70.

WILDER, W.
1964 "Confusion versus Classification in the Study of Purum Society." *American Anthropologist*, 66:1365-71.

WILKINSON, SIR J. G.
1878 *The Manners and Customs of the Ancient Egyptians*. New York: Scribner and Welford.

WILLEY, G.

1953 "Archaeological Theories and Interpretation: New World." A. Kroeber, ed., *Anthropology Today*. Chicago: University of Chicago Press, 361-85.

WILLIAMS, ELGIN

1947 "Anthropology for the Common Man." *American Anthropologist*, 49:84-89.

WILLIAMS, ERIC

1945 *Capitalism and Slavery*. Chapel Hill: University of North Carolina Press.

WILLIAMS, J. L.

1936 "Boas and American Ethnologists." *Thought*, 11:194-209.

WILLIAMS, R.

1958 *Culture and Society: 1780-1950*. New York: Columbia University Press.

WILSON, G. and M. HUNTER

1939 "The Study of African Society." Rhodes-Livingstone Institute. Rhodes-Livingstone Papers 2.

1945 *The Analysis of Social Change*. Cambridge: Cambridge University Press.

WISSLER, C.

1913 "Doctrine of Evolution and Anthropology." *American Anthropologist*, 15:355-56.

1917 *The American Indian; An Introduction to the Anthropology of the New World*. New York: D. C. McMurtrie.

1926 *The Relation of Nature to Man in Aboriginal America*. New York: Oxford University Press.

1929 *An Introduction to Social Anthropology*. New York: Holt.

1933 "The American Aborigines." Unpublished Collected Writings.

1938 (orig. 1922) *The American Indian*. New York: Oxford University Press.

WITTFOGEL, K.

1929 "Geopolitik, geographischer Materialismus and Marxismus." *Unter dem Banner der Marxismus*, 3:17-51;485-522;698-735.

1931 *Wirtschaft und Gesellschaft Chinas*. Leipzig: C. L. Hirschfeld.

1935 "The Foundations and Stages of Chinese Economic History." *Zeitschrift für sozial Forschung* (Paris), 4:26-60.

1938 "Die Theorie der Orientalischen Gesellschaft." *Zeitschrift für sozial Forschung* (Paris), 7:90-122.

1953 "The Ruling Bureaucracy of Oriental Despotism: A Phenomenon that Paralyzed Marx." *The Review of Politics*, 15:350-59.

1957 *Oriental Despotism*. New Haven: Yale University Press.

1960 "A Stronger Oriental Despotism." *China Quarterly*, 1-6.

1964 "Ideas and the Power Structure." W. T. de Bary and A. T. Embree, eds., *Approaches to Asian Civilizations*. New York: Columbia University Press, 86-97.

WITTKOWER, E. D. and J. FRIED (eds.)

1963 *Transcultural Psychiatric Research*. Montreal: McGill University Press.

WOLF, A.

1966 "Childhood Association, Sexual Attraction, and the Incest Taboo: A Chinese Case." *American Anthropologist*, 68:883-98.

WOLF, E.

1957 "Closed Corporate Peasant Communities in Mesoamerica and Central Java." *Southwestern Journal of Anthropology*, 1-18.

1959 *Sons of the Shaking Earth*. Chicago: University of Chicago Press.

1960 "Review of White's *The Science of Culture*." *American Anthropologist*, 62:148-51.

1966 *Peasants*. Englewood Cliffs: Prentice-Hall.

WOOD, J. G.

1874-1880 *Natural History of Man*. London: George Routledge.

WORSAAE, J. J. A.

1849 *The Primeval Antiquities of Denmark*. W. J. Thomas, trans. London.

WORSELEY, P.M.

1956 "The Kinship System of the Tallensi: A Revaluation." *Journal of the Royal Anthropological Institute*, 86:37-77.

1957 *The Trumpet Shall Sound: A Study of 'Cargo' Cults in Melanesia*. London: MacGibbon and Kee.

1961 "The Analysis of Rebellion and Revolution in British Social Anthropology." *Science and Society*, 21:26-37.

ZANNOLI, V.

1910 *Le Tèorie da A. Bastian e l'Etnologia Moderna*. Padova: Accademia Scientifica Veneto-Trentino-Istriana.

ZETTERBERG, H.

1965 *On Theory and Verification in Sociology*. Totowa, N. J.: The Bedminster Press.

ZHUKOV, E.

1960 "The Periodization of World History." *Rapporte*, 1:74-88. Stockholm: International Historical Congress.

ZIPF, G. K.

1935 *The Psycho-Biology of Language; An Introduction of Dynamic Philology*. Boston: Houghton-Mifflin.

ZIRKLE, C.

1959 *Evolution, Marxian Biology and the Social Sciences*. Philadelphia: University of Pennsylvania Press.

Index